## The Editors

JENNIFER HARRIS is Associate Professor of English at Mount Allison University and visiting faculty at University of Waterloo, Canada. Her essays have appeared in *African American Review*, *Journal of American Culture*, and *Resources for American Literary Study*. Her editorial work includes eight volumes of the Alphabet City cultural studies book series for MIT Press. She has also been a Fulbright Fellow and a Social Science and Humanities Resource Council of Canada grant recipient.

BRYAN WATERMAN is Associate Professor of English at New York University. He is the author of *Republic of Intellect: The Friendly Club of New York City and the Making of American Literature* (2007) and editor of the Norton Critical Edition of Charles Brockden Brown's *Wieland* and *Memoirs of Carwin the Biloquist*. His essays have appeared in *Early American Literature*, *American Literary History*, and *The William and Mary Quarterly*.

## W. W. NORTON & COMPANY, INC.
*Also Publishes*

ENGLISH RENAISSANCE DRAMA: A NORTON ANTHOLOGY
*edited by David Bevington et al.*

THE NORTON ANTHOLOGY OF AFRICAN AMERICAN LITERATURE
*edited by Henry Louis Gates Jr. and Nellie Y. McKay et al.*

THE NORTON ANTHOLOGY OF AMERICAN LITERATURE
*edited by Nina Baym and Robert Levine et al.*

THE NORTON ANTHOLOGY OF CHILDREN'S LITERATURE
*edited by Jack Zipes et al.*

THE NORTON ANTHOLOGY OF DRAMA
*edited by J. Ellen Gainor, Stanton B. Garner Jr., and Martin Puchner*

THE NORTON ANTHOLOGY OF ENGLISH LITERATURE
*edited by Stephen Greenblatt et al.*

THE NORTON ANTHOLOGY OF LATINO LITERATURE
*edited by Ilan Stavans et al.*

THE NORTON ANTHOLOGY OF LITERATURE BY WOMEN
*edited by Sandra M. Gilbert and Susan Gubar*

THE NORTON ANTHOLOGY OF MODERN AND CONTEMPORARY POETRY
*edited by Jahan Ramazani, Richard Ellmann, and Robert O'Clair*

THE NORTON ANTHOLOGY OF POETRY
*edited by Margaret Ferguson, Mary Jo Salter, and Jon Stallworthy*

THE NORTON ANTHOLOGY OF SHORT FICTION
*edited by R. V. Cassill and Richard Bausch*

THE NORTON ANTHOLOGY OF THEORY AND CRITICISM
*edited by Vincent B. Leitch et al.*

THE NORTON ANTHOLOGY OF WORLD LITERATURE
*edited by Martin Puchner et al.*

THE NORTON FACSIMILE OF THE FIRST FOLIO OF SHAKESPEARE
*prepared by Charlton Hinman*

THE NORTON INTRODUCTION TO LITERATURE
*edited by Kelly J. Mays*

THE NORTON READER
*edited by Linda H. Peterson and John C. Brereton*

THE NORTON SAMPLER
*edited by Thomas Cooley*

THE NORTON SHAKESPEARE, BASED ON THE OXFORD EDITION
*edited by Stephen Greenblatt et al.*

For a complete list of Norton Critical Editions, visit
www.wwnorton.com/webnce

A NORTON CRITICAL EDITION

Hannah Webster Foster

# THE COQUETTE

## *and*

# THE BOARDING SCHOOL

AUTHORITATIVE TEXTS
SOURCES AND CONTEXTS
CRITICISM

*Edited by*

JENNIFER HARRIS
MOUNT ALLISON UNIVERSITY

BRYAN WATERMAN
NEW YORK UNIVERSITY

W · W · NORTON & COMPANY · *New York* · *London*

W. W. Norton & Company has been independent since its founding in 1923, when William Warder Norton and Mary D. Herter Norton first published lectures delivered at the People's Institute, the adult education division of New York City's Cooper Union. The firm soon expanded its program beyond the Institute, publishing books by celebrated academics from America and abroad. By midcentury, the two major pillars of Norton's publishing program—trade books and college texts—were firmly established. In the 1950s, the Norton family transferred control of the company to its employees, and today—with a staff of four hundred and a comparable number of trade, college, and professional titles published each year—W. W. Norton & Company stands as the largest and oldest publishing house owned wholly by its employees.

This title is printed on permanent paper containing 30 percent post-consumer waste recycled fiber.

The text of this book is composed in Fairfield Medium with the display set in Bernhard Modern.
Book design by Antonina Krass.
Composition by Westchester.
Manufacturing by Maple Press.
Production manager: Sean Mintus.

Library of Congress Cataloging-in-Publication Data

Foster, Hannah Webster, 1759–1840.

The coquette, and The boarding school : authoritative texts sources and contexts, criticism / Hannah Webster Foster ; edited by Jennifer Harris, Bryan Waterman. — 1st ed.
        p.   cm. — (A Norton critical edition)
    Includes bibliographical references.
    **ISBN 978-0-393-93167-9 (pbk.)**
    I. Harris, Jennifer, date.   II. Waterman, Bryan, 1970–   III. Foster, Hannah Webster, 1759–1840. Boarding school.   IV. Title.
    PS744.F7C63 2012
    813'.2—dc23

                                                                2012016308

W. W. Norton & Company, Inc., 500 Fifth Avenue, New York, NY 10110-0017
wwnorton.com

W. W. Norton & Company Ltd., Castle House, 75/76 Wells Street, London
W1T 3QT

1  2  3  4  5  6  7  8  9  0

# Contents

# List of Illustrations

# Preface

In 1866, when Hannah Webster Foster's 1797 novel *The Coquette: or, The History of Eliza Wharton; a Novel; Founded on Fact* was republished as *The Coquette; or the Life and Letters of Eliza Wharton* in "Peterson's Dollar Series of Good Novels," it had been a steady seller for almost seventy years, in more than ten editions—including a newspaper serial—with copies circulated among friends and passed down through families who lovingly annotated and inscribed them. In 1855 the popular poet Jane E. Locke, introducing her own edition, went so far as to claim that *The Coquette* "took precedence in interest . . . of all American novels, at least throughout New England, and was found, in every cottage within its borders, beside the family Bible, and though pitifully, yet almost as carefully treasured." The name of the novel's heroine, Eliza Wharton, was better known than that of the novel's author—who until 1855 was listed only as "A Lady of Massachusetts"—and became attached to a number of popular items, from a touring waxwork exhibit to an antebellum racehorse. By contrast, as of 1866, Foster's second novel, *The Boarding School* (1798), had faded into relative obscurity, with only one subsequent printing, in 1829, the year Foster's husband died.

The difference in the fate of the novels might be attributed in part to their divergent genres. First and foremost *The Coquette* is a novel of seduction, composed of a series of letters, what literary historians call an epistolary novel. In form it draws on numerous British novels of seduction that had proven enormously popular in the colonies, such as Samuel Richardson's *Pamela* (1740) and *Clarissa* (1748). Like these books, it presents itself as multiple correspondences, almost always between members of the same sex, apparently gathered and arranged by some unseen editorial hand after the fact. *The Boarding School* is also an epistolary novel, but instead of illustrating how a woman might go wrong and sacrifice her honor, it instructs female readers how to avoid such traps and live a virtuous life. Even more than *The Coquette*, it can be categorized as a conduct novel: it advises readers how to comport themselves in public and private, in speech and thought, and in reading and writing. Episodes that demonstrate the cost of veering from the correct path

are embedded throughout, informing but not intruding on the narrative. While both books remain eminently readable, the seduction novel generally contains more emotional highs and lows than a novel composed of letters between a boarding school mistress and her students about the challenges they will face in navigating the wider world. Though both novels aim to promote virtuous behavior, only one of them has sex—or at least a hint of it, with earlier readers filling in the blanks, much as we do today. Particularly in *The Coquette*, the epistolary format also requires readers to make judgments between competing accounts, deciding which, if any, letter writers have a corner on moral truths or even on the facts of the matter at hand.

If *The Coquette* has sex, it also had something else: scandal, and real-life scandal at that. As Foster's readers were aware, Eliza Wharton was a thinly veiled portrait of Elizabeth Whitman (1752–1788), whose death had occasioned much commentary for nearly a decade by the time Foster wrote her novel. Whitman was one of four children born to Reverend Elnathan Whitman, pastor of the Second Church of Christ in Hartford, Connecticut, and a fellow of the corporation of Yale College. Her mother was Abigail Stanley, daughter of Colonel Nathaniel Stanley, treasurer of the Connecticut Colony. Whitman's extended family tree was populated by well-known New England ministers and educators, including the Great Awakening religious leader Jonathan Edwards, revolutionary poet John Trumbull, and Reverend Aaron Burr, second president of Princeton, whose son, Aaron Burr, Jr., was later third vice president of the United States. As Foster's readers probably also knew, Whitman was a poet, albeit unpublished in her lifetime, and a friend of Connecticut's most prominent writers, including Yale's President Timothy Dwight and Joel Barlow, famed for his long poem *The Vision of Columbus* (1787), as well as the mock epic *The Hasty Pudding* (1793). Whitman's own poetry entered newspaper circulation alongside accounts of her death in the summer and fall of 1788.

Whitman would have lived her life in relative obscurity had it not been for the circumstances of her premature death. In late May or early June 1788, she left her family's Connecticut home, ostensibly bound for Boston. Instead, she switched carriages, arriving twenty miles north of Boston at the Bell Tavern, in Danvers, Massachusetts. There she secured lodgings under an assumed name, "Mrs. E. Walker," and told those who inquired that she was waiting for her husband. Locals later remembered her as well bred, engaging in genteel and ladylike pursuits—reading, writing, needlework—but evading personal questions. Of course, the most notorious fact about her wasn't her penmanship, but her pregnancy. When she gave birth to a stillborn child, her husband hadn't yet arrived. Her Danvers friends

wished to send for her family; instead, she burned any letters that might lead to her identification before dying two weeks later, on July 25, of complications from childbirth. She was thirty-six years old. On her death, a notice was placed in the local newspaper, asking for help in identifying the mysterious stranger. The public's curiosity was aroused as other papers throughout New England and as far south as Charleston, South Carolina, reprinted the item and other bits of commentary on her case. These included a much-reprinted excerpt of a letter from the Reverend Jeremy Belknap in Boston—printed anonymously—to the physician Benjamin Rush in Philadelphia suggesting that the story might make a powerful "moral lecture for young Ladies" (see page 303 in this volume). Soon, Mrs. Walker was unmasked as Elizabeth Whitman, and the scandal began: who was Elizabeth Whitman and why was she hiding in Danvers?

The question persists to this day. Providing details about the "real" Elizabeth Whitman is particularly difficult beyond her basic genealogy: what scant writings exist about her are invariably tainted by the knowledge of her fate, dying alone, seemingly abandoned by her lover. Those who fell into what we might call the Belknap camp derided her as coquettish, grasping, and manipulative; those with a more romantic bent memorialized Whitman as above average in beauty, intellectually and poetically gifted. The slim record of evidence suggests the latter is probably more accurate, if exaggerated. As one family member recalled, "With all her impulse and love of social life she was the idol of her friends." Her few extant letters (see 269–300 in this volume) suggest a vibrant and generous woman, intellectually playful and well read. The idiosyncrasy of her spelling seems less a matter of lack of education and more a matter of the conventions of the time. Her father's house was said by a relative to boast a "rare library" that "was a centre for scholars and distinguished people." But she did not spend all her time or even most of it in the library: she frequently traveled to visit friends throughout New England for extended stays, probably to help defray her mother's expenses following her father's death in 1777. These friends included the daughters of Yale's president during the American Revolution, Ezra Stiles, young women who turned composing poetry into a household game when not entertaining a stream of Yale students (all male, of course) who were eager to impress female company. When Whitman was at home she, like the Stiles women, no doubt participated in the household economy, gardening and setting away stores for winter. Indeed, one reality of life in the Whitman family was constant thrift, the result of Elnathan's meager salary and the church's frequent tardiness in paying it. At the same time, the family's social status demanded they keep up appearances, creating a constant tension. And so Elizabeth might attend the Hartford

Dancing Academy, but she also knew how to make her own clothes. The family might commission paintings of various members, but they also sent their children to stay with others, reducing their own household costs. As Elnathan's own health faltered, there would have been more pressure on his daughters to marry for economic reasons, a pressure accelerated with his death. Elizabeth entertained multiple suitors in the 1770s and early 1780s and was engaged once to a young minister, Joseph Howe, who died in her father's home in 1775. Yet a decade after Elnathan Whitman's death, Elizabeth and her sisters were well on their way to being old maids when she embarked on a drastic course, one that would make her a subject of gossip and speculation for more than a hundred years.

What set tongues and moralists equally aflame was that despite having borne a child, she was definitely known not to be married. The public was transfixed. Soon writings attributed to her—from fragments of letters (some written in code) to poetic pronouncements on her own desperate situation—appeared in newspapers, alongside comments on her conduct and habits (See "The Elizabeth Whitman Paper Trail" on pages 302–07 of this volume). While her poetry and the circumstances of her death garnered sympathy from many, others imposed a less favorable reading. Belknap, who does not seem to have known her personally, wrote to Rush that "She was handsome genteel & sensible but vain & coquettish, a *great reader of Romances.* She refused two as good offers of Marriage as she deserved because she aspired to higher than a Clergyman's wife & having coqueted it till past her bloom, fell into criminal indulgencies, proved *enceinte* & then eloped." While Belknap's sources were misinformed on at least one count—her first fiancé had in fact died—this depiction of Whitman as a vain coquette would come to be the dominant one in public circulation, finding its way into the first American novel, William Hill Brown's *The Power of Sympathy,* early the next year (1789; see pages 307–14 of this volume). Whitman's story would inevitably be assigned a moral meaning.

When Hannah Webster Foster decided to fictionalize the story of Elizabeth Whitman via the figure of Eliza Wharton, she was intervening in an existing narrative. It's not surprising that she tread carefully: William Hill Brown had angered many in his Boston social circle when his novel exposed another recent neighborhood scandal. Foster, as the wife of a respectable minister, could not afford such controversy. And so she had to navigate the Whitman family's privacy—one evident concession being the novel's appearance only after the death of Elizabeth's mother in 1795. Likewise, Foster had to balance the feelings of Whitman's friends, who would not have appreciated a slanderous portrait, against the need to maintain the story's moral. If this were not enough, Foster also faced an audience

that was familiar with the story's major plot points. What we would now call a spoiler was common knowledge at the time: Foster's readers picked up the novel knowing not only that the heroine would die, but also where she would die, and how. Still, not unlike today, when celebrity scandals sell newspapers and magazines, what curious spectators wanted was more. In *The Coquette* Foster gives it to them, letter by letter, detail by detail, so that readers can participate in the unfolding of events, presuming to understand exactly how it happened.

Foster's decision to plot the novel in first-person letters would prove crucial to its popularity. Even though her work is fiction, she presents it in such a way that many readers, well into the next century, believed it was real. The marketing of the book furthers this: "A Novel: Founded on Fact" announces the title page, a claim reproduced in subsequent reviews, notices, and editions. Foster deliberately forwards this perception, including details that suggest she had some privileged access to Whitman or her friends. Notably, she opens the novel with a letter that corrects the most potent rumor circulating about Whitman: that she had declined offers of marriage in favor of coquetry. Instead, we learn, the first suitor of Eliza Wharton has died, nursed by her to the end, a case that parallels an actual episode in Whitman's life. Foster continues to use such tactics. For instance, Whitman's friends and family believed she was going to visit Henry and Anna Barrett Hill in Boston when she detoured to Danvers: the Hills lived in Boston on Summer Street; in the novel, they are refashioned as the Sumners. Other congruencies suggest that Foster had a more than passing acquaintance with someone who knew Whitman, though she clearly draws on the public paper trail as well. More insider allusions may be lost to us today. Given the degree of verisimilitude seemingly embedded in the text, it is probably not surprising that some readers of *The Coquette* presumed that Foster was related to Whitman; a few even trusted the letters were authentic. "Her correspondence as published," writes a reviewer as late as 1878, "point a moral and adorn a tale it were well our modern belle should heed." One early twentieth-century writer, Charles Bowles Knowlton, assumed that Anna Barrett Hill and Hannah Webster Foster had collaborated to produce the epitaph for Whitman's headstone, which was later reproduced, with subtle alterations, in Foster's novel. In reality, Foster's connection to Whitman was tenuous at best—they were related via John Foster by the marriage of two distant cousins—and her sources seem to have been points in the same gossip networks that ran up and down the coast.

While readers might attribute the novel's perceived authenticity to Foster's insider information, it is her convincing representation

of Eliza Wharton's struggle that makes *The Coquette* resonate as true. Many readers from 1797 to the present have found it difficult not to sympathize with the energetic Wharton when she expresses her frustration at being confined to houses filled with the sick, the dying, and the generally old. We feel for her when her friends urge her to marry a man she sees as boring and uptight. When Wharton follows the counsel of many an advice manual in assessing frankly what life would be like married to a particular suitor, in this case a minister—declaring "There are duties arising from the station, which I fear I should not be able to fulfill; cares and restraints to which I could not submit"—we nod compassionately. It's hard not to cheer Wharton when she argues her right to make her own decisions and imagines herself as free, invoking all of the recent Revolution's celebrated rhetoric. That it all comes to naught isn't the point; any alternative ending we imagine for Wharton doesn't look so bright either. As Foster shows us, a husband and babies aren't a guarantee of happiness. If anything, the fate of the novel's married women might make us regard Eliza Wharton as reasonably suspicious of marriage and maternity.

Modern criticism of Foster's novel frequently turns on the question of the degree to which Foster shows such sympathy for her heroine. Feminist critics have often pointed out that Wharton's dilemma is more complicated than simply choosing between virtue and vice: neither of her suitors seems ideal. Other critics, reading Foster as less than sympathetic to Eliza, read the novel as an indictment of licentiousness and luxury in the post-Revolutionary period, a case study of what happens when liberty is taken too far. It seems true that, if Foster displays definite sympathy to her heroine, she stops short of condoning her illicit actions. Indeed, she goes so far as to script a tearful admission of guilt and repentance by Wharton. This is important, as it imposes the moral of the narrative, without which the novel would lack any posture to respectability. It also ensures the heroine continues to be read as sympathetic. One charge that might be laid against Whitman is that there is no record of her expressing regret; instead, until the very end, she was, according to the first newspaper report of her death, "agreeable; her deportment, amiable and engaging; and though in a state of anxiety and suspense, she preserved a cheerfulness which seemed to be not the effect of instability, but of a firm and patient temperament." Foster paraphrases this report near the novel's close (see Letter LXXI, pages 126–28), but her emphasis on Wharton's penitence, though probably drawn from imagination, seems calculated to protect Whitman from her harshest critics. It also lends depth to the story's believability. With luck, most of us will get through life without ever having done something so utterly destructive to our own well being.

But some of us won't, or have narrowly escaped some supremely foolish action only to realize it after the fact, and for those this scene is a moment of instant recognition. Readers of the late eighteenth and early nineteenth centuries were no different. For young women, the seduction novel generally, and Eliza and Elizabeth more specifically, might serve as an additional reminder of the consequences. No one wants to be Eliza Wharton when she proclaims "my sun has set at noon"—meaning, essentially, my life as I know it is over, just when it should be at its peak.

Whether or not the novel is factually accurate is immaterial. For an inestimable number of readers it felt emotionally true, and that was what mattered. Because of this it seems irrelevant to what degree Foster was able to draw on actual details of Whitman's life; it is more important that many readers thought she did. Accordingly, a disproportionate number of surviving copies of the novel are annotated with the names of individuals believed—rightly or wrongly—to have inspired various characters. It is not just the Sumners who are "revealed": Reverend Haly is Joseph Howe (1747–1775), and Boyer is Joseph Buckminster (1751–1812), another of Whitman's ministerial suitors. Some readers cut and pasted relevant materials from newspapers into their volumes, including obituary notices for other Whitman family members; at least one reader sketched an image of the Bell Tavern where Whitman had died onto the novel's flyleaf, suggesting it had been used as a travel companion. Such activities were not confined to communion with the book itself. Inspired by Foster's novel, throughout the nineteenth century readers debated the identity of the father of Elizabeth Whitman's child, one of the few characters for whom a "real-life" counterpart could not be immediately verified—though her cousin Pierpont Edwards, the youngest son of Jonathan Edwards, was a popular candidate by midcentury, probably due to his already profligate reputation. Some Hartford gossips whispered that Jeremiah Wadsworth, commissary general during the Revolution, was her lover. Others had additional "pet candidates": Joel Barlow, Aaron Burr, a local Hartford miller by the name of Burt, and James Watson, later a U.S. senator, were all proposed over the course of the next century. Select readers and some residents of Danvers maintained a residual belief in Whitman's claims to have been married; some accounts in travel books, magazines, and even a few ostensibly nonfiction accounts of the case mounted a tradition in explicit contention with Foster's seduction tale.

Regardless of the identity of her suitor or her marital state, Whitman's faithfulness to her lover, even when he didn't arrive, protecting his name to her death, was seen as a sign of her fidelity. Accordingly, her grave became a site of pilgrimage where courting couples might pledge their love. Men and women alike wept over it, and at least

one poet, John Patch, wrote an ode to it. Thus Whitman/Wharton became an indigenous American folk hero, her gravestone turned into relics, chipped away by romantic pilgrims—by midcentury it had already been substantially reduced. Nineteenth-century tour guides advertised it as an attraction, while newspaper articles continued to revisit her story, collapsing Whitman and Wharton with impunity and even claiming that she inspired Hawthorne's *The Scarlet Letter*. Other items associated with Whitman were treasured and exhibited, from scraps of wallpaper and a dress, to a dance card, to the inventory of items taken at her death, to artifacts recovered at the demolition of the Bell—including the doorstep itself. Those who undertook such acts of romantic preservation weren't simply positioning themselves as active readers of *The Coquette*; rather they became participants in the novel, agents in its world. None of this would have happened without the currency bestowed on Whitman's story by Foster's novel. With each republication, both Wharton and Whitman were recirculated, reinscribed, and reintroduced into American popular culture. *The Coquette* even inspired other literary efforts. In 1802, J. Horatio Nichols published a play, *The New England Coquette*, clearly calculated to profit on the success of Foster's novel. In 1851, an enterprising magazine editor published a sequel, *Clara Wharton*. These unauthorized works testify to readers' affection for Eliza Wharton in capitalizing on their desire to see her death avenged; both works scripted an extended repentance for her suitor, as well as a suitable punishment for him—something absent from *The Coquette*.

The success of Foster's novel was, in some ways, its own undoing. Notably, it introduced a conundrum for other readers via the Wharton/Whitman figure in that some found Wharton so sympathetic that they refused to believe Whitman guilty of the sexual fall that first brought her to the public's attention. This view retained currency well into the late nineteenth and early twentieth centuries, as evidenced in book-length studies on the topic by Caroline Wells Healey Dall (1875) and Charles Knowles Bolton (1912). Dall accused Foster of being an "unprincipled woman" with a "warm imagination" and positioned herself in opposition to the novel: "I have been trying all my life to defend the purity of Elizabeth Whitman," she wrote in 1907. In the process of defending Whitman, Dall's own principles were questionable, as she manipulated evidence, rewriting some of Whitman's surviving letters for publication and possibly withholding others. Claiming she had succeeded in uncovering new evidence that would clear Whitman's name—a family tradition that suggested Whitman had indeed been married—Dall asserted: "My work is done."

Ironically, Dall and Bolton accused Foster of portraying Whitman negatively by representing her as guilty, eliding the degree to which Foster herself had created a sympathetic heroine. Likewise, they ignore the degree to which public sympathy for Whitman had long been grounded in Foster's novel, though readers like Dall made more of Whitman's poetic abilities than Foster did. That these competing traditions continue to be interwoven is evident in Danvers, where Whitman died, and where in the early twenty-first century citywide book clubs read *The Coquette*, amateur historians continue to debate the identity of Whitman's seducer, and the local historical society has erected a new gravestone—which names Whitman as "Heroine of *The Coquette*"—beside the decimated original.

It might seem odd that the woman who wrote *The Coquette*, a book that has inspired such passion, would author *The Boarding School* a year later. Whereas *The Coquette* invites intense sympathy with an individual, *The Boarding School* diffuses our attention among a number of young women. While *The Coquette* proffers a rake we can despise, *The Boarding School* doesn't introduce such characters at all. And even as *The Coquette* gives us an independent Eliza, who takes action without consulting her friends, *The Boarding School* provides a network of women who see themselves as accountable to the whole. One is the story of an individual in tension with a community; the other is a novel about a community striving for harmony, as the name of the school—Harmony Grove—suggests. What binds these novels together, aside from a common author, is their concern with female propriety in post-Revolutionary America. While the Revolution was celebrated for emancipating Americans from British tyranny, some feared the very arguments that undergirded it—against unjust exercises of power and limitations on personal freedoms— might be taken up by others within the new nation for the purposes of rebellion. Of particular concern was the possibility that women might be motivated to demand concessions. Although Abigail Adams famously counseled her husband to "Remember the ladies," for if ignored "we are determined to foment a Rebellion," the founding fathers moved to counter expressions of female independence. At its most ridiculous, the question of women's political status in the new republic played out in early national debates about currency design: the loose hair of Lady Liberty was judged "too convulsive" and was accordingly tied back. As the artist, Gilbert Stuart, commented, "Liberty on the other coins had run mad. . . . We will bind it up and thus render her a steady matron." Even as women might wish to experience personal freedom, such liberties were condoned only insofar as they would support the national desire for stable wives and mothers.

*The Coquette* and *The Boarding School* represent two currents in the era: a desire for women to participate in the promise and opportunities of the new nation, and the need to do so in a way that did not shift a gendered status quo—one that defined women first and foremost as virtuous wives, mothers, and daughters. Certainly, in penning such novels, Foster herself was navigating exactly this terrain, entering into a print sphere deemed masculine and intervening in public debates about women's learning, their place in the nation, and the right to speak authoritatively. Modern readers tend to forget that women who published in the late eighteenth century might be deemed morally suspect. We tend to assume that educating women—white middle- and upper-class women at least—was perceived as a universal good in the nation. True, many leading male citizens, like Benjamin Rush, supported female education, but there was no agreed-upon standard as to what that might mean. Some felt it was enough for women to be able to read the Christian Bible and keep household accounts; on the other end of the spectrum were those perceived radicals, avid readers of Mary Wollstonecraft, who advocated for equality in access to learning. In *The Boarding School*, Foster reveals herself to be somewhere in between, promoting the practical acquisition of domestic skills as well as familiarity with a variety of historical, philosophical, religious, and poetic tomes—albeit for the purpose of assisting in self-reflection on one's conduct and character. Conduct, she believes, cannot be sacrificed to character. However, in making this argument, Foster reveals her own extensive learning through a variety of quotes and allusions, which some might have deemed promiscuous at the time, even if deployed in the cause of advocating female virtue or advising women (and men) what not to read. To a certain extent, such learning is justified in the figure of an enterprising widow who wishes to support her own daughters honestly and ensure their financial future. But Foster was no widow writing out of necessity; she was a well-off wife and mother. It is not surprising that she chose to publish anonymously, asserting her right to do so according to her status: "A Lady of Massachusetts." Anonymity not only shielded her from criticism of her novels, but also protected her reputation from charges of vanity and impropriety.

Oddly, if Foster's *Coquette* ensured the preservation of stories associated with Whitman, the practice of publishing anonymously meant that Foster lacked the same reputation, and many materials relating to her own life have been lost or were destroyed by her. Little is known about Hannah Webster Foster. We know her mother was Hannah Wainwright, the daughter of Captain John Wainwright, and her father, Grant Webster, a Boston moneylender and

commission merchant. Webster epitomized the possibilities of eighteenth-century America: the son of a mariner, he attended Harvard and rose to a position of financial prominence, first in Haverhill then later in Salisbury, Massachusetts. Hannah was born either there or in nearby Amesbury in September 1758. When Hannah was not quite seven, her mother died, and it has been suggested (though without firm foundation) that she was then sent to boarding school. Whatever the case, Hannah acquired an education and eventually established herself in the literary circles of Boston, where her father had relocated in the early 1760s. Not a coquette, she was certainly something of a belle, as her granddaughter recounted in the 1870s: "she was quite celebrated as a young lady, for her wit as well as beauty, she took great interest in politics, and her articles in the papers attracted the attention of many gentlemen." While no such articles have been identified, she could very well have published anonymously, following conventions of a gendered print sphere that subordinated individual aggrandizement to communal order. Without specific evidence, modern scholars have often assumed and asserted that Foster wrote for contemporary periodicals. The famed Mercy Otis Warren, who also published at the same time, was reluctant to have her authorship of works known, though she and others, including the poet Sarah Wentworth Morton, issued volumes under their own names in the 1790s.

In 1785, Hannah Webster married the "mild-eyed" Reverend John Foster, a graduate of Dartmouth and the newly appointed minister at Brighton, Massachusetts, near Boston. By all accounts, the young bride—described in the marriage announcement as "a young lady of superior sence [sic] and merit"—received a warm welcome in her new community, "the whole parish going out to meet them when they came from their bridal, escorting them home with much ceremony." Foster was busy over the next dozen years, bearing six children, overseeing the building of a new home, and fulfilling the duties of a minister's wife. Yet, she managed to maintain an active intellectual profile, devouring the latest publications New England had to offer, as references in her writings demonstrate.

Evidence suggests that Foster's novels were composed and published in a relatively short period. From comments on current events in *The Boarding School* we learn, for instance, that Foster was writing in April 1798; just over two months later the work was being typeset. How she found time to write, given her domestic commitments, is unknown. Given its episodic and fragmentary nature, the novel's epistolary format may have been well-suited to composing in stolen moments. Still, the original poetic compositions Foster included in *The Boarding School* clearly required reflection and revision, something a busy mother was probably hard pressed to

find. It is possible she used the opportunity of the novel to include verse she had written before, but not published.

Foster appears to have applied the lessons she advocated in *The Boarding School* to the rearing of her own children; her daughters, in their own careers as writers and editors, remembered their youth in idyllic terms. While domestic help was not beyond Foster's reach, especially as she appears to have inherited substantial wealth from her father, the children assisted in various household tasks. The girls had additional time to devote to the cultivation of the flowering shrubs and plants that surrounded their impressive home. The Foster household was also known for its large collection of books, and neighborhood children were encouraged to use it as a lending library. As Foster's children aged, it is likely that she took an active interest in their education, and local schoolteachers are said to have been somewhat in awe of her. Three of Foster's daughters became writers, while her sons openly supported female education, as is evident in the opportunities they eventually afforded their own daughters. Yet Foster's commitment to education extended beyond her own family. According to Boston folklore, she became the patron of an apprentice papermaker, Phineas Adams, enabling him to enter Harvard at the age of twenty. Following Adams's graduation in 1801, he founded and edited *The Monthly Anthology or Magazine of Polite Literature*, later the *North American Review*. Though anonymous authorship is difficult to attribute with any certainty, tradition holds that Adams enlisted Foster as an anonymous contributor to the magazine. That it is Hannah Webster Foster and not her husband who is remembered as Adams's patron demonstrates not just that she had the power to dispose of her income as she chose, but also that her reputation as a patron of literary and intellectual culture persisted for decades.

Despite her literary ties to nearby Boston, Foster's life centered on Brighton, and in turn she was at its center. In Brighton's 1929 centenary celebrations, Foster's influence and presence were recalled as important to the founding of the Ladies Association of the First Parish Church of Brighton, the first such association in the state. As John Foster was initially the town's only minister, he and his wife were "situated in the high life" according to one chronicler, with a perceived preference for socializing among local gentry. When they did venture outside of their circle, such visits might produce substantial anxiety; the daughter of one parishioner recounts her family spending at least a week preparing for a call. The perception of arrogance and aristocratic pretensions on the part of the Fosters was enhanced by the "elaborate mansion" they built and occupied as of 1810, implying Foster's motivation for writing was more personal than financial. That the Fosters were considered emotionally distant

by some parishioners would later become a source of contention, cited in the division of the church membership.

While parishioners might have wished for a more humble minister and wife, Hannah Webster Foster perhaps unsurprisingly preferred to socialize with those who shared a similar educational background, and by extension, cultural and literary interests. As the wife of a minister, Foster would not have been in a position to defend herself openly against charges of elitism or arrogance. Any telltale signs of dissatisfaction with her situation might be found in the confession of *The Coquette*'s Eliza Wharton who, in considering a marriage proposal from a minister, admits her lack of enthusiasm for "forming a connection, which must confine me to the duties of domestic life, and make me dependent for happiness, perhaps too, for subsistence, upon a class of people, who will claim the right of scrutinizing every part of my conduct." Foster knew firsthand what that meant.

Following her husband's death in September 1829, Foster relocated to Montreal, where two of her daughters, Eliza Lanesford Cushing and Harriet Vaughn Cheney, then resided, alongside another daughter's widower and their children. As novelists themselves, contributors to Canada's premier cultural magazine, the *Literary Garland*, and the editors of the *Snow Drop*, a magazine for children, the sisters were beacons of Montreal's literary life. A family member describes their shared home as "the centre of intellectual activity" and its residents as "diligent readers of the best books. Often one of them would read aloud, and then they would fall into animated conversation as to the quality of the thought and the characteristics of the author. . . . So often the talk became a spirited discussion of free, independent, active minds." Foster ended her life amid a community of intelligent, engaged women, one she herself had facilitated, and which bore more than a passing resemblance to *The Boarding School*'s Harmony Grove. It was there she died on April 17, 1840, at the age of eighty-one.

Foster's legacy as an author is evident in a generation and more of professional female writers she inspired and, in some cases, nurtured. They, in turn, passed down her lessons for generations more, asserting over and over again women's competency as writers, editors, and even publishers. If Foster had not destroyed her own papers like Whitman, we might know even more about her and those indebted to her for inspiration as well as practical guidance. Instead, she retained her anonymity until the end, her name finally appearing on *The Coquette* only after her death. Yet the success and power of her novels draws us back to her for what she accomplished. *The Coquette* and *The Boarding School* provide compelling portraits of women at the turn of the nineteenth century as they traverse new

social and political territory, attempt to articulate their own ambitions, and search for personal fulfillment even as currents of thought, social mores, and movements surge around them. Some of those currents are apparent to the heroines; others we can see only in hindsight. It is because Foster manages to capture it all, from convictions to uncertainties, with remarkable power, that the novels retain their force more than two centuries later.

This Norton Critical Edition contains materials selected to enhance an understanding of the period in which the novels were written, the contexts in which they were produced, the real-life events that inspired them, and recent critical appraisals. Of significant import are new and corrected transcriptions of Elizabeth Whitman's letters to Joel Barlow and his wife Ruth, allowing readers to draw comparisons between Foster's rendering of female voices in both novels and an actual example of the period (from the prototype of one novel's heroine, no less). An inventory of the items found in Whitman's room at her death invites readers to reflect on what life was like for a middle-class woman of the period, if this is the sum total of her effects. Images of Eliza Wharton might provoke consideration of how she was perceived over time, as she becomes less a moralizing example and more a romantic heroine. Selections from popular representations of Whitman, as well as unauthorized sequels to *The Coquette*, also force us to think about shifting responses and the nature of readers' desires. The same can be said of the contemporary critical pieces we have selected, which position themselves variously to the novels, staking diverse and sometimes contradictory claims about their function, their readers, their politics, and their reception. Most of these pieces were written without recourse to the original documents we include, and some are worth revisiting in light of these and other materials. Foster's work may be fixed on the page, but as the example of Elizabeth Whitman shows us, interpretation is open, fluid, and always up for discussion.

In conducting the research for such a volume and shepherding it through the publication process, inevitable debts have accrued. We are particularly thankful to Carol Bemis and Rivka Genesen at W. W. Norton. William Marchione deserves thanks for sharing primary source research into local perceptions of the Fosters. In New York, Blevin Shelnutt provided research assistance and help preparing materials for the manuscript. Librarians at the Huntington Library, the Massachusetts Historical Society, the Boston Public Library, the Peabody Essex Museum, the Andover-Harvard Theological Library, the American Antiquarian Society, Fales Library and Special Collections at NYU, the Beinecke Library at Yale, and

the Houghton Library at Harvard all provided invaluable assistance in tracing and accessing primary documents and other materials. The staff of the Peabody Historical Society and Museum was particularly kind in letting Jennifer rummage through their closets. As always, the interlibrary loan departments of our individual institutions exhibited notable resilience and dedication. A grant from the Social Science and Humanities Resource Council of Canada (SSHRC) facilitated some of the primary source research undertaken (Harris), as did fellowship assistance from the Massachusetts Historical Society, the American Society for Eighteenth-Century Studies, the Houghton Library, and the Huntington Library (Waterman). Finally, we thank our families for their patient support: Jennifer thanks Daniel Vogel and Emil Harris Vogel, and Bryan thanks Charlie, Molly, and Anna Waterman, and especially Stephanie Smith-Waterman.

# A Note on the Texts

This Norton Critical Edition uses the first edition of each of Foster's novels as its copy texts. *The Coquette* was printed in Boston by Samuel Etheridge for Ebenezer Larkin in 1797. *The Boarding School* was published in Boston by Isaiah Thomas and Ebenezer Andrews in 1798. For both novels we have retained original spelling, punctuation, and usage, including the variant spellings for Laurence/Lawrence in *The Coquette* and some archaic uses of quotation marks. We have silently corrected a small number of obvious printer's errors (inverted type, missing letters, etc.) and have eliminated the use of the long "s" that was still in use at the end of the eighteenth century.

The Texts of
# THE COQUETTE
and
# THE BOARDING SCHOOL

THE

COQUETTE;

OR, THE

HISTORY OF ELIZA WHARTON;

A

N O V E L;

FOUNDED ON FACT.

By a *LADY of* MASSACHUSETTS.

[Hannah Foster]

Boston :

PRINTED BY SAMUEL ETHERIDGE,
FOR E. LARKIN,
No. 47, CORNHILL.

1797.

# L  E  T  T  E  R    I.

TO MISS LUCY FREEMAN.[1]

*NEW-HAVEN.*

An unusual sensation possesses my breast; a sensation, which I once thought could never pervade it on any occasion whatever. It is *pleasure;* pleasure, my dear Lucy, on leaving my paternal roof! Could you have believed that the darling child of an indulgent and dearly beloved mother would feel a gleam of joy at leaving her? but so it is. The melancholy, the gloom, the condolence, which surrounded me for a month after the death of Mr. Haly,[2] had depressed my spirits, and palled[3] every enjoyment of life. Mr. Haly was a man of worth; a man of real and substantial merit. He is therefore deeply, and justly regreted by *his* friends; he was chosen to be a future guardian, and companion for me, and was, therefore, beloved by *mine.* As their choice; as a good man, and a faithful friend, I esteemed him. But no one acquainted with the disparity of our tempers and dispositions, our views and designs, can suppose my heart much engaged in the alliance. Both nature and education had instilled into my mind an implicit obedience to the will and desires of my parents. To them, of course, I sacrificed my fancy in this affair; determined that my reason should concur with theirs; and on that to risk my future happiness. I was the more encouraged, as I saw, from our first acquaintance, his declining health; and expected, that the event would prove as it has. Think not, however, that I rejoice in his death. No; far be it from me; for though I believe that I never felt the passion of love for Mr. Haly; yet a habit of conversing with him, of hearing daily the most virtuous, tender, and affectionate sentiments from his lips, inspired emotions of the sincerest friendship, and esteem.

He is gone. His fate is unalterably, and I trust, happily fixed. He lived the life, and died the death of the righteous. O that my last end may be like his! This event will, I hope, make a suitable and abiding impression upon my mind; teach me the fading nature of all sublunary[4] enjoyments, and the little dependence which is to be placed on earthly felicity. Whose situation was more agreeable; whose prospects more flattering, than Mr. Haly's? Social, domestic,

---

1. Believed by nineteenth-century readers to be based on Anna Barrett (1739–1822), who married Henry Hill (1737–1828) of Boston. Portraits of the Hills by John Singleton Copley survive. His portrait of Mrs. Hill is on the cover of this Norton Critical Edition.
2. Believed to be based on the Reverend Joseph Howe (1747–1775), a suitor of Elizabeth Whitman's, who died while staying with the Whitman family.
3. Paled, decreased in sharpness.
4. Between the earth and moon; earthly.

and connubial[5] joys were fondly anticipated, and friends, and fortune seemed ready to crown every wish! Yet animated by still brighter hopes, he cheerfully bid them all adieu. In conversation with me, but a few days before his exit; "There is" said he, "but one link in the chain of life, undissevered;[6] that, my dear Eliza, is my attachment to you. But God is wise and good in all his ways; and in this, as in all other respects, I would cheerfully say, His will be done."

You, my friend, were witness to the concluding scene; and therefore, I need not describe it.

I shall only add, on the subject, that if I have wisdom and prudence to follow his advice and example; if his prayers for my temporal and eternal welfare be heard and answered, I shall be happy indeed.

The disposition of mind, which I now feel, I wish to cultivate. Calm, placid, and serene; thoughtful of my duty, and benevolent to all around me, I wish for no other connection than that of friendship,

This Letter is all egotism, I have even neglected to mention the respectable, and happy friends, with whom I reside; but will do it in my next. Write soon, and often; and believe me sincerely yours,

<div align="right">ELIZA WHARTON.[7]</div>

# L  E  T  T  E  R   II.

## TO THE SAME.

<div align="right">*NEW-HAVEN.*</div>

Time, which effaces every occasional impression,[1] I find gradually dispelling the pleasing pensiveness,[2] which the melancholy event, the subject of my last, had diffused over my mind. Naturally cheerful, volatile, and unreflecting, the opposite disposition, I have found to contain sources of enjoyment, which I was before unconscious of possessing.

My friends, here, are the picture of conjugal[3] felicity. The situation is delightful. The visiting parties perfectly agreeable. Every thing tends to facilitate the return of my accustomed vivacity. I have written to my mother, and received an answer. She praises my fortitude,

---

5. Relating to marriage.
6. Not separated.
7. A fictional version of Elizabeth Whitman (1752–1788).
1. This phrase echoes a familiar gravestone inscription from the era.
2. Dwelling on thoughts, potentially tinged with sadness.
3. Relating to marriage.

and admires the philosophy which I have exerted, under, what she calls, my heavy bereavement.[4] Poor woman! She little thinks that my heart was untouched; and when that is unaffected, other sentiments and passions make but a transient impression. I have been, for a month or two, excluded from the gay world; and, indeed, fancied myself soaring above it. It is now that I begin to descend, and find my natural propensity for mixing in the busy scenes and active pleasures of life returning. I have received your letter; your moral lecture rather; and be assured, my dear, your monitorial lessons and advice shall be attended to. I believe I shall never again resume those airs, which you term *coquettish*,[5] but which I think deserve a softer appellation; as they proceed from an innocent heart, and are the effusions of a youthful, and cheerful mind. We are all envited to spend the day, to morrow, at Col. Farington's,[6] who has an elegant seat in this neighbourhood. Both he and his Lady are strangers to me; but the friends, by whom I am introduced, will procure me a welcome reception. Adieu.

ELIZA WHARTON.

# L  E  T  T  E  R  III.

## TO THE SAME.

*NEW-HAVEN.*

Is it time for me to talk again of conquests? or must I only enjoy them in silence? I must write to you the impulses of my mind; or I must not write at all. You are not so morose, as to wish me to become a nun, would our country, and religion allow it. I ventured yesterday to throw aside the habiliments[1] of mourning, and to array myself in those more adapted to my taste. We arrived at Col. Farington's about one o'clock. The Col. handed me out of the carriage, and introduced me to a large company assembled in the Hall. My name was pronounced with an *emphasis*; and I was received with the most flattering tokens of respect. When we were summoned to dinner, a young gentleman in a clerical dress offered me his hand, and led me to a table furnished with an elegant, and sumptuous repast,[2] with more

---

4. Being deprived of something; grief.
5. Flirting with and arousing the feelings of men without the intent of reciprocating their attentions.
6. The military title suggests he served in the American Revolutionary War (1775–83).
1. Forms, dress.
2. A splendid meal.

gallantry,[3] and address than commonly fall to the share of students. He sat opposite me at table; and whenever I raised my eye, it caught his. The ease, and politeness of his manners, with his particular attention to me, raised my curiosity, and induced me to ask Mrs. Laiton who he was? She told me that his name was Boyer;[4] that he was descended from a worthy family; had passed with honor and applause through the university where he was educated; had since studied divinity with success; and now had a call to settle as a minister in one of the first parishes in a neighbouring state.

The gates of a spacious garden were thrown open, at this instant; and I accepted with avidity an invitation to walk in it. Mirth, and hilarity prevailed, and the moments fled on downy wings; while we traced the beauties of art and nature, so liberally displayed, and so happily blended in this delightful retreat. An enthusiastic admirer of scenes like these, I had rambled[5] some way from the company, when I was followed by Mrs. Laiton to offer her condolence on the supposed loss, which I had sustained, in the death of Mr. Haly. My heart rose against the woman, so ignorant of human nature, as to think such conversation acceptable at such a time. I made her little reply, and waved the subject, though I could not immediately dispel the gloom which it excited.

The absurdity of a custom, authorising people at a first interview to revive the idea of griefs, which time has lulled; perhaps obliterated, is intolerable. To have our enjoyments arrested by the empty compliments of unthinking persons, for no other reason, than a compliance with fashion is to be treated in a manner, which the laws of humanity forbid.

We were soon joined by the gentlemen, who each selected his partner, and the walk was prolonged.

Mr. Boyer offered me his arm, which I gladly accepted; happy to be relieved from the impertinence of my female companion. We returned to tea, after which the ladies sung, and played by turns on the Piano Forte;[6] while some of the gentlemen accompanied with the flute, the clarinet, and the violin, forming in the whole a very decent concert. An elegant supper, and half an hour's conversation after it, closed the evening; when we returned home, delighted with our entertainment and pleased with ourselves and each other. My imagination is so impressed with the festive scenes of the day, that Morpheus[7] waves his ebon-wand in vain. The evening is fine beyond the

3. Exaggerated chivalry.
4. Believed by nineteenth-century readers to be based on the Reverend Joseph Buckminster (1751–1812), a Yale tutor and suitor of Whitman's after Reverend Howe's death.
5. Walked without definite route or aim, excepting pleasure.
6. Piano.
7. Greek god of dreams.

power of description! all nature is serene and harmonious;[8] in per-
fect unison with my present disposition of mind. I have been taking
a retrospect of my past life; and a few juvenile follies[9] excepted,
which I trust the recording angel has blotted out with the tear of
charity,[1] find an approving conscience, and a heart at ease. Fortune,
indeed, has not been very liberal of her gifts to me; but I presume on
a large stock in the bank of friendship, which, united with health and
innocence, give me some pleasing anticipations of future felicity.

Whatever my fate may be, I shall always continue your

ELIZA WHARTON.

# L E T T E R  IV.

### TO MR. SELBY.

*NEW HAVEN.*

You ask me, my friend, whether I am in pursuit of truth, or a lady?
I answer, both. I hope and trust they are united; and really expect
to find truth and the virtues and graces besides in a fair form. If you
mean by the first part of your question whether I am searching into
the sublimer doctrines of religion? To these I would by no means be
inattentive; but to be honest, my studies of that kind have been very
much interrupted of late. The respectable circle of acquaintances
with which I am honored here, has rendered my visits very frequent
and numerous. In one of these I was introduced to Miss Eliza Whar-
ton; a young lady whose elegant person, accomplished mind, and
polished manners have been much celebrated. Her fame has often
reached me; but, as the queen of Sheba said to Solomon, the half
was not told me.[1] You will think, that I talk in the style of a lover. I
confess it, nor am I ashamed to rank myself among the professed
admirers of this lovely fair one. I am in no danger, however, of
becoming an enthusiastic devotee. No, I mean to act upon just and
rational principles.[2] Expecting soon to settle in an eligible situation,
if such a companion as I am persuaded she will make me, may fall to
my lot, I shall deem myself as happy as this state of imperfection will
admit. She is now resident at Gen. Richman's. The general and his

8. A familiar construction or cliché in writing of the period.
9. Foolish actions.
1. Cf. 1 Peter 4:8 (King James Version): And above all things have fervent charity among
   yourselves: for charity shall cover the multitude of sins.
1. In the Biblical story (1 Kings 10:7), the Queen of Sheba had heard wondrous things
   about Solomon's wisdom and wealth, but on meeting him she realized the "half was not
   told," that they exceeded accounts.
2. I.e., to choose reason over emotion.

lady are her particular friends. They are warm in her praises. They tell me, however, that she is naturally of a gay disposition. No matter for that; it is an agreeable quality, where there is discretion sufficient for its regulation. A cheerful friend, much more a cheerful wife is peculiarly necessary to a person of a studious and sedentary life. They dispel the gloom of retirement, and exhilerate the spirits depressed by intense application. She was formerly addressed by the late Mr. Haly of Boston. He was not, it seems, the man of her choice; but her parents were extremely partial to him, and wished the connection to take place. She, like a dutiful child, sacrificed her own inclination to their pleasure, so far as to acquiesce in his visits. This she more easily accomplished, as his health, which declined from their first acquaintance, led her to suppose, as the event has proved, that he would not live to enter into any lasting engagements. Her father, who died some months before him, invited him to reside at his house, for the benefit of a change of air, agreeably to the advice of his physicians. She attended him during his last illness, with all the care and assiduity of a nurse;[3] and with all the sympathising tenderness of a sister.

I have had several opportunities of conversing with her. She discovers[4] an elevated mind, a ready apprehension,[5] and an accurate knowledge of the various subjects which have been brought into view. I have not yet introduced the favorite subject of my heart. Indeed she seems studiously to avoid noticing any expression which leads towards it. But she must hear it soon. I am sure of the favor and interest of the friends with whom she resides. They have promised to speak previously in my behalf. I am to call as if accidentally this afternoon, just as they are to ride abroad. They are to refer me to Miss Wharton for entertainment, till their return. What a delightful opportunity for my purpose! I am counting the hours, nay, the very moments. Adieu. You shall soon hear again from your most obedient,

J. BOYER.

3. A common phrase of the period. "Assiduity": attentive care.
4. Displays, exhibits.
5. Quickness in grasping ideas.

# L E T T E R   V.

TO MISS LUCY FREEMAN.

*NEW-HAVEN.*

These bewitching charms of mine have a tendency to keep my mind in a state of perturbation.[1] I am so pestered with these admirers; not that I am so very handsome neither; But I dont know how it is, I am certainly very much the taste of the other sex. Followed, flattered, and caressed; I have cards and compliments in profusion. But I must try to be serious; for I have, alas! one serious lover. As I promised you to be particular in my writing, I suppose I must proceed methodically. Yesterday we had a party to dine. Mr. Boyer was of the number. His attention was immediately engrossed; and I soon perceived that every word, every action, and every look was studied to gain my approbation. As he sat next me at dinner, his assiduity and politeness were pleasing; and as we walked together afterwards, his conversation was improving. Mine was sentimental and sedate; perfectly adapted to the taste of my gallant.[2] Nothing, however, was said particularly expressive of his apparent wishes. I studiously avoided every kind of discourse which might lead to this topic. I wish not for a declaration from any one, especially from one whom I could not repulse and do not intend to encourage at present. His conversation, so similar to what I had often heard from a similar character, brought a deceased friend to mind, and rendered me somewhat pensive. I retired directly after supper. Mr. Boyer had just taken leave.

Mrs. Richman came into my chamber as she was passing to her own. Excuse my intrusion, Eliza, said she; I thought I would just step in and ask you if you have passed a pleasant day?

Perfectly so, madam; and I have now retired to protract the enjoyment by recollection. What, my dear, is your opinion of our favorite Mr. Boyer? Declaring him your favorite, madam, is sufficient to render me partial to him. But to be frank, independent of that, I think him an agreeable man. Your heart, I presume, is now free? Yes, and I hope it will long remain so. Your friends, my dear, solicitous for your welfare, wish to see you suitably and agreeably connected.[3] I hope my friends will never again interpose in my concerns of that nature. You, madam, who have ever known my heart, are sensible, that had the Almighty spared life, in a certain instance, I must have sacrificed my own happiness, or incurred their censure. I am young,

---

1. Mental agitation.
2. A man of fashion and pleasure, particularly attentive to women; a flatterer.
3. Married to an equal of her choice. Mrs. Richman wishes her not to become a spinster, considered an unattractive fate.

gay, volatile. A melancholy event has lately extricated me from those shackles, which parental authority had imposed on my mind. Let me then enjoy that freedom[4] which I so highly prize. Let me have opportunity, unbiassed by opinion, to gratify my natural disposition in a participation of those pleasures which youth and innocence afford. Of such pleasures, no one, my dear, would wish to deprive you. But beware, Eliza!—Though strowed[5] with flowers, when contemplated by your lively imagination, it is, after all, a slippery, thorny path. The round of fashionable dissipation[6] is dangerous. A phantom is often pursued, which leaves its deluded votary the real form of wretchedness. She spoke with an emphasis, and taking up her candle, wished me a good night. I had not power to return the compliment. Something seemingly prophetic in her looks and expressions, cast a momentary gloom upon my mind! But I despise those contracted ideas which confine virtue to a cell. I have no notion of becoming a recluse. Mrs. Richman has ever been a beloved friend of mine; yet I always thought her rather prudish. Adieu,

ELIZA WHARTON.

# L  E  T  T  E  R   VI.

TO THE SAME.

*NEW-HAVEN.*

I had scarcely seated myself at the breakfast table this morning, when a servant entered with a card of invitation from Major Sanford, requesting the happiness of my hand this evening, at a ball, given by Mr. Atkins, about three miles from this. I shewed the billet[1] to Mrs. Richman, saying, I have not much acquaintance with this gentleman, madam; but I suppose his character sufficiently respectable to warrant an affirmative answer. He is a gay man, my dear, to say no more, and such are the companions we wish, when we join a party avowedly formed for pleasure. I then stepped into my apartment, wrote an answer, and dispatched the servant. When I returned to the parlour, something disapprobating[2] appeared in the countenances of both my friends. I endeavored without seeming to observe, to dissipate it by chit chat; but they were better pleased with each other

---

4. In the context of the American Revolution, the invocation of freedom has additional resonance.
5. Strewn.
6. Waste of moral powers by overindulgence in pleasure.
1. A note or short letter.
2. Disapproving.

than with me; and soon rising, walked into the garden, and left me to amuse myself alone. My eyes followed them through the window. Happy pair, said I. Should it ever be my fate to wear the hymenial chain,[3] may I be thus united! The purest and most ardent affection, the greatest consonance of taste and disposition, and the most congenial virtue and wishes distinguish this lovely couple. Health and wealth, with every attendant blessing preside over their favored dwelling, and shed their benign influence without alloy. The consciousness of exciting their displeasure gave me pain; but I consoled myself with the idea that it was ill founded.

They should consider, said I, that they have no satisfaction to look for beyond each other.

There every enjoyment is centered; but I am a poor solitary being, who need some amusement beyond what I can supply myself. The mind, after being confined at home for a while, sends the imagination abroad in quest of new treasures, and the body may as well accompany it, for ought I can see.

General Richman and lady have ever appeared solicitous to promote my happiness since I have resided with them. They have urged my acceptance of invitations to join parties, though they have not been much themselves, of late; as Mrs. Richman's present circumstances[4] render her fond of retirement. What reason can be assigned for their apparent reluctance to this evening's entertainment is to me incomprehensible; but I shall apply the chymical[5] powers of friendship, and extract the secret from Mrs. Richman to morrow if not before. Adieu. I am now summoned to dinner, and after that shall be engaged in preparation till the wished for hour of hilarity and mirth engrosses every faculty of your

ELIZA WHARTON.

# L  E  T  T  E  R  VII.

TO MR. SELBY.

*NEW-HAVEN.*

Divines need not declaim,[1] nor philosophers expatiate on the disappointments a human life! Are they not legibly written on every page of our existence? Are they not predominantly prevalent over every period of our lives?

---

3. Firm ties of marriage; derived from Hymen, the Greek god of marriage.
4. I.e., she is pregnant.
5. Chemical. I.e., potent, and designed to elicit a specific effect as if by scientific principle.
1. Ministers need not criticize.

When I closed my last letter to you, my heart exulted in the pleasing anticipation of promised bliss; my wishes danced on the light breezes of hope, and my imagination dared to arrest the attention, and even claim a return of affection from the lovely Eliza Wharton! But imagination only, it has proved; and that dashed with the bitter ranklings of jealousy and suspicion.

But to resume my narrative. I reached the mansion of my friend about four. I was disagreeably struck with the appearance of a carriage at the door, as it raised an idea of company which might frustrate my plan; but still more disagreeable were my sensations, when, on entering the parlour, I found Major Sanford evidently in a waiting posture. I was very politely received; and when Eliza entered the room with a brilliance of appearance and gaiety of manner, which I had never before connected with her character, I rose, as did Major Sanford who offered his hand, and led her to a chair. I forgot to sit down again, but stood transfixed by the pangs of disappointment. Miss Wharton appeared somewhat confused; but soon resuming her vivacity, desired me to be seated; inquired after my health, and made some common place remarks on the weather. Then apologizing for leaving me, gave her hand again to Major Sanford, who had previously risen, and reminded her that the time and their engagements made it necessary to leave the good company; which, indeed, they both appeared very willing to do. General Richman and lady took every method in their power to remove my chagrin, and atone for the absence of my fair one, but ill did they succeed. They told me that Miss Wharton had not the most distant idea of my visiting there, this afternoon; much less of the design of my visit; that for some months together, she had been lately confined by the sickness of Mr. Haly, whom she attended during the whole of his last illness; which confinement had eventually increased her desire of indulging her natural disposition for gaiety. She had, however, they said, an excellent heart and reflecting mind, a great share of sensibility, and a temper peculiarly formed for the enjoyments of social life. But this gentleman, madam, who is her gallant this evening—is his character unexceptionable? Will a lady of delicacy associate with an immoral, not to say profligate[2] man? The rank and fortune of Major Sanford, said Mrs. Richman, procure him respect.

His specious[3] manners render him acceptable in public company; but I must own that he is not the person with whom I wish my cousin to be connected, even for a moment. She never consulted me so little on any subject as on that of his card this morning. Before I had time to object, she dismissed the servant; and I forbore to destroy her

2. Wasteful, ruinous, or destructive.
3. Seemingly convincing but in reality false.

expected happiness, by acquainting her with my disapprobation of her partner. Her omission was not design; it was juvenile indiscretion. We must, my dear sir, continued she, look with a candid eye on such excentricities. Faults, not foibles,[4] require the severity of censure. Far, madam, be it from me to censure any conduct, which as yet I have observed in Miss Wharton; she has too great an interest in my heart to admit of that.

We now went into more general conversation. Tea was served; and I soon after took leave. General Richman, however, insisted on my dining with him on Thursday, which I promised. And here I am again over head and ears in the hypo.[5] A disease, you will say, peculiar to students. I believe it peculiar to lovers; and with that class I must now rank myself, though I did not know, until this evening, that I was so much engaged as I find I really am. I knew, indeed, that I was extremely pleased with this amiable girl; that I was interested in her favor; that I was happier in her company than any where else, with innumerable other circumstances, which would have told me the truth, had I examined them. But be that as it may; I hope, and trust that I am, and ever shall be a reasonable creature; and not suffer my judgment to be misled by the operations of a blind passion.

I shall now lay aside this subject, endeavor to divest even my imagination of the charmer, and return until Thursday, to the contemplation of those truths and duties, which have a happy tendency to calm the jarring elements which compose our mortal frame. Adieu.

J. BOYER.

# L E T T E R  VIII.

TO MR. CHARLES DEIGHTON.

*NEW-HAVEN.*

We had an elegant ball, last night, Charles; and what is still more to the taste of your old friend, I had an elegant partner; one exactly calculated to please my fancy; gay, volatile, apparently thoughtless of every thing but present enjoyment. It was Miss Eliza Wharton, a young lady, whose agreeable person, polished manners, and refined talents, have rendered her the toast of the country around for these two years; though for half that time she has had a clerical[1] lover

4. Weaknesses.
5. An abbreviation of hypochondria, meaning depression.
1. Relating to the clergy or a clergyman.

imposed on her by her friends; for I am told it was not agreeable to her inclination. By this same clerical lover of hers, she was for several months confined as a nurse. But his death has happily relieved her, and she now returns to the world with redoubled lustre.[2] At present she is a visitor to Mrs. Richman, who is a relation. I first saw her on a party of pleasure at Mr. Frazier's where we walked, talked, sung, and danced together. I thought her cousin watched her with a jealous eye; for she is, you must know, a prude: and immaculate, more so than you or I must be the man who claims admission to her society. But I fancy this young lady is a coquette; and if so, I shall avenge my sex, by retaliating the mischiefs, she meditates against us. Not that I have any ill designs; but only to play off her own artillery, by using a little unmeaning gallantry. And let her beware of the consequences. A young clergyman came in at Gen. Richman's yesterday, while I was waiting for Eliza, who was much more cordially received by the general and his lady, than was your humble servant: but I lay that up.

When she entered the room, an air of mutual embarrassment was evident. The lady recovered her assurance much more easily than the gentleman. I am just going to ride, and shall make it in my way to call and inquire after the health of my dulcinea.[3] Therefore, adieu for the present.

<div style="text-align: right">PETER SANFORD.</div>

# L E T T E R   IX.

TO MISS LUCY FREEMAN.

<div style="text-align: right"><em>NEW-HAVEN.</em></div>

I am not so happy to day in the recollection of last evening's entertainment, as I was in the enjoyment.

The explanation which I promised you from Mrs. Richman yesterday, I could not obtain. When I went down to dinner, some friends of General Richman's had accidentally dropped in, which precluded all particular conversation. I retired soon to dress, and saw Mrs. Richman no more, till I was informed that Major Sanford waited for me. But I was surprised on going into the parlour to find Mr. Boyer there. I blushed and stammered; but I know not why; for certain I am, that I neither love nor fear the good man yet, whatever I may do some

---

2. Luminous or shining properties.
3. Dulcinea is the name given by Don Quixote to his mistress in Miguel de Cervantes's seventeenth-century romance of the same name; hence, a romantic name for a mistress or sweetheart.

future day. I would not be understood that I do not respect and esteem him; for I do both. But these are calm passions, which sooth rather than agitate the mind. It was not the consciousness of any impropriety of conduct; for I was far from feeling any. The entertainment for which I was prepared was such as virtue would not disapprove, and my gallant was a man of fortune, fashion, and for ought I knew, of unblemished character.

But Mr. Boyer was much more disconcerted than myself. Indeed he did not recover his philosophy while I staid. I believe, by some hints I have received since, that he had some particular views, in which he was disappointed.

Our ball had every charm which could render a ball delightful. My partner was all ease, politeness, and attention; and your friend was as much flattered and caressed as vanity itself could wish. We returned to General Richman's about two. Major Sanford asked leave to call and inquire after my health, this morning, and I am now expecting him. I rose to breakfast. The late hour of retiring to rest had not depressed, but rather exhilerated my spirits. My friends were waiting for me in the parlor. They received me sociably, inquired after my health, my last evening's entertainment, the company, &c. When, after a little pause, Mrs. Richman said, and how do you like Major Sanford, Eliza? Very well indeed, madam: I think him a finished gentleman. Will you, who are a connoisieur, allow him that title? No, my dear: in my opinion, he falls far below it; since he is deficient in one of the great essentials of the character, and that is, *virtue*. I am surprised, said I: but how has he incurred so severe a censure? By being a professed libertine;[1] by having but too successfully practised the arts of seduction; by triumphing in the destruction of innocence and the peace of families!

O, why was I not informed of this before? But, perhaps these are old affairs; the effects of juvenile folly; crimes of which he may have repented, and which charity ought to obliterate. No, my dear, they are recent facts; facts which he dares not deny; facts for which he ought to be banished from all virtuous society. I should have intimated this to you before, but your precipitate[2] acceptance of his invitation deprived me of an opportunity, until it was too late to prevent your going with him; and we thought it best to protract your enjoyment as long as possible, not doubting but your virtue and delicacy would, in future, guard you against the like deception.

Must I then become an avowed prude[3] at once; and refuse him admission, if he call, in compliance with the customary forms? By

1. A man who is not restrained by moral law, especially with regards to sexual morality.
2. Sudden.
3. One professing to exhibit excessively proper behavior, especially with regards to sex.

no means. I am sensible, that even the false maxims of the world must be complied with in a degree. But a man of Major Sanford's art can easily distinguish between a forbidding, and an encouraging reception. The former may, in this case, be given without any breach of the rules of politeness. Astonished, and mortified, I knew not what further to say. I had been so pleased with the man, that I wished to plead in his favor; but virtue and prudence forbade. I therefore rose and retired. He is this moment, I am told, below stairs. So that I must bid you adieu, until the next post.

ELIZA WHARTON.

# L E T T E R  X.

## TO THE SAME.

*NEW-HAVEN.*

Upon closing my last, I walked down, and found Major Sanford alone. He met me at the door of the parlor; and taking my hand with an air of affectionate tenderness, led me to a seat, and took one beside me. I believe the gloom of suspicion had not entirely forsaken my brow. He appeared, however, not to notice it; but after the compliments of the day had passed, entered into an easy and agreeable conversation on the pleasures of society: a conversation perfectly adapted to my taste, and calculated to dissipate my chagrin,[1] and pass the time imperceptibly. He inquired the place of my native abode; and having informed him, he said he had thoughts of purchasing the seat of Capt. Pribble, in that neighborhood, for his residence; and could he be assured of my society and friendship, his resolution would be fixed. I answered his compliment only by a slight bow. He took leave, and I retired to dress for the day, being engaged to accompany my cousin to dine at Mr. Laurence's, a gentleman of fortune and fashion, in this vicinity. Mr. Laurence has but one daughter, heiress to a large estate, with an agreeable form, but a countenance, which to me, indicates not much soul. I was surprised in the afternoon to see Major Sanford alight at the gate. He entered with the familiarity of an old acquaintance; and, after accosting each of the company, told me, with a low bow, that he did not expect the happiness of seeing me again so soon. I received his compliment with a conscious awkwardness. Mrs. Richman's morning lecture still rung in my head; and her watchful eye now traced every turn of mine, and

---

1. Vexation, troubled mind.

every action of the major's. Indeed, his assiduity[2] was painful to me; yet I found it impossible to disengage myself a moment from him, till the close of the day brought our carriage to the door; when he handed me in, and pressing my hand to his lips, retired.

What shall I say about this extraordinary man? Shall I own to you, my friend, that he is pleasing to me? His person, his manners, his situation, all combine to charm my fancy; and to my lively imagination, strew the path of life with flowers. What a pity, my dear Lucy, that the graces and virtues are not oftner united![3] They must, however, meet in the man of my choice; and till I find such a one, I shall continue to subscribe[4] my name

ELIZA WHARTON.

# L  E  T  T  E  R  XI.

### TO MR. CHARLES DEIGHTON.

*NEW-HAVEN.*

Well, Charles, I have been manœuvring to day, a little revengefully. That, you will say, is out of character. So baleful[1] a passion does not easily find admission among those softer ones, which you well know I cherish. However, I am a mere Proteus,[2] and can assume any shape that will best answer my purpose.

I called this forenoon, as I told you I intended, at Gen. Richman's. I waited some time in the parlor alone, before Eliza appeared; and when she did appear, the distant reserve of her manner and the pensiveness of her countenance convinced me that she had been vexed, and I doubted not but Peter Sanford was the occasion. Her wise cousin, I could have sworn, had been giving her a detail of the vices of her gallant; and warning her against the danger of associating with him in future. Notwithstanding, I took no notice of any alteration in her behavior; but entered with the utmost facetiousness[3] into a conversation which I thought most to her taste. By degrees, she assumed her usual vivacity; cheerfulness and good humor again animated her countenance. I tarried[4] as long as decency would admit. She having intimated that they were to dine at my friend Lawrence's,

2. Over-attentiveness.
3. A common phrase in the period; "graces": fashionable manners; "virtues": moral uprightness.
4. Sign.
1. Menacing.
2. A Greek sea god capable of changing form.
3. Lightheartedness.
4. Waited.

I caught at this information; and determined to follow them, and teaze the jealous Mrs. Richman, by playing off all the gallantry I was master of in her presence.

I went, and succeeded to the utmost of my wishes, as I read in the vexation, visible in the one; and the ease and attention displayed by the other. I believe too, that I have charmed the eye at least, of the amiable Eliza. Indeed, Charles, she is a fine girl. I think it would hurt my conscience to wound her mind or reputation. Were I disposed to marry, I am persuaded she would make an excellent wife; but that you know is no part of my plan, so long as I can keep out of the noose. Whenever I do submit to be shackled, it must be from a necessity of mending my fortune. This girl would be far from doing that. However, I am pleased with her acquaintance, and mean not to abuse her credulity[5] and good nature, if I can help it.

<div style="text-align: right;">PETER SANFORD.</div>

# L E T T E R   XII.

TO MISS LUCY FREEMAN.

<div style="text-align: right;"><i>NEW-HAVEN.</i></div>

The heart of your friend is again besieged. Whether it will surrender to the assailants or not, I am unable at present to determine. Sometimes I think of becoming a predestinarian,[1] and submitting implicitly to fate, without any exercise of free will; but, as mine seems to be a wayward one, I would counteract the operations of it, if possible.

Mrs. Richman told me this morning, that she hoped I should be as agreeably entertained this afternoon, as I had been the preceding; that she expected Mr. Boyer to dine, and take tea; and doubted not but he would be as attentive and sincere to me, if not as gay and polite as the gentleman who obtruded his civilities yesterday. I replied that I had no reason to doubt the sincerity of the one, or the other, having never put them to the test, nor did I imagine I ever should. Your friends, Eliza, said she, would be very happy to see you united to a man of Mr. Boyer's worth; and so agreeably settled, as he has a prospect of being. I hope, said I, that my friends are not so weary of my company, as to wish to dispose of me. I am too happy in my present connections to quit them for new ones. Marriage is the tomb of

---

5. Readiness to believe.
1. One who believes that fate is predetermined by God. Calvinism extends the concept to include the doctrine that God has willed salvation for some and damnation for others.

friendship. It appears to me a very selfish state. Why do people, in general, as soon as they are married, centre all their cares, their concerns, and pleasures in their own families? former acquaintances are neglected or forgotten. The tenderest ties between friends are weakened, or dissolved; and benevolence itself moves in a very limited sphere. It is the glory of the marriage state, she rejoined, to refine, by circumscribing our enjoyments. Here we can repose in safety.

> "The friendships of the world are oft
> Confed'racies in vice, or leagues in pleasure:
> Our's has the purest virtue for its basis;
> And such a friendship ends not but with life."[2]

True, we cannot always pay that attention to former associates, which we may wish; but the little community which we superintend[3] is quite as important an object; and certainly renders us more beneficial to the public. True benevolence, though it may change its objects, is not limited by time or place. Its effects are the same, and aided by a second self, are rendered more diffusive and salutary.

Some pleasantry passed, and we retired to dress. When summoned to dinner, I found Mr. Boyer below. If what is sometimes said be true, that love is diffident,[4] reserved, and unassuming, this man must be tinctured[5] with it. These symptoms were visible in his deportment when I entered the room. However, he soon recovered himself, and the conversation took a general turn. The festive board was crowned with sociability, and we found in reality, "The feast of reason, and the flow of soul."[6] After we rose from table, a walk in the garden was proposed, an amusement we are all peculiarly fond of. Mr. Boyer offered me his arm. When at a sufficient distance from our company, he begged leave to congratulate himself on having an opportunity which he had ardently desired for some time, of declaring to me his attachment; and of soliciting an interest in my favor; or, if he might be allowed the term, affection. I replied, that, Sir, is indeed laying claim to an important interest. I believe you must substitute some more indifferent epithet[7] for the present. Well then, said he, if it must be so, let it be esteem, or friendship. Indeed, Sir, said I, you are intitled to them both. Merit has always a share in that bank; and I know of none, who has a larger claim on that score, than Mr.

2. Spoken by Portius to Marcus in Act 2, Scene 1 of Joseph Addison's *Cato: A Tragedy* (1712), an extremely popular play in Revolutionary America. The subsequent portion of the speech concerns the dangers of loving unwisely.
3. Supervise.
4. Timid, unassuming.
5. Dyed or stained.
6. From Alexander Pope's *Imitations of Horace* (1733–38), Book 2. Pope celebrates an elevated society while also critiquing the shallowness of his contemporary world.
7. Adjective meant to be characteristic of the person being described.

Boyer. I suppose my manner was hardly serious enough for what he considered a weighty cause. He was a little disconcerted; but soon regaining his presence of mind, entreated me, with an air of earnestness, to encourage his suit, to admit his addresses, and, if possible, to reward his love. I told him, that this was rather a sudden affair to me; and that I could not answer him without consideration. Well then, said he, take what time you think proper, only relieve my suspense, as soon as may be. Shall I visit you again to morrow? O, not so soon, said I. Next Monday, I believe will be early enough. I will endeavor to be at home. He thanked me even for that favor, recommended himself once more to my kindness; and we walked towards the company, returned with them to the house, and he soon took leave. I immediately retired to write this letter, which I shall close, without a single observation on the subject, until I know your opinion.

<div align="right">ELIZA WHARTON.</div>

# L E T T E R  XIII.

### TO MISS ELIZA WHARTON.

<div align="right">*HARTFORD.*</div>

And so you wish to have my opinion before you know the result of your own. This is playing a little too much with my patience. But, however, I will gratify you this once, in hopes that my epistle[1] may have a good effect. You will ask, perhaps, whether I would influence your judgment? I answer, no; provided you will exercise it yourself: but I am a little apprehensive that your fancy will mislead you. Methinks I can gather from your letters, a predilection[2] for this Major Sanford. But he is a rake, my dear friend; and can a lady of your delicacy and refinement, think of forming a connection with a man of that character? I hope not. Nay, I am confident you do not. You mean only to exhibit a few more girlish airs, before you turn matron. But I am persuaded, if you wish to lead down the dance of life with regularity, you will not find a more excellent partner than Mr. Boyer. Whatever you can reasonably expect in a lover, husband, or friend, you may perceive to be united in this worthy man. His taste is undebauched,[3] his manners not vitiated,[4] his morals uncorrupted. His situation in life is, perhaps, as elevated as you have a right to

---

1. Letter.
2. Preference.
3. Not seduced from duty or virtue.
4. Morally wasted, spoiled.

claim. Forgive my plainness, Eliza. It is the task of friendship, some-times to tell disagreeable truths. I know your ambition is to make a distinguished figure in the first class of polished society; to shine in the gay circle of fashionable amusements, and to bear off the palm[5] amidst the votaries[6] of pleasure. But these are fading honors, unsat-isfactory enjoyments; incapable of gratifying those immortal princi-ples of reason and religion, which have been implanted in your mind by nature; assiduously cultivated by the best of parents, and exerted, I trust, by yourself. Let me advise you then, in conducting this affair; an affair, big, perhaps, with your future fate, to lay aside those coquettish airs which you sometimes put on; and remember that you are not dealing with a fop,[7] who will take advantage of every conces-sion; but with a man of sense and honor, who will properly estimate your condescension, and frankness. Act then with that modest free-dom, that dignified unreserve which bespeaks conscious rectitude[8] and sincerity of heart.

I shall be extremely anxious to hear the process and progress of this business. Relieve my impatience, as soon as possible, and believe me yours, with undissembled affection.

LUCY FREEMAN.

# L  E  T  T  E  R   XIV.

### TO MISS LUCY FREEMAN.

*NEW-HAVEN.*

I have received, and read again and again, your friendly epistle. My reason and judgment entirely coincide with your opinion; but my fancy claims some share in the decision: and I cannot yet tell which will preponderate.[1] This was the day fixed for deciding Mr. Boyer's cause. My friends here gave me a long dissertation[2] on his merits. Your letter, likewise, had its weight, and I was candidly summing up the *pros* and *cons* in the garden, whither I had walked (Gen. Rich-man and lady having rode out) when I was informed that he was waiting in the parlor. I went immediately in (a good symptom, you will say) and received him very graciously. After the first compli-ments were over, he seemed eager to improve the opportunity to

5. To win the prize.
6. Worshipers.
7. A fool or dandy, overly attentive to appearance, dress, and manners.
8. Moral uprightness.
1. Outweigh the other.
2. An extended discussion or treatise.

enter directly on the subject of his present visit. It is needless for me to recite to you, who have long been acquainted with the whole process of courtship, the declarations, propositions, protestations, intreaties, looks, words and actions of a lover. They are, I believe, much the same, in the whole sex, allowing for their different dispositions, educations, and characters. But you are impatient I know for the conclusion. You have hastily perused the preceding lines, and are straining your eye forward to my part of the farce; for such it may prove after all. Well then, not to play too long with the curiosity, which I know to be excited, and actuated[3] by real friendship, I will relieve it. I think you would have been pleased to have seen my gravity, on this important occasion. With all the candor and frankness which I was capable of assuming, I thus answered his long harangue,[4] to which I had listened, without interrupting him. Self-knowledge, sir, that most important of all sciences, I have yet to learn. Such have been my situations in life, and the natural volatility[5] of my temper, that I have looked but little into my own heart, in regard to its future wishes and views. From a scene of constraint and confinement, ill suited to my years and inclination, I have just launched into society. My heart beats high in expectation of its fancied joys. My sanguine[6] imagination paints, in alluring colors, the charms of youth and freedom, regulated by virtue and innocence. Of these, I wish to partake. While I own myself under obligations for the esteem which you are pleased to profess for me, and in return, acknowledge, that neither your person nor manners are disagreeable to me, I recoil at the thought of immediately forming a connection, which must confine me to the duties of domestic life, and make me dependent for happiness, perhaps too, for subsistence, upon a class of people, who will claim the right of scrutinising every part of my conduct; and by censuring those foibles, which I am conscious of not having prudence to avoid, may render me completely miserable. While, therefore, I receive your visits, and cultivate towards you sentiments of friendship and esteem, I would not have you consider me as confined to your society, or obligated to a future connection. Our short acquaintance renders it impossible for me to decide what the operations of my mind may hereafter be. You must either quit the subject, or leave me to the exercise of my free will, which perhaps may coincide with your present wishes. Madam, said he, far is the wish from me to restrain your person or mind. In your breast I will repose my cause. It shall be my study to merit a return of affection; and I doubt not, but generosity and honor will influence your conduct towards

3. Motivated or caused.
4. A vehement speech.
5. Instability; in chemistry, a tendency to evaporate quickly.
6. Hopeful.

me. I expect soon to settle among a generous and enlightened people, where I flatter myself I shall be exempt from those difficulties, and embarrassments, to which too many of my brethren are subject. The local situation is agreeable, the society refined and polished; and if, in addition, I may obtain that felicity which you are formed to bestow, in a family connection, I shall be happy indeed.

He spoke with emphasis. The tear of sensibility sparkled in his eye. I involuntarily gave him my hand, which he pressed with ardor to his lips. Then rising, he walked to the window to conceal his emotion. I rang the bell and ordered tea; during, and after which, we shared that social converse, which is the true zest of life, and which, I am persuaded, none but virtuous minds can participate. General Richman and lady returned with the shades of the evening. The penetrating eye of my cousin traced in *our* countenances the progress of the cause, and the smile of approbation animated *hers*. Mr. Boyer asked the favor of my company to ride to morrow morning, which was granted. He tarried to supper, and took his leave. I retired immediately to my chamber, to which I was followed by Mrs. Richman. I related to her the conversation, and the encouragement which I had given to Mr. Boyer. She was pleased; but insisted that I should own myself somewhat engaged to him. This, I told her I should never do to any man, before the indissoluble knot was tied. That, said I, will be time enough to resign my freedom. She replied that I had wrong ideas of freedom, and matrimony; but she hoped that Mr. Boyer would happily rectify them.

I have now, my dear friend, given you an account of my present situation, and leave you to judge for yourself concerning it. Write me your opinion, and believe me ever yours.

ELIZA WHARTON.

# L E T T E R   XV.

TO MISS ELIZA WHARTON.

*HARTFORD.*

I congratulate you, my dear Eliza, on the stability of your conduct towards Mr. Boyer. Pursue the system which you have adopted, and I dare say, that happiness will crown your future days. You are indeed very tenacious of your freedom, as you call it; but that is a play about words. A man of Mr. Boyer's honor and good sense will never abridge any privileges which virtue can claim.

When do you return to embellish our society, here? I am impatient to see you, and likewise this amiable man. I am much interested in

his favor. By the way, I am told that Major Sanford has been to look at the seat of Captain Pribble, which is upon sale. It is reported that he will probably purchase it. Many of our gentry[1] are pleased with the prospect of such a neighbor. As an accomplished gentleman, say they, he will be an agreeable addition to our social parties; and as a man of property, and public spirit, he will be an advantage to the town; but, from what I have heard of him, I am far from supposing him a desirable acquisition in either of these respects. A man of a vicious character cannot be a good member of society. In order to that, his principles and practice must be uncorrupted: in his morals, at least, he must be a man of probity, and honor. Of these qualifications, if I mistake not, this gallant of yours cannot boast. But I shall not set up for a censor. I hope neither you nor I shall have much connection with him. My swain[2] interests himself very much in your affairs. You will possibly think him impertinent; but I give his curiosity a softer name. Should I own to you that I place great confidence in his integrity and honor, you would, perhaps, laugh at my weakness; but, my dear, I have pride enough to keep me above coquettry, or prudery; and discretion enough, I hope, to secure me from the errors of both. With him I have determined to walk the future round of life. What folly then would it be to affect reserve and distance, relative to an affair in which I have so much interest? Not that I am going to betray your secrets. These I have no right to divulge; but I must be the judge what may, and what may not be communicated. I am very much pressed for an early day of consummation; but I shall not listen to a request of that kind, till your return. Such is my regard for you, that a union of love would be imperfect, if friendship attended not the rites. Adieu.

LUCY FREEMAN.

# L  E  T  T  E  R   XVI.

### TO MISS LUCY FREEMAN.

*New-Haven.*

We go on charmingly here; almost as soft and smooth as your ladyship. It seems to me that love must stagnate, if it have not a light breeze of discord once in a while to keep it in motion. We have not tried any yet, however. We had a lovely tour this forenoon; were out three long hours, and returned to dinner in perfect harmony.

1. Rank by birth; gentlemen.
2. A suitor, not of the highest standing.

Mr. Boyer informed me that he should set out to morrow morning, for his future residence, and soon put on the sacred bands.[1] He solicited an epistolary correspondence, at the same time, as an alleviation of the care which that weighty charge would bring on his mind. I consented; telling him, that he must not expect any thing more than general subjects from me.

We were somewhat interrupted in our confidential intercourse, in the afternoon, by the arrival of Major Sanford. I cannot say that I was not agreeably relieved. So sweet a repast, for several hours together, was rather sickening to my taste. My enamorato[2] looked a little mortified at the cheerful reception which I gave the intruder, and joined not so placidly in the social conversation, as I could have wished.

When Mr. Boyer, after the Major took leave, pressed me to give him some assurance of my constancy, I only reminded him of the terms of our engagement. Seeing me decided, he was silent on the subject, and soon bid me an affectionate adieu; not expecting, as he told me, the pleasure of a personal interview again, for two or three months.

Thus far we have proceeded in this sober business. A good beginning, you will say. Perhaps it is. I do not, however, feel myself greatly interested in the progress of the negociation. Time may consolidate my affections, and enable me to fix them on some particular object. At present the most lively emotions of my heart are those of friendship; that friendship which I hope you will soon participate with your faithful

<div align="right">Eliza Wharton.</div>

# L E T T E R  XVII.

<div align="center">TO MR. SELBY.</div>

<div align="right"><i>New-Haven.</i></div>

I have succeeded in my addresses to the lovely Eliza Wharton; as far at least as I had any reason to expect from our short acquaintance. I find the graces of her person and mind rise in my esteem; and have already enjoyed, in her society, some of the happiest hours of my life. She is kind, affable, and condescending; yet I must own that I have not been able to infuse into her bosom, the ardor which I feel in my own. I know that the native modesty of the sex would

1. I.e., take up his clerical duties.
2. *From Italian*: A lover.

restrain the discovery; but there is an animation of countenance, which betrays the sensations of the heart, that I find wanting in hers on this occasion.

I have just taken leave of my fair, and propose returning to morrow morning; to take upon me the solemn charge, which lies with such weight upon my mind, that I need every support, both human and divine. Eliza has promised to correspond with me. From this I anticipate a source of pleasure, which alone can atone for her absence. I am, &c.

<div align="right">J. BOYER.</div>

# L  E  T  T  E  R  XVIII.

<div align="center">TO MR. CHARLES DEIGHTON.</div>

<div align="right">*NEW-HAVEN.*</div>

Do you know, Charles, that I have commenced lover? I was always a general one; but now I am somewhat particular. I shall be the more interested, as I am likely to meet with difficulties; and it is the glory of a rake, as well as a christian to combat obstacles.[1] This same Eliza, of whom I have told you, has really made more impression on my heart, than I was aware of; or than the sex, take them as they rise, are wont to do. But she is besieged by a priest (a likely[2] lad though). I know not how it is, but they are commonly successful with the girls, even the gayest of them. This one, too, has the interest of all her friends, as I am told. I called yesterday, at General Richman's, and found this pair together, apparently too happy in each other's society for my wishes. I must own, that I felt a glow of jealousy, which I never experienced before; and vowed revenge for the pain it gave me, though but momentary. Yet Eliza's reception of me was visibly cordial; nay, I fancied my company as pleasing to her as that which she had before. I tarried not long, but left him to the enjoyment of that pleasure which I flatter myself will be short-lived. O, I have another plan in my head; a plan of necessity, which, you know, is the mother of invention. It is this: I am very much courted and caressed by the family of Mr. Lawrence, a man of large property in this neighborhood. He has only one child; a daughter, with whom I imagine the old folks intend to shackle me in the bonds of matrimony. The girl looks very well. She has no soul though, that I can discover. She is heiress, nevertheless, to a great fortune; and that is all the soul I wish for in a wife. In

1. Referring to trials of Christian faith.
2. Suitable.

truth, Charles, I know of no other way to mend my circumstances. But lisp[3] not a word of my embarrassments for your life. Show and equipage[4] are my hobby-horse;[5] and if any female wish to share them with me, and will furnish me with the means of supporting them, I have no objection. Could I conform to the sober rules of wedded life, and renounce those dear enjoyments of dissipation, in which I have so long indulged, I know not the lady in the world with whom I would sooner form a connection of this sort than with Eliza Wharton. But it will never do. If my fortune, or hers were better, I would risk a union; but as they are, no idea of the kind can be admitted. I shall endeavor, notwithstanding, to enjoy her company as long as possible. Though I cannot possess her wholly myself, I will not tamely see her the property of another.

I am now going to call at General Richman's, in hopes of an opportunity to profess my devotion to her. I know I am not a welcome visitor to the family; but I am independent of their censure[6] or esteem, and mean to act accordingly.

<div align="right">Peter Sanford.</div>

# L    E    T    T    E    R    XIX.

TO MISS LUCY FREEMAN.

<div align="right">*New-Haven.*</div>

I find the ideas of sobriety, and domestic solitude, I have been cultivating for three days past, somewhat deranged by the interruption of a visitor, with whom, I know, you will not be pleased. It is no other than Major Sanford. I was walking alone in the garden yesterday, when he suddenly appeared to my view. How happy am I, said he, seizing my hand, in this opportunity of finding you alone; an opportunity, Miss Wharton, which I must improve in expatiating[1] on a theme, that fills my heart, and solely animates my frame.

I was startled at his impetuosity, and displeased with his freedom. Withdrawing my hand, I told him, that my retirement was sacred. He bowed submissively; begged pardon for his intrusion, alledged, that he found no body but the servants in the house; that they informed him, I was alone in the garden, which intelligence was too pleasing for him to consult any forms of ceremony for the regulation

3. Whisper.
4. Fittings, accessories.
5. Favorite pursuit or pastime.
6. Judgment, criticism.
1. Elaborating.

of his conduct. He then went on rhapsodically to declare his passion, his suspicions, that I was forming a connection with Mr. Boyer, which would effectually destroy all his hopes of future happiness. He painted the restraint, the confinement, the embarrassments to which a woman, connected with a man of Mr. Boyer's profession, must be subjected; however agreeable his person might be. He asked if my generous mind could submit to cares and perplexities like these; whether I could not find greater sources of enjoyment in a more elevated sphere of life, or share pleasures better suited to my genius and disposition, even in a single state? I listened to him involuntarily. My heart did not approve his sentiments, but my ear was charmed with his rhetoric, and my fancy captivated by his address.

He invited my confidence, by the most ardent professions of friendship, and labored to remove my suspicions by vows of sincerity. I was induced by his importunity,[2] gradually to disclose the state of affairs between Mr. Boyer and myself. He listened eagerly; wished not, he said, to influence me unduly; but if I were not otherwise engaged, might he presume to solicit a place in my friendship and esteem; be admitted to enjoy my society, to visit me as an acquaintance, and to attend my excursions and amusements, as a brother, if no more? I replied, that I was a pensioner of friendship,[3] at present; that my friends were extremely refined in their notions of propriety, and that I had no right to receive visitants independent of them. I understand you, madam, said he. You intimate that my company is not agreeable to them: but I know not why. Surely my rank in life is as elevated; and my knowledge of, and acceptance in the world, are as extensive as General Richman's. I hope, said I, since we are engaged in the conversation, that you will excuse my frankness, if I tell you, that the understanding and virtue of this worthy couple, induce them, without any regard to rank, to bestow their esteem wherever it is merited. I cannot say that you are not a sharer. Your own heart can best determine, whether upon their principles, you are, or not! He appeared mortified, and chagrined; and we had walked some distance without exchanging a word, or a look. At last, he rejoined, I plead guilty to the charge, madam, which they have undoubtedly brought against me, of imprudence and folly in many particulars; yet of malignancy and vice I am innocent. Brought up in affluence; innured from my infancy to the gratification of every passion; the indulgence of every wish, it is not strange, that a life of dissipation and gaiety should prove alluring to a youthful mind, which had no care but to procure what it deemed enjoyment. In this pursuit

2. Won over or obliged by his persistent or pressing demand.
3. Recipient of friendship; one maintained or supported by friendship.

I have perhaps deviated from the rigid rules of discretion, and the harsher laws of morality.

But let the veil of charity be drawn over my faults;[4] let the eye of candor impartially examine my present behavior; let the kind and lenient hand of friendship assist in directing my future steps; and, perhaps, I may not prove unworthy of associating with the respectable inhabitants of this happy mansion; for such I am sure it must be, while honored with Miss Wharton's presence. But, circumstanced as you and I are, at present, I will not sue for your attention, as a lover; but rest contented, if possible, with that share of kindness, and regard, which your benevolence may afford me as a friend. I bowed in approbation of his resolution. He pressed my hand with ardor to his lips; and at that instant General Richman entered the garden. He approached us cheerfully, offered Major Sanford his hand with apparent cordiality, and told us pleasantly, that he hoped he should not be considered as an intruder. By no means, sir, said Major Sanford. It is I who have incurred that imputation.[5] I called this afternoon to pay you my respects; when being informed that you and your lady were abroad, and that Miss Wharton was in the garden, I took the liberty to invade her retirement. She has graciously forgiven my crime, and I was just affixing the seal to my pardon as you entered.

We then returned into the house. Mrs. Richman received us politely. During tea, the conversation turned on literary subjects, in which I cannot say that the Major bore a very distinguished part. After he was gone, Mrs. Richman said, I hope you have been agreeably entertained, Miss Wharton? I did not chuse my company, madam, said I. Nor, said she, did you refuse it, I presume. Would you not have me respect the rights of hospitality towards your guests, when you are absent, madam? If you had acted from that motive, I own my obligations to you, my dear; but even that consideration can hardly reconcile me to the sacrifice of time, which you have made to the amusement of a seducer. I hope, madam, you do not think me an object of seduction! I do not think you seducible; nor was Richardson's Clarissa,[6] till she made herself the victim, by her own indiscretion. Pardon me, Eliza, this is a second Lovelace.[7] I am alarmed by his artful intrusions. His insinuating attentions to you

---

4. Cf. 1 Peter 4:8.
5. Insinuation.
6. The epistolary novel *Clarissa* (1748) by Samuel Richardson features a heroine who is subject to multiple trials, including assaults on her virtue, but who remains firm in her principles, eventually dying. Her "indiscretion" was initially to trust her seducer. Though British, the novel was extremely popular in eighteenth- and nineteenth-century America.
7. The seducer in *Clarissa*, who pretends to be honorable but proceeds to drug and rape the heroine.

are characteristic of the man. Come, I presume you are not inter-
ested to keep his secrets, if you know them. Will you give me a little
sketch of his conversation? Most willingly, said I; and, accordingly,
related the whole. When I had concluded, she shook her head, and
replied, beware, my friend, of his arts. Your own heart is too sincere
to suspect treachery and dissimulation[8] in another; but suffer not
your ear to be charmed by the syren voice of flattery; nor your eye to
be caught by the phantom of gaiety and pleasure. Remember your
engagements to Mr. Boyer. Let sincerity and virtue be your guides,
and they will lead you to happiness and peace. She waited not for an
answer, but immediately rising, begged leave to retire, alledging that
she was fatigued. Gen. Richman accompanied her, and I hastened
to my apartment, where I have written thus far, and shall send it on
for your comments. I begin to think of returning soon to your circle.
One inducement is, that I may be free from the intrusions of this
man. Adieu.

ELIZA WHARTON.

# L  E  T  T  E  R   XX.

## TO MRS. M. WHARTON.

*NEW-HAVEN.*

From the conversation of the polite, the sedate, the engaging and
the gay; from corresponding with the learned, the sentimental and
the refined, my heart and my pen turn with ardor and alacrity[1] to a
tender and affectionate parent, the faithful guardian and guide of my
youth; the unchanging friend of my riper years. The different dispo-
sitions of various associates, sometimes perplex the mind, which
seeks direction; but in the disinterested affection of the maternal
breast, we fear no dissonance of passion, no jarring interests, no dis-
union of love. In this seat of felicity[2] is every enjoyment which fancy
can form, or friendship, with affluence, bestow; but still my mind
frequently returns to the happy shades of my nativity. I wish there to
impart my pleasures, and share the counsels of my best, my long
tried and experienced friend. At this time, my dear mamma, I am
peculiarly solicitous for your advice. I am again inportuned[3] to listen

---

8. Artifice or deception.
1. Cheerful readiness.
2. Happiness.
3. Asked persistently.

to the voice of love; again called upon to accept the addresses of a gentleman of merit and respectability. You will know the character of the man, when I tell you, it is Mr. Boyer. But his situation in life! I dare not enter it. My disposition is not calculated for that sphere. There are duties arising from the station, which I fear I should not be able to fulfil; cares and restraints to which I could not submit. *This* man is not disagreeable to me; but if I must enter the connubial state, are there not *others*, who may be equally pleasing in their persons, and whose profession may be more conformable to my taste? You, madam, have passed through this scene of trial, with honor and applause. But alas! can your volatile daughter ever acquire your wisdom; ever posses your resolution, dignity and prudence?

I hope soon to converse with you personally upon the subject, and to profit by your precepts and example. I anticipate the hour of my return to your bosom, with impatience. My daily thoughts and nightly dreams restore me to the society of my beloved mamma; and, till I enjoy it in reality, I subscribe myself your dutiful daughter,

ELIZA WHARTON.

# L  E  T  T  E  R  XXI.

TO MISS ELIZA WHARTON.

*HARTFORD.*

How welcome to me, my dear Eliza, are the tidings of your return? My widowed heart has mourned your absence, and languished for the company of its now, dearest connection. When stript of one dependence, the mind naturally collects, and rests itself in another. Your father's death deprived me, for a while, of every enjoyment. But a reviving sense of the duties which I owed to a rising family, roused me from the lethargy of grief. In my cares I found an alleviation of my sorrows. The expanding virtues of my children soothed and exhilerated my drooping spirits; and my attention to their education, and interest, was amply rewarded by their proficiency and duty. In them, every hope, every pleasure now centres. They are the axis on which revolves the temporal felicity of their mother. Judge then, my dear, how anxiously I must watch, how solicitously I must regard every circumstance which relates to their welfare and prosperity! Exquisitely alive to these sensations, your letter awakens my hopes and my fears. As you are young and charming, a thousand dangers lurk unseen around you. I wish you to find a friend and protector, worthy of being rewarded by your love and your society. Such a one,

I think, Mr. Boyer will prove. I am, therefore, sorry, since there can be no other, that his profession should be an objection in your mind. You say, that I have experienced the scenes of trial, connected with that station. I have, indeed; and I will tell you the result of this experience. It is, that I have found it replete with happiness. No class of society has domestic enjoyment more at command, than clergymen. Their circumstances are generally a decent competency. They are removed alike from the perplexing cares of want, and from the distracting parade of wealth. They are respected by all ranks, and partakers of the best company. With regard to its being a dependent situation, what one is not so? Are we not all links in the great chain of society, some more, some less important; but each upheld by others, throughout the confederated[1] whole? In whatever situation we are placed, our greater or less degree of happiness must be derived from ourselves. Happiness is in a great measure the result of our own dispositions and actions. Let us conduct uprightly and justly; with propriety and steadiness; nor servilely cringing for favor, nor arrogantly claiming more attention and respect than our due; let us bear with fortitude the providential, and unavoidable evils of life, and we shall spend our days with respectability and contentment, at least.

I will not expatiate on the topic of your letter, till we have a personal interview, for which I am, indeed, impatient. Return, my daughter, as soon as politeness will allow, to your expecting friends; more especially, to the fond embraces of your affectionate mother,

M. WHARTON.

# L E T T E R  XXII.

TO MISS ELIZA WHARTON.

*Hampshire.*

Can time, can distance, can absence allay, or extinguish the sentiments of refined affection, the ardor of true love? No, my dear Eliza. If I may judge by my own heart, I shall say they cannot. Amidst the parade which has attended me, the interesting scenes in which I have been engaged, and the weighty cares, which have occupied my attention, your idea has been the solace of my retired moments; the soother of every anxious thought. I recal, with pleasure, the

_____
1. United.

conversation which we have shared. I dwell with rapture on the marks of favor which I have received from you. My first wish is the continuance and increase of these favors; my highest ambition, to deserve them. I look forward and anticipate with impatience, the future enjoyment of your society; and hope we shall one day experience the reality of those beautiful lines of Thompson:

> —— "An elegant sufficiency,
> Content, retirement, rural quiet, friendship;
> Books, ease and alternate labor, useful life;
> Progressive virtue, and approving heaven;
> These are the matchless joys of virtuous love."[1]

Mr. Selby, my particular friend, will have the honor of delivering this letter. He will be able to give you any information, relative to our public transactions, which you may wish. May I solicit the favor of a line, through him, in return? It will relieve, in some measure, the tediousness of this separation. I intend to pay my respects to you personally, in about a fortnight; till when, I subscribe myself your sincere and affectionate friend,

<div align="right">J. BOYER.</div>

# L  E  T  T  E  R   XXIII.

## TO THE REV. J. BOYER.

<div align="right">*NEW-HAVEN.*</div>

I have executed your commission, and been amply rewarded for my trouble, by the pleasure I enjoyed in the society of the agreeable family to which I was introduced; especially of the amiable and accomplished lady, who is the object of your particular regard. I think she fully justifies your partiality to her. She appears to possess both the virtues and the graces. Her form is fine, and her countenance interests us at once in her favor. There is a mixture of dignity and ease, which commands respect, and conciliates affection. After these encomiums,[1] will you permit me to say, there is an air of gaiety in her appearance and deportment, which favors a little of coquetry. I am persuaded, however, that she has too much good sense to practice its

---

1. From James Thomson's discussion of "Connubial Life" in the "Spring" section of *The Seasons* (1726–30). *The Seasons*, a collection of poems, was groundbreaking in its simple yet romantic treatment of nature, and Foster draws heavily on it throughout her writing. Note that she omits the last line of this stanza—"And thus their moments fly"—implying the fleeting nature even of pure joys.
1. High praises.

arts. She received your letter very graciously, asked leave to retire a few moments; and returned with a smile of complacency on her brow, which I construe favorably to you.

There was a Mr. Laurence, with his lady and daughter, and a certain Major Sanford, at the house. The latter, I believe, in the modern sense of the phrase, *is much of a gentleman*, that is, a man of show and fashion.

Miss Wharton asked me, when I should leave town, and when I should return, or have an opportunity of conveyance to Hampshire?[2] I told her I should write by the next post, and if she had any commands, would be happy to execute them. She would send a line to her friend, she said, if I would take the trouble to inclose it in my letter. I readily consented; and told her, that I would call and receive her favor to morrow morning. This chit-chat was a little aside; but I could not but observe, that the foresaid Major Sanford had dropped his part in the conversation of the rest of the company, and was attending to us, though he endeavored to conceal his attention, by looking carelessly over a play, which lay on the window by him. Yet he evidently watched every word and action of Miss Wharton, as if he were really interested in her movements.

It is said she has many admirers, and I conceive it very possible that this may be one of them; though, truly, I do not think that she would esteem such a conquest any great honor. I now joined in the general topic of conversation, which was politics. Mrs. Richman and Miss Wharton judiciously, yet modestly bore a part; while the other ladies amused themselves with Major Sanford, who was making his sage remarks on the play, which he still kept in his hand. General Richman at length observed, that we had formed into parties. Major Sanford, upon this, laid aside his book. Miss Laurence simpered; and looked as if she was well pleased with being in a party with so fine a man; while her mother replied, that she never meddled with politics; she thought they did not belong to ladies. Miss Wharton and I, said Mrs. Richman, must beg leave to differ from you, madam. We think ourselves interested in the welfare and prosperity of our country; and, consequently, claim the right of inquiring into those affairs, which may conduce to, or interfere with the common weal. We shall not be called to the senate or the field to assert its privileges, and defend its rights, but we shall feel for the honor and safety of our friends and connections, who are thus employed. If the community flourish and enjoy health and freedom, shall we not share in the happy effects? if it be oppressed and disturbed, shall we not endure our proportion of the evil? Why then should the love of our country be a masculine passion only? Why should government, which involves

2. I.e., New Hampshire.

the peace and order of the society, of which we are a part, be wholly
excluded from our observation? Mrs. Laurence made some slight
reply and waved the subject. The gentlemen applauded Mrs. Rich-
man's sentiments as truly Roman; and what was more, they said,
truly republican.[3]

I rose to take leave, observing to Miss Wharton, that I should call
to morrow as agreed. Upon this, Gen. Richman politely requested
the favor of my company at dinner. I accepted his invitation, and bid
them good night. I shall do the same to you for the present; as
I intend, to morrow to scribble the cover, which is to inclose your
Eliza's letter.

<div style="text-align:right">T. SELBY.</div>

# L   E   T   T   E   R   XXIV.

<div style="text-align:center">TO THE REV. J. BOYER.</div>

<div style="text-align:right"><em>NEW-HAVEN.</em></div>

I resume my pen, having just returned from Gen. Richman's; not
with an expectation, however, of your reading this, till you have
perused, and reperused the inclosed. I can bear such neglect, in this
case, as I have been alike interested myself.

I went to Gen. Richman's at twelve o'clock. About a mile from
thence, upon turning a corner, I observed a gentleman and lady on
horseback, some way before me, riding a very moderate pace, and
seemingly in close conversation. I kept at the same distance from
them, till I saw them stop at the General's gate. I then put on, and
coming up with them, just as they alighted, and was surprised to find
them no other than Major Sanford and Miss Wharton. They were
both a little disconcerted at my salutation; I know not why. Miss
Wharton invited him in, but he declined, being engaged to dine.
Gen. Richman received us at the door. As I handed Miss Wharton
in, he observed jocosely,[1] that she had changed company. Yes sir, she
replied, more than once, since I went out, as you doubtless observed.
I was not aware, said Mrs. Richman, that Major Sanford was to be of
your party to day. It was quite accidental, madam, said Miss Whar-
ton. Miss Laurence and I had agreed last evening, to take a little
airing, this forenoon. A young gentleman, a relation of her's, who is
making them a visit, was to attend us. We had not rode more than

---

3. Revolutionary and post-Revolutionary Americans idealized the ancient Roman repub-
   lic as a model representative government.
1. Playfully.

two miles, when we were overtaken by Major Sanford, who very politely asked leave to join our party. Miss Laurence very readily consented; and we had a very sociable ride. The fineness of the day induced me to protract the enjoyment of it abroad; but Miss Laurence declined riding so far as I proposed, as she had engaged company to dine. We therefore parted till evening, when we are to meet again. What, another engagement! said Mrs. Richman. Only to the assembly,[2] madam. May I inquire after your gallant, my dear? But I have no right, perhaps, to be inquisitive, said Mrs. Richman. Miss Wharton made no reply; and the conversation took a general turn. Miss Wharton sustained her part with great propriety. Indeed, she discovers a fund of useful knowledge,[3] and extensive reading, which render her peculiarly entertaining; while the brilliancy of her wit, the fluency of her language, the vivacity and ease of her manners, are inexpressibly engaging. I am going myself to the assembly this evening, though I did not mention it to General Richman; I therefore took my leave soon after dinner.

I have heard so much in praise of Miss Wharton's penmanship, in addition to her other endowments, that I am almost tempted to break the seal of her letter to you; but I forbear. Wishing you much happiness in the perusal of it, and more in the possession of its writer, I subscribe myself, yours, &c.

T. SELBY.

# L E T T E R  XXV.

## TO THE REV. J. BOYER.

*NEW-HAVEN.*

SIR,

Your favor of the 4th inst.[1] came to hand yesterday. I received it with pleasure, and embrace this early opportunity of contributing my part to a correspondence, tending to promote a friendly and social intercourse. An epistolary communication between the sexes has been with some, a subject of satire and censure; but unjustly, in my opinion. With persons of refinement and information, it may be a source

2. A sanctioned social gathering, common in large towns in the period.
3. A fundamental component of democratic education in late-eighteenth-century America, "useful knowledge" encompassed everything from farm management to ancient languages. As Benjamin Franklin defined it, such knowledge "let light into the nature of things tend[ing] to increase the power of man over matter, and multiply the conveniences and pleasures of life."
1. I.e., instant; "favor of the 4th inst.": letter written on the fourth day of the present month.

of entertainment and utility. The knowledge and masculine virtues of your sex may be softened, and rendered more diffusive by the inquisitiveness, vivacity, and docility of ours; drawn forth and exercised by each other.

In regard to the *particular* subject of your's I shall be silent. Ideas of that kind are better conveyed, on my part, by words, than by the pen.

I congratulate you on your agreeable settlement, and hope it will be productive of real and lasting happiness. I am convinced that felicity is not confined to any particular station, or condition in life; yet methinks some are better calculated to afford it to me, than others.

Your extract from a favorite poet[2] is charmingly descriptive; but is it not difficult to ascertain what we can pronounce "an elegant sufficiency?" Perhaps you will answer as some others have done, We can attain it by circumscribing our wishes within the compass of our abilities. I am not very avaricious; yet I must own that I should like to enjoy it without so much trouble as that would cost me.

Excuse my seeming levity. You have flattered my cheerfulness by commending it; and must, therefore, indulge me in the exercise of it. I cannot conveniently be at the pains of restraining its sallies, when I write in confidence.

Is a sprightly disposition, in your view, indicative of a giddy mind, or an innocent heart? Of the latter, I presume; for I know you are not a misanthrope.

We expect the pleasure of Mr. Selby's company to dinner. You are, certainly, under obligations to his friendship for the liberal encomiums he bestowed on you, and your prospects yesterday. Mrs. Richman rallied me after he was gone, on my listening ear. The General and she unite in requesting me to present their respects. Wishing you health and happiness, I subscribe myself your friend,

Eliza Wharton.

# LETTER XXVI.

### TO MISS LUCY FREEMAN.

*New-Haven.*

I am perplexed and embarrassed, my friend, by the assiduous attentions of this Major Sanford. I shall write circumstantially, and frankly to you, that I may have the benefit of your advice. He came

2. I.e., James Thompson. See letter XXII on p. 34.

here, last Monday, in company with Mr. Laurence, his wife, and daughter, to make us a visit. While they were present, a Mr. Selby, a particular friend of Mr. Boyer, came in, and delivered me a letter from him. I was really happy in the reception of this proof of his affection. His friend gave a very flattering account of his situation and prospects.

The watchful eye of Major Sanford traced every word and action, respecting Mr. Boyer, with an attention, which seemed to border on anxiety. That, however, did not restrain, but rather accellerate my vivacity and inquisitiveness on the subject; for I wished to know whether it would produce any real effect upon him, or not.

After Mr. Selby's departure, he appeared pensive, and thoughtful, the remainder of the evening; and evidently sought an opportunity of speaking to me aside; which I studiously avoided. Miss Laurence and I formed an engagement to take an airing in the morning on horseback; attended by a relation of hers, who is now with them. They called for me about ten, when we immediately set out upon our preconcerted excursion. We had not proceeded far, before we were met by Major Sanford. He was extremely polite, and finding our destination was not particular, begged leave to join our party. This was granted, and we had an agreeable tour for several miles; the time being passed in easy, and unstudied remarks upon obvious occurrences. Maj. Sanford could not, however, conceal his particular attention to me, which rather nettled Miss Laurence. She grew somewhat serious, and declined riding so far as we had intended; alledging that she expected company to dine.

Major Sanford understanding that she was going to the assembly in the evening with Mr. Gordon, solicited me to accept a ticket and form a party with them. The entertainment was alluring, and I consented. When we had parted with Miss Laurence, Major Sanford insisted on my riding a little farther; saying, he must converse with me on a particular subject; and if I refused him this opportunity, that he must visit me, at my residence, let it offend whom it would. I yielded to his importunity; and we rode on. He then told me that his mind was in a state of suspense and agitation, which was very painful to bear; and which I only could relieve; that my cheerful reception of Mr. Boyer's letter, yesterday, and deportment[1] respecting him, had awakened in his breast all the pangs of jealousy, which the most ardent love could feel; that my treatment of Mr. Boyer's friend convinced him that I was more interested in his affairs than I was willing to own; that he foresaw himself to be condemned to an eternal separation; and the total loss of my favor and society, as soon as time and circumstances would allow.

1. Conduct.

His zeal, his pathos, alarmed me. I begged him to be calm. To you, said I, as a friend, I have intrusted my situation in relation to Mr. Boyer. You know that I am under no special obligation to him; and I do not intend to form any immediate connection. Mr. Boyer must have different ideas, madam; and he has reason for them, if I may judge by appearances. When do you expect another visit from him? In about a fortnight. And is my fate to be then decided; and so decided, as I fear it will be, through the influence of your friends, if not by your own inclination? My friends, sir, will not control; they will only advise to what they think most for my interest; and I hope, that my conduct will not be unworthy of their approbation.[2] Pardon me, my dear Eliza, said he, if I am impertinent; it is my regard for you which impels me to the presumption. Do you intend to give your hand to Mr. Boyer? I do not intend to give my hand to any man at present. I have but lately entered society; and wish, for a while, to enjoy my freedom, in the participation of pleasures, suited to my age and sex. These, said he, you are aware, I suppose, when you form a connection with that man, you must renounce; and content yourself with a confinement to the tedious round of domestic duties, the pedantic conversation of scholars, and the invidious criticisms of a whole town. I have been accustomed, said I, and am therefore attached to men of letters; and as to the praise or censure of the populace, I hope always to enjoy that approbation of conscience, which will render me superior to both. But you forget your promise, not to talk in this style; and have deviated far from the character of a friend and brother, with which you consented to rest satisfied. Yes, but I find myself unequal to the task. I am not stoic enough, tamely to make so great a sacrifice. I must plead for an interest in your favor, till you banish me from your presence, and tell me plainly that you hate me. We had by this time reached the gate; and as we dismounted, were unexpectedly accosted by Mr. Selby, who had come agreeably to his promise, to dine with us, and receive my letter to Mr. Boyer.

Major Sanford took his leave as General Richman appeared at the door. The General and his lady rallied me on my change of company; but very prudently concealed their sentiments of Major Sanford, while Mr. Selby was present. Nothing material occurred before, and during dinner; soon after which, Mr. Selby went away. I retired to dress for the assembly; and had nearly completed the labor of the toilet, when Mrs. Richman entered. My friendship for you, my dear Eliza, said she, interests me so much in your affairs, that I cannot repress my curiosity to know who has the honor of your

2. Approval.

hand, this evening. If it be any honor, said I, it will be confered on
Major Sanford. I think it far too great to be thus bestowed, returned
she. It is perfectly astonishing to me, that the virtuous part of my
sex will countenance, caress, and encourage those men, whose pro-
fession it is to blast their reputation, destroy their peace, and triumph
in their infamy! Is this, madam, the avowed design of Major Sanford?
I know not what he avows; but his practice too plainly bespeaks his
principles and views. Does he now practice the arts you mention; or
do you refer to past follies? I cannot answer for his present conduct;
his past has established his character. You, madam, are an advocate
for charity; that, perhaps, if exercised in this instance might lead you
to think it possible for him to reform; to become a valuable member
of society; and, when connected with a lady of virtue and refinement,
to be capable of making a good husband. I cannot conceive that such
a lady would be willing to risk her all upon the slender prospect of his
reformation. I hope the one with whom I am conversing, has no
inclination to so hazardous, an experiment. Why, not much. Not
much! If you have any, why do you continue to encourage Mr. Boyer's
addresses? I am not sufficiently acquainted with either yet, to deter-
mine which to take. At present, I shall not confine myself in any
way. In regard to these men, my fancy and my judgment are in
scales.[3] Sometimes one preponderates, sometimes the other. Which
will finally outweigh, time alone can reveal. O my cousin, beware of
the delusions of fancy! Reason must be our guide, if we would expect
durable happiness. At this instant a servant opened the door, and
told me that Major Sanford waited in the parlor. Being ready, I
wished Mrs. Richman a good evening, and went down. Neither Gen-
eral Richman nor his lady appeared. He therefore handed me imme-
diately into his phaeton,[4] and we were soon in the assembly room.

   I was surprised, on my entrance, to find Mr. Selby there, as he did
not mention, at dinner, his intention of going. He attached himself
to our party; and, in the intervals of dancing, took every opportunity
of conversing with me. These, however, were not many; for Major
Sanford assiduously precluded the possibility of my being much
engaged by any one else. We passed the evening very agreeably; but
the Major's importunity was rather troublesome, as we returned
home. He insisted upon my declaring whether Mr. Boyer really pos-
sessed my affections; and whether I intended to confer myself on
him or not. If, said he, you answer me in the affirmative, I must
despair; but if you have not absolutely decided against me, I will still
hope, that my persevering assiduity, my faithful love, may at last be

3. I.e., her imaginative and rational faculties are being weighed against one another.
4. A light, open carriage.

rewarded. I told him that I was under no obligation to give him any account of my disposition towards another; and that he must remember the terms of our present association, to which he had subscribed. I therefore begged him to wave the subject now, if not forever. He asked my pardon, if he had been impertinent; but desired leave to renew his request, that I would receive his visits, his friendly visits. I replied, that I could not grant this; and that he must blame himself, not me, if he was an unwelcome guest at General Richman's. He lamented the prejudices which my friends had imbibed against him; but flattered himself that I was more liberal than to be influenced by them, without any positive proof of demerit; as it was impossible that his conduct towards me should ever deviate from the strictest rules of honor and love.

What shall I say now, my friend? This man, to an agreeable person has superadded, graceful manners, an amiable temper, and a fortune sufficient to ensure the enjoyments of all the pleasing varieties of social life. Perhaps a gay disposition, and a lax education may have betrayed him into some scenes of dissipation. But is it not an adage generally received, that *"a reformed rake makes the best husband?"*[5] My fancy leads me for happiness to the festive haunts of fashionable life. I am at present, and know not but I ever shall be, too volatile for a confinement to domestic avocations,[6] and sedentary pleasures. I dare not, therefore, place myself in a situation where these must be indispensable. Mr. Boyer's person, and character are agreeable. I really esteem the man. My reason and judgment, as I have observed before, declare for a connection with him, as a state of tranquillity and rational happiness. But the idea of relinquishing those delightful amusements and flattering attentions, which wealth and equipage bestow, is painful. Why were not the virtues of the one, and the graces and affluence of the other combined? I should then have been happy indeed! But, as the case now stands, I am loath to give up either; being doubtful which will conduce most to my felicity.

Pray write me impartially; let me know your real sentiments, for I rely greatly upon your opinion.

I am, &c.

ELIZA WHARTON.

---

5. This claim—and its falsity—would be familiar to readers of Richardson's *Clarissa*, though it had been inspired by Richardson's earlier novel, *Pamela* (1740), in which the rake does reform and marry his would-be victim.
6. Hobbies, distractions.

# L  E  T  T  E  R   XXVII.

*NEW-HAVEN.*

I am quite a convert to Pope's assertion, that "Every woman is, at heart, a rake."[1] How else can we account for the pleasure which they evidently receive from the society, the flattery, the caresses of men of that character? Even the most virtuous of them seem naturally prone to gaiety, to pleasure, and, I had almost said, to dissipation! How else shall we account for the existence of this disposition, in your favorite fair? It cannot be the result of her education. Such a one as she has received, is calculated to give her a very different turn of mind. You must forgive me, my friend, for I am a little vexed, and alarmed on your account. I went last evening to the assembly, as I told you in my last that I intended. I was purposely without a partner, that I might have the liberty to exercise my gallantry, as circumstances should invite. Indeed, I must own, that my particular design was, to observe Miss Wharton's movements, being rather inclined to jealousy in your behalf. She was handed into the assembly room by Major Sanford. The brilliance of their appearance, the levity[2] of their manners, and the contrast of their characters I found to be a general subject of speculation. I endeavored to associate with Miss Wharton, but found it impossible to detach her a moment from the coxcomb[3] who attended her. If she has any idea of a connection with you, why does she continue to associate with another, especially with one of so opposite a description? I am seriously afraid, that there is more intimacy between them, than there ought to be, considering the encouragement she has given you.

I hope you will not be offended by my freedom in this matter. It originates in a concern for your honor and future happiness. I am anxious, lest you should be made the dupe of a coquette, and your peace of mind fall a sacrifice to an artful debauchee. Yet I must believe, that Miss Wharton has, in reality, all that virtue and good sense of which she enjoys the reputation; but her present conduct is mysterious.

I have said enough (more than I ought, perhaps) to awaken your attention to circumstances, which *may* lead to important events. If they appear of little, or no consequence to you, you will at least

1. Excerpted from Alexander Pope's "Epistle to a Lady" (1735), which demonstrates the qualities of an ideal woman by contrast with her opposite.
2. Lightness; freedom of conduct.
3. Fool; superficial pretender.

ascribe the mention of them to motives of sincere regard, in your
friend and humble servant,

T. SELBY.

# L E T T E R   XXVIII.

*NEW-HAVEN.*

I go on finely with my amour. I have every encouragement that I
could wish. Indeed my fair one does not verbally declare in my favor;
but then, according to the vulgar proverb, *that actions speak louder
than words*, I have no reason to complain; since she evidently
approves my gallantry, is pleased with my company, and listens to my
flattery. Her sagatious[1] friends have undoubtedly given her a detail of
my vices. If, therefore, my past conduct has been repugnant to her
notions of propriety, why does she not act consistently, and refuse at
once to associate with a man whose character she cannot esteem?
But no; that, Charles, is no part of the female plan: our entrapping a
few of their sex, only discovers the gaiety of our dispositions, the
insinuating graces of our manners, and the irresistible charms of our
persons and address. These qualifications are very alluring to the
sprightly fancy of the fair. They think to enjoy the pleasures which
result from this source; while their vanity and ignorance prompt
each one to imagine herself superior to delusion; and to anticipate
the honor of reclaiming the libertine, and reforming the rake! I dont
know, however, but this girl will really have that merit with me; for
I am so much attached to her, that I begin to suspect I should
sooner become a convert to sobriety than lose her. I cannot find that
I have made much impression on her heart as yet. Want of success
in this point mortifies me extremely, as it is the first time I ever
failed. Besides, I am apprehensive that she is prepossessed in favor
of the other swain, the clerical lover, whom I have mentioned to you
before. The chord, therefore, upon which I play the most, is the dis-
similarity of their dispositions and pleasures. I endeavor to detach
her from him, and disaffect her towards him; knowing, that if I can
separate them entirely, I shall be more likely to succeed in my plan.
Not that I have any thoughts of marrying her myself; that will not do
at present. But I love her too well to see her connected with another
for life. I must own myself a little revengeful too in this affair. I wish

1. I.e., sagacious, or acute in perception; intelligent.

to punish her friends, as she calls them, for their malice towards me; for their cold and negligent treatment of me whenever I go to the house. I know that to frustrate their designs of a connection between Mr. Boyer and Eliza would be a grievous disappointment. I have not yet determined to seduce her, though, with all her pretensions to virtue, I do not think it impossible. And if I should, she can blame none but herself, since she knows my character, and has no reason to wonder if I act consistently with it. If she will play with a lion, let her beware of his paw, I say. At present, I wish innocently to enjoy her society; it is a luxury which I never tasted before. She is the very soul of pleasure. The gayest circle is irradiated by her presence, and the highest entertainment receives its greatest charm from her smiles. Besides, I have purchased the seat[2] of Capt. Pribble, about a mile from her mother's; and can I think of suffering her to leave the neighborhood, just as I enter it? I shall exert every nerve to prevent that, and hope to meet with the usual success of

PETER SANFORD.

# L E T T E R   XXIX.

### TO MISS ELIZA WHARTON.

*HARTFORD.*

You desire me to write to you, my friend; but if you had not, I should by no means have refrained. I tremble at the precipice on which you stand; and must echo, and re-echo the seasonable admonition of the excellent Mrs. Richman, "Beware of the delusions of fancy!" You are strangely infatuated by them! Let not the magic arts of that worthless Sanford lead you, like an *ignis fatuus*[1] from the path of rectitude and virtue!

I do not find, in all your conversations with him, that one word about marriage drops from his lips. This is mysterious? No, it is characteristic of the man. Suppose, however, that his views are honorable; yet what can you expect, what can you promise yourself from such a connection? "A reformed rake," you say, "makes the best husband;" a trite, but a very erroneous maxim, as the fatal experience of thousands of our sex can testify. In the first place, I believe that rakes very seldom *do* reform, while their fortunes and constitutions enable them to pursue their licentious pleasures. But even allowing this to happen, can a woman of refinement and delicacy enjoy the society

2. Estate.
1. *Latin*; a ghostly and misleading light.

of a man, whose mind has been corrupted, whose taste has been vitiated, and who has contracted a depravity both of sentiment and manners, which no degree of repentance can wholly efface? Besides, of true love they are absolutely incapable. Their passions have been too much hackneyed to admit so pure a flame. You cannot anticipate sincere and lasting respect from them. They have been so long accustomed to the company of those of our sex, who observe no esteem; that the greatest dignity and purity of character can never excite it in their breasts. They are naturally prone to jealousy. Habituated to an intercourse with the baser part of the sex, they level the whole, and seldom believe any to be incorruptible. They are always hard hearted and cruel. How else could they triumph in the miseries which they frequently occasion? Their specious manners may render them agreeable companions abroad; but at home the evil propensities of their minds will invariably predominate. They are steeled against the tender affections, which render domestic life delightful; strangers to the kind, the endearing sympathies of husband, father, and friend! The thousand nameless attentions which soften the rugged path of life, are neglected, and deemed unworthy of notice by persons who have been inured to scenes of dissipation and debauchery! and is a man of this description to be the partner, the companion, the bosom friend of my Eliza? Forbid it heaven! Let not the noble qualities, so lavishly bestowed upon her, be thus unworthily sacrificed!

You seem to be particularly charmed with the fortune of Major Sanford; with the gaiety of his appearance; with the splendor of his equipage; with the politeness of his manners; with what you call the graces of his person! These, alas! are superficial, ensnaring endowments. As to fortune, prudence, economy, and regularity are necessary to preserve it, when possessed. Of these Major Sanford is certainly destitute; unless common fame (which more frequently tells truth than some are willing to allow) does him great injustice. As to external parade, it will not satisfy the rational mind, when it aspires to those substantial pleasures for which yours is formed. And as to the graces of person and manners, they are but a wretched substitute for those virtues which adorn and dignify human life. Can you, who have always been used to serenity and order in a family, to rational, refined and improving conversation, relinquish them, and launch into the whirlpool of frivolity, where the correct taste and the delicate sensibility which you possess must constantly be wounded by the frothy and illiberal sallies of licentious wit?[2]

2. Inappropriate or risqué humor.

This, my dear, is but a faint picture of the situation to which you seem inclined! Reverse the scene, and you will perceive the alternative, which is submitted to your option, in a virtuous connection with Mr. Boyer. Remember that you are acting for life; and that your happiness in this world; perhaps in the next, depends on your present choice!

I called, last evening, to see your mamma. She is fondly anticipating your return; and rejoicing in the prospect of your agreeable and speedy settlement. I could not find it in my heart to distress her by intimating that you had other views. I wish her benevolent bosom never more to feel the pangs of disappointed hope.

I am busily engaged in preparing for my nuptials. The solemn words "as long as ye both shall live," render me thoughtful and serious. I hope for your enlivening presence soon; which will prove a seasonable cordial to the spirits of your

LUCY FREEMAN.

# L  E  T  T  E  R   XXX.

### TO MISS LUCY FREEMAN.

*NEW-HAVEN.*

I believe your spirits need a cordial indeed, my dear Lucy; after drawing so dreadful a portrait of my swain. But I call him mine no longer. I renounce him entirely. My friends shall be gratified. And if their predictions are verified, I shall be happy in a union with the man of their choice. General Richman and lady have labored abundantly to prove that my ruin was inevitable if I did not immediately break all intercourse with Major Sanford. I promised a compliance with their wishes; and have accomplished the task, though a hard one I found it. Last Thursday he was here, and desired leave to spend an hour with me. I readily consented, assuring my friends it should be the last hour, which I would ever spend in his company.

He told me that he was obliged to leave town for a few days; and, as I should probably see Mr. Boyer, before his return, he could not depart in peace without once more endeavoring to interest me in his favor; to obtain some token of esteem, some glimpse of hope, that I would not utterly reject him, to support him in his absence. I thanked him for the polite attention he had paid me, since our acquaintance; told him that I should ever retain a grateful sense of his partiality to me; that he would ever share my best wishes; but that all connection of the kind, to which he alluded, must from that time, for ever cease.

He exerted all his eloquence to obtain a retraction of that sentence, and ran, with the greatest volubility,[1] through all the protestations, prayers, entreaties, professions and assurances which love could feel or art contrive. I had resolution, however, to resist them, and to command my own emotions on the occasion, better than my natural sensibility gave me reason to expect.

Finding every effort vain, he rose precipitately, and bade me adieu. I urged his tarrying to tea; but he declined, saying, that he must retire to his chamber, being, in his present state of mind, unfit for any society, as he was banished from mine. I offered him my hand, which he pressed with ardor to his lips, and bowing in silence, left the room.

Thus terminated this affair; an affair, which, perhaps, was only the effect of mere gallantry on his part, and of unmeaning pleasantry on mine; and which, I am sorry to say, has given my friends so much anxiety and concern. I am under obligations to them for their kind solicitude, however causeless it may have been.

As an agreeable companion, as a polite and finished gallant, Major Sanford is all that the most lively fancy could wish. And as you have always affirmed that I was a little inclined to coquetry, can you wonder at my exercising it upon so happy a subject? Besides, when I thought more seriously, his liberal fortune[2] was extremely alluring to me, who, you know, have been hitherto confined to the rigid rules of prudence and economy, not to say, necessity in my finances.

Miss Laurence called on me yesterday, as she was taking the air, and asked me whether Major Sanford took leave of me when he left town? He was here last week, said I, but I did not know that he was gone away. O yes, she replied, he is gone to take possession of his seat, which he has lately purchased of Captain Pribble. I am told it is superb; and it ought to be, if it have the honor of his residence. Then you have a great opinion of Major Sanford, said I. Certainly; and has not every body else? said she. I am sure he is a very fine gentleman. Mrs. Richman smiled rather contemptuously, and I changed the subject.

I believe that the innocent heart of this simple girl is a little taken in.

I have just received a letter from Mr. Boyer, in the usual style. He expects the superlative happiness of kissing my hand next week. O dear! I believe I must begin to fix my phiz.[3] Let me run to the glass and try if I can make up one that will look *madamish*. Yes, I succeed very well.

1. Ready flow of speech.
2. Substantial wealth.
3. Face; expression.

I congratulate you on your new neighbor; but I advise friend George to have the guardian knot[4] tied immediately, lest you should be ensnared by this bewitching 'squire.

I have been trying to seduce General Richman to accompany me to the assembly, this evening, but cannot prevail. Were Mrs. Richman able to go with us, he would be very happy to wait on us together; but to tell the truth, he had rather enjoy her company at home, than any which is to be found abroad. I rallied him on his old fashioned taste; but my heart approved and applauded his attachment. I despise the married man or woman, who harbors an inclination to partake of separate pleasures.

I am told, that a servant man inquires for me below; the messenger of some enamoured swain, I suppose. I will step down and learn what message he brings————

Nothing extraordinary; it is only a card of compliments from a Mr. Emmons, a respectable merchant of this city, requesting the honor to wait on me to the assembly this evening. A welcome request, which I made no hesitation to grant. If I must resign these favorite amusements, let me enjoy as large a share as possible, till the time arrive. Adieu. I must repair to the toilet and adorn for a new conquest, the person of

ELIZA WHARTON.

# L  E  T  T  E  R  XXXI.

TO MISS ELIZA WHARTON.

*HARTFORD.*

I am very happy to find you are in so good spirits, Eliza, after parting with your favorite swain. For I perceive that he is really the favorite of your fancy, though your heart cannot esteem him; and, independent of that, no sensations can be durable.

I can tell you some news of this strange man. He has arrived, and taken possession of his seat. Having given general invitations, he has been called upon and welcomed by most of the neighboring gentry. Yesterday he made an elegant entertainment. Friend George (as you call him) and I were of the number, who had cards. Twenty one couple went, I am told. We did not go. I consider my time too valuable to be spent in cultivating acquaintance with a person from whom

---

4. I.e., marital bond. Eliza puns on the phrase "Gordian Knot," or an extremely complicated problem or situation.

neither pleasure nor improvement are to be expected. His profuseness may bribe the unthinking multitude to show him respect; but he must know, that though

> "Places and honors have been bought for gold,
> Esteem and love were never to be sold."[1]

I look upon the vicious habits, and abandoned character of Major Sanford, to have more pernicious[2] effects on society, than the perpetrations of the robber and the assassin. These, when detected, are rigidly punished by the laws of the land. If their lives be spared, they are shunned by society, and treated with every mark of disapprobation and contempt. But to the disgrace of humanity and virtue, the assassin of honor; the wretch, who breaks the peace of families, who robs virgin innocence of its charms, who triumphs over the ill placed confidence of the inexperienced, unsuspecting, and too credulous fair, is received, and caressed, not only by his own sex, to which he is a reproach, but even by ours, who have every conceivable reason to despise and avoid him. Influenced by these principles, I am neither ashamed nor afraid openly to avow my sentiments of this man, and my reasons for treating him with the most pointed neglect.

I write warmly on the subject; for it is a subject in which I think the honor and happiness of my sex concerned. I wish they would more generally espouse their own cause. It would conduce to the public weal, and to their personal respectability. I rejoice, heartily, that you have had resolution to resist his allurements, to detect and repel his artifices. Resolution, in such a case, is absolutely necessary; for,

> "In spite of all the virtue we can boast,
> The woman that deliberates is lost."[3]

As I was riding out, yesterday, I met your mamma. She wondered that I was not one of the party at our new neighbor's. The reason, madam, said I, is that I do not like the character of the man. I know nothing of him, said she; he is quite a stranger to me, only as he called at my house, last week, to pay me his respects, as he said, for the sake of my late husband, whose memory he revered; and because I was the mother of Miss Eliza Wharton, with whom he had the honor of some little acquaintance. His manners are engaging, and I am sorry to hear that his morals are corrupt.

---

1. Foster amends Pope's *An Essay on Man* (1733–34): "Judges and senates have been bought for gold; / Esteem and love were never to be sold." Pope's poem instructs readers that God, not man, is the center of life, and that it behooves mortals to behave virtuously.
2. Destructive.
3. From Addison's *Cato*, Act 4, Scene 1, wherein a young woman cannot decide which man to love.

This, my dear, is a very extraordinary visit. I fear that he has not yet laid aside his arts. Be still on your guard, is the advice of your sincere and faithful friend,

LUCY FREEMAN.

# L E T T E R   XXXII.

TO MR. CHARLES DEIGHTON.

*HARTFORD.*

I am really banished and rejected; desired never more to think of the girl I love, with a view of indulging that love, or of rendering it acceptable to its object! You will perhaps, dispute the propriety of the term, and tell me it is not love, it is only gallantry, and a desire to exercise it with her, as a favorite nymph.[1] I neither know, nor care by what appellation you distinguish it, but it truly gives me pain. I have not felt one sensation of genuine pleasure since I heard my sentence; yet I acquiesced in it, and submissively took my leave; though I doubt not but I shall retaliate the indignity one time or other.

I have taken possession of my new purchase, an elegant and delightful residence. It is rendered more so by being in the vicinity of my charmer's native abode. This circumstance will conduce much to my enjoyment, if I can succeed in my plan of separating her from Mr. Boyer. I know that my situation and mode of life are far more pleasing to her than his, and shall therefore trust to my appearance and address for a reestablishment in her favor. I intend, if possible, to ingratiate myself with her particular friends. For this purpose, I called last week at her mother's, to pay my respects to her (so I told the good woman) as an object of my particular regard; and as the parent of a young lady, whom I had the honor to know and admire. She received me very civilly, thanked me for my attention, and invited me to call whenever I had opportunity; which was the very thing I wanted. I intend likewise, to court popularity. I don't know but I must accept, by and by, some lucrative office in the civil department.[2] Yet I cannot bear the idea of confinement to business. It appears to me quite inconsistent with the character of a gentleman; I am sure it is, with that of a man of pleasure. But something I must do; for I tell you, in confidence, that I was obliged to mortgage this place, because I had not wherewithal to pay for it. But I shall manage matters very well, I have no doubt, and keep up the appearance of

1. In Greek mythology, a semi-divine beautiful maiden.
2. A government position.

affluence, till I find some lady in a strait for a husband, whose fortune will enable me to extricate myself from these embarrassments. Do come and see me, Charles; for, notwithstanding all my gaiety and parade, I have some turns of the hypo, some qualms of conscience, you will call them; but I meddle not with such obsolete words. And so good bye to you, says

<div align="right">Peter Sanford.</div>

# L  E  T  T  E  R  XXXIII.

## TO MISS LUCY FREEMAN.

<div align="right"><em>New-Haven.</em></div>

MY DEAR FRIEND,

I believe I must begin to assume airs of gravity; and they will not be quite so foreign to my feelings now, as at some other times. You shall know the reason. I have been associated for three days, with sentiment and sobriety, in the person of Mr. Boyer. I don't know but this man will seduce me into matrimony. He is very eloquent upon the subject; and his manners are so solemn, that I am strongly tempted, yet I dare not to laugh. Really, Lucy, there is something extremely engaging and soothing too, in virtuous and refined conversation. It is a source of enjoyment which cannot be realised by the dissolute and unreflecting. But then, this particular theme of his, is not a favorite one to me; I mean, as connected with its consequences, care and confinement. However, I have compounded the matter with him, and conditioned that he shall expatiate on the subject, and call it by what name he pleases, *platonic* or *conjugal*, provided he will let me take my own time for the consummation. I have consented that he shall escort me, next week, to see my mamma and my Lucy. O, how the idea of returning to that revered mansion, to those beloved friends, exhilarates my spirits!

General Richman's politeness to me has induced him to invite a large party of those gentlemen and ladies who have been particularly attentive to me, during my residence here, to dine and take tea, to morrow. After that, I expect to be engaged in making farewell visits, till I leave the place. I shall, therefore, forego the pleasure of telling you any occurrences, subsequent to this date, until you see and converse with your sincere friend,

<div align="right">Eliza Wharton.</div>

# L  E  T  T  E  R  XXXIV.

*HARTFORD.*

DEAR MADAM,

The day after I left your hospitable dwelling, brought me safe to that of my honored mamma; to the seat of maternal and filial affection; of social ease and domestic peace; of every species of happiness which can result from religion and virtue; from refinement in morals, and manners.

I found my brother and his wife, with Lucy Freeman and Mr. Sumner, waiting to receive and bid me welcome. I flew with extacy[1] to the bosom of my mamma, who received me with her accustomed affection, testified by the expressive tears of tenderness which stole silently down her widowed cheek. She was unable to speak. I was equally so. We therefore indulged, a moment, the pleasing emotions of sympathising sensibility. When disengaged from her fond embrace, I was saluted by the others in turn; and having recovered myself, I presented Mr. Boyer to each of the company, and each of the company to him. He was cordially received by all, but more especially by my mamma.

The next day I was called upon and welcomed by several of my neighboring acquaintance; among whom I was not a little surprised to see Major Sanford. He came in company with Mr. Stoddard and Lady, whom he overtook, as he told me, near by; and, as they informed him that the design of their visit was to welcome me home, he readily accepted their invitation to partake of the pleasure which every one must receive on my return. I bowed slightly at his compliment, taking no visible notice of any peculiarity of expression either in his words or looks.

His politeness to Mr. Boyer, appeared to be the result of habit. Mr. Boyer's to him, to be forced by respect to the company to which he had gained admission. I dare say, that each felt a conscious superiority; the one on the score of merit; the other on that of fortune. Which ought to outweigh, the judicious mind will easily decide. The scale, as I once observed to you, will turn as fancy or reason preponderates. I believe the esteem which I now have for Mr. Boyer, will keep me steady; except, perhaps, some little excentricities, now and then, just by way of variety. I am going to morrow morning to spend a few days with Lucy Freeman; to assist in the preparation for, and the

---

1. I.e., ecstasy.

solemnization of her nuptials. Mr. Boyer, in the mean time, will tarry among his friends in town. My mamma is excessively partial to him; though I am not yet jealous that she means to rival me. I am not certain, however, but it might be happy for him if she should. For I suspect, notwithstanding the disparity of her age, that she is better calculated to make him a good wife than I am or ever shall be.

But to be sober. Please, madam, to make my compliments acceptable to those of your neighbors, whose politeness and attention to me, while at your house, have laid me under particular obligations of gratitude and respect. My best regards attend General Richman. Pray tell him, that though I never expect to be so good a wife as he is blessed with; yet I intend, after a while (when I have sowed all my wild oats) to make a tolerable one.

I am anxious to hear of a wished for event, and of your safety. All who know you, feel interested in your health and happiness; but none more warmly than your obliged and affectionate

<div align="right">ELIZA WHARTON.</div>

# L E T T E R   XXXV.

<div align="center">TO MISS ELIZA WHARTON.</div>

<div align="right">*NEW-HAVEN.*</div>

I write a line, at Mrs. Richman's request, just to inform you, Eliza, that yesterday, that lovely and beloved woman presented me with a daughter. This event awakens new sensations in my mind; and calls into exercise a kind of affection which had before lain dormant. I feel already the tenderness of a parent; while imagination fondly traces the mother's likeness in the infant form. Mrs. Richman expects to receive your congratulations, in a letter by the next post. She bids me tell you, moreover, that she hopes soon to receive an invitation, and be able to attend to the consummation you talk of. Give Mrs. Richman's and my particular regards to your excellent mother; and to the worthy Mr. Boyer. With sentiments of esteem and friendship, I am, &c.

<div align="right">S. RICHMAN.</div>

# L  E  T  T  E  R  XXXVI.

### TO MRS. RICHMAN.

*HARTFORD.*

From the scenes of festive mirth, from the conviviality[1] of rejoicing friends, and from the dissipating amusements of the gay world, I retire with alacrity, to hail my beloved friend on the important charge which she has received; on the accession to her family, and, may I not say, on the addition to her care; since that care will be more than counterbalanced by the pleasure it confers. Hail happy babe! Ushered into the world by the best of mothers; entitled by birth-right to virtue and honor; defended by parental love, from the weakness of infancy and childhood, by guardian wisdom from the perils of youth, and by affluent independence from the griping hand of poverty, in more advanced life! May these animating prospects be realised by your little daughter; and may you long enjoy the rich reward of seeing her all that you wish!

Yesterday, my dear friend, Lucy Freeman gave her hand to the amiable and accomplished Mr. George Sumner. A large circle of congratulating friends were present. Her dress was such as wealth and elegance required. Her deportment was every thing that modesty and propriety could suggest. They are, indeed, a charming couple. The consonance of their dispositions, the similarity of their tastes, and the equality of their ages are a sure pledge of happiness. Every eye beamed with pleasure on the occasion, and every tongue echoed the wishes of benevolence. Mine only was silent. Though not less interested in the felicity of my friend than the rest, yet the idea of a separation; perhaps, of an alienation of affection, by means of her entire devotion to another, cast an involuntary gloom over my mind. Mr. Boyer took my hand, after the ceremony was past. Permit me, Miss Wharton, said he, to lead you to your lovely friend; her happiness must be heightened by your participation of it. Oh no; said I, I am too selfish for that. She has conferred upon another that affection which I wished to engross. My love was too fervent to admit a rival. Retaliate then, said he, this fancied wrong, by doing likewise. I observed that this was not a proper time to discuss that subject; and, resuming my seat, endeavored to put on the appearance of my accustomed vivacity. I need not relate the remaining particulars of the evening's entertainment. Mr. Boyer returned with my mamma, and I remained at Mrs. Freeman's.

---

1. Jovial company.

We are to have a ball here, this evening. Mr. Boyer has been with us, and tried to monopolize my company; but in vain. I am too much engaged by the exhilerating scenes around, for attending to a subject which affords no variety. I shall not close this till to morrow.

————I am rather fatigued with the amusements of last night, which were protracted to a late hour. Mr. Boyer was present; and I was pleased to see him not averse to the entertainment, though his profession prevented his taking an active part. As all the neighboring gentry were invited, Mr. Freeman would, by no means, omit Major Sanford, which his daughter earnestly solicited. It happened (unfortunately, shall I say?) that I drew him for a partner. Yet I must own, that I felt very little reluctance to my lot. He is an excellent dancer, and well calculated for a companion in the hours of mirth and gaiety. I regretted Mr. Boyer's being present, however; because my enjoyment seemed to give him pain. I hope he is not inclined to the passion of jealousy. If he is, I fear it will be somewhat exercised.

Lucy Freeman, now Mrs. Sumner, removes, next week, to Boston. I have agreed to accompany her, and spend a month or two in her family. This will give variety to the journey of life. Be so kind as to direct your next letter to me there.

Kiss the dear little babe for me. Give love, compliments, &c. as respectively due; and believe me, with every sentiment of respect, your affectionate

ELIZA WHARTON.

# L E T T E R   XXXVII.

### TO MR. CHARLES DEIGHTON.

*HARTFORD.*

DEAR CHARLES,

My hopes begin to revive. I am again permitted to associate with my Eliza; invited to the same entertainment! She does not refuse to join with me in the mazy dance,[1] and partake the scenes of festive mirth. Nay, more; she allows me to press her hand to my lips; and listens to the sighing accents of love. Love her, I certainly do. Would to heaven I could marry her! Would to heaven I had preserved my fortune; or she had one to supply its place! I am distracted at the idea of losing her forever. I am sometimes tempted to solicit her hand in serious

---

1. A jocular dance; alternately, resembling a maze. An allusion to Alexander Pope's *The Dunciad*; Thomson also writes of the mazy dance in "Autumn," *The Seasons*, which Foster cites throughout the novel.

earnest; but if I should, poverty and want must be the consequence. Her disappointment in the expectation of affluence and splendor, which I believe her ruling passion,[2] would afford a perpetual source of discontent and mutual wretchedness.

She is going to Boston with her friend, Mrs. Sumner. I must follow her. I must break the connection, which is rapidly forming, between her and Mr. Boyer; and enjoy her society a while longer, if no more.

I have had a little intimation from New-Haven, that Miss Laurence is partial to me, and might easily be obtained, with a handsome property into the bargain. I am neither pleased with, nor averse to the girl. But she has money, and that may supply the place of love, by enabling me to pursue independent pleasures. This she must expect, if she marries a man of my cast. She doubtless knows my character; and if she is so vain of her charms or influence, as to think of reforming or confining me, she must bear the consequences.

However, I can keep my head up, at present, without recourse to the noose of matrimony; and shall, therefore, defer any particular attention to her, till necessity requires it.

<div align="center">I am, &c.</div>

<div align="right">PETER SANFORD.</div>

# L E T T E R   XXXVIII.

<div align="center">TO MRS. M. WHARTON.</div>

<div align="right">*BOSTON.*</div>

You commanded me, my dear mamma, to write you. That command, I cheerfully obey, in testimony of my ready submission and respect. No other avocation could arrest my time, which is now completely occupied in scenes of amusement.

Mrs. Sumner is agreeably settled and situated. She appears to be possessed of every blessing which can render life desirable. Almost every day, since our arrival, has been engrossed by visitants. Our evenings, we have devoted to company abroad; and that more generally than we should otherwise have done, as my stay is limited to so short a period. The museum, the theatres, the circus and the assemblies have been frequented.

Mrs. Sumner has made me several presents, notwithstanding which, the articles requisite to a fashionable appearance, have involved me in considerable expense. I fear that you will think me extravagant when you are told how much.

---

2. A preoccupation or dominant concern.

Mr. Boyer tarried in town about a week, having business. He appeared a little concerned at my taste for dissipation, as he once termed it. He even took the liberty to converse seriously on the subject.

I was displeased with his freedom; and reminded him that I had the disposal of my own time, as yet; and that while I escaped the censure of my own heart, I hoped that no one else would presume to arraign it.[1] He apologised, and gave up his argument.

I was much surprised, the first time I went to the play, to see Major Sanford in the very next box.[2] He immediately joined our party; and wherever I have been since, I have been almost sure to meet him.

Mr. Boyer has taken his departure; and I do not expect to see him again, till I return home.

O mamma! I am embarrassed about this man. His worth I acknowledge; nay, I esteem him very highly. But can there be happiness with such a disparity of dispositions?

I shall soon return to the bosom of domestic tranquillity, to the arms of maternal tenderness, where I can deliberate and advise at leisure, about this important matter. Till when,

<div align="center">I am, &c.</div>

<div align="right">ELIZA WHARTON.</div>

# L  E  T  T  E  R    XXXIX.

<div align="center">TO MR. T. SELBY.</div>

<div align="right">*HAMPSHIRE.*</div>

DEAR SIR,

I believe that I owe you an apology for my long silence. But my time has been much engrossed of late; and my mind much more so. When it will be otherwise, I cannot foresee. I fear, my friend, that there is some foundation for your suspicions respecting my beloved Eliza. What pity it is, that so fair a form, so accomplished a mind, should be tarnished, in the smallest degree, by the follies of coquetry! If this be the fact, which I am loth to believe, all my regard for her shall never make me the dupe of it.

When I arrived at her residence, at New-Haven, where I told you in my last, I was soon to go, she gave me a most cordial reception.

---

1. To examine, find fault with, or call to trial.
2. An anachronism in Foster's adaptation of the Whitman story. When Elizabeth Whitman died in 1788, the theater was still six years away from being legalized in Boston, and only after much public debate.

Her whole behavior to me was correspondent with those sentiments of esteem and affection which she modestly avowed. She permitted me to accompany her to Hartford, to restore her to her mother, and to declare my wish to receive her again from her hand. Thus far, all was harmony and happiness. As all my wishes were consistent with virtue and honor, she readily indulged them. She took apparent pleasure in my company, encouraged my hopes of a future union, and listened to the tender accents of love.

But the scenes of gaiety, which invited her attention, reversed her conduct. The delightful hours of mutual confidence, of sentimental converse, and of the interchange of refined affection, were no more! Instead of these, parties were formed, unpleasing to my taste; and every opportunity was embraced to join in diversions, in which she knew I could not consistently take a share. I, however, acquiesced in her pleasure, though I sometimes thought myself neglected, and even hinted it to her mother. The old lady apologised for her daughter, by alledging that she had been absent for a long time; that her acquaintances were rejoiced at her return, and welcomed her by striving to promote her amusement.

One of her most intimate friends was married during my stay; and she appeared deeply interested in the event. She spent several days in assisting her, previous to the celebration. I resided, in the mean time, at her mamma's, visiting her at her friend's, where Major Sanford, among others, was received as a guest. Mrs. Sumner acquainted me that she had prevailed on Miss Wharton to go and spend a few weeks with her at Boston, whither she was removing; and urged my accompanying them. I endeavored to excuse myself, as I had been absent from my people a considerable time, and my return was now expected. But their importunity was so great, and Eliza's declaration that it would be very agreeable to her, so tempting, that I consented. Here I took lodgings and spent about a week, taking every opportunity to converse with Eliza, striving to discover her real disposition towards me. I mentioned the inconvenience of visiting her so often as I wished, and suggested my desire to enter, as soon as might be, into a family relation. I painted in the most alluring colours the pleasures resulting from domestic tranquillity, mutual confidence, and conjugal affection; and insisted on her declaring frankly whether she designed to share this happiness with me, and when it should commence. She owned that she intended to give me her hand; but when she should be ready, she could not yet determine. She pretended a promise from me to wait her time; to consent that she should share the pleasures of the fashionable world, as long as she chose, &c.

I then attempted to convince her of her mistaken ideas of pleasure; that the scenes of dissipation, of which she was so passionately fond,

afforded no true enjoyment; that the adulation[1] of the coxcomb could not give durability to her charms, or secure the approbation of the wise and good; nor could the fashionable amusements of brilliant assemblies, and crouded theatres furnish the mind with

> "That which nothing earthly gives, or can destroy,
> The soul's calm sunshine, and the heart felt joy."[2]

These friendly suggestions, I found were considered as the theme of a priest; and my desire to detach her from such empty pursuits, as the selfishness of a lover. She was even offended at my freedom; and warmly affirmed, that no one had a right to arraign her conduct. I mentioned Major Sanford who was then in town, and who (though she went to places of public resort with Mr. and Mrs. Sumner) always met and gallanted her home. She rallied me upon my jealousy, as she termed it; wished that I would attend her myself, and then she should need no other gallant. I answered that I had rather resign that honor to another; but wished, for her sake, that he might be a gentleman whose character would not disgrace the company with which he associated. She appeared mortified and chagrined in the extreme. However, she studiously suppressed her emotions; and even soothed me with the blandishments[3] of female softness. We parted amicably. She promised to return soon, and prepare for a compliance with my wishes. I cannot refuse to believe her! I cannot cease to love her! My heart is in her possession. She has a perfect command of my passions. Persuasion dwells on her tongue. With all the boasted fortitude and resolution of our sex, we are but mere machines. Let love once pervade our breasts; and its object may mould us into any form that pleases her fancy, or even caprice![4]

I have just received a letter from Eliza, informing me of her return to Hartford. To morrow I shall set out on a visit to the dear girl; for, my friend, notwithstanding all her foibles, she is very dear to me. Before you hear from me again, I expect that the happy day will be fixed; the day which shall unite, in the most sacred bands, this lovely maid, and your faithful friend,

J. Boyer.

1. Fawning praise.
2. Pope, *Essay on Man*, Epistle 4.
3. Gentle flattery, intended to persuade.
4. Whim.

# L E T T E R  XL.

TO MR. T. SELBY.

*HAMPSHIRE.*

I have returned; and the day, indeed, is fixed; but Oh! how different from my fond expectations! It is not the day of union, but the day of final separation; the day which divides me from my charmer; the day which breaks asunder the bands of love; the day on which my reason assumes its empire, and triumphs over the arts of a finished coquette! Congratulate me, my friend, that I have thus overcome my feelings, and repelled the infatuating wiles of a deceitful girl. I would not be understood to impeach Miss Wharton's virtue; I mean her chastity. Virtue in the common acceptation of the term, as applied to the sex, is confined to that particular, you know. But in my view, this is of little importance, where all other virtues are wanting!

When I arrived at Mrs. Wharton's, and inquired for Eliza, I was told that she had rode out; but was soon expected home. An hour after, a phaeton stopped at the door, from which my fair one alighted, and was handed into the house by Major Sanford, who immediately took leave. I met her and offered my hand, which she received with apparent tenderness.

When the family had retired after supper, and left us to talk on our particular affairs, I found the same indecision, the same loathness to bring our courtship to a period, as formerly. Her previous excuses were renewed, and her wishes to have a union still longer delayed, were zealously urged. She could not bear the idea of confinement to the cares of a married life at present; and begged me to defer all solicitation on that subject to some future day. I found my temper rise, and told her plainly, that I was not thus to be trifled with; that if her regard for me was sincere; if she really intended to form a connection with me, she could not thus protract the time, try my patience, and prefer every other pleasure to the rational interchange of affection, to the calm delights of domestic life. But in vain did I argue against her false notions of happiness; in vain did I represent the dangerous system of conduct, which she now pursued, and urge her to accept, before it was too late, the hand and heart which were devoted to her service. That, she said, she purposed, ere long to do; and hoped amply to reward my faithful love; but she could not fix the time this evening. She must consider a little further; and likewise consult her mother. Is it not Major Sanford whom you wish to consult, madam? said I. She blushed, and gave me no answer. Tell me, Eliza, I continued, tell me frankly, if he has not supplanted me in your affections; if he be not the cause of my being

thus evasively, thus cruelly treated? Major Sanford, sir, replied she, has done you no harm. He is a particular friend of mine; a polite gentleman, and an agreeable neighbor; and therefore I treat him with civility; but he is not so much interested in my concerns, as to alter my disposition towards any other person. Why, said I, do you talk of friendship with a man of his character? Between his society and mine, there is a great contrast. Such opposite pursuits and inclinations cannot be equally pleasing to the same taste. It is therefore necessary, that you renounce the one, to enjoy the other. I will give you time to decide which. I am going to a friend's house to spend the night; and will call on you to morrow, if agreeable, and converse with you further upon the matter. She bowed assent, and I retired.

The next afternoon I went as agreed; and found her mamma and her alone in the parlor. She was very pensive and appeared to have been in tears. The sight affected me. The idea of having treated her harshly, the evening before, disarmed me of my resolution to insist on her decision that day. I invited her to ride with me and visit a friend, to which she readily consented. We spent our time agreeably. I forebore to press her on the subject of our future union; but strove rather to soothe her mind, and inspire her with sentiments of tenderness towards me. I conducted her home, and returned early in the evening to my friend's, who met me at the door; and jocosely told me, that he expected I should now rob them of their agreeable neighbor. But, added he, we have been apprehensive that you would be rivalled, if you delayed your visit much longer. I did not suspect a rival, said I. Who can the happy man be? I can say nothing from personal observation, said he; but fame, of late, has talked loudly of Major Sanford and Miss Wharton. Be not alarmed, continued he, seeing me look grave. I presume no harm is intended. The Major is a man of gallantry, and Miss Wharton is a gay lady; but I dare say that your connection will be happy, *if it be formed.* I noticed a particular emphasis on the word *if;* and as we were alone, I followed him with questions, till the whole affair was developed. I informed him of my embarrassment; and he gave me to understand that Eliza's conduct had, for some time past, been a subject of speculation in the town; that formerly, her character was highly esteemed; but that her intimacy with a man of Sanford's known libertinism; more especially as she was supposed to be engaged to another, had rendered her very censurable; that they were often together; that wherever she went, he was sure to follow, as if by appointment; that they walked, talked, sung and danced together in all companies; that some supposed he would marry her; others, that he only meditated adding her name to the black catalogue of deluded wretches, whom he had already ruined!

I rose, and walked the room in great agitation. He apologized for his freedom; was sorry if he had wounded my feelings; but friendship

alone had induced him frankly to declare the truth, that I might guard against duplicity and deceit.

I thanked him for his kind intensions; and assured him that I should not quit the town till I had terminated this affair, in one way or another.

I retired to bed, but sleep was a stranger to my eyes. With the dawn I rose; and after breakfast walked to Mrs. Wharton's, who informed me, that Eliza was in her chamber, writing to a friend, but would be down in a few minutes. I entered into conversation with the old lady on the subject of her daughter's conduct; hinted my suspicions of the cause, and declared my resolution of knowing my destiny immediately. She endeavored to extenuate, and excuse her as much as possible; but frankly owned that her behavior was mysterious; that no pains had been wanting, on her part, to alter and rectify it; that she had remonstrated, expostulated, advised and entreated, as often as occasion required. She hoped that my resolution would have a good effect, as she knew that her daughter esteemed me very highly.

In this manner we conversed till the clock struck twelve; and Eliza, not appearing, I desired her mamma to send up word that I waited to see her. The maid returned with an answer that she was indisposed, and had lain down. Mrs. Wharton observed, that she had not slept for several nights, and complained of the head ache in the morning. The girl added, that she would wait on Mr. Boyer in the evening. Upon this information I rose and abruptly took my leave. I went to dine with a friend, to whom I had engaged myself the day before; but my mind was too much agitated to enjoy either the company or the dinner. I excused myself from tarrying to tea, and returned to Mrs. Wharton's. On inquiry, I was told that Eliza had gone to walk in the garden; but desired that no person might intrude on her retirement. The singularity of the request awakened my curiosity, and determined me to follow her. I sought her in vain, in different parts of the garden, till, going towards an arbor, almost concealed from sight, by surrounding shrubbery, I discovered her, sitting in close conversation with Major Sanford! My blood chilled in my veins, and I stood petrified with astonishment, at the disclosure of such baseness and deceit. They both rose in visible confusion. I dared not trust myself to accost them. My passions were raised, and I feared that I might say or do something unbecoming my character. I therefore gave them a look of indignation and contempt, and retreated to the house. I traversed the parlor hastily, overwhelmed with chagrin and resentment! Mrs. Wharton inquired the cause. I attempted to tell her, but my tongue refused utterance! While in this situation, Eliza entered the room. She was not less discomposed than myself. She sat down at the window and wept. Her mamma wept likewise. At length she recovered herself, in a

degree, and desired me to sit down. I answered no; and continued walking. Will you, said she, permit me to vindicate my conduct and explain my motives? Your conduct, said I, cannot be vindicated; your motives need no explanation; they are too apparent! How, Miss Wharton, have I merited this treatment from you? But I can bear it no longer. Your indifference to me proceeds from an attachment to another; and forgive me, if I add, to one, who is the disgrace of his own sex, and the destroyer of yours. I have been too long the dupe of your dissimulation and coquetry. Too long has my peace of mind been sacrificed to the arts of a woman, whose conduct has proved her unworthy of my regard; insensible to love, gratitude and honor!

To you, madam, said I, turning to her mother, I acknowledge my obligations for your friendship, politeness and attention. I once hoped for the privilege of rocking for you the cradle of declining age. I am deprived of that privilege; but I pray that you may never want a child, whose love and duty shall prove a source of consolation and comfort!

Farewell! If we never meet again in this life, I hope and trust we shall in a better; where the parent's eye shall cease to weep for the disobedience of a child; and the lover's heart to bleed for the infidelity of his mistress!

I turned to Eliza, and attempted to speak; but her extreme emotion softened me, and I could not command my voice. I took her hand, and bowing, in token of an adieu, went precipitately out of the house. The residence of my friend, with whom I lodged, was at no great distance, and thither I repaired. As I met him in the entry, I rushed by him, and betook myself to my chamber.

The fever of resentment, and the tumult of passion began now to give place to the softer emotions of the soul. I found myself perfectly unmanned. I gave free scope to the sensibility of my heart; and the effeminate relief of tears materially lightened the load which oppressed me.

After this arduous struggle I went to bed; and slept more calmly than for several nights before. The next morning I wrote a farewell letter to Eliza (a copy of which I shall inclose to you) and ordering my horse to be brought, left town immediately.

My resentment of her behavior has much assisted me in erasing her image from my breast. In this exertion I have succeeded beyond my most sanguine expectations. The more I reflect on her temper and disposition, the more my gratitude is enlivened towards the wise Disposer of all events for enabling me to break asunder the snares of the deluder. I am convinced, that the gaiety and extravagance of her taste, the frivolous levity of her manners disqualify her for the station in which I wished to have placed her. These

considerations, together with that resignation to an overruling Providence[1] which the religion I profess, and teach, requires me to cultivate, induce me cheerfully to adopt the following lines of an ingenious poet:

"Since all the downward tracts of time,
　God's watchful eye surveys,
Oh, who so wise to choose our lot,
　Or regulate our ways?

Since none can doubt his equal love,
　Unmeasurably kind,
To his unerring gracious will,
　Be every wish resign'd.

Good, when he gives, supremely good,
　Not less when he denies;
E'en crosses from his sovereign hand,
　Are blessings in disguise."[2]

I am, &c.

J. BOYER.

TO MISS ELIZA WHARTON.

*Enclosed in the foregoing.*

HARTFORD.

MADAM,

Fearing, that my resolution may not be proof against the eloquence of those charms, which have so long commanded me, I take this method of bidding you a final adieu. I write not as a lover. That connection between us is for ever dissolved; but I address you as a friend; a friend to your happiness, to your reputation, to your temporal and eternal welfare. I will not rehearse the innumerable instances of your imprudence and misconduct, which have fallen under my observation. Your own heart must be your monitor! suffice it for me to warn you against the dangerous tendency of so dissipated a life; and to tell you that I have traced (I believe aright) the cause of your dissimulation and indifference to me. They are an aversion to the

1. The hand of God.
2. Hymn attributed to James Hervey (1714–1758), appearing in his *Meditations and Contemplations* (1748), though it has earlier roots in the writings of the seventeenth-century Carmelite, Brother Lawrence.

sober, rational, frugal mode of living, to which my profession leads; a fondness for the parade, the gaiety, not to say, the licentiousness of a station calculated to gratify such a disposition; and a prepossession for Major Sanford, infused into your giddy mind by the frippery, flattery and artifice of that worthless and abandoned man. Hence you preferred a connection with him, if it could be accomplished; but a doubt, whether it could, together with the advice of your friends, who have kindly espoused my cause, have restrained you from the avowal of your real sentiments, and led you to continue your civilities to me. What the result of your coquetry would have been, had I waited for it, I cannot say, nor have I now any desire or interest to know. I tear from my breast the idea which I have long cherished of future union and happiness with you in the conjugal state. I bid a last farewell to these fond hopes, and leave you for ever!

For your own sake, however, let me conjure you to review your conduct, and before you have advanced beyond the possibility of returning to rectitude and honor, to restrain your steps from the dangerous path in which you now tread!

Fly Major Sanford. That man is a deceiver. Trust not his professions. They are certainly insincere; or he would not affect concealment; he would not induce you to a clandestine intercourse! Many have been the victims of his treachery! O Eliza! add not to the number! Banish him from your society, if you wish to preserve your virtue unsullied, your character unsuspicious! It already begins to depreciate. Snatch it from the envenomed tongue of slander, before it receive an incurable wound!

Many faults have been visible to me; over which my affection once drew a veil.[3] That veil is now removed. And, acting the part of a disinterested friend, I shall mention some few of them with freedom. There is a levity in your manners, which is inconsistent with the solidity and decorum becoming a lady who has arrived to years of discretion. There is also an unwarrantable extravagance betrayed in your dress. Prudence and economy are such necessary, at least, such decent virtues, that they claim the attention of every female, whatever be her station or her property. To these virtues you are apparently inattentive. Too large a portion of your time is devoted to the adorning of your person.

Think not that I write thus plainly from resentment. No; It is from benevolence. I mention your foibles, not to reproach you with them, but that you may consider their nature and effects, and renounce them.

3. Cf. 1 Peter 4:8.

I wish you to regard this letter as the legacy of a friend; and to improve it accordingly. I shall leave town before you receive it. O, how different are my sensations at going, from what they were when I came! but I forbear description.

Think not, Eliza, that I leave you with indifference! The conflict is great; the trial is more than I can calmly support! Yet the consciousness of duty, affords consolation. A duty I conceive it to be, which I owe to myself; and to the people of my charge, who are interested in my future connection.

I wish not for an answer; my resolution is unalterably fixed. But should you hereafter be convinced of the justice of my conduct; and become a convert to my advice, I shall be happy to hear it.

That you may have wisdom to keep you from falling, and conduct you safely through this state of trial to the regions of immortal bliss, is the fervent prayer of your sincere friend, and humble servant,

<div align="right">J. BOYER.</div>

# L  E  T  T  E  R   XLI.

## TO MRS. LUCY SUMNER.

<div align="right">*HARTFORD.*</div>

The retirement of my native home is not so gloomy, since my return from Boston, as I expected, from the contrast between them.

Indeed, the customs and amusements of this place are materially altered, since the residence of Major Sanford among us. The dull, old fashioned sobriety which formerly prevailed, is nearly banished; and cheerfulness, vivacity, and enjoyment are substituted in its stead. Pleasure is now diffused through all ranks of the people, especially the rich; and surely it ought to be cultivated, since the wisest of men informs us, that "a merry heart doth good like a medicine."[1] As human life has many diseases, which require medicines, are we not right in selecting the most agreeable and palatable? Major Sanford's example has had great influence upon our society in general; and though some of our old dons think him rather licentious; yet, for ought I can see, he is as strict an observer of decorum,[2] as the best of them. True, he seldom goes to church; but what of that? The

1. Proverbs 17:22.
2. Proper behavior.

Deity is not confined to temples made with hands. He may worship him as devoutly elsewhere, if he chuses; and who has a right to say he does not?

His return from Boston was but a day or two after mine. He paid me an early visit; and, indeed, has been very attentive ever since. My mamma is somewhat precise in her notions of propriety; and of course, blames me for associating so freely with him. She says, that my engagements to Mr. Boyer ought to render me more sedate; and more indifferent to the gallantry of mere *pleasure-hunters*, to use her phrase. But I think otherwise. If I am to become a recluse, let me, at least, enjoy those amusements, which are suited to my taste, a short time first. Why should I refuse the polite attentions of this gentleman? They smoothe the rugged path of life, and wonderfully accelerate the lagging wheels of time.

Indeed, Lucy, he has an admirable talent for contributing to vary, and increase amusement. We have few hours unimproved. Some new plan of pleasure, and sociability is constantly courting our adoption. He lives in all the magnificence of a prince; and why should I, who can doubtless share that magnificence if I please, forego the advantages and indulgences it offers, merely to gratify those friends who pretend to be better judges of my happiness than I am myself.

I have not yet told my mamma that he entertains me with the lover's theme; or, at least, that I listen to it. Yet I must own to you, from whom I have never concealed an action or idea, that his situation in life charms my imagination; that the apparent fervor and sincerity of his passion affect my heart. Yet there is something extremely problematical in his conduct. He is very urgent with me to dissolve my connection with Mr. Boyer, and engage not to marry him without his consent; or knowledge, to say no more. He warmly applauds my wish, still longer to enjoy the freedom and independence of a single state; and professedly adopts it for his own. While he would disconnect me from another, he mysteriously conceals his own intentions and views. In conversation with him yesterday, I plainly told him that his conduct was unaccountable; that if his professions and designs were honorable he could not neglect to mention them to my mamma; that I should no longer consent to carry on a clandestine intercourse with him; that I hourly expected Mr. Boyer, whom I esteemed, and who was the favorite of my friends; and that unless he acted openly in this affair before his arrival, I should give my hand to him.

He appeared thunderstruck at this declaration. All his words and actions were indicative of the most violent emotions of mind. He entreated me to recall the sentence; for I knew not, he said, his motives for secrecy; yet he solemnly swore that they were honorable. I replied in the words of the poet,

> "Trust not a man, they are by nature cruel,
> False, deceitful, treacherous, and inconstant.
> When a man talks of love, with caution hear him;
> But if he swear, he'll certainly deceive you."[3]

He begged that he might know by what means he had provoked my suspicions; by what means he had forfeited my confidence? His importunity vanquished my fortitude; and before we parted, I again promised to make him acquainted, from time to time, with the progress of my connection with Mr. Boyer.

Now, my dear friend, I want your advice more than ever. I am inadvertently embarrassed by this man; and how to extricate myself, I know not. I am sensible that the power is in my hands; but the disposition (shall I confess it) is wanting!

> "I know the right, and I approve it too;
> I know the wrong, and yet the wrong pursue!"[4]

I have just received a card from Major Sanford, inviting me to ride this afternoon. At first I thought of returning a negative answer; but recollecting that Mr. Boyer must soon be here, I concluded it best to embrace this opportunity, of talking further with him. I must now prepare to go; but shall not close this letter, for I intend writing in continuation, as events occur, till this important business is decided.

*Tuesday evening.* The little tour which I mentioned to you this afternoon, was not productive of a final determination. The same plea was repeated over, and over again, without closing the cause. On my return I found Mr. Boyer waiting to receive me. My heart beat an involuntary welcome. I received him very cordially, though with a kind of pleasure mixed with apprehension. I must own that his conversation and manners are much better calculated to bear the scrutinising eye of a refined understanding and taste, than Major Sanford's. But whether the fancy ought not to be consulted about our settlement for life, is with me a question.

When we parted last, I had promised Mr. Boyer, to inform him positively, at this visit, when my hand should be given. He therefore came, as he told me in the course of our conversation, with the resolution of claiming the fulfilment of this promise.

I begged absolution; told him, that I could not possibly satisfy his claim; and fought still to evade, and put off the important decision. He grew warm; and affirmed that I treated him ungenerously, and

---

3. A rewording of Thomas Otway, *The Orphan, or, The Unhappy Marriage: A Tragedy* (1680), Act 2, Scene 1. In the original, the male speaker addresses his sister, and includes himself in the condemnation of men's actions.
4. Medea speaks these words in Book 7 of *Metamorphoses*, by the Roman poet Ovid (43 B.C.–A.D. 17/18).

made needless delays. He even accused me of indifference towards him; and of partiality to another. Major Sanford he believed, was the man who robbed him of the affection which he had supposed his due. He warned me against any intercourse with him, and insisted that I must renounce the society of the one or the other immediately. He would leave me, he said, this evening and call to morrow to know the result of my determination. It was late before he bade me good night; since which I have written these particulars. It is now time to lay aside my pen, and deliberate what course to take.

*Wednesday Evening.* Last night I closed not my eyes. I rose this morning with the sun, and went into the garden till breakfast. My mamma doubtless saw the disorder of my mind, but kindly avoided any inquiry about it. She was affectionately attentive to me, but said nothing of my particular concerns. I mentioned not my embarrassment to her. She had declared herself in favor of Mr. Boyer; therefore I had no expectation, that she would advise impartially. I retired to my chamber, and remained in a kind of reverie, for more than an hour; when I was roused by the rattling of a carriage at the door. I hastened to the window, and saw Major Sanford just driving away. The idea of his having been to converse with my mamma, gave me new sensations. A thousand perplexities occurred to my mind relative to the part most proper for me to act in this critical situation. All these might have been avoided, had I gone down and inquired into the matter; but this I delayed till dinner. My mamma then informed me, that Major Sanford had been with her, and inquired for me; but that she thought it unnecessary to call me, as she presumed I had no particular business with him. I knew the motives by which she was actuated, and was vexed at her evasions. I told her plainly, that she would never carry her point in this way; that I thought myself capable of conducting my own affairs; and wished her not to interfere, except by her advice, which I should always listen to, and comply with when I could possibly make it consistent with my inclination and interest. She wept at my undutiful anger (of which I have severely repented since) and affectionately replied, that my happiness was the object of her wishes and prayers; conformably to which she felt constrained, freely to speak her mind, though it incurred my displeasure. She then went through again with all the comparative circumstances and merits of the two candidates for my favor, which have perpetually rung in my ears for months. I shed tears at the idea of my embarrassment; and in this condition Mr. Boyer found us. He appeared to be affected by my visible disorder; and without inquiring the cause, endeavored to dissipate it. This was kindly done. He conversed upon indifferent subjects; and invited me to ride, and take tea with your mamma, to which I readily consented. We found her at home; and passed the time agreeably, excepting the

alloy of your absence. Mr. Boyer touched lightly on the subject of our last evening's debate; but expatiated largely on the pleasing power of love; and hoped that we should one day both realize and exemplify it in perfection. When we returned, he observed that it was late, and took his leave; telling me that he should call to morrow; and begged that I would then relieve his suspense. As I was retiring to bed, the maid gave me a hint that Major Sandford's servant had been here and left a letter. I turned instantly back to my mamma, and telling her my information, demanded the letter. She hesitated, but I insisted on having it; and seeing me resolute, she reluctantly gave it into my hand. It contained the following words:

"Am I forsaken? Am I abandoned? Oh my adorable Eliza, have you sacrificed me to my rival? Have you condemned me to perpetual banishment, without a hearing?

I came this day, to plead my cause at your feet; but was cruelly denied the privilege of seeing you! My mind is all anarchy and confusion! My soul is harrowed up with jealousy! I will be revenged on those who separate us, if that distracting event take place! But it is from your lips only that I can hear my sentence! You must witness its effects! To what lengths my despair may carry me, I know not! You are the arbitress of my fate!

Let me conjure you to meet me in your garden to morrow at any hour you shall appoint. My servant will call for an answer in the morning. Deny me not an interview; but have pity on your faithful                                                   *Sanford*."

I wrote for answer, that I would meet him to morrow, at five o'clock in the afternoon.

I have now before me another night for consideration; and shall pass it in that employment. I purpose not to see Mr. Boyer, till I have conversed with Major Sanford.

*Thursday Morning.* The morning dawns, and ushers in the day; a day, perhaps big with the fate of your friend! What that fate may be is wrapped in the womb of futurity; that futurity which a kind Providence has wisely concealed from the penetration of mortals!

After mature consideration; after revolving and re-revolving every circumstance on both sides of the question, I have nearly determined, in compliance with the advice of my friends, and the dictates of my own judgment, to give Mr. Boyer the preference, and with him to tread the future round of life.

As to the despair of Major Sanford, it does not much alarm me. Such violent passions are seldom so deeply rooted, as to produce lasting effects. I must, however, keep my word, and meet him according to promise.

Mr. Boyer is below. My mamma has just sent me word that he wished to see me. My reply was that I had lain down, which was a fact.

*One o'Clock.* My mamma, alarmed by my indisposition, has visited my apartment. I soon convinced her that it was but trifling, owing principally to the want of sleep; and that an airing in the garden, which I intended towards night, would restore me.

*Ten o'clock, at night.*—The day is past! and such a day it has been, as I hope never more to see!

At the hour appointed, I went tolerably composed and resolute into the garden. I had taken several turns, and retired into the little arbor, where you and I have spent so many happy hours, before Major Sanford entered. When he appeared, a consciousness of the impropriety of this clandestine intercourse suffused my cheek, and gave a coldness to my manners. He immediately penetrated the cause, and observed that my very countenance told him he was no longer a welcome guest to me. I asked him if he ought so to be; since his motives for seeking admission, were unworthy of being communicated to my friends? That he said was not the case, but that prudence in the present instance required a temporary concealment.

He then undertook to exculpate himself from blame, assuring me that as soon as I should discountenance the expectations of Mr. Boyer, and discontinue the reception of his address, his intentions should be made known. He was enlarging upon this topic, when we heard a footstep approaching us; and looking up saw Mr. Boyer within a few paces of the arbor.—Confusion seized us both! We rose involuntarily from our seats, but were mute as statues! He spoke not a word, but casting a look of indignant accusation at me, a glance which penetrated my very soul, turned on his heel, and walked hastily back to the house.

I stood a few moments, considering what course to take, though shame and regret had almost taken from me the power of thought.

Major Sanford took my hand. I withdrew it from him. I *must* leave you, said I. Where will you go? said he. I will go and try to retrieve my character. It has suffered greatly by this fatal interview.

He threw himself at my feet and exclaimed, leave me not, Eliza, I conjure you not to leave me. Let me go now, I rejoined, or I bid you farewell for ever. I flew precipitately by him, and went into the parlor, where I found Mr. Boyer and my mamma, the one traversing the room in the greatest agitation; the other in flood of tears! Their appearance affected me; and I wept like an infant! when I had a little recovered myself, I begged him to sit down; He answered no. I then told him, that however unjustifiable my conduct might appear, perhaps I might explain it to his satisfaction, if he would hear me; that

my motives were innocent, though they doubtless wore the aspect of criminality, in his view. He sternly replied, that no palliation[5] could avail; that my motives were sufficiently notorious! He accused me of treating him ill, of rendering him the dupe of coquetting artifice, of having an intrigue with Major Sanford, and declared his determination to leave me for ever, as unworthy of his regard, and incapable of love, gratitude, or honor!—There was too much reason in support of his accusations for me to gainsay them, had his impetuosity suffered me to attempt it.

But in truth I had no inclination to self defence. My natural vivacity had forsaken me; and I listened without interrupting him to the fluency of reproachful language, which his resentment inspired. He took a very solemn and affectionate leave of my mamma; thanking her for her politeness, and wishing her much future felicity. He attempted to address me, I suppose somewhat in the same way; but his sensibility overcome him; and he only took my hand, and bowing in silence, departed.

The want of rest for two long nights together, the exercise of mind, and conflict of passions, which now tortured my breast, were too much for me to support!

When I saw that he was gone; that he had actually forsaken me, I fainted. My mamma, with the assistance of the maid, soon restored me.

When I opened my eyes, and beheld this amiable and tender parent, watching and attending me with the most anxious concern; without one reproachful word, without one accusing look, my reflections upon the part I had acted, in defeating her benevolent wishes, were exquisitely afflictive! But we mutually forbore to mention the occasion of my illness; and I complied with her advice to take some refreshment, and retire to my chamber. I am so much fatigued by the exertions of the day, that rest is absolutely necessary; and I lay aside my pen to seek it.

*Friday Morning.* When I shall again receive the balmy influence of sleep, I know not. It has absolutely forsaken me at present. I have had a most restless night. Every awakening idea presented itself to my imagination; whether I had sustained a real loss in Mr. Boyer's departure; reflections on my own misconduct, with the censure of my friends, and the ill-natured remarks of my enemies, excited the most painful anxiety in my mind!

I am going down, but how shall I see my mamma? To her will I confess my faults, in her maternal breast repose my cares, and by her friendly advice regulate my conduct. Had I done this before, I might

5. Effort to make less conspicuous.

have escaped this trouble, and saved both her and myself many distressing emotions!

*Friday Evening.* I have had a long conversation with my mamma, which has greatly relieved my mind. She has soothed me with the most endearing tenderness.

Mr. Atkins, with whom Mr. Boyer lodged, while in town, called here this afternoon. I did not see him, but he told my mamma that Mr. Boyer had returned home, and left a letter for me, which he had promised to convey with his own hand. By this letter I am convinced that the dye is absolutely cast, with respect to him, and that no attempts on my part to bring about a reconciliation would be either prudent or successful. He has penetrated the cause of my proceedings; and such is his resentment, that I am inclined not much to regret his avoiding another interview.

My excuses would be deemed utterly insufficient, and truth would not befriend and justify me.

As I know you are impatient to hear from me, I will now dispatch this long letter without any other addition, than that I am your sincere friend,

ELIZA WHARTON.

# L  E  T  T  E  R   XLII.

### TO MR. CHARLES DEIGHTON.

*HARTFORD.*

Well, Charles, the show is over, as we yankees say; and the girl is my own. That is, if I will have her. I shall take my own time for that, however. I have carried my point, and am amply revenged on the whole posse of those dear friends of her's. She was entangled by a promise (not to marry this priest without my knowledge,) which her conscience would not let her break. Thank God, I have no conscience. If I had, I believe it would make wretched work with me! I suppose she intended to have one, or the other of us; but preferred me. I have escaped the noose, this time, and I'll be fairly hanged, if I ever get so near it again. For indeed Charles, I was seriously alarmed. I watched all their motions; and the appearances of harmony between them awakened all my activity and zeal. So great was my infatuation, that I verily believe I should have asked her in marriage, and risked the consequences, rather than to have lost her!

I went to the house, while Mr. Boyer was in town, but her mamma refused to call her, or to acquaint her that I was there. I then wrote a despairing letter, and obtained a conference with her in the garden.

This was a fortunate event for me. True, Eliza was very haughty, and resolutely insisted on immediate declaration or rejection. And I cannot say what would have been the result, if Mr. Boyer had not surprized us together. He gave us a pretty harsh look and retired without speaking a word.

I endeavored to detain Eliza, but in vain. She left me on my knees, which are always ready to bend on such occasions.

This finished the matter, it seems. I rose, and went into a near neighbor's to observe what happened; and in about half in hour saw Mr. Boyer come out, and go to his lodgings.

This, said I to myself, is a good omen. I went home, and was informed next day, that he had mounted his horse and departed.

I heard nothing more of her till yesterday, when I determined to know how she stood affected towards me. I therefore paid her a visit, her mamma being luckily abroad.

She received me very placidly, and told me, on inquiry, that Mr. Boyer's resentment at her meeting me in the garden was so great, that he had bid her a final adieu. I congratulated myself on having no rival; hoped that her favor would now be unbiassed, and that in due time I should reap the reward of my fidelity. She begged me not to mention the subject; said she had been perplexed by our competition, and wished not to hear any thing further about it at present. I bowed in obedience to her commands and changed the discourse.

I informed her, that I was about taking a tour to the southward; that I should be absent several months, and trusted that on my return her embarrassments would be over.

I left her with regret. After all, Charles, she is the *summum bonum*[1] of my life. I must have her in some way or other. No body else shall, I am resolved.

I am making preparations for my journey; which between you and me, is occasioned by the prospect of making a speculation, by which I hope to mend my affairs. The voyage will at least lessen my expenses, and screen me from the importunity of creditors till I can look about me.

<div style="text-align: right">PETER SANFORD.</div>

---

1. *Latin*: Highest good.

# L  E  T  T  E  R   XLIII.

*NEW-HAVEN.*

MY DEAR ELIZA,

Through the medium of my friends at Hartford I have been informed of the progress of your affairs, as they have transpired. The detail which my sister gave me of your separation from Mr. Boyer was painful; as I had long contemplated a happy union between you. But still more disagreeable sensations possessed my breast, when told that you had suffered your lively spirits to be depressed, and resigned yourself to solitude and dejection!

Why, my dear friend, should you allow this event thus to affect you? Heaven, I doubt not, has happiness still in store for you greater than you could have enjoyed in that connection. If the conviction of any misconduct on your part, give you pain, dissipate it by the reflection, that unerring rectitude is not the lot of mortals, that few are to be found who have not deviated in a greater or less degree from the maxims of prudence. Our greatest mistakes may teach lessons which will be useful through life.

But I will not moralize. Come and see us; and we will talk over the matter once, and then dismiss it for ever. Do prevail on your mamma to part with you a month or two, at least. I wish you to witness how well I manage my nursery business. You will be charmed with little Harriot. I am already enough of the mother to think her a miniature of beauty and perfection.

How natural, and how easy the transition from one stage of life to another! Not long since I was a gay, volatile girl; seeking satisfaction in fashionable circles and amusements; but now I am thoroughly domesticated. All my happiness is centered within the limits of my own walls; and I grudge every moment that calls me from the pleasing scenes of domestic life. Not that I am so selfish as to exclude my friends from my affection or society. I feel interested in their concerns, and enjoy their company. I must own, however, that conjugal and parental love are the main springs of my life. The conduct of some mothers in depriving their helpless offspring of the care and kindness which none but a mother can feel, is to me unaccountable. There are many nameless attentions which nothing short of maternal tenderness, and solicitude can pay; and for which the endearing smiles, and progressive improvements of the lovely babe are an ample reward.

How delightful to trace from day to day the expansion of reason and the dawnings of intelligence! Oh, how I anticipate the time, when these faculties shall be displayed by the organs of speech; when the lisping accent shall heighten our present pleasure, and the young idea be capable of direction "how to shoot"![1] General Richman is not less interested by these enjoyments than myself. All the father beams in his eye! All the husband reigns in his heart, and pervades his every action!

Miss Lawrence is soon to be married to Mr. Laiton. I believe he is a mere fortune-hunter. Indeed she has little to recommend her to any other. Nature has not been very bountiful, either to her body, or mind. Her parents have been shamefully deficient in her education; but have secured to her what they think the chief good; not considering that happiness is by no means the invariable attendant of wealth.

I hope this incoherent scroll will amuse, while it induces you speedily to favor us with another visit.

My best wishes attend your honored mamma; while I subscribe myself, &c.

A. RICHMAN.

# L E T T E R XLIV.

TO MRS. LUCY SUMNER.

*HARTFORD.*

I am extremely depressed, my dear Lucy! The agitating scenes, through which I have lately passed, have broken my spirits, and rendered me unfit for society.

Major Sanford has visited me, and taken his leave. He is gone to the southward on a tour of two or three months. I declined any further conversation with him, on the subject of love. At present, I wish not to hear it mentioned by any one.

I have received a very friendly and consolatory letter from Mrs. Richman. She invites me to spend a few months with her; which with my mamma's consent I shall do. I hope the change of situation and company will dissipate the gloom which hangs over my mind.

It is a common observation, that we know not the value of a blessing but by deprivation.

---

1. In "Spring," from *The Seasons*, Thomson writes: "Delightful task! to rear the tender thought, / To teach the young idea how to shoot."

This is strictly verified in my case. I was insensible of my regard for Mr. Boyer, till this fatal separation took place. His merit and worth now appear in the brightest colors. I am convinced of that excellence which I once slighted; and the shade of departed happiness haunts me perpetually! I am sometimes tempted to write him, and confess my faults; to tell him the situation of my mind, and to offer him my hand. But he has precluded all hopes of success, by the severity of his letter to me. At any rate, I shall do nothing of the kind, till my return from New-Haven.

I am the more willing to leave home, as my affairs are made a town talk. My mamma persuades me to disregard it. But how can I rise superior to "The world's dread laugh, which scarce the firm philosopher can scorn?"[1]

Pray remember me to Mr. Sumner. You are happy, my friend, in the love and esteem of a worthy man; but more happy still, in deserving them. Adieu.

ELIZA WHARTON.

## L  E  T  T  E  R   XLV.

TO THE SAME.

*HARTFORD.*

I have returned to the once smiling seat of maternal affection; but I find not repose and happiness, even there!

In the society of my amiable friends at New-Haven, I enjoyed every thing that friendship could bestow; but rest to a disturbed mind was not in their power.

I was on various parties of pleasure, and passed through different scenes of amusement; but with me they have lost their charms. I relished them not as formerly.

Mrs. Richman advises me to write to Mr. Boyer, and I have concluded to act accordingly. If it answer no other purpose, it will be a relief to my mind. If he ever felt for me the tenderness and regard which he professed, methinks they cannot be entirely obliterated. If they still remain, perhaps I may rekindle the gentle flame, and we may both be happy. I may at least recal his esteem, and that will be a satisfaction to my conscious mind.

---

1. An amendment of Thomson: "For still the world prevail'd, and its dread laugh, / Which scarce the firm philosopher can scorn." From "Autumn," *The Seasons.*

I wonder what has become of Major Sanford! Has he too forsaken me? Is it possible for him wilfully to neglect me? I will not entertain so injurious a suspicion.

Yet, if it were the case, it would not affect me like Mr. Boyer's disaffection; for I frankly own, that my fancy, and a taste for gaity of life, induced me to cherish the idea of a connection with Major Sanford; while Mr. Boyer's real merit has imprinted those senti-ments of esteem and love in my heart, which time can never efface.

Instead of two, or three, more than twelve months have elapsed, and I have not received a line from Major Sanford in all that time, which I fully expected, though he made no mention of writing; nor have I heard a syllable about him, except a report circulated by his servants, that he is on the point of marrying, which I do not believe. No, it is impossible! I am persuaded that his passion for me, was sincere, however deceitful he may have been with others. But I will not bestow an anxious thought upon him. My design relative to Mr. Boyer, demands my whole attention.

My hopes and fears alternately prevail, and my resolution is extremely fluctuating. How it finally terminates you shall hear in my next. Pray write to me soon. I stand in need of the consoling power of friendship. Nothing can beguile my pensive hours, and exhilerate my drooping spirits, like your letters.

Let me know how you are to be entertained this winter at the the-atre. That, you know, is a favorite amusement of mine. You see I can step out of myself a little. Afford an assisting hand, and perhaps I may again be fit for society.

ELIZA WHARTON.

# L E T T E R   XLVI.

TO THE REV. J. BOYER.

*HARTFORD.*

SIR,

It is partly in compliance with your desire, in your last letter to me, in which you tell me, "that when I am convinced of the justice of your conduct, and become a convert to your advice, you shall be happy to hear it;" and partly from a wish to inform you, that such is in truth my present state of mind, that I now write to you.

I cannot but hope that this letter coming from the hand which you once sought, will not be unacceptable.

Pope very justly observes, "that every year is a critic on the last."[1] The truth of this observation is fully exemplified in my years! How severely this condemns the follies of the preceding, my own heart alone can testify!

I shall not offer any palliation, or apology for my misconduct. You told me it admitted none. I frankly confess it; and if the most humble acknowledgement of my offences, with an assurance that they have cost me the deepest repentance, can in any degree atone for them, I now make that atonement. Casting off the veil of dissimulation, I shall write with frankness; believing you possessed of more honor than to make any ungenerous use of the confidence reposed in you.

To say that I ever esteemed you, may, perhaps, appear paradoxical, when compared with certain circumstances which occurred during our acquaintance; but to assert that I loved you, may be deemed still more so. Yet these are real facts, facts of which I was then sensible, and by which I am now more than ever affected.

I think you formerly remarked, that absence served but to heighten real love. This I find by experience. Need I blush to declare these sentiments, when occasion like this, calls for the avowal? I will go even further, and offer you that heart which once you prized; that hand which you once solicited. The sentiments of affection, which you then cultivated, though suppressed, I flatter myself are not wholly obliterated. Suffer me then to rekindle the latent flame; to revive that friendship and tenderness, which I have so foolishly neglected. The endeavor of my future life shall be to reward your benevolence, and perhaps we may yet be happy together.

But let not this offer of myself constrain you. Let not pity influence your conduct. I would have you return, if that pleasing event take place, a voluntary act. Receive or consent not to confer happiness.

I thought it a duty which I owed to you, and to myself, to make this expiation; this sacrifice of female reserve, for the wrongs I have done you. As such I wish you to accept it; and if your affections are intirely alienated, or otherwise engaged; if you cannot again command the respect and love which I would recal, do not despise me for the concessions I have made. Think as favorably of my past faults, and of my present disposition, as charity will allow. Continue, if possible, to be my friend, though you cease to be my lover.

Should this letter find you in the full possession of happiness, let not the idea of your once loved Eliza, thus intruding itself again upon your thoughts, interrupt your enjoyments. May some distinguished female, as deserving, as fair, partake with you of that bliss which I have forfeited.

---

1. In *An Essay on Criticism* (1711), Pope writes: "But you, with Pleasure own your Errors past, / And make each Day a Critique on the last."

Whatever may be my destiny, my best wishes shall ever attend you, and a pleasing remembrance of your honorable attentions preside, till death, in the breast of,

ELIZA WHARTON.

# L E T T E R   XLVII.

TO MISS ELIZA WHARTON.

*HAMPSHIRE.*

MADAM,

As I was sitting last evening in my study, a letter was handed me by a servant; upon which I no sooner cast my eye, than I recognized, with surprise, the hand and seal of my once loved, but to me long lost Eliza! I opened it hastily, and with still greater surprise, read the contents!

You write with frankness. I shall answer in the same manner.

On reviewing our former intercourse, be assured, that I have not an accusing thought in my heart. The regard which I felt for you was tender and animated, but it was not of that passionate kind which ends in death or despair. It was governed by reason, and had a nobler object in view, than mere sensual gratification. It was excited by the appearance of excellent qualities. Your conduct, at length, convinced me it was misplaced; that you possessed not, in reality, those charms which I had fondly ascribed to you. They were inconsistent, I conceived, with that artifice and dissimulation, of which you strove to render me the dupe. But thank heaven, the snare was broken. My eyes were opened to discover your folly; and my heart, engaged, as it was, exerted resolution and strength to burst asunder the chain by which you held me enslaved, and to assert the rights of an injured man.

The parting scene, you remember. I reluctantly bade you adieu. I tore myself from you, determined to eradicate your idea from my breast! Long and severe was the struggle. I at last vanquished, as I thought, every tender passion of my soul, (for they all centered in you) and resigned myself to my God, and my duty; devoting those affections to friendship, which had been disappointed in love. But they are again called into exercise. The virtuous, the amiable, the accomplished Maria Selby possesses my entire confidence and esteem; and I trust I am not deceived, when I think her highly deserving of both. With her I expect soon to be united in the most

sacred and endearing of human relations; with her to pass my future days in serenity and peace.

Your letter, therefore, came too late; were there no other obstacle to the renewal of our connection. I hope at the close of life, when we take a retrospect of the past, that neither of us shall have reason to regret our separation.

Permit me to add, that for your own sake, and for the sake of your ever valued friends, I sincerely rejoice that your mind has regained its native strength and beauty; that you have emerged from the shade of fanciful vanity. For although to adopt your own phrase, I cease to style myself your lover, among the number of your friends, I am happy to be reckoned. As such, let me conjure you, by all that is dear and desirable, both in this life, and another, to adhere, with undeviating exactness, to the path of rectitude and innocence; and to improve the noble talents, which heaven has liberally bestowed upon you, in rendering yourself amiable, and useful to your friends. Thus will you secure your own, while you promote the happiness of all around you.

I shall ever cherish sentiments of kindness towards you, and with gratitude remember your condescension, in the testimony of regard, which you have given me in your last letter.

I hope soon to hear that your heart and hand are bestowed on some worthy man, who deserves the happiness you are formed to communicate. Whatever we may have called errors, will, on my part, be for ever buried in oblivion; and for your own peace of mind, I entreat you to forget that any idea of a connection between us ever existed.

I shall always rejoice at the news of your welfare, and my ardent prayers will daily arise for your temporal and eternal felicity.

I am, &c.

J. BOYER.

# L  E  T  T  E  R   XLVIII

### TO MRS. LUCY SUMNER.

*HARTFORD.*

Health, placid serenity, and every domestic pleasure, are the lot of my friend; while I, who once possessed the means of each, and the capacity of tasting them, have been tossed upon the waves of folly, till I am shipwrecked on the shoals of despair!

Oh my friend, I am undone! I am slighted, rejected by the man who once sought my hand, by the man who still retains my heart!

and what adds an insupportable poignancy to the reflection, is self-condemnation! From this inward torture, where shall I flee? Where shall I seek that happiness which I have madly trifled away?

The inclosed letters,[1] will show you whence this tumult of soul arises. But I blame not Mr. Boyer. He has acted nobly. I approve his conduct, though it operates my ruin!

He is worthy of his intended bride, and she is what I am not, worthy of him. Peace and joy be their portion, both here and hereafter! But what are now my prospects? what are to be the future enjoyments of my life?

Oh that I had not written to Mr. Boyer! by confessing my faults, and by avowing my partiality to him, I have given him the power of triumphing in my distress; of returning to my tortured heart all the pangs of slighted love! and what have I now to console me? my bloom is decreasing; my health is sensibly impaired. Those talents, with the possession of which I have been flattered, will be of little avail when unsupported by respectability of character!

My mamma, who knows too well the distraction of my mind, endeavors to sooth and compose me, on christian principles; but they have not their desired effect. I dare not converse freely with her on the subject of my present uneasiness, lest I should distress her. I am therefore, obliged to conceal my disquietude, and appear as cheerful as possible in her company, though my heart is ready to burst with grief!

Oh that you were near me, as formerly, to share and alleviate my cares! to have some friend in whom I could repose confidence, and with whom I could freely converse, and advise, on this occasion, would be an unspeakable comfort!

Such a one, next to yourself, I think Julia Granby to be. With your leave and consent I should esteem it a special favor if she would come and spend a few months with me. My mamma joins in this request. I would write to her on the subject, but cannot compose myself at present. Will you prefer my petition for me?

If I have not forfeited your friendship, my dear Mrs. Sumner, write to me, and pour its healing balm into the wounded mind of your

ELIZA WHARTON.

---

1. See the two preceding letters. [*Foster's note.*] I.e., Eliza has sent Lucy the preceding exchange with Boyer.

# L   E   T   T   E   R   XLIX.

### TO MISS ELIZA WHARTON.

*BOSTON.*

Your truly romantic letter came safe to hand. Indeed, my dear, it would make a very pretty figure in a novel. A bleeding heart, slighted love, and all the *et ceteras* of romance, enter into the composition!

Excuse this raillery;[1] and I will now write more seriously. You refer yourself to my friendship for consolation. It shall be exerted for the purpose. But I must act the part of a skilful surgeon, and probe the wound, which I undertake to heal.

Where, O Eliza Wharton! Where is that fund of sense, and sentiment which once animated your engaging form? Where that strength of mind that independence of soul, that alacrity and sprightliness of deportment, which formerly raised you superior to every adverse occurrence? Why have you resigned these valuable endowments, and suffered yourself to become the sport of contending passions?

You have now emerged from that mist of fanciful folly, which, in a measure obscured the brilliance of your youthful days.

True, you figured among the first rate coquettes; while your friends, who knew your accomplishments, lamented the misapplication of them; but now they rejoice at the returning empire of reason.

True, you have erred; mislead by the gaiety of your disposition, and that volatility, and inconsideration, which were incident to your years; but you have seen, and nobly confessed your errors. Why do you talk of slighted love? True, Mr. Boyer, supposing you disregarded him, transferred his affections to another object; but have you not your admirers still, among men of real merit? Are you not esteemed, and caressed by numbers, who know you capable of shining in a distinguished sphere of life? Turn then, my friend, from the gloomy prospect, which your disturbed imagination has brought into view. Let reason and religion erect their throne in your breast; obey their dictates and be happy. Past experience will point out the quicksands which you are to avoid in your future course.

Date then, from this, a new æra of life; and may every moment be attended with felicity. Follow Mr. Boyer's advice, and forget all former connections.

---

1. Banter.

Julia accepts your invitation. Nothing short of your request could induce me to part with her. She is a good girl; and her society will amuse and instruct you.

<div style="text-align:center">I am, &c.</div>

<div style="text-align:right">LUCY SUMNER.</div>

# L   E   T   T   E   R   L.

TO MRS. LUCY SUMNER.

<div style="text-align:right"><em>HARTFORD.</em></div>

My Julia Granby has arrived. She is all that I once was; easy, sprightly, debonair. Already has she done much towards relieving my mind. She endeavors to divert, and lead my thoughts into a different channel from that to which they are now prone. Yesterday, we had each an invitation to a ball. She labored hard to prevail on me to go; but I obstinately refused. I cannot yet mix with gay and cheerful circles. I therefore alledged that I was indisposed, and persuaded her to go without me.

The events of my life have always been unaccountably wayward. In many instances I have been ready to suppose that some evil genius presided over my actions, which has directed them contrary to the sober dictates of my own judgment.

I am sometimes tempted to adopt the sentiment expressed in the following lines of the poet,

> "To you, great gods, I make my last appeal;
> O, clear my conscience, or my crimes reveal!
> If wand'ring through the paths of life I've run;
> And backward trod the steps, I sought to shun,
> Impute my errors to your own decree;
> My feet were guilty, but my heart was free."[1]

I suppose you will tell me, that the fate I accuse, through the poet, is only the result of my own imprudence. Well, be it what it may; either the impulse of my own passions, or some higher efficiency; sure I am, that I pay dear for its operation.

I have heard it remarked, that experience is the preceptor of fools; but that the wise need not its instruction. I believe I must be content to rank accordingly, and endeavor to reap advantage from its tuition.

---

1. The hero speaks these lines in John Dryden's 1679 adaptation of Sophocles' *Oedipus*, Act 3, before departing the stage. However, in this instance, Foster likely invokes Richardson's use in *Clarissa*, in which the lines are spoken by the heroine.

Julia urges me to revisit the scenes of amusements and plea-
sure; in which she tells me, she is actuated by selfish motives. She
wishes it for her own sake. She likes neither to be secluded from
them, nor to go alone. I am sometimes half inclined to seek, in
festive mirth, a refuge from thought and reflection. I would
escape, if possible, from the idea of Mr. Boyer. This I have never
been able to accomplish, since he dropped a tear upon my hand,
and left me. I marked the spot with my eye; and twenty times in a
day, do I view it, and fondly imagine it still there! How could I give
him pain! I hope his happy Maria never will! I hope she will
reward that merit, which I have slighted! but I forbear. This theme
carries away my pen, if I but touch upon it. And no wonder; for it
is the sole exercise of my thoughts! Yet I will endeavor to divert
them. Send me some new books; not such, however, as will require
much attention. Let them be plays or novels, or any thing else,
that will amuse and extort a smile.

Julia and I have been rambling in the garden. She insisted upon
my going with her into the arbor, where I was surprised with Major
Sanford. What a croud of painful ideas rushed upon my imagina-
tion! I believe she repented her rashness. But no more of this. I must
lay aside my pen; for I can write nothing else!

ELIZA WHARTON.

# L  E  T  T  E  R  LI.

### TO MRS. LUCY SUMNER.

*HARTFORD.*

DEAR MADAM,

You commanded me to write you respecting Miss Wharton; and
I obey. But I cannot describe to you the surprising change, which
she has undergone. Her vivacity has entirely forsaken her; and she
has actually become, what she once dreaded above all things, a
recluse! She flies from company, as eagerly as she formerly sought
it! Her mamma is exceedingly distressed by the settled melan-
choly which appears in her darling child; but neither of us think it
best to mention the subject to her. We endeavor to find means to
amuse her; and we flatter ourselves that the prospect of success
rather increases. It would add greatly to my happiness, to contrib-
ute, in any degree, to restore her to herself, to her friends, and to
society.

We are all invited to dine abroad to morrow; and to oblige me, she
has consented to go.

Pray madam, write to her often. Your letters may do much for her. She is still feelingly alive to the power of friendship; and none can exercise it upon her to greater acceptance, or with more advantage than yourself.

Major Sanford's house is undergoing a complete repair. The report is, that he is soon to be married. Miss Wharton has heard, but does not believe it. I hope, for her sake, it will prove true. For, at any rate, he is about returning; and from her mamma's account of his past conduct towards Eliza, were he to return unconnected, he would probably renew his attentions; and though they might end in marriage, her happiness would not be secured. She has too nice a sense of love and honor, to compound with his licentious principles. A man, who has been dissolute before marriage, will very seldom be faithful afterwards.

I went into Eliza's chamber the other day, and found her with a miniature picture in her hand. You pretend to be a physiognomist,[1] Julia, said she. What can you trace in that countenance? I guessed whose it was; and looking wistfully at it, replied, I believe the original is an artful, designing man. He looks to me like a Chesterfieldian.[2] Pray who is he? Major Sanford, said she; and I am afraid you have hit his character exactly. Sure I am, that the appearance of those traits in it has made my heart ache! She wept, as she spoke it.

Poor girl! I wish he may never give you greater cause to weep! She is strongly blind to the vices and imperfections of this man. Though naturally penetrating, he has some how or other, cast a deceptious mist over her imagination, with respect to himself. She professes neither to love, nor esteem him; and owns that his ungenerous artifice mislead her in her treatment of Mr. Boyer. Yet she has forgiven him, and thinks him a pleasing companion!

How prone to error is the human mind! How much lighter than the breath of zephyrs[3] the operations of fancy! Strange then, it should ever preponderate over the weightier powers of the understanding![4]

But I will not moralize. My business here is to dissipate, not to collect ideas; and I must regulate myself accordingly.

---

1. One who studies the face to determine character.
2. Characteristic of Philip Dormer Stanhope, Earl of Chesterfield (1694–1773) or his writings; elegant; suave. Chesterfield's *Letters to His Son* (1774) were popular in Revolutionary America but also controversial, especially for his demeaning attitude toward women and his endorsement of insincerity in the service of ambition.
3. Light breezes, named for Zephyrus, Greek god of the west wind.
4. In eighteenth-century theories of the mind, the "understanding" denoted faculties of awareness and sensory perception. Julia asserts that Eliza's "fancy," or imagination, has outweighed her grasp on actuality.

I am endeavoring to prepare Eliza, by degrees, to accompany me
to Boston, the ensuing winter; but think it doubtful whether I shall
succeed. I shall, however, return myself; till when, I am, &c.

JULIA GRANBY.

# L  E  T  T  E  R  LII.

TO MISS ELIZA WHARTON.

*BOSTON.*

MY DEAR ELIZA,

I received yours of the 24th. ult.[1] and thank you for it; though it
did not afford me those lively sensations of pleasure, which I usually
feel at the perusal of your letters. It inspired me both with concern,
and chagrin. With concern, lest your dejection of mind should affect
your health; and with chagrin at your apparent indulgence of melan-
choly. Indeed, my friend, your own happiness and honor, require you
to dissipate the cloud which hangs over your imagination.

Rise then above it; and prove yourself superior to the adverse
occurrences which have befallen you. It is by surmounting difficul-
ties, not by sinking under them, that we discover our fortitude. True
courage consists not in flying from the storms of life; but in braving
and steering through them with prudence. Avoid solitude. It is the
bane of a disordered mind; though of great utility to a healthy one.
Your once favorite amusements court your attention. Refuse not
their solicitations. I have contributed my mite,[2] by sending you a few
books; such as you requested. They are of the lighter kind of read-
ing; yet perfectly chaste; and if I mistake not, well adapted to your
taste.

You wish to hear from our theatre. I believe it will be well supplied
with performers this winter. Come and see whether they can afford
you any entertainment. Last evening I attended a tragedy; but never
will I attend another. I have not yet been able to erase the gloom
which it impressed upon my mind. It was Romeo and Juliet. Distress-
ing enough to sensibility this! Are there not real woes (if not in our
own families, at least among our own friends, and neighbors) suffi-
cient to exercise our sympathy and pity, without introducing ficti-
tious ones into our very diversions? How can that be a diversion,
which racks the soul with grief, even though that grief be imaginary.

1. Short for ultimo (*Latin*); in the preceding month.
2. Small bit.

The introduction of a funeral solemnity, upon the stage, is shocking indeed!

Death is too serious a matter to be sported with! An opening grave cannot be a source of amusement to any considerate mind! The closing scene of life can be no pastime, when realized! it must therefore awaken painful sensations, in the representation!

The circus is a place of fashionable resort of late, but not agreeable to me. I think it inconsistent with the delicacy of a lady, even to witness the indecorums, which are practiced there; especially, when the performers of equestrian feats are of our own sex. To see a woman depart so far from the female character, as to assume the masculine habit and attitudes; and appear entirely indifferent, even to the externals of modesty, is truly disgusting, and ought not to be countenanced by our attendance, much less by our approbation. But setting aside this circumstance, I cannot conceive it to be a pleasure to sit a whole evening, trembling with apprehension, lest the poor wight[3] of a horseman, or juggler, or whatever he is to be called, should break his neck in contributing to our entertainment.

With Mr. Bowen's museum,[4] I think you were much pleased. He has made a number of judicious additions to it, since you were here. It is a source of rational and refined amusement. Here the eye is gratified, the imagination charmed, and the understanding improved. It will bear frequent reviews without palling on the taste. It always affords something new; and for one, I am never a weary spectator.

Our other public, and private places of resort, are much as you left them.

I am happy in my present situation; but when the summer returns, I intend to visit my native home. Again, my Eliza, will we ramble together in those retired shades which friendship has rendered so delightful to us. Adieu, my friend, till then. Be cheerful, and you will yet be happy.

LUCY SUMNER.

---

3. A living creature, often implying contempt or commiseration.
4. Daniel Bowen (1760–1856) was the proprietor of the Columbian Museum, which included a waxwork show featuring figures from British and American history, as well as patriotic and Biblical scenes. Bowen arrived in Boston in 1791. Like Foster, he resided in Brighton. In the wake of Foster's novel, select nineteenth-century wax museums and traveling shows featured a likeness of Eliza Wharton.

# L   E   T   T   E   R   LIII.

*HARTFORD.*

Gracious Heaven! What have I heard? Major Sanford is married! Yes, the ungrateful, the deceitful wretch, is married! He has forsworn, he has perjured, and given himself to another! That, you will say, is nothing strange. It is characteristic of the man. It may be so; but I could not be convinced of his perfidy,[1] till now!

Perhaps it is all for the best. Perhaps, had he remained unconnected, he might still have deceived me; but now I defy his arts!

They tell me, he has married a woman of fortune. I suppose he thinks, as I once did, that wealth can ensure happiness. I wish he may enjoy it.

This event would not affect me at all, were it not for the depression of spirits which I feel, in consequence of a previous disappointment; since which, every thing of the kind agitates and overcomes me. I will not see him. If I do, I shall betray my weakness, and flatter his vanity; as he will doubtless think he has the power of mortifying me by his connection with another.

Before this news discomposed me, I had attained to a good degree of cheerfulness. Your kind letter, seconded by Julia's exertions, had assisted me in regulating my sensibility. I have been frequently into company, and find my relish for it gradually returning.

I intend to accept the pleasure to which you invite me, of spending a little time with you, this winter. Julia and I will come together. Varying the scene may contribute effectually to dissipate the gloom of my imagination. I would fly to almost any resort, rather than my own mind. What a dreadful thing it is to be afraid of one's own reflections, which ought to be a constant source of enjoyment! But I will not moralize. I am sufficiently melancholy, without any additional cause to increase it!

ELIZA WHARTON.

---

1. Treacherousness.

# L E T T E R  LIV.

*HARTFORD.*

DEAR DEIGHTON,

Who do you think is writing to you? Why, it is your old friend, metamorphosed into *a married man!* You stare, and can hardly credit the assertion. I cannot realize it myself; yet, I assure you, Charles, it is absolutely true! Necessity, dire necessity, forced me into this dernier[1] resort. I told you, some time ago, it would come to this.

I stood aloof, as long as possible; but in vain did I attempt to shun the noose. I must either fly to this resource; or give up all my show, equipage, and pleasure, and degenerate in to a downright plodding money-catcher, for a subsistence. I chose the first; and who would not? yet I feel some remorse at taking the girl to wife, from no better motives. She is really too good for such an imposition. But she must blame herself, if she suffer hereafter; for she was visibly captivated by my external appearance; and wanted but very little solicitation to confer herself, and fortune on so charming a fellow. Her parents opposed her inclination, for a while, because I was a stranger, and rather too gay for their taste. But she had not been used to contradiction, and could not bear it; and therefore they ventured not to cross her. So I bore off the prize; and a prize she really is. Five thousand pounds in possession, and more in reversion,[2] if I do not forfeit it. This will compensate for some of my past mistakes, and set matters right for the present. I think it doing much better than to have taken the little Laurence girl, I told you of, with half the sum. Besides, my Nancy is a handsomer, and more agreeable person. But that is of little consequence to me, you know. "Beauty soon grows familiar to the lover."[3] Were I a lover, it would be of no great avail. A lover I am; yet not of my wife. The dart which I received from Miss Wharton, sticks fast in my heart; and I assure you, I could hardly persuade myself even to appear unfaithful to her. O, Eliza, accuse me not of infidelity; for your image is my constant companion! A thousand times have I cursed the unpropitious[4] stars, which withheld from her a fortune. That would have enabled me to marry her; and with her, even wedlock would have been supportable.

---

1. *French*: Last.
2. The total amount the individual has banked, and the amount that will be due upon the conclusion of some event.
3. From Addison's *Cato*, Act 1, Scene 4.
4. Unfavorable.

I am told, that she is still single. Her sober lover never returned. Had he loved as I did, and do, he could not have been so precipitate. But these stoic souls are good for nothing, that I know of, but

> "Fix'd like a plant, to one peculiar spot,
> To draw nutrition, propagate, and rot."[5]

I want to see Eliza, and I must see her; yet I dread an interview. I shall frankly confess my motives for marrying; and the reasons of my conduct, before I went away. I shall own that my circumstances would not allow me to possess her; and yet that I could not resign her to another.

When I make up the matter with her, I shall solicit her friendship for my wife. By this mean I may enjoy her society, at least, which will alleviate the confinement of a married state. To my spouse I must be as civil as possible. I really wish she had less merit, that I might have a plausible excuse for neglecting her.

To morrow I shall go to Mrs. Wharton's. I am very much taken up with complimental visits, at present. What deference is always paid to equipage! They may talk of this virtue, their learning, and what not; but without either of them, I shall bear off the palm of respect from those, who have them, unadorned with gold, and its shining appendages.

Every thing hereabouts recals Eliza to my mind. I impatiently anticipate the hour, which will convey me to her presence.

<div align="right">PETER SANFORD.</div>

# L  E  T  T  E  R  LV.

<div align="center">TO MRS. LUCY SUMNER.</div>

<div align="right">HARTFORD.</div>

A new scene has opened upon us to day, my dear Mrs. Sumner; a visit from Major Sanford. My mamma, Miss Granby, and myself, were sitting together in the chamber. Miss Granby was entertaining us by reading aloud in Millot's elements of history,[1] when a servant rapped at the door, and handed in the following billet.

---

5. A minor amendment of Pope's couplet in *An Essay on Man*, Epistle 2. Mary Wollstone-craft also invoked this quote in *Thoughts on the Education of Daughters* (1787), in the section titled "Matrimony."
1. Claude François Xavier Millot, *Elements of History. Translated from the French of the Abbé Millot*, 5 vols., printed in Worcester, Mass., by Isaiah Thomas in 1789.

"Will Miss Wharton condescend to converse a few moments with her once favored Sanford? He is but too sensible that he has forfeited all claim to the privilege. He therefore presumes not to request it on the score of merit, or of former acquaintance; but solicits it from her benevolence, and pity."

I read and showed it to my mamma, and Julia. What, said I, shall I do? I wish not to see him. His artifice has destroyed my peace of mind; and his presence may open the wounds which time is closing. Act, said my mamma, agreeably to the dictates of your own judgment. I see no harm in conversing with him, said Julia. Perhaps it may remove some disagreeable thoughts, which now oppress and give you pain. And as he is no longer a candidate for your affections, added she, with a smile, it will be less hazardous than formerly. He will not have the insolence to speak; nor you the folly to hear, the language of love.

He was accordingly invited in. When I rose to go down, I hessitated, and even trembled. I fear, said I, to myself, it will be too much for me; yet why should it? Conscious innocence will support me. This he has not. When I entered the room he stepped forward to meet me. Confusion and shame were visibly depicted in his countenance. He approached me hastily; and without uttering a word, took my hand. I withdrew it. O! Miss Wharton, said he, despise me not. I am convinced that I deserve your displeasure, and disdain; but my own heart has avenged your cause. To your own heart, then, said I, I will leave you! But why do you again seek an interview with one whom you have endeavored to mislead; with one whom you have treated with unmerited neglect? Justice to myself required my appearing before you; that by confessing my faults, and obtaining your forgiveness, I might soften the reproaches of my own mind. Will you be seated, sir? said I. Will you, rejoined he, condescend to sit with me, Eliza? I will, sir, answered I. The rights of hospitality I shall not infringe. In my own house, therefore, I shall treat you with civility. Indeed, said he, you are very severe; but I have provoked all the coldness and reserve which you can inflict!

I am a married man, Eliza. So I understand, said I; and I hope you will never treat your wife with that dissimulation and falsehood, which you have exercised towards me. Would to heaven, exclaimed he, that you were my wife! I should not then fail in my love or duty as a husband! Yet she is an amiable girl; and, had I a heart to give her, I might still be happy! but that, alas! I can never recal. Why, then, said I, did you marry her? You were doubtless master of your own actions. No, said he, I was not. The embarrassed state of my affairs precluded the possibility of acting as I wished. Loving you most ardently, I was anxious to prevent your union with another, till

I could so far improve my circumstances, as to secure you from poverty and want in a connection with me. My regard was too sincere to permit me to deceive you, by a marriage which might have proved unhappy for us both. My pride forbad my telling you the motives of my delay; and I left you to see if I could place myself in a situation worthy of your acceptance. This I could not effect; and therefore have run the risk of my future happiness, by marrying a lady of affluence. This secures to me the externals of enjoyment; but my heart, I fear, will never participate it. Yet it affords me some degree of satisfaction that I have not involved you in distress. The only alleviation of which my banishment from you is capable, is your forgiveness. In compassion, then, refuse it not! It cannot injure you! To me it will be worth millions! He wept! Yes, Lucy, this libertine; this man of pleasure and gallantry wept! I really pitied him from my heart. I forgive you, said I, and wish you happy; yet, on this condition only, that you never again pollute my ears with the recital of your infamous passion. Yes, infamous, I call it, for what softer appellation can be given to such professions from a married man? Harbor not an idea of me, in future, inconsistent with the love and fidelity which you owe your wife; much less, presume to mention it, if you wish not to be detested by me; and for ever banished from my presence. He expressed gratitude for his absolution even upon these terms; and hoped his future conduct would entitle him to my friendship and esteem. That, I replied, time only can determine.

One favor more he begged leave to solicit; which was, that I would be a neighbor to his wife. She was a stranger, he said, and would deem my society a particular privilege. This, I told him, I could not grant, at present, whatever I might do hereafter. He did not urge it any further, but inquired after my mamma, and expressed a wish to see her. I rung the bell, and ordered her and Miss Granby to be called. When they came, he was very polite to them both; and, after usual compliments, told my mamma that he was happy in having obtained my forgiveness, to which he was anxious to have her seal affixed. My daughter, said she, is the injured party; and if she be satisfied, I shall not complain. He thanked her for her condescention; informed her that he was married, and requested her to visit his wife. We then conversed upon different subjects for a short time, and he took his leave. A sigh escaped him as he departed; and a gloom was visible in his countenance, which I never observed before.

I must acknowledge that this interview has given me satisfaction. I have often told you that if I married Major Sanford, it would be from a predilecton for his situation in life. How wretched must have been my lot, had I discovered, too late, that he was by no means possessed of the independence, which I fondly anticipated. I knew not my own heart, when I contemplated a connection with him. Little

did I think that my regard for Mr. Boyer was so deeply rooted, as I now find it. I foolishly imagined that I could turn my affections into what channel I pleased. What then must have been my feelings, when I found myself deprived both of inward peace, and outward enjoyment! I begin now to emerge from the darkness, in which I have been long benighted! I hope the tragic comedy, in which I have acted so conspicuous a part, will come to a happy end.

Julia and I talk, now and then, of a journey to Boston. As yet I have not resolution to act with much decision upon the subject. But, wherever I am, and whatever may be my fate, I shall always be your's in truth,

ELIZA WHARTON.

# L E T T E R  LVI.

TO MRS. LUCY SUMNER.

*HARTFORD.*

I begin to hope we shall come to rights here, by and by. Major Sanford has returned; has made us a visit; and a treaty of peace, and amity (but not of commerce,) is ratified.[1]

Eliza appears to be rapidly returning to her former cheerfulness, if not gaity. I hope she will not diverge too far from her present sedateness and solidity; yet I am not without apprehensions of danger, on that score. One extreme commonly succeeds another. She tells me, that she assiduously cultivates her natural vivacity; that she finds her taste for company and amusements increasing; that she dreads being alone, because past scenes arise to view which vex and discompose her.

These are indications of a mind not perfectly right. I flatter myself, however, that the time is not far distant, when her passions will vibrate with regularity.[2]

I need not repeat to you any thing relative to Major Sanford's conciliatory visit. Eliza has given you a particular, and I believe, a faithful detail. I was called down to see this wonderful man; and disliked him exceedingly. I am astonished that Eliza's penetrating

---

1. Julia puns on the language of diplomatic treaties in wartime, familiar to Foster's characters and audience because of the Revolution. The Treaty of Amity and Commerce of 1778 established an alliance of American colonists and the French. "Commerce" could, in this context, have a light sexual connotation.
2. I.e., when her mind and body will be appropriately tuned and regulated, or her passions will be in harmony with her best interests. The image is of a stringed instrument that vibrates in sympathy when a similarly attuned instrument is played.

eye, has not long since read his vices in his very countenance. I am
told by a friend, who has visited them, that he has an agreeable wife;
and I wish she may find him a husband of the same description; but
I very much doubt the accomplishment of my wish. For I have no
charity for these reformed rakes.

We were walking abroad the other afternoon, and met Major San-
ford and lady. Eliza did not see them till they were very near us. She
started, turned pale, and then colored like crimson. I cannot but
think, a little envy rankled in her heart. Major Sanford very politely
accosted us; and congratulated Mrs. Sanford on this opportunity of
introducing her to a particular friend; presenting Eliza. She received
her with an easy dignity, and bid her welcome to this part of the
country. Mrs. Sanford answered her modestly; hoped for the plea-
sure of a further acquaintance; and urged us, as we were not far from
their house, to return with them to tea. We declined; and, wishing
each other a good evening, parted. Major Sanford's eyes were rivet-
ted on Eliza, the whole time we were together; and he seemed loath
to remove them, when we separated. I suspect there is some truth in
his tale of love. I shall therefore discourage Eliza from associating
with him under any pretext whatever. She appeared more pensive
and thoughtful than common, as we returned home; and said little
the rest of the evening; but next morning was as chatty as ever.

She is warm in the praises of Mrs. Sanford, thinks her an accom-
plished woman, and wonders that the major could suggest an idea of
marrying her for her money. She intends, she says, to visit her soon;
and wishes me to accompany her. This, for her own sake, I shall
defer, as long as possible.

I am, &c.

JULIA GRANBY.

# L  E  T  T  E  R   LVII.

TO MRS. LUCY SUMNER.

*Hartford.*

By Julia's advice, we have neglected the repeated invitations of Major
Sanford, to visit and commence neighborhood with them, till yester-
day; when we received a polite billet, requesting the honor of our
company to dine. My mamma declined going; but said she had no
objection to our compliance with the message, if we thought proper.
Julia and I accordingly went. We found a large company assembled in
a spacious hall, splendidly furnished and decorated. They were all
very polite and attentive to me; but none more so than Major San-

ford and his lady, who jointly strove to dissipate the pensiveness of
my mind, which I found it impossible to conceal. When we were
summoned to dinner, the major being near me, offered his hand,
and leading me into the dining room, seated me at a table furnished
with all the variety which could please the eye, or regale the taste of
the most luxurious epicure. The conversation turned on various
subjects, literary, political, and miscellaneous. In the evening we
had a ball. Major Sanford gave the hand of his wife to a Mr. Grey,
alledging that he was a stranger, and therefore, entitled to particu-
lar attention; and then solicited mine for himself. I was on the point
of refusing him, but recollecting that it might have the appearance of
continued resentment, contrary to my declaration of forgiving what
was past, I complied. He was all kindness, and assiduity; the more so,
I imagine, with a view to make amends for his former ingratitude
and neglect. Tenderness is now peculiarly soothing to my wounded
heart. He took an opportunity of conversing with his wife and me
together; hoped she would be honored with my friendship, and
acquaintance; and begged, for her sake, that I would not be a stranger
at his house. His Nancy, he said, was far removed from her maternal
friends; but I could supply their place, if I would generously under-
take the task. She joined in expressing the same sentiments and
wishes. Alas! Sir, said I, Eliza Wharton is not now what she once
was! I labor under a depression of spirits, which must render my com-
pany rather painful than pleasing to my friends. The idea of what I
had been, contrasted with what I then was, touched my sensibility;
and I could not restrain the too officious tear from stealing down my
cheek. He took me by the hand, and said, you distress me, Miss
Wharton, indeed, you distress me! Happiness must, and shall attend
you! Cursed be the wretch, who could wound a heart like your's!

Julia Granby now joined us. An inquisitive concern was visible in
her countenance.

I related this conversation to her, after we returned home; but
she approved it not.

She thought Major Sanford too particularly attentive to me, con-
sidering what had previously happened. She said it would be noticed
by others, and the world would make unfavorable remarks upon any
appearance of intimacy between us. I care not for that, said I. It is an
ill-natured, misjudging world; and I am not obliged to sacrifice my
friends to its opinion. Were Major Sanford a single man I should
avoid his society; but since he is married; since his wife is young,
beautiful and lovely, he can have no temptation to injure me. I there-
fore see no evil, which can arise from the cultivation of friendship
with *her*, at least. I relish company so little, that I may surely be
indulged in selecting that which is most agreeable to my taste, to
prevent my becoming quite a misanthrope.

I thank you, my dear Mrs. Sumner, for your kind letter. It was a seasonable cordial[1] to my mind; and I will endeavor to profit by your advice.

Your remarks on the public entertainments are amusing, and as far as I am a judge, perfectly just.

I think it a pity they have not female managers for the theatre. I believe it would be under much better regulations, than at present.

With cordial respects to Mr. Sumner, I subscribe myself, yours in sincerity,

ELIZA WHARTON.

# L  E  T  T  E  R  LVIII.

### TO MR. CHARLES DEIGHTON.

*HARTFORD.*

Rejoice with me, my friend, that I have made my peace with the mistress of my heart. No devotee could have been more sincere in his penitence, than I was in mine. Indeed, Charles, I never knew I had so much sensibility before! Why, I was as much a woman as the very weakest of the sex!

But I dealt very plainly and sincerely with her, to be sure; and this atones for all past offences, and procures absolution for many others yet to be committed.

The dear girl was not inexorable;[1] she was as placable[2] and condescending as I could expect, considering the nature of the crime, which was apparently slighting her person and charms, by marrying another. This you know is one of the nicest points with the ladies. Attack their honor, that is their chastity, and they construe it to be the effect of excessive love, which hurries you a little beyond the bounds of prudence. But touch their vanity, by preferring another, and they will seldom pardon you. You will say I am very severe upon the sex. And have I not reason to be so, since I have found so many frail ones among them. This, however, is departing from my subject.

Eliza is extremely altered! Her pale dejected countenance, with the sedateness of her manners, so different from the lively glow of health, cheerfulness and activity which formerly animated her appearance and deportment, struck me very disagreeably.

---

1. A sweet drink generally taken after meals.
1. Incapable of being moved by entreaty.
2. Pleasing.

With all my gallantry, and fluency in love matters, I was unable to acquit myself tolerably; or to address her with any degree of ease and confidence. She was very calm; and spoke with great indifference about my marriage, &c. which mortified me exceedingly. Yet I cannot consent to believe that her present depression of spirits arises solely from Mr. Boyer's infidelity. I flatter myself that I am of sufficient consequence to her, to have contributed in a degree.

When I inquired after her health, she told me she had been indisposed; but was now much better. This indisposition, I am informed, was purely mental; and I am happy to observe her recovering from it. I frequently visit her, sometimes with, and sometimes without my wife; of whom, through my mediation, she has become a favorite. I have married, and according to the general opinion, reformed. Yet I suspect my reformation, like most others of the kind, will prove instable as "the baseless fabric of a vision;"[3] unless I banish myself entirely from her society. But that I can never do; for she is still lovely in my eyes, and I cannot control my passions. When absent from her, I am lost to every thing but her idea. My wife begins to rally me on my fondness for Miss Wharton. She asked me the other day if she had a fortune? No, said I, if she had I should have married her. This wounded her sensibility. I repented of my sincerity, and made my peace for that time. Yet, I find myself growing extremely irritable, and she must take heed how she provokes me; for I do not love her; and I think the name of wife becomes more and more distasteful to me every day.

In my mind Eliza has no competitor. But I must keep up appearances, though I endeavor to regain her love. I imagine that the enjoyment of her society, as a neighbor and friend may content me for the present, and render my condition supportable.

Farewell, Charles. I hope you will never be embarrassed with a wife, nor lack some favorite nymph to supply the place of one.

PETER SANFORD.

# L E T T E R   LIX.

TO MRS. LUCY SUMNER.

*Hartford.*

DEAR LUCY,

I intended, this week, to have journeyed to Boston with Julia Granby; but my resolution fails me. I find it painful even to think

---

3. Shakespeare, *The Tempest*, Act 4, Scene 1.

of mixing again with the gay multitude. I believe the melancholy reflections, by which I am oppressed, will be more effectually, if not more easily surmounted, by tarrying where they are rendered familiar, than by going from them awhile, and then returning.

Julia will therefore go without me. I envy her no enjoyment there, except your company.

The substitution of friendship in the place of love for Major Sanford, I find productive of agreeable sensations. With him, he assures me, it is a far more calm, and rational pleasure. *He* treats me with the affection and tenderness of a brother; and his *wife*, who exceeds him in professions of regard, with all the consoling softness, and attention of a sister. Indeed, their politeness has greatly contributed to revive the cheerfulness of my natural disposition.

I believe the major's former partiality to me, as a lover, is intirely obliterated; and for my part, I feel as little restraint in his company, and his lady's, as in that of any other in the neighborhood.

I very much regret the departure of Julia; and hope you will permit her to return to me again, as soon as possible. She is a valuable friend. Her mind is well cultivated; and she has treasured up a fund of knowledge and information, which renders her company both agreeable and useful in every situation of life. We lately spent the afternoon and evening at Mr. Smith's. They had a considerable number of visitants; and among the rest, Major Sanford. His wife was expected, but did not come, being indisposed.

I believe, my friend, you must excuse me if my letters are shorter than formerly. Writing is not so agreeable to me as it used to be. I love my friends as well as ever; but I think they must be weary of the gloom and dulness which pervades my present correspondence. When my pen shall have regained its original fluency and alertness, I will resume and prolong the pleasing task.

I am, my dear Lucy, your's most affectionately,

ELIZA WHARTON.

# L  E  T  T  E  R  LX.

TO THE SAME.

*HARTFORD.*

DEAR MADAM,

Agreeably to your desire, every art has been tried, every allurement held out, every argument used, and every plan adopted which Mrs. Wharton and I could devise to induce Eliza to accompany me to Boston; but all in vain. Sometimes she has been almost persuaded to a

compliance with our united request; but soon has resolutely determined against it. I have observed her sentiments to be suddenly changed after being in company with Major Sanford. This alarms us exceedingly. Indeed the major seems to have insinuated himself into her good opinion more than ever. She is flattered into the belief that his attention to her is purely the result of friendship and benevolence.

I have not so favorable an opinion of the man, as to suppose him capable of either. He has become very familiar here. He calls in almost every day. Sometimes he but just inquires after our health; and sometimes makes long visits. The latter is his invariable practice, when he finds Eliza alone. Mrs. Wharton always avoids seeing him if she can. She dreads, she says, his approaching the house.

I entered the parlor the other day, somewhat suddenly, and found him sitting very near Eliza, in a low conversion. They both rose in apparent confusion, and he soon retired.

When he was gone; I suspect, said I, that the major was whispering a tale of love, Eliza? Do you imagine, said she, that I would listen to such a theme from a married man? I hope not, said I; but his conduct towards you indicates a revival of his former sentiments, at least. I was not aware of that, said she. As yet I have observed nothing in his behavior to me, inconsistent with the purest friendship.

We drank tea not long since at Mr. Smith's. Late in the afternoon, Major Sanford made his appearance to apologize, as he said, for Mrs. Sanford, who was indisposed, and could not enjoy the pleasure of the visit she had contemplated. He was very gay, the whole evening; and when the company separated, he was the first to present his arm to Eliza, who accepted it without hesitation. A Mr. Newhall attended me, and we endeavored to keep them company; but they evidently chose to walk by themselves. Mr. Newhall observed, that if Major Sanford were not married, he should suspect he still intended a union with Miss Wharton. I replied, that their former intercourse having terminated in friendship, rendered them more familiar with each other, than with the generality of their acquaintance.

When we reached the house, Mr. Newhall chose not to go in, and took his leave. I waited at the door for Eliza and Major Sanford. At some little distance I saw him press her hand to his lips. It vexed me exceedingly; and no sooner had they come up, than I sullenly bade him good night, and walked directly in. Eliza soon followed me. I sat down by the fire in a thoughtful posture. She did the same. In this situation we both remained for some time, without speaking a word. At length she said, you seem not to have enjoyed your walk, Miss Granby; did you not like your gallant? Yes, said I, very well; but I am mortified that you were not better provided for. I make no complaint,

rejoined she; I was very well entertained. That is what displeases me, said I; I mean your visible fondness for the society of such a man. Were you averse to it, as you ought to be, there would be no danger. But he has an alluring tongue, and a treacherous heart. How can you be pleased and entertained by his conversation? to me it appears totally repugnant to that refinement and delicacy for which you have always been esteemed.

His assiduity, and obtrusion ought to alarm you. You well know what his character has been. Marriage has not changed his disposition. It is only a cloak which conceals it. Trust him not then, my dear Eliza! If you do, depend upon it, you will find his professions of friendship to be mere hypocricy, and deceit! I fear that he is acting over again the same unworthy arts, which formerly mislead you. Beware of his wiles! Your friends are anxious for you. They tremble at your professed regard, and apparent intimacy with that unprincipled man. My friends, said she, are very jealous of me, lately. I know not how I have forfeited their confidence, or incurred their suspicion. By encouraging that attention, I warmly replied, and receiving those caresses from a married man, which are due from him to none but his wife! He is a villian, if he deceived her into marriage by insincere professions of love. If he had then an affection for her, and has already discarded it, he is equally guilty! Can *you* expect sincerity from the man, who withholds it from an amiable, and deserving wife? no, Eliza; it is not love, which induces him to entertain you with the subject! It is a baser passion; and if you disdain not his artifice; if you listen to his flattery, you will, I fear, fall a victim to his evil machinations! If he conducted like a man of honor, he would merit your esteem; but his behavior is quite the reverse! Yet vile as he is, he would not dare to lisp his insolent hopes of your regard, if you punished his presumption with the indignation it deserves; if you spurned from your presence the ungrateful wretch, who would requite your condescension by triumphing in your ruin!

She now burst into tears, and begged me to drop the subject. Her mind, she said, was racked by her own reflections. She could bear but little. Kindness deceived, and censure distressed her!

I assured her of my good intentions; that as I saw her danger, I thought it a duty of the friendship and affection I bore her, solemnly to warn her against it before we parted. We talked over the matter more calmly, till she professed herself resolved in future to avoid his company, and reject his insinuations.

The next day, as I walked out, I met Major Sanford. He accosted me very civilly. I barely bid him good morning, and passed on.

I made it in my way to call at his house, and bid Mrs. Sanford adieu; not expecting another opportunity equally favorable. When I entered the parlor, she was playing a melancholy air on the harpsi-

cord. She rose, and gave me a polite and graceful reception. I told her, as I was soon to leave town, I called to take my leave of her; a compliment, which her attention to me required. Are you going to leave us then, Miss Granby? said she. I shall regret your departure exceedingly. I have so few friends in this part of the country, that it will give me sensible pain to part with one I so highly value.

I told her in the course of conversation, that I expected the pleasure of seeing her yesterday at Mr. Smith's; and was very sorry for the indisposition, which prevented her favoring us with her company. Indeed, said she, I did not know I was expected there! Were you there pray? Yes, said I; and Major Sanford excused your not coming, on the account I have mentioned. Well, said she, this is the first word I ever heard about it; he told me that business led him abroad! Did he gallant any lady? O, said I, he was with us all together. We had no particular gallants.

Seeing her curiosity excited, I heartily repented saying any thing of the matter, and waved the subject. Little did I suspect him to have been guilty of so base an artifice! It was evidently contrived to facilitate an interview with Eliza.

When I returned I related this affair to Mrs. Wharton and her daughter. The old lady and I expatiated largely on the vileness of this conduct; and endeavored to expose it to Eliza's view in its true colors. She pretended not to justify it. Yet she looked as if she wished it in her power.

I am now preparing for my journey to Boston; which I must however defer another week, for the sake of a more agreeable passage in the stage. I regret leaving Eliza! I tremble at her danger! She has not the resolution to resist temptation, which she once possessed. Her mind is surprisingly weakened! She appears sensible of this; yet adds to it by yielding to her own imbecility. You will receive a letter from her with this; though I had much difficulty to persuade her to write. She has unfortunately become very averse to this, her once favorite amusement.

As I shall soon have the pleasure of conversing with you personally, I conclude without any other addition to this scroll, than the name of your obliged

JULIA GRANBY.

# L  E  T  T  E  R   LXI.

*BOSTON.*

MY DEAR FRIEND,

I have received your letters, and must own to you that the perusal
of them gave me pain. Pardon my suspicions, Eliza: they are excited
by real friendship. Julia, you say, approves not Major Sandford's par-
ticular attention to you. Neither do I. If you recollect, and examine
his conversation in his conciliatory visit, you will find it replete with
sentiments, for the avowal of which, he ought to be banished from all
virtuous society.

Does he not insidiously declare that you are the only object of
his affections; that his union with another was formed from
interested views; and though that other is acknowledged to be
amiable and excellent, still he has not a heart to bestow, and
expects not happiness with her? Does this discover even the
appearance of amendment? Has he not, by false pretensions, mis-
lead a virtuous woman, and induced her to form a connection
with him? She was a stranger to his manner of life; and doubtless
allured, as you have been, by flattery, deceit, and external appear-
ance, to trust his honor; little thinking him wholly devoid of that
sacred tie! What is the reward of her confidence? Insensibility to
her charms, neglect of her person, and professed attachment to
another!

Is he the man, my dear Eliza, whose friendship you wish to culti-
vate? Can that heavenly passion reside in a breast, which is the seat
of treachery, duplicity, and ingratitude? You are too sensible of its
purity and worth, to suppose it possible. The confessions of his own
mouth condemn him. They convince me that he is still the aban-
doned libertine; and that marriage is but the cloak of his intrigues.
His officious[1] attentions to you are alarming to your friends. You
own your mind weakened, and peculiarly susceptible of tender
impressions. Beware how you receive them from him. Listen not a
moment to his flattering professions. It is an insult upon your under-
standing for him to offer them. It is derogatory to virtue for you to
hear them.

Slight not the opinion of the world. We are dependent beings; and
while the smallest traces of virtuous sensibility remain, we must feel
the force of that dependence, in a greater or less degree. No female,
whose mind is uncorrupted, can be indifferent to reputation. It is an

---

1. Characterized by an eagerness to please.

inestimable jewel, the loss of which can never be repaired. While retained, it affords conscious peace to our own minds, and ensures the esteem and respect of all around us.

Blessed with the company of so disinterested and faithful a friend, as Julia Granby, some deference is certainly due to her opinion and advice. To an enlarged understanding a cultivated taste, and an extensive knowledge of the world, she unites the most liberal sentiments, with a benevolence, and candor of disposition, which render her equally deserving of your considence and affection.

I cannot relinquish my claim to a visit from you this winter. Marriage has not alieniated, or weakened my regard for my friends. Come, then, to your faithful Lucy. Have you sorrows? I will sooth, and alleviate them. Have you cares? I will dispel them. Have you pleasures? I will heighten them. Come then, let me fold you to my expecting heart. My happiness will be partly suspended till your society render it complete. Adieu.

LUCY SUMNER.

# L E T T E R  LXII.

### TO MISS JULIA GRANBY.

*HARTFORD.*

DEAR JULIA,

I hope Mrs. Sumner and you will excuse my writing but one letter, in answer to the number I have received from you both. Writing is an employment, which suits me not at present. It was pleasing to me formerly, and therefore, by recalling the idea of circumstances and events which frequently occupied my pen in happier days, it now gives me pain. Yet I have just written a long consolatory letter to Mrs. Richman. She has buried her babe; her little Harriot, of whom she was doatingly fond.

It was a custom with some of the ancients, we are told, to weep at the birth of their children.

Often should we be impelled to a compliance with this custom, could we foresee the future incidents of their lives. I think, at least, that the uncertainty of their conduct and condition in more advanced age, may reconcile us to their removal to a happier state, before they are capable of tasting the bitterness of woe.

"Happy the babe, who, privilege'd by fate,
To shorter labors, and a lighter weight,

Receiv'd but yesterday the gift of breath;
Order'd to morrow, to return to death."[1]

Our domestic affairs are much as when you left us. Nothing
remarkable has occurred in the neighborhood, worth communicat-
ing. The company and amusements of the town are as usual, I sup-
pose. I frequent neither of them. Having incurred so much censure
by the indulgence of a gay disposition, I am now trying what a recluse
and solitary mode of life will produce. You will call me splenetic.[2] I
own it. I am pleased with nobody; still less with myself. I look around
for happiness, and find it not. The world is to me a desart! If I indulge
myself in temporary enjoyment, the consciousness or apprehension
of doing amiss, destroys my peace of mind. And, when I have recourse
to books, if I read those of serious description, they remind me of an
awful futurity, for which I am unprepared; if history, it discloses
facts in which I have no interest; if novels, they exhibit scenes of
pleasure which I have no prospect of realizing!

My mamma is solicitously attentive to my happiness; and though
she fails of promoting it; yet I endeavor to save her the pangs of dis-
appointment, by appearing what she wishes.

I anticipate, and yet I dread your return; a paradox this, which
time alone can solve.

Continue writing to me, and intreat Mrs. Sumner, in my name, to
do likewise. Your benevolence must be your reward.

ELIZA WHARTON.

# L   E   T   T   E   R   LXIII.

### TO MISS ELIZA WHARTON.

*BOSTON.*

A paradox, indeed, is the greater part of your letter to us, my dear
Eliza. We had fondly flattered ourselves that the melancholy of your
mind was exterminated. I hope no new cause has revived it. Little
did I intend, when I left you, to have been absent so long; but Mrs.
Sumner's disappointment, in her plan of spending the summer at
Hartford induced me, in compliance with her request, to prolong my
residence here.

1. From Matthew Prior's *Solomon on the Vanity of the World* (1718), also quoted by Hervey
   in *Meditations*, Foster's likely source. The verse can also be found on the tombstones of
   children in late-eighteenth-century New England.
2. Melancholic or ill-tempered. The term was sometimes used in the period to connote an
   old maid or spinster.

But for your sake, she now consents to my leaving her, in hopes I may be so happy as to contribute to your amusement.

I am both pleased and instructed by the conduct of this amiable woman. As I always endeavored to imitate her discreet and modest behavior in a single state; so likewise shall I take her for a pattern, should I ever enter a married life. She is most happily united. Mr. Sumner, to all the graces and accomplishments of the gentleman, adds the still more important and essential properties of virtue, integrity and honor. I was once present when a person was recommended to her for a husband. She objected that he was a rake. True, said the other, he has been, but he has reformed. That will never do for me, rejoined she; I wish my future companion to need no reformation: a sentiment worthy the attention of our whole sex; the general adoption of which, I am persuaded, would have a happy influence upon the manners of the other.

I hope neither you, nor I, Eliza, shall ever be tried by a man of debauched principles. Such characters I conceive to be totally unfit for the society of women, who have any claim to virtue and delicacy.

I intend to be with you, in about a month. If agreeable to you, we will visit, and spend a few weeks with the afflicted Mrs. Richman. I sincerely sympathize with her, under her bereavement. I know her fondness for you will render your company very consoling to her; and I flatter myself that I should not be an unwelcome guest.

Make my respects to your mamma; and believe me ever your's,

<div style="text-align:right">JULIA GRANBY.</div>

# L E T T E R  LXIV.

<div style="text-align:center">TO MRS. LUCY SUMNER.</div>

<div style="text-align:right"><em>HARTFORD.</em></div>

DEAR MADAM,

I have arrived in safety, to the mansion of our once happy and social friends. But I cannot describe to you, how changed, how greatly changed this amiable family appears since I left it. Mrs. Wharton met me at the door; and tenderly embracing, bade me a cordial welcome. You are come, Julia, said she, I hope, to revive and comfort us. We have been very solitary during your absence. I am happy madam, said I, to return; and my endeavors to restore cheerfulness and content, shall not be wanting. But, where is Eliza? By this time we had reached the back parlor, whither Mrs. Wharton led me; and the door being open, I saw Eliza, reclined on a settee, in a very thoughtful posture. When I advanced to

meet her, she never moved; but sat "like patience on a monument, smiling at grief!"[1]

I stopped involuntarily, and involuntarily raising my eyes to heaven, exclaimed, is that Eliza Wharton! She burst into tears; and attempted to rise, but sunk again into her seat. Seeing her thus affected, I sat down by her; and throwing my arm about her neck, why these tears? said I. Why this distress, my dear friend? Let not the return of your Julia give you pain! She comes to sooth you with the consolations of friendship! It is not pain, said she, clasping me to her breast; it is pleasure, too exquisite for my weak nerves to bear! See you not, Julia, how I am altered? Should you have known me for the sprightly girl, who was always welcome at the haunts of hilarity and mirth? Indeed, said I, you appear indisposed, but I will be your physician. Company, and change of air will, I doubt not, restore you. Will these cure disorders of the mind, Julia? They will have a powerful tendency to remove them, if rightly applied; and I profess considerable skill in that art. Come, continued I, we will try these medicines in the morning. Let us rise early, and step into the chaise; and after riding a few miles, call and breakfast with Mrs. Freeman. I have some commissions from her daughter. We shall be agreeably entertained there, you know.

Being summoned to supper, I took her by the hand, and we walked into another room, where we found her brother, and his wife, with her mamma waiting for us. We were all very chatty; even Eliza resumed, in a degree, her former sociability. A settled gloom, notwithstanding, brooded on her countenance; and a deep sigh often escaped her, in spite of her evident endeavors to suppress it. She went to bed before us; when her mamma informed me that her health had been declining for some months, that she never complained, but studiously concealed every symptom of indisposition. Whether it were any real disorder of body, or whether it arose from her depression of spirits, she could not tell; but supposed they operated together, and mutually heightened each other.

I inquired after Major Sanford; whether he and Eliza had associated together during my absence? Sometimes, she said, they seemed on good terms; and he frequently called to see her; at others, they had very little, if any correspondence at all. She told me that Eliza never went abroad, and was very loath to see company at home; that her chief amusement consisted in solitary walks; that the dreadful idea of her meeting Major Sanford in these walks, had now and then intruded upon her imagination; that she had not the least evi-

---

1. Viola, meditating on women's fate to suppress their desires and accept pain without complaint, in William Shakespeare's *Twelfth Night*, Act 2, Scene 4. In this context, "monument" suggests a tombstone.

dence of the fact, however; and indeed, was afraid to make any inquiries into the matter, lest her own suspicions should be discovered; that the major's character was worse than ever; that he was much abroad, and frequently entertained large parties of worthless bacchanalians[2] at his house; that common report said he treated his wife with indifference, neglect, and ill nature; with many other circumstances, which it is not material to relate.

Adieu, my dear friend, for the present. When occasion requires, you shall hear again from your affectionate

JULIA GRANBY.

# L   E   T   T   E   R   LXV.

TO MR. CHARLES DEIGHTON.

*HARTFORD.*

Good news, Charles, good news! I have arrived to the utmost bounds of my wishes; the full possession of my adorable Eliza! I have heard a quotation from a certain book; but what book it was I have forgotten, if I ever knew. No matter for that; the quotation is, that "stolen waters are sweet, and bread eaten in secret is pleasant."[1] If it has reference to the pleasures, which I have enjoyed with Eliza, I like it hugely, as Tristram Shandy's father said of Yorick's sermon;[2] and I think it fully verified.

I had a long and tedious siege. Every method which love could suggest, or art invent, was adopted. I was sometimes ready to despair, under an idea that her resolution was unconquerable, her virtue impregnable. Indeed, I should have given over the pursuit long ago, but for the hopes of success I entertained from her parlying[3] with me, and in reliance upon her own strength, endeavoring to combat, and counteract my designs. Whenever this has been the case, Charles, I have never yet been defeated in my plan. If a lady will consent to enter the lists[4] against the antagonist of her honor, she may be sure of loosing the prize. Besides, were her delicacy genuine, she would banish the man at once, who presumed to doubt, which he certainly does, who attempts to vanquish it!

---

2. Drunken partygoers.
1. Proverbs 9:17.
2. Laurence Sterne's *The Life and Opinions of Tristram Shandy, Gentleman* (1759–67) was a popular British novel characterized by sexual humor and ridicule. Parson Yorick is a witty clergyman, whose sermon on conscience is referred to here.
3. Conferring, especially between warring parties.
4. To accept a challenge or engage in combat.

But, far be it from me to criticise the pretensions of the sex. If I gain the rich reward of my dissimulation and gallantry, that you know is all I want.

To return then to the point. An unlucky, but not a miraculous accident, has taken place, which must soon expose our amour.[5] What can be done? At the first discovery, absolute distraction seized the soul of Eliza, which has since terminated in a fixed melancholy. Her health too is much impaired. She thinks herself rapidly declining; and I tremble when I see her emaciated form!

My wife has been reduced very low, of late. She brought me a boy a few weeks past, a dead one though.

These circumstances give me neither pain nor pleasure. I am too much ingrossed by my divinity, to take an interest in any thing else. True, I have lately suffered myself to be somewhat engaged here and there, by a few jovial lads, who assist me in dispelling the anxious thoughts, which my perplexed situation excites. I must, however, seek some means to relieve Eliza's distress. My finances are low; but the last fraction shall be expended in her service, if she need it.

Julia Granby is expected at Mrs. Wharton's every hour. I fear that her inquisitorial eye will soon detect our intrigue, and obstruct its continuation. Now there's a girl, Charles, I should never attempt to seduce; yet she is a most alluring object, I assure you. But the dignity of her manners forbid all assaults upon her virtue. Why, the very expression of her eye, blasts in the bud, every thought, derogatory to her honor; and tells you plainly, that the first insinuation of the kind, would be punished with eternal banishment and displeasure! Of her there is no danger! But I can write no more, except that I am, &c.

PETER SANFORD.

# LETTER LXVI.

### TO MRS. LUCY SUMNER.

*HARTFORD.*

Oh, my friend! I have a tale to unfold; a tale which will rend every nerve of sympathizing pity, which will rack the breast of sensibility, and unspeakably distress your benevolent heart! Eliza—Oh the ruined, lost Eliza!

---

5. I.e., she is pregnant.

I want words to express the emotions of indignation, and grief which oppress me! But I will endeavor to compose myself; and relate the circumstances as they came to my knowledge.

After my last letter, Eliza remained much in the same gloomy situation as I found her. She refused to go, agreeably to her promise, to visit your mamma; and under one pretext or another, has constantly declined accompanying me any where else, since my arrival.

Till last Thursday night she slept in the same bed with me; when she excused herself, by saying she was restless, and should disturb my repose. I yielded to her humor of taking a different apartment, little suspecting the real cause! She frequently walked out; and though I sometimes followed, I very seldom found her. Two or three times, when I happened to be awake, I heard her go down stairs; and on inquiry in the morning, she told me that she was very thirsty, and went down for water. I observed a degree of hesitancy in her answers, for which I could not account. But last night, the dreadful mystery was developed! A little before day, I heard the front door opened with great caution. I sprang from my bed, and running to the window, saw by the light of the moon, a man going from the house. Soon after I perceived a footstep upon the stairs, which carefully approached and entered Eliza's chamber.

Judge of my astonishment, my surprise, my feelings, upon this occasion! I doubted not but Major Sanford was the person I had seen; and the discovery of Eliza's guilt, in this infamous intrigue, almost deprived me of thought and recollection! My blood thrilled with horror at this sacrifice of virtue! After a while I recovered myself, and put on my clothes. But what to do, I knew not; whether to go directly to her chamber, and let her know that she was detected; or to wait another opportunity.

I resolved on the first. The day had now dawned. I tapped at her door; and she bid me come in. She was sitting in an easy chair by the side of her bed. As I entered she withdrew her handkerchief from her face; and looking earnestly at me, said, what procures me the favor of a visit, at this early hour, Miss Granby? I was disturbed, said I, and wished not to return to my bed. But what breaks your rest; and calls you up so unseasonably, Eliza? Remorse, and despair, answered she, weeping. After what I have witnessed, this morning, rejoined I, I cannot wonder at it! Was it not Major Sanford whom I saw go from the house some time ago? She was silent, but tears flowed abundantly. It is too late, continued I, to deny or evade. Answer my question sincerely; for, believe me, Eliza, it is not malice, but concern for you, which prompts it. I will answer you, Julia, said she. You have discovered a secret, which harrows up my very soul!

A secret, which I wished you to know, but could not exert resolution to reveal! Yes! It was Major Sanford; the man who has robbed me of my peace; who has triumphed in my destruction; and who will cause my sun to sit at noon![1]

I shudder, said I, at your confession! Wretched, deluded girl! Is this a return for your parent's love, and assiduous care; for your friends' solicitude, and premonitory advice? You are ruined, you say! You have sacrificed your virtue to an abandoned, despicable profligate! And you live to acknowledge and bear your infamy! I do, said she; but not long shall I support this burden! See you not, Julia, my decaying frame, my faded cheek, and tottering limbs? Soon shall I be insensible to censure and reproach! Soon shall I be sequestered in that mansion, "where the wicked cease from troubling, and where the weary are at rest!"[2] Rest! said I, can you expect to find rest either in this world, or another, with such a weight of guilt on your head? She exclaimed, with great emotion, add not to the upbraidings of a wounded spirit! Have pity upon me, Oh! my friend, have pity upon me!

Could you know what I suffer, you would think me sufficiently punished! I wish you no other punishment, said I, than what may effect your repentance and reformation. But your mother, Eliza! She cannot long be ignorant of your fall; and I tremble to think of her distress! It will break her widowed heart! How has she loved; how has she doated upon you! Dreadful is the requital which you have made! My mother, rejoined she—Oh, name her not! The very sound is distraction to me! Oh! my Julia, if your heart be not shut against mercy and compassion towards me, aid me through this trying scene! Let my situation call forth your pity, and induce you, undeserving as I am, to exert it in my behalf!

During this time, I had walked the chamber. My spirits had been raised above their natural key, and were exhausted. I sat down, but thought I should have fainted, till a copious flood of tears gave me relief. Eliza was extremely affected. The appearance of calamity which she exhibited would have softened the most obdurate anger. Indeed, I feared some immediate and fatal effect. I therefore seated myself beside her; and assuming an air of kindness, compose yourself, Eliza, said I; I repeat what I told you before, it is the purest friendship, which thus interests me in your concerns. This, under the direction of charity, induces me again to offer you my hand. Yet you have erred against knowledge and reason; against warning and counsel. You have forfeited the favor of your friends; and reluctant will be their forgiveness. I plead guilty, said she, to all your charges.

1. Amos 8:9 "And it shall come to pass in that day, Saith the Lord GOD, that I will cause the sun to go down at noon, and I will darken the earth in the clear day." The verse suggests a premature demise as punishment for deviating from God's principles.
2. Adapted from Job 3:17.

From the general voice I expect no clemency.[3] If I can make my peace with my mother, it is all I seek or wish on this side the grave.

In your benevolence I confide for this. In you, I hope to find an intercessor. By the remembrance of our former affection and happiness, I conjure you, refuse me not. At present, I entreat you to conceal from her this distressing tale. A short reprieve is all I ask. Why, said I, should you defer it? When the painful task is over, you may find relief in her lenient kindness. After she knows my condition, I cannot see her, resumed she, till I am assured of her forgiveness. I have not strength to support the appearance of her anger and grief. I will write to her what I cannot speak. You must bear the melancholy message, and plead for me, that her displeasure may not follow me, to the grave; whither I am rapidly hastening. Be assured, replied I, that I will keep your secret as long as prudence requires. But I must leave you now: your mamma will wonder at our being thus closetted together. When opportunity presents, we will converse further on the subject. In the mean time, keep yourself as composed as possible, if you would avoid suspicion. She raised her clasped hands, and with a piteous look, threw her handkerchief over her face, and reclined in her chair, without speaking a word. I returned to my chamber, and endeavored to dissipate every idea which might tend to disorder my countenance, and break the silence I wished to observe, relative to what had happened.

When I went down, Mrs. Wharton desired me to step up, and inform Eliza that breakfast was ready. She told me she could not yet compose herself sufficiently to see her mamma; and begged me to excuse her absence as I thought proper. I accordingly returned for answer to Mrs. Wharton, that Eliza had rested but indifferently, and being somewhat indisposed, would not come down, but wished me to bring her a bowl of chocolate, when we had breakfasted. I was obliged studiously to suppress even my thoughts concerning her, lest the emotions they excited might be observed. Mrs. Wharton conversed much of her daughter, and expressed great concern about her health and state of mind. Her return to this state of dejection, after having recovered her spirits and cheerfulness, in a great degree, was owing, she feared, to some cause unknown to her; and she entreated me to extract the secret, if possible. I assured her of my best endeavors, and doubted not, I told her, but I should be able in a few days to effect what she wished.

Eliza came down and walked in the garden before dinner; at which she commanded herself much better than I expected. She said that a little ride might, she imagined, be of service to her; and asked me if I would accompany her a few miles in the afternoon. Her mamma

3. Leniency.

was much pleased with the proposition; and the chaise was accordingly ordered.

I observed to Eliza, as we rode, that with her natural and acquired abilities, with her advantages of education, with her opportunities of knowing the world, and of tracing the virtues and vices of mankind to their origin, I was surprised at her becoming the prey of an insidious libertine, with whose character she was well acquainted, and whose principles she was fully apprised would prompt him to deceive and betray her. Your surprise is very natural, said she. The same will doubtless be felt and expressed by every one to whom my sad story is related. But the cause may be found in that unrestrained levity of disposition, that fondness for dissipation and coquetry which alienated the affections of Mr. Boyer from me. This event fatally depressed, and enfeebled my mind. I embraced with avidity the consoling power of friendship, ensnaringly offered by my seducer; vainly inferring from his marriage with a virtuous woman, that he had seen the error of his ways, and forsaken his licentious practices, as he affirmed, and I, fool that I was, believed it!

It is needless for me to rehearse the perfidious arts, by which he insinuated himself into my affections, and gained my confidence. Suffice it to say, he effected his purpose! But not long did I continue in the delusive dream of sensual gratification. I soon awoke to a most poignant sense of his baseness, and of my own crime and misery. I would have fled from him; I would have renounced him for ever; and by a life of sincere humility and repentance, endeavored to make my peace with heaven, and to obliterate, by the rectitude of my future conduct, the guilt I had incurred; but I found it too late! My circumstances called for attention; and I had no one to participate my cares, to witness my distress, and to alleviate my sorrows, but him. I could not therefore prevail on myself, wholly to renounce his society. At times I have admitted his visits; always meeting him in the garden, or grove adjoining; till of late, the weather, and my ill health induced me to comply with his solicitations, and receive him into the parlor.

Not long, however, shall I be subject to these embarrassments. Grief has undermined my constitution. My health has fallen a sacrifice to a disordered mind. But I regret not its departure! I have not a single wish to live. Nothing which the world affords can restore my former serenity and happiness!

The little innocent I bear, will quickly disclose its mother's shame! God Almighty grant it may not live as a monument of my guilt, and a partaker of the infamy and sorrow, which is all I have to bequeath it! Should it be continued in life, it will never know the tenderness of a parent; and, perhaps, want and disgrace may be its wretched portion! The greatest consolation I can have, will be to carry it with me to a

state of eternal rest; which, vile as I am, I hope to obtain, through the infinite mercy of heaven, as revealed in the gospel of Christ.

I must see Major Sanford again. It is necessary to converse further with him, in order to carry my plan of operation into execution. What is this plan of operation, Eliza? said I. I am on the rack of anxiety for your safety. Be patient, continued she, and you shall soon be informed. To morrow I shall write my dreadful story to my mother. She will be acquainted with my future intentions; and you shall know, at the same time, the destination of your lost friend. I hope, said I, that you have formed no resolution against your own life. God forbid, rejoined she. My breath is in his hands, let him do what seemeth good in his sight! Keep my secret one day longer, and I will never more impose so painful a silence upon you.

By this time we had reached home. She drank tea with composure, and soon retired to rest. Mrs. Wharton eagerly inquired whether I had found out the cause of Eliza's melancholy. I have urged her, said I, on the subject; but she alledges that she has particular reasons for present concealment. She has, notwithstanding, promised to let me know, the day after to morrow. Oh, said she, I shall not rest till the period arrives. Dear, good woman, said I to myself, I fear you will never rest afterwards!

This is our present situation. Think what a scene rises to the view of your Julia! She must share the distresses of others, though her own feelings, on this unhappy occasion are too keen to admit a moment's serenity! My greatest relief is in writing to you; which I shall do again by the next post. In the mean time, I must beg leave to subscribe myself, sincerely yours,

<div style="text-align: right">JULIA GRANBY.</div>

# L  E  T  T  E  R    LXVII.

<div style="text-align: center">TO THE SAME.</div>

<div style="text-align: right">HARTFORD.</div>

All is now lost; lost, indeed! She is gone! Yes, my dear friend, our beloved Eliza is gone! Never more shall we behold this once amiable companion, this once innocent and happy girl. She has forsaken, and, as she says, bid an everlasting adieu to her home, her afflicted parent and her friends! But I will take up my melancholy story where I left it in my last.

She went, as she told me she expected, into the garden, and met her detestable paramour. In about an hour she returned, and went directly to her chamber. At one o'clock I went up, and found her

writing, and weeping. I begged her to compose herself, and go down to dinner. No; she said, she could not eat; and was not fit to appear before any body. I remonstrated against her immoderate grief; represented the injury she must sustain by the indulgence of it, and conjured her to suppress the violence of its emotions.

She entreated me to excuse her to her mamma; said she was writing to her, and found it a task too painful to be performed with any degree of composure; that she was almost ready to sink under the weight of her affliction; but hoped and prayed for support, both in this, and another trying scene, which awaited her. In compliance with her desire, I now left her; and told her mamma that she was very busy in writing; wished not to be interrupted at present; but would take some refreshment, an hour or two hence. I visited her again, about four o'clock; when she appeared more calm and tranquil.

It is finished, said she, as I entered her apartment, it is finished. What said I, is finished? No matter, replied she; you will know all to morrow, Julia. She complained of excessive fatigue, and expressed an inclination to lie down; in which I assisted her, and then retired. Some time after her mamma went up, and found her still on the bed. She rose, however, and accompanied her down stairs. I met her at the door of the parlor, and taking her by the hand, inquired how she did? Oh, Julia, miserably indeed, said she. How severely does my mother's kindness reproach me! How insupportably it increases my self-condemnation! She wept; she wrung her hands, and walked the room in the greatest agony! Mrs. Wharton was exceedingly distressed by her appearance. Tell me, Eliza, said she, tell me the cause of your trouble! Oh, kill me not by your mysterious concealment! My dear child, let me, by sharing, alleviate your affliction! Ask me not, madam, said she; O my mother, I conjure you not to insist on my divulging to night, the fatal secret which engrosses and distracts my mind! To morrow I will hide nothing from you. I will press you no further, rejoined her mamma. Chuse your own time, my dear; but remember, I must participate your grief, though I know not the cause.

Supper was brought in; and we endeavored to prevail on Eliza to eat, but in vain. She sat down, in compliance with our united importunities; but neither of us tasted food. It was removed untouched. For a while, Mrs. Wharton and I gazed in silent anguish upon the spectacle of woe, before us! At length, Eliza rose to retire. Julia, said she, will you call at my chamber, as you pass to your own? I assented. She then approached her mamma, fell upon her knees before her, and clasping her hand, said, in broken accents, Oh madam! can you forgive a wretch, who has forfeited your love, your kindness, and your compassion? Surely, Eliza, said she, you are not that being! No, it is impossible! But however great your transgression, be assured of my

forgiveness, my compassion, and my continued love! Saying this, she threw her arms about her daughter's neck, and affectionately kissed her. Eliza struggled from her embrace, and looking at her with wild despair, exclaimed, this is too much! Oh, this unmerited goodness is more than I can bear! She then rushed precipitately out of the room, and left us overwhelmed in sympathy and astonishment!

When Mrs. Wharton had recovered herself a little, she observed, that Eliza's brain was evidently disordered. Nothing else, continued she, could impel her to act in this extraordinary manner. At first she was resolved to follow her; but I dissuaded her from it, alledging, that as she had desired me to come into her chamber, I thought it better for me to go alone. She acquiesced; but said she should not think of going to bed; but would, however, retire to her chamber, and seek consolation there. I bade her good night; and went up to Eliza, who took me by the hand and led me to the toilet, upon which she laid the two inclosed letters, the one to her mamma, and the other to me. These, said she, contain what I had not resolution to express. Promise me, Julia, that they shall not be opened till to-morrow morning. I will, said I. I have thought and wept, continued she, till I have almost exhausted my strength, and my reason. I would now obtain a little respite, that I may prepare my mind for the account I am one day to give at a higher tribunal than that of earthly friends. For this purpose, what I have written, and what I shall yet say to you, must close the account between you and me. I have certainly no balance against you, said I. In my breast you are fully acquitted. Your penitential tears have obliterated your guilt, and blotted out your errors with your Julia. Henceforth, be they all forgotten. Live, and be happy. Talk not, said she, of life. It would be a vain hope, though I cherished it myself.

> "That I must die, it is my only comfort;
> Death is the privilege of human nature;
> And life without it were not worth our taking.
> Thither the poor, the prisoner and the mourner
> Fly for relief, and lay their burdens down!"[1]

You have forgiven me, Julia; my mother has assured me of her forgiveness, and what have I more to wish? my heart is much lightened by these kind assurances; they will be a great support to me in the dreadful hour which awaits me! What mean you, Eliza? said I. I fear some desperate purpose labors in your mind. Oh, no, she replied; you may be assured your fear is groundless. I know not what I say; my brain is on fire; I am all confusion! Leave me, Julia; when

---

1. From Nicholas Rowe's *The Fair Penitent* (1703). The play concerns a wife's seduction by another man. The next line, not included here, is an invitation to death.

I have had a little rest, I shall be composed. These letters have
almost distracted me; but they are written, and I am comparatively
easy. I will not leave you, Eliza, said I, unless you will go directly to
bed, and endeavor to rest. I will, said she, and the sooner the better.
I tenderly embraced her, and retired, though not to bed. About an
hour after, I returned to her chamber, and opening the door very
softly, found her apparently asleep. I acquainted Mrs. Wharton with
her situation, which was a great consolation to us both; and encour-
aged us to go to bed. Having suffered much in my mind, and being
much fatigued, I soon fell asleep; but the rattling of a carriage,
which appeared to stop at a little distance from the house, awoke
me. I listened a moment, and heard the door turn slowly on its
hinges. I sprang from my bed, and reached the window just in time
to see a female handed into a chaise by a man who hastily followed
her, and drove furiously away! I at once concluded they could be no
other than Eliza and Major Sanford. Under this impression I made
no delay, but ran immediately to her chamber. A candle was burning
on the table; but Eliza was not there! I thought it best to acquaint
her mamma with the melancholy discovery; and steping to her
apartment for the purpose, found her rising. She had heard me
walk, and was anxious to know the cause. What is the matter, Julia,
said she; what is the matter? Dear madam, said I, arm yourself with
fortitude! What new occurrence demands it? rejoined she. Eliza has
left us! Left us! what mean you? She is just gone! I saw her handed
into a chaise, which instantly disappeared!

At this intelligence she gave a shriek, and fell back on her bed! I
alarmed the family, and by their assistance soon recovered her. She
desired me to inform her of every particular relative to her elope-
ment, which I did; and then delivered her the letter which Eliza had
left for her. I suspect, said she, as she took it; I have long suspected;
what I dared not believe! The anguish of my mind has been known
only to myself, and my God! I could not answer her, and therefore
withdrew. When I had read Eliza's letter to me, and wept over the
sad fall; and, as I fear, the total loss of this once amiable and accom-
plished girl, I returned to Mrs. Wharton. She was sitting in her easy
chair; and still held the fatal letter in her hand. When I entered, she
fixed her streaming eyes upon me, and exclaimed, O Julia, this is
more than the bitterness of death! True, madam, said I, your afflic-
tion must be great; yet that all-gracious Being, who controls every
event, is able, and I trust, disposed to support you! To Him, replied
she, I desire humbly to resign myself; but I think I could have borne
almost any other calamity with greater resignation and compo-
sure than this. With how much comparative ease could I have
followed her to the grave, at any period since her birth! Oh, my
child, my child! dear, very dear hast thou been to my fond heart!

Little did I think it possible for you to prepare so dreadful a cup of sorrow for your widowed mother! But where, continued she, where can the poor fugitive have fled? Where can she find that protection and tenderness, which, notwithstanding her great apostacy,[2] I should never have withheld? From whom can she receive those kind attentions, which her situation demands.

The agitation of her mind had exhausted her strength; and I prevailed on her to refresh, and endeavor to compose herself to rest; assuring her of my utmost exertions to find out Eliza's retreat, and restore her to a mother's arms.

I am obliged to suppress my own emotions; and to bend all my thoughts towards the alleviation of Mrs. Wharton's anxiety and grief.

Major Sanford is from home, as I expected; and I am determined, if he return, to see him myself, and extort from him the place of Eliza's concealment. Her flight, in her present state of health, is inexpressibly distressing to her mother; and, unless we find her soon, I dread the effects!

I shall not close this, till I have seen or heard from the vile miscreant who has involved a worthy family in wretchedness!

*Friday Morning*—Two days have elapsed without affording us much relief. Last evening, I was told that Major Sanford was at home. I immediately wrote him a billet, entreating and conjuring him to let me know where the hapless Eliza had fled. He returned me the following answer.

"Miss Granby need be under no apprehensions, respecting the situation of our beloved Eliza. She is well provided for, conveniently accommodated, and has every thing to make her happy, which love or affluence can give.

Major Sanford has solemnly sworn not to discover her retreat. She wishes to avoid the accusations of her friends, till she is better able to bear them.

Her mother may rest assured of immediate information, should any danger threaten her amiable daughter; and also of having seasonable notice of her safety."

Although little dependence can be placed upon this man; yet these assurances have, in a great degree, calmed our minds. We are, however, contriving means to explore the refuge of the wanderer; and hope, by tracing his steps, to accomplish our purpose. This we have engaged a friend to do.

I know, my dear Mrs. Sumner, the kind interest you will take in this disastrous affair. I tremble to think what the event may be! To relieve your suspense, however, I shall write you every circumstance, as it occurs. But at present, I shall only enclose Eliza's letters to her

---

2. Abandonment of one's morals or faith.

mamma, and me, and, subscribe myself your sincere and obliged friend,

JULIA GRANBY.

# L   E   T   T   E   R   LXVIII.

## TO MRS. M. WHARTON.

*TUESDAY.*

MY HONORED AND DEAR MAMMA,

In what words, in what language shall I address you? What shall I say on a subject which deprives me of the power of expression? Would to God I had been totally deprived of that power before so fatal a subject required its exertion! Repentance comes too late, when it cannot prevent the evil lamented. For your kindness, your more than maternal affection towards me, from my infancy to the present moment, a long life of filial duty and unerring rectitude could hardly compensate. How greatly deficient in gratitude must I appear then, while I confess, that precept and example, counsel and advice, instruction and admonition, have been all lost upon me!

Your kind endeavors to promote my happiness have been repaid by the inexcusable folly of sacrificing it. The various emotions of shame, and remorse, penitence and regret, which torture and distract my guilty breast, exceed description. Yes, madam, your Eliza has fallen; fallen, indeed! She has become the victim of her own indiscretion, and of the intrigue and artifice of a designing libertine, who is the husband of another! She is polluted, and no more worthy of her parentage! She flies from you, not to conceal her guilt, that she humbly and penitently owns; but to avoid what she has never experienced, and feels herself unable to support, a mother's frown; to escape the heart-rending sight of a parent's grief, occasioned by the crimes of her guilty child!

I have become a reproach and disgrace to my friends. The consciousness of having forfeited their favor, and incurred their disapprobation and resentment, induces me to conceal from them the place of my retirement; but, lest your benevolence should render you anxious for my comfort in my present situation, I take the liberty to assure you that I am amply provided for.

I have no claim even upon your pity; but from my long experience of your tenderness, I presume to hope it will be extended to me. Oh, my mother, if you knew what the state of my mind is, and has been, for months past, you would surely compassionate my case! Could

tears efface the stain, which I have brought upon my family, it would, long since have been washed away! But, alas, tears are vain; and vain is my bitter repentance! It cannot obliterate my crime, nor restore me to innocence and peace! In this life I have no ideas of happiness. These I have wholly resigned! The only hope which affords me any solace, is that of your forgiveness. If the deepest contrition can make an atonement; if the severest pains, both of body and mind, can restore me to your charity, you will not be inexorable! Oh, let my sufferings be deemed a sufficient punishment; and add not the insupportable weight of a parent's wrath! At present, I cannot see you. The effect of my crime is too obvious to be longer concealed, to elude the invidious eye of curiosity. This night, therefore, I leave your hospitable mansion! This night I become a wretched wanderer from thy paternal roof! Oh, that the grave were this night to be my lodging! Then should I lie down and be at rest! Trusting in the mercy of God, through the mediation of his son; I think I could meet my heavenly father with more composure and confidence, than my earthly parent!

Let not the faults and misfortunes of your daughter oppress your mind. Rather let the conviction of having faithfully discharged your duty to your lost child, support and console you in this trying scene.

Since I wrote the above, you have kindly granted me your forgiveness though you knew not how great, how aggravated was my offence! You forgive me, you say: Oh, the harmonious, the transporting sound! It has revived my drooping spirits; and will enable me to encounter, with resolution, the trials before me!

Farewell, my dear mamma! pray and pray for your ruined child; and be assured, that affection and gratitude will be the last sentiments, which expire in the breast of your repenting daughter,

<div align="right">ELIZA WHARTON.</div>

# L  E  T  T  E  R   LXIX.

<div align="center">TO MISS JULIA GRANBY.</div>

<div align="right">*TUESDAY.*</div>

MY DEAR FRIEND,

By that endearing title you permit me still to address you, and such you have always proved yourself, by a participation of my distresses, as well as by the consoling voice of pity and forgiveness. What destiny Providence designs for me, I know not; but I have my forebodings that this is the last time I shall ever accost you! Nor does this apprehension arise merely from a disturbed imagination. I have

reason to think myself in a confirmed consumption, which commonly proves fatal to persons in my situation. I have carefully concealed every complaint of the kind from my mamma, for fear of distressing her; yet I have never been insensible of their probable issue, and have bidden a sincere welcome to them, as the harbingers of my speedy release from a life of guilt and woe!

I am going from you, Julia. This night separates us, perhaps, for ever! I have not resolution to encounter the tears of my friends; and therefore seek shelter among strangers; where none knows, or is interested in my melancholy story. The place of my seclusion I studiously conceal; yet I shall take measures that you may be apprized of my fate.

Should it please God to spare and restore me to health, I shall return, and endeavor, by a life of penitence and rectitude, to expiate my past offences. But should I be called from this scene of action; and leave behind me a helpless babe, the innocent sufferer of its mother's shame, Oh, Julia, let your friendship for me extend to the little stranger! Intercede with my mother to take it under her protection; and transfer to it all her affection for me; to train it up in the ways of piety and virtue, that it may compensate her for the afflictions which I have occasioned!

One thing more I have to request. Plead for me with my two best friends, Mrs. Richman and Mrs. Sumner. I ask you not to palliate[1] my faults; that cannot be done; but to obtain, if possible, their forgiveness. I cannot write all my full mind suggests on this subject. You know the purport; and can better express it for me.

And now, my dear Julia, recommending myself again to your benevolence, to your charity and (may I add?) to your affection; and entreating that the fatal consequences of my folly, now fallen upon my devoted head, may suffice for my punishment; let me conjure you to bury my crimes in the grave with me, and to preserve the remembrance of my former virtues, which engaged your love and confidence; more especially of that ardent esteem for you, which will glow till the last expiring breath of your despairing

ELIZA WHARTON.

1. To ease or reduce the resulting harm.

# L E T T E R   LXX.

I have, at last, accomplished the removal of my darling girl, from a place where she thought every eye accused, and every heart condemned her.

She has become quite romantic in her notions. She would not permit me to accompany her, lest it should be reported that we had eloped together. I provided amply for her future exigencies, and conveyed her by night to the distance of ten or twelve miles, where we met the stage, in which I had previously secured her a seat. The agony of her grief at being thus obliged to leave her mother's house, baffles all description.

It very sensibly affected me, I know. I was almost a penitent. I am sure I acted like one, whether I were sincere or not. She chose to go where she was totally unknown. She would leave the stage, she said, before it reached Boston, and take passage in a more private carriage to Salem, or its vicinity, where she would fix her abode; chalking the initials of my name over the door, as a signal to me of her residence.[1]

She is exceedingly depressed; and says she neither expects nor wishes to survive her lying in. Insanity, for aught I know, must be my lot, if she should die. But I will not harbor the idea. I hope, one time or other, to have the power to make her amends, even by marriage. My wife may be provoked, I imagine, to sue for a divorce. If she should, she would find no difficulty in obtaining it; and then I would take Eliza in her stead. Though I confess that the idea of being thus connected with a woman whom I have been able to dishonor would be rather hard to surmount. It would hurt even my delicacy, little as you may think me to possess, to have a wife whom I know to be seducible.[2] And, on this account, I cannot be positive that even Eliza would retain my love.

My Nancy and I have lived a pretty uncomfortable life, of late. She has been very suspicious of my amour with Eliza; and now and then expressed her jealous sentiments a little more warmly than my

---

1. Here and elsewhere in the details of Eliza's flight, Foster draws on widely circulated newspaper accounts of Elizabeth Whitman's disappearance and death a decade earlier. See "The Elizabeth Whitman Paper Trail" in this Norton Critical Edition, pp. 302–07.
2. A reference to a similar scenario in *Don Quixote*, in which a husband tests a wife's fidelity by arranging her seduction by his friend.

patience would bear. But the news of Eliza's circumstances and retirement, being publicly talked of, have reached her ears, and rendered her quite outrageous. She tells me she will no longer brook my indifference and infidelity; intends soon to return to her father's house, and extricate herself from me intirely. My general reply to all this, is, that she knew my character before we married, and could reasonably expect nothing less than what has happened. I shall not oppose her leaving me, as it may conduce to the execution of the plan I have hinted above.

To morrow I shall set out to visit my disconsolate fair one. From my very soul I pity her; and wish I could have preserved her virtue consistently with the indulgence of my passion. To her I lay not the principal blame, as in like cases, I do to the sex in general. My finesse was too well planned for detection, and my snares too deeply laid for any one to escape who had the least warmth in her constitution, or affection in her heart. I shall, therefore, be the less whimsical about a future connection, and the more solicitous to make her reparation, should it ever be in my power.

Her friends are all in arms about her. I dare say I have the imprecations[3] of the whole fraternity. They may thank themselves in part; for I always swore revenge for their dislike and coldness towards me. Had they been politic, they would have conducted more like the aborigines of the country, who are said to worship the devil out of fear.

I am afraid I shall be obliged to remove my quarters; for Eliza was so great a favorite in town, that I am looked upon with an evil eye. I plead with her before we parted last to forgive my seducing her; alledged my ardent love, and my inability to possess her in any other way. How, said she, can that be love which destroys its object? But granting what you say, you have frustrated your own purpose. You have deprived yourself of my society, which might have been innocently enjoyed. You have cut me off from life in the midst of my days. You have rendered me the reproach of my friends, the disgrace of my family, and a dishonor to virtue and my sex! but I forgive you, added she. Yes, Sanford, I forgive you; and sincerely pray for your repentance and reformation. I hope to be the last wretched female, sacrificed by you to the arts of falsehood and seduction!

May my unhappy story serve as a beacon to warn the American fair of the dangerous tendency and destructive consequences of associating with men of your character, of destroying their time, and risking their reputation by the practice of coquetry and its attendant follies! But for these, I might have been honorably connected; and capable, at this moment, of diffusing and receiving happiness! But

3. Ill wishes.

for your arts, I might have remained a blessing to society, as well as the delight and comfort of my friends!

Your being a married man unspeakably aggravates both your guilt and mine. This circumstance annexes indelible shame to our crime! You have rent asunder the tenderest ties of nature! You have broken the bonds of conjugal love, which ought ever to be kept sacred and inviolate! You have filled with grief and discontent the heart of your amiable wife, whom gratitude, if no other principle, should have induced you to cherish with tenderness; and I, wretch that I am, have been your accomplice!

But I cease to reproach you. You have acted but too consistently with the character, which I was sufficiently apprised you sustained. The blame then may be retorted on myself, for disregarding the counsels, warnings and admonitions of my best friends. You have prided yourself in the character of a libertine. Glory no longer in your shame! You have accomplished your designs; your dreadful designs against me! Let this suffice. Add not to the number of those deluded creatures, who will one day rise up in judgment against you, and condemn you.

By this time we had nearly reached the inn, and were soon to part. I seized her hand and exclaimed, you must not leave me, Eliza, with that awful anathema[4] on your lips! Oh, say that you will forget my past faults. That, said she, I shall soon do; for in the grave there is no remembrance! This to my mind, was a harsher sentence than the other; and almost threw me into despair. Never was so wrought upon before! I knew not what to say or do! She saw my distress, and kindly softened her manner. If I am severe, said she, it is because I wish to impress your mind with such a sense of your offences against your Maker, your friends and society in general, as may effect your repentance and amendment. I wish not to be your accuser, but your reformer. On several accounts, I view my own crime in a more aggravated light than yours; but my conscience is awakened to a conviction of my guilt. Yours, I fear is not. Let me conjure you to return home, and endeavor by you future kindness and fidelity to your wife, to make her all the amends in your power. By a life of virtue and religion, you may yet become a valuable member of society, and secure happiness both here and hereafter.

I begged leave to visit her retirement next week, not in continuation of our amour, but as a friend, solicitous to know her situation and welfare. Unable to speak, she only bowed assent. The stage being now ready, I whispered some tender things in her ear, and kissing her cheek, which was all she would permit, suffered her to depart.

4. Consignment to damnation.

My body remains behind; but my soul, if I have any, went with her!

This was a horrid lecture, Charles! She brought every charge against me, which a fruitful and gloomy imagination could suggest! But I hope, when she recovers, she will resume her former cheerfulness, and become as kind and agreeable as ever. My anxiety for her safety is very great. I trust, however, it will soon be removed; and peace and pleasure be restored to your humble servant,

PETER SANFORD.

# L  E  T  T  E  R  LXXI.

## TO MRS. LUCY SUMNER.

*HARTFORD.*

The drama is now closed! A tragical one indeed it has proved!

How sincerely, my dear Mrs. Sumner, must the friends of our departed Eliza, sympathize with each other; and with her afflicted, bereaved parent!

You have doubtless seen the account, in the public papers, which gave us the melancholy intelligence. But I will give you a detail of circumstances.

A few days after my last was written, we heard that Major Sanford's property was attached,[1] and he a prisoner in his own house. He was the last man, to whom we wished to apply for information respecting the forlorn wanderer; yet we had no other resource. And after waiting a fortnight in the most cruel suspense, we wrote a billet, entreating him, if possible, to give some intelligence concerning her. He replied, that he was unhappily deprived of all means of knowing himself; but hoped soon to relieve his own, and our anxiety about her.

In this situation we continued, till a neighbor (purposely, we since concluded) sent us a Boston paper. Mrs. Wharton took it, and inconscious of its contents, observed that the perusal might divert her, a few moments. She read for some time; when it suddenly dropped upon the floor. She clasped her hands together, and raising her streaming eyes to heaven, exclaimed, It is the Lord; let him do what he will! Be still, O my soul, and know that he is God!

---

1. Seized by the courts with the intent of being sold to pay the owner's debts.

What, madam, said I, can be the matter? She answered not; but with inexpressible anguish depicted in her countenance, pointed to the paper. I took it up, and soon found the fatal paragraph. I shall not attempt to paint our heart felt grief and lamentation upon this occasion; for we had no doubt of Eliza's being the person described, as a stranger, who died at Danvers, last July. Her delivery of a child; her dejected state of mind; the marks upon her linen; indeed, every circumstance in the advertisement convinced us beyond dispute, that it could be no other.[2] Mrs. Wharton retired immediately to her chamber, where she continued overwhelmed with sorrow that night and the following day. Such, in fact, has been her habitual frame ever since; though the endeavors of her friends, who have sought to console her, have rendered her somewhat more conversable. My testimony of Eliza's penitence, before her departure, is a source of comfort to this disconsolate parent. She fondly cherished the idea, that having expiated her offence by sincere repentance and amendment, her deluded child finally made a happy exchange of worlds. But the desperate resolution, which she formed, and executed of becoming a fugitive; of deserting her mother's house and protection, and of wandering and dying among strangers, is a most distressing reflection to her friends; especially to her mother, in whose breast so many painful ideas arise, that she finds it extremely difficult to compose herself to that resignation, which she evidently strives to exemplify.

Eliza's brother has been to visit her last retreat; and to learn the particulars of her melancholy exit. He relates, that she was well accommodated, and had every attention and assistance, which her situation required. The people where she resided appear to have a lively sense of her merit and misfortunes. They testify her modest deportment, her fortitude under the sufferings to which she was called, and the serenity and composure, with which she bid a last adieu to the world. Mr. Wharton has brought back several scraps of her writing, containing miscellaneous reflections on her situation, the death of her babe, and the absence of her friends. Some of these were written before, some after her confinement. These valuable testimonies of the affecting sense, and calm expectation she entertained of her approaching dissolution, are calculated to sooth and comfort the minds of mourning connections. They greatly alleviate the regret occasioned by her absence, at this awful period.

Her elopement can be equalled only by the infatuation which caused her ruin.

2. See "The Elizabeth Whitman Paper Trail" in this Norton Critical Edition, pp. 302–07.

> "But let no one reproach her memory.
> Her life has paid the forfeit of her folly.
> Let that suffice."[3]

I am told that Major Sanford is quite frantic. Sure I am that he has reason to be. If the mischiefs he has brought upon others return upon his own head, dreadful indeed must be his portion! His wife has left him, and returned to her parents. His estate, which has been long mortgaged, is taken from him; and poverty and disgrace await him! Heaven seldom leaves injured innocence unavenged! Wretch, that he is, he ought for ever to be banished from human society! I shall continue with Mrs. Wharton, till the lenient hand of time has assuaged her sorrows; and then make my promised visit to you. I will bring Eliza's posthumous papers with me, when I come to Boston, as I have not time to copy them now.

I foresee, my dear Mrs. Sumner, that this disastrous affair will suspend your enjoyments, as it has mine. But what are our feelings, compared with the pangs which rend a parent's heart? This parent, I here behold, inhumanly stripped of the best solace of her declining years, by the ensnaring machinations of a profligate debauchee! Not only the life, but what was still dearer, the reputation and virtue of the unfortunate Eliza, have fallen victims at the shrine of *libertinism!* Detested be the epithet! Let it henceforth bear its true signature, and candor itself shall call it *lust* and *brutality!*

Execrable is the man, however arrayed in magnificence, crowned with wealth, or decorated with the external graces and accomplishments of fashionable life, who shall presume to display them, at the expense of virtue and innocence! Sacred names! attended with real blessings; blessings too useful and important to be trifled away! My resentment at the base arts, which must have been employed to complete the seduction of Eliza, I cannot suppress. I wish them to be exposed, and stamped with universal ignominy! Nor do I doubt but you will join with me in execrating the measures by which *we* have been robbed of so valuable a friend; and *society*, of so ornamental a member.

I am, &c.

JULIA GRANBY.

---

3. No source has been found for this citation, though it seems to echo passages in John Ford's 1633 play, *'Tis Pity She's a Whore*, Act 4, Scene 2. If Foster was indeed drawing on the play, its controversial subject matter would have made it inappropriate for her to do so directly. The text also foreshadows the tombstone inscription at the novel's close.

# L   E   T   T   E   R   LXXII.

*HARTFORD.*

Confusion, horror and despair are the portion of your wretched, unhappy friend! Oh, Deighton, I am undone! Misery irremediable is my future lot! She is gone; yes, she is gone for ever! The darling of my soul, the centre of all my wishes and enjoyments is no more! Cruel fate has snatched her from me; and she is irretrievably lost! I rave, and then reflect: I reflect, and then rave! I have not patience to bear this calamity, nor power to remedy it! Where shall I fly from the upbraidings of my mind, which accuses me as the murderer of my Eliza! I would fly to death, and seek a refuge in the grave; but the forebodings of a retribution to come, I cannot away with! Oh, that I had seen her; that I had once more asked her forgiveness! But even that privilege, that consolation was denied me! The day on which I meant to visit her, most of my property was attached, and to secure the rest, I was obliged to shut my doors, and become a prisoner in my own house! High living, and old debts, incurred by extravagance, had reduced the fortune of my wife to very little, and I could not satisfy the clamorous demands of my creditors.

I would have given millions, had I possessed them, to have been at liberty to see, and to have had power to preserve Eliza from death! But in vain was my anxiety; it could not relieve; it could not liberate me! When I first heard the dreadful tidings of her exit, I believe I acted like a madman! Indeed, I am little else now!

I have compounded with my creditors, and resigned the whole of my property.

Thus, that splendor and equipage, to secure which, I have sacrificed a virtuous woman, is taken from me; that poverty, the dread of which prevented my forming an honorable connection with an amiable and accomplished girl, the only one I ever loved, has fallen, with redoubled vengeance, upon my guilty head; and I must become a vagabond in the earth!

I shall fly my country as soon as possible; I shall go from every object which reminds me of my departed Eliza! But never, never shall I eradicate from my bosom the idea of her excellence; or the painful remembrance of the injuries I have done her! Her shade will perpetually haunt me! The image of her, as she appeared when mounting the carriage which conveyed her for ever from my sight, she waved her hand in token of a last adieu, will always be present to my imagination! The solemn counsel she gave me before we parted, never more to meet, will not cease to resound in my ears!

While my being is prolonged, I must feel the disgraceful, and torturing effects of my guilt in seducing her! How madly have I deprived her of happiness, of reputation, of life! Her friends, could they know the pangs of contrition, and the horror of conscience which attend me, would be amply revenged!

It is said, she quitted the world with composure and peace. Well she might! She had not that insupportable weight of iniquity, which sinks me to despair! She found consolation in that religion, which I have ridiculed as priestcraft and hypocrisy! But whether it be true, or false, would to heaven I could now enjoy the comforts, which its votaries evidently feel!

My wife has left me. As we lived together without love, we parted without regret.

Now, Charles, I am to bid you a long, perhaps, a last farewell. Where I shall roam in future, I neither know nor care; I shall go where the name of Sanford is unknown; and his person and sorrows unnoticed.

In this happy clime I have nothing to induce my stay. I have not money to support me with my profligate companions; nor have I any relish, at present, for their society. By the virtuous part of the community, I am shunned as the pest and bane of social enjoyment. In short I am debarred from every kind of happiness. If I look back, I recoil with horror from the black catalogue of vices, which have stained my past life, and reduced me to indigence and contempt. If I look forward, I shudder at the prospects which my foreboding mind presents to view, both in this and a coming world! This is a deplorable, yet just picture of myself! How totally the reverse of what I once appeared!

Let it warn you, my friend, to shun the dangerous paths which I have trodden, that you may never be involved in the hopeless ignominy and wretchedness of

PETER SANFORD.

# L   E   T   T   E   R   LXXIII.

TO MISS JULIA GRANBY.

*BOSTON.*

A melancholy tale have you unfolded, my dear Julia; and tragic indeed is the concluding scene!

Is she then gone! gone in this most distressing manner! Have I lost my once loved friend; lost her in a way which I could never have conceived to be possible.

Our days of childhood were spent together in the same pursuits, in the same amusements. Our riper years encreased our mutual affection, and maturer judgment most firmly cemented our friendship. Can I then calmly resign her to so severe a fate! Can I bear the idea of her being lost to honor, to fame, and to life! No; she shall still live in the heart of her faithful Lucy; whose experience of her numerous virtues and engaging qualities, has imprinted her image too deeply on the memory to be obliterated. However she may have erred, her sincere repentance is sufficient to restore her to charity.

Your letter gave me the first information of this awful event. I had taken a short excursion into the country, where I had not seen the papers; or if I had, paid little or no attention to them. By your directions I found the distressing narrative of her exit. The poignancy of my grief, and the unavailing lamentations which the intelligence excited, need no delineation. To scenes of this nature, you have been habituted in the mansion of sorrow, where you reside.

How sincerely I sympathize with the bereaved parent of the dear, deceased Eliza, I can feel, but have not power to express. Let it be her consolation, that her child is at rest. The resolution which carried this deluded wanderer thus far from her friends, and supported her through her various trials, is astonishing! Happy would it have been, had she exerted an equal degree of fortitude in repelling the first attacks upon her virtue! But she is no more; and heaven forbid that I should accuse or reproach her!

Yet, in what language shall I express my abhorrence of the monster, whose detestable arts have blasted one of the fairest flowers in creation? I leave him to God, and his own conscience! Already is he exposed in his true colors! Vengeance already begins to overtake him! His sordid mind must now suffer the deprivation of those sensual gratifications, beyond which he is incapable of enjoyment!

Upon your reflecting and steady mind, my dear Julia, I need not inculcate the lessons which may be drawn from this woe-fraught tale; but for the sake of my sex in general, I wish it engraved upon every heart, that virtue alone, independent of the trappings of wealth, the parade of equipage, and the adulation of gallantry, can secure lasting felicity. From the melancholy story of Eliza Wharton, let the American fair learn to reject with disdain every insinuation derogatory to their true dignity and honor. Let them despise, and for ever banish the man, who can glory in the seduction of innocence and the ruin of reputation. To associate, is to approve; to approve, is to be betrayed!

<div align="center">I am, &c.</div>

<div align="right">LUCY SUMNER.</div>

# L E T T E R   LXXIV.

TO MRS. M. WHARTON.

*Boston.*

DEAR MADAM,

We have paid the last tribute of respect to your beloved daughter. The day after my arrival, Mrs. Sumner proposed that we should visit the sad spot which contains the remains of our once amiable friend. The grave of Eliza Wharton, said she, shall not be unbedewed by the tears of friendship.

Yesterday we went accordingly, and were much pleased with the apparent sincerity of the people, in their assurances that every thing in their power had been done to render her situation comfortable. The minutest circumstances were faithfully related; and from the state of her mind, in her last hours, I think much comfort may be derived to her afflicted friends.

We spent a mournful hour, in the place where she is intered, and then returned to the inn, while Mrs. Sumner gave orders for a decent stone to be erected over her grave, with the following inscription:[1]

1. This text varies slightly from the actual inscription on Whitman's grave:

> This humble stone, in memory of
> ELIZABETH WHITMAN,
> Is inscribed by her weeping friends,
> To whom she endeared herself.
> By uncommon tenderness and affection.
> Endowed with superior genius and accomplishments,
> She was still more distinguished by humility and benevolence.
> Let Candour throw a veil over her frailties,
> For great was her charity to others.
> She lived an example of calm resignation,
> And sustained the last painful scene,
> Far from every friend.
> Her departure was on the 25th of July, A.D. 1788.
> In the 37th year of her age;
> The tears of strangers watered her grave.

"THIS HUMBLE STONE,

*IN MEMORY OF*

## ELIZA WHARTON,

*IS INSCRIBED BY HER WEEPING FRIENDS,*
*TO WHOM SHE ENDEARED HERSELF BY UNCOMMON*
*TENDERNESS AND AFFECTION.*
*ENDOWED WITH SUPERIOR ACQUIREMENTS,*
*SHE WAS STILL MORE DISTINGUISHED BY HUMIL-*
*ITY AND BENEVOLENCE.*
*LET CANDOR THROW A VEIL OVER HER FRAILTIES,*
*FOR GREAT WAS HER CHARITY TO OTHERS.*
*SHE SUSTAINED THE LAST*
*PAINFUL SCENE, FAR FROM EVERY FRIEND;*
*AND EXHIBITED AN EXAMPLE*
*OF CALM RESIGNATION.*
*HER DEPARTURE WAS ON THE 25th DAY OF*
*JULY, A. D. ——,*
*IN THE 37th YEAR OF HER AGE,*
*AND THE TEARS OF STRANGERS WATERED HER*
*G R A V E."*

I hope, madam, that you will derive satisfaction from these exertions of friendship, and that, united to the many other sources of consolation with which you are furnished, they may alleviate your grief; and while they leave the pleasing remembrance of her virtues, add the supporting persuasion, that your Eliza is happy.

I am, &c.

JULIA GRANBY.

F  I  N  I  S.

THE

# BOARDING SCHOOL;

OR,

# LESSONS

OF A

PRECEPTRESS TO HER PUPILS:

CONSISTING OF

INFORMATION, INSTRUCTION, AND ADVICE,

Calculated to improve the Manners, and form the Character of

## YOUNG LADIES.

TO WHICH IS ADDED,

A Collection of LETTERS, written by the PUPILS, to their INSTRUCTOR, their FRIENDS, and each other.

BY A LADY OF MASSACHUSETTS;

AUTHOR OF THE COQUETTE.

*Hannah Foster*

Published according to Act of Congress.

PRINTED AT *BOSTON*,

By I. THOMAS AND E. T. ANDREWS.

Sold by them, by C. BINGHAM, and the other Booksellers in *Boston*; by I. THOMAS, *Worcester*; by THOMAS, ANDREWS & PENNIMAN, *Albany*; and by THOMAS, ANDREWS & BUTLER, *Baltimore.*——JUNE, 1798.

# Dedication.

To the YOUNG LADIES of AMERICA the following sheets are affectionately inscribed.

Convinced of the many advantages of a good education, and the importance of improving those advantages; or of counterbalancing the want of them by exerting the mental powers which nature has bestowed; sensible, too, that the foundation of a useful and happy life must be laid in youth, and that much depends on the early infusion of virtuous principles into the docile mind, the author has employed a part of her leisure hours in collecting and arranging her ideas on the subject of female deportment.

How far she has succeeded in her design, the voice of a candid public will pronounce.

THE
# BOARDING SCHOOL, &C.

On the delightful margin of the Merimac,[1] in one of the most pleasant and beautiful situations, which that fertile and healthful part of America affords, lived Mrs. Williams, the virtuous relict[2] of a respectable clergyman.

She had two daughters, lovely and promising as ever parent could boast.

Mrs. Williams's circumstances were easy. She possessed a little patrimony,[3] to which she retired, after her husband's decease; but a desire of preserving this for her children, and a wish to promote their advantage and enlarge their society, induced her to open a Boarding School.

As she had an eye, no less to the social pleasure, than to the pecuniary profit of the undertaking, she admitted only seven, at a time, to the privilege of her tuition.

These were all young ladies, who had previously received the first rudiments of learning, and been initiated into the polite accomplishments, which embellish virtue and soften the cares of human life. They had generally lived in the metropolis, and had acquired the graces of a fashionable deportment; but they possessed different tempers and dispositions, which had been variously, and, in some respects, erroneously managed.

To cultivate the expanding flowers, and to prune the juvenile eccentricities, which were disseminated among these tender plants; or, to speak without a figure, to extend and purify their ideas, to elevate and refine their affections, to govern and direct their passions, required an eye, watchful, and a hand, skilful as those of the judicious Mrs. Williams.

While her judgment and prudence aided the useful acquisitions of the mind, a sprightly fancy and a cheerful disposition, regulated by experience and discretion, qualified her to enter, at once, with becoming dignity and condescending ease, into all their concerns; to participate their pleasures; while, with candour and mildness, she reproved their errors, detected their follies, and facilitated their amendment.

As the young ladies had finished their school education, before Mrs. Williams received them to her mansion, her instructions were

1. The Merrimack River, which begins in New Hampshire and flows through Massachusetts to Newburyport. The Merrimack Valley includes Concord, New Hampshire, and Lowell, Massachusetts.
2. Widow.
3. Paternal inheritance.

more especially designed to polish the mental part, to call forth the dormant virtues, to unite and arrange the charms of person and mind, to inspire a due sense of decorum and propriety, and to instil such principles of piety, morality, benevolence, prudence and economy, as might be useful through life.

Their time was, accordingly, disposed in a manner most conducive to the attainment of these objects. Every part of it was employed to some valuable purpose; "for idleness," Mrs. Williams observed, "is the rust of the mind."[4]

Whatever tended to enlarge, inform, improve, or amuse, she supposed worthy their attention.

She particularly endeavoured to domesticate them; to turn their thoughts to the beneficial and necessary qualifications of private life; often inculcating, that

> "Nothing lovelier can be found in woman,
> Than to study household good;"[5]

and labouring to convince them of the utter insignificance and uselessness of that part of the sex, who are

> "Bred only and completed to the taste
> Of lustful appetence;[6] to sing, to dance,
> To dress, and troll the tongue, and roll the eye."[7]

Early rising she recommended, both by precept and example. This, she said, would not only promote their health, but render them mistresses of many hours, which must otherwise be lost in enervating sloth and inaction. "And should we," continued she, "who have so much cause for exertion, thus sacrifice the best part of our time?"

> "Falsely luxurious, will not man awake,
> And, starting from the bed of sloth, enjoy
> The cool, the fragrant, and the silent hour,
> To meditation due, and sacred song?
> And is there aught in sleep can charm the wise?
> To lie in dead oblivion, losing half
> The fleeting moments of too short a life?
> Total extinction of th' enlighten'd soul!
> Or else to feverish vanity alive,
> Wilder'd and tossing through distemper'd dreams?
> Who would in such a gloomy state remain,

4. Common maxim of unknown origin.
5. John Milton, *Paradise Lost* (1667), Book 9, lines 232–33. Milton's poem addresses the fall of man from Christian Grace, and his expulsion from Eden.
6. Appetite or desire.
7. *Paradise Lost*, Book 11, lines 618–20.

> Longer than nature craves; when every muse,
> And every blooming pleasure wait without.
> To bless the wildly devious morning walk?"[8]

Another laudable practice of Mrs. Williams, was perfect regularity in the government of her pupils, and in the arrangement of their daily exercises. "When," said she, "we observe the order of the natural world, and admire the consistency and harmony of every part, we may hence derive a lesson, for the regulation of our conduct, in the sphere assigned to us."

Pursuant to this plan of operation, the young ladies arose at five; from which they had two hours at their own disposal, till the bell summoned them at seven, to the hall, where, the ceremonies of the morning salutation over, they breakfasted together; their repast being seasoned with the unrestrained effusions of good humour and sociability. On these occasions, Mrs. Williams suspended the authority of the matron, that, by accustoming her pupils to familiarity in her presence, they might be free from restraint; and, feeling perfectly easy and unawed, appear in their genuine characters. By this mean she had an opportunity of observing any indecorum of behaviour, or wrong bias; which she kept in mind, till a proper time to mention, and remonstrate[9] against it; a method, the salutary[1] effects of which were visible in the daily improvement of her pupils.

The breakfast table removed, each took her needle-work,[2] except one, who read some amusing and instructive book, for the benefit and entertainment of the rest. The subject was selected by Mrs. Williams, who conferred the reading upon them in rotation.

At twelve o'clock, they were dismissed till one, when dinner again called them together, which was conducted in the same manner as the morning repast.

Having resumed their occupations, the reader of the day produced some piece of her own composition, either in prose, or verse, according to her inclination, as a specimen of her genius and improvement. This being submitted to Mrs. Williams's inspection, and the candid perusal and criticism of her companions; and the subject canvassed with great freedom of opinion, they withdrew from the tasks of the day to seek that relaxation and amusement, which each preferred. No innocent gratification was denied them. The sprightly dance, the sentimental song, and indeed every species of pastime, consistent

---

8. From James Thomson's *The Seasons*, "Summer" (1726–30). See p. 34 n. 1 in this Norton Critical Edition.
9. To protest against or reproach.
1. Wholesome.
2. An important part of traditional female education in eighteenth-century America. Finer girls' schools included advanced needlework in the curriculum, and students produced decorative samplers.

with the decorum of the sex, was encouraged, as tending to health, cheerfulness, and alacrity.

In these pleasing pursuits and enjoyments, the present class of happy companions had nearly completed the term allotted them by their parents, and were soon to leave the peaceful shades in which they delighted, when, being assembled on the Monday morning of their last week, their revered Preceptress thus accosted them:

"As the period is approaching, my dear pupils, when I must resign your society, and quit the important charge of instructor and friend, which I have sustained with so much pleasure, and, I trust, with some degree of fidelity, I shall sum up the counsels, admonitions, and advice, which I have frequently inculcated, and endeavour to impress them on your minds, as my valedictory address. For this purpose, during this last week of your residence with me, I shall dispense with your usual exercises, and substitute a collection of my own sentiments, enforced by the pathos of the occasion.

"Your docility, and cheerful diligence in attending to my instructions; your modest, affectionate, and respectful behaviour, together with the laudable progress you have made in every branch, which you have pursued, have well rewarded my care, and engaged my approbation and love. To me, therefore, a separation will be painful. To you the period is important. It is a period, which, while it relieves you from the confinement of scholastic rules, introduces you to new scenes of cares, of pleasures, of trials, and of temptations, which will call for the exercise of every virtue, and afford opportunity for improving the endowments, both natural and acquired, which you possess. Think not, then, that your emancipation from schools, gives you liberty to neglect the advantages which you have received from them. The obligations under which you are laid to your parents for the education they have given you, require a diligent improvement of every talent committed to your trust.

"Of needle-work you are complete mistresses, from the most delicate and highly finished, to the most ordinary, though perhaps not less useful, economy of mending and making the coarser garments of family use. Many, I am aware, suppose *this last* a species of learning, which is beneath the attention of a lady: but Clara will tell you how valuable it has proved to her; and how valuable it *may* prove to you.

"Nursed in the lap of affluence, and accustomed to unbounded expense, Clara little thought, at your age, that she should ever depend on her needle for the livelihood and decent appearance of a rising family. A discreet and prudent mother early inculcated the lessons of industry and economy, which she now practices; and taught her that the knowledge could be of no disservice, though she never had occasion for it. She married with the brightest prospects. But a series of

unavoidable disasters, such as no human wisdom could foresee or prevent, reduced her to narrow circumstances; and, to complete her misfortune, she was left a widow with four small children. Her parents were in the grave; her patrimony[3] was gone! In this exigence,[4] what was her resource? Not fruitless lamentations, and unavailing complaints. She immediately summoned her resolution; and by the use of her needle has ever since supported herself and family with decency, and been highly respected for her prudent exertions and exemplary industry. Directly the reverse of this amiable character is that of Belinda. She was educated in the same way with Clara; the same schools gave them tuition; and similar prospects awaited their entrance into life. Calamities attended the progress of each; but different as their tempers and dispositions was their conduct under them. The falling fortunes of Clara were awhile suspended by her discretion and frugality; while the ruin of Belinda was hastened by her extravagance, dissipation, and idleness. View them, now, in their reduced state! Neatness, cheerfulness, and activity preside in the dwelling of Clara; negligence, peevishness,[5] and sloth[6] are legibly stamped on that of Belinda. The ear is pained by her complaints of poverty; the eye is disgusted by her slatternly[7] appearance, and ostentatious display of the tattered remnants of finery, which bespeak the pride and indolence of their owner; who will neither convert them into more comfortable garments, nor, by repairing, render them becoming.

"I hope, however, that occasions like these may never call for your exertions. But there may be cases, when, to know the use of your needles will answer important purposes, even in an exalted station, and amidst the splendor of affluence and plenty.

"Matilda dignified a princely fortune by the exercise of every virtue which can adorn a lady. Among these, charity shone conspicuous. Her maid said to her, one day, Madam, would you have me lay aside these cast-clothes for some poor person? Yes, replied Matilda; but sit down, and mend them first. Don't you see they need it? Why, Madam, rejoined the girl, is it not enough for you to give them away? I should think the least they can do is to mend them for themselves! In that case, said Matilda, my bounty would be greatly diminished. People, who need charity have not the necessary materials for putting such articles into repair; and should I furnish them, perhaps they have never been taught to use their needles. No more have I, returned the maid. Have you not? said Matilda. Well then, sit down,

---

3. Inheritance.
4. State of need.
5. Irritability.
6. Laziness.
7. Untidy, careless.

and I will direct your ingenuity upon these clothes. By this mean you may learn a very useful lesson, I assure you; a lesson, which by practising for yourself, will enable you to lay up part of your wages against the time when sickness or old age shall take you from your labours.

"Such examples of condescension and benevolence to inferiors, are of more real and lasting use than pounds prodigally bestowed.

"Do you seek higher testimonies of the honor and utility of this employment? You may collect many from the histories which you have read during the last year. Among the Romans, and several other nations of antiquity, a scarf, wrought by the needle of a favourite fair, was received as an honorable token of respect, and improved as an invincible stimulus to heroic deeds. Ladies of the first rank and station considered it as no derogation[8] from the dignity or delicacy of their character, to make their own apparel, and that of their families. The virtuous Panthea, when her husband was going to fight in the cause of Cyrus,[9] her generous deliverer, magnificently adorned his person, and decorated his armour with her own needle-work.

"We ought never to be idle. No moment should be unoccupied. Some employment, salutary, either to body or mind, or both, should be constantly pursued; and the needle is always at hand to supply the want of other avocations. The listless vacuity, which some young ladies indulge, renders them extremely unhappy, though they are insensible of the cause, and seek to beguile the time in frivolous amusements.

"A still more endearing motive remains to be suggested; and that is the pleasure, which your accomplishments in this ornamental and useful art must afford your parents; and the pain, which your neglect of it hereafter must occasion them.

"But your faithful and assiduous improvement of time, since you have been with me, is a sure pledge of your perseverance in the path of duty, and your progress in every virtue. I trust, therefore, that what I have said will be engraved on your memories; and that some useful ideas will be selected by each of you for your future advantage.

"Your minds are a good soil; and may I not flatter myself, that the seeds of instruction which I have sown, "will spring up, and yield fruit abundantly?"[1]

With one voice, they most affectionately assured Mrs. Williams, that it should be their daily study to profit by her lessons; and withdrew.

---

8. Lessening of reputation or honor.
9. A tale from the writings of Xenophon of Athens (430–354 B.C.), an historian and contemporary of Socrates. The beauty of the virtuous Panthea, taken captive by enemy forces, generates a debate between the enemy leader Cyrus and his friend Araspes on whether human passion is stronger than human will.
1. A familiar paraphrase of the parable of the sower in Matthew 13.

## Monday, P. M.

### READING.

Being assembled, this afternoon, Mrs. Williams thus resumed her discourse.

"Reading is so common a part of education, that the value of it is not duly estimated; nor the manner of performing it, sufficiently attended to. It is not the mere propriety of pronunciation, accent, and cadence, which constitutes good reading. You must enter into the spirit of the subject, and feel interested in the matter, before you can profit by the exercise.

"But you are so well acquainted with the manner of reading, that the quality of books most worthy of your perusal is the only point on which I need to enlarge.

"Romances, the taste of former times, are now so far out of vogue, that it is hardly necessary to warn you against them. They exhibit the spirit of chivalry, knight-errantry, and extravagant folly, which prevailed in the age they depict. But they are not interesting; nor can they be pleasing to the correct taste and refined delicacy of the present day.

"Novels are the favourite, and the most dangerous kind of reading, now adopted by the generality of young ladies. I say dangerous, because the influence, which, with very few exceptions, they must have upon the passions of youth, bears an unfavourable aspect on their purity and virtue. The style in which they are written is commonly captivating; and the luxuriance of the descriptions with which they abound, extremely agreeable to the sprightly fancy, and high expectations of the inexperienced and unreflecting. Their romantic pictures of love, beauty, and magnificence, fill the imagination with ideas which lead to impure desires, a vanity of exterior charms, and a fondness for show and dissipation, by no means consistent with that simplicity, modesty, and chastity, which should be the constant inmates of the female breast. They often pervert the judgment, mislead the affections, and blind the understanding.

"A melancholy example of this sort is exhibited in Juliana. Juliana was the only daughter of a wealthy merchant, who grudged no expense which could please or embellish his darling child. He, however, possessed neither leisure nor abilities "to teach the young idea how to shoot;"[1] but thought it sufficient that he gave her every advantage, which could be derived from the various schools, to which she was consigned. She had a brilliant fancy, and a fondness for books,

---

1. From Thomson, *The Seasons*, "Spring."

which, properly directed, might have proved of great use to her. But, having no better principles instilled into her mind, she indulged herself in the unlimited reading of novels, and every light publication which a circulating library could furnish.

"Hence her imagination took wing, and carried her far above the scenes of common life. The excessive refinement of her mind admitted no ordinary amusements or avocations. Plain truth from her own sex was an insult; and from the other, nothing less than adoration would satisfy her unbounded vanity. Her beauty (of which she really had a considerable share) and the large fortune which she would probably inherit, gained her many admirers; some of whom were men of unquestionable merit. But a sober, rational courtship could not answer her ideas of love and gallantry. The swain, who would not die for her, she deemed unworthy of notice.

"Her father strongly recommended a gentleman, as well calculated, in his opinion, to make her happy, and as having his entire approbation; but she rejected him with disdain, though she could produce no one objection against his person, or character.

"Her father acquiesced; expressing, however, his regret at the mistaken notions she had imbibed; and warning her most pathetically against the indulgence of so romantic a disposition; yet all in vain. He was considered as an illiterate plodder after wealth, which she had a right to bestow as she pleased.

"At last the lovely youth whom she had so long contemplated, made his appearance. A military captain entered the town on the recruiting service. Young, handsome, easy, bold and assuming; with all the *bon ton*[2] of the coxcomb, and all the insolence of the novice. He saw Juliana; he sacrificed to her charms, and conquered. She could not resist the allurements of his gallantry. His affectation of dying love was received with apparent pleasure; while art and duplicity took advantage of her weakness, to precipitate her into engagements to pity and relieve him. Her friends saw her danger, and warmly remonstrated against her imprudent conduct, in receiving the addresses of a man, destitute of property to support her, and void of every kind of personal merit. Her father entreated and implored the rejection of her lover, till, finding every other method vain, he at length resolutely forbade him the house, and his daughter's company. This was viewed as persecution; and, consistently with her sentiments of adventurous love, a clandestine amour was commenced. Her father surprised them together; and, enraged at their disgraceful intrigue, seized the captain, and endeavoured to turn him out of doors. He violently resented this ungentlemanlike treatment, as he

---

2. *French*: Fashionable society, literally "good tone."

termed it, and defended himself with his sword. The old gentleman received a slight wound, in the scuffle; but accomplished his purpose. Juliana was terrified at this rencounter,[3] and, dreading her father's displeasure, ran out with her paramour. His lodgings were near, and thither, favoured by the darkness of the night, he instantly led her. She involuntarily followed him, without considering the impropriety of her conduct. Here he drew his sword, and, throwing himself at her feet, professed his despair, and declared himself resolved to put an immediate end to his life. She endeavoured to reason him into calmness; but in vain. He was sensible, that, if he now relinquished her to her father, he should lose her forever. His apparent agony overcame her, and she gave him her hand.

"Her father was almost distracted at her elopement. He traced her steps, and, following her to the house, condescended to soothe her with parental kindness; and promised her pardon and continued affection, if she would renounce her worthless lover, and return. She confessed it was too late; that she was his wife.

"Petrified with astonishment, he looked at her, for some time, with speechless grief; and, showing his arm, bound up with the wound he had received, left her with every token of anguish and indignation!

"When the fever of passion had abated, a returning sense of duty in Juliana, and, in the captain, the fear of losing the property which he sought, induced them to seek a reconciliation, and make submissive efforts to obtain it. But her father was too highly incensed to grant it to him, on any terms; or to her, on any other than the utter rejection of her unworthy companion. These terms were not complied with.

"Sorrow and vexation preyed so deeply upon the mind of this afflicted parent, that they brought on a rapid decline; and he died without again seeing his undutiful and ruined daughter. His estate was divided between Juliana and her four brothers. Her portion was received by her husband, and soon spent in dissipation and excess. Having rioted on the fortune of his wife, while she often pined at home for want of the common necessaries of life, he left her, to join his regiment, promising remittances from time to time, for her support. This promise, however, was but ill performed; and she now feels the dreadful effects of her folly, in the accumulated ills of poverty and neglect. Yet she still cherishes the most passionate fondness for what has proved her bane. A friend called to see her, not long since, and found her the emblem of wretchedness and sloth. Her emaciated form, her squalid appearance, the disorder of her house, and her tattered raiment, bespoke the shameful negligence of the owner. Yet she was sitting with a novel in her hand, over which she had apparently been weeping. She expatiated largely on

---

3. An unplanned encounter or hostile exchange.

the tale it contained, while her children, who exhibited a picture of real woe, engaged not her attention. Her friend enquired how she could be thus interested and distressed by mere fiction, while every thing about her was calculated to arouse the keenest feelings of her soul! She coolly replied, I have fortitude sufficient to support my own calamity, but I must sympathize with the heroine of adversity. I have not lost my sensibility with my fortune. My only luxury is now imagination! How ill-timed, and how improperly exerted, was this kind of sensibility, in Juliana! Where, and what was her sensibility, when she disobeyed an indulgent parent, sacrificed her reputation, and threw herself into the arms of a worthless man for protection—from what? from the kindness and love of her best friends!

"But I would not be understood to condemn all novels indiscriminately; though great prudence is necessary to make a useful selection. Some of them are fraught with sentiment; convey lessons for moral improvement; and exhibit striking pictures of virtue rewarded; and of vice, folly, and indiscretion punished; which may prove encouragements to imitate, or warnings to avoid similar practices. I shall not descend to particulars. Those, which are sanctioned by the general voice of delicacy and refinement, may be allowed a reading; yet none should engross your minds, to the neglect of more important objects; nor be suffered to monopolize too large a portion of your time.

"Novels are a kind of light reading, on which the imagination feasts, while the more substantial food which is requisite to the nourishment of the understanding, is either untasted or undigested. Imagination is a sportive faculty, which should be curbed by the reins of prudence and judgment. Its sallies are delightful in youth, provided they be not too excursive.

"Poetry is, by some, ranked with novels; but I think injudiciously. Good poetry is certainly a sublime[4] source of entertainment and instruction. What music is to the ear, poetry is to the heart. There must, indeed, be a natural taste for it, before it can be highly relished or enjoyed; and this taste, wherever it exists, should be cultivated. I know of no kind of reading more richly formed for the mental repast of a liberal and polished young lady, than the poetical productions of true genius. The trifling and indelicate cantos of ordinary witlings,[5] and everyday poetasters, are unworthy your attention. But the species of poetry which I now recommend, is peculiarly adapted to soften the passions, excite sympathy, and meliorate the affections. It soothes the jarring cares of life, and, pervading the secret recesses of the soul, serves to rouse and animate its dormant powers.

4. Elevated.
5. Petty wits.

"Many essays, written by monitors of both sexes, are extant, which you may find profitable and pleasing, both in youth and more advanced age. Among the foremost of these, I mention Mrs. Chapone's letters to her niece,[6] which contain a valuable treasure of information and advice.

"But among your hours devoted to reading, history must not be without a place. Here an extensive field of ages and generations, which have gone before you, is opened to your view. Here your curiosity may be gratified by a retrospection of events, which, by conducting your thoughts to remotest climes and periods, interests and enlarges the mind. Here the various revolutions, the rise, fall, and dismemberment of ancient kingdoms and states may be traced to the different springs of action, in which they originated. Hence you may gain a competent acquaintance with human nature in all its modifications, from the most rude and barbarous, to the most civilized and polished stages of society. This is a species of knowledge, which will not only be of constant use to you, in the government of your own temper and manners, but highly ornamental in your intercourse with the polite and learned world.

"But let your reading of every description be regular and methodical. Never confuse your minds by a variety of subjects at once. When you turn your attention to any one in particular, finish, and lay that aside, before you take up another. Let what you read be well understood at the time, and well digested afterwards. Possess yourselves, at least, of the leading traits: otherwise your labour will be totally lost. If convenient, always recapitulate what you have been perusing, and annex to it your own sentiments and remarks, to some friend. If you have no friend at hand, who will be disposed to hear, recollect, and run it over in your own thoughts. This will be a great assistance to memory. But whatever be the kind of reading which you undertake, select such authors as good judges esteem the best, upon the subject. Have a particular regard to the morality and delicacy of the books you peruse.

"When you read for mere amusement, (which should seldom happen) be careful not to corrupt and vitiate[7] your taste by frothy and illiberal performances, which will degrade the dignity and sully the purity of your minds. That time is very greatly mispent, which is bestowed in reading what can yield no instruction. Not a moment's attention should be given to books which afford not some degree of improvement. Always have an eye, therefore, to profit, as well as to

---

6. Hester Mulso Chapone (1727–1801), an early bluestocking and friend of Samuel Richardson, published *Letters on the Improvement of the Mind* in 1773, covering topics such as "The Study of the Holy Scriptures," "The Regulation of the Heart and Affections," "Politeness and Accomplishments," and "Reading History."
7. To spoil or waste.

pleasure. Remember that youth is the seed-time of life.[8] You are now to cultivate that knowledge, which future years must ripen. Free from those domestic cares, which will engross and occupy your minds, when placed at the head of families, a most inestimable price is now put into your hands to get wisdom. Now you may learn; then you must practice.

"Now, therefore, lay up in store some provision for every exigence, some embellishment for every station.

"Look upon Elvira. Her acquirements in a single state have qualified her for a shining pattern of matronal[9] duties. Her husband's business abroad prevents him from attending to domestic avocations; nor need he be anxious respecting the management of his household affairs. Elvira is present to every occasion. The superintendence of her family, and the education of her children is her delight. Capable of instructing them in every needful branch of science, and of furnishing them with every requisite endowment, she is, at once, their guide, their example, and their friend. When her husband returns from the cares and fatigues of business, with what becoming ease and cheerfulness does she dissipate the anxiety which sometimes hangs upon his brow, and exhilerate his spirits by the enlivening charms of rational and refined conversation! In the entertainment of their friends, how distinguished a part she sustains! Her powers of mind have been so happily improved, that she is able to discuss every subject with ease and propriety. To an enlarged understanding and a cultivated taste, to an extensive knowledge of the world and an acquaintance with polite literature, she superadds those amiable virtues, which give society its highest relish; while the elegance of her manners and the modesty of her deportment are a proof of the greatness of her mind, and render her esteemed, beloved, and respected by all who know her.

"But I flatter myself that each of you, my dear pupils, will be an Elvira. Then will you do justice to the superior advantages of your education; be the delight of your friends, and the ornaments of your country.

"Religious subjects must, by no means, be neglected in the course of your reading. Let the BIBLE be the rule of your faith and practice. If you wish an explanation of any particular passages, seek it from some judicious and pious friend, or in the writings of some judicious and learned commentator. But always attend chiefly to those points which serve to mend the heart, rather than to those knotty, metaphysical disquisitions, which tend only to perplex the understanding,

---

8. A popular maxim in eighteenth-century sermons and advice manuals. See, for an early example, Samuel Wesley, *Poems on Several Occasions* (London, 1736).
9. Appropriate to a married woman.

and involve the inquirer in such labyrinths of abstrusity,[1] as are above human comprehension, and beyond human concern. The essential doctrines and precepts of the gospel are level to every capacity; and upon a life and conversation governed by these, our hopes, both of present peace and future glory, must be founded. "He hath shewed thee what is good; and what doth the Lord require of thee, but to do justly, and to love mercy, and to walk humbly with thy God?"[2]

## Tuesday, A. M.

### WRITING AND ARITHMETIC.

The young ladies being seated, this morning, their Preceptress addressed them as follows.

"Writing is productive both of pleasure and improvement. It is a source of entertainment which enlarges the mental powers more, perhaps, than any other. The mind is obliged to exertion for materials to supply the pen. Hence it collects new stores of knowledge, and is enriched by its own labours. It imperceptibly treasures up the ideas, which the hand impresses. An opportunity is furnished of reviewing our sentiments before they are exposed; and we have the privilege of correcting or expunging such as are erroneous. For this purpose, you will find it a good method to collect and write your thoughts upon any subject that occurs; for by repeatedly arranging and revising your expressions and opinions, you may daily improve them, and learn to think and reason properly on every occasion. By this mean you may likewise provide yourselves with a fund of matter for future use, which, without this assistance, the memory would not retain. It will be of great service to note down in your common-place book[1] such particulars as you may judge worth remembering, with your own observations upon them. This will be a kind of amusement which will exercise your thinking powers at the time, and, by recurring to it afterwards, it may afford you many useful hints.

"The frequent use of the pen is calculated to refine and enlarge your understandings. Have you any talent at composition? it will be increased by cultivation.

"Neglect no opportunity, therefore, which your leisure affords, of delighting your friends, and accomplishing yourselves by the exercise of your genius in this way.

"Thrice blessed are we, the happy daughters of this land of liberty, where the female mind is unshackled by the restraints of tyrannical

1. Obscurity or abstraction.
2. Micah 6:8.
1. A notebook into which the keeper entered useful or important information, recipes, biblical or literary passages, and the like.

custom, which in many other regions confines the exertions of genius to the usurped powers of lordly man! Here virtue, merit, and abilities are properly estimated under whatever form they appear. Here the widely extended fields of literature court attention; and the American fair are invited to cull the flowers, and cultivate the expanding laurel.

"But the species of writing, which is open to every capacity, and ornamental to every station, is the epistolary.[2] This, between particular friends, is highly agreeable and interesting. It is a method of interchanging sentiments, and of enjoying intercourse with those from whom you are far removed, which is a happy substitute for personal conversation. In a correspondence of this sort, all affectation, formality, and bombast[3] should be laid aside.

"Ease, frankness, simplicity, and sincerity should be its leading traits. Yet let not your letters be composed of mere founding terms, and verbose egotism; but intermix sentiment with expression, in such a manner as may be improving as well as pleasing. Letters of friendship should conduce[4] no less to the advantage than entertainment of the person addressed; and mere cursory letters, of general acquaintance, must, at least, be written with propriety and accuracy. The formation of the characters, the spelling, the punctuation, as well as the style and sense, must be attended to.

"Never omit noticing the receipt of letters, unless you mean to affront the writers. Not to answer a letter, without being able to assign some special reason for the neglect, is equally unpardonable as to keep silence when conversation is addressed to you in person.

"By habituating[5] yourselves to writing, what may, at first, appear a task, will become extremely pleasant. Refuse not, then, to improve this part of your education, especially by your frequent and dutifully affectionate epistles to your parents, when absent from them. Express your gratitude for their care, and convince them it has not been lost upon you.

"Always employ your pens upon something useful and refined. Let no light or loose compositions occupy your time and thoughts; but remember that what you utter in this way is in some measure the picture of your hearts. Virtue forbid, that this favourite employment should be disgraced by impurity, indelicacy, or the communication of vicious and ignoble sentiments!

"One of the sages of antiquity being asked why he was so long in writing his opinion, replied, 'I am writing for futurity.'[6]

---

2. Pertaining to letter-writing.
3. Inflated talk.
4. Contribute.
5. Accustoming.
6. Unidentified.

"Your characters during life, and even when you shall sleep in the dust, may rest on the efforts of your pens. Beware then how you employ them. Let not the merit of your attainments in this noble art be degraded by improper subjects for its exercise. Suffer not the expectation of secrecy to induce you to indulge your pens upon subjects, which you would blush to have exposed. In this way your characters may be injured, and your happiness destroyed.

"Celia and Cecilia were companions at a boarding school. When separated, they commenced an epistolary correspondence, on which each valued herself. Their former intimacy, which they termed friendship, prompted them to write with unlimited confidence; and, without the least reserve, to reveal every dictate of levity and thoughtless folly. They imagined themselves perfectly secure from the censure of the critic. Their education had not taught them, that a virtuous mind should shrink even from ideal indelicacy. Celia was courted by Silvander, a young man of whom she was passionately fond; but she had art and resolution enough to conceal her letters from his inspection, though he often solicited a communication of her correspondence. At length he became impatient for a perusal of letters which appeared so pleasing and interesting to the parties, and suspicious that some particular cause directed their privacy. Influenced by these motives, Silvander bribed a market-boy, who came from the village where Cecilia lived, and always conveyed the letters to and from her, to give them first into his hand. How astonished was he to find the lightness of mind exemplified in them! Purity of sentiment, delicacy of thought, and refinement of taste were entirely laid aside; and illiberal wit, frothy jests, double entendres, and ridiculous love-tales were substituted in their place. His name was used with so much freedom, and every circumstance relative to his intercourse, and proposed connexion with Celia, was bandied with such familiarity, that he was mortified, disgusted, and chagrined, in the extreme. He had the policy, however, to conceal the discovery till he had copied a considerable number of Celia's letters, leaving out whatever had reference to his own affairs. He then revenged himself by disclosing his knowledge to her, avowing his indignation at her weakness, duplicity and folly, and taking an immediate and final leave. Not content with this, he even circulated her letters among his acquaintance. This fixed the stamp of ignominy[7] on the correspondents; and their names and characters were rendered as ridiculous as scandal and malicious wit could desire.

"Celia was almost distracted at the loss of her lover; but when she found the method he had taken to punish her indiscretion, and that her reputation was thus materially injured, she secluded herself, in

7. Dishonor.

a great measure, from society. Her sensibility received a wound which could never be healed; and she lived and died in melancholy, regret, and obscurity.

"However censurable the unjust and ungenerous conduct of Silvander may be deemed, yet no adequate excuse can be offered for the young ladies, who dishonored their pens and their talents by a most improper and unbecoming use of both.

"Next to writing, arithmetic usually claims attention. This is absolutely necessary in every department, and in every stage of life. Even in youth, the proper arrangement of your expenses will conduce greatly to your advantage; and when placed at the head of families, it will be very friendly to the order and economy of your domestic affairs. But, leaving your matronal conduct to future admonition, many benefits result from keeping regular accounts in a single state. Your parents allow you a certain sum for your own private use. Fashion and folly are always busy in creating innumerable imaginary wants, which must exceed your finances, if you do not attend to an exact adjustment of your expenditures. For this purpose, always calculate your immediate and most necessary demands. Let these be first supplied, and then, if your funds be not exhausted, more superfluous ones may occupy your thoughts. There is one claim, however, which must not be neglected, and that is CHARITY. You will, therefore, manage your expenses in such a manner as to reserve some portion of your income for the necessitous. Should you think your allowance insufficient to admit the children of want to a share, let your benevolence plead for the retrenchment of some trifling article which you may dispense with, without much inconvenience; and the exquisite pleasure resulting from the bestowment, will more than counterbalance the sacrifice. In these, and many other particulars, a knowledge of arithmetic will enable you to conduct the affairs of youth with ease, advantage, and usefulness. And, perhaps, as you advance in years, and are called to fill more important stations, you may find it of still greater utility.

"The father of Lucinda was in easy circumstances, while he could perform the duties and enjoy the profits of a lucrative business. He was the affectionate parent of a numerous family, to whose education and improvement he attended with unwearied diligence and pleasure; till repeated losses in trade, and disappointments in his worldly expectations embarrassed his affairs, depressed his spirits, and impaired his health. In the midst of these difficulties, his amiable and beloved wife was removed by death. This trial was greater than he could support. He sunk under the affliction, and lost his reason. Lucinda was the eldest of six children, the care of whom, with the melancholy task of attending and ministering to the necessities of her unhappy father, devolved on her. She looked upon the

woe-fraught[8] scene, and wept. Her heart was sinking under the weight of grief; and hope, the best soother of the unfortunate, had nearly abandoned her. She advised with her friends, who proposed to relieve the family by means of a subscription. Lucinda thanked them for their proffered kindness, and returned to her disconsolate habitation. She deliberated on the projected measure; which she considered must be slow, uncertain, and, at any rate, inadequate to their future exigences. She could not reconcile herself to the idea of her father's depending on charity for subsistence. Yet what could be done? One resource only remained;—her own exertions. By these she flattered herself, that she might save the family from suffering want, and discharge the obligations she owed to her revered parent. Her education, by which, among other branches of learning, she had been well instructed in arithmetic, (that being her father's favourite study) qualified her for this undertaking. She therefore devoted herself to the business without delay; examined her father's accounts, collected whatever remained that was valuable; sold the superfluous moveables, and purchased a small stock for trade. All who knew her motives and merit frequented her shop, and encouraged her by their custom and kindness. By this mean, together with her judicious management, and engaging behaviour, she increased her business to such a degree, as to support the family with ease and reputation.

"Her discreet and dutiful conduct to her father, soon restored him to his reason.

"When he found how prudently and affectionately Lucinda had exerted herself in his behalf, he exclaimed, "Many daughters have done virtuously, but thou excellest them all!"

"He resumed his former business, and lived to see his children all well provided for, and happily settled around him."

*Tuesday, P. M.*

MUSIC AND DANCING.

Her pupils having taken their places, Mrs. Williams proceeded.

"In music and dancing you have made such proficiency that your performances must be very pleasing to your friends, before whom you occasionally exhibit.

"As dancing is an accomplishment merely external, let not the vanity of excellence in it betray itself in an air of conscious superiority, when you shine at the ball, and perceive yourselves to have attracted the attention and applause of the gay assembly. But in the midst of hilarity and mirth, remember that modesty, diffidence,[1]

---

8. Heavy with sadness.
1. Modesty, sometimes implying self-doubt.

discretion, and humility are indispensable appendages of virtue and decency.

"Music is a talent which nature has bestowed, and which your application has considerably improved. It has a powerful influence over the heart; wonderfully soothes and humanizes the passions, and is a source of refined pleasure to a mind capable of tasting its charms.

"Never refuse gratifying your friends by the exertion of your abilities in performing, unless for some very special reason. Though I would not have you vain of your skill, and officiously forward to display it; yet the affectation of uncommon modesty, and ignorance, is truly ridiculous. To plead inability to exercise powers, which you are conscious of possessing, and for which you wish to be esteemed and honored by others, is false delicacy, and will never gain admission to the breast where that which is genuine resides. How perfectly absurd it is for a young lady, who is politely requested to entertain a company with her musical talents, to declare them so small that she is really ashamed to expose herself before such good judges; or that she has neglected playing, or singing, for some time, and cannot immediately revive her dormant skill; or that she has forgotten her tunes, or songs; or that she has a bad cold, (which none but herself perceives) and is unable to sing; or that she is loath to begin this amusement, and must insist upon some other lady's setting the example; which other lady has, in her turn, an equal number of excuses! Thus the time of the company is engrossed, and their pleasure suspended, till a long train of arguments, entreaties, and compliments are run through, and her vanity fully gratified by the most flattering and importunate solicitations.

"Then, elate with pride and self importance, she condescends to grant their request; not considering how far she has derogated from her own merit by the futile artifice she has employed; an artifice unworthy of an ingenuous mind, and disgraceful to any lady who has arrived to years of discretion.

"Let us view this evasive manner of seeking compliments a little nearer. When a person is known to be mistress of this delightful art, what can be her motive for delaying the gratification of her friends by its exercise, and refusing a compliance with their wishes, till their patience is exhausted? I believe that excuses, in this case, are very seldom sincere. The youthful mind is not insensible to praise, nor indifferent to the means of obtaining it.

"Why then should it not be received and increased by a ready and obliging compliance? A desire to please is usually attended with success; and for what reason should the power and disposition be artfully concealed?

"Always preserve a frankness and sincerity in your actions and designs. These will add dignity to your condescensions, and gracefulness to your deportment.

"Rise superior to those little arts which bespeak the finesse of a childish folly, or a narrow mind. Do honor to this, as well as to every other part of your education, by acting conformably to the precepts which have been given you, the knowledge which you have acquired, and the opportunities with which you may be furnished for the purpose.

"Music and dancing, though polite and elegant accomplishments, are, perhaps, the most fascinating, and, of course, the most dangerous of any that fall under that description. When indulged to excess, beside engrossing much time which ought to be employed in the execution of more necessary and useful designs, they sometimes allure their fond votaries from that purity and rectitude which are the chief embellishments of the female character. They lay the mind open to many temptations, and, by nourishing a frivolous vanity, benumb the nobler powers both of reflection and action.

"Levitia was endowed, by the joint influence of nature and art, with these pleasing charms. Symmetry was perfected in her form; and her voice was melody itself. Her parents were not in affluent circumstances; yet their taste led them to distinguish those graces and talents in their daughter, which they injudiciously flattered themselves might, one day, raise her to affluence and fame. Hence they spared no pains nor expense, in their power to bestow, to assist her inclination and gratify her wishes. As she advanced in years, she assiduously cultivated and diligently improved those endowments which she had been erroneously encouraged, and even taught, to consider most valuable. To adorn her person, regulate her movements, and practise her music, was all her care. Nor had she a wish beyond the pleasures, which she fancied they could yield. Her mind resembled a garden, in which the useful plants are overrun and choaked by noxious[2] weeds. Here and there a gaudy flower rears its brilliant head, and proudly dares to arrest the eye; while the delicate and useful lie buried and concealed in the surrounding waste!

"Flattery was pleasing to her ear, in whatever form it was presented. The gay and licentious sought her society; and vanity with its attendant train of follies led her imagination far from the sphere of life which Providence had assigned her. Her parents saw their own mistake, and were alarmed at her's: but, alas! too late were their endeavours to prevent the mischiefs which impended. They could not supply her unbounded wants; and therefore to gratify her ruling passion, she deemed means of her own invention indispensable.

2. Harmful.

Among her admirers was a foreigner, who, failing of success in his own country, sought a subsistence in ours, from the stage. He knew Levitia's talents. These might give her the palm of applause, and in his way of life, render her conspicuous. This plan he communicated to her, insidiously offering to become her guardian, and to put her under the protection of such friends as should defend her honor, and ensure her success. She was pleased with the project. Wholly unacquainted with the world, and unsuspicious of the subtle arts of the deluding libertine, she scrupled not his veracity,[3] but listened to his insinuating declarations of love and friendship. She was deceived by the vanity of appearing where her fancied merit would meet with the encouragement and reward it deserved; and vainly imagining that her beauty might secure her elevation and affluence, she readily consented to the fatal experiment, eloped[4] from her father's house, and became a professed actress.

"Her parents were overwhelmed with grief and anxiety, at the discovery; but to no purpose were all their exertions to reclaim her. She had left them, no more to return; left them, too, with the heart-rending reflection, that they themselves had heedlessly contributed to her disgrace and ruin. But bitter indeed were the fruits of her disobedience and folly!

"She made her appearance on the stage. She sung and danced, for which she was caressed, flattered, and paid. A licentious mode of life quadrating[5] with the levity of her heart, soon left her a prey to seduction. Her gaiety and beauty gained her many votaries, and she became a complete courtezan.[6]

"In the midst of this career, her mother died of a broken heart, evidently occasioned by her undutiful and vicious conduct. A sense of her ingratitude to her parents, and her shameless manner of life struck her mind, not naturally unfeeling, with such force, as to throw her into a fever which undermined her constitution, deprived her of her beauty, ruined her voice, and left her without means of support. Her pretended lover, finding she could no longer be useful to him, perfidiously abandoned her to poverty and shame. She returned, like the prodigal, to her unhappy father, who received, but could not assist her. Her behaviour, with its consequences in the death of her mother, had impaired his health, depressed his spirits, and rendered him incapable of providing for himself.

"She is now despised and avoided by all her former acquaintance, and must inevitably spend the remainder of her days in wretchedness.

3. Did not doubt his sincerity.
4. Ran away.
5. Harmonizing with.
6. A high-end prostitute.

"Let us turn from this disgusting picture, and behold its contrast in the amiable Florella. To beauty of person she superadds delicacy, sensibility, and every noble quality of the mind. Respectful to her superiors, affable, cheerful, and polite to her equals, and condescendingly kind to her inferiors, Florella is universally esteemed, beloved, and admired. Of the pleasing accomplishments of music and dancing she is a consummate mistress. Yet she is superior to the vain arts of flattery, while the dignity of conscious virtue raises her far above the affectation of false modesty and diffidence. To please and oblige those friends who are interested in her happiness, and gratified by her performances, is her delight. Nor does she think it necessary, by feigned excuses, to delay the pleasure, which she is able to afford; but willingly enhances that pleasure by a ready and cheerful compliance. This she thinks the best return she can make for their kind attention. Though delighted with these amusements herself, she, nevertheless, considers them as amusements *only*; and assiduously cultivates the more solid branches of her education. These, she is wont to say, may render me useful and happy, when the voice of music shall be brought low, and when the sprightly limbs shall become languid and inactive.

"How happy her parents in her filial duty and affection! How rich the reward of their care and expense in contributing to her improvements! How happy Florella in their complacency and love, and in the consciousness of deserving them!

"She was, not long since, addressed by a gentleman, who was pleasing to her fancy; but, determined never to indulge a sentiment of partiality without the entire approbation of her parents, she referred him to their decision. For particular reasons, they disapproved of his suit. She acquiesced without reserve, and immediately dismissed him. Who would not rather be a resembler of Florella, than a vain, imprudent, and ruined Levitia?

"True, indeed, the acquirements and graces of Florella are not attainable by every one; but the virtues of discretion, modesty, and kindness are within the reach of the humblest sphere, and the most moderate abilities."

*Wednesday, A. M.*

### MISCELLANEOUS DIRECTIONS *for the* GOVERNMENT *of the* TEMPER *and* MANNERS.

"I shall now," said Mrs. Williams, "endeavour to sketch out for you the plan of conduct, which I think will be most conducive to your honor and happiness while in a single state. Hitherto you have been under the direction of parents, guardians, and instructors, who have

regulated your deportment, and laboured to give you just ideas upon every subject and occasion. That period is now over. You are now launching into life, where you will think and act more for yourselves.

"The path of rectitude, my dear young friends, is narrow and intricate. Temptations lurk around to beguile your feet astray; and dangers which appear insurmountable will often arise to affright you from the ways of virtue.

"But remember that a crown of honor and happiness awaits the undeviating pursuit of truth and duty. Let religion be your guide, and discretion your handmaid. Thus attended, you will escape the snares of youth, and surmount the perplexing cares of more advanced age. At your entrance on the stage of action, the allurements of pleasure will spread innumerable charms to court your acceptance. Beware of their fascinating wiles; and whatever course you adopt, be sure it is such as will bear the test of examination and reflection. Let these be the criterion of all your pursuits and enjoyments. Make it an invariable practice to re-trace the actions and occurrences of the day, when you retire to rest; to account with your own hearts for the use and improvement of the past hours; and rectify whatever you find amiss, by greater vigilance and caution, in future; to avoid the errors into which you have fallen, and to discharge the duties incumbent upon you.

"To neglect this, will be a source of great inadvertencies and failings.

"To know yourselves, in every particular, must be your constant endeavour. This knowledge will lead you to propriety and consistency of action. But this knowledge cannot be obtained without a thorough and repeated inspection of your various passions, affections, and propensities. When obtained, however, it will prevent the ill effects of flattery, by which you will doubtless be endangered, as you advance into the scenes of fashionable life. It will enable you to distinguish flattery from that generous praise which is the effusion of a feeling heart, affected by the perception of real merit. A young lady, unskilled in the deceitful arts of a giddy world, is very apt to be misled by the adulation which is offered at the shrine of vanity. She is considered as a mark for the wit of every coxcomb, who wishes to display his gallantry.

"Flattery is a dazzling meteor, which casts a delusive glare before the eye; and which seduces the imagination, perverts the judgment, and silences the dictates of sound reason. Flattery is, therefore, the poison and bane of the youthful mind. It renders the receiver blind to those defects which she ought to see and rectify, and proud of imaginary graces which she never yet possessed. Self-knowledge, as before observed, will facilitate the detection of this

disguised adversary, by enabling you to investigate your real accomplishments and merits.

"That praise which is the result of deserved approbation from those, whose good opinion you wish to enjoy, is worthy your attention and grateful acceptance: but the fulsome compliments and hyperbolical[1] professions of unmeaning and empty pretenders, calculated only to fill the imagination with the inflammable air of self-conceit and arrogant pride, should be rejected with disdain, and cordially despised by every lady of sense and sentiment, as an insult upon her understanding, and an indignity to her sensibility.

"Let it, therefore, be known to those who court your favour by an ostentatious parade of admiration and obsequiousness,[2] that their dissimulation and duplicity are discovered, and that you are superior to such futility.

"In order to discriminate between flattery and merited praise, critically examine your own heart and life. By this mean you will ascertain what is really your due, and what is merely the effect of this insidious art. But let no ideas of your own endowments, however just, elate you with an opinion of your superior powers of pleasing.

"Be not ostentatious of your charms, either of person or mind. Let modesty, diffidence, and propriety regulate you, in regard to each. Exalted advantages will render you an object of envy to the weak minded of your own sex, and of satire to the ill-natured part of the other. Never obtrude even your real graces and accomplishments upon the world. The penetrating and judicious will see and applaud them, while retiring from the gaze of a misjudging and misrepresenting throng.

> "Naked in nothing should a woman be,
> But veil her very wit with modesty;
> Let man discover; let her not display;
> But yield her charms of mind with sweet delay."[3]

"Those who are solicitous for beauty should remember that the expression of the countenance, in which its very essence consists, depends on the disposition of the mind.

> "What's female beauty, but an air divine,
> Thro' which the mind's all gentle graces shine?
> These, like the sun, irradiate[4] all between;
> The body charms, because the soul is seen.

1. Exaggerated.
2. Eagerness to please.
3. From Edward Young's *Love of Fame, the Universal Passion* (1728), Satire 6. In his satires, Young ridicules women who lack strength of character.
4. Illuminate.

Hence men are often captives of a face,
They know not why; of no peculiar grace.
Some forms, tho' bright, no mortal man can bear;
Some, none resist, tho' not exceeding fair."[5]

"Beauty, my dear girls, is indeed a desirable quality. Neither the pen of the moralist, nor the spleen[6] of the satyrist, nor the envy of such as want it, could ever bring it into contempt or neglect. Yet mere external beauty is transient as the meteor, and frail as the bubble, which floats on the surface of the watery element.

"Behold the disconsolate and despised Flirtilla! and from her fate learn not to trust in the effects or duration of this adventitious quality.

"Early in life, Flirtilla was taught that her charms were irresistible; that she might aspire to an absolute ascendency over the hearts and passions of her votaries. A superficial, but fashionable education added the allurements of art to those of person, and rendered her a finished coquette.

"Her beauty and the gaiety of her manners gained her numerous admirers, who swarmed around, like the insect tribe, eager to sip the fragrance of the equally fair and fading rose. The incense of flattery, in every form, was her tribute.

"Elated by this, she gave free scope to her ruling passions, the love of pleasure and dissipation. Her best days were spent in the chase of vanity; and she culled the flowers of life, without considering, that substantial fruit would be required at a more advanced period, as a substitute for the fading blossoms of youth. Her mind was barren of improvement, and consequently destitute of resources.

"She vainly imagined the triumphs of beauty to be permanent, till its declared enemy, the small-pox[7] convinced her of the egregious[8] mistake. By this she found her empire suddenly overturned. The merciless disorder had reduced her to a level with the generality of her sex, in appearance, and, in enjoyment, far below them. Her glass faithfully represented this insupportable reduction. Regret and chagrin heightened the apparent calamity. She was remembered only as the contrast of what she once had been. Her lovers were disgusted with the change, and sought more pleasing objects of attention; while men of sentiment could not find a similarity of disposition, in her, to induce a connexion.

5. From Young's *Love of Fame, the Universal Passion*, Satire 6.
6. Ill humor.
7. An infectious disease that frequently left scars on the face of survivors.
8. Remarkably bad.

"Her female acquaintance, who had envied her as a rival, or feared her as a superior, now insulted her with their pity, or mortified her by remarks on the surprising alteration in her appearance.

"Finding no alleviation from society, she retired from the world to nurse, in solitude, the vexation and disappointment she experienced.

"View her now, peevish, discontented, and gloomy! Her ideas of pleasure were centered in that person, which is now neglected; in those endowments which have now forsaken her forever!

"Thought she studiously shuns; for she has nothing pleasing to occupy her reflections, but what is irretrievably lost!

"Miserable Flirtilla! thou trustedst in vanity, and vanity is thy recompense![9] How happy mightest thou have been, even in this change, if thy heart had been rectified, thy understanding improved, and thy mind liberally stored with useful sentiments, knowledge, and information!

"Cultivate, then, my young friends, those dispositions and attainments, which will yield permanent and real satisfaction, when sickness, adversity, or age shall have robbed your eyes of their lustre, and diminished the bloom and sprightliness of your forms.

"You are doubtless sensible that your happiness, in life, does not depend so much on your external, as your internal graces.

"The constitutional temper of your minds was given you by nature; but reason is added for its regulation.

> "On life's vast ocean diversely we sail;
> Reason the chart; but passion is the gale."[1]

"Our passions were certainly implanted for wise and benevolent purposes; and, if properly directed, may be of great utility. This direction nature will teach, and education improve. To their precepts we must implicitly listen, if we would become respectable or contented.

"Examine yourselves, therefore, with impartial scrutiny. Find out your particular faults in this respect, and exert your unwearied industry to amend them.

"Possibly you may be naturally hasty, passionate, or vindictive. If so, how wretched, at times, must the indulgence of this temper render you! When reason, awhile suspended, resumes its empire, and calm reflection succeeds the riot of passion, how severe must be your self-condemnation, and how keen your sensations of regret! Perhaps an unkindness of expression to some particular friend, disrespectful treatment of an honored superior, ill-timed resentment to a beloved

9. Repayment.
1. From Pope, *Essay on Man*.

equal, or imperious and unbecoming severity to a deserving infe-
rior, may give you the most painful emotions, and degrade you in
your own, as well as in the estimation of every observer! To prevent
this evil, accustom yourselves to check the first risings of anger, and
suspend every expression of displeasure, till you can deliberate on
the provocation, and the propriety of noticing it. It may have been
undesigned, and, therefore, not justly provoking. You may have mis-
understood the word, or action of offence, and inquiry may remove
the grounds of your suspicion: or the person offending may be one
with whom prudence and honor require you not to enter the lists.
But if neither of these considerations occur, reflect a moment, that
your own reputation and consequent happiness are at stake; and that
to lose the command of yourselves and your passions is inconsistent
with the delicacy of ladies, the moderation of christians, and the
dignity of rational beings.

"Let every sally[2] alarm, and excite you to rally and new-discipline
your forces; and to be more strictly on your guard against the assaults
of your foe.

"The character of Camilla is a pattern worthy of your imitation.
While very young, Camilla was unfortunately deprived of the instruc-
tion and regulating hand of a discreet and judicious mother. Her
father was too much immersed in business to attend to the cultiva-
tion of his daughter's mind.

"He gave her the means of a genteel education, praised her
excellencies, and chid[3] her faults, without being at the pains of
teaching her how to amend them. The irritability of her temper he
rather indulged, considering her as a girl of *spirit*, who would make
her way in the world, in spite of obstacles. She was naturally gener-
ous, tender-hearted, and humane; but her temper was as uncon-
trollable as the whirlpool, and as impetuous as the wind. Happily
for her, she had an uncommon strength of mind, a ready apprehen-
sion, a quick perception, and a depth of understanding, seldom
equalled. She saw her errors, was conscious of her failings, and a
severe sufferer for her faults. But such was the extreme quickness
of her feelings, and so passionate her resentment of any thing
which appeared injurious or affrontive,[4] that she could not always
repress them. She married a gentleman of a similar temper, and of
equal prudence. In the union of such violent spirits, great har-
mony could not be presaged.[5] Their passions were lively, their
affections ardent.

2. Witticism.
3. Scolded.
4. Insulting.
5. Predicted.

"The honey-moon in raptures flew,
A second brought its transports too;
The third, the fourth, were not amiss;
The fifth was friendship, mix'd with bliss;
But ere a twelvemonth pass'd away,
They found each other made of clay."[6]

"Inadvertencies gave offence; frequent altercations arose; both were tenacious[7] of their rights, and averse to condescension. Camilla saw the impending danger; she became sensible that the happiness of her life depended on amendment and caution; she resolved to avoid giving or taking offence, with the greatest diligence; to suppress every emotion of anger; and when she thought herself injured, to retire, or be silent, till passion had subsided, and she could regain her calmness.

"This was a hard task, at first; but perseverance rendered it effectual to a thorough reformation in each.

"Her example and pathetic admonitions[8] induced her husband to adopt her prudent plan. They found their mutual endeavours productive of real satisfaction, and happiness the reward of their exertions to secure it.

"To be vindictive is equally, perhaps more fatal to our own, and the peace of others, than to be passionate. Violent passions of all kinds are generally transient; but revenge is the offspring of malice, the parent of discord, and the bane of social love. It is an evidence of a weak and sickly mind. True greatness will rise superior to this ignoble spirit, so peculiarly ungraceful in a lady, and inconsistent with that delicacy and softness, which ought ever to characterize the sex.

"But an envious temper is, of all others, the most degrading and miserable. Envy is a malignant poison, which rankles in the heart, and destroys the inward peace; even while there is an outward appearance of serenity. That mind, which cannot rejoice in the happiness of others, is capable of very little in itself. To look with a grudging and evil eye on the enjoyments of our neighbour, must be a source of perpetual chagrin and mortification.

"Envy indulged, is a punishment to its possessor. Eradicate, then, the first, and every emotion of so corroding and destructive a nature; and endeavour to excel only by that virtuous emulation, which is productive of improvement and respectability.

---

6. Foster amends Oliver Goldsmith's 1765 poem "The Double Transformation" to reflect less the husband's perspective than a mutual experience: "But, when a twelvemonth passed away, / Jack found his goddess made of clay."
7. Adhesive.
8. Dramatic reproofs.

"A kind, compassionate, benevolent, humane disposition is an invaluable treasure. It will render you blessings to society, and objects of universal esteem.

> "In *you* 'tis graceful to dissolve at woe;
> With every motion, every word, to wave
> Quick o'er the kindling cheek the ready blush;
> And from the smallest violence to shrink,"—[9]

"This amiable temper, however, may sometimes degenerate into weakness.

"Prudence should be exercised, even in the indulgence of the most engaging qualities. In the progress of life, occasions may call for that resolution and fortitude, which admit not of apparent softness; but such occasions very seldom occur.

"How alluring are the charms of sympathy and charity! Happy are they who always feel the one, and have power and inclination to exemplify the other!

> "The diamond, and the ruby's blaze
> Dispute the palm with beauty's queen;
> Not beauty's queen demands such praise,
> Devoid of virtue, if she's seen.
> But the soft tear in pity's eye
> Outshines the diamond's brightest beam,
> And the sweet blush of modesty
> More beauteous than the ruby's seen."[1]

*Wednesday, P. M.*

DRESS.

"Dress" continued Mrs. Williams to her re-assembled and attentive pupils, "is an important article of female economy. By some it is doubtless considered as too essential. This is always the case, when it becomes the ruling passion, and every other excellence is made subordinate to it. A suitable attention to the etiquette of appearance is necessary to render us respectable in the eyes of the world; and discovers an accommodating disposition, which is, at once, engaging and useful in the commerce of society. Females are taxed with being peculiarly attached to, and captivated by the glare of splendor and show. But I believe superficial minds are not confined to sex. Whatever form they actuate, to beautify and adorn it will be the principal object.

---

9. Thomson's *The Seasons*, "Autumn."
1. Dr. James Fordyce (1720–1796), "True Beauty." Fordyce was the British author of the popular book *Sermons to Young Women* (1766).

"A certain species of gaiety and airiness is becoming in youth. Young ladies, therefore, act perfectly in character, when, under proper restraint, they indulge their taste in the decoration of their persons. But they should be especially careful that their taste be correct; consistent with the modest delicacy which is the glory and ornament of woman.

"It is laudable[1] to follow fashions, so far as they are governed by these rules; but whenever they deviate, quit them with express disapprobation and disgust. Any assumptions of the masculine habit are unbecoming. Dress and manners should be correspondent; and the engaging softness and artless simplicity, which grace my pupils, must be quite inconsistent with the air and attire of the other sex.

"A gaudy and fantastical mode of decoration is by no means a recommendation. It bespeaks a lightness of mind and a vanity of disposition, against which a discreet and modest girl should guard with the utmost vigilance. Extravagance is a great error, even where fortune will allow the means of supporting it. Many are the claims which the children of affliction and want have upon the superfluous plenty of the rich. How much better expended would some part of their redundance be, in relieving the necessities of such, than in decorating their own persons, with every ornament which art can contrive to create expense!

"Neatness and propriety should be the main objects; for loveliness needs no foreign aid to give it a passport. Neatness is too often connected with the idea of a prudish singularity; but no gaudiness of apparel, no richness of attire, no modishness of appearance can be an equivalent for it. Propriety is that garb which becomes our situation and circumstances in life. There certainly ought to be a difference between different ages and conditions, in this respect. Many articles, ornamental to Miss in her teens, would appear absurd, fantastical, and ridiculous in maturer years. Neither should the matronal robes, and the close cap hide the natural ringlets, and easy shapes of the blooming girl.

"It is a very false taste which induces people in dependent and narrow circumstances, to imitate the expensive mode of dress which might be very decent for those who move in a higher sphere.

"To endeavour to conceal indigence[2] by the affectation of extravagance, is committing a great offence, both against ourselves, and the community to which we belong. The means of support should always be attended to. A conformity to these will render you more respected for prudence, than a deviation for the sake of show without substance, can make you admired.

1. Praiseworthy.
2. Poverty.

"Louisa and Clarinda are striking examples. They were both the daughters of reputable parents, whose situations in the world were easy and comfortable, though not affluent. They were able to give their children a good education, but no other portion. Gay, volatile, and ambitious, Louisa was the votary of fashion. A superior in dress excited the keenest sensations of envy in her bosom; and a rival in appearance gave her unspeakable mortification. Dissatisfied with her natural charms, cosmetics and paints added to her expenses, and betrayed her folly. She had many professed admirers, who found her a willing dupe to flattery, and who raised her vanity by praising her excellent taste.

"Leander, a gentleman of liberal education, superior merit, and handsome property, cast his eye around for a companion to share and enjoy these advantages with him. Louisa caught his attention. The elegance of her person, and splendor of her appearance, charmed his imagination, and inspired the idea of a fortune sufficient to support her expensive style of living. He paid his addresses, and was received with the most flattering encouragement. But how great was his disappointment, when he discovered the smallness of her resources, and the imprudence of her management! This, said he to himself, will never do for me. Were my income far superior to what it is, it would not be adequate to such unbounded extravagance. Besides, where so little economy is practised, while under parental government, what must be the consequence of that unlimited indulgence, which the confidence due to a wife demands? Were I to abridge her expenses, and endeavour to rectify her fantastical taste, it would doubtless foment dissension,[3] discord, and animosity, which must terminate in wretchedness. He resolved, however, to try her real disposition, by gently hinting his disapprobation of her gaiety. This she resented; and a rupture, which ended in a final separation, ensued. She found, too late, the value of the man, whom she had slighted; and ever after regretted that folly which had irretrievably alienated his affections.

"The modesty and neatness of Clarinda's garb next caught Leander's eye. Conversing with her on the subject of dress, the justness of her sentiments gave him the highest ideas of the rectitude and innocence of her mind. A costly article was offered for her purchase; but she refused it. It would not become me, said she, nor any other person who has not an affluent fortune. If I had a sufficiency to buy it, I would procure something more simple and necessary for myself; and the overplus might render an object of distress contented and happy.

"Yet was Clarinda always elegantly neat; always genteelly fashionable. Frugality and economy; free from profusion and extravagance,

---

3. Encourage disagreement.

enabled her to indulge her own taste entirely; and while she enjoyed that, she repined not at the fancied superiority of others. Leander found her all he wished, in appearance; all he hoped for, in reality. As their tastes were correspondent, and their highest aim, when united, to please each other, they were not dependent on the breath of fashion for their happiness. A compliance with its forms did not elate their pride, nor a departure from them, fill their hearts with peevishness and discontent."

## Thursday, A. M.

### POLITENESS.

"Still more important than your habit, is your air and deportment. It is not sufficient that these are pleasing to the eye of the superficial observer. Your behaviour and conversation must be uniformly governed by the laws of politeness, discretion, and decorum. Else you will be disgusting to people of refinement; and the judicious and discerning will discover the weakness of your minds, notwithstanding the showy ornaments, intended to conceal it from public view.

"Inattention in company is a breach of good manners. Indeed, it is a downright insult; being neither more nor less, than declaring that you have not the least respect for any who are present. Either you do not value their good opinion, or you have something more important than their conversation to occupy your minds.

"You should always be attentive to those with whom you are conversant, let their rank and standing be what they may. Your superiors will esteem you for your respectful treatment of them; your equals will love you for your kindness and familiarity; your inferiors will respect you for your condescension and meekness.

"Attention in company will be advantageous to yourselves. Like the industrious bee, which sips honey from every plant, you may derive some benefit or instruction from all kinds of society. Some useful remark or information; some sentiment which may allure you to the practice of virtue, or deter you from a vicious perpetration, may repay your labour, and be serviceable through life.

"But should there be no other motive than that of pleasing your associates, and rendering them happy, by making yourselves agreeable, it may be considered as a sufficient inducement to the practice of this branch of good-breeding. Many girls, in the thoughtless levity of their hearts, divert themselves at the expense of others; and, with the utmost glee, point out any thing peculiar in the appearance, words, or actions of some one in the company, whom they select for a subject of merriment and ridicule. This, by shrewd looks, ironical gestures, or tittering whispers, is kept up, to the great mortification

of the unhappy victim, and to the reproach and dishonor of the offenders. Such conduct is a breach, not only of the rules of common civility, but of humanity; besides being directly repugnant to the precept of doing to others as we would that they should do to us.

"Be particularly careful, then, not to mortify, or give pain to an inferior.

"Let the question, 'who maketh thee to differ?'[1] suppress every emotion of ridicule, contempt, or neglect; and induce you to raise and encourage depressed merit by your notice and approbation.

"As far as propriety, delicacy, and virtue will allow, conform to the taste, and participate in the amusements and conversation of the company into which you have fallen. If they be disagreeble to you, avoid a supercilious[2] avowal of your dislike. This, instead of reforming, would probably give them a disgust to you, and perhaps subject you to affronts. Yet where a disapprobating word or hint may be seasonable, neglect not the opportunity of contributing to their benefit and amendment.

"Are you conscious of superior advantages, either mental or external, make no ostentatious display of them. Vanity too often leads young ladies to obtrude their acquirements on the eyes of observers, inconsiderately apprehending they may otherwise be unnoticed. Such forwardness always subjects them to censure, ridicule, and envy; the expressions of which destroy that self-approbation which retiring merit invariably enjoys. However, exert that dignity of virtue which will render you independent of caprice, calumny,[3] and unprovoked satire.

"Make no ungenerous, or ill-natured remarks on the company, or on the individuals of which it is composed.

"If you dislike them, avoid them in future. If you witness errors, faults, or improprieties, conceal, or at least extenuate them, as much as possible.

"Make just allowances for those who may differ from you in opinion; and be cautious never to misrepresent, or circulate what appears amiss to you, and must, if exposed, be injurious to others. Charity hides a multitude of faults. Certainly then, charity will never aggravate nor create them.

"To give currency to a report, which tends to the disadvantage and dishonor of another, is defaming; and defamation is a species of cruelty, which can never be expiated.

"Of this the unhappy, though imprudent Eudocia, is an exemplification.

---

1. 1 Corinthians 4:7.
2. Disdainful.
3. Slander.

"Eudocia was young, gay, and charming. A levity of disposition, which the innocence of her heart attempted not to restrain, sometimes gave the tongue of slander pretence to aim its envenomed shafts at her character, and to misrepresent her sprightliness.

"Independent in fortune; still more so in mind, calumny gave her no pain, while she was conscious of the rectitude of her intentions.

"Leontine was a gentleman of property; agreeable in his person and manners; of strict honor, and extremely tenacious of it; but of a severe and unforgiving temper. He paid his addresses to Eudocia; was accepted, approved, and beloved. Yet, though he had gained her affections, he had not sufficient influence to regulate her conduct, and repress her gaiety. Her fondness for show and gallantry, in some instances, induced her to countenance the attentions, and receive the flattery, of men, whose characters were exceptionable, in Leontine's estimation. He remonstrated against her imprudence, and gave her his ideas of female delicacy. She laughed at his gravity, and rallied[4] him on his implicit subjection to the opinions of others.

"Towards the close of a fine day, Eudocia rambled along a retired road, to enjoy the air. She was alone; but the hope of meeting her beloved Leontine, whom she expected that evening, imperceptibly led her beyond her intended excursion. The rattling of a carriage caused her to stop; and, thinking it to be Leontine's, she approached it before she perceived her mistake. A gentleman of an elegant appearance alighted, and accosting her politely, expressed his surprise at finding her so far from home without an attendant. She found it was Florio, with whom she had a slight acquaintance, having once met with him in company. She frankly owned her motive for walking thus far; and refused his invitation to return in his carriage. He renewed his request; and his importunity, seconded by her fatigue, at last prevailed. At this moment the detracting Lavina passed by. She saw Eudocia, and with a sneering smile, wished her a good night. Eudocia was unconscious of fault, and therefore fearless of censure. But the artful Florio, desirous of protracting the pleasure of her company, took a circuitous route, which considerably increased the distance to her father's house. However, he conveyed her safely home, though not so soon as she wished. She found that Leontine had been there, and had gone to visit a friend; but would soon return. Leontine was just seated at his friend's, when Lavina entered.

"She told the circle, that Florio had just passed her, and that he had company she little expected to see with him. They inquired if it was his former mistress? No, said she, he has discarded her some time ago, and if we may judge by appearances, has chosen a new

4. Ridiculed with good humor.

one. Upon being asked who, she presumed to name Eudocia. Every countenance expressed surprise and regret. In Leontine's, rage and resentment were visibly depicted. He rose, and stepping hastily to Lavina, told her he was a party concerned, and demanded an explanation of what she had insinuated. She perceived that she had given offence, and endeavoured to excuse herself; but he resolutely told her that no evasions would avail; that he insisted on the real truth of her scandalous report. Finding him thus determined, she related the simple fact of seeing Eudocia in a carriage with Florio, who was a known libertine, and accustomed to the society of loose women. Leontine asked her how she came to associate the ideas she had mentioned with Eudocia's name? She replied that the lightness of her behaviour had sometimes rendered her censurable; and she thought this instance, in particular, authorized suspicion. Leontine could not deny that she was culpable[5] in appearance; yet made answer, that though scandal might feast on the failings of virtue, he believed Eudocia's innocence much purer, and her heart much better than her detracters'; and, taking his hat, he wished the company a good evening, and left them.

"His passions were on fire. He could not comprehend the mysterious conduct of Eudocia. Her absence from home, at a time when he expected her to receive him, and her being seen at a distance, in company with a professed debauchee, were a labyrinth which he could not explore. Though he doubted not Eudocia's honor, yet her folly and imprudence, in subjecting her character to suspicion and reproach, he thought unpardonable. His resentment determined him to break the proposed connexion immediately; and, lest his love should get the better of his resolution, he went directly to the house.

"As he could not command his temper, he appeared extremely agitated, and angrily told Eudocia that she had caused him great uneasiness; and that he came to claim the satisfaction of knowing, why she had avoided his society, and made an assignation with a man who had involved her in infamy? Eudocia was astonished, and justly offended at this address. With all the dignity of conscious innocence, she replied, that as yet he had no right to challenge an account of her conduct; but for her own sake, she would condescend to give it. This she did, by a faithful and undisguised relation of facts. She then asked him, if he was satisfied. He answered, No. For, said he, though you have cleared yourself of guilt, in my apprehension, you will find it very difficult to free your character from the blemish it has received in the opinion of the world. Saying this, he told her, that, however highly he esteemed her, so opposite were their dispositions, that they must often be at variance; and so nice was his sense of honor,

5. Guilty.

that his wife, like Cæsar's, must not only be virtuous, but unsuspected. She rejoined, that his sentiments were apparent; and if what he then expressed were his opinion of her, it was best they should part.

"Some further conversation passed; when, promising to call, the next day, and satisfy her parents, and wishing Eudocia all possible happiness in life, he took his leave.

"The impropriety of her conduct, and her losing the affections of a man she too ardently loved, together with the cruel treatment she had just received from him, overwhelmed her with grief, and produced the most violent emotions of regret. She walked her room in all the anguish of disappointed hope. Her parents used every argument to soothe and console her; but in vain.

"She yielded to their persuasions so far as to retire to bed; but rest she found not; and the morning presented her in a burning fever. Leontine called in the course of the day; but the friends of Eudocia refused to see him. An account of her disorder had roused him to a sense of his rashness, and he begged to be admitted to her chamber; but this she utterly denied.

"Her fever left her; but the disease of her mind was beyond the power of medicine. A settled melancholy still remains; and she lives the victim of calumniation!

"To detract from the merit of others, beside the want of politeness which it betrays, and beside the injuries which it always occasions, is extremely impolitic. It is to confess your inferiority, and to acknowledge a wish, not to rise to greater respectability; but to bring down those about you to your own level! Ill-natured remarks are the genuine offspring of an envious and grovelling mind.

"Call yourselves to a severe account, therefore, whenever you have been guilty of this degrading offence; and always check the first impulses towards it.

"Accustom yourselves to the exercise of sincerity, benevolence, and good-humour, those endearing virtues, which will render you beloved and respected by all.

"To bestow your attention, in company, upon trifling singularities in the dress, person, or manners of others, is spending your time to little purpose. From such a practice you can derive neither pleasure nor profit; but must unavoidably subject yourselves to the imputation of incivility and malice."

*Thursday, P. M.*

AMUSEMENTS.

"Amusement is impatiently desired, and eagerly sought by young ladies in general. Forgetful that the noblest entertainment arises from a placid and well cultivated mind, too many fly from themselves, from thought and reflection to fashionable dissipation, or what they call pleasure, as a mean of beguiling the hours which solitude and retirement render insupportably tedious.

"An extravagant fondness for company and public resorts is incompatible with those domestic duties, the faithful discharge of which ought to be the prevailing object of the sex. In the indulgence of this disposition, the mind is enervated, and the manners corrupted, till all relish for those enjoyments, which, being simple and natural, are best calculated to promote health, innocence, and social delight, is totally lost.

"It is by no means amiss for youth to seek relaxation from severer cares and labours, in a participation of diversions, suited to their age, sex, and station in life. But there is great danger of their lively imaginations' hurrying them into excess, and detaching their affections from the ennobling acquisitions of moral improvement, and refined delicacy. Guard, then, against those amusements which have the least tendency to sully the purity of your minds.

"Loose and immoral books; company, whose manners are licentious, however gay and fashionable; conversation, which is even tinctured with profaneness or obscenity; plays, in which the representation is immodest, and offensive to the ear of chastity; indeed, pastimes of every description, from which no advantage can be derived, should not be countenanced; much less, applauded. Why should those things afford apparent satisfaction in a crowd, which would call forth the blush of indignation in more private circles? This question is worthy the serious attention of those ladies, who, at the theatre, can hardly restrain their approbation of expressions and actions, which, at their houses, would be intolerably rude and indecent, in their most familiar friends!

"Cards are so much the taste of the present day, that to caution my pupils against the too frequent use of them, may be thought old-fashioned in the extreme. I believe it, however, to be a fascinating game, which occupies the time, without yielding any kind of pleasure or profit. As the satyrist humourously observes,

> "The love of gaming is the worst of ills;
> With ceaseless storms the blacken'd soul it fills;

> Inveighs[1] at Heaven, neglects the ties of blood;
> Destroys the power and will of doing good;
> Kills health, pawns honor, plunges in disgrace;
> And, what is still more dreadful—spoils your face."[2]

"One thing at least is certain; it entirely excludes all rational conversation. That delightful interchange of sentiment, which the social meeting of friends is calculated to afford, and from which many advantages might be derived, is utterly excluded.

"Reading, writing, drawing, needle-work, dancing, music, walking, riding, and conversation, are amusements well adapted to yield pleasure and utility. From either of these, within proper bounds, there is no danger of injury to the person, or mind; though to render even our diversions agreeable, they must be enjoyed with moderation, and variously and prudently conducted. Such as are peculiarly exhilarating to the spirits, however innocent in themselves, should be more cautiously and sparingly indulged.

"When once the mind becomes too much relaxed by dissipating pastimes, it is proportionably vitiated, and negligent of those nice attentions to the rules of reserve and decorum, which ought never to be suspended. Intoxicating is the full draught[3] of pleasure to the youthful mind; and fatal are the effects of unrestrained passions.

"Flavia was the daughter of a gentleman, whose political principles obliged him to leave his country, at the commencement of the American revolution. At that time she was at nurse in a neighbouring village; between which and the metropolis, all communication being cut off, he was reduced to the necessity of leaving her to the mercy of those to whom she was entrusted. Having received her from pecuniary[4] motives only, they no sooner found themselves deprived of the profits of their labour and care, than they sought relief by an application to the town for her support. A wealthy farmer in the vicinity, who had often seen and been pleased with the dawning charms of Flavia, pitied her condition; and having no children of his own, resolved to shelter her from the impending storm, till she could be better provided for. At his house, she was brought up in a homely, though comfortable manner. The good man and his wife were excessively fond of her, and gave her every instruction and advantage in their power. Plain truths were liberally inculcated, and every exertion made to give her a habit of industry and good nature. Flavia requited their kindness by an obliging and cheerful, a docile and

---

1. Denouces.
2. From Young, *Love of Fame*, Satire 6.
3. Quantity of drink.
4. Related to money.

submissive deportment. As she advanced in years, she increased in beauty. Her amiable disposition rendered her beloved, and her personal accomplishments made her admired by all the village swains. The approbating smile of Flavia was the reward of their toils, and the favour of her hand in the rustic dance was emulously sought.

"In this state, Flavia was happy. Health and innocence were now her portion; nor had ambition as yet taught her to sigh for pleasures beyond the reach of her attainment.

"But the arrival of her father, who had been permitted to return, and re-possess the estate which he had abandoned, put a period to the simplicity and peace of Flavia's mind. He sought, and found her; and though sensible of his obligations to her foster-parents for snatching her from want and distress, still he could not prevail on himself to make so great a sacrifice to gratitude as they wished, by permitting his daughter to spend her days in obscurity. The lively fancy of Flavia was allured by the splendid promises and descriptions of her father; and she readily consented to leave the friends of her childhood and youth, and explore the walks of fashionable life.

"When she arrived in town, what new scenes opened upon the dazzled eyes of the admiring, and admired Flavia!

"Wealth, with its attendant train of splendid forms and ceremonies, courted her attention, and every species of dissipating amusement, sanctioned by the name of pleasure, beguiled the hours and charmed the imagination of the noviciate.[5] Each enchanting scene she painted to herself in the brightest colours; and her inexperienced heart promised her happiness without allay. Flattery gave her a thousand charms which she was hitherto inconscious of possessing, and the obsequiousness of the gaudy train around raised her vanity to the highest pitch of arrogance and pride. Behold Flavia, now, launched into the whirlpool of fashionable folly! Balls, plays, cards, and parties engross every portion of her time.

"Her father saw, too late, the imprudence of his unbounded indulgence; and his egregious mistake, in so immediately reversing her mode of life, without first furnishing her mind with sufficient knowledge and strength to repel temptation. He endeavoured to regulate and restrain her conduct; but in vain. She complained of this, as an abridgment of her liberty, and took advantage of his doating fondness to practise every excess. Involved in expenses (of which losses at play composed a considerable part) beyond her power to defray, in this embarrassing dilemma, she was reduced to the necessity of accepting the treacherous offer of Marius to advance money for the support of her extravagance. Obligated by his apparent kindness, she could not refuse the continuance of his acquaintance, till his delusive arts had

5. Or novitiate; Beginner.

obtained the reward he proposed to himself, in the sacrifice of her honor. At length she awoke to a trembling sense of her guilt, and found it fatal to her peace, reputation, and happiness.

"Wretched Flavia! no art could conceal thy shame! The grief of her mind, her retirement from company, and the alteration in her appearance, betrayed her to her father's observation. Highly incensed at the ingratitude and baseness of her conduct, he refused to forgive her; but sent her from the ensnaring pleasures of the town, to languish out the remainder of life in solitude and obscurity."

### *Friday, A. M.*

#### FILIAL[1] AND FRATERNAL[2] AFFECTION.

"The filial and fraternal are the first duties of a single state. The obligations you are under to your parents cannot be discharged, but by a uniform and cheerful obedience; an unreserved and ready compliance with their wishes, added to the most diligent attention to their ease and happiness. The virtuous and affectionate behaviour of children is the best compensation, in their power, for that unwearied care and solicitude which parents, only, know. Upon daughters, whose situation and employments lead them more frequently into scenes of domestic tenderness; who are often called to smooth the pillow of sick and aged parents, and to administer with a skilful and delicate hand the cordial,[3] restorative to decaying nature, an endearing sensibility, and a dutiful acquiesence in the dispositions, and even peculiarities of those from whom they have derived existence, are indispensably incumbent.

"Such a conduct will yield a satisfaction of mind more than equivalent to any little sacrifices of inclination or humour which may be required at your hands.

"Pope, among all his admired poetry, has not six lines more beautifully expressive than the following:

"Me, let the pious office long engage,
To rock the cradle of declining age;
With lenient arts extend a mother's breath,
Make languor[4] smile, and smooth the bed of death;
Explore the thought, explain the asking eye,
And keep awhile one parent from the sky!"[5]

---

1. The condition of a child in relation to a parent.
2. Relating to a brother or sibling.
3. Comforting medicine or restorative drink.
4. Illness, distress.
5. Alexander Pope, "Epistle to Dr. Arbuthnot" (1734). In this poem Pope justifies why certain subjects deserve to be satirized. Note that Foster substitutes "pious" for Pope's word choice, "tender."

"Next in rank and importance to filial piety, is fraternal love. This is a natural affection which you cannot too assiduously cultivate. How delightful to see children of the same family dwell together in unity; promoting each other's welfare, and emulous only to excel in acts of kindness and good will. Between brothers and sisters the connexion is equally intimate and endearing. There is such a union of interests, and such an undivided participation of enjoyments, that every sensible and feeling mind must value the blessings of family friendship and peace.

"Strive, therefore, my dear pupils, to promote them, as objects which deserve your particular attention; as attainments which will not fail richly to reward your labour.

"Prudelia, beside other amiable endowments of person and mind, possessed the most lively sensibility, and ardent affections.

"The recommendations of her parents, united to her own wishes, had induced her to give her hand to Clodius, a gentleman of distinguished merit. He was a foreigner; and his business required his return to his native country.

"Prudelia bid a reluctant adieu to her friends, and embarked with him. She lived in affluence, and was admired and caressed by all that knew her, while a lovely family was rising around her. Yet these pleasing circumstances and prospects could not extinguish or alienate that affection, which still glowed in her breast for the natural guardians and companions of her childhood and youth.

"With the deepest affliction she heard the news of her father's death, and the embarrassed situation in which he had left his affairs. She was impatient to console her widowed mother, and to minister to her necessities. For these purposes, she prevailed on her husband to consent that she should visit her, though it was impossible for him to attend her. With all the transport of dutiful zeal, she flew to the arms of her bereaved parent. But how great was her astonishment and grief, when told that her only sister had been deluded by an affluent villain, and by his insidious arts, seduced from her duty, her honor, and her home! The emotions of pity, indignation, regret, and affection, overwhelmed her, at first; but recollecting herself, and exerting all her fortitude, she nobly resolved, if possible, to snatch the guilty, yet beloved Myra, from ruin, rather than revenge her injured family by abandoning her to the infamy she deserved. To this intent she wrote her a pathetic letter, lamenting her elopement, but entreating her, notwithstanding, to return and receive her fraternal embrace. But Myra, conscious of her crime, and unworthiness of her sister's condescension and kindness, and above all, dreading the superiority of her virtue, refused the generous invitation. Prudelia was not thus to be vanquished in her benevolent undertaking. She even followed her to her lodgings, and insisted on an interview. Here she painted,

in the most lively colours, the heinousness of her offence, and the ignominy and wretchedness that awaited her. Her affection allured, her reasoning convinced her backsliding sister. Upon the promise of forgiveness from her mother, Myra consented to leave her infamous paramour, and retrace the paths of rectitude and virtue.

"Her seducer was absent on a journey. She, therefore, wrote him a farewell letter, couched in terms of sincere penitence for her transgression, and determined resolution of amendment in future, and left the house. Thus restored and reconciled to her friends, Myra appeared in quite another character.

"Prudelia tarried with her mother till she had adjusted her affairs, and seen her comfortably settled and provided for. Then taking her reclaimed sister with her, she returned to her anxiously expecting family. The uprightness and modesty of Myra's conduct, ever after, rendered her universally esteemed, though the painful consciousness of her defection was never extinguished in her own bosom.

"A constant sense of her past misconduct depressed her spirits, and cast a gloom over her mind; yet she was virtuous, though pensive, during the remainder of her life.

"With this, and other salutary effects in view, how necessary, how important are filial and fraternal affection!"

*Friday, P. M.*

FRIENDSHIP.

"Friendship is a term, much insisted on by young people; but, like many others, more frequently used than understood. A friend, with girls in general, is an intimate acquaintance, whose taste and pleasures are similar to their own; who will encourage, or at least connive at their foibles and faults, and communicate with them every secret; in particular those of love and gallantry, in which those of the other sex are concerned. By such friends, their errors and stratagems are flattered and concealed, while the prudent advice of real friendship is neglected, till they find, too late, how fictitious a character, and how vain a dependence they have chosen.

"Augusta and Serena were educated at the same school, resided in the same neighbourhood, and were equally volatile in their tempers, and dissipated in their manners. Hence every plan of amusement was concerted and enjoyed together. At the play, the ball, the cardtable, and every other party of pleasure, they were companions.

"Their parents saw that this intimacy strengthened the follies of each; and strove to disengage their affections, that they might turn their attention to more rational entertainments, and more judicious advisers. But they gloried in their friendship, and thought it

a substitute for every other virtue. They were the dupes of adulation, and the votaries of coquetry.

"The attentions of a libertine, instead of putting them on their guard against encroachments, induced them to triumph in their fancied conquests, and to boast of resolution sufficient to shield them from delusion.

"Love, however, which, with such dispositions, is the pretty plaything of imagination, assailed the tender heart of Serena. A gay youth, with more wit than sense, more show than substance, more art than honesty, took advantage of her weakness to ingratiate himself into her favour, and persuade her they could not live without each other. Augusta was the confident of Serena. She fanned the flame, and encouraged her resolution of promoting her own felicity, though at the expense of every other duty. Her parents suspected her amour, remonstrated against the man, and forbad her forming any connexion with him, on pain of their displeasure. She apparently acquiesced; but flew to Augusta for counsel and relief. Augusta soothed her anxiety, and promised to assist her in the accomplishment of all her wishes. She accordingly contrived means for a clandestine intercourse, both personal and epistolary.

"Aristus was a foreigner, and avowed his purpose of returning to his native country, urging her to accompany him. Serena had a fortune, independent of her parents, left her by a deceased relation. This, with her hand, she consented to give to her lover, and to quit a country, in which she acknowledged but one friend. Augusta praised her fortitude, and favoured her design. She accordingly eloped and embarked. Her parents were almost distracted by her imprudent and undutiful conduct; and their resentment fell on Augusta, who had acted contrary to all the dictates of integrity and friendship, in contributing to her ruin; for ruin it proved. Her ungrateful paramour, having rioted on the property which she bestowed, abandoned her to want and despair. She wrote to her parents, but received no answer. She represented her case to Augusta, and implored relief from her friendship; but Augusta alleged that she had already incurred the displeasure of her family on her account, and chose not again to subject herself to censure by the same means.

"Serena at length returned to her native shore, and applied in person to Augusta, who coolly told her that she wished no intercourse with a vagabond, and then retired. Her parents refused to receive her into their house; but from motives of compassion and charity, granted her a small annuity, barely sufficient to keep her and her infant from want.

"Too late she discovered her mistaken notions of friendship; and learned by sad experience, that virtue must be its foundation, or sincerity and constancy can never be its reward.

"Sincerity and constancy are essential ingredients in virtuous friendship. It invariably seeks the permanent good of its object; and in so doing, will advise, caution and reprove, with all the frankness of undissembled affection. In the interchange of genuine friendship, flattery is utterly excluded. Yet, even in the most intimate connexions of this kind, a proper degree of respect, attention, and politeness, must be observed. You are not so far to presume on the partiality of friendship, as to hazard giving offence, and wounding the feelings of persons, merely because you think their regard for you will plead your excuse, and procure your pardon. Equally cautious should you be, of taking umbrage at circumstances which are undesignedly offensive.

"Hear the excellent advice of the wise son of Sirach, upon this subject:

"'Admonish thy friend; it may be he hath not done it; and if he have done it, that he do it no more. Admonish thy friend; it may be he hath not said it; and if he have, that he speak it not again. Admonish thy friend; for many times it is a slander; and believe not every tale. There is one that slippeth in his speech, but not from his heart; and who is he that offendeth not with his tongue?'[1]

"Be not hasty in forming friendships; but deliberately examine the principles, disposition, temper, and manners, of the person you wish to sustain this important character. Be well assured: that they are agreeable to your own, and such as merit your entire esteem and confidence, before you denominate her your friend. You may have many general acquaintances, with whom you are pleased and entertained; but in the chain of friendship there is a still closer link.

> "Reserve will wound it, and distrust destroy.
> Deliberate on all things with thy friend:
> But since friends grow not thick on ev'ry bough,
> Nor ev'ry friend unrotten at the core,
> First, on thy friend, deliberate with thyself:
> Pause, ponder, sift; not eager in the choice,
> Nor jealous of the chosen: fixing, fix:
> Judge before friendship; then confide till death."[2]

"But, if you would have friends, you must show yourselves friendly; that is, you must be careful to act the part you wish from another. If

---

1. Ecclesiasticus 19:13–16. Ecclesiasticus is also known as *The Wisdom of Sirach*, written by Jesus ben Sirach approximately 200 B.C. This book is not included in Hebrew or Protestant scripture but was recognized as part of the Old Testament canon by Roman Catholic and Eastern Orthodox churches. Foster seems to cite it as having moral but not scriptural authority.

2. From Edward Young, *The Complaint: or, Night-Thoughts on Life, Death, & Immortality*, published through the 1740s and popularly known as *Night Thoughts*. The poem is melancholic, dwelling on the deaths of Young's loved ones.

your friend have faults, mildly and tenderly represent them to *her*; but conceal them as much as possible from the observation of the world. Endeavour to convince her of her errors, to rectify her mistakes, and to confirm and increase every virtuous sentiment.

"Should she so far deviate, as to endanger her reputation and happiness; and should your admonitions fail to reclaim her, become not, like Augusta, an abettor of her crimes. It is not the part of friendship to hide transactions which will end in the ruin of your friend. Rather acquaint those who ought to have the rule over her of her intended misteps, and you will have discharged your duty; you will merit, and very probably may afterwards receive, her thanks.

"Narcissa and Florinda were united in the bonds of true and generous friendship. Narcissa was called to spend a few months with a relation in the metropolis, where she became acquainted with, and attached to a man who was much her inferior; but whose specious manners and appearance deceived her youthful heart, though her reason and judgment informed her, that her parents would disapprove the connexion. When she returned home, the consciousness of her fault, the frankness which she owed to her friend, and her partiality to her lover, wrought powerfully upon her mind, and rendered her melancholy. Florinda soon explored the cause, and warmly remonstrated against her imprudence in holding a moment's intercourse with a man, who, she knew, would be displeasing to her parents. She searched out his character, and found it far inadequate to Narcissa's merit. This she represented to her in its true colours, and conjured her not to sacrifice her reputation, her duty, and her happiness, by encouraging his addresses: but to no purpose were her expostulations.[3] Narcissa avowed the design of permitting him to solicit the consent of her parents, and the determination of marrying him without it, if they refused.

"Florinda was alarmed at this resolution; and, with painful anxiety, saw the danger of her friend. She told her plainly, that the regard she had for her demanded a counteraction of her design; and that if she found no other way of preventing its execution, she should discharge her duty by informing her parents of her proceedings. This Narcissa resented, and immediately withdrew her confidence and familiarity; but the faithful Florinda neglected not the watchful solicitude of friendship; and when she perceived that Narcissa's family were resolutely opposed to her projected match, and that Narcissa was preparing to put her rash purpose into execution, she made known the plan which she had concerted, and by that mean prevented her destruction. Narcissa thought herself greatly injured, and declared that she would never forgive so flagrant a

---

3. Arguments.

breach of fidelity. Florinda endeavoured to convince her of her good intentions, and the real kindness of her motives; but she refused to hear the voice of wisdom, till a separation from her lover, and a full proof of his unworthiness, opened her eyes to a sight of her own folly and indiscretion, and to a lively sense of Florinda's friendship, in saving her from ruin without her consent. Her heart overflowed with gratitude to her generous preserver. She acknowledged herself indebted to Florinda's benevolence, for deliverance from the baneful impetuosity[4] of her own passions. She sought and obtained forgiveness; and ever after lived in the strictest amity[5] with her faithful benefactress."

### Saturday, A. M.

#### LOVE.

"The highest state of friendship which this life admits, is in the conjugal relation. On this refined affection, love, which is but a more interesting and tender kind of friendship, ought to be founded. The same virtues, the same dispositions and qualities which are necessary in a friend, are still more requisite in a companion for life. And when these enlivening principles are united, they form the basis of durable happiness. But let not the mask of friendship, or of love, deceive you. You are now entering upon a new stage of action, where you will probably admire, and be admired. You may attract the notice of many, who will select you, as objects of adulation, to discover their taste and gallantry; and perhaps of some whose affections you have really and seriously engaged. The first class your penetration will enable you to detect; and your good sense and virtue will lead you to treat them with the neglect they deserve. It is disreputable for a young lady to receive and encourage the officious attentions of those mere pleasure-hunters, who rove from fair to fair, with no other design than the exercise of their art, address, and intrigue. Nothing can render their company pleasing, but a vanity of being caressed, and a false pride in being thought an object of general admiration, with a fondness for flattery which bespeaks a vitiated mind. But when you are addressed by a person of real merit, who is worthy your esteem, and may justly demand your respect, let him be treated with honor, frankness, and sincerity. It is the part of a prude, to affect a shyness, reserve, and indifference, foreign to the heart. Innocence and virtue will rise superior to such little arts, and indulge no wish which needs disguise.

4. Injurious haste.
5. Friendship.

"Still more unworthy are the insidious and deluding wiles of the coquette. How disgusting must this character appear to persons of sentiment and integrity! how unbecoming the delicacy and dignity of an uncorrupted female!

"As you are young and inexperienced, your affections may possibly be involuntarily engaged, where prudence and duty forbid a connexion. Beware, then, how you admit the passion of love. In young minds, it is of all others the most uncontrollable. When fancy takes the reins, it compels its blinded votary to sacrifice reason, discretion and conscience to its impetuous dictates. But a passion of this origin tends not to substantial and durable happiness. To secure this, it must be quite of another kind, enkindled[1] by esteem, founded on merit, strengthened by congenial dispositions and corresponding virtues, and terminating in the most pure and refined affection.

"Never suffer your eyes to be charmed by the mere exterior; nor delude yourselves with the notion of unconquerable love. The eye, in this respect, is often deceptious, and fills the imagination with charms which have no reality. Nip, in the bud, every particular liking, much more all ideas of love, till called forth by unequivocal tokens, as well as professions of sincere regard. Even then, harbour them not without a thorough knowledge of the temper, disposition, and circumstances of your lover, the advice of your friends; and, above all, the approbation of your parents. Maturely weigh every consideration for and against, and deliberately determine with yourselves, what will be most conducive to your welfare and felicity in life. Let a rational and discreet plan of thinking and acting, regulate your deportment, and render you deserving of the affection you wish to insure. This you will find far more conducive to your interest, than the indulgence of that romantic passion, which a blind and misguided fancy paints in such alluring colours, to the thoughtless and inexperienced.

"Recollect the favourite air you so often sing:

> "Ye fair, who would be bless'd in love,
>     Take your pride a little lower;
> Let the swain that you approve,
>     Rather like you than adore.
>
> Love that rises into passion,
>     Soon will end in hate, or strife;
> But from tender inclination
>     Flow the lasting joys of life."[2]

1. Lit up.
2. In his novel *The History of Sir Charles Grandison* (1753), Samuel Richardson introduces these verses as a common song in which a female heroine is kidnapped and must preserve her virtue.

"I by no means undervalue that love which is the noblest principle of the human mind; but wish only to guard you against the influence of an ill-placed and ungovernable passion, which is improperly called by this name.

"A union, formed without a refined and generous affection for its basis, must be devoid of those tender endearments, reciprocal attentions, and engaging sympathies, which are peculiarly necessary to alleviate the cares, dispel the sorrows, and soften the pains of life. The exercise of that prudence and caution which I have recommended, will lead you to a thorough investigation of the character and views of the man by whom you are addressed.

"Without good principles, both of religion and morality, (for the latter cannot exist independent of the former) you cannot safely rely, either upon his fidelity or his affection. Good principles are the foundation of a good life.

"If the fountain be pure, the streams which issue from it will be of the same description.

"Next to this, an amiable temper is essentially requisite. A proud, a passionate, a revengeful, a malicious, or a jealous temper, will render your lives uncomfortable, in spite of all the prudence and fortitude you can exert.

"Beware, then, lest, before marriage, love blind your eyes to those defects, to a sight of which, grief and disappointment may awaken you afterwards. You are to consider marriage as a connexion for life; as the nearest and dearest of all human relations; as involving in it the happiness or misery of all your days; and as engaging you in a variety of cares and duties, hitherto unknown. Act, therefore, with deliberation, and resolve with caution: but, when once you have come to a choice, behave with undeviating rectitude and sincerity.

"Avarice[3] is not commonly a ruling passion in young persons of *our* sex. Yet some there are, sordid enough to consider wealth as the chief good, and to sacrifice every other object to a splendid appearance. It often happens, that these are miserably disappointed in their expectations of happiness. They find, by dear-bought experience, that external pomp is but a wretched substitute for internal satisfaction.

"But I would not have outward circumstances entirely overlooked. A proper regard should always be had to a comfortable subsistence in life. Nor can you be justified in suffering a blind passion, under whatever pretext, to involve you in those embarrassing distresses of want, which will elude the remedies of love itself, and prove fatal to the peace and happiness at which you aim.

"In this momentous affair, let the advice and opinion of judicious friends have their just weight in your minds. Discover, with candor

3. Greed.

and frankness, the progress of your amour, so far as is necessary to enable them to judge aright in the cause; but never relate the love-tales of your suitor, merely for your own, or any other person's amusement. The tender themes, inspired by love, may be pleasing to you; but, to an uninterested person, must be insipid and disgusting, in the extreme.

"Never boast of the number, nor of the professions of your admirers. That betrays an unsufferable vanity, and will render you perfectly ridiculous in the estimation of observers. Besides, it is a most ungenerous treatment of those who may have entertained, and expressed a regard for you. Whatever they have said upon this subject, was doubtless in confidence, and you ought to keep it sacred, as a secret you have no right to divulge.

"If you disapprove the person, and reject his suit, that will be sufficiently mortifying, without adding the insult of exposing his overtures.

"Be very careful to distinguish real lovers from mere gallants. Think not every man enamoured with you, who is polite and attentive. You have no right to suppose any man in love with you, till he declares it in plain, unequivocal, and decent terms.

"Never suffer, with impunity, your ear to be wounded by indelicate expressions, double entendres,[4] and insinuating attempts to seduce you from the path of rectitude. True love will not seek to degrade its object, much less to undermine that virtue which ought to be its basis and support. Let no protestations induce you to believe that person your friend, who would destroy your dearest interests, and rob you of innocence and peace. Give no heed to the language of seduction; but repel the insidious arts of the libertine, with the dignity and decision of insulted virtue. This practice will raise you superior to the wiles of deceivers, and render you invulnerable by the specious flattery of the unprincipled and debauched.

"Think not the libertine worthy of your company and conversation, even as an acquaintance.

"That reformed rakes make the best husbands," is a common, and I am sorry to say, a too generally received maxim.[5] Yet I cannot conceive, that any lady, who values, or properly considers her own happiness, will venture on the dangerous experiment. The term *reformed* can, in my opinion, have very little weight; since those, whose principles are vitiated, and whose minds are debased by a course of debauchery and excess, seldom change their pursuits, till necessity, or interest requires it; and, however circumstances may alter or restrain their conduct, very little dependence can be placed

4. *French*: Double meanings, often with a lewd or sexual connotation.
5. See p. 42, n. 5, in this Norton Critical Edition.

on men whose disposition is still the same, but only prevented from indulgence by prudential motives. As a rake is most conversant with the dissolute and abandoned of both sexes, he doubtless forms his opinion of others by the standard to which he has been accustomed, and therefore supposes all women of the same description. Having been hackneyed[6] in the arts of the baser sort, he cannot form an idea, that any are in reality superior to them. This renders him habitually jealous, peevish, and tyrannical. Even if his vicious inclinations *be* changed, his having passed his best days in vice and folly, renders him a very unsuitable companion for a person of delicacy and refinement.

"But whatever inducements some ladies may have to risk themselves with those who have the reputation of being reformed, it is truly surprising that any should be so inconsiderate as to unite with such as are still professed libertines. What hopes of happiness can be formed with men of this character?

"Vice and virtue can never assimilate; and hearts divided by them can never coalesce. The former is the parent of discord, disease, and death; the latter, of harmony, health, and peace. A house divided against itself cannot stand; much less can domestic felicity subsist between such contrasted dispositions.

"But however negligent or mistaken many women of real merit may be, relative to their own interest, I cannot but wish they would pay some regard to the honor and dignity of their sex. Custom only has rendered vice more odious in a woman than in a man. And shall we give our sanction to a custom, so unjust and destructive in its operation; a custom which invites and encourages the enemies of society to seek our ruin? Were those who glory in the seduction of innocence, to meet with the contempt they deserve, and to be pointedly neglected by every female of virtue, they would be ashamed of their evil practices, and impelled to relinquish their injurious designs.

"But while they are received and caressed in the best companies, they find restraint altogether needless; and their being men of spirit and gallantry (as they style themselves) is rather a recommendation than a reproach!

"I cannot help blushing with indignation, when I see a lady of sense and character gallanted and entertained by a man who ought to be banished from society, for having ruined the peace of families, and blasted the reputation of many, who, but for him, might have been useful and happy in the world but who, by his insidious arts, are plunged into remediless insignificance, disgrace, and misery."

6. Worn-out, made commonplace.

## Saturday, P. M.

### RELIGION.

"Having given you my sentiments on a variety of subjects which demand your particular attention, I come now to the closing and most important theme; and that is Religion. The virtuous education which you have received, and the good principles which have been instilled into your minds from infancy, will render the enforcement of Christian precepts and duties a pleasing lesson.

"Religion is to be considered as an essential and durable object; not as the embellishment of a day; but an acquisition which shall endure and increase through the endless ages of eternity.

"Lay the foundation of it in youth, and it will not forsake you in advanced age; but furnish you with an adequate substitute for the transient pleasures which will then desert you; and prove a source of rational and refined delight; a refuge from the disappointments and corroding cares of life, and from the depressions of adverse events. "Remember now your Creator, in the days of your youth, while the evil days come not, nor the years draw nigh, when you shall say, we have no pleasure in them."[1] If you wish for permanent happiness, cultivate the divine favour as your highest enjoyment in life, and your safest retreat when death shall approach you.

"That even the young are not exempt from the arrest of this universal conqueror the tombstone of Amelia will tell you. Youth, beauty, health and fortune, strewed the path of life with flowers, and left her no wish ungratified. Love, with its gentlest and purest flame, animated her heart, and was equally returned by Julius. Their passion was approved by their parents and friends; the day was fixed, and preparations were making for the celebration of their nuptials. At this period, Amelia was attacked by a violent cold, which, seating on her lungs, baffled the skill of the most eminent physicians, and terminated in a confirmed hectic.[2] She perceived her disorder to be incurable, and with inexpressible regret and concern anticipated her approaching dissolution. She had enjoyed life too highly to think much of death; yet die she must! "Oh," said she, "that I had prepared, while in health and at ease, for this awful event! Then should I not be subjected to the keenest distress of mind, in addition to the most painful infirmities of body! Then should I be able to look forward with hope, and to find relief in the consoling expectation of being united, beyond the grave, with those dear and beloved connexions,

---

1. Ecclesiastes 12:1.
2. A hectic fever recurred daily and was believed to be caused by a number of factors, including an indulgence in passions and luxurious living. A confirmed hectic was not expected to recover, but to decline until dying.

which I must soon leave behind! Let my companions and acquaintance learn from me the important lesson of improving their time to the best of purposes; of acting at once as becomes mortal and immortal creatures!"

"Hear, my dear pupils, the solemn admonition, and be ye also ready!

"Too many, especially of the young and gay, seem more anxious to live in pleasure, than to answer the end of their being by the cultivation of that piety and virtue which will render them good members of society, useful to their friends and associates, and partakers of that heart-felt satisfaction which results from a conscience void of offence both towards God and man.

"This, however, is an egregious mistake; for in many situations, piety and virtue are our only source of consolation; and in all, they are peculiarly friendly to our happiness.

"Do you exult in beauty, and the pride of external charms? Turn your eyes, for a moment, on the miserable Flirtilla.[3] Like her, your features and complexion may be impaired by disease: and where then will you find a refuge from mortification and discontent, if destitute of those ennobling endowments which can raise you superior to the transient graces of a fair form; if unadorned by that substantial beauty of mind which can not only ensure respect from those around you, but inspire you with resignation to the divine will, and a patient acquiescence in the most painful allotments of a holy Providence? Does wealth await your command, and grandeur with its fascinating appendages beguile your fleeting moments? Recollect, that riches often make themselves wings and fly away. A single instance of mismanagement; a consuming fire, with various other misfortunes which no human prudence can foresee or prevent, may strip you of this dependence; and, unless you have other grounds of comfort than earth can boast, reduce you to the most insupportable wretchedness and despair. Are you surrounded by friends, and happy in the society of those who are near and dear to you? Soon may they be wrested from your fond embrace, and consigned to the mansions of the dead!

"Whence, then, will you derive support, if unacquainted with that divine Friend, who will never fail nor forsake you; who is the same yesterday, to-day, and forever?

"Health and youth, my dear girls, are the seasons for improvement. Now you may lay up a treasure which neither sickness nor adversity can impair.

"But the hour of distress is not the only time, in which religion will be advantageous to you. Even in prosperity, it will prove the best

---

3. See page 160. [*Foster's note.*]

solace, and the highest ornament of your lives. What can be more dignified, respectable, and lovely, than the Christian character? The habitual practice of those duties which the gospel inculcates will give lustre to your beauty and durability to your charms. By correcting your passions, it will improve your joys, endear you to your friends and connexions, and render you contented, happy, and useful in every stage and condition of life.

Religion will not deprive you of temporal enjoyments; it will heighten and increase them. It will not depress, but exhilarate your spirits. For it consists not in a gloomy, misanthropic[4] temper, declining the social and innocent delights of life; but prepares the mind to partake with satisfaction of every pleasure which reason approves, and which can yield serenity and peace in the review. Be not ashamed then of appearing religious, and of rising by that mean above the vain, unthinking crowd.

"Let not the idle jests of heedless and unprincipled companions deter you from a stedfast adherence to the path of truth and righteousness. 'Follow not the multitude to do evil.'[5] Never conform to fashion, even though it claim the patronage of politeness, so far as to countenance irreligion in any of its modifications.

"Jesting upon sacred subjects, ridiculing the professors of Christianity, light and irreverent conduct upon solemn occasions, ought to be cautiously avoided and decidedly condemned. Too many girls are so extremely thoughtless as to carry the levity of their manners even to the sanctuary; and by whispering, winking, tittering, and other indecent actions, display their folly to their own disgrace, and to the great disgust of all judicious and sober people. Such behaviour is not only offensive to the Deity, but insulting to all who would worship him free from interruption. It is not only an indignity offered to religion, but a flagrant breach of the rules of good breeding. Content not yourselves, therefore, with a bare attendance on the institutions of religion; but conduct with propriety, decorum, and seriousness, while engaged in the solemn service. Bear in mind, that you assemble with a professed purpose of paying homage to the Supreme; and consider yourselves as in his immediate presence!

"The offices of devotion demand your attention in private, as well as in public.

"Accustom yourselves, therefore, to stated periods of retirement for meditation and prayer; and adopt every other mean which is calculated to keep alive in your minds a due sense of your dependence and obligations, and to inspire you with that uniform love to

---

4. Hating mankind.
5. A paraphrase of Exodus 23:2.

God and benevolence to the human kind, which will prove your greatest glory here, as well as your crown of rejoicing hereafter."

The hour of departure having arrived, on Monday morning, Mrs. Williams assembled with her pupils; when the regret, visibly depicted on every countenance, was variously expressed. The tear of grateful regard stole silently down the bloomy cheeks of some: others betrayed their sensibility by audible sobs, which they could not repress: and all united in testifying the sense they entertained of the advantages they had received from Mrs. Williams's tuition, the happiness they had enjoyed in each other's society, and their determination to remember her counsels, cultivate continued friendship among themselves, and endeavour to be worthy of her's.

Mrs. Williams then took an affectionate leave of each one, and left them with her daughters. The most cordial good wishes were mutually interchanged, till their carriages received and separated them.

The friendship and unity thus commenced and confirmed, were never obliterated. They always cherished the most sincere affection for their Preceptress, and each other; which they displayed in an unreserved and social correspondence, both personal and epistolary. The residence of Mrs. Williams they denominated HARMONY-GROVE, which it ever after retained, and by which it is designated in the following selection of their letters.

# LETTERS.

*To Mrs.* M. WILLIAMS.

BOSTON.

RESPECTED AND DEAR MADAM,

Conformably to my promise, when I left your abode, the first efforts of my pen are dedicated to you. The pleasure which arises from the recollection of your more than maternal kindness to me, especially your unwearied endeavours to refine and embellish my mind, and to lay the foundation of right principles and practices, is interwoven with my existence; and no time or circumstances can erase my gratitude.

I arrived last evening safely; and was affectionately received by my honored parents, and beloved brothers and sisters. The emotions of regret which I felt in the morning, at the painful separation from you and my dear school-mates, with whom I have lived so happily, had not wholly subsided. I could not help listening, now and then, for some judicious observation from my Preceptress; and frequently cast my eyes around in search of some of the amiable companions, among whom I had been used to unbend every thought.

The splendor of the apartments gave me ideas of restraint that were painful; and I looked abroad for the green, where we were wont to gambol,[1] and the lawn where we so often held our twilight sports, and almost fancied that we sometimes caught a glimpse of the attendant Sylphs[2] who played around us; but in vain. Stately domes, crowded streets, rattling carriages, and all the noise and confusion of a commercial city were substituted. I retired to bed, and was awaked in the night by the riotous mirth of a number of Bachanalians, reeling from the haunts of intemperance and excess.

Alas! said I, this is not the Æolian harp[3] that used to soothe our slumbers at the boarding school. I composed myself again; but awoke at the accustomed hour of five. I arose; and, having praised

1. Play.
2. Beings or spirits of the air.
3. A stringed instrument played by the breeze.

191

my Maker for the preservations of the night, walked down. Not a living creature was stirring in the house.

I took a turn in the garden. Here art seemed to reign so perfectly mistress, that I was apprehensive lest I should injure her charms by viewing them.

I accordingly retired to the summer-house, and, having a book in my hand, sat down and read till the clock struck seven. I then thought it must be breakfast time, and returned to the house; but was much disappointed to find none of the family up, except one man-servant and the housemaid, who had just crept down.

They appeared perfectly astonished to see me come in from abroad; and the girl respectfully inquired if indisposition had occasioned my rising so early. I told her no; that the wish to preserve my health had called me up two hours before. Well, rejoined she, you will not find any body to keep you company here, for two hours to come. I was chagrined at the information, and asked her for a bowl of milk, it being past my usual breakfast time. The milk man had just arrived, and I drank some; but it had lost its flavour on the road. It was not like that which was served us at Harmony-Grove. I stepped to the harpsichord, and having sung and played a morning hymn, returned to my chamber, where, taking my work, I sat down by the window to view the listless tribe of yawning mortals who were beginning to thicken in the streets. One half of these appeared to be dragged forth by necessity, rather than any inclination to enjoy the beauties of a fine morning.

At nine, I was summoned into the parlour to breakfast. My sisters gently chid me for disturbing their repose with my music. I excused myself by alleging that I had been so long accustomed to early rising that I should find it difficult to alter the habit.

Here, madam, you have an account of my first night and morning's occupation. Were I to proceed with every new occurrence, through the year, and subjoin my own remarks, I must write volumes instead of letters.

Please to communicate this scroll to your amiable daughters, and remind them of their promise to write.

A line from Harmony-Grove would be a luxury to me.

Meanwhile, permit me still to subscribe myself, with the utmost respect, your grateful pupil,

HARRIOT HENLY.

## *To Miss* MATILDA FIELDING.

BOSTON.

DEAR MATILDA,

I did not intend, when we parted at the boarding school, that a whole month should have elapsed without bearing you some testimony of my continued friendship and affection; but so numerous have been my avocations, and so various my engagements, that I have scarcely called a moment my own since I returned home. Having been from town a year, I was considered as too antique to appear in company abroad, till I had been perfectly metamorphosed. Every part of my habit has undergone a complete change, in conformity to the present fashion. It was with extreme regret that I parted with the neatness and simplicity of my country dress; which, according to my ideas of modesty, was more becoming. But, I trust, this alteration of appearance will have no tendency to alienate those sentiments from my heart, which I imbibed under the tuition of Mrs. Williams.

I went, last evening, to the assembly;[1] but though dazzled, I was by no means charmed, by the glare of finery and tinselled decorations that were displayed.

There were some ladies, whose gentility and fashionable dress were evidently the product of a correct taste; but others were so disguised by tawdry gewgaws,[2] as to disgust me exceedingly.

Mrs. Williams used to say, that the dress was indicative of the mind. If this observation be just, what opinion am I to form of the gay multitudes who trip along the streets, and throng the places of public resort in this metropolis; the lightness and gaudiness of whose appearance, bespeak a sickly taste, to say no more!

I am furnished with feathers, flowers, and ribbons, in profusion. I shall, however, use them very sparingly; and though I would not be entirely singular, yet I *must* insist on consulting my own fancy a little, and cannot willingly sacrifice my own opinion to the capricious whimsy of fashion, and her devotees. My aunt Laurence, who, you know, is extravagantly genteel, is making us a visit. She laughs very heartily at my silly notions, as she calls them, and styles me a novice in the ways of the world; but hopes, notwithstanding, that I shall acquire a better taste, when I am more acquainted with fashionable life. That I may be much improved by a more extensive knowledge of the world, I doubt not; yet may I never be corrupted by that levity and folly, which are too prevalent among a part of my sex.

---

1. A publicly sanctioned gathering for dancing or other social activities.
2. Tacky baubles or trinkets.

I will not, however, censure and condemn others; but attend to myself and be humble. Adieu.

LAURA GUILFORD.

## *To Miss* MATILDA FIELDING.

HARMONY-GROVE.

DEAR MATILDA,

The tear of regret for your departure is scarcely dried from the cheek of your Maria; and the pleasing remembrance of the happiness I have enjoyed in your society is accompanied with a sigh, whenever I reflect that it exists no more.

My mamma has often observed, that those friendships which are formed in youth, provided they be well founded, are the most sincere, lively, and durable. I am sure that the ardency of mine can never abate; my affectionate regards for you can never decay.

We have another class of boarders; but you and your amiable companions had so entirely engrossed my confidence and esteem, that I shall find it difficult to transfer them, in any degree, to others. The sensations of Anna are very different, though she is capable of the most refined friendship. The natural vivacity, and, as I tell her, the volatility of her disposition, renders a variety of associates pleasing to her.

In order to recal your ideas to the exercises of Harmony-Grove, I enclose the sallies of my pen for this morning, fully assured of your candour and generosity in the perusal.

Pray omit no opportunity of writing, and favour me with your observations on the polite world. I shall receive every line as a pledge of your continued love to your

MARIA WILLIAMS.

## An ODE on SPRING.

*Enclosed in the preceding Letter.*

Hail, delight-restoring Spring!
Balmy pleasures with thee bring;
Aromatic gales dispense,
Misty vapours banish hence.
Blithe the jocund hinds appear,
Joy supports returning care,

Mirth the ready hand attends,
Pleasing hope the toil befriends.
Hark! the shady groves resound,
Love and praise re-echo round;
Music floats in every gale,
Peace and harmony prevail.
Here no stormy passions rise;
Here no feuds impede our joys;
Here ambition never roams,
Pride or envy never comes.
Come, Matilda; ruddy morn
Tempts us o'er the spacious lawn;
Spring's reviving charms invite
Every sense to taste delight.
Such delights as never cloy,
Health and innocence enjoy.
Youth's the spring-time of our years,
Short the rapid scene appears:
Let's improve the fleeting hours!
Virtue's noblest fruits be ours.

## *To Miss* CAROLINE LITTLETON.

BOSTON.

You have left—you have forsaken me, Caroline! But I will haunt
you with my letters; obtrude[1] myself upon your remembrance; and
extort from you the continuance of your friendship!

What do I say? Obtrude and extort! Can these harsh words be
used when I am addressing the generous and faithful Caroline?

But you have often encouraged my eccentricities by your smile,
and must therefore still indulge them.

Nature has furnished me with a gay disposition; and happy is it
for me, that a lax education has not strengthened the folly too com-
monly arising from it.

Mrs. Williams's instructions were very seasonably interposed to
impress my mind with a sense of virtue and propriety. I trust they
have had the desired effect; and that they will prove the guardian of
my youth, and the directory of maturer age. How often has the dear,
good woman taken me into her chamber, and reminded me of inde-
corums of which I was unconscious at the time; but thankful after-
wards that they had not escaped her judicious eye; as her observations

1. Intrude.

tended to rectify my errors, and render me more cautious and circumspect in future. How salutary is advice like her's; conveyed, not with the dogmatic[2] air of supercilious wisdom; but with the condescending ease and soothing kindness of an affectionate parent, anxiously concerned for the best good of those under her care!

I was very happy at Harmony-Grove; and the result of that happiness, I hope, will accompany me through life.

Yet I find the gaiety of the town adapted to my taste; nor does even Mrs. Williams condemn the enjoyment of its pleasures.

I was, last evening, at a ball; and I assure you, the attention I gained, and the gallantry displayed to attract my notice and approbation, were very flattering to my vanity; though I could not forbear inwardly smiling at the futile arts of the pretty fellows who exhibited them.

Their speeches appeared to have been so long practised, that I was on the point of advising them to exercise their genius, if they had any, in the invention of something new. But a polite conformity to the *ton*[3] restrained my satire. Adieu.

<div align="right">JULIA GREENFIELD.</div>

## To *Miss* CLEORA PARTRIDGE.

<div align="right">NEWBURY-PORT.</div>

I am disappointed and displeased, Cleora! I have long been anxious to procure the Marchioness de Sevignè's letters,[1] having often heard them mentioned as standards of taste and elegance in the epistolary way. This excited my curiosity, and raised my hopes of finding a rich entertainment of wit and sentiment. I have perused, and perused in vain; for they answer not my ideas of either. They are replete with local circumstances, which, to indifferent readers, are neither amusing nor interesting. True, the style is easy and sprightly; but they are chiefly composed of family matters, such as relate to her own movements and those of her daughter; many of which are of too trifling a nature to be ranked in the class of elegant writing. I own myself, however, not a competent judge of their merit as a whole, even in my own estimation; for I have read the two first volumes only.

---

2. Asserted in an arrogant or inflexible manner.
3. Fashion, shortened from the French phrase *Bon Ton.*
1. The *Lettres nouvelles ou nouvellement recouvrées, de la marquise de Sévigné et de la marquise de Simiane, sa petite-fille* by Marie de Rabutin-Chantal, marquise de Sévigné (1626–1696) were first excerpted for publication in 1725. Caroline is reading them in the original French, given that an extensive multiple-volume English translation did not appear until 1811.

That letters ought to be written with the familiarity of personal conversation, I allow; yet many such conversations, even between persons of taste and refinement, are unworthy the public attention.

Equal was my chagrin, not long since, on reading Pope's letters.[2] He, said I to myself, who bears the palm from all contemporary poets, and who is so consummate a master of this divine art, must surely furnish a source of superior entertainment, when he descends to friendly and social communications.

Indeed, there are good sentiments and judicious observations, interspersed in his letters; but the greater part of them have little other merit than what arises from the style.

Perhaps you will charge me with arrogance, for presuming to criticise, much more to condemn, publications which have so long been sanctioned by general approbation. Independent in opinion, I write it without reserve, and censure not any one who thinks differently. Give me your sentiments with the same freedom upon the books which you honor with a perusal, and you will oblige your affectionate

<div align="right">CAROLINE LITTLETON.</div>

## *To Miss* CAROLINE LITTLETON.

<div align="right">SALEM.</div>

DEAR CAROLINE,

I received your's with those lively sensations of pleasure which your favours always afford. As I was perusing it, my papa came into the room. He took it out of my hand, and read it; then returning it with the smile of approbation; I think, said he, that your correspondent has played the critic very well. Has she played it justly, Sir? said I. Why, it is a long time, said he, since I read the Marchioness de Sevignè's letters. I am not, therefore, a judge of their merit. But, with regard to Pope, I blame not the sex for retaliating upon him; for he always treated them satirically. I believe revenge was no part of my friend's plan, said I. She is far superior to so malignant a passion; though, were she capable of seeking it, it would be in behalf of her sex.

Company now coming in, the conversation shifted.

I have often smiled at the pitiful wit of those satirists and essayists, who lavish abundant eloquence on trifling foibles, the mere whims of a day; and of no consequence to the body natural, moral, or political. The extension of a hoop,[1] the contraction of the waist,

---

2. *Letters of Mr. Alexander Pope* (1737).
1. Hoops changed the shape of a woman's skirt.

or the elevation of the head-dress, frequently afford matter for pages of elaborate discussion. These reformers, too, always aim at the good of our sex! I think it a great pity they do not lop off some of their own exuberant follies; though, perhaps, they wish us to exchange labours; and, in return for their benevolent exertions, that we endeavour to expose and correct their errors. I have sometimes thought their satire to be tinctured with malice; and that the cause of their disaffection may generally be found in personal resentment. Had Pope and his coadjutors[2] been favourites with the ladies, I doubt not but they would have found more excellencies in them than they have ever yet allowed.

I have lately been reading the generous and polite Fitzosborne's[3] letters; and I need not tell you how much I was pleased and charmed with them.

The justness of his sentiments, and the ease and elegance of his diction are at once interesting and improving. His letter and ode to his wife on the anniversary of their marriage, surpass any thing of the kind I have ever read. I verily think, that, had I the offer of a heart capable of dictating such manly tenderness of expression, and such pathetic energy of generous love, I should be willing to give my hand in return, and assent to those solemn words, "love, honor, and—(I had almost said) obey." Adieu.

CLEORA PARTRIDGE.

## To Miss CLEORA PARTRIDGE.

NEWBURY-PORT.

DEAR CLEORA,

I agree with you, that the habits of the weak and vain are too insignificant to employ the pens of those, whose literary talents might produce great and good effects in the political, moral, and religious state of things. Were absurd fashions adopted only by those whose frivolity renders them the dupes of folly, and whose example can have no effect on the considerate and judicious part of the community, I should think them below the attention of statesmen, philosophers, and divines: but this is not the case. The votaries and the inventors of the most fantastical fashions are found in the ranks of, what is called, refined and polished society; from whom we might

---

2. Colleagues or assistants, especially in religious or legal situations.
3. *The Letters of Sir Thomas Fitzosborne on Several Subjects* (1748), a popular work by British author William Melmoth (1710–1799). Melmoth particularly addressed matters of taste and beauty.

hope for examples of elegance and propriety, both in dress and behaviour. By these, luxury and extravagance are sanctioned. Their influence upon the poorer class is increased; who, emulous of imitating their superiors, think *that* the most eligible appearance, (however beyond their income, or unsuitable to their circumstances and condition in life) which is preferred and countenanced by their wealthier neighbours.

Absurd and expensive fashions, then, are injurious to society at large, and require some check; and why is not satire levelled against them, laudable in its design, and likely to produce a good effect? Adieu.

<div style="text-align: right">CAROLINE LITTLETON.</div>

## *To Miss* MATILDA FIELDING.

<div style="text-align: right">HARMONY-GROVE.</div>

DEAR MATILDA,

Notwithstanding the coldness of the season, every heart seems to be enlivened, and every mind exhilarated by the anniversary of the new year. Why this day is so peculiarly marked out for congratulations, I shall not now inquire; but in compliance with the prevailing custom of expressing good wishes on the occasion, send you mine in a scribble.

> Early I greet the opening year,
> While friendship bids the muse appear,
>     To wish Matilda bless'd.
> The muse, devoid of selfish art,
> Obeys the dictates of a heart,
>     Which warms a friendly breast.
>
> The rolling earth again has run
> Her annual circuit round the sun,
>     And whirl'd the year away:
> She now her wonted[1] course renews,
> Her orbit's track again pursues;
>     Nor feels the least decay.
>
> How soon the fleeting hours are gone!
> The rapid wheels of time glide on,
>     Which bring the seasons round.

---

1. Accustomed.

Winter disrobes the smiling plain,
But spring restores its charms again,
   And decks the fertile ground.

The sweet returns of cheerful May
Come with a vivifying[2] ray,
   Inspiring new delight:
Beclad with every various charm
To please the eye, the fancy warm,
   And animate the sight.

But youth no kind renewal knows;
Swiftly the blooming season goes,
   And brings the frost of age!
No more the vernal[3] sun appears,
To gild the painful round of years,
   And wintry damps assuage!

With rapid haste the moments fly
Which you and I, my friend, enjoy;
   And they return no more!
Then let us wisely now improve
The downy moments, as they rove,
   Which nature can't restore.

O Source of wisdom! we implore
Thy aid to guide us safely o'er
   The slippery paths of youth:
O deign to lend a steady ray
To point the sure, the certain way
   To honor and to truth!

Let thy unerring influence shed
Its blessings on Matilda's head,
   While piety and peace,
Thy genuine offspring, round her wait,
And guard her thro' this transient state,
   To joys that never cease!

May constant health its charms extend,
And fortune every blessing lend,
   To crown each passing day:
May pleasures in succession shine,

2. Giving life to.
3. Relating to spring.

And every heart-felt bliss be thine,
Without the least allay.[4]

<div align="right">MARIA WILLIAMS.</div>

*To Miss* CLEORA PARTRIDGE.

<div align="right">BOSTON.</div>

DEAR CLEORA,

I have this week engaged in the celebration of the nuptials of my friend, Amanda South. A splendid wedding, a gay company, an elegant supper, and a magnificent ball, were the sum of our entertainment.

I imagine such exhilarating scenes designed to dispel the anxiety and thoughtfulness, which every reflecting person must feel on this solemn occasion. This untried state presents to the apprehensive mind such a variety of new cares and duties, that cheerfulness, festivity, and hilarity seem necessary to banish the thought of them, so far as to render a delicate and sensible female sufficiently composed to conduct with propriety. But I must confess, that, were I called to the trial, I should choose to retire from the observation of those indifferent and unfeeling spectators, to whom the blushing modesty of a bride is often a pastime.

Indeed, Cleora, when we look around the world and observe the great number of unhappy marriages, which were contracted with the brightest prospects, yet, from some unforeseen cause, have involved the parties in wretchedness for life, we may well indulge a diffidence of our own abilities to discharge the duties of the station, and be solicitous that our future companion should in all respects be qualified to assist in bearing the burdens of the conjugal state.

Experience only can determine how far we are right in the judgment we form of ourselves, and of the person of our choice. So many are the deceptions which love and courtship impose upon their votaries, that I believe it very difficult for the parties concerned to judge impartially, or to discern faults, where they look only for virtues. Hence they are so frequently misled in their opinions, and find, too late, the errors into which they have been betrayed.

---

4. Foster attributed her original verses to her characters, though she may have printed some elsewhere anonymously. This poem, for instance, is included unattributed (minus the first stanza and with a new verse and minor revisions) as "The New Year" in Daniel Sewall's *An Astronomical Diary, or Almanack, for the Year of Our Lord, 1809,* suggesting Sewall recopied it from a newspaper or journal or from Foster's novel, or that she submitted it elsewhere for publication.

When do you come to Boston, Cleora? I am impatient for your society; because your friendship is void of flattery, and your sincerity and cheerfulness are always agreeable and advantageous. Adieu.

<div align="right">HARRIOT HENLY.</div>

## To Miss HARRIOT HENLY.

<div align="right">SALEM.</div>

Indeed, Harriot, I open your letters with as much gravity as I would a sermon; you have such a knack of moralizing upon every event! What mortal else would feel serious and sentimental at a wedding? Positively, you shall not come to mine. Your presence, I fear, would put such a restraint upon me, as to render me quite foolish and awkward in my appearance.

However, I must acknowledge it a weighty affair; and what you say has, perhaps, too much truth in it to be jested with. I believe, therefore, we had better resolve not to risk the consequences of a wrong choice, or imprudent conduct; but wisely devote ourselves to celibacy. I am sure we should make a couple of very clever old maids. If you agree to this proposition, we will begin in season to accustom ourselves to the virtues and habits of a single life. By observing what is amiss in the conduct of others in the same state, and avoiding their errors, I doubt not but we may bring even the title into repute. In this way we shall be useful to many of our own sex, though I am aware it would be a most grievous dispensation to a couple of the other; but no matter for that.

The world needs some such examples as we might become; and if we can be instrumental of retrieving *old-maidism* from the imputation of ill-nature, oddity, and many other mortifying charges, which are now brought against it, I believe we shall save many a good girl from an unequal and unhappy marriage. It might have a salutary effect on the other sex too. Finding the ladies independent in sentiment, they would be impelled to greater circumspection of conduct to merit their favour.

You see that my benevolence is extensive. I wish to become a general reformer. What say you to my plan, Harriot? If you approve it, dismiss your long train of admirers immediately, and act not the part of a coquette, by retaining them out of pride or vanity. We must rise above such narrow views, and let the world know that we act from principle, if we mean to do good by our example. I shall continue to receive the addresses of this same Junius,[1] till I hear that

1. Junius was the anonymous yet influential author of letters in eighteenth-century Britain which exposed the corruption of King George III's officers and highlighted the constitutional rights of English subjects. He was known for his persuasive wit.

you have acceded to my proposal; and then, display my fortitude by renouncing a connexion which must be doubtful as to the issue, and will certainly expose me to the mortification of being looked at, when I am married. Farewell.

CLEORA PARTRIDGE.

## *To Miss* CAROLINE LITTLETON.

BOSTON.

DEAR CAROLINE,

I have just returned from a rural excursion, where, in the thicket of a grove, I enjoyed all the luxury of solitude. The sun had nearly finished his diurnal[1] course, and was leaving our hemisphere to illuminate the other with his cheering rays.

The sprightly songsters had retired to their bowers,[2] and were distending their little throats with a tribute of instinctive gratitude and praise.

The vocal stains re-echoed from tree to tree, and invited me to join the responsive notes. My heart expanded with devotion and benevolence. I wished the whole human kind to share the feelings and the happiness which I enjoyed; while the inanimate creation around seemed to partake of my satisfaction! Methought the fields assumed a livelier verdure;[3] and the zephyrs were unusually officious in wafting the fragrance of aromatic gales. I surveyed the surrounding scenery with rapturous admiration; and my heart glowed with inexpressible delight at the lovely appearance of nature, and the diffusive bounties of its almighty Author!

Let others, said I, exult in stately domes, and the superfluities of pomp; immerse themselves in the splendid novelties of fashion, and a promiscuous crowd of giddy amusements! I envy them not.

> Give me a mind to range the sylvan[4] scene,
>   And taste the blessings of the vernal day;
> While social joys, and friendly, intervene
>   To chase the gloomy cares of life away.[5]

I wish not to abandon society, nor to resign the pleasures which it affords; but it is a select number of friends, not a promiscuous crowd, which I prefer.

1. Daily.
2. Spaces enclosed by branches.
3. Greenness.
4. Being of the woods.
5. Young's *Love of Fame*, Satire 1.

When the mind is much engrossed by dissipating pleasures, it is apt to forget itself, and neglect its own dignity and improvement. It is necessary often to retreat from the noise and bustle of the world, and commune with our own hearts. By this mean we shall be the better qualified both to discharge the duties and participate the enjoyments of life.

Solitude affords a nearer and more distinct view of the works of creation; elevates the mind, and purifies its passions and affections.

> O Solitude! in thee the boundless mind
> Expands itself, and revels unconfin'd;
> From thee, each vain, each grov'lling passion flies,
> And all the virtues of the soul arise![6]

Adieu.

JULIA GREENFIELD.

## To Miss LAURA GUILFORD.

BOSTON.

MY DEAR LAURA,

Rambling in the garden, I have picked a nosegay,[1] which I transmit to you as a token of my remembrance. Though the poetical bagatelle[2] which accompanies it is not equal to the elegance of the subject; yet I confide in your candour to excuse its futility, and give a favourable interpretation to its design.

> Laura, this little gift approve,
> Pluck'd by the hand of cordial love!
> With nicest care the wreath I've dress'd,
> Fit to adorn your friendly breast.
> The rose and lilly are combin'd,
> As emblems of your virtuous mind!
> Pure as the first is seen in thee
> Sweet blushing sensibility.
> Carnations here their charms display,
> And nature shines in rich array,
> Od'rous, as virtue's accents sweet,
> From Laura's lips with wit replete.
> The myrtle with the laurel bound,
> And purple amaranthus crown'd,
> Within this little knot unite,

6. Unknown source.
1. Bunch of flowers.
2. A light piece of verse.

Like Laura's charms, to give delight!
Fair, fragrant, soft, like beauty dress'd;
So she unrivall'd stands confess'd;
While blending still each finish'd grace,
Her virtues in her mien we trace;
Virtues, which far all tints outshine,
And, verdant, brave the frost of time.

           I am, &c.

<div align="right">SOPHIA MANCHESTER.</div>

### To Miss MARIA WILLIAMS.

<div align="right">BOSTON.</div>

DEAR SISTER,

I am not so far engaged by the new scenes of fashionable gaiety which surround me, as to forget you and the other dear friends, whom I left at Harmony-Grove. Yet so great is the novelty which I find in this crowded metropolis, that you cannot wonder if my attention is very much engrossed. Mr. and Mrs. Henly, with their amiable daughters, are extremely polite and attentive to me; and have taken every method to contribute to my amusement. I went, yesterday, in their company, to Commencement at Cambridge;[1] and was very much entertained with the exhibition. I pretend not to be a judge of the talents displayed by the young gentlemen who took an active part; or of the proficiency they had made in science. I have an opinion of my own, notwithstanding; and can tell how far my eye and ear were gratified.

I never knew before that dress was a classical study; which I now conclude it must be, or it would not have exercised the genius of some of the principal speakers on this public occasion!

The female garb too, seemed to claim particular attention. The *bon ton*, taste, and fashions of our sex, afforded a subject of declamation to the orator; and of entertainment to the audience, composed, in part, of our legislators, politicians, and divines! I could not but think that those scholars who employ their time in studying, investigating, and criticising the ladies' dresses, might as well be occupied in the business of a frizeur[2] or the man-milener;[3] either of

---

1. In the late eighteenth century, ceremonies at Harvard were held in July and were the occasion for lavish festivities, including orations and a dinner for faculty and alumni, paid for by the graduates.
2. Hairdresser.
3. Tailor.

which would afford them more frequent opportunities for the display of their abilities, and render their labours more extensively useful to the sex. Others might then improve the time, which *they* thus frivolously engrossed on this anniversary, in contributing to the entertainment of the *literati*, who doubtless expect to be gratified by the exertions of genius, and an apparent progress in those studies, which are designed to qualify the rising youth of America for important stations both in church and state.

The assembly was extremely brilliant; the ladies seemed to vie with each other in magnificent decorations. So much loveliness was visible in their native charms, that, without any hint from the speakers of the day, I should have thought it a pity to add those foreign ornaments, which rather obscure than aid them.

I was a little displeased by the unbecoming levity of some of my sex; and apprehensive lest it might induce misjudging and censorious people to imagine that they were led thither more by the vanity of attracting notice, than to receive any mental entertainment.

Without our consent, we ran a race back to town, which endangered our necks. The avaricious hackman,[4] desirous of returning for another freight, had no mercy on his passengers or horses. However, we arrived safely, though much fatigued by the pleasure of the day.

Pleasure carried to excess degenerates into pain. This I actually experienced; and sighed for the tranquil enjoyments of Harmony-Grove, to which I propose soon to return, and convince you how affectionately I am your's.

ANNA WILLIAMS.

*To Miss* ANNA WILLIAMS.

HARMONY-GROVE.

DEAR ANNA,

Your enlivening letter restored us, in some measure, to your society; or at least alleviated the pain of your absence.

I am glad you attended Commencement. It was a new scene, and consequently extended your ideas. I think you rather severe on the classical gentlemen. We simple country-folks must not presume to arraign *their* taste, whose learning and abilities render them conspicuous on the literary stage. They, doubtless, write on subjects best adapted to their capacities. As for the follies of fashion, I think

---

4. Driver of a rental carriage.

the gentlemen are under obligations to the ladies for adopting them; since it gives exercise to their genius and pens.

You were tired, you say, with pleasure. I believe those dissipating scenes, which greatly exhilarate the spirits, call for the whole attention, and oblige us to exert every power, are always fatiguing.

Pleasures of a calmer kind, which are moderately enjoyed, which enliven rather than exhaust, and which yield a serenity of mind on reflection, are the most durable, rational, and satisfying. Pleasure is the most alluring object which is presented to the view of the young and inexperienced. Under various forms it courts our attention; but, while we are still eager in the pursuit, it eludes our grasp. Its fascinating charms deceive the imagination, and create a bower of bliss in every distant object. But let us be careful not to fix our affections on any thing which bears this name, unless it be founded on virtue, and will endure the severest scrutiny of examination.

Our honored mamma, and all your friends here, are impatient for your return. They unitedly long to embrace, and bid you welcome to these seats of simplicity and ease: but none more ardently, than your affectionate sister,

MARIA WILLIAMS.

### To Miss MATILDA FIELDING.

BOSTON.

DEAR MATILDA,

Anxious to make the best possible use of the education I have received; and fully impressed with the idea, that the human mind is capable of continual improvements, it is my constant endeavour to extract honey from every flower which falls in my way, or, to speak without a figure, to derive advantage from every incident. Pursuant to the advice of our excellent Preceptress, I keep this perpetually in view; and am therefore disappointed when defeated in the attempt.

This afternoon I have been in company with three ladies, celebrated for their beauty and wit. One of them, I think, may justly claim the reputation of beauty. To a finished form, a fair complexion, and an engaging, animating countenance are added. Yet a consciousness of superior charms was apparent in her deportment; and a supercilious air counteracted the effects of her personal accomplishments. The two others were evidently more indebted to art than to nature for their appearance. It might easily be discovered that paint constituted all the delicacy of their complexion!

What a pity, that so many are deceived in their ideas of beauty! Certain it is, that artificial additions serve rather to impair than increase its power. "Who can paint like nature?"[1] What hand is skilful enough to supply her defects? Do not those who attempt it always fail, and render themselves disgusting? Do they not really injure what they strive to mend; and make it more indifferent than usual, when divested of its temporary embellishments? Beauty cannot possibly maintain its sway over its most obsequious votaries, unless the manners and the mind unitedly contribute to secure it. How vain then is this subterfuge! It may deceive the eye, and gain the flattery of the prattling coxcomb;[2] but accumulated neglect and mortification inevitably await those who trust in the wretched alternative.

From their good sense, I had been led to expect the greatest entertainment. I therefore waited impatiently till the first compliments were over, and conversation commenced.

But, to my extreme regret, I found it to consist of ludicrous insinuations, hackneyed jests, and satirical remarks upon others of their acquaintance who were absent. The pretty fellows of the town were criticized; and their own adventures in shopping were related with so much minuteness, hilarity, and glee, that I blushed for the frivolous levity of those of my sex, who could substitute buffoonery[3] for wit, and the effusions of a perverted imagination for that refined and improving conversation, which a well cultivated mind and a correct taste are calculated to afford!

If, said I to myself, this be the beauty and the wit of polished society, restore me again to the native simplicity and sincerity of Harmony-Grove!

I took my leave as soon as politeness would allow; and left them to animadvert[4] upon me. Independent for happiness on the praise or censure of superficial minds, let me ever be conscious of meriting approbation, and I shall rest contented in the certain prospect of receiving it. Adieu.

SOPHIA MANCHESTER.

## *To Miss* SOPHIA MANCHESTER.

BEVERLY.

I sympathize with you, my dear Sophia, in the disappointment you received in your expectations from beauty and wit.

1. Thomson's *The Seasons*, "Spring."
2. Chattering dandy.
3. Foolish behavior.
4. Find fault.

You may nevertheless derive advantage from it. Your refined and delicate ideas raise you too far above the scenes of common life. They paint the defects of your inferiors in such lively colours, that the greater part of the community must be displeasing to you. Few, you should remember, have had the advantages which you have enjoyed; and still fewer have your penetrating eye, correct taste, and quick sensibility. Let charity then draw a veil over the foibles of others, and candour induce you to look on the best and brightest side.[5]

It is both our duty and interest to enjoy life, as far as integrity and innocence allow; and, in order to this, we must not soar above, but accommodate ourselves *to* its ordinary state. We cannot stem the torrent of folly and vanity; but we can step aside and see it roll on, without suffering ourselves to be borne down by the stream.

Empty conversation must be disgusting to every rational and thinking mind; yet, when it partakes not of malignity, it is harmless in its effects, as the vapour which floats over the mead in a summer's eve. But, when malice and envy join to give scope to detraction, we ought to avoid their contagion, and decidedly condemn the effusions of the ill-natured merriment which they inspire.

Our sex have been taxed as defamers. I am convinced, however, that they are not exclusively guilty; yet, for want of more substantial matter of conversation, I fear they too often give occasion for the accusation! A mind properly cultivated, and stored with useful knowledge, will despise a pastime which must be supported at the expense of others. Hence only the superficial and the giddy are reduced to the necessity of filling the time in which they associate together, with the degrading and injurious subjects of slander. But I trust that our improved countrywomen are rising far superior to this necessity, and are able to convince the world, that the American fair are enlightened, generous, and liberal. The false notions of sexual disparity, in point of understanding and capacity, are justly exploded; and each branch of society is uniting to raise the virtues and polish the manners of the whole.

I am, &c.

MATILDA FIELDING.

## *To Miss* JULIA GREENFIELD.

SALEM.

DEAR JULIA,

From your recommendation of Mrs. Chapone's letters; and, what is still more, from the character given them by Mrs. Williams, I was

---

5. Cf. the epitaph on Eliza Wharton's headstone in *The Coquette*, p. 133 in this Norton Critical Edition.

anxious to possess the book; but, not being able to procure it here, my clerical brother, who was fortunately going to Boston, bought and presented it to me.

I am much gratified by the perusal, and flatter myself that I shall derive lasting benefit from it.

So intricate is the path of youth, and so many temptations lurk around to beguile our feet astray, that we really need some skilful pilot to guide us through the delusive maze. To an attentive and docile mind, publications of this sort may afford much instruction and aid. They ought, therefore, to be carefully collected, and diligently perused.

Anxious to make my brother some acknowledgment for his present, I wrought and sent him a purse, accompanied with a dedication which I thought might amuse some of his solitary moments; and which, for that purpose, I here transcribe and convey to you.

> The enclosed, with zeal and with reverence due,
> Implor'd my permission to wait upon you;
> And begg'd that the muse would her favour extend,
> To briefly her worth and her service commend.
> The muse, who by dear-bought experience had known
> How little her use to the clergy had grown,
> With officious advice thus attack'd the poor purse:
> Why, you novice! 'tis plain that you cannot do worse!
> If the end of your being you would ever attain,
> And honor, preferment, and influence gain,
> Go quick to the pocket of some noble knave,
> Whose merit is wealth, and his person its slave:
> Or enter the mansion, where splendour appears,
> And pomp and eclat[1] are the habit she wears:
> Or hie to the court, where so well you are known,
> So highly esteem'd and so confident grown,
> That without your assistance and recommendation,
> None claims any merit, or fills any station!
> Seek either of these; and with joy you'll behold
> Yourself crown'd with honor, and filled with gold.
> But to wait on a priest: How absurd is the scheme:
> His reward's in reversion; the future's his theme.
> Will these, for the present, your cravings supply;
> Or soften the din of necessity's cry?
> Of hunger and want the loud clamours repel;
> Or crush the poor moth that would on you revel?
> For poets and prophets, the world has decreed,
> On fame and on faith may luxuriously feed!
> Here the purse interpos'd with a strut and a stare,

1. Acclaim.

Pray, good madam muse, your suggestions forbear!
On virtue and worth I'm resolv'd to attend,
A *firm*, if I am not a *plentiful* friend.
Tho' not swell'd with gold, and with metal extended,
What little I have shall be rightly expended:
And a trifle, by justice and wisdom obtain'd,
Is better than millions dishonestly gain'd!
Yet I hope and presume, that I never shall be
Excluded his pocket for the lack of a fee!

    Thus the muse and the purse—till I took the direction,
And destin'd the latter to your kind protection.
My wishes attend her, with fervour express'd,
That in yellow or white she may always be dress'd;
And e'er have the power each dull care to beguile;
Make the summer more gay, and the bleak winter smile!
But if Fortune be blind; or should she not favour
These wishes of mine, you must scorn the deceiver;
And, rising superior to all she can do,
Find a bliss more substantial than she can bestow!

<div align="right">CLEORA PARTRIDGE.</div>

## *To Miss* LAURA GUILFORD.

<div align="right">WORCESTER.</div>

DEAR LAURA,

I have spent a very agreeable summer in the country; but am now preparing to return to town. I anticipate, with pleasure, a restoration to your society, and that of my other friends there. I should, however, quit these rural scenes with reluctance, were it not that they are giving place to the chilling harbingers of approaching winter. They have afforded charms to me, which the giddy round of fashionable amusements can never equal. Many, however, think life insupportable, except in the bustle and dissipation of a city. Of this number is the volatile Amelia Parr, whom you know as well as I. So extreme is her gaiety, that the good qualities of her mind are suffered to lie dormant; while the most restless passions are indulged without restraint. I have just received a letter from her, which you will see to be characteristic of her disposition. I enclose that, and my answer to it for your perusal. Read both with candour; and believe me ever your's.

<div align="right">HARRIOT HENLY.</div>

### *To Miss* HARRIOT HENLY.

[*Enclosed in the preceding.*]

BOSTON.

Where are you, Harriot; and what are you doing? Six long months absent from the town! What can you find to beguile the tedious hours? Life must be a burden to you! How can you employ yourself? Employ, did I say? Pho! I will not use so vulgar a term! I meant amuse! Amusement surely is the prime end of our existence! You have no plays, no card-parties, nor assemblies that are worth mentioning! Intolerably heavy must the lagging wheels of time roll on! How shall I accelerate them for you? A new novel may do something towards it! I accordingly send you one, imported in the last ships. Foreign, to be sure; else it would not be worth attention. They have attained to a far greater degree of refinement in the old world, than we have in the new; and are so perfectly acquainted with the passions, that there is something extremely amusing and interesting in their plots and counter-plots, operating in various ways, till the dear creatures are jumbled into matrimony in the prettiest manner that can be conceived!

*We*, in this country, are too much in a state of nature to write good novels yet. An American novel is such a moral, sentimental thing, that it is enough to give any body the vapours to read one. Pray come to town as soon as possible, and not dream away your best days in obscurity and insignificance.

But this boarding school; this Harmony-Grove, where you formerly resided, has given you strange ideas of the world. With what raptures I have heard you relate the dull scenes in which you were concerned there! I am afraid that your diseased taste has now come to a crisis, and you have commenced prude in earnest! But return to your city friends; and we will lend our charitable assistance, in restoring you to gaiety and pleasure.

AMELIA PARR.

### *The Answer.*

WORCESTER.

DEAR AMELIA,

Your letter——your rattle, rather, came to hand yesterday. I could not avoid smiling at your erroneous opinions; and, in my turn, beg

leave to express my wonder at your entertainments in town. True, we have no plays. We are not obliged by fashion to sit, half suffocated in a crowd, for the greater part of the night, to hear the rantings, and see the extravagant actions of the buskin heroes,[1] (and those not always consistent with female modesty to witness!) We have no card-parties, avowedly formed for the purpose of *killing time!* But we have an agreeable neighbourhood; among which we can easily collect a social circle; and persons of taste, politeness and information compose it. Here we enjoy a rational and enlivening conversation, which is at once refined and improving. We have no assemblies, composed of a promiscuous crowd of gaudy belles and beaux; many of whom we should despise in a private company, and deem unworthy our notice. But we have genteel balls, the company of which is select, none being admitted but such as do honor to themselves and each other. The amusement is not protracted till the yawning listlessness of the company proclaims their incapacity for enjoyment; but we retire at a seasonable hour, and add to the pleasure of the evening that of undisturbed rest through the night. Of course, we can rise with the sun, and sip the nectarious dews, wafted in the aromatic gale. We breakfast before the heat of the day has brought on a languor, and deprived us of appetite; after which, we amuse ourselves with our needles, books, or music; recline on the sofa, or ramble in the grove, as fancy or convenience directs. In the shady bower we enjoy either the luxury of solitude, or the pleasures of society; while you are, the whole time, in the midst of hurry and bustle. Eager in the chase, *you* fly from one scene of dissipation to another; but the fatigue of this ceaseless round, and the exertion of spirits necessary to support it, render the objects of pursuit tasteless and insipid.

Which mode of life, yours or mine, do you now think the most rational, and productive of the greatest happiness? The boarding school, which you affect to despise, has, it is true, formed my taste; and I flatter myself that I shall never wish it altered.

I shall soon return to town; but not for pleasure. It is not in crowds that I seek it.   Adieu.

HARRIOT HENLY.

1. Heroes dressed in the high boots worn by tragic actors.

## *To Miss* SOPHIA MANCHESTER.

CONCORD.

DEAR SOPHIA,

Having been with my aunt Burchel for a fortnight past, I have indulged myself in reading novels; with which her library is well supplied.

Richardson's works have occupied a large portion of the time. What a surprising command has this great master of the passions over our feelings! It is happy for his own and succeeding ages, that he embarked in the cause of virtue. For his influence on the affections of his readers is so great, that it must have proved very pernicious, had he enlisted on the side of vice. Though I am not much of a novel reader, yet his pen has operated like magic on my fancy; and so extremely was I interested, that I could have dispensed with sleep or food for the pleasure I found in reading him.

By this circumstance I am more than ever convinced of the great caution which ought to be used in perusing writings of the kind. How secretly, and how insidiously may they undermine the fabric of virtue, by painting vice and folly in the alluring colours, and with the lively style of this ingenious author. The mind should be well informed, and the judgment properly matured, before young people indulge themselves in the unrestrained perusal of them.

The examples of virtue and noble qualities, exhibited by the author I have mentioned, are truly useful; but every writer of novels is not a Richardson: and what dreadful effects might the specious manners of a Lovelace have on the inexperienced mind, were they not detected by a just exhibition of his vices!

The noble conduct of Clementina and Miss Byron[1] are worthy of imitation; while the indiscretion of Clarissa, in putting herself under the protection of a libertine, is a warning to every fair. But both examples are often overlooked. While the ear is charmed with the style, and the fancy riots on the luxuriance of description, which so intimately blend the charms of virtue and the fascinations of vice; they are not readily distinguished by all.

I am not equally pleased with all Richardson's writings; yet so multifarious[2] are his excellencies, that his faults appear but specks, which serve as foils to display his beauties to better advantage.

---

1. Clementina della Porretta and Harriet Byron appear in Samuel Richardson's *The History of Sir Charles Grandison*. Miss Byron preserves her virtue while under assault, while Clementina sacrifices her love out of religious conviction. Their action is contrasted with Clarissa's unwise behavior in trusting Lovelace in Richardson's earlier novel.
2. Having great variety.

Before I went from home I was engaged in reading a course of history; but I fear I shall not return from this flowery field to the dry and less pleasing path of more laborious studies. This is one disadvantage of novel reading. It dissipates the ideas, relaxes the mind, and renders it inattentive to the more solid and useful branches of literature. Adieu.

LAURA GUILFORD.

## To Mrs. WILLIAMS.

BOSTON.

DEAR MADAM,

Neither change of place nor situation can alienate my affections from you, or obliterate my grateful remembrance of your kindness.

Your admonitions and counsels have been the guide of my youth. The many advantages which I have already received from them, and the condescending readiness with which they were always administered, embolden me to solicit your direction and advice in a still more important sphere. The recommendation of my parents and friends, seconded by my own inclination, have induced me to yield my heart and engage my hand to Mr. Sylvanus Farmington, with whose character you are not unacquainted. Next Thursday is the era fixed for our union. O madam, how greatly shall I need a monitor like you! Sensible of my own imperfections, I look forward with diffidence and apprehension, blended with pleasing hopes, to this new and untried state!

Your experienced pen can teach me how to discharge the duties, divide the cares, and enjoy the pleasures, peculiar to the station on which I am entering. Pray extend your benevolence, and communicate your sentiments on female deportment in the connubial relation. Practising upon such a model, I may still be worthy the appellation, which it will ever be my ambition to deserve, of your affectionate friend and pupil,

HARRIOT HENLY.

## To Miss HARRIOT HENLY.

HARMONY-GROVE.

Indeed, my dear Harriot, you are making an important change of situation; a change interesting to you and your friends; a change which involves, not only your own happiness, but the happiness of the worthy man whom you have chosen, of the family, over which

you are to preside, and perhaps, too, of that with which you are to be connected.

I rejoice to hear that this connexion, on which so much depends, is not hastily formed; but that it is the result of long acquaintance, is founded on merit, and consolidated by esteem. From characters like yours, mutually deserving and excellent, brilliant examples of conjugal virtue and felicity may be expected. Yet as human nature is imperfect, liable to errors, and apt to deviate from the line of rectitude and propriety, a monitorial guide may be expedient and useful. Your partiality has led you to request this *boon* of me; but diffidence of my own abilities compels me to decline the arduous task. Nevertheless, I have it happily in my power to recommend an abler instructor, who has written professedly upon the subject. The AMERICAN SPECTATOR, or MATRIMONIAL PRECEPTOR,[1] lately published by Mr. David West, of Boston, contains all you can wish. The judicious compiler has collected and arranged his materials with admirable skill and address. Peruse this book, and you will be at no loss for counsels to direct, and cautions to guard you through the intricate cares and duties of the connubial life. The essays are, chiefly, extracted from the most approved English writers. The productions of so many able pens, properly disposed, and exhibited in a new and agreeable light, must not only be entertaining, but useful to every reader of taste and judgment. I wish this publication to be considered as a necessary piece of furniture by every housekeeper. The editor has certainly deserved well of his country; and Hymen[2] should crown him with unfading garlands.

I shall visit you, my dear Harriot, after the happy knot (for such I flatter myself it will prove) is tied. In the mean time, I subscribe myself, with the most ardent wishes for your prosperity and happiness, your sincere friend,

MARY WILLIAMS.

1. David West, compiler, *The American spectator, or Matrimonial preceptor. A collection (with additions and variations) of essays, epistles, precepts and examples, relating to the married state, from the most celebrated writers, ancient and modern. Adapted to the state of society in the American republic* (Boston: Manning & Loring, 1797). West's anthology of marriage advice included comments on writing from classical texts alongside such English authors as Addison, Steele, and Johnson. It concluded with a declaration that America's "free government, and fertile regions" were particularly hospitable to marriage.
2. God of marriage.

## *To Miss* CLEORA PARTRIDGE.

NEWBURY-PORT.

What think you of wit, Cleora? If you estimate it by the worth of your own, you think it an invaluable jewel. But this jewel is variously set. Yours is in the pure sterling gold of good sense: yet, as displayed by some, it glistens on the mere tinsel of gaiety, which will not bear the scrutinizing eye of judgment.

Yesterday I received a visit from a young lady, lately moved into this neighbourhood, who is reputed a wit. Her conversation reminded me of Pope's satirical remark:

> "There are, whom Heaven has bless'd with store of wit;
> But want as much again to manage it."[1]

I found her's to consist in smart sayings, lively repartees, and ludicrous allusions.

So strong was her propensity to display this talent, that she could not resist any temptation which offered, though it led her to offend against the rules of politeness and generosity. As some persons of real genius were present, topics of literature and morality were discussed. Upon these she was mute as a statue; but whenever the playfulness of her fancy could find a subject, she was extremely loquacious. This induced me to suspect that the brilliance of her imagination had dazzled her understanding, and rendered her negligent of the more solid and useful acquisitions of the mind.

Is it not often the case, that those who are distinguished by any superior endowment, whether personal or mental, are too much elated by the consciousness of their pre-eminence, and think it sufficient to counterbalance every deficiency?

This, Mrs. Williams used to say, is owing to the want of self-knowledge; which, if once possessed, will enable us properly to estimate our own characters, and to ascertain with precision wherein we are defective, as well as wherein we excel. But it is the misfortune of *us*, young people, that we seldom attain this valuable science, till we have experienced many of the ills which result from the want of it. Ambition, vanity, flattery, or some such dazzling meteor, engrosses our attention, and renders us blind to more important qualifications.

But to return to this same wit, of which I was speaking. It is certainly a very dangerous talent, when imprudently managed. None that we can possess tends so directly to excite enmity, or destroy friendship.

1. Pope, *Essay on Criticism.*

An ill-natured wit is of all characters the most universally dreaded. People of this description are always feared, but rarely loved. Humanity and benevolence are essentially necessary to render wit agreeable. Accompanied by these, it cannot fail to please and entertain.

> "Wit, how delicious to man's dainty taste!
> 'Tis precious as the vehicle of sense;
> But as its substitute, a dire disease!
> Pernicious talent! flatter'd by mankind,
> Yet hated too.————
> Sense is the diamond, weighty, solid, sound:
> When cut by wit, it casts a brighter beam;
> Yet, wit apart, it is a diamond still.
> Wit, widow'd of good sense, is worse than nought;
> It hoists more sail to run against a rock."[2]

But I believe I cannot give a better proof of my own wit, than to conclude this scribble before your patience is quite exhausted by the perusal. Adieu.

CAROLINE LITTLETON.

## To Miss HARRIOT HENLY.

HARMONY-GROVE.

DEAR HARRIOT,

The first moment which I have been able to snatch from the affectionate embraces of my honored mamma, and my dear sister Maria, is devoted to you. Judging by the anxious solicitude of my own heart, I know you are impatient to hear of my safe arrival. It is needless to tell you how cordially I was received. You have witnessed the mutual tenderness which actuates our domestic circle. Where this is the governing principle, it is peculiarly interesting to sensibility. It is extremely exhilarating to the mind to revisit, after the shortest absence, the place of our nativity and juvenile happiness. "There is something so seducing in that spot, in which we first had our existence, that nothing but it can please. Whatever vicissitudes we experience in life, however we toil, or wheresoever we wander, our fatigued wishes still recur to home for tranquillity. We long to die in that spot which gave us birth, and in that pleasing expectation opiate every calamity."[1]

2. Young, *The Complaint.*
1. Goldsmith [*Foster's note*]. From Oliver Goldsmith, *The Citizen of the World* (1760–61), in which a foreign narrator comments on the state of English morals.

The satisfaction of returning home, however, has not obliterated the pleasure which I enjoyed on my visit to you. Does not a change of scene and situation contribute to the happiness of life? The natural love of this variety seems wisely implanted in the human breast; for it enables us to accommodate ourselves with facility to the different circumstances in which we are placed. I believe that no pleasures make so deep an impression on the memory, as those of the first and most innocent period of our lives. With what apparent delight do persons, advanced in years, re-trace their puerile[2] feats and diversions! "The hoary head looks back with a smile of complacency, mixed with regret, on the season when health glowed on the cheek, when lively spirits warmed the heart, and when toil strung the nerves with vigour."[3]

The pleasures of childhood and youth, when regulated by parental wisdom, and sweetened by filial affection and obedience, must be grateful to the recollection at any age: and for this plain reason, because innocence and simplicity are their leading traits. How soothing, how animating, then, must be reflection, at the evening of a life, wholly spent in virtue and rectitude!

Pope observes that "Every year is a critique on the last. The man despises the boy, the philosopher the man, and the Christian all."[4] Happy are those who can take a retrospect of all, with the supporting consciousness, that each part has been rightly performed! Adieu.

ANNA WILLIAMS.

## To Miss MATILDA FIELDING.

BOSTON.

I am impatient for an opportunity of returning your civilities, my dear Matilda; and if possible, of repaying you some part of the pleasure, which you so liberally afforded me, during my late visit to your hospitable mansion. For this purpose, I must insist on the performance of your promise to spend the winter in town. It is true that I cannot contribute to your amusement in kind. Yet, according to the generally received opinion, that variety is necessary to the enjoyment of life, we may find *our's* mutually heightened by the exchange. Delightful rambles, and hours of contemplative solitude, free from the interruptions of formality and fashion, I cannot insure; but you may depend on all that friendship and assiduity can substitute; and while the bleak winds are howling abroad, a cheerful

2. Childish.
3. Knox [*Foster's note*]. Vicesimus Knox, from "An Essay on the Pleasures of Reflection," in *Essays, Moral and Literary* (1778).
4. Pope, *Essay on Criticism*.

HANNAH WEBSTER FOSTER

fireside, and a social circle, may dispel the gloom of the season. The pleasures of our family are very local. Few are sought, in which the understanding and affections can have no share. For this reason, a select, not a promiscuous acquaintance is cultivated. And however unfashionable our practice may be deemed, we can find entertainment, even in the dull hours of winter, without recourse to cards. Almost every other recreation affords some exercise and improvement to the body or mind, or both; but from this neither can result. The whole attention is absorbed by the game. Reason lies dormant, and the passions only are awake. However little is depending, the parties are frequently as much agitated by hope and fear, as if their all were at stake. It is difficult for the vanquished not to feel chagrin; while the victors are gratified at the expense of their friends. But the principal objection with me, is the utter exclusion of conversation; a source of pleasure, and of profit too, for which I can admit nothing as an equivalent. Winter evenings are peculiarly adapted to this rational and refined entertainment. Deprived of that variety of scenery, and those beauties of nature, which the vernal and autumnal seasons exhibit, we are obliged to have recourse to the fire-side for comfort. Here we have leisure to collect our scattered ideas, and to improve, by social intercourse, and the exertion of our mental powers.

Our sex are often rallied on their volubility:[1] and, for myself, I frankly confess, that I am so averse to taciturnity,[2] and so highly prize the advantages of society and friendship, that I had rather plead guilty to the charge than relinquish them.

> "Hast thou no friend to set thy mind a-broach?
> Good sense will stagnate. Thoughts shut up, want air,
> And spoil, like bales unopen'd to the sun.
> Had thought been all, sweet speech had been deny'd;
> Speech, thought's canal! Speech, thought's criterion too.
> Thought, in the mine, may come forth gold or dross;
> When coin'd in word, we know its real worth:
> If sterling, store it for thy future use;
> 'Twill buy thee benefit, perhaps renown.
> Thought, too, deliver'd, is the more possess'd;
> Teaching, we learn; and giving, we retain
> The births of intellect: when dumb, forgot.
> Speech ventilates our intellectual fire;
> Speech burnishes our mental magazine;
> Brightens for ornament, and whets for use."[3]

1. Chattiness; loquaciousness.
2. Reticence; unsociable silence.
3. Young, *The Complaint.*

Come then, Matilda, participate the pleasures, and accelerate the improvement, of your affectionate friend,

LAURA GUILFORD.

## To Miss LAURA GUILFORD.

BEVERLY.

DEAR LAURA,

Your's of the 9th ult. has just come to hand. It gave me renewed experience of the truth of the observation, that next to the personal presence and conversation, is the epistolary correspondence of a friend. I am preparing, with the most lively sensations of pleasure, to gratify my own wishes, and comply with your polite invitation. The romantic beauty of the rural scenes has forsaken me; and what can so amply compensate for their absence, as the charms you offer?

I envy you nothing which the town affords, but the advantages you derive from the choice of society adapted to your own taste. Your sentiments of the fashionable diversion of card-playing, are, in my view, perfectly just. I believe that many people join in it, because it is the *ton*, rather than from any other motive. And as such persons generally pay the greatest deference to Lord Chesterfield's opinions and maxims, I have often wondered how they happened to overlook, or disregard his animadversions upon this subject; and have felt a strong inclination to tell them, that this *all-accomplished* master of politeness, and oracle of pleasure, expressly says, "All amusements, where neither the understanding nor the senses can have the least share, I look upon as frivolous, and the resources of little minds, who either do not think, or do not love to think."[1]

We had a pretty party here, last evening; and a party it literally was; for it consisted entirely of ladies. This singular circumstance was remarked by one of the company, who, at least, pretended to think it agreeable, because, said she, we can now speak without restraint, or the fear of criticism. I confess that I was not prude enough to acquiesce in her opinion.

Ladies of delicacy and refinement will not countenance or support a conversation, which gentlemen of sense and sentiment can disapprove. As each were formed for social beings, and depend on the other for social happiness, I imagine that society receives its greatest charm from a mutual interchange of sentiment and knowledge.

"Both sexes are reciprocal instruments of each other's improvement. The rough spirit of the one is tempered by the gentleness of

1. Chesterfield, *Letters to His Son* (1774).

the other, which has likewise its obligations to that spirit. Men's sentiments contract a milder turn in the company of women, who, on the other hand, find their volatility abated in that of the men. Their different qualities, intermingling, form a happy symphony. From their intimate conjunction, their real advantages must be common and inseparable; and as for those ridiculous wranglings about superiority, they may be reckoned insults to nature, and betray a want of a due sense of its wise and gracious dispensations."[2]

Many ladies affect to think it inconsistent with female reserve, to acknowledge themselves pleased with the company of the other sex; but while such are the objects and advantages of a mixed society, I blush not to own myself desirous of its cultivation.        Adieu.

<div align="right">MATILDA FIELDING.</div>

### To Miss CAROLINE LITTLETON.

<div align="right">BOSTON.</div>

DEAR CAROLINE,

I take the liberty to send you Bennet's Letters.[1] When my mamma put them into my hand, Sophia, said she, I recommend this book to your attentive perusal. It highly deserves it, and will richly reward your labour. You have, indeed, completed your school education; but you have much yet to learn. Improvements in knowledge are necessarily progressive. The human mind is naturally active and eager in pursuit of information; which we have various and continual means of accumulating: but never will *you* have a more favourable opportunity for the cultivation of your mind, than you now enjoy. You are now free from those domestic cares and avocations, which may hereafter fall to your lot, and occupy most of your time. Speculation must then give place to practice. Be assiduous, therefore, to increase the fund, that it may yield you a competent interest, and afford you a constant resource of support and enjoyment.

With these words she withdrew, while I was still listening to the sweet accents of maternal tenderness and discretion, which vibrated on my ear, even after her departure.

2. The Ladies' Friend [*Foster's note*]. An American edition of Pierre-Joseph Boudier de Villemert's *The Ladies Friend: Being a Treatise on the Virtues and Qualifications Which are the Brightest Ornaments of the Fair Sex, and Render them Most Agreeable to the Sensible part of Mankind* was first published in Philadelphia, 1771. New editions appeared from Matthew Carey in 1793 and N. Douglas of Danbury in 1794. De Villemart celebrates female authors as the equal of males ("women can do whatever they dare undertake") and expresses a belief that the best way to reform women is first to reform men.
1. Reverend John Bennett, *Letters to a Young Lady, on a variety of Useful and Interesting Subjects calculated to improve the heart, to form the manners and enlighten the understanding* (1789). Bennett's enormously popular work was also serialized in the *American Museum or Universal Magazine* in 1792.

I find it worthy the recommendation of so good a judge. As a moral writer, the precepts and observations of its author are excellent; as a religious one, his piety is exemplary, and his instructions improving. His selection of books, which he deems most proper for our sex, though too numerous, perhaps, may, notwithstanding, assist and direct the young, in their course of reading.

Who would not imitate his Louisa?[2] In her he has forcibly displayed the beauties of an amiable disposition, and the advantages which even *that* may derive from a virtuous and religious education.

These letters are not scholastic and elaborate dissertations; they are addressed to the heart; they are the native language of affection: and they can hardly fail to instil the love of virtue into every mind susceptible of its charms.

If you have not read them, I will venture to predict that they will afford you entertainment, as well as instruction; and if you *have*, they will bear a second perusal. Indeed, every valuable book should be re-perused. On a first reading, our curiosity to know something of all it contains, hurries us forward with a rapidity which outstrips both the memory and judgment.

When this predominant passion is gratified, an attentive review will commonly furnish many useful and important lessons, which had nearly or quite escaped our notice before.

This, by some, is deemed too laborious a task. They prefer company and conversation to reading of any kind; and allege, in defence of their opinion, that a knowledge of the world, and of human nature, together with that ease and gracefulness of manners, which are of the utmost consequence to all who would make a respectable figure in life, are much better obtained in this way, than by the cold and unimpassioned perusal of books.

But is not every acquisition of this sort merely superficial? Need we not a guide, superior to our own judgment and experience, to point out the line of duty and propriety, in the various conditions and relations of our existence?

Our acquaintance with living characters and manners can afford us but a very limited view of mankind, in the different periods and stages of society. The inquisitive mind labours to extend its knowledge to the most distant climes and remote antiquity; and craves other materials for the exercise of its reflecting powers, than can be derived from occasional and desultory conversation. Now, by what means can this laudable curiosity be so effectually satisfied, as by the perusal of judicious and well chosen books? Not that I would depreciate the value of good company (for I esteem it highly;) but add its many advantages to those which reading affords. This combination

2. The humble yet accomplished heroine of Bennett's work.

must have a happy tendency to give us possession, both of the virtues and graces; and to render our attainments at once solid and ornamental.

What think you, Caroline? Do you agree with me in opinion? Let me hear from you by the first opportunity; and believe me your's most sincerely.

SOPHIA MANCHESTER.

## To Miss SOPHIA MANCHESTER.

NEWBURY-PORT.

I thank you, my dear friend, for the book you were so obliging as to send me; and for the letter which accompanied it. The book I had read; but, as you justly observe, I must be a gainer by a second perusal.

Upon the subject of reading, I perfectly accord with you in sentiment. It is an amusement, of which I was always enthusiastically fond. Mrs. Williams regulated my taste; and, by directing and maturing my judgment, taught me to make it a source of refined and substantial pleasure. I do not wish to pursue study as a profession, nor to become a learned lady; but I would pay so much attention to it, as to taste the delights of literature, and be qualified to bear a part in rational and improving conversation. Indeed, I would treasure up such a fund of useful knowledge, as may properly direct my course through life, and prove an antidote against the vexations and disappointments of the world. I think, Sophia, that our sex stand in special need of such a resource to beguile the solitary hours which a domestic station commonly imposes. Is it not for want of this that some females furnish a pretext for the accusation (which is illiberally brought against all) of having recourse to scandal, and the sallies of indelicate mirth? Conversation requires a perpetual supply of materials from the mind: and, accordingly as the mind has been cultivated or neglected, dignified or degrading subjects will be introduced.

I received a letter, yesterday, from our lively and lovely friend, Anna Williams. How delightfully blended in this charming girl, are vivacity and sentiment, ease and propriety. Adieu.

CAROLINE LITTLETON.

## *To Miss* MARIA WILLIAMS.

So often, my dear Maria, has the pen of the divine, the moralist, and the novelist been employed on the subject of female frailty and seduction; and so pathetically has each described the folly and misery of the fatal delusion which involves many in disgrace, that I am astonished when I see those, who have the best means of information, heedlessly sacrificing their reputation, peace and happiness, to the specious arts of the libertine! In this case, it is common for our sex to rail against the other, and endeavour to excite the pity of the world by painting the advantage which has been taken of their credulity and weakness. But are we not sufficiently apprised of the enemies we have to encounter? And have we not adequate motives to circumspection and firmness?

I am generally an advocate for my own sex; but when they suffer themselves to fall a prey to seducers, their pusillanimity[1] admits no excuse. I am bold to affirm that every woman, by behaving with propriety on all occasions, may not only resist temptation, but repel the first attempts upon her honor and virtue.

That levity of deportment, which invites and encourages designers, ought studiously to be avoided. Flattery and vanity are two of the most dangerous foes to the sex. A fondness for admiration insensibly throws them off their guard, and leads them to listen and give credit to the professions of those who lie in wait to deceive.

The following remarks, though severe, perhaps, can hardly be deemed inconsistent with the character which their author assumes.[2] "Women would do well to forbear their declamations against the falsity and wickedness of men; the fault is theirs, to fall into such coarse-spun snares as are laid for them.

"That servile obsequiousness which women should immediately look upon as the mark of fraud, and which should make them apprehend a surprise, is the very thing which allures them, and renders them soon the victims of perjury and inconstancy; the just punishment of a disposition which fixes their inclinations on superficial qualities. It is this disposition which draws after them a crowd of empty fops, who, if they have any meaning at all, it is only to deceive. Something pleasing in a man's person, a giddy air, a perpetual levity, supply the place of valuable endowments."

1. Cowardliness.
2. The Ladies' Friend. [*Foster's note.*]

A recent, and singular adventure has rendered observations of this sort peculiarly striking to my mind; which may account for the subject and the length of this letter.

I will give you a detail of it, though I must conceal the real names of the parties concerned.

Yesterday, the weather being very fine, and the sleighing excellent, several of our family, with two or three friends, were induced to make an excursion a few miles into the country. We stopped at a house which had formerly been a tavern, and in which we had often been well entertained on similar occasions. As we were in haste to receive the benefit of a good fire, we did not notice the removal of the sign, nor advert to the possibility of its being converted to a private mansion. Being very cold, I stepped first out of the sleigh, and ran hastily in; leaving the gentlemen to exercise their gallantry with the other ladies. The room I entered had no fire. I therefore opened the door which led to the next apartment, when I beheld the beautiful and admired Clarinda sitting in an easy chair, pale and wan, with an infant in her arms! I stood mute and motionless, till the woman of the house appeared to conduct me to another room. Confusion and shame were visibly depicted in Clarinda's countenance; and, unable to meet my eye, she threw her handkerchief over her face, and fell back in her chair.

I followed the good woman, and, apologizing for my intrusion, told her the cause. She recollected my having been there before, and readily excused my freedom.

By this time the rest of the company, who had been shown into a decent parlour, were inquiring for me; and I could scarcely find opportunity to request my conductress to ask Clarinda's forgiveness in my name, and to assure her of my silence, before I had joined them. I assumed an appearance of cheerfulness very foreign to the feelings of my heart, and related my mistake without any mention of the melancholy discovery I had made. We prevailed on the woman to accommodate us with tea and coffee, as we wished to ride no further. While preparations were making, she came in to lay the table, and as she withdrew gave me a token to follow her; when she informed me that Clarinda had been extremely overcome by my detecting her situation; but being somewhat recovered, desired a private interview. I accordingly repaired to her apartment, where I found her bathed in tears. Pity operated in my breast, and with an air of tenderness I offered her my hand; but she withheld her's, exclaiming in broken accents, O no! I am polluted—I have forfeited your friendship—I am unworthy even of your compassion!

I begged her to be calm, and promised her that she should suffer no inconvenience from my knowledge of her condition.

She thanked me for my assurances, and subjoined[3] that, since she knew the candour and generosity of my disposition, she would entrust me with every circumstance relative to her shameful fall; when, after a considerable pause, she proceeded nearly in the following words.

"Though our acquaintance has been for some time suspended, and though we have lived in different parts of the town, yet common fame has doubtless informed you that I was addressed by the gay, and to me, too charming Florimel! To the most captivating form, he superadded the winning graces of politeness, and all those insinuating arts which imperceptibly engage the female heart.

"His flattering attentions, and apparent ardour of affection were to my inexperienced and susceptible mind proofs of his sincerity; and the effusions of the most lively passion were returned with unsuspecting confidence.

"My father, strict in his principles, and watchful for my real welfare, disapproved his suit; alleging that although Florimel was calculated to please in the gayer moments of life, he was nevertheless destitute of those sentiments of religion and virtue, which are essentially requisite to durable felicity. But I could not be persuaded that he lacked any perfection which maturer years would not give him; and therefore finding my attachment unconquerable, my father reluctantly acquiesced in the proposed connexion. My ill-judged partiality for this ungenerous man absorbed every other passion and pursuit; while he took advantage of my yielding fondness, and assumed liberties which I knew to be inconsistent with delicacy, but had not resolution to repel. One encroachment succeeded another, and every concession was claimed and granted as a proof of love, till at length he became absolute master of my will and my person! Shame and remorse soon roused me to a sense of my guilt, and I demanded an immediate performance of his promise of marriage. This, under one pretext or another, he constantly evaded. His visits daily became less frequent, and his attentions less assiduous; while the most poignant anguish of mind deprived me of every comfort. I found myself reduced to the humiliating alternative of entreating my seducer to screen me from infamy by the name of wife, though he should never consider or treat me as such. To this he insultingly replied, that my situation must necessarily detect our illicit commerce; and his pride could never brook the reputation of having a wife whose chastity had been sacrificed. As soon as rage and resentment, which at first took from me the power of utterance, would permit, Wretch! exclaimed I, is it not to you the sacrifice has been

3. Added.

made? Who but you has triumphed over my virtue, and subjected me to the disgrace and wretchedness I now suffer? Was it not in token of my regard for you that I yielded to your solicitations? And is this the requital I am to receive? Base, ungrateful man! I despise your meanness! I detest the ungenerous disposition you betray, and henceforth reject all intercourse and society with you! I will throw myself on the mercy of my injured parents, and renounce you forever.

"Seeing me almost frantic, he endeavoured to soothe and appease me. He apologized for the harshness of his language, and even made professions of unabated affection; but gave as a reason for deferring the conjugal union, at present, that commercial affairs obliged him to sail immediately for Europe; assuring me at the same time that on his return he would not fail to renew and consummate the connexion. To this I gave no credit, and therefore made no reply. He then requested me to accept a purse to defray my expenses, during his absence, which I rejected with disdain; and he departed. The distress and despair of my mind were inexpressible. For some days, I resigned myself entirely to the agonizing pangs of grief. My parents imputed my dejection to Florimel's departure, and stove to console me. It was not long, however, before my mother discovered the real cause. In her, resentment gave place to compassion; but the anger of my father could not be appeased. He absolutely forbad me his presence for some time; but my mother at length prevailed on him to see, and assure me of forgiveness and restoration to favour, if I would consent to renounce and disown my child; to which, not then knowing the force of maternal affection, I readily consented. This place was privately procured for me, and hither, under pretence of spending a month or two with a friend in the country, I retired. Tomorrow my dear babe is to be taken from me! It is to be put to nurse, I know not where! All I am told is, that it shall be well taken care of! Constantly will its moans haunt my imagination, while I am deprived even of the hope of ministering to its wants; but must leave it to execrate the hour which gave it birth, and deprived it of a parent's attention and kindness.

"As soon as possible, I shall return to my father's house; and as I am unknown here, and you are the only person, out of our family, who shares the dreadful secret, I flatter myself that my crime may still be concealed from the world. The reproaches of my own mind I can never escape. Conscious guilt will give the aspect of accusation to every eye that beholds me; and however policy may compel me to wear the mask of gaiety and ease, my heart will be wrung with inexpressible anguish by the remembrance of my folly, and always alive to the distressing sensations of remorse and shame! Oh Julia! you have witnessed my disgrace! pity and forgive me! Perhaps I once appeared as virtuous and respectable, as you now do; but how changed! how

fallen! how debased! Learn from my fate to despise the flattery of the worthless coxcomb, and the arts of the abandoned libertine."

By this time I was summoned to tea; when, giving all the consolation in my power to the unhappy Clarinda, I rejoined my company; and to prevent their inquisitiveness about my absence, told them I had been with a sick woman, upon whom I accidentally intruded when I first came in; and that she had detained me, all this time, by a recital of her complaints and misfortunes. This account satisfied their curiosity; but the melancholy into which my mind had been thrown was not easily dissipated; nor could I, without doing violence to my feelings, put on the appearance of my usual cheerfulness and ease.

Here, my dear Maria, is a picture of the frailty and weakness of our sex! How much reason have we then to "watch and pray that we enter not into temptation!"[4]

With affectionate regards to your mamma and sister, I subscribe myself your's most sincerely,

<div align="right">JULIA GREENFIELD.</div>

## To Miss JULIA GREENFIELD.

<div align="right">HARMONY-GROVE.</div>

MY DEAR FRIEND,

I was much affected by the woe-fraught tale which you gave me in your last. We cannot too much regret that such instances of duplicity and folly are ever exhibited. They are alike disgraceful to both sexes, and demonstrate the debasing and fatal tendency of the passions, when suffered to predominate.

Your observations upon our sex I believe to be just, though many would probably deem them severe. However, I think it not much to the honor of the masculine character, which the God of nature designed for a defence and safeguard to female virtue and happiness, to take advantage of the tender affection of the unsuspecting and too credulous fair; and, in return for her love and confidence, perfidiously to destroy her peace of mind, and deprive her of that reputation, which might have rendered her a useful and ornamental member of society. True, we ought to take warning by such examples of treachery and deceit; yet, how much more conducive to the honor and happiness of our species, were there no occasion to apprehend such ungenerous requitals of our sincerity and frankness!

---

4. Matthew 26:41. Foster's paraphrase of Jesus' instructions to Peter in the Garden of Gethsemane, just prior to his arrest and crucifixion. Before the night is through, Peter denies his association with Jesus.

Yesterday, my mamma took the liberty to read that part of your letter, which contains the story of Clarinda, to her pupils, and to make such comments upon it as the subject suggested; during which we could not but observe the extreme emotion of one of the misses, a most amiable girl of about sixteen. When the paragraph respecting Clarinda's disowning her child was read, she hastily rose, and in broken accents begged leave to withdraw. This was granted, without any inquiry into the cause; though our curiosity, as you may well suppose, was much excited. After we were dismissed, my mamma prevailed on her to tell the reason of her agitation.

"I am," said she, "the illegitimate offspring of parents, whom I am told are people of fortune and fashion. The fear of disgrace overcame the dictates of natural affection, and induced my mother to abandon me in my infancy. She accordingly gave me away, with a large sum of money, which she vainly imagined would procure me kind and good treatment. But, unhappily for me, the people to whom I was consigned, availing themselves of their security from inspection and inquiry, abused the trust reposed in them, and exposed me to the greatest hardships. As they were persons of vulgar minds and unfeeling hearts, they did not commiserate my friendless condition. My quick sensibility incurred their displeasure or derision. I was often insultingly reproached with the misfortune of my birth; while the tears which these ungenerous reflections extorted from me, were either mocked or punished. I had a thirst for knowledge; but they allowed me no time for acquiring it, alleging that they could not support me in idleness, but that I must earn my living, as they did their's, by hard labour. Oppressed by these insults, I bore the galling yoke of their authority with the utmost impatience. When screened from observation, my tears flowed without restraint; and the idea of my parents' cruelty, in thus subjecting me to infamy and wretchedness, continually haunted my imagination. Sometimes I fancied my mother in view, and; exposing my tattered raiment, expostulated with her concerning the indignities I suffered, and the unreasonable hardship of leaving me to bear all the punishment of my guilty birth! At other times I painted to myself a father, in some gentleman of pleasing aspect; and fondly indulged the momentary transport of throwing myself at the feet of one, whom I could call by that venerable and endearing name! Too soon, however, did the reverse of parental tenderness awake me from my delusive reveries.

"In this manner I lingered away my existence, till I was twelve years old; when going, one day, to the house of a gentleman in the neighbourhood, to which I was often sent to sell herbs, and other trifles, I was directed into the parlour, where the most beautiful sight in nature opened to my view; while the contrast between my own situation, and that of children blessed with affectionate parents, gave

me the most painful sensations. The lady of the house was surrounded by her four sons, the eldest of whom was reading lessons, which she most pathetically inculcated upon all. As the door was open, I stood some minutes unobserved; and was so delighted with the tender accents in which her instructions were imparted, and the cheerful obedience with which they were received, that I had no disposition to interrupt them.

"At length I was seen, and bid to come in. But, when questioned about my errand, I was so absorbed in the contemplation of maternal and filial love, exhibited in this happy group, that my tongue refused utterance, and I burst into tears. The children gathered around, and inquired what ailed the poor little girl? But when the lady took me by the hand, and kindly asked what was the matter, I could not restrain or conceal my feelings. When my tears had relieved me, I related the cause of my grief; describing my own situation, and the effect which its contrast had produced on my mind.

"She was affected by my story, and seemed pleased with my sensibility; while the children lamented my misfortunes, and artlessly requested their mamma to let me come and live with them.

"Little did I then expect so great a favour; but to my surprise, as well as joy, Mrs.——, the lady of whom I have been speaking, and by whom I am put under your care, came, a few days after, and asked the people where I lived, if they were willing to part with me. By their consent she took me home, and has ever since treated me like a child.

"I am now happy beyond expression. My gratitude to my benefactress, who, guided by a wise and good Providence, has snatched me from obscurity and misery, and given me so many advantages for improvement, is unbounded.

"But the idea that any helpless innocent should be unnaturally exposed to the sufferings which I have experienced, is insupportably distressing to my imagination.

"Let my story, if possible, be told to Clarinda, that she may be induced to have compassion upon her defenceless offspring."

You are at liberty, therefore, my dear Julia, to make what use you please of this letter. I shall make no comments upon the subject of it, nor add any thing more to its length, but that I am affectionately your's.

MARIA WILLIAMS.

## To Miss ANNA WILLIAMS.

<div align="right">SALEM.</div>

DEAR ANNA,

My contemplated visit to Harmony-Grove must be deferred. A severe illness has lately confined my mamma to her chamber. This claimed all my time and attention, and called me to a new scene of care; that of a family, which I was obliged to superintend during her indisposition. Her recovery has, at length, restored tranquillity and joy to our abode; but she has not yet resumed the direction of her household affairs. To this, she tells me, she is reconciled by the hope, that experience may render me an adept in domestic economy. Indeed, Anna, I think this an essential branch of female education; and I question whether it can be acquired by mere speculation. To me it is plain, that every lady ought to have some practice in the management of a family, before she takes upon herself the important trust.

Do not many of the mistakes and infelicities of life arise from a deficiency in this point?

Young ladies of fashion are not obliged to the task, and have too seldom any inclination to perform duties which require so much time and attention; and with which, perhaps, they have injudiciously been taught to connect the idea of servility. Hence it is, that when called to preside over families, they commit many errors, during their novitiate,[1] at least, which are alike detrimental to their interest and happiness. How necessary is it, then, to avoid this complication of evils by a seasonable application to those offices of housewifery, which may one day become our province.

Early rising, I find a great assistance in my present occupation. It is almost incredible how much may be gained by a diligent improvement of those hours which are but too commonly lost in sleep. I arose this morning with the dawn. The serenity of the sky and the fragrance of the air invited me abroad. The calmness which universally prevailed served to tranquillize my mind, while the receding shades of night, and the rising beams of day formed a contrasted assemblage of the beautiful, the splendid, the solemn, and the sublime. The silence which pervaded the surrounding scenery was interrupted only by the melody of the feathered songsters, who seemed to rejoice in this undisturbed opportunity of praising their Maker. My heart expanded with gratitude and love to the all-bountiful Author of nature; and so absorbed was I in the most delightful meditations, that I saw with regret the hour approaching which must again call

---

1. Training period; time spent as a novice.

me to the active duties of domestic and social life. These, however, are objects of real moment, and cannot innocently be disregarded. They give a relish to amusement, and even to devotion, which neither the dissipated nor the recluse can know. Adieu.

CLEORA PARTRIDGE.

### To Miss HARRIOT HENLY.

BEVERLY.

DEAR HARRIOT,

I sincerely thank you for your affectionate letter, by the last post, and for the book with which it was accompanied. The very title is sufficient to rouse the feelings and attract the attention of the patriotic mind. Beacon-Hill[1] claims a conspicuous place in the history of our country. The subject of this poem must be highly interesting to every true American; while the genius it displays cannot fail to gratify every poetical taste. Philenia's[2] talents justly entitle her to a rank among the literary ornaments of Columbia.[3]

I have been reviewing Millot's Elements of Ancient and Modern History;[4] and recommend it to your re-perusal. It is undoubtedly the most useful compendium extant. The tedious minuteness and prolix[5] details of sieges and battles, negociations and treaties, which fatigue the reader and oppress the memory, in most works of the kind, are happily avoided in this; while the elegance, simplicity, conciseness and perspicuity of the style, render it intelligible to every capacity, and pleasing to every taste. To those who have a relish for history, but want leisure to give it full scope, Millot is well calculated to afford both information and entertainment. It is an objection, commonly made by our sex to studies of this nature, that they are dry and elaborate; that they yield little or no exercise to the more sprightly faculties of the mind; that the attention is confined to an uninteresting and barren detail of facts, while the imagination pants in vain for the flowery wreaths of decoration.

---

1. A historic neighborhood of Boston on property settled by William Blaxton in the 1620s; Blaxton later sold his property to Puritan settlers.
2. Harriot has sent Matilda a copy of *Beacon Hill. A Local Poem* (1797), dedicated to Revolutionary soldiers and attributed to Philenia, a pseudonym for American author Sarah Wentworth Morton (1759–1846). Morton was at the center of a well-known scandal when her husband and sister had an illicit affair, leading to the latter's suicide and a public inquest. The novel *The Power of Sympathy* (1789) was loosely based on these events, and was for some time believed to be penned by Morton; in reality, the author was William Hill Brown. See an excerpt on pp. 307–14 of this Norton Critical Edition.
3. I.e., the United States.
4. Claude-François-Xavier Millot (1726–1785) published his *Éléments d'histoire générale ancienne et moderne* between 1772 and 1783.
5. Lengthy.

This is a plausible excuse for those who read only for amusement, and are willing to sacrifice reason, and the enlargement of their minds, to the gaudy phantom of a day; but it can never be satisfactory to the person, who wishes to combine utility with pleasure, and dignity with relaxation. History improves the understanding, and furnishes a knowledge of human nature and human events, which may be useful; as well as ornamental, through life. "History," says the late celebrated Ganganelli, "brings together all ages and all mankind into one point of view. Presenting a charming landscape to the mental eye, it gives colour to the thoughts, soul to the actions, and life to the dead; and brings them again upon the stage of the world, as if they were again living; but with this difference, that it is not to flatter, but to judge them."[6]

The duties and avocations of our sex will not often admit of a close and connected course of reading. Yet a general knowledge of the most necessary subjects may undoubtedly be gained, even in our leisure hours; provided we bestow them not on works of mere taste and fancy, but on the perusal of books calculated to enrich the understanding with durable acquisitions.

The sincerest wishes for your health and happiness glow in the breast of your affectionate

MATILDA FIELDING.

## To Miss MARIA WILLIAMS.

BOSTON.

MY DEAR MARIA,

Since I wrote you last, I have made an agreeable visit to my good friend, Sylvia Star. After rambling in the fields and gardens till we were fatigued, we went into her brother's library. He was in a studious attitude, but gave us a polite reception. We are come to solicit a portion of your repast, Amintor,[1] said I. Be so kind as to furnish us with some instructive page, which combines entertainment and utility; and while it informs the mind, delights the imagination. I am not happy enough to know your taste respecting books, said he; and, therefore, may not make a proper selection. Here, however, is an author highly spoken of by a lady, who has lately added to the number of literary publications; handing me Sterne's Sentimental Journey.[2] I

---

6. Ganganelli, Pope Clement XIV (1705–1774), *Interesting Letters of Pope Clement XIV* (1777).
1. *Daphne and Amintor*, a 1765 comic opera by Isaac Bickerstaff, had been performed in Massachusetts during the 1790s. "Amintor": defender.
2. Laurence Sterne's novel *A Sentimental Journey Through France and Italy* (1768) includes several amorous episodes.

closed and returned the book. You have indeed mistaken my taste, said I. Wit, blended with indelicacy, never meets my approbation. While the fancy is allured, and the passions awakened, by this pathetic humourist, the foundations of virtue are insidiously undermined, and modest dignity insensibly betrayed. Well, said he, smiling, perhaps you are seriously inclined. If so, this volume of sermons may possibly please you. Still less, rejoined I. The serious mind must turn with disgust from the levity which pervades these discourses, and from the indecent flow of mirth and humour, which converts even the sacred writings, and the most solemn subjects of religion, into frolic and buffoonery. Since such is your opinion of this celebrated writer, said he, I will not insult your feelings by offering you his Tristram Shandy.[3] But here is another wit, famous for his *"purity."* Yes, said I, if obscene and vulgar ideas, if ill-natured remarks and filthy allusions be purity, Swift[4] undoubtedly bears the palm from all his contemporaries. As far as grammatical correctness and simplicity of language can deserve the epithet, his advocates may enjoy their sentiments unmolested; but, in any other sense of the word, he has certainly no claim to *"purity."* I conceive his works, notwithstanding, to be much less pernicious in their tendency, than those of Sterne. They are not so enchanting in their nature, nor so subtle in their effects. In the one, the noxious insinuations of licentious wit are concealed under the artful blandishments of sympathetic sensibility; while we at once recoil from the rude assault which is made upon our delicacy, by the roughness and vulgarity of the other.

Choose then, said Amintor, for yourself. I availed myself of his offer, and soon fixed my eyes upon Doctor Belknap's History of New-Hampshire, and American Biography;[5] both of which I have since read with the greatest satisfaction.

By this judicious and impartial historian, we are led, from its first settlement, to trace the progress of the infant colony. We accompany its inhabitants in their enterprizes, their dangers, their toils, and their successes. We take an interest in their prosperity; and we tremble at the dreadful outrages of the barbarous foe. Our imagination is again recalled to the gradual advance of population and agriculture. We behold the wilderness blooming as the rose, and the haunts of savage beasts, and more savage men, converted into fruitful fields and pleasant habitations. The arts and sciences flourish; peace and harmony are restored; and we are astonished at the amazing contrast, produced in little more than a single century!

3. Laurence Sterne, *The Life and Opinions of Tristram Shandy, Gentleman* (1759–67).
4. Jonathan Swift (1667–1745), a satirist and novelist best remembered today for such works as *Gulliver's Travels* (1726) and *A Modest Proposal* (1729).
5. Jeremy Belknap (1744–1798) published the three-volume *History of New Hampshire* (1784, 1791, 1792), followed by the two-volume *American Biography* (1794, 1798).

When we turn to the American Biography, gratitude glows in our bosoms towards those intrepid and active adventurers, who traversed a trackless ocean, explored an unknown region, and laid the foundation of empire and independence in this western hemisphere. The undaunted resolution, and cool, determined wisdom of Columbus,[6] fill us with profound admiration. We are constrained to pay a tribute of just applause to the generosity of a female mind, exemplified in Isabella,[7] who, to surmount every obstacle, nobly consented to sacrifice even her personal ornaments to the success of this glorious expedition.

The daring spirit of Captain Smith,[8] and the prudence, policy, and magnanimity of his conduct to the treacherous natives, and to his equally treacherous and ungrateful countrymen, exhibit an example of patriotism and moderation, which at once commands our applause, and interests our feelings. While we tremble and recoil at his dreadful situation, when bending his neck to receive the murderous stroke of death, the native virtues of our sex suddenly reanimate our frame; and, with sensations of rapture, we behold compassion, benevolence, and humanity triumphant even in a savage breast; and conspicuously displayed in the conduct of the amiable, though uncivilized Pocahontas![9] Nor are the other characters in this work uninteresting: and I am happy to find that the same masterly pen is still industriously employed for the public good;[1] and that a second volume of American Biography is now in the press.

In reviewing this letter, I am astonished at my own presumption, in undertaking to play the critic. My imagination has outstripped my judgment; but I will arrest its career, and subscribe myself most affectionately your's.

SOPHIA MANCHESTER.

## To Miss ANNA WILLIAMS.

BOSTON.

DEAR ANNA

I retired, after breakfast this morning, determined to indulge myself in my favourite amusement, and write you a long letter. I had just

---

6. Christopher Columbus (1451–1506).
7. Isabella I (1451–1504), Queen of Castile and León, responsible for funding Columbus's expedition.
8. Captain John Smith (1580–1631), a leader of the Virginia Colony at Jamestown between 1608 and 1609.
9. Pocahontas (c. 1595–1617), a member of the Powhatan Confederacy credited with assisting European settlers at Jamestown in what is now Virginia.
1. How vain are our expectations! While the types were setting for this very page, Dr. Belknap suddenly expired in a fit.—*Printer.* [*Original publisher's note*]. Rev. Jeremy Belknap died June 20, 1798. Foster and Belknap shared a publisher in Thomas and Andrews.

mended my pen and folded my paper, when I was informed that three ladies waited for me in the parlour. I stepped down and found Lucinda P——, Fulvia F——, and Delia S——. They were gaily dressed, and still more gaily disposed. "We called," said they, "to invite you, Miss Maria, to join our party for a shopping tour." Loath to have the ideas dissipated, which I had collected in my pericranium,[1] for the purpose of transmitting to a beloved sister, I declined accepting their invitation; alleging that I had no occasion to purchase any thing to-day; and therefore begged to be excused from accompanying them. They laughed at my reason for not engaging in the expedition. "Buying," said their principal speaker, "is no considerable part of our plan, I assure you. Amusement is what we are after. We frankly acknowledge it a delightful gratification of our vanity to traverse Cornhill,[2] to receive the obsequious congees,[3] and to call forth the gallantry and activity of the beaux behind the counter; who, you must know, are extremely alert when we belles appear. The waving of our feathers, and the attractive airs we assume, command the profoundest attention, both of master and apprentices; who, duped by our appearance, suffer less brilliant customers to wait, or even to depart without notice, till we have tumbled over and refused half the goods in the shop. We then bid a very civil adieu; express our regret at having given so much trouble; are assured, in return, that it has been rather a pleasure; and leave them their labour for their pains."

A most insignificant amusement this, said I to myself! How little can it redound to the honor and happiness of these unthinking girls, thus to squander their time in folly's giddy maze! They undoubtedly wish to attract eclat;[4] but they would do well to remember those words of the satirist, which, with the alteration of a single term, may be applied to them:

> "*Columbia's* daughters, much more fair than nice,
> Too fond of admiration, lose their price;
> Worn in the public eye, give cheap delight
> To throngs, and tarnish to the sated sight."[5]

Viewing their conduct in this light, I withstood their solicitations, though I palliated my refusal in such a manner as to give no umbrage.[6]

1. In popular usage, the skull or brain generally.
2. A Boston shopping district from the eighteenth century onward.
3. Ceremonious bows.
4. Publicity.
5. Foster amends Young's lines "Britannia's daughters, much more fair, than nice" to reflect her American audience. See *Love of Fame*, Satire 5.
6. Offense.

Of all expedients to kill time, this appears to me, as I know it will to you, the most ridiculous and absurd.

What possible satisfaction can result from such a practice? It certainly fatigues the body; and is it any advantage to the mind? Does it enlarge the understanding, inspire useful ideas, or furnish a source of pleasing reflection? True, it may gratify a vitiated imagination, and exhilarate a light and trifling mind. But these ought to be restrained and regulated by reason and judgment, rather than indulged.

I wish those ladies, who make pleasure the supreme object of their pursuit, and argue in vindication of their conduct, that

"Pleasure is good, and *they* for pleasure made,"

would confine themselves to that species which

"Neither blushes, nor expires."[7]

The domestic virtues, if duly cultivated, might certainly occupy those hours, which they are now solicitous to dissipate, both with profit and delight. "But it is time enough to be domesticated," say they, "when we are placed at the head of families, and necessarily confined to care and labour."

Should not the mind, however, be seasonably inured to the sphere of life which Providence assigns us?

"To guide the pencil, turn th' instructive page;
To lend new flavour to the fruitful year,
And heighten nature's dainties; in their race
To rear their graces into second life;
To give society its highest taste;
Well-ordered home man's best delight to make;
And, by submissive wisdom, modest skill,
With every gentle care-eluding art,
To raise the virtues, animate the bliss,
And sweeten all the toils of human life:
This be the female dignity and praise."[8]

A proper attention to these necessary duties and embellishments would not only correct this rambling disposition, but happily leave neither leisure nor temptation for its indulgence.

I intended to have given you some account of my agreeable visit here; but the *chit-chat* of the ladies I have mentioned, has occupied a large portion of my time this morning, and an engagement to dine abroad claims the rest.

---

7. An adaptation from Young's *The Complaint*: "Pleasure is good, and Man for Pleasure made; / But Pleasure full of Glory, as of Joy; / Pleasure, which neither blushes, nor expires."
8. Thomson, *The Seasons,* "Autumn."

I hope soon to embrace you in our beloved retirement, and again to enjoy the sweets of my native home.

"Had I the choice of sublunary good,
What could I wish that I possess not there?
Health, leisure, means t' improve it, friendship, peace."[9]

My most dutiful affections await mamma; and my kind regards attend the young ladies residing with her. How great a share of my ardent love is at your command need not be renewedly testified by

MARIA WILLIAMS.

### *To Miss* SOPHIA MANCHESTER.

NEWBURY-PORT.

The extracts which you transmitted to me in your last kind letter, my dear Sophia, from your favourite author, Doctor Young,[1] corresponded exactly with the solemnity infused into my mind by the funeral of a neighbour, from which I had just returned.

I agree with you, that the Night-Thoughts are good devotional exercises. It is impossible to read them with that degree of attention which they merit, without being affected by the important and awful subjects on which they treat. But Young, after all, is always too abstruse,[2] and in many instances, too gloomy for me. The most elaborate application is necessary to the comprehension of his meaning and design; which, when discovered, often tend rather to depress than to elevate the spirits.

Thompson is much better adapted to my taste. Sentiment, elegance, perspicuity, and sublimity are all combined in his Seasons. What an inimitable painter! How admirably he describes the infinitely variegated beauties and operations of nature! To the feeling and susceptible heart they are presented in the strongest light. Nor is the energy of his language less perceivable, when he describes the Deity riding on the wings of the wind, and directing the stormy tempest.

"How chang'd the scene! In blazing height of noon,
The sun, oppress'd, is plung'd in thickest gloom;
Still horror reigns, a dismal twilight round,
Of struggling night and day malignant mix'd.

9. From William Cowper, *The Task: A Poem in Six Books* (1785).
1. In both *The Coquette* and *The Boarding School*, Foster quotes extensively from works by Edward Young (c. 1683–1765), a British poet, dramatist, and churchman. Young was a favorite writer of the devout but is also generally understood as a precursor to the Romantics.
2. Difficult.

Far to the hot equator crowding fast,
Where, highly rarefy'd, the yielding air
Admits their stream, incessant vapours roll,
Amazing clouds on clouds continual heap'd;
Or whirl'd tempestuous by the gusty wind,
Or silent, borne along, heavy and slow,
With the big stores of steaming oceans charg'd.
Meantime, amid these upper seas, condens'd
Around the cold aërial mountain's brow,
And by conflicting winds together dash'd,
The thunder holds his black tremendous throne.
From cloud to cloud the rending lightning rage;
Till, in the furious elemental war
Dissolv'd, the whole precipitated mass
Unbroken floods and torrents pours."[3]

Conscious of our own weakness and dependence, we can hardly fail to adore and to fear that Divine Power, whose agency this imagery exhibits to our minds. Nor are the devout affections of our hearts less excited, when we behold the same glorious Being arrayed in love, and accommodating the regular succession of summer and winter, feed-time and harvest to our convenience and comfort. When nature, obedient to his command, revives the vegetable world, and diffuses alacrity[4] and joy throughout the animal, and even rational creation, we involuntarily exclaim with the poet,

"HAIL, SOURCE OF BEING! UNIVERSAL SOUL
Of heaven and earth! Essential Presence, hail!
To Thee I bend the knee; to THEE my thoughts
Continual climb; who, with a master hand,
Hast the great whole into perfection touch'd.
By THEE the various vegetative tribes,
Wrapt in a filmy net, and clad with leaves,
Draw the live ether, and imbibe the dew.
By THEE, dispos'd into congenial soils,
Stands each attractive plant, and sucks, and swells
The juicy tide; a twining mass of tubes.
At THY command, the vernal sun awakes
The torpid sap, detruded to the root
By wintry winds; which now in fluent dance,
And lively fermentation, mounting, spreads
All this innumerous-colour'd scene of things."[5]

---

3. Thomson, *The Seasons*, "Summer."
4. Cheerful readiness.
5. Thomson, *The Seasons*, "Spring."

Aided in our observations by this pathetic and pious writer, our hearts beat responsive to the sentiments of gratitude, which he indirectly, yet most forcibly inculcates in that devout address to the Supreme Parent:

> "——Were every faultering tongue of man,
> ALMIGHTY FATHER! silent in thy praise,
> Thy works themselves would raise a general voice,
> Even in the depth of solitary woods,
> By human foot untrod; proclaim thy power,
> And to the quire celestial THEE resound,
> Th' eternal Cause, Support, and End of all!"[6]

By this beautiful poem we are allured to the study of nature, and to the contemplation of nature's God. Our hearts glow with devotion and love to the sovereign Lord and Benefactor of the universe; and we are drawn, by the innumerable displays of his goodness, to the practice of virtue and religion.

You may, possibly, call me an enthusiast. Be it so. Yet I contend for the honor, but especially for the privilege, of being a cheerful one. For I think we dishonor our heavenly Father by attaching any thing gloomy or forbidding to his character. In the participation of divine blessings, let us rather exercise a thankful, and contented disposition.

I remain your's most affectionately.

CAROLINE LITTLETON.

## To Mrs. WILLIAMS.

BOSTON.

DEAR MADAM,

By *her* desire, in conjunction with my own inclination, I inform you that Harriot Henly is no more——Yesterday she gave her hand, and renounced her name together; threw aside the sprightly girl we have been so long accustomed to admire, and substituted in her place the dignified and respectable head of a family, in Mrs. Farmington.

Have I not lost my amiable friend and associate? Will not her change of situation tend to lessen our intercourse, and to alienate our affections?

When I contemplate the social circle, so firmly cemented in the bands of friendship, at the boarding school, where the most perfect harmony, ease and satisfaction presided, I recoil at the idea of

---

6. Thomson, *The Seasons*, "Summer."

becoming less dear, less interesting, and less necessary to each other. It is with the utmost reluctance that I admit the idea of rivals to that affection and benevolence which we have, so long, and so sincerely interchanged.

The charm however is broken. Harriot is already married; and my friends are extremely solicitous that I should follow her example. But in a connexion which requires so many precautions before it is formed, and such uninterrupted circumspection and prudence afterwards; the great uncertainty of the event inspires me with timidity and apprehension.

Harriot put into my hands, and I read with pleasure, the book which you recommended to her on the subject. But still we wished for your instruction and advice. The sentiments of a person so dear and interesting to us, are particularly calculated to engage our attention, and influence our conduct. Relying, too, on your judgment and experience, your forming pen may render us more worthy objects of attachment.

We, however, unite in assuring you of our gratitude for all past favours; and in presenting our sincere regards to the young ladies.

I am, with great respect, your affectionate and grateful

LAURA GUILFORD.

## To Miss LAURA GUILFORD.

HARMONY-GROVE.

DEAR LAURA,

The obligations under which you lay me, by your generous confidence, and affectionate expressions of regard, induce me again to assume the Preceptress towards you, and to gratify your wishes, by imparting my sentiments on your present situation and prospects.

I am told by my daughter, who had the honor of bearing your letter, that you are, what I always expected you would be, an object of general admiration. Yet, I trust, your good sense will enable you duly to distinguish and treat the several candidates for your favour.

It is, indeed, my young friend, a matter of the most serious consequence, which lies upon your mind, and awakens your anxiety. Your friends are studious of your welfare, and kindly concerned that the important die on which the happiness of your life depends, should be judiciously cast. You doubtless remember, that I discoursed upon this subject in my concluding lessons to your class.

Disparity of tempers, among other things which were then suggested, and which you will doubtless recollected, was represented,

as tending to render life uncomfortable. But there are other dispari-
ties which may be equally hostile to your peace.

Disparity of years is very apt to occasion the indulgence of pas-
sions destructive of conjugal felicity. The great difference between
the sprightly fancy, vivacity, and enterprize of youth, and the deliber-
ate caution, phlegmatic[1] coldness, and sententious[2] wisdom of age,
render them very unpleasant companions to each other. Marriage
between persons of these opposite descriptions is commonly the
result of pecuniary motives, with one party, at least: the suspicion of
this, in the other, must necessarily produce discontent, uneasiness,
and disaffection.

Age is naturally jealous of respect, and apprehensive of being
slighted. The most trifling and unmeaning inattentions will there-
fore be construed amiss. For an excessive desire of being objects of
supreme regard is almost invariably accompanied with a strong per-
suasion of being the reverse. Hence accusations, reproaches, and
restraints, on the one side, produce disgust, resentment and alien-
ation on the other, till mutual and unceasing wretchedness ensue.
Indeed, where interest alone, without this inequality of years, is
the principal inducement, marriage is seldom happy. Esteem and
love are independent of wealth and its appendages. They are not to
be sold or bought. The conjugal relation is so near and interesting;
the mind, as well as the person, is so intimately concerned in it,
that something more substantial and engaging than gold is requi-
site to make it a blessing.

Marriage, being the commencement of a domestic life, beside the
many agreeable circumstances attending it, has its peculiar cares
and troubles, which require the solace of a companion actuated by
better principles, and possessed of more amiable endowments than
outward splendour and magnificence can afford. In the hour of sick-
ness and distress, riches, it is true, can bestow bodily comforts and
cordials; but can they be made an equivalent for the tender sympa-
thy, the endearing kindness, and the alleviating attention of a bosom
friend, kindly assiduous to ease our pains, animate our prospects,
and beguile the languid moments which elude all other consolations?
The sorrows as well as the joys of a family state, are often such as
none but a bosom friend can participate. The heart must be engaged
before it can repose with ease and confidence. To a lady of sensibility,
the confinement of the body, without the consent and union of
according minds, must be a state of inexpressible wretchedness.

Another situation, not less to be deplored, is a connexion with
the immoral and profane.

1. Self-possessed, unemotional.
2. Moralizing.

How shocking must it be, to hear that sacred NAME, which you revere and love, constantly treated with levity and irreverence! And how painful the necessity of being constrained, for the sake of peace, to witness in silence; and without even the appearance of disapprobation, the most shameful outrages upon religion and virtue! May you never taste the bitterness of this evil!

Intemperance[3] is a vice, which one would imagine no lady would overlook in a suitor. But, strange to tell! there are those, even among our own sex, who think and speak of inebriation in the other, at the jovial and well-furnished board,[4] as a mark of conviviality and good fellowship!

What, then, is the distinguishing badge of humanity? Can that reason, which alone raises us superior to the brute creation, be wantonly sacrificed with impunity; yea, with reputation?

How degrading and how dreadful must this enormity appear to an interested, affectionate, and virtuous wife! What agonizing pangs of mortification and anguish must she endure, when she meets him, in whose society she delights, whose return she has anticipated with impatience, and whose happiness and honor are the moving springs of her life, intoxicated with wine; the powers of his mind suspended by the poisonous cup, and every faculty absorbed in the deadly draught! What a perpetual source of dread and apprehension must hence arise; and how often must the blush of indignant virtue and wounded delicacy be called forth!

The gamester[5] is an equally dangerous companion. His family is robbed, not only of his company and his talents, but of that property, to the benefit of which they have an indisputable claim. His earnings are squandered among worthless and profligate associates abroad; while the faithful partner of his life, and perhaps, too, a rising offspring, languish at home for want of bread!

How fatal is the tendency of such examples! How can that father inculcate the duties of piety, virtue and decency, who exhibits the reverse of each in his own conduct? And under what an unspeakable disadvantage must that mother labour, in the instruction and education of her children, whose admonitions, counsels, and directions are practically counteracted by him who ought to bear an equal share of the burden! The government and superintendence of a family are objects of such magnitude and importance, that the union and co-operation of its heads are indispensably necessary. It is a little commonwealth;[6] and if internal feuds and dissensions arise, anarchy and confusion must ensue.

---

3. Lacking moderation, commonly used as a synonym for drunkenness.
4. A table with plentiful food.
5. Gambler.
6. A body founded for the common good.

Domestic happiness is the foundation of every other species. At times, indeed, we may enjoy ourselves abroad, among our friends; but a good heart will return home, as to the seat of felicity.

> "————Home is the resort
> Of love, of joy, of peace and plenty, where,
> Supporting and supported, polish'd friends
> And dear relations mingle into bliss."[7]

Since so much, then, depends upon a judicious choice, how important is it, that you examine well before you decide; and that you dispense with no quality in the man to whom you shall give your hand, which is essential to the virtue and happiness of your life. For this purpose, consult your judgment, rather than your fancy; and suffer not superficial accomplishments, but solid merit to preponderate.

I have now endeavoured to point out the most apparent and threatening dangers to which you may be exposed. But though these are avoided, many unforeseen accidents will doubtless occur to cloud your sanguine hopes. These, when there are no vices to produce them, may arise from follies, and from the indulgence of erroneous expectations. Little misunderstandings sometimes occasion disagreements which terminate in coldness and disaffection, and plant a root of bitterness which can hardly be eradicated.

Let prudence, therefore, be your pole-star,[8] when you enter the married state. Watch with the greatest circumspection over yourself; and always exercise the tenderest affection, the most unwearied patience, and the most cheerful acquiescence in the treatment of your companion. Guard especially against being affected by those little inattentions and foibles, which too often give pain and umbrage without design; and produce those remonstrances,[9] criminations, and retorts, which are the great inlets of strife, and bane of love.

You must bear, with calmness, every thing that the sincerest desire of peace can dictate; and studiously avoid every expression, and even look, which may irritate and offend. Your own happiness, you will consider so intimately connected with that of your husband, as to be inseparable; and consequently, that all your hopes of comfort in this life, and perhaps, too, in the next, depend upon your conducting with propriety and wisdom towards him.

I take the liberty, through you, to convey my congratulations to Mrs. Farmington. May her change of condition be happy, to the full extent of our most sanguine expectations, and benevolent wishes. I fully intended writing her on the subject, but have unwarily

---

7. Thomson, *The Seasons*, "Autumn."
8. Guide.
9. Protests.

bestowed so much time upon you, that for the present, I must forego the pleasure. Some things in this letter, which you will doubtless communicate, are applicable to her case. These she will receive as friendly hints from me; and I am confident that her known discretion will continue to shed a benign and engaging influence upon her whole deportment, and render her uniformly respected and beloved.

The bearer is waiting, and I can only add, that I remain your sincere and affectionate friend.

MARY WILLIAMS.

### *To Miss* CLEORA PARTRIDGE.

BOSTON.

DEAR CLEORA,

The pleasing hope with which you inspired me, when we parted last, of receiving a visit from you in town, has been constantly cherished. I have anticipated your arrival with the utmost impatience; but have endeavoured, notwithstanding, to beguile the slow-paced hours by a useful and pleasing occupation; the revision of my geographical studies.

My papa has kindly procured me Doctor Morse's last, and much improved edition of Universal Geography,[1] which, with the assistance of a pair of globes he possessed, has afforded me the most delightful entertainment. When at school, I thought this the most agreeable study allotted me; never deeming it a task, but an amusement.

It affords me, as it must every true American, the sincerest pleasure to be furnished with the means of acquiring this favourite science, by my own countryman; and the spirit of Columbian independence exults in my bosom, at the idea of being able to gain an accurate acquaintance with my own and other countries, without recourse to the labours of foreigners.

I think the present generation under special obligations to the active industry of Dr. Morse, in providing us with that necessary and rich fund of information, which his Geography and Gazetteer contain. From these sources we may derive a sufficient knowledge of the world we inhabit, without departing from our domestic sphere.

Come, then, my dear Cleora, and without fatigue or expense, we will make the tour of the globe together. After investigating the

---

1. Jedidiah Morse (1761–1826) published his *American Geography* (1789) as a nationalist enterprise, to reflect the values and needs of American citizens. He followed this in 1797 with *Universal Geography of the United States*, accompanied by a gazetteer, i.e., a geographical directory.

local situation of different and distant climes, we will turn to the historic page, and examine the manners, government, character, and improvements of their inhabitants. We will traverse the frozen wastes of the frigid zones, and the burning sands of the equatorial region; then return and bless the temperate and happy medium in which we are placed; and, casting an eye around, exult in our peculiar advantages of soil and situation, peace and good government, virtue and religion.

The fine mornings of this season afford many delightful hours, before the heat of the day relaxes the mind and enervates[2] the body. Come, then, enjoy and improve these, in concert with your faithful and affectionate friend,

JULIA GREENFIELD.

*To Miss* MATILDA FIELDING.

HARMONY-GROVE.

DEAR MATILDA,

Last Thursday, after having concluded the usual occupations and sedentary amusements of the day, I walked out, towards evening, to enjoy the benefit of a cool and fragrant air, and the serenity and beauty of those rural scenes which have a powerful tendency to soothe and tranquillize the mind. When I had rambled in the fields, to a considerable distance, I crossed into the road, to return home free from the inconvenience of the dew, which had begun to fall.

I had not proceeded far, when I observed a female, who had the appearance of youth and misfortune, sitting by the wall in a pensive attitude, with an infant in her lap. When I approached her, she arose, and in the most humble and pathetic accents, besought me to direct her to some shelter, where she might repose her weary limbs for the night. The aspect and language of distress awakened my compassion. To know she really needed charity, was a sufficient inducement with me to bestow it, without scrupulously inquiring whether she deserved it or not. I therefore told her to follow me, and I would conduct her to a lodging.

As we walked on, I questioned her respecting the place of her nativity, her parentage, and the reason of her being reduced to the situation in which I had found her. She informed me that she was born in Ireland; that her parents brought her into this country, before her remembrance; that while she was very young, they both died, and left her to the protection and mercy of strangers; that she

2. Weakens.

was bandied[1] from one to another, in the village where Providence had cast her lot, till she was able to earn her own living: "and since that time," said she, "I believe the character of an honest and industrious girl will not be refused me." How then, said I, came you by this incumbrance? pointing to the child. "In that," replied she, "I am verily guilty. Brought up in ignorance of those principles of decency, virtue and religion, which have kept *you* innocent, Madam, I was ruined by a deceitful man, who, under the mask of love, and with the most solemn promises of marriage, betrayed my confidence, and left me to reap the bitter fruits of my credulity. The woman where I lived, when she discovered my situation, ordered me to leave her house immediately. It was no matter, said she, how much I suffered, or what became of me. On my own head, she told me, my iniquity should fall; she would not lighten the burden, if it were in her power.

"Some of the neighbours informed me, that she had reason to be severe upon my fault, being once in the same condemnation herself.

"Having no friend who could assist me, I applied to the selectmen[2] of the town, who provided for me till I was able to work, and then told me I must shift for myself; offering, however, to keep the child, which I refused, being determined it should never suffer for want of a mother's care, while I had life.

"I am now wandering in pursuit of employment, that the labour of my hands may support myself and little one. This has been often denied me, either for fear my child should be troublesome, or because my character was suspected. I have sometimes suffered so much from fatigue and want, that I have despaired of relief, and heartily wished both myself and my babe in the grave."

On examination, I found her knowledge confined entirely to domestic drudgery; that she had never been taught either to read or write. She appears, notwithstanding, to have good natural sense; and a quickness of apprehension, and readiness of expression, seldom equalled in her sphere of life.

I conducted her into the kitchen, and desired she might have supper, and a bed provided for her. My mamma, whose benevolent heart and liberal hand are always ready to relieve the necessitous, was pleased to approve my conduct; and having kept her through the next day, and observed her disposition and behaviour, hired her as a servant; and we have reason to believe, from her apparent fidelity and grateful exertions, that our kindness will be well repaid. I have even extended my charity further, and undertaken to teach

1. Passed.
2. Elected officials who helped govern New England towns.

her to read. She is very tractable;[3] and I expect to be amply rewarded for my labour, by her improvements.

Indeed, Matilda, it is melancholy to see our fellow-creatures reared up, like the brute creation; neither instructed how to live above their animal appetites, nor how to die as Christians, when they have finished their toilsome career!

This girl is only seventeen. Her age, therefore, as well as her docility and submissiveness, encourage the pleasing hope of restoring her to the paths of rectitude and peace. I shall endeavour, as opportunity offers, to instil into her susceptible mind, the principles of virtue and religion; and, perhaps, I may lead her to the love and practice of both, and render her a useful member of society. Her fate impresses, more forcibly than ever, on my mind, the importance of a good education, and the obligations it confers. Had you or I been subjected to the same ignorance, and the same temptations, who can say that we should have conducted better? How many fall for want of the directing hand of that parental love and friendship, with which we are blessed! Contrasting our situation with her's, how much have *we* to account for, and how inexcusable shall *we* be, if we violate our duty, and forfeit our dignity, as reasonable creatures!

That extreme bitterness and acrimony,[4] which is sometimes indulged, against persons who are unhappily seduced from the way of virtue, may operate as a discouragement to all designs and endeavours to regain it: whereas, the soothing voice of forgiveness, and the consequent prospect of being restored to reputation and usefulness, might rouse the attention, and call forth the exertions of some, at least, who, through despair of retrieving their characters, abandon themselves to vice, and adopt a course, alike disgraceful to their sex, and to human nature.

But, though I advocate the principles of philanthropy and Christian charity, as extending to some very special cases, I am far from supposing this fault generally capable of the least extenuation. Whatever allowance may be made for those, whose ignorance occasions their ruin, no excuse can be offered for others, whose education, and opportunities for knowing the world and themselves, have taught them a better lesson.

I need not, however, be at the pains to enforce this truth upon you: and, as my head is so full of the subject, that I have no disposition to write upon any thing else, I will put an end to this incoherent scroll, by annexing the name of your sincere and faithful friend,

MARIA WILLIAMS.

3. Compliant.
4. Biting sharpness.

## To Miss CAROLINE LITTLETON.

<div align="right">BOSTON.</div>

DEAR CAROLINE,

Happening to be in my chamber, this morning, the maid came running up stairs in such violent haste, as to put herself fairly out of breath. Will you be so kind, Miss Sophia, said she, as to lend me a quarter of a dollar? I put my hand into my pocket, and found I had no small change. I have nothing less than a dollar, Susan, said I; but, if it is a matter of consequence to you, I will go to my mamma, and procure it for you. She was loath to give me that trouble; but, if I would, it would really oblige her very much indeed. Her solicitude excited my curiosity. Will you inform me what you want it for? said I. O yes; she believed it was no harm—But there was a woman in the wood-house, who told fortunes; and she wished to know her's, but could not without the money. A woman who tells fortunes! said I. What fortunes? the past, or the future? The future, to be sure, Ma'am, rejoined she. Ay, how does she know them? said I. Has she been let into the secret designs of Providence? or can she divine the mysteries of fate? She tells fortunes by cards, Ma'am, said she; and I really believe she tells true. Can you imagine, said I, that a knowledge of your destiny in life, is to be gained from any possible arrangement of a pack of cards? Why not, Ma'am? Many people have been told exactly what was to happen. You may depend on it, Susan, said I, you are deceived. The Almighty, who disposes all events according to his sovereign pleasure, does not unveil futurity to mortals, especially to *such* mortals, who, by an idle vicious course of life, counteract his laws, and disregard his authority. I would willingly give you the money, twice told, if you needed it; but I cannot consent to your being imposed on, by this worthless vagrant, who has no other design than to pick your pocket.

The girl departed at these words; and, though I felt an emotion of regret at refusing to gratify her, yet my reason and conscience forbad my being accessary to the fraud.

This curiosity to explore the hidden counsels of the Most High, prevails not only among servants, but even many, from whom better things might be expected, are under its infatuating influence.

The Supreme Being has, for wise and benevolent reasons, concealed from us the future incidents of our lives. A humble reliance on his power and goodness, accompanied with a cheerful submission to the dispensations of his providence, is what the Lord our God requireth of us.

I have heard my mamma relate an anecdote of a particular friend of her's, who was imposed on very seriously in this way.

A gentleman, whom I shall call Sylvander, was very deeply in love with her; but his person, and, much more, his disposition and manners, were extremely disgusting to her. Averse to the very idea of a connexion with him, she accordingly refused his addresses. Yet he had art sufficient to interest her friends in his behalf; who, pitying his situation, endeavoured to soften the heart of the obdurate fair. But in vain they strove to conciliate her affections.

In defiance of all opposition, however, he incessantly obtruded his visits, till she reluctantly admitted them; and being somewhat coquettish, she at times received him more benignly; which flattered his hopes of ultimately accomplishing his wishes. Finding his ardent suit of but little avail, and perceiving that he made but small progress towards gaining her favour, he had recourse to art. Surprising her, one day; in close confabulation[1] with a fortune-teller, the idea immediately struck him, that he might effect, through this mean, what all his assiduity and solicitations could never insure. He communicated his plan to a female friend, who was equally the confident of both parties. Directed by him, she conversed with Sylvia on the subject; professed her belief in the skill of these jugglers; and appeared desirous of taking this measure to learn her fate. Sylvia joined in her opinion and wishes; and away they tripped together on the important errand. Meanwhile, Sylvander had been to the fellow who was to reveal their destinies; and, bribing him to favour the design, left him, instructed what answers to make to their interrogations.

They arrived, and proposed their business. The mediums of information, a pack of cards, were brought forth, and mysteriously arranged. Sylvia's curiosity was on tip-toe. She listened with profound attention to his oracular wisdom; and believed him really inspired, when he told her, that her former lover, for whom she had a great regard, was gone to a foreign country. This she knew to be true, and therefore gave him full credence, when he added, that he would never live to return; and when he proceeded still further to observe, that another gentleman of great merit now courted her; that she was not fond of his addresses, but would soon see his worth and her own error; give him her hand, and be happy.

In short, he so artfully blended the past and present, which she knew, with the future which Sylvander wished, and had therefore dictated, that she was firmly persuaded he dealt with some invisible power, and that fate had, indeed, predestined her to the arms of Sylvander. Convinced of this, she attended to his overtures more

1. Familiar conversation.

placidly, contemplated his person and endowments with less aversion, and endeavoured to reconcile herself to the unavoidable event.

This she effected; and not long after, he obtained her in marriage, and triumphed in the success of his duplicity.

In process of time, her other lover returned. Disappointment and despair presided in his breast. He saw Sylvia, upbraided her with her inconstancy, and declared himself utterly ruined. Pity and returning love operated in her mind, and rendered her completely wretched. She most severely condemned her own folly, in listening to the dictates of a misguided curiosity; and acknowledged herself justly punished, for presuming to pry into the secret designs of Heaven.

These strolling pretenders to foreknowledge are peculiarly dangerous to the weak-minded and credulous part of the community; and how it happens that they are ever encouraged, is to me inconceivable. Did they actually give the information they promise, how much reason should we have to avoid them! How many sources of grief would be opened, by the anticipation of future evils, of which, now, we have no apprehension! and how often should we be deprived of the consolatory hope of a speedy deliverance from present sufferings!

With every sentiment of respect and affection, I am most sincerely your's.

SOPHIA MANCHESTER.

*To Miss* ANNA WILLIAMS.

BOSTON.

DEAR ANNA,

A most melancholy and distressing event has spread a gloom over the face of the metropolis. Every heart heaves the sympathetic sigh, and every eye drops the tear of regret. The very sudden death of Doctor Clarke,[1] who was seized with an apoplectic fit, in the midst of his sermon, yesterday afternoon, and expired this morning, is a subject of universal lamentation.

Not only we, who had the happiness to sit under his ministry, and to enjoy his particular friendship and attention, but the whole town; and, indeed, the public at large have sustained a great loss in his departure. Amiable in his disposition, engaging in his manners, and benevolent in his whole deportment, he conciliated the affections of every class. His talents as a scholar, philosopher, and divine, commanded the respect of the most judicious and learned;

---

1. Dr. John Clarke was pastor of the First Church in Boston from 1778 to his death on April 2, 1798, at the age of forty-two.

while the elegance, perspicuity and delicacy of his style, joined with the undissembled seriousness of his manner, rendered him uniformly acceptable to the devout. In every condition and relation of life, he was exemplary as a Christian; and as a preacher, an air of persuasion invariably accompanied him, which arrested the attention of the most heedless auditors.

> ———"By him, in strains as sweet
> As angels use, the gospel whisper'd peace.
> Grave, simple and sincere; in language plain;
> And plain in manner.   Decent, solemn, chaste,
> And natural in gesture.   Much impress'd
> Himself, as conscious of his awful charge,
> And anxious mainly that the flock he fed
> Might feel it too.   Affectionate in look,
> And tender in address, as well becomes
> A messenger of grace to guilty men."[2]

He was particularly attractive to young people. While he charmed their ear, he convinced their understanding, and excited them to the love and practice of virtue.

A striking example of this occurred some years ago, which I will take the liberty to relate. He preached in a neighbouring church on these words, "She that liveth in pleasure is dead while she liveth."[3] In this discourse he painted those allurements of pleasure which surround the young and gay; more especially of our sex, in the most just and lively colours. He represented, in pathetic, engaging and refined language, the snares to which they are exposed, and the most probable means of escaping them. He exhibited, with all their attractions, the native charms of virtue, and pourtrayed vice in its true deformity. He described, in the most animating terms, the respectability, usefulness, and happiness of those who undeviatingly adhere to the path of rectitude and innocence; and, with the most energetic and affectionate tenderness, warned the youth to avoid the devious walks of vice and dissipation.

A number of young ladies, who had been his hearers, happening to be together in the evening, united in the wish to express their gratitude to him; but not having a personal acquaintance with him, could devise no better method than writing. The following anonymous letter was accordingly penned by one of the company, and privately conveyed to the Doctor, at the request of all.

———————

2. Cowper, *The Task*.
3. 1 Timothy, v.6. [*Foster's note.*] The passage from 1 Timothy 5:6 is taken from the King James Version.

BOSTON.

"REVEREND SIR,

"The well known candour of your disposition, and your apparent zeal for the promotion of religion and virtue, embolden us to flatter ourselves, that you will pardon this method of conveying to you our sincere and united thanks for your very seasonable, judicious, and useful discourse, delivered last Sunday morning, at our meeting.

"It is much to be lamented, that the depravity of the age is such, as to render sermons of this nature just and necessary; and it is almost matter of equal regret, that we have so seldom opportunities of being benefited by them.

"That we oftener hear than receive instruction, is a truth which can neither be denied, nor evaded; and can only be accounted for, by that passionate fondness for pleasure, which prevails to such a degree of enthusiasm, as to precipitate its votaries into whatever presents itself under this deluding aspect, without considering whether it be durable, or fleeting.

"It is certainly a most humiliating reflection, that our sex (which is the female) should ever take more pains to gain the qualifications of agreeable triflers than of rational friends; or be more anxious to become *amusing*, than useful companions. But, Sir, does not such conduct in ladies too often receive the most flattering encouragement from the gentlemen? How seldom is intrinsic merit distinguished; and the serious, prudent female preferred, even by those who style themselves men of sense and penetration, to the airy flaunting coquette!

"The constant attention which is paid to those who make the gayest appearance, and the applause which is lavished upon her who has the largest portion of external graces and fashionable embellishments, induce many who entertain the good-natured desire of pleasing, to bestow more of their time and care on the cultivation of those superficial accomplishments, which they find necessary to render them acceptable to most circles into which they fall, than upon the acquisition of those substantial virtues, which they daily see neglected and ridiculed; though, at the same time, perhaps, they are convinced of the superior satisfaction which the latter would afford.

"But it is needless for one sex to criminate the other. We allow, that, generally speaking, they are equally to blame. In this instance, however, as the male assume the prerogative of superior judgment and intellectual abilities, they ought to prove the justice of their claim by setting nobler examples, and by endeavouring to reform whatever tends to vitiate the taste and corrupt the morals of society.

"Yet, after all, the evil cannot be effectually remedied, but by the concurrent exertions of both: and we are humbly of opinion, that if this reformation were more frequently inculcated from the pulpit, in the delicate, engaging, and pious manner of the discourse which now excites our gratitude to you, and our resolutions to conduct accordingly, it would be efficacious in bringing about so desirable an event.

"We entreat your pardon, Reverend Sir, for the freedom, prolixity, and errors of this epistle.

"Though personally unknown to you, we doubt not you will readily grant it, when we assure you, that we are actuated by a sincere regard to the interests of religion and morality, and by a grateful sense of your exertions in the glorious cause.

"The united sentiments of a number of young ladies, who heard and admired your sermon, last Sunday morning, are expressed above.

REV. JOHN CLARKE."[4]

It is much to be regretted, that Dr. Clarke did not publish more of his literary labours.

The universal approbation bestowed upon those, which he suffered to see the light, is an unequivocal evidence of his merit, as an author. His "Letters to a Student in the University of Cambridge,"[5] are written in a most pleasing style, and contain instruction and advice, of which no person in pursuit of a public education ought to be ignorant. His "Answer to the question, Why are you a Christian?"[6] which has already had three editions in Boston, and three in England, is one of the best compendiums of the external and internal evidences of our holy religion, extant. It is plain and intelligible to the lowest capacity, and may enable every one without much study, to give a reason for the hope that is in him.

From these specimens we may form an opinion of what the world has lost by his early exit.

I shall make no other apology for the length of this letter, than the interest which I feel in the subject; and this, I am persuaded, you will deem sufficient.

My affectionate regards wait on your mamma and sister, while I subscribe myself your's most sincerely,

JULIA GREENFIELD.

4. In formal letters of this period, the addressee is named at the letter's close.
5. John Clarke, *Letters to a Student in the University of Cambridge, Massachusetts* (1796), published by Samuel Hall.
6. John Clarke, *An Answer to the Question Why are You a Christian* (1795), printed by Joseph Belknap.

## *To Miss* CLEORA PARTRIDGE.

BEVERLY.

DEAR CLEORA,

The shortness of time is a very common subject of complaint; but I think the misuse of it, a much more just one. Its value is certainly under-rated by those who indulge themselves in morning sloth.

Sweet, indeed, is the breath of morn; and after the body has been refreshed by the restoring power of sleep, it is peculiarly prepared to procure and participate the pleasures of the mind. The jarring passions are then composed, and the calm operations of reason succeed of course; while

> "———— Gentle gales,
> Fanning their odoriferous wings, dispense
> Native perfumes, and whisper whence they stole
> These balmy spoils."[1]

The morning is undoubtedly a season, of all others, most favourable to useful exertions. Those, therefore, who lose three or four hours of it, in slumbering inaction, make a voluntary sacrifice of the best part of their existence. I rose to-day, not with the sun, but with the dawn; and after taking a few turns in the garden, retired to the summer-house. This, you know, is a favourite hour with me.

> "To me be nature's volume broad display'd;
> And to peruse its all-instructing page,
> Or, haply catching inspiration thence,
> Some easy passage, raptur'd, to translate,
> My sole delight; as thro' the falling glooms
> Pensive I stray, or with the rising dawn
> On fancy's eagle-wing excursive soar."[2]

Having a memorandum-book and pencil in my pocket, I descended from the lofty heights to which the immortal bard, my beloved Thompson, had insensibly raised my imagination, to the humble strains of simple rhyme, in order to communicate my sensations to you. These I enclose, without attempting to tell you, either in prose or verse, how affectionately I am your's.

MATILDA FIELDING.

———

1. Milton, *Paradise Lost*.
2. Thomson, *The Seasons*, "Summer."

The morning dawns, the russet grey
Slowly avoids the opening day:
Receding from the gazing eye,
The misty shades of twilight fly.
The ruddy streaks of light appear,
To guide our western hemisphere;
While tuneful choirs responsive join
To praise the gracious Pow'r Divine,
Whose mighty hand, with sov'reign sway,
Restores, alternate, night and day.
   Hail, opening morn! thy sober rays
Demand the contemplative gaze;
Unnumber'd beauties please the sight,
And give the mental eye delight.
   O dawn! thy sombre shades I love;
With thee in solitude I'll rove;
While health expansive gives the mind
To taste thy pleasures unconfin'd.
   Here, free from fashions artful forms,
Benevolence the bosom warms;
Persuasive virtue charms the soul,
And reason's laws alone control.
   Let others, lost in sloth, forego
The joys thy early hours bestow;
Thy zephyrs far more sweets dispense,
Than *Somnus*[3] yields to drowsy sense!
   Mild as thy beams of radiance shine,
May piety my powers refine;
Pure as thy mimic pearls, that spread
Their liquid beauties o'er the mead;
And, like yon rising orb of day,
May wisdom guide my dubious way.

### *To Miss* MATILDA FIELDING.

HARMONY-GROVE.

DEAR MATILDA,

I was, last week, at Boston; and, having occasion for a new hat, stepped into a milliner's shop to inquire the mode. The milliner replied, that it was not yet in her power to answer my question.

---

3. The Roman god of sleep.

"The spring ships," said she "are later than common; but their arrival
is hourly expected, when we shall be furnished with memorandum-
books which will ascertain and determine the fashion for the sea-
son." What she meant by memorandum-books, I could not conceive.
I had always supposed them blanks, designed for noting whatever
occurred, without inconvenience. Unwilling, however, to be thought
a simple country-girl, totally unacquainted with the world, I sought
no explanation from her; but repaired to a particular friend for
instruction. From whom I learned that the chief value of these
same memorandum-books consists in their containing imported
cuts of ladies' head-dresses, hats, and other habiliments, which are
always sure to be admired and imitated, as the perfection of taste
and propriety!

This discovery mortified me exceedingly. It justified, beyond any
thing which I had ever suspected to exist as a fact, what I once
heard a European assert, "that Americans had neither character nor
opinion of their own."

With due deference to those better judges, who despite the sim-
plicity of our ancestors, and labour to introduce the corrupt man-
ners and customs of the old world into our country, I cannot but
think it extremely ridiculous for an independent nation, which dis-
cards all foreign influence, glories in its freedom, and boasts of its
genius and taste, servilely to ape exotic fashions, even in articles of
dress and fanciful ornaments.

Have not the daughters of Columbia sufficient powers of inven-
tion to decorate themselves? Must we depend upon the winds and
waves for the form, as well as the materials of our garb? Why may
we not follow our own inclination; and not be deemed finical[1] or
prudish in our appearance, merely because our habit is not exactly
correspondent with the pretty pictures in the memorandum-books,
last imported?

It is sincerely to be regretted that this subject is viewed in so
important a light. It occupies too much of the time, and engrosses
too much of the conversation of our sex. For one, I have serious
thoughts of declaring independence.

ANNA WILLIAMS.

---

1. Overly particular, finicky.

## *To Miss* CAROLINE LITTLETON.

[*On the Death of her Mother.*]

HARMONY-GROVE.

MY DEAR CAROLINE,

To tell you that I am sorry for your loss, or that I sympathize with you in your affliction, would be but the language you daily hear; and often, perhaps, from the unfeeling and indifferent. But you will do me the justice to believe, that I take a particular interest in your concerns, and really share your grief. A holy Providence has wounded you by a stroke, which is extremely painful and severe. Your best friend is shrouded in the grave. In the maternal breast, your fondest affections, and most unsuspecting confidence have hitherto concentred; and who can provide you with an equivalent substitute? To the almighty Father and Friend of creation, it becomes you to repair for comfort and support.

The dying advice and counsel of your dear mamma, which, you inform me, were pathetic,[1] instructive and consolatory, will be a guide to your feet. Often realize the solemn scene, and remember, that, "though dead, she yet speaketh."[2]

You have great cause of thankfulness, that she was spared to direct you so far through the intricate and dangerous path of youth; to complete your education, to teach you, by her example, how to acquit yourself with usefulness and honor; and, above all, to furnish you with that important knowledge, to which every thing else should be made subservient—how to die!

An era of your life has now commenced, which is no less important than affecting. That assisting hand, which formerly led you, is now cold and lifeless! Those lips, from which you have been accustomed to receive information and advice, are sealed in perpetual silence! And that heart, which always glowed with the warmest solicitude for your happiness, has ceased to palpitate![3]

You must now think and act for yourself. As the eldest daughter, you will be placed at the head of your father's family. You must, therefore, adopt a plan of conduct, conducive to its harmony, regularity, and interest.

Filial duty to your surviving parent, more tenderly inculcated by your participation of his heavy bereavement, will lead you to

---

1. I.e., pitiable, or exciting sympathy.
2. A popular adaptation of Hebrews 11:4: "By faith Abel offered unto God a more excellent sacrifice than Cain, by which he obtained witness that he was righteous, God testifying of his gifts: and by it he being dead yet speaketh."
3. Beat.

consult his inclination, and sedulously[4] contribute all in your power to lighten the burden of domestic arrangements devolved upon him. While he laments the death of a prudent, affectionate, and beloved wife, give him reason to rejoice, that he is blessed with a daughter, capable of soothing the pains, alleviating the cares, and heightening the enjoyments of his life.

Your brothers and sisters will look up to you as the guide of their tender years. While their weeping eyes and pathetic accents are directed towards you, let kindness, discretion, and patience, characterize your deportment, and engage their confidence and love.

Having mentioned your duty to others, I cannot dismiss the subject without dropping a few hints for your direction, in regard to your personal behaviour.

A very important charge is committed to you, as well in the duties which you owe to yourself, as in the superintendence of your father's family.

The sovereign Disposer of all things has, at an early age, made you, in a measure, your own guardian. Your father's business calls him much abroad. With you, therefore, he is obliged to entrust, not only his domestic concerns; but, what is still more dear to his heart, the care of your own person and mind; of your own reputation and happiness.

Circumstanced as you are, company has the most powerful charms. Your's is now the prerogative of receiving and returning visits in your own name. At home, you are sole mistress of ceremonies. This is extremely alluring to the sprightly fancy of youth. But time, you will remember, is too important a blessing to be sacrificed to a promiscuous crowd of unimproving companions. Besides, the character of a young lady will necessarily be sullied by the imputation of being constantly engaged in parties of pleasure, and exhilarating amusement. Flattery often avails itself of the unguarded moments of gaiety; and, insinuating its insidious charms into the heedless and susceptible mind, inflates it with pride and vanity, and produces an affectation and air of self-importance, which are peculiarly disgusting, because easily distinguished from that true dignity of manners, which results from conscious rectitude. Genuine merit is always modest and unassuming; diffident of itself, and respectful to others.

Your father has a right to your unlimited confidence. You will, therefore, make him your chief friend and counsellor. Though he may not possess all the winning softness of a mother, he doubtless has as ardent an affection for you, and as sincere a desire to promote your welfare. Hence you may safely repose your dearest concerns in his paternal breast, and receive, with the utmost deference, his

4. Attentively.

kind instruction and advice. Let his judgment have an entire ascendency over your mind and actions, especially in your intercourse and society with the other sex. Consider him as better acquainted with their merit, circumstances, and views, than you can be; and, should you contemplate a connexion for life, let his opinion determine your choice.

Watch over your dear little sisters, with all the tenderness of fraternal affection; be their protector and friend; instil into their minds the principles of virtue and religion; arm them against the snares and temptations by which they will be surrounded; and lead them, by your own conduct, in the way of truth and peace.

When you have leisure and inclination to write, the effusions of your pen will always be acceptable to your sincere and faithful friend,

MARY WILLIAMS.

THE END.

# SOURCES AND CONTEXTS

# On Coquetry

## A modern Coquette's account of herself.[†]

I am, you must know, a young woman, whose whole dependence is on my person and accomplishments, and as I would willingly be married to a man of fortune, a description of both may be pretty necessary. In the first place, I have a sweet figure, charming teeth, and the finest eyes in the world; my face has a good deal of wholesome flesh and blood about it, and I fancy myself possessed of a constitution very little favourable to the physicians. Then, as for my accomplishments, I can sing all the songs in the opera of *Artaxerxes*,[1] have a mutual taste for extravagance and pleasure, am passionately fond of running into debt, and have an utter aversion to going to church. I am in the strictest sense of the word, a bewitching girl, and very happily calculated to break a husband's heart. If any gentleman, therefore, has the least inclination to be made both a beggar and a cuckold, he can by no means apply to a person more devoted to his service.—But then I expect settlements pretty considerable—for making a man unhappy, I could not think of less than two thousand a year, tho' fifteen hundred might be accepted. You may perhaps, laugh at hearing me talk of making a man miserable who shall honour me with his hand as an argument in my favour; but you do not remember that the more universal any custom is, the more fashionable it must be considered, and that making each other wretched is one of the politest accomplishments amongst the married people of distinction. Not but that I can preserve appearances very well; I could say—"My life!" to a husband, at the same time I was winking at another man in company, and call him a "dear creature!" at the very time I was convinced he was the greatest brute in the universe.

---

† Anonymous, "A modern Coquette's account of herself," *The Salem Chronicle, and Essex Advertiser* (April 7, 1786).
1. Persian King from 465 to 424 B.C. An opera based on his life, written by the English composer Thomas Arne (1710–1778), premiered in London in 1762 and was popular for decades. Although the opera was not particularly controversial, the implication here seems to be that the coquette's taste runs toward the popular and ephemeral.

# FOR THE *MASSACHUSETTS GAZETTE.*

## On Coquetry.[†]

In the course of my observations on COQUETRY, I am sensible that many reflections must be thrown out not at all to the honour of my own sex; but the consideration of this shall not stint my production, as I mean every performance shall be grounded on the basis of impartiality.

Coquetry took its rise from foppery[1]—and indeed every female folly owes its origin in some measure to that detestable source. To a fop, sentiment is not agreeable, and delicacy and natural ease are too much to cope with. Something must be done to amuse this phantom—he can *ogle*, *whistle* and *smile*. The airs of coquetry answer the purpose completely: the fop is delighted with jilting airs and affectation, he can, in the management of them, *display his* TALENTS *to advantage*. In proportion as foppery gains ground, coquetry prevails;

> And ev'ry mental beauty's laid aside,
> To flatter fops and sooth the coxcombs pride.
> Miss, flirts her fan, Sir, twirls his watch-key round,
> Ogling and whistling in their turns abound.
> How *nobly* are the moments thus employ'd,
> Or, rather, how ignobly time's destroy'd.

A very considerable number of the fair sex despise coquetry in all its shapes; but not a few study to acquire its arts; to the last mentioned only will my observations apply.

The restraint which coquettish airs puts on conversation, renders those hours painful which are set apart to be devoted to pleasure; unless it should happen that the company consisted entirely of coquets and fops, which I believe is seldom the case. Coquetry is as great a blemish to the actions of a female, as paint is to the natural beauty of her features. A lady not only gives pain to others by laying an unnatural restraint upon her manners and conversation, but she gives pain also to herself, for it is impossible for any one to be happy when absorbed in affectation.—Natural ease, vivacity and freedom in the fair, render their company in the highest degree agreeable,

> And when of those accomplishments possest,
> The fair are courted and they are carest:

---

[†] Anonymous, "For the *Massachusetts Gazette*. On Coquetry," *Massachusetts Gazette* (April 22, 1788), 4.

1. The behavior of a fop, or a man too consumed with his clothing and personal appearance.

> But if coquettish airs are e'er put on,
> And frankness banish'd for detested *ton*,
> The scene is chang'd, and merit shuns the fair,
> And all their charms disperse like empty air.

Coquetry is attended with many disadvantages, as the external garb must comport with the character assumed: a considerable part of the day must be devoted to the toilet, and after miss is equipped with her hat awry, and all the ornaments of art, the part of a coquet must be acted over and over again, before the looking-glass, in order to be perfect in every role. What a dire mortification must it be to coquet, who, after having spent the greatest part of the day in decorating her sweet person to bestow or receive a visit, should a shower of rain prevent the accomplishment of either. O! the disappointment,—this lovely face to be unseen! Was ever any thing so unfortunate?—Cruel, cruel, cruel fate! On the contrary, a lady who makes it her rule to dress decently gay, whose object in going into company is to enjoy and partake of the agreeable converse of friends, if she has spent an hour or more at her dressing table, to visit or be visited, if a disappointment takes place, she calmly retires to engage in the domestic duties of life, or employ her leisure time in reading a sentimental novel or some entertaining history. What a contrast betwixt a lady possest of affability, and governed by good humour, and a flirting coquette.

As the foppery of the male sex induces many females to practice coquetry, it is hoped that the fair will not any longer suffer their conduct to be influenced by the foibles of those who reflect disgrace on the human mind. What exultation must fill the heart of a fop if he perceives his actions tend in the least degree to influence those of a lady's. But what mortification must he feel if he is sensible that his manners are copied and despised by the fairest part of the creation.

> Ye fair, relinquish all coquettish airs,
> Employ your minds about far nobler cares;
> Learn all the duties of domestick life,
> Which shine in virgins and adorn a wife,
> Then will the hours of thought procure you bliss,
> And worth extol you, though a fop may hiss.

*JUVENIS*[2]

---

2. *Latin*: Youthful or young.

# The Life and Death of Elizabeth Whitman

## The Letters of Elizabeth Whitman to Joel and Ruth Barlow, 1779–1783[†]

EDITORIAL STATEMENT

Fifteen letters from Elizabeth Whitman to Joel and Ruth Baldwin Barlow survive in the Baldwin Family Papers at the Henry E. Huntington Library. The Baldwin collection, made up largely of Barlow letters and the correspondence of Joel's sister-in-law, Clara Baldwin Bomford, came to the Huntington in 1956, having been stored for generations in a portable writing desk Joel Barlow had taken with him to Europe during his diplomatic missions in the early nineteenth century. In 1936, three letters from Mary Wollstonecraft and one from Helen Maria Williams, all to Joel Barlow's wife, Ruth, were removed from this collection without the owner's knowledge, donated to the library at UC-Berkeley, and published by a Berkeley professor and the graduate student who had stumbled upon them. The owner secured the remaining papers in a bank vault until 1955, when Barlow's biographer, James Woodress, tracked them down and helped bring them to the Huntington.[1] Nearly seventy-five years

† Reprinted from Bryan Waterman, ed., "The Letters of Elizabeth Whitman to Joel and Ruth Barlow, 1779–1783" *Early American Literature* 46.3 (2011): 565–600. Reprinted by permission of the U of North Carolina P. Footnotes throughout this selection are by Bryan Waterman.

    I wish to thank Tim Cassedy, Kara Zavarella, and Stephanie Smith-Waterman for their assistance in double-checking my transcriptions against photocopies of the originals and Caroline W. H. Dall's published versions. Jennifer Harris gave useful advice on notes and Blevin Shelnutt assisted with citation formats. Thanks to the Henry E. Huntington Library and the Massachusetts Historical Society for fellowship support in 2006 and 2007 that made this editorial work possible and for permission to publish this material from their collections. [*Waterman's note.*]

1. The account in Kurtz and Autrey obscures the questionable means by which the letters made their way to Berkeley. For the account above see Woodress. Thanks to Nancy Peterson for bringing Woodress's essay to my attention.

    The Wollstonecraft letters taken from this collection tell us much of what little we know about Wollstonecraft's ill-fated relationship with Gilbert Imlay, the American father of her first child, who had been one of Joel Barlow's business partners in Paris in

earlier, the Whitman letters had been loaned by Ruth Bomford Paine (Ruth Barlow's niece) to the novelist and reformer Caroline Wells Healey Dall, who published bowdlerized versions of some of them in her 1875 book *The Romance of the Association; or, One Last Glimpse of Charlotte Temple and Eliza Wharton*. Dall apparently had more letters in her possession than are currently in the Huntington's collection, since she excerpts some that are not in the Baldwin Family Papers. For roughly a decade after Dall published *The Romance of the Association*, she stalled every time Ruth Bomford Paine asked her to return them. Dall feared that the literary executor of one of the writers represented in the family collection intended to have much of it burned.[2] Fearing she would lose the letters eventually, Dall hired someone to copy several of them into a notebook that now is housed with her papers at the Massachusetts Historical Society. Once Dall had supposedly returned everything to Paine, the collection passed through two more generations before it made its way to California in 1911, packed inside Barlow's desk.

Fourteen of the extant Whitman letters are addressed to Joel Barlow; the final one is addressed to Ruth. Whitman met both Joel and Ruth in late 1778 in New Haven, where she stayed with the family of Yale's president, Ezra Stiles. The exchange seems to have ended when the Barlows settled near Whitman's family in Hartford in 1782. Not much is known of the interactions between the Barlows and Whitman from 1783 to 1788, when Joel departed for Europe on business and Whitman fled Hartford for Massachusetts, where she gave birth to a stillborn child while hiding in a country tavern, only to die a few weeks after. Her story was publicized in newspapers and memorialized a decade later in Hannah Webster Foster's steadily selling novel, *The Coquette*.

If Caroline Dall's valiant preservation of parts of the Baldwin Papers suggests she valued historical transparency, her editing of the letters in *Romance of the Association* indicates otherwise. She wrote her book about Whitman primarily to argue that, contrary to the plot of Foster's novel, Whitman had secretly been married when she arrived, quite pregnant, at the Bell Tavern in Danvers, Massachusetts, in the summer of 1788. For some reason, Dall believed, Whitman's secret spouse had neither arrived before her child was born, nor cleared the air when, after her death, she was routinely framed as a coquette or a victim of seduction. Dall marshals Whitman's letters to the Barlows in support of this case, but only after

---

the 1790s (Kurtz and Autrey). On Imlay and Wollstonecraft see especially Verhoeven. Gordon makes more than any other Wollstonecraft biographer of her relationship with the Barlows.
2. See especially Dall, letter.

editing out much of their flirtatious content and explaining away some peculiar features she couldn't easily omit.

Perhaps even more problematic from an editorial standpoint, Dall printed selections from some letters that no longer exist in the original, and in one case she inserted whole paragraphs that do not appear in the letter's manuscript original, making these portions of her text particularly unreliable.[3] In spite of the very clear evidence that Dall freely altered the letters she printed, I have chosen to include here Dall's published versions of two letters that are not present in the Baldwin Family Papers or in her MHS notebook. Another letter included here comes from a transcription, found in the Baldwin Family Papers, of a letter that does not appear to exist in the original, and yet another missing letter is printed here using Dall's MHS notebook as the copy text.[4]

Headnotes, in italics, identify source locations and indicate whether the letter survives in multiple versions. I give priority to materials in Whitman's hand, collected at the Huntington Library. (No other manuscript documents by her are known to survive.) Comparison of Dall's published versions with both the MHS notebook transcriptions and the originals indicates that she significantly amended the letters she included in *Romance*, though her copyist aimed for accurate transcriptions in the MHS notebook. Therefore, I give transcriptions in her MHS notebook priority over *Romance*. Headnotes also include any markings on the letter's exterior, including addressee, postage, or personal conveyance.

I have retained original spelling and punctuation in most cases; insertions in brackets are mine and have been used sparingly to provide clarity and ease the reader's experience. Such insertions fall into specific categories: First, when an obvious word or letter has been accidentally omitted, I have inserted it. Second, when a word is misspelled so severely as to be nearly unintelligible (e.g., "spept" where she means "stepped"), I have provided the clarifying word in brackets following the word as it appears in the original. Third, when a letter has been damaged and portions of a word or phrase are missing, I provide the most reasonable guess suggested by the context; if at all uncertain about such suggestions I include a question mark within the brackets. If the missing word cannot be recovered by

3. See Whitman, letter to J. Barlow, Feb. 16, 1779. The inserted material includes the names of several prominent associates of Whitman's: Joseph Buckminster, Aaron Burr, Ezra Stiles, and a "Captain Wooster." The density of this name dropping makes it tempting to think that Dall fabricated the material whole cloth in an effort to place Whitman in a constellation of Connecticut high society, though she could also have lifted these paragraphs from another letter, now lost.

4. See Whitman's letters to J. Barlow from 1779 of Feb. 22, July 1, and November and her letter of May 12, 1781. Versions of the first two are preserved in Dall's MHS notebook, making letters 13 and 18 the only two for which we depend entirely on Dall's printed version in *Romance*.

contextual implications, it appears as [*missing*]. Fourth, in rare instances I have inserted a punctuation mark in brackets when I felt the reader would be confused without it, though by no means have I sought to standardize her usage. Whitman's punctuation, like that of most eighteenth-century letter writers, is irregular at best. She often omitted punctuation or used a variety of dashes to indicate that she had concluded a sentence or thought. I have rendered her dashes in varying lengths as they appear in the original letters; in some cases she seems to use a long dash at the end of a sentence or paragraph to indicate that she is unable to express herself fully. I have silently omitted words written at the foot of one page used to indicate the first word that will appear at the top of the next. Insertions using carats have been silently adopted. Strikethroughs appear ~~so~~ and all <u>underlined</u> material using a single line.

### THE LETTERS

*1. February 9, 1779—Elizabeth Whitman to Joel Barlow*

*Baldwin Papers, Huntington Library. Not included in Dall's Romance.*

On exterior fold: "1 // Mr. Joel Barlow // New-Haven // Favour by Miss Thomson"

Feb. 9th–79

Dear Joel

    I had like to have said jewel, where do you think your wife is now? no further of[f] than Chesshire[5] I assure you where she is very happy at present sitting beside our friend Sally,[6] which make her think of you, & of those days so much admird when Hymen first united us O joel! I know not when we shall have opportunity to enjoy again the pleasures of that delightfu[l] union————

    I took my pen only just to give you a short account of our perils in getting here, which were manifold—as we journeyd along the pleasant streets of Carmel,[7] we had the misfortune to break one of our carriage wheels, so we were obligd to walk, which was very pleasant. I went into a house but there my heart would not let me stay long, as one [of] my fellow creatures was in great distress, with the cholic— the next stage we made was a Blacksmiths shop, where [we] made out to get the carriage mended what would you have said joel could you have seen your wife standing on the forge to warm & dry herself, as she did for half an hour, she really made a droll figure & could

---

5. Chesshire, CT, between New Haven and Hartford.
6. Possibly Sally Bradley, who married Dudley Baldwin, Barlow's future brother-in-law.
7. Presumably Mount Carmel, near Hamden, CT, north of New Haven.

not help laughing at herself the whole time, you would have laughd too ~~had~~ could you have seen how quick she spept [stepped] from the forge & ran into what Billy[8] call'd the counting room, when the Smith came with his Hammer, & began to blow the fire O dear O dear [wha]t[9] a time we had—from this place we proceeded to the Tavern tho we found only fifteen or twenty men drinking & talking— here we staid all night & had a mortification to observe thier was a fi[re?] two or three doors off. & there our Sa[lly] was. I wish I could just have look[ed in?] upon them, but I heard all abo[ut it?] this morning—& so may you f[rom?] Sally—I must bid you adeau for we are going to have the pleasure of rideing a few miles in the rain this morning—be sure [to] write me by the post & tell me all that I want to know be particular in informing me how my friends do & let me know all your motions—if you can read this letter 'tis more than I can do myself[1] but it shall pass for a letter wheather you can or not I trust you will make necessary excuses for this written in the mids[t] of company—I am your faithful wife——

### 2. February 16, 1779—Elizabeth Whitman to Joel Barlow

*Baldwin Papers, Huntington Library. This letter appears abridged and edited in Dall,* Romance, *80–82, minimizing the flirtatiousness and references to Barlow's "tender words" to her. Dall also includes several paragraphs not present in the Huntington ms letter (see p. 275, n. 9) and misdates it February 19, from Hartford.*

On exterior in another hand: "E.W. Feb 16 '79," and beneath that, in very faded pencil, in yet another hand: "Betsy Whitman"; in a third hand: "Postage 2√/"; in Whitman's hand: "2 // Mr. Joel Barlow // Redding"[2]

Ma Chere ame,[3]
    You will easily beleave me when I tell you your letter was the most welcome thing imaginable—I had just been lamenting that the Post did not arrive at the usual time, & feard I should have no

---

8. Probably William Whitman, Elizabeth Whitman's younger brother (1758–1846; Yale 1779), who was admitted to the Connecticut bar in 1785 but made a living as an apothecary and, later, as clerk of city courts in Hartford (Dexter 131–32). I rely on Dexter for biographical information on most of Whitman's male acquaintances.
9. The manuscript is torn here and again along the right margin of this page where bracketed words or portions of words appear in the text.
1. Her handwriting decreases in size from this point as she runs out of space on the sheet.
2. Redding, CT, Barlow's hometown. The "2" indicates Whitman's numbering system for her letters.
3. Whitman uses rudimentary French throughout and often mistakenly uses the feminine gender when addressing Barlow. This may be a sign that her French writing instruction was preparing her for same-sex correspondence, or perhaps her models were love letters written from men to women.

letters this week—when somebody was so good as to call & leave me five—which do you think I read first? but I will not mortify you so much as to leave you in doubt one moment, yours had as it ought that preference—what can I say in return to all the fond tender things it contains? What but that my heart beats in delightful unison to every tender sentiment, and that I am inexpresibly oblig'd to you.—O you are certainly the paragon of Husbands—were all married men like you what a happy world for our Sex! but I hope as many as see you & know of your excellence, will take pattern by you— think of you, that I shall, & to you, as often as possable I am vexed to think that the night is almost out or rather that the morning approaches very fast, & that the Post will ride in a few hours I would willingly spend the whole time in writing but suppose I must for decencys sake go thro' the ceremony of going to bed before I am too tired & stupid to say any thing intertaing.[4] when I sat down to write I was so much so, I could scarce hold my pen, but the thoughts of you has enlivend me a little I will tell you how I came to be very tired, I have been walking half a mile in the mud this evening I beleave you will think that the mud is my element, & that I have a particular delight in it, to emerge myself in it again so soon, when what I had contracted in my journey was hardly brushd off—I ought to inform you I did not get home 'till friday. nor would I have come so soon, for the roads were inlotterable [intolerable], but I grew impatient for letters, & knew I could have none where I was, nor could I bear to think of them waiting for me one moment at Harford[5]—I stay'd three or four days at Southington, to rest and recriait after my troublesome adventures, there could not be a better place for this purpose, to eat & drink is all we have to do—I found the scene much changd at Southington[6] from N.H.[7] & the alteration was all for the wor[s]e—yet the peaceful unruffled life one leads in such a place has its charms—to rise in the morning & lay your plan for the day, knowing almost to a certainty that nothing will happen to interupt it, to read & work alternately, then for diversion perhaps some country sport amongst your family & neighbours—to find yourself quite out of ambition's way, & in the very bosom of contentment this certainly is agreeable, & never more so than when one has met with trouble in a busier scene—I relishd it highly—but what principally pleased me, was I found myself no longer afraid if a certain subject was started, I neither trembled nor turnd pale, I sat at my ease & felt as if nobody would hurt me—I know you will laugh at me for a pusilinemous creature for being ever so afraid as you have seen me——but I could

4. Unclear whether she means to write "interesting" or "entertaining."
5. Hartford.
6. Southington, CT, between New Haven and Hartford.
7. New Haven.

not help it—if Mr. B——[8] is with you give my kindest love to him you
wont be jealous that is my foiable[9]—I suppose because I have the
most love—Joel, I am really ashamd of this letter, I have trifled thro'
the whole of it indeed I was fit for nothing else—I will endeavour to
write one next Post more worthy your perusal—before let me hear
from you by him if you love me—Adieu, mon cher

Mr. Barlow Feb[y] 16[th]–79

### 3.February 22, 1779—Elizabeth Whitman to Joel Barlow

*The original of this letter is not included in the Baldwin Papers at the
Huntington. The text here comes from a transcript, in an unknown
hand, found in the Baldwin Papers, box 8, "Miscellaneous and Ephem-
era." Another transcription, with some variants, is found in Dall's MHS
notebook. A third, truncated version appears in Dall, Romance, 83–84.
Because the Baldwin Papers transcript sticks most closely to Whitman's
stylistic idiosyncrasies and preserves irregularities, I have chosen to use it
as source text.*

Addressed to "Mr. Joel Barlow // Reading"

8. Abraham Baldwin (1754–1807; Yale 1772), Barlow's future brother-in-law. Baldwin
   would move to Augusta, GA, in 1784, where he would serve as founder and first presi-
   dent (1786–1801) of the University of Georgia, as well as a member of the Continental
   Congress, Constitutional Convention, and US Senate.
9. Dall inserts several paragraphs here; the source for the inserted material is unclear, as
   these paragraphs do not appear in the original of any of the extant letters. Though it
   remains possible that she interpolates another letter (dated Feb. 19?) that does not
   survive in the Baldwin Papers, we should still assume these paragraphs have been
   altered as elsewhere in her edition or perhaps even wholly fabricated, though that pos-
   sibility seems extreme even for Dall:

   > Thank you for writing at that late hour when you must have been fatigued with *dis-
   > simulation*. Was the question you mention agitated at your meeting? I don't believe
   > there was a clergyman there, or he would have got it determined in a different man-
   > ner. I wish the ladies would get up a disputing club!
   >      You are my constant boast among my married acquaintance. Tell my little rogue of
   > a brother that I think he takes too much upon himself in laughing at our connection.
   >      As to Mr. Baldwin, if he were at the door, I would not run into the cupboard to
   > avoid him. He may mean well, in writing all to Buckminster and nothing to me; but
   > I do not think it.
   >      You mention in one of your letters, your having been at Mr. Burr's. Why did you
   > not tell me how you liked those good folks, and whether you could divine how they
   > liked you? Make my compliments to all the President's family, not forgetting Dr. Ezra
   > Stiles, to whom I esteem myself under the greatest obligation. Tell Mr. Baldwin that
   > Captain Wooster was told *here* of my having had the small-pox, which he would
   > desire him not to mention, if it is not too late. I hope it will not get much about, for I
   > shall want to go to New Haven again some time. Did you have an agreeable ball last
   > evening? I was there in imagination: did you see anything of me? I had an invitation,
   > but it was rather too muddy to come in any other way. (*Romance* 81–82)

   Mentioned in these paragraphs: William Whitman (see p. 273, n. 8); Abraham Bald-
   win (see n.8, above); Joseph Buckminster (1751–1812; Yale 1771), who served as tutor
   from 1774 to 1778 before moving to Portsmouth, NH, in January 1779, and who
   nineteenth-century tradition holds was the model for the Reverend Boyer in Foster's
   *Coquette.* "Mr. Burr" is possibly Aaron Burr (1756–1836), Whitman's cousin. Ezra
   Stiles (1727–95), president of Yale College from 1778 to 1795, was the father of Whit-
   man's friend Betsey (1758–95), with whom she lived while in New Haven. "Captain
   Wooster" is probably Thomas Wooster (1752–92; Yale 1768).

Mon Cher,

You see I can't forget my favourite[1] appelation, the week has rolled round so quick amongst my old friends, & acquaintance whom I had not seen for a long time—that—don't think I am going to say I have not thought of you, but I have not wrote that good letter which I promised—& I do not know wheather[2] I ever shall, but if I don't it will not be for want of attempting it, tho I must confess that has been one cause this week.———

I wish I had the letter which I trust the Post has for me from you, that would I doubt not inspire me with something more agreeable— to say—than ought I can think of at present. I hope mon cher you have written by the post, I am anxious to know whether you recieve my letters safe where you are—if I find you do I shall write with the most perfect freedom—you may remember we talked of a cor- rispondence of that unreserved kind which you are so happy as to enjoy with a certain improving friend of yours[3]—in which all dis- guises are thrown aside & you mention every good or ill quallity[4] to each other, which either is possest of, in the same terms that you consider them in your own Souls—I confess I was struck at first thought with the advantages which must result from such a correspondence if it could be maintained without destroying friendship—& I am willing to believe in hearts so well regulated as yours this is probable—besides in you—the virtues so far prevail that you cannot have much disagreeable to hear but with the gen- erallity of the world you are sensible that this would not do—for very few can bear to be told of their faults, & fewer still have sin- cerity to tell them to one's own ear I confess to you tho perhaps you will think it a foolish diffidence I am always loathe to risk this trial of the friend I love—besides it would look too much like arrogance in me to censure & pick flaws in my friends—who as kind fortune would have it—& as you very justly observe are some of the worthi- est, & most amiable people in the world & too much my superiors to come under my observation all this you will see is written to excuse me from a condition you would have me agree too yet I could wish you to perform your part of it, as I can certainly bear to hear my faults tho I do not like to search for yours. lay aside there- fore for a little time all partiality for the wife of your talk & I tell her the faults you have observed in her character & conduct & may it

1. The "u" is inserted with a carat as if to match Whitman's spelling.
2. The "a" inserted with a carat, presumably to match Whitman's original.
3. Dall replaces "a certain improving friend of yours" with "Mr. Swift." Zephaniah Swift (1759–1823; Yale 1778) represented Connecticut in the US House from 1793 to 1797 and later served as a Connecticut State Supreme Court justice.
4. Second "l" inserted with a carat.

happen to you as it did to Mirabel[5] in the play who studied the faults of his mistress 'till they grew so familiar to him he could think of them without the least unhappiness & liked her ne'er the less for them. Pray how does our family of muses do? & what do they do? I hope you do not keep them in idleness. I know you have other cares & more interesting concerns, that is concerns of interests to attend to, but you know I always told you & must say still I wish you to superintend them a little at your leisure by way of relaxation & amusement & above all things I wish you to send me a smapple [sample] of the work they produce whether great or small.

I have not yet told you that I have had the pleasure of seeing your friend Jacob's[6] poetry & Smith's oration[7] the first was read with particular pleasure with which I [always][8] peruse the production of the Muses, particularly [American][9] Muses. But the proud girl could not [help saying][1] in her heart this Poet cannot write like my Husband yet it is a pretty peace but has some flat lines in it which I dare say you observed & could wish you had altered[.] apropos to poetry I have just been reading the prospect of peace[2] which you gave me but it wants to make it compleat the commendatory verses which you promise pray send them to me—I should be obliged to you too for the bright rosy morning B——[3] can sing it if he has the lines—but do not let these take up all your next letter have you seen your favorite friend yet or heard anything from your second wife[4] those two I am afraid rival me a little in your affections yet I love them exceedingly because you do & wish to hear all you know about them, mon cher I must bid you adieu I am ever your fond & faithful wife.

Feb. 22th 79

---

5. Mirabell, a character from William Congreve's comedy *The Way of the World* (1700). By identifying Barlow with Mirabell she places him in the role of loveable rake.
6. Stephen Jacob (1755–1817; Yale 1778), author of *A Poetical Essay*. Jacob was a US attorney for Vermont in the 1790s and a state Supreme Court justice in 1801–02. See also Webster.
7. Noah Smith (1756–1812; Yale 1778), author of *A Speech*. Like Stephen Jacob's poem, cited above, the oration marked the first anniversary of the Battle of Bennington, in which the British general John Burgoyne's army was defeated by the Green Mountain Boys of Vermont.
8. The Huntington transcription has "(have?)" here, indicating that the original was damaged by the time that copy was made. The version in Dall's MHS notebook, which was transcribed earlier, has "always."
9. The Huntington transcription indicates two missing words here. Dall's MHS notebook has "American."
1. The Huntington transcription indicates two missing words here. Dall's MHS notebook has "help saying."
2. Barlow, *Prospect*.
3. "The Bright Rosy Morning," a popular song. For a nineteenth-century version see *Universal Songster* 124–25. "B——" is probably Abraham Baldwin.
4. I.e., Ruth Baldwin (1756–1818), Barlow's eventual wife. They married clandestinely on January 21, 1781.

### 4. March 17, 1779—Elizabeth Whitman to Joel Barlow

*Baldwin Papers, Huntington Library. Dall includes a version, edited, in Romance, 84–86.*

Wensday Eve March 17[th]–79[5]

Mon cher,

I am unspeakably obligd to you—I have just been reading over your last charming pacquet & know not how to thank you as I ought, but could you be sensable of the delight it gave me you would think yourself in some measure rewarded for I know that benevolent heart of yours loves to give pleasure to every one—& I would hope, nay am almost certain, that your wife has so much interest in it that it cannot but rejoice in her satisfaction—I longd to write you by the Post but was forced to write several letters to Boston—half the letters I write are tasks from which I could fly with pleasure to scribble down my heart to you, to talk to you of that enchanting art which I so much admire, & in which you so much excel and of ten thousand things that occur to my mind whenever I think of you, but it must not be—our acquaintance tho not so much endeard have a claim upon our time & gratitude & nature forbids us to neglect those with whom we have spent many of our social hours—before I go any further I must tell you how sorry I am that you should be so ill receavd at Mr B——[6] through a mistake & on my account I will have that mistake rectified so say nothing against it. I cannot bear that your character should suffer so much for my sake—I cannot conceave where Mrs B——[7] got her intelligence or who gave you yours some medling or malicious as well as misinformd person was the first no doubt but I will not trouble myself too much about it since you do not—am happy the affair is like to make so little noise could wish I had it in my power to recompense you & one other friend for the kind part you have taken in it.——I am excessive sorry for Mr. Baldwin[8] tell him so but that will not do him much good. I wish I were near enough to pay back a little of his tender care don't you think. I sometimes wish to make one again with my little family O I think I could content myself tho I were not to see a W——[9] for many days—do you know I think my Brother[1] improves greatly under your auspices—let me bespeak your kind attention to him, form his taste if you can to those things

---

5. In pencil in another hand below the date: "whole."
6. Michael Baldwin (1719–87), a North Guilford, CT, blacksmith who was Ruth and Abraham Baldwin's father. Baldwin opposed Barlow's courting his daughter.
7. Theodora Wolcot Baldwin (1746–1814), Michael Baldwin's second wife and Ruth's step-mother, though only ten years her senior.
8. Presumably Abraham Baldwin.
9. Possibly "Whitman," if "my little family" refers to her mother and siblings.
1. Her younger brother was apparently being tutored in some capacity by Barlow.

which you yourself admire to books to Study these besides being improveing, afford a rational amusement to the mind, these are safe pleasure but oh what deceitful ones lurk in the world to catch the unwary youth my poor boy will be particularly disposed to be led astray by these unless his friends protect him he is uncommonly influenced by the company he keeps. I can perceave already since you have been with him his taste for study & the beauties of composition are improv'd.——you have been so extreamly good I am sorry I cannot gratify you in everything you ask. I have searchd a great deal for the lines I wrote on P. E.[2] death but cannot find it them I gave it to Mr. Dwight[3] & I beleave never took a coppy of it but will get it for you if I can you must not expect however to find in it one of those thousand beauties I admire in yours you really make me ashamed to attempt poetry tho you have revivd the wish in me & 'tis stronger than ever but I have more judgement to controul it——I shall be more fond of Shenstone[4] than ever since he has raised a spirit of emulation in you did I ever tell you that I thought your genius & character a little resembled his tho' the first I beleave has more elevation may your life be longer & happier than that of poet of the Leasowes if these are your first attempts in elegy you certainly succeed to admiration yet I have been trying to find some fault & perhaps I could for I read with all the malice of a friend, but I will not tell you what faults I find unless you will promise to return the compliment to my peace when you get it—apropos to finding fault I am resolved you shall find fault with me in person for I have a thousand faults & if you will not find them out I will tell them to you & I on my part will either find or make some in you to prove my sincerity ever since I knew of the correspondence betwixt S——t[5] & you I dyed to have such a one & who so proper to hold it with as ones Husband—so rub up your memory & find out as many of my faults as you can I daresay you will find some either of my friends or enemies that will help you & for my part if you will promise to accept it as kindly as 'tis meant I promise to be perfectly sincear & to tell you all I can hear of you good or bad & ~~almost~~ all I think——'tis so excessive late I cannot write much more am ashamd to send this rambled letter but you must excuse it Bushnell[6] thretend to see it & I almost

2. Possibly "President Edwards," i.e., Jonathan Edwards, her paternal relation and briefly president of the College of New Jersey (later Princeton) from 1757 to his death in 1758, though Whitman would have been only a child when he died.
3. Timothy Dwight (1752–1817; Yale 1769), was a tutor from 1771 to 1777, coinciding with Barlow's college years. He later served as Yale's president from 1795 to 1817. Dwight was Jonathan Edwards's grandson.
4. William Shenstone (1714–63), English poet of the "Graveyard School." His estate, the Leasowes, was a favorite destination of sentimental travelers.
5. Zephaniah Swift.
6. Dall substitutes "Matt" here for "Bushnell" (*Romance* 86). I have not identified a Matthew Bushnell in other records from the era. It may be Ebenezer Bushnell (Yale 1777).

destroyd it in defending it from him I would not care if it had been quite had I time to write a better—my love to all friends pray tell me what is become of Dudly Baldwin?[7] pray how do you come on with french, & can you understand mine I could say a thousand things to you yet had I time but late as it is I must write to my Brother my plan for meating is not quite ripe but I hope we shall not be disappointed—where is S——t & when do you intend to see him————O mon cher I must bid you adeau—[8]

### 5. March 29, 1779—Elizabeth Whitman to Joel Barlow

*Baldwin Papers, Huntington Library. Printed, with some editing, in Dall, Romance, 86–88.*

On leaf: "7 // Mr. Joel Barlow // New Haven // To the care of Whitman"[9]

Ma cher

All that ever I have heard or read of the pleasures & advantages of a married life is nothing to what I have experienced since my connexion with you, 'tis now about three months since we enterd that happy state & I do not perceave but that it gives me as much joy as at the first moment your letters seem to express the same sentiment—indeed <u>ma cher</u> I beleave we are peculiarly fortunate some of my friends this way will have it 'tis only because we are separated that we agree so well, & say so many soft things to each other—but I am not oblig'd to beleave them. & am sure could they see us together they would find cause to alter thier opinion. nay Rochfacoult[1] himself would own that our marriage was rather delightful than convenient—but I must leave this charming subject to make room for one next to it most agreeable, poetry—the liberty which you allow me of criticizing upon yours is very flattering more so than even your compliments & knowing all apology unnecessary to you I shall make use of it with the same freedom with which you granted it—I do believe you are sincear or tho you are my Husband you would not have so large a share of my heart as you have

There are so many beauties in your Elegies that it looks like envy or ill-nature to pop them and dwell upon the few faults but you know I do not pass them unnoticed or unadmired if you will have me find fault then I can do it in a few instances with the expression

<hr>

7. Dudley Baldwin (1753–94), Abraham and Ruth's older brother.
8. She writes to the very lower right corner, filling the entire final page.
9. I.e., to be delivered via her brother, William.
1. La Rochefoucauld's *Les Maximes* (1664) was printed in translation in Philadelphia in 1778. Maxim number 300 held that "[t]here are convenient marriages, but no happy ones." La Rochefoucauld's maxims are debated in William Hill Brown's 1789 novel *The Power of Sympathy* in a scene (letter 40) that contains an extended digression on Elizabeth Whitman's disappearance and death.

only the sentiments are every w[h]ere beautiful, just, & above all criticism. I do not like the word which introduces the first elegy, yet I do not very well know what I would have substituted in its place, or why I dislike it perhaps you can tell—from thence to the fourth verse I like entirely—& the last couplet of that is certainly extremely beautiful in the first the thought is good but I do not think it so happily expressed this I think the case with the 5 too the last lines beautiful the first I think might be mended. The three last verses are so exceeding fine that if I were to say half what I think of them you would accuse me of flattery. but the other elegy is my favourite perhaps because of the subject which you have touchd so tenderly that while it melts me into tears it charms—I have made two or three slight alterations in it too trifling to mention only of single words. I will show you when I see you O joel when will that be—I must tell you I have ventur'd so far as to give one coppy of this elegy to the mother of that sweet Child, but without your name—& she seemed disposed to give your wife the credit of writing it I wish she were capable of it——you excuse yourself in a very flattering & at the same time ingenious manner from finding fault with your wife but indeed you shall not be excusd her faults are too many to need pointing out & she will provoke you to notice them by her severity to yours—I have about a thousand things to say & it is too late to say many more why are you gloomy you must not be by any means hope every thing, expect every thi[ng][2] & do what you can to make your circumstances agreeable tell Mr. B ——[3] I am half uneasy that I do not hear from him & sometimes fear he is offended with me if 'tis only because he is always taken up with writing Buckminster I forgive him my kind love to Ruthie let me know when she is to return—I begin to languish already for some more poetry & O I would give a great deal to hear you sing Dealia[4] as you did the first time I saw—[5] how does your Brother joel do[6] & all the little circle we used to be so sociable with remember me to them ever—what you say of my Brother pleases me—but is it possable for him to be steady in any thing that is good? he is a flighty little fellow & I am afraid will be ruind adeau <u>Ma cher</u>.
March 29–79

2. MS torn here but the word seems clear from context.
3. Abraham Baldwin.
4. Several popular songs and poems from the eighteenth century include the name Delia. For instance, William Shenstone, a favorite poet of Whitman's, addressed his Elegy XXV "To Delia, with some flowers" (94). In a later letter, dated July 1, 1779, she refers again to the song as "my . . . Dealia," which may indicate that she had written a song by this title.
5. This dash is ambiguous; it could simply be punctuation but the mark is low enough on the line that it could be another indication of an omitted name, as in "the first time I saw——."
6. Unclear which of Barlow's brothers this indicates.

### 6. April 15, 1779—Elizabeth Whitman to Joel Barlow

*Baldwin Papers, Huntington Library. A transcription appears in Dall's MHS notebook; Dall also prints it in* Romance, *88–89, though she abridges it significantly and says she only preserves its "triviality" because it alludes to Joseph Buckminster, by Dall's time long believed to have been one of Whitman's rejected suitors.*

On leaf: "8 // Mr Joel Barlow // New Haven"

<div align="center">April 15<sup>th</sup>–79</div>

Ma chere ame,

I have not been quite well for some days past or I should feare have been silent to you. your last letter was one of the most agreeable things I have met with for a great while. I began to fear before I received it that absence had at last coold your affection, or that your second wife[7] was returnd, & the first forgotten, or that you had found another, or, in short my head was full of a thousand disagreeable apprehensions, but now I have no room for complaint & am resolvd no idle jealousies shall again have power to disturb the uncommon felicity which has fallen to my lot in you—who are certainly the faithfulest & best of Husbands, if you must know who I think you resemble or rather who you sometimes by something in your manner put me in mind of 'tis Buckminster, if you remember what you said or did at the time I made you that promise you will know what this is better than I can tell you. I am glad you have at last been so sincear with your wife as to tell her one of her faults I beleave what you observe is extremely just that I do not make a proper difference in my conduct toward the worthless & the worthy of my acquaintance, but trust me in my heart I make the due distinction—your plan pleases me exceedingly—whether it is romantic or not. I am as yet scarce able to judge, it has made me so much so I have done nothing but fancy fine things for you ever since I saw it—I expect it will all be realized & a great deal more—but if I were to give the soberest opinion that I can frame of it I should say that the foundation is laid in reason & reallity but that your romantic imagination had a little share in the finishing and success of it that it will succeed in a degree that will please tho perhaps not satisfy you I have not a doubt I hope & expect that you will always let me into the minutia of your schemes—especially poetical ones. I long to know what story & plan you will fix on for a poem of some emmenence it will not do for you much longer only to coquet it with the muses—but pray let me know all that you write—I am happy that my remarks met your approbation it will induce me to be always free of them—pray what is

---

7. Ruth Baldwin.

the reason that neither Ruthe nor her Brother write me one word for so long a time—give my love to them if you please & to all my acquaintance—tell Betsy Styles[8] that within a few days she will see somebody that I love dearly & that she does not hate pray tell her this & tell her that I say so——if my letter is very dull you must excuse it for really I am not well besides 'tis very late & I am tired. I shall write again tomorrow if the Deacon does not go too soon for me. [I am][9] sorry you have lost Swift for a correspondent tho', I know it cannot be for any long time for wherever he is he will make his letters find their way to you I can but ill supply his place as a correspondent tho I will not yeald to anyone in friendship for you—

you may expect a little volume of satire upon your life conversation behaviour &c as soon as I can get time & spirits to write it. I intend to be very severe tell you all the faults you have & more. I do not know but part of this peace will accompany this, hope it will please you Adieu mon cher—I should have wrote you again but found myself yesterday unwell as to be too stupid I am better this morning but now have not time to say much I shall not fail to improve the erliest opportunity in the meantime let me hear from you. adeau

### 7. April 23, 1779—Elizabeth Whitman to Joel Barlow

*Baldwin Papers, Huntington Library. Dall includes this letter in* Romance, *89–90, abridged and misdated as April 29.*

On leaf: "9 // Mr. Jocl Barlow // New Haven"

Ma cher,

I cannot wholly neglect writing by so inviting an opportunity tho I assure you I have very little time & that little I am obligd to steal from some of the most agreeable company in the world, I mean my Weathersfield[1] friends with whom I am so happy as to be at present on a visit, for the first time since my return—but O Joel to see Sammy,[2] & to see him bending his course towards N.H. is enough to make me wish to leave even this agreeable place & to join once more my dear Family & friends there. I told you in my last that I would no more be jealous—but I promised too much. I find I cannot help having a thousand doubts & fears that you will forget me—forget at least

---

8. Betsey Stiles (1758–95), daughter of Yale president Ezra Stiles.
9. MS damaged; missing words suggested from context.
1. Wethersfield, CT, just south of Hartford.
2. Perhaps Sammy Lyman, a Litchfield native, who is mentioned in the letter of Joel Barlow to Ruth Barlow, July 26, 1779, as staying with Mr. or Mrs. Ellsworth, in Wethersfield or Hartford. But his dates in New Haven were much earlier. (Yale 1770; US House of Representatives from Massachusetts, 1795–1800.) The reference later in the letter to "Brother Sammy" is unclear. Joel had an older brother named Samuel, born in 1752, who died in battle in 1776. Whitman's only brother was named William.

that particular tenderness which used to make us the ~~envy~~ admiration[3] & envy of all married pairs—but why should I doubt you—tis certain this tenderness is natural to you—tis as certain I shall never do anything to deserve the loss, as that I never can, to merit the continuance of it—so much for love & jealousy—which I hope you will excuse in so fond a wife—but now after all this soft nonsense to talk a little like folks of the world—I suppose you will be very glad to see Brother Sammy—I suppose nobody will be sorry—for he is in truth a most amiable creature. I suppose I shall have a great pacquet of letters when he returns if I do not I leave you to suppose how much I shall be disappointed—do you think I do not want to hear from you. I assure you I do extremely & particularly from our dear Muses pray send me word how they do, & what they do or rather let them speak for themselves on paper—I want to know your plans about poetry I intended to send you with this a peace which I beleave will please you if you have not read it—it is a poem calld the Shipwreck[4] not very correct & written by an unlearned author but full of native beauties—I find I cannot borrow it at present as the gentleman is not at home but will send it you the first opportunity—ma cher I have heard one peace of news from N.H. that supprises me this is that our french Master Mr. Beautonaux[5] is married if this is true we may I presume take all the credit of it to our selves. Sure nothing but the sight of our uncommon happiness could wrought such a miracle in the old man as at last to make him alter his resolution & determine upon matrimony if it is so pray send me word wh[o][6] he has married & whether Styles marr[ied] hi[m]. I said I would write but a few lines bu[t] that is scarce possable to you I have yet a thousand things to say I know not when I shall get time to find fault with you—but I could find a great deal with Mr. Baldwin—give my love to him & tell him I am really afraid he either has, or thinks he has some cause to be displeasd with me, & that I am uneasy upon the subject—Ruthe too is silent to me & this give me a great deal of pain my heart is still too greatful for past kindness to bear this neglect without suffering— pray let me hear from my dear friend by you—let me know what they think if they think at all of me—adeau Ma cher I am yours ever— Weathersfield April 23–79

3. Here she overwrites the word "envy" with "admiration."
4. Falconer. The poem was addressed to "the sentimentalists of America" by the printer. If this is, indeed, the poem Whitman cites, she must mean something by "native beauties" other than originating in the American colonies.
5. Probably Beautineau or Batineau. Not identified.
6. MS damaged; in the next few lines, insertions in brackets are determined by context.

## 8. *May 10, 1779—Elizabeth Whitman to Joel Barlow*

*Baldwin Papers, Huntington Library. Dall includes this, abridged and edited, in* Romance, *90–91.*

On leaf: "10 // Mr. Joel Barlow // New Haven // favour by Mr. Whiting"[7]

Mon, cher,

I study so little French I can not get one new phrase for you—I do not know but you will think me wanting in my duty as a wife that I have not answered your kind letters sooner or at least made some acknowledgment for them—that is all I can pretend to do at this time—for it is one Oclock & I am very tired have spent the evening in company besides walking half a mile judge then if I can pretend to find fault with you at present—no really I am too tired & too good humourd—but for your encouragement I will tell you I have got a sheet full of hints and sketches in that way which I have taken down when I felt most disposed to be severe & intend to work them into a part of a satire the first leisure opportunity you cant think how sorry I am to hear you do not intend comeing to Election[8] I flattered myself you would—'tis not to[o] late yet pray alter your plans & come there is one at least here who wants to see you exceedingly that you cannot doubt. & she has made many more wish to see you—I heard last week from Mr. Dwight that he would soon take journey to Come he will certainly either go or return by the way of N. Haven & in that case you will see him & be able to consult him your self I sincearly wish you may for I know of no person so capable of advising or assisting you either in fixing on a plan or executing—your wifes opinion you may always command on every subject. & she wishes for your sake she were more worthy to advise you I think your plan a good one so far as I am able to judge I have but one objection to it that I think of at present & that is a selfish one I confess I do not like to have you go so far but go where you will I depend upon that our connexion will not be forgotten—I wish in my Soul you would come to Election but if you do not I shall depend upon seeing you before you put out on your Tour—you must know that this Election is a very hurrying time with us which is one reason you have not a better letter—Adieu mon cher. 'tis almost morning remember me to all friends
May 10th–79

---

7. Probably William Joseph Whiting, who would graduate from Yale in 1780.
8. The day on which the governor and assembly were elected; many festivities accompanied the actual election.

### 9. May 12, 1779—Elizabeth Whitman to Joel Barlow

*Baldwin Papers, Huntington Library. Not included in Dall.*

On leaf: "11 // Mr. Joel Barlow // New Haven // Favourd by Mr. Tracy"[9]

Ma chere ame

I really look upon it as a misfortune that I should always be forced to write you in a hurry but I had rather say something tho ever so insipid than nothing—I hope you have before this receavd my last hasty letter which I sent by Mr. Whiting[1] I was extreamly disappointed in not seeing you or any of my dear friends from N. Haven at Election. I heard from you yesterday by Mr. Leavenworth[2] but how could you let him come without a letter 'tis true I cannot pretend my last was worth an answer but I hoped & expected that you would improve every opportunity but your other wife is returnd well Joel I am willing you should pay a share of your attention to her. but I must not be neglected—give my love to Ruthe & tell her I try to be as generous as possible & do not bequeath you to her but a little I will write the dear girl the very first opportunity when I can command a moment leasure—you enquired in one of yours about Mr. Dwight he will be at N. Haven I beleave sometime next week—

I have no poetry or any thing else to send you at present but will send you every thing that I think will please you by Billy[3] among the rest I will not fail to send the critical observation you seem so desireous of adeau Tracy waits
May 12

### 10. June 8, 1779—Elizabeth Whitman to Joel Barlow

*Baldwin Papers, Huntington Library. Dall leaves out almost the whole first paragraph and the last half of the second. See* Romance, *91.*

On leaf: "12 // Mr. Joel Barlow // New Haven"[4]

Ma chere ame,

Your letters came very seasonable to save me from a fit of despair do you know that your last before these were dated in april—twas a great while indeed for you to be silent—but I accept your excuses—& if I did not, must forgive you after the receipt of two such kind &

9. Uriah Tracy (1755–1807; Yale, 1778), a future US senator from Connecticut (1796–1807).
1. Letter 8 here.
2. Mark Leavenworth (1752–1812; Yale 1771) would join Barlow in French business ventures in the 1790s.
3. Presumably her brother, William.
4. This appears to be the last numbered letter before Whitman discontinued her system.

agreeable letters I am ashamed of the poor return I am going to make to them, I say going to, for I can not make any other 'tis late at night & I am fatigued to death with the hot weather & a great deal of company which we have had this week, I think they pressed me because I wanted to be at leasure, & have a little time to devote to you—I must again disappoint you of my long letter but you shall have it finally—& the longer I keep it the more I will make—there is policy in this for I expect the more fault I find with you the better you will love me—I wish you could have found no one to bring your letters & then I should before this have had the satisfaction to see you I absolutely depend upon your promise of comeing here this summer—if one time will but suit you as well as another I will tell you in my next when I wish you to come if not come when you can with most convenience & be assured come when you will I shall rejoice to see you— Betsy Styles is in town & you will easily beleave it gives me a great deal of pleasure to see her, but it makes me wish more than ever for you & a few other New Haven friends with whom we used to spend our sociable evenings—

What you say on the subject of jealousy is extreamly agreeable, but you must not expect to cure me entirely of mine, since jealousy is my foiable—the very kind & tender interest which you appear to take in whatever concerns me merits my warmest gratitude you shall have some account of my affairs before long——make me no apology for your letters, & by no means alter the style of them. I like your principle subject & your manner of treating it extreamly—you will see Mr. Dwight before I shall—when I do see him I shall not forget you—nor at any other time I am sorry Swift is mad with the world but you must get his fit over as soon as you can—come & see him, & me, & you will put us both into good humour—pray keep your promise & write oftner I wish there had been a dozen Miss Salmonses[5] if you would have given each of them a letter—remember my love to Mr. Atwater[6] & all our acquaintance O how I long to hear you sing the new tune that you tell of, & my ou Dealia—I know you will not approve of a pacquet without poetry & therefore send the little peice of which you used to like the first verse so well pray what is become of our muses? have you wrote nothing lately give me leave to say you must make me acquainted with all you write if you do not send it to me—I owe letters to Mr. Baldwin, & Ruthe but can only write to you to night excuse me to them. I will write soon—<u>adieu mon cher</u> I am as ever <u>yours</u>

5. Not identified, though Salmon was a familiar Connecticut surname.
6. Noah Atwater (1752–1802), Yale tutor from 1778 to 1781. Barlow mentions, in a 1779 letter to Noah Webster, Atwater (and William Lockwood; see below, p. 288) as allies and advocates with the president in his attempt to win a tutor's position at Yale (Todd 20).

### 11. July 1, 1779, Elizabeth Whitman to Joel Barlow

*This letter is not included in the Baldwin Papers at the Huntington. The copy text is Dall's MHS notebook. Dall includes an abbreviated version of this letter in* Romance, *91–92.*

July 1st 1779

Ma Chere,

I wish I could ever know of an opportunity to write you more than half an hour beforehand. I would not then send you such worthless insignificant letters as I do. but as it is I judge you by myself in sending them, for any thing suits me better than neglect. I should have replyd to your last letter which was dearly welcome among my friends and my pleasures and made a part of the last,—but till this I have not known of an opportunity when I could command a moment's time, I desired however Mr. Baldwin and Lockwood[7] to say every thing kind and affectionate for me to my dear husband—and Mr. Lockwood as a married man certainly knew how to treat the subject—We live here especially in the summer season a life of pleasurable disapation and have so much company that it is almost impossible how much so ever one may think of an absent friend to steal a moments time for him—I am quite impatient for you to come and see us—I only wait for my sister Polly[8] to return to urge you to it with all the ardor that suits my connexion with you—the poor girl has spent a dull summer at Westbury[9]—we have had a world of good company in her absence and I am a mind to reserve some for her at her return—I know she wants exceedingly to see her new brother[1]—What is become of the Muses? I begin to grow very impatient for some account from Parnassus[2]—you have seen Mr. Dwight I hope, it is as much as I can do to say I have, he made so short a stay here, and his friends were almost [*missing*][3] to pull him to pieces—tis almost a misfortune to be so very good, and so much beloved—let me hear from you soon. You should not wait for me, you have ten times my leisure for writing. I must bid you adieu.

Ma cher—
E. W.

---

7. William Lockwood (1753–1828); Yale tutor from 1779 to 1780.
8. Elizabeth's younger sister, Mary (1754–1834).
9. Now Watertown, CT, northwest of Waterbury.
1. I.e., Barlow, playing on the marital conceit Whitman maintains throughout several of the letters.
2. Mount Parnassus, associated in Greek mythology with Apollo, the Muses, and Orpheus. She may be using the reference as a nickname for New Haven or for Yale College itself.
3. Word erased.

*12. October 17, 1779—Elizabeth Whitman to Joel Barlow*

*Baldwin Papers, Huntington Library. Included in Dall's MHS notebook and in Dall, Romance, 92–94, where it appears with some commentary.*

On leaf: "Mr. Joel Barlow // New Haven"[4]

Ma chare ame,

I am extreamly pleased with the dependence you put upon my friendship nor shall it ever disappoint you—I will write you all I know of the affair you mention I wish it was more, & better, indeed I know nothing particular—those Gentlemen to whom your friends have mention your plan[5] approve of it, & say you shall be encouraged. I wish God would give some one of them a heart to do all that you want or rather I wish he would give some of us who have hearts the means—. I must own to you dear joel I have no great expectation that those to whom the affair has been mention will do any thing affectual about it—I have had much conversation with Webster[6] about it, & he is still sanguine he will write you all his thoughts on the subject & advise you to stay at N.H. 'till he can tell you with certainty what to depend upon in this I join him. as in a short time he will probably be able to inform you.

Let me beg of you my dear Friend not to be discouraged with regard to your design tho it should not succeed at this time. & above all things not to give yourself any uneasiness about what your friends have attempted, if it should not succeed it cannot possably be any disadvantage to you that I can think of—your friends will be proud to avow that it originated from them. & it has at least made you known to some worthy men who will wish you well. & possably do you some service if not in the way & at the time I wish—yet, I feel for your delicacy which I know is wounded by the idea you entertain of the matter—be assured I have not mentioned it to any mortal, nor shall I & I beleave Webster has mentioned it only to those who he thought would be of service how far they may mention it is impossable to say, but I beg you would give yourself no trouble about it—And now let me intreat you once more not to be dejected on any account, 'tis true you are in a disagreeable situation on some accounts but it will be mended soon Fortune owes you much, & she will pay you—you are placed at the bottom of her wheel & every change must be for the better—you have every thing to hope & nothing to fear I know you despise the favours of fortune any further

---

4. Marked in pencil, in another hand, at top of letter: "Whole."
5. I.e., his plan for *Vision of Columbus*, the patriotic epic he would publish in 1787.
6. Noah Webster (1758–1843; Yale 1778). Webster was one of Barlow's most frequent correspondents in this period.

than they are necessary—the prosecution of your noble & benevo-
lent designs I know you have a Soul as much superior to the sordid
love of welth as your Genius is to that of the generallity of men—all
I wish you is a decent independance that shall enable you to gratify
~~your~~ & persue your favourite inclinations. If [those][7] who can help
you to this will not you mu[st] help yourself for you can you will
certainly meet with some assistance—write to me as often as pos-
sable while you continue at N.H. I will write you again by next
weeks post or sooner if I have opportunity preserve your spirits & be
certain of the constant affection of your friends, in me you will
always find a true one as I will shew you by more than words if I ever
have it in my power—Adieu mon cher——
October 17[th]–79

### 13. November 1779—Elizabeth Whitman to Joel Barlow

*The copy text is Dall's version in* Romance, *95. This letter is not included
in the Baldwin Papers and does not appear in Dall's MHS notebook.*

November, 1779.

What time I have, I steal from our dear Northampton friends. Mr.
and Mrs. Dwight, Sally,[8] and Mrs. Storrs[9] speak of you with a great
deal of affection, and hoped to have met you here.

I am sorry that I cannot now inform you with respect to Colonel
Broom.[1] I will take the earliest opportunity, but it might not be
proper to mention it just at present, as the family are overwhelmed
with affliction at the loss of a dear sister. The use you make of that
melancholy event is just and rational. I always feel that the loss of
one friend binds the rest closer to my heart. I am sorry for Ruthe's
misfortune. Tell her that I love her, and will write by the first
opportunity, I find at last your long-sought letter from Mr. Baldwin,
Mr. Dwight found it at Northampton, and brought it here. I hope it
will make some amends for your disappointment in not seeing him.
Providence will throw something in your way before long. I have
very little expectation of your coming to Colonel Broom, because
his children are so young.[2] I can hardly think he wants an instruc-

---

7. MS damaged; this insertion and the next are implied from context.
8. Not identified, though possibly the same Sally as in letter 1 here.
9. Not identified. Seth Storrs of Northampton, MA, was involved with Dwight (and Bar-
low briefly) in establishing a preparatory school in Northampton. Storrs was not mar-
ried, however, until the late 1780s. Dwight's sister, Sarah, married Nathan Storrs of
Northampton, date unknown.
1. Zunder, in *Early Days of Joel Barlow*, speculates that Dall may have misread the name
of Col. John Brown of Northampton (262). However, Whitman probably refers to Lt.
Col. John Broome (1738–1810), who fled New York City for Hartford during the Revo-
lution and ran his merchant business out of Wethersfield. See Mather 664. Thanks to
Jennifer Harris for help with this identification.
2. John Broome's oldest child was born in 1771.

tor. If he should, I believe you would be acceptable to him, and have no doubt the place would suit you.

*14. December 18, 1779—Elizabeth Whitman to Joel Barlow*

*Baldwin Papers, Huntington Library. Printed in Dall*, Romance, 95.

On leaf: "Mr. Joel Barlow // New-Haven"[3]

Ma Chere,

I have been wishing for an opportunity of writing you this long time but not one could I find & now I know of none but will neglect writing no longer. I thought you were not in quite so good spirits when you wrote last as I could wish it is not come to that yet that the world has nothing for you to do besides your friends will always want you one of those on whom you used to say you had the least dependance has found an employment for you that I think will be agreeable this is Mr D——t his School[4] is like to succeed & with him I think you must be happy, & will have some advantages for Study that you can have no where else Watson[5] will write you more about the matter I am much pleasd with the prospect of haveing you [settled?][6] at Northampton at least for a time what an excellent man is our friend! I never think of him but with gratitude to Heaven for haveing made him so worthy & so amiable—I have just been reading a pretty observation in the Guardian which I apply to him "It is a tribute that ought to be paid to Providence by men of distinguished faculties to praise & adore the author of their being with a spirit suitable to those faculties & rouse slower men by their word, actions & writing to a participation of their transports & thanksgivings"[7]

Thus does our admirable friend & it is almost impossable for any one to be in his company & not grow both wiser & better—you'll think me in a grave humour but 'tis Saturday night I love to be grave some times & whatever humour I am in I love to indulge it to you— Does not this Storm make you think of one we had last Christmas I am I am[8] afraid I shall not be so warm this winter as I was then—I hope this will find you at New Haven & if you stay there long I hope to see you there—how do the Muses this winter? & what do they do? I design to send them a little work soon—I know a Song of which

3. The outer leaf also includes what appears to be a "4," perhaps a postal mark.
4. Dwight had opened a day school in Northampton, MA, where he had returned from New Haven to care for his aging mother in 1778. Barlow had already taught for Dwight that summer, and Whitman seems to think the position could be regained.
5. James Watson (1750–1806; Yale 1776) would become a prosperous merchant in New York City after the war and a member of the US Senate from 1798 to 1800.
6. Word unclear. Could also be fitted. In either case the t's are not crossed.
7. A passage from Addison and Steele 87, also included in Addison 221.
8. Repetition in original.

the tune is excellent but the words very indifferent the subject a parting scene between two lovers what could be better, I will send you a coppy of it. now if you will let Quammeny[9] take it & work it up in a more elligiable form I shall be much obligd to you—I have not your letter by me & forget whether you mention receiving one from me by Mr. Hopkins[1]—I am dull to night & therefore bid you adeau in all humours[2] & tenses I am yours———
Dec[br] 18[th] very Stormy–79

## 15. December 28, 1779—Elizabeth Whitman to Joel Barlow

*Baldwin Papers, Huntington Library; also in Dall's MHS Notebook.*

On leaf: "Mr. Joel Barlow // New Haven // Hon[d] by Doct. Northrop"[3]

Ma Chere,

I suppose this letter will reach New Haven almost as soon as youself but so good an opportunity I would improve tho' it had hapned on Saturday besides I am determined to leave you no room for complaint any longer—I had no opportunity for conversation when you were here 'twas only literally seeing you so that I know nothing about you that I want to know I mean of the situation of your mind your prospects & your Poem I was happy however to observe you appeard in better spirits than for some time past—Hope is said to be the best blessing indulgd to mortals if this be true you are certainly not unhappy for you have much to hope—&, as I think, who you know am never sanguine you have at present good reason to hope almost all that you can wish—

I made in my last a request to you to make a new song that will go to the tune of the enclosed if you will be so good at some leasure hour as to write one & send me I shall be extreamly obligd to you I will get the tune which is a fine one Prickd & send it to you.——Webster was here the afternoon you left us he was very sorry that he could not see you but say he will write you soon.

Pray let me hear from you as often as possable The Song you see on the other side 'tis a mere jargon of sentiment & nonsense will serve excellently as a foil for Quominies—pray keep Quamminy in

---

9. Tyler suggests this is a nickname Barlow had given himself (142). It was also a name frequently given to slaves. Barlow would "set Quamminy to work" on poetry, as he wrote in a letter to Ruth Baldwin of Oct. 10, 1780. In Whitman's next letter (letter 15) she refers to Quamminy using a female pronoun and in letter 16 she refers to Quamminy in terms that imply both servitude and that Quamminy is one of her and Barlow's daughters, the Muses.

1. Lemuel Hopkins (1750–1801), who with Dwight, Barlow, and a few others would form the circle later known as the Hartford or Connecticut Wits, was at this time a physician in Litchfield, CT.

2. Dall substitutes "moods" for "humours" and makes other minor changes throughout.

3. Dr. Joel Northrop (1753–1807; Yale 1776), who lived and practiced in New Haven.

employ dont let her be idle this cold weathers Watson is afraid she will freeze in spight of all he has done for her—I intend to slip down & see your Quomany[4] this winter if possable remember me to all friends particularly Ruthe—Watson & Billy desire love to you adeau Ma Chere I
     am yours————
Dec 28th–79
[Enclosure]

## A Parting Scenes [*sic*]

### 1

Hark! the trumpet sounds to arms, O fatal noise!
Hark! the trumpet sounds to arms, adeau all joys
Cares, & fears, all round me move,
For your sake my charming love.
Midst alarms, & bloody arms,
Ye Gods preserve the man I love.

### 2

Hark the General gives command, ye brave obey
Hark! the General gives command, march march away;
Cannons roar & bullets fly,
Oh I sigh, I faint, & die;
While such sorrows fill my heart
May heaven defend my better part.

### 3

Amidst blood & wounds & terrers while he goes,
Those cruel scenes of war, create my woes;
Ye angels who protect the brave
Guard my hero from the grave
I your praises will prolong
While life remains in every song.

### 4

Cease complaints, & dry your tears my lovely maid
Cease complaint, & dry your tears dont be afraid;
Heaven that hath made mankind its care,
Saves the brave to guard the fair

---

4. She may distinguish here between two imaginary servants/muses, Quamminy and Quomany, though it remains unclear.

Cruel fate my life may close
But shall never change my vows.

5

Those kind words do charm my Soul thou lovely youth
Those kind words do charm my soul for they are truth
But when dangers round the[e] fly
I in fear for you shall die
And if you your life should lose
What avail your faithful vows

6

Cease complaints & dry your tears you lovely maid
Cease complaints & dry your tears dont be afraid
Coward Souls the fair despise,
Heroes are the men they prize
Honor calls I must obey
You'd despise me should I stay.———

## 16. *February 25, 1780—Elizabeth Whitman to Joel Barlow*

*Baldwin Papers, Huntington Library. Also printed in Dall*, Romance, 98.
On leaf: "Mr. Joel Barlow // N.H."

<p style="text-align:center">Hartford Feb<sup>y</sup> 25<sup>th</sup> 1780</p>

Ma Cher,

   This is just to inform you that I am not at Boston I do not chuse
that the report of my being there should deprive me of any more let-
ters I must own I am in your debt & shall be for I cannot write any
thing to night worth the least attention but as I wish to keep up a
constant correspondence with you I mean to write every opportunity
such stuff as I can think of without any trouble & expect in return
the wit of the Muses—is not it a very modest Bargain that I make
with you? but you know I can & do write better than this sometime
either by luck or study—I hear but very little from you this winter but
I will not complain for I suppose you are employd in taking care of
the family however there was a time when no cares could have made
you so long unmindful of your dearest, I mean one of your dearest
wifes, but we have been married more than a year & if we are not
quite so attentive to each other as at first few of our cotemperaries
will be able to reproach us———for my own part I feel no decline of
affection but beleave that I shall love you as in duty bound all the
days of my life.———I have just receavd a letter from Ruthy which I

fear I shall not have time to answer by this opportunity in that case I beg you would give my love to her I am extreamly obliged to her. if this letter is not quite so good as it should be I do not much care for you have got a fine long large one from Mr. Lyman[5] so I judge by the outside which I assure you is all I have seen—I wish I were with you to help you read it I had a good mind to have made use of the preveleges of a wife & opend it so great was my desire to see the productions of so fine a pen as Mr. Lymans.———

Pray what has Quamany done with my Song. if she has not finishd it she is an idle hussy & I beg you would set her immediately about it I am sure that her Sisters had rather she should do their work over after them than be idle as the[y] are all <u>Spinsters</u>—I have rattled away at a great rate & got together a collection of words which you may put any friendly meaning too—you must if you please excuse this writing but if you were to write half so bad I should scold at you like a true wife I designd to have made my letter a little longer but the Deacon is going & you must excuse it Mr. Watson & Polly send their love to you I am as ever yours

### 17. March 21, 1780—Elizabeth Whitman to Joel Barlow

*Baldwin Papers, Huntington Library. A transcript appears in Dall's MHS notebook but it is not included in* Romance.

On leaf: "Mr. Joel Barlow // New Haven // Favour by Mr. Blakely"[6]
In another hand: "Betsy Whitman's letters to Mr. Barlow 1779–80 (heroine of the novel called Eliza Wharton)"[7]

Ma Cher,

There was a time when two months would not have elaps'd without bringing me a line from you but—"What does not change? The Tower that long has stood, &c.["][8] Ma vie, mon amour, & mon bel ange, seem already to be forgotten for the credit of love you ought to write a little oftner—I designd to have wrote you however—but company comeing in has prevented me, & I can only desire you to give the enclosed to Ruthy—I am extreamly impatient to hear a little news from Parnassus—I know you have Friend there pray forward some intelligence to me—I am as ever yours—

———

March 21[th] 80

5. Possibly Samuel Lyman (see p. 283, n.2), who lived and practiced law in Hartford.
6. Possibly David Blakely (1750–1821), a native of Woodbury, CT, who served in the Revolutionary army and later farmed in Vermont.
7. Hannah Webster Foster's *The Coquette*, based on Whitman's life and death, was known to many nineteenth-century readers as *Eliza Wharton*.
8. Close quote omitted in original. The quotation is from John Armstrong (1709–79), Scottish poet and physician. See *Art of Preserving Health*.

## 18. May 12, 1781—Elizabeth Whitman to Joel Barlow

*Dall includes this fragment in* Romance, 99; *it is not in the Baldwin Papers at the Huntington Library or in Dall's MHS notebook.*

### May 12, 1781.

I heard from you by Mr. Levengsworth,[9] but why did you let him come without a letter? Give my love to Ruthe, and tell her that I do try to be as generous as possible, and do not begrudge you to her but a little.[1] I will write the dear girl by the very first opportunity. You enquire about Mr. Dwight. He will be in New Haven next week.

## 19. November 25, 1782—Elizabeth Whitman to Ruth Barlow

*Baldwin Papers, Huntington Library; printed in* Romance, 99–102. *In the margin of the last page, in pencil: "E. Whitman."*

### Hartford Nov^br 25^th 1782

My Dear Ruthe,

I thank you a thousand times for your letter, & the agreeable news it contains, will we admit you do you ask into this excellent town of Hartford?[2] yes with as much pleasure as a Lawyer does his client, or a Lady her lover, & rather than you should not have room I should be willing to turn out several that I know of—notwithstanding I always thought my self very publick spirited—& know that the riches of a community consists in the number of its inhabitents. but I hope that we shall not be obligd to impoverish ourselvs on your account—but that you will add to our <u>strenth</u> & riches, by comeing amongst us, for Goodrich[3] has I suppose by this time secured you, as perhaps he has wrote you word, a very good place, I beleave it will be in Trumbulls[4] neighbourhood but when I last saw Goodrich he was not quite certain as to what you tell of your poverty, I am glad of it with all my heart, for many reason. I beleave I shall not here mention more than three or four, & leave the rest 'till some other opportunity—in the first place, then, I love you so well as to be willing to share any fortune with you, & we are poor & always have been so, & are contriving to become still more poor if we can—in this we are no ways singuler, most of the people of merit

9. I.e., Mark Leavenworth.
1. Joel and Ruth had been secretly married at the end of January.
2. The Barlows settled in Hartford in 1782 and lived there for the next several years. Joel left for England in the spring of 1788.
3. Chauncey Goodrich (1759–1815; Yale 1776) was a tutor from 1779 to 1781, practiced law in Hartford in the 1780s, and served as a US senator from 1808 to 1813.
4. John Trumbull (1750–1831; Yale 1767), was a tutor from 1771 to 1773 and practiced law in New Haven after 1774. He was also Whitman's cousin and another member of the Hartford Wits.

that I have ever know, or heard of, are, & were so before us. now I do not mean to imply because that we are poor that we must be absolutely be people of merit, but I think as the world goes the sign is very much in our favour—then as for poets, & men of Genius with whom you have a right to class your Husband, they have always been poor from time immemoreal, I need not mention Homer, the prince of them, who sung his Epic poem about the Streets, nor a thousand others whose historys I dare say you have at your tongues end for my part I am apt to imagine poverty to be a peculiar mark of the favour of Heaven, as the ancients used to esteem it to be struck with lightning—I only wish my dear that you were half so well convinced of the blessings & advantages of poverty as I am, you would then be perfectly contented if it should be your lot, which however you are by no means certain of unless you take great pains to deserve it. Polly is in a great hurry about some work & therefore the agreeable task of writing for both devolves upon me, I do not doubt she will set her hand to all I have said or can say about poverty.——

I am heartily glad to hear my dear friend that you are treated at home with kindness, & attention, not that I by any means think that enough for so diserving a Child as you have ever been, but I could not bear, as I have sometimes told you, to have you on other than friendly terms with your own father, I cant but hope he will yet do you justice sometime or other—& I think we ought to suffer any thing but absolute slavery, from so revered a character rather than shew resentment.——

The walking has been so extreamly bad I have been able to make but little enquery about crokery, there is I beleave considerable queensware in town, I am not certain about China I will look for this & the other articles & let you know as soon as possable, I beleave such things are not less high here than at New Haven but then you would save the trouble of bringing them—pray give my love to joel if he is returnd, Mr Wadsworth[5] send his to you & thanks you for remembering him when you were at Ridgefield—Mama,[6] Abby,[7] every body send love to you, & wish to see you—you see my dear I have not less propensity to write long letters than you have—don't you think it is the sign of a fertile genius? but I must bid you adeau for the present whatever inclination I may have to continue writing

    Yours always E W

5. Jeremiah Wadsworth (1743–1804), Hartford merchant and banker, was another of Whitman's cousins. He was later a member of the Continental Congress and the US House of Representatives (1789–95).
6. Abigail Stanley Whitman (1719–95), Elizabeth's mother.
7. Whitman's sister Abigail. Sources differ on whether she was older (b. 1746?) or younger than Elizabeth.

WHITMAN'S LETTERS

20. Poem: "To Mr. Barlow, by his friend, Miss Whitman, on New-Year's Day, 1783"

*Published in the* New York Daily Advertiser, *October 4, 1788;* Worcester Magazine, *October 2, 1788; and the Northampton, Massachusetts,* Hampshire Gazette, *October 15, 1788.*[8]

Should every wish the breast of friendship knows,
Be to your ear convey'd in rustick prose,
Lost in the wonders of your eastern clime,
Or wrapt in vision to some unborn time;
The unartful tale might no attention gain,
For friendship knows not like the muse to feign.
Forgive her then, if in this weak essay,
She tries to emulate thy daring lay,
And give to truth, and warm affection's glow,
The charms that from the tuneful sisters flow,
On this bless'd morning's most auspicious rise,
Which finds thee circled with domestic joys;
May thy glad heart in grateful tribute pay,
To him who shap'd thy course and smooth'd thy way;
That Guardian power, who, to thy merit kind,
Bestow'd the bliss most suited to thy mind;
Retirement, friendship, leisure; learned ease,
All that the philosophic soul can please;
All that the muses love, the harmonious nine,
Inspire thy lays and aid each great design:
But more than all the world could else bestow,
To fix secure in bliss thy future life,
Heaven crown'd thy blessings with a lovely wife;
Wise, gentle, good—O! every grace combin'd,
That charms the sense or captivates the mind!
Skill'd every soft emotion to improve,
The joy of friendship, and the wish of love;
To sooth the heart which pale misfortunes train,
Invades with grief or agonizing pain;
To point through devious paths, the narrow road
That leads the soul to virtue and to God.
O friend! O sister! to my bosom dear,
By every tie that binds the soul sincere;
O, while I fondly dwell upon thy name,
Why sinks my soul unequal to the theme.

8. Published following Whitman's death in July 1788, amid other newspaper commentary on the matter. See Waterman.

But though unskill'd thy various worth to praise,
Accept my wishes and excuse my lays.
May all thy future days like this be gay,
And love and fortune blend thy kindest ray:
Long in their various gifts may thou be blest,
And late ascend the endless realms of rest.

### WORKS CITED

Addison, Joseph. *The Evidences of the Christian Religion*. London: Tonson, 1730.

Addison, Joseph, and Richard Steele. *The Guardian, vol. 1*. London: Tonson, 1714.

Armstrong, John. *The Art of Preserving Health: A Poem*. 1744.

Baldwin Family Papers, 1779–81. Box 1, BN 434–48, Henry E, Huntington Lib., San Marino.

Barlow, Joel. *The Prospect of Peace: A Poetical Composition, Delivered in Yale-College, at the Public Examination, of the Candidates for the Degree of Bachelor of Arts; July 23, 1778*. New Haven: Green, 1778.

——. Letter to Ruth Barlow. 26 July 1779. Barlow Papers. Houghton Lib., Harvard U, Cambridge.

——. Letter to Ruth Barlow. 10 Oct. 1780. Barlow Papers. Houghton Lib., Harvard U, Cambridge.

Dall, Caroline W. H. Letter to John Rand. 11 Feb. 1892. BN 181. Henry E. Huntington Lib., San Marino.

——. Notebook [MHS notebook]. Dall Papers. Reel 43, vol. N5. Massachusetts Historical Soci., Boston.

——. *The Romance of the Association; or, One Last Glimpse of Charlotte Temple and Eliza Wharton, A Curiosity of Literature and Life*. Cambridge: Wilson, 1875.

Dexter, Franklin Bowditch. *Biographical Sketches of the Graduates of Yale College with Annals of the College History, July, 1778–June, 1792*. Vol. 4. New York: Holt, 1907.

Falconer, William. *The Shipwreck: A Sentimental and Descriptive Poem. In Three Cantos. By William Falconer. An English Sailor*. Philadelphia: Bell, 1774.

Gordon, Lyndall. *Vindication: A Life of Mary Wollstonecraft*. New York: Harper Collins, 2005.

Jacob, Stephen. *A Poetical Essay, Delivered at Bennington, on the Anniversary of the 16th of August, 1777*. Hartford: Watson, 1779.

Kurtz, Benjamin Putnam, and Carrie Cobb Autrey, eds. *Four New Letters of Mary Wollstonecraft and Helen M. Williams*. Berkeley: U of California P, 1937.

Mather, Frederick Gregory. *The Refugees of 1776 from Long Island to Connecticut*. Albany: Lyon, 1913.

Shenstone, William. *The Works in Verse and Prose*. London: Dodsley, 1764.

Smith, Noah. *A Speech, Delivered at Bennington, on the Anniversary of the 16th of August, 1777*. Hartford: Watson, 1779.

Todd, Charles Burr. *The Life and Letters of Joel Barlow, LLD, Poet, Statesman, Philosopher, with Extracts from His Works and Hitherto Unpublished Poems*. New York: Putnam, 1886.

"To Mr. Barlow, by His Friend, Miss Whitman, on New-Year's Day, 1783." *Worcester Magazine* 2 Oct. 1788: 4. Reprinted as "Pegasus of Apollo! . . . To Mr. Barlow, by His Friend, Miss Whitman, on New-Year's Day, 1783." *New York Daily Advertiser* 4 Oct. 1788: 2. Reprinted as "To Mr. Barlow, by His Friend, Miss Whitman, on New-Year's Day, 1783." *Hampshire Gazette* [Northampton] 15 Oct 1788: 4.

Tyler, Moses Colt. *Three Men of Letters*. New York: Putnam, 1895.

*The Universal Songster and Museum of Mirth: A Collection of Popular Songs*. Boston: Gaylor, 1835.

Verhoeven, Wil. *Gilbert Imlay: Citizen of the World*. London: Pickering, 2008.

Waterman, Bryan. "Elizabeth Whitman's Disappearance and Her 'Disappointment.'" *William and Mary Quarterly* 3rd ser. 66.2 (2009): 325–64.

Webster, Noah. Letter to Stephen Jacob. 3 Oct. 1803. *The Letters of Noah Webster*. Ed. Harry R. Warfel. New York: Library Publishers, 1953, 253.

Woodress, James. "The Writing of Biography." *The Continuing Quest*. Ed. Martha Boaz. Metuchen: Scarecrow, 1967. 82–96. Vol. 2 of *The Quest for Truth*.

Zunder, Theodore A. *The Early Days of Joel Barlow, a Connecticut Wit: Yale Graduate, Editor, Lawyer and Poet, Chaplain during the Revolutionary War; His Life and Works from 1754 to 1787*. New Haven: Yale UP, 1934.

# Inventory of Whitman's Belongings on Her Death[†]

2 ginneys, 1 crown, 2-4 pistoreens dollars.[1]

6 silver teaspoons, Marked E. W.

[†] From Charles Knowles Bolton, *The Elizabeth Whitman Mystery at the Old Bell Tavern in Danvers* (Peabody, MA: Peabody Historical Society, 1912), 39–41.

1. "Ginney": or guinea, a British gold coin valued at 21 shillings; "crown": a British silver coin valued at five shillings or 25 pence; "pistoreen": or pistareen, a small Spanish silver coin used in American colonies and the West Indies.

1 pinch back ring set with a Stone, 1 gold twisted ring.

1 quilt working pocket book, 1 small chiney green Box.

1 silver probe, & 1 pr. Silver Fosseps, 1 pr. Sizers, 1 doble Bladed Knife.[2]

4 Musslen Tuckers,[3] 1 black lace, 2 ribbens.

1 pr. Muslen ruffles, 2 Lawn[4] and 1 Muzlen apron.

1 Black Mode apron, 1 gause apron, 2 gause Handkerchiefs.

2 Lace Handkerchiefes, 1 black Silk do, 1 Shaul cotten.

1 Mizlen cloke, 1 remnant of gauze, 2 gilt Fanns.

2 ribbons, 3 pr. cloath & 1 pr. Leather gloves.

1 figured Lutstring[5] gound, 1 lite patch—found in ye trunks with other triffling small things.

3 cloath capps, 2 calico gounds & 1 skirt ditto.

2 pr. fustin[6] Pokets, 4 pr. cotten & 1 pr. thread Hose.

4 Linen Shifts, 1 Mercilions quilt.

1 pr. Russels Shoes, 1 cotten shaul found wrapted in Draper cloth.

1 calash, 1 black Bonet, 1 black Satten cloke.

1 camblet Riding hood, 1 pr. Stays, 1 pr. old leather and 1 pr. of old calimico Shoes,

1 Japand Qt Kenister[7] of green Tea.

1 Ink case with Sealing wax, wafers, etc.

1 work bag and kniting worker, etc.

1 pr. white Mettle Shoe Buckles.

1 old Silk Handkerchief, including Sundry Babe cloths.

1 Box with Sundry pieces of Ribbons, Small Looking glass, a gauze capp, etc.,

Ten sheets of paper.

---

2. "Fosseps": i.e., forceps; "Sizers," i.e., scissors. Sewing or, perhaps, obstetrical equipment.
3. "Muslin," a popular woven fabric, brought to Europe from the Middle East; "tucker": a protective piece of linen worn around the neck and shoulders or tucked into a low-cut dress.
4. A tightly woven, glossy fabric.
5. I.e., lustering, a glossy silk.
6. I.e., fustian, a durable cloth of cotton and flax.
7. Japanned: polished; "Kenister," i.e. canister.

# BRYAN WATERMAN

## The Elizabeth Whitman Paper Trail[†]

The *Salem Mercury*'s notice of Whitman's death was reprinted, with
minor variations on occasion, in at least fourteen newspapers, mostly
up and down the East Coast, though not in New Haven or Hartford,
where she was best known. The *Salem Mercury* did not reprint any of
the additional items on Whitman that originated elsewhere.

> Last Friday, a female stranger died at the Bell Tavern, in Dan-
> vers; and on Sunday her remains were decently interred. The
> circumstances relative to this woman are such as excite curios-
> ity, and interest our feelings. She was brought to the Bell in a
> chaise, from Watertown, as she said, by a young man whom she
> had engaged for that purpose. After she had alighted, and taken
> a trunk with her into the house, the chaise immediately drove
> off. She remained at this inn till her death, in expectation of the
> arrival of her husband, whom she expected to come for her, and
> appeared anxious as his delay. She was averse to being interro-
> gated concerning herself or connexions; and kept much retired
> to her chamber, employed in needle-work, writing, &c. She said,
> however, that she came from Westfield, in Connecticut; that her
> parents lived in that State; that she had been married only a few
> months; and, that her husband's name was Thomas Walker;—
> but always carefully concealed her family name. Her linen was
> all marked E.W. About a fortnight before her death, she was
> brought to bed of a lifeless child. When those who attended her
> apprehended her fate, they asked her, whether she did not wish
> to see her friends: She answered, that she was very desirous of
> seeing them. It was proposed that she should send for them; to
> which she objected, hoping in a short time to be able to go to
> them. From what she said, and from other circumstances, it
> appeared probable to those who attended her, that she belonged
> to some country town in Connecticut: Her conversation, her
> writings and manners, bespoke the advantage of a respectable
> family & good education. Her person was agreeable; her deport-
> ment, amiable & engaging; and, though in a state of anxiety and
> suspense, she preserved a cheerfulness, which seemed not the
> effect of insensibility, but of a firm and patient temper. She was
> supposed to be about 35 years old. Copies of letters, of her writ-

[†] Adapted from Bryan Waterman, "The Elizabeth Whitman Paper Trail," *The William and Mary Quarterly* (April 2009): 359–64. Reprinted by permission. All footnotes in this selection are by Bryan Waterman. Images of the original newspaper articles as well as the poem "Disappointment" as it appeared in William Hill Brown's 1789 *Power of Sympathy* are available on http://oieahc.wm.edu/wmq/Apr09/waterman.html.

ing, dated at Hartford, Springfield, and other places, were left among her things.—This account is given by the family in which she resided; and it is hoped the publication of it will be a means of ascertaining her friends of her fate.[1]

The following article from the *Pennsylvania Mercury*, based on Jeremy Belknap's letter to Benjamin Rush of August 16, 1788, was reprinted in at least nine other newspapers, none in Whitman's native Connecticut.

> In one of our papers* there is an account from Danvers, of a woman who died at an inn, of a puerperal fever—a stranger, supposed to be from Connecticut, &c.—I need not repeat the whole, as you will doubtless see it—What I mention it for is, that I think the story may serve as a good moral lecture to young ladies—for this lady, whose conduct appeared so mysterious, proves to be the daughter of a deceased clergyman in Connecticut—She was handsome, genteel, and sensible, but vain and coquettish; *a great reader of Romances.* She refused two as good offers of marriage as she deserved, because she aspired higher than to be a clergyman's wife: And having coquetted it 'till past her bloom, fell into criminal indulgences, proved pregnant, and then eloped—pretending (where she lodged and died,) to be married, and carried on the deception 'till death.
> *See Pennsylvania Mercury of August 7th, 1788.[2]

1. "Salem, July 29," *Salem* [Mass.] *Mercury*, July 29, 1788, [3]. The item was repr. on its own in the [Boston] *Independent Chronicle and the Universal Advertiser*, July 31, 1788, [3]; *Boston Gazette, and the Country Journal*, Aug. 4, 1788, [1]; [Middletown, Conn.] *Middlesex Gazette*, Aug. 4, 1788, [1]; as "Portsmouth, August 5," [Portsmouth] *New-Hampshire Spy*, Aug. 5, 1788, 119; as "Salem, July 29," [New York] *Daily Advertiser*, Aug. 7, 1788, [2]; [Philadelphia] *Pennsylvania Mercury and Universal Advertiser*, Aug. 7, 1788, [4]; [Providence, R.I.] *United States Chronicle: Political, Commercial and Historical*, Aug. 7, 1788, [3]; [Philadelphia] *Pennsylvania Packet, and Daily Advertiser*, Aug. 8, 1788, [2]; *Norwich* [Conn.] *Packet, Or, The Country Journal*, Aug. 14, 1788, [3]; [New London] *Connecticut Gazette and the Universal Intelligencer*, Aug. 15, 1788, [3]; [Portland, Maine] *Cumberland Gazette*, Aug. 21, 1788, [2]; [Bennington] *Vermont Gazette or Freemen's Depository*, Aug. 25, 1788, [2]; [Pittsfield, Mass.] *Berkshire Chronicle*, Aug. 28, 1788, [3]; [Charleston, S.C.] *City Gazette and Daily Advertiser*, Sept. 10, 1788, [2]. I rely on multiple searches with varying keywords in Readex's Early American Newspapers digital database for discussions of newspaper circulation throughout this article. If the search is not exhaustive or is hampered by the limitations of the database and search engine software, the trends in circulation, at least, should be clear from the search results.
2. Printed just one week after Jeremy Belknap wrote the letter to Benjamin Rush (and three weeks after the same Philadelphia newspaper had repr. the original notice of Whitman's death), Belknap's interpretation of Whitman's story was repr. over the course of a month in at least nine more newspapers, slightly fewer than carried the original death notice. (Of these nine only five had run the earlier notice from the *Salem Mercury*.) See "Extract of a Letter from Boston," *Pennsylvania Mercury and Universal Advertiser*, Aug. 23, 1788, [4]; [Philadelphia] *Independent Gazetteer*, Aug. 25, 1788, [2]; *Pennsylvania Packet, and Daily Advertiser*, Aug. 25, 1788, [3]; "New-York, Aug. 30," [New York] *Impartial Gazetteer, and Saturday Evening's Post*, Aug. 30, 1788, [3]; "New-York, Sept. 3. Extract of a Letter from Boston," [New York] *Independent Chronicle and the Universal Advertiser*, Sept. 11, 1788, [3]; "United Columbia. Pennsylvania. Philadelphia, August 25," *Worcester* [Mass.] *Magazine*, Sept. 4, 1788, [2]; "Charleston, September 13, 1788," *City Gazette and Daily Advertiser*, Sept. 13, 1788, [3]; "Extract of a Letter from Boston," [Windsor] *Vermont*

The next letter, to Benjamin Russell, editor of the *Massachusetts Centinel*, was followed by the poem "Disappointment" and "A Letter in Characters Decyphered." The letter and accompanying texts were submitted by the correspondent Curiosos as a correction to the poem's first appearance, two days earlier, in another newspaper, the *Herald of Freedom*, where it and the deciphered letter had been attributed to the late "F——s T——e A——p" (Frances Theodora Apthorp).[3] Only minor variations exist between the two versions of the poem, with the exception of the name change in the penultimate line from "T——e's early tomb" in the *Herald of Freedom* to "E—A's early tomb" in the *Massachusetts Centinel*. On September 24 the *Massachusetts Centinel* again published a letter by Curiosos, this time with errata for the poem: "In the 10th line for *future*, read *useless*—In the 18th line for *kiss'd thee smiling*, read *kiss'd thy token*—the sense is not complete without the alteration—In the 24th line for *show* read *shower*—In the 31st line for *But, ah!* read *And each*." Brown's version in *The Power of Sympathy* follows Curiosos' suggested revisions. The *Herald of Freedom* version of "Disappointment" was reprinted, with corrected attribution given elsewhere in the same editions, in two other New England newspapers. The *Massachusetts Centinel* version was reprinted in four additional newspapers in New England and the mid-Atlantic.[4]

<hr/>

*Journal, and the Universal Advertiser*, Sept. 15, 1788, [2]; *Vermont Gazette or Freemen's Depository*, Sept. 22, 1788, [2]; "Newyork, September 3," *Cumberland Gazette*, Sept. 25, 1788, [1]. I have not been able to locate the New York reprinting dated September 3 that apparently supplied the source for some of these reprintings. In any case the circulation of this extract was more circumscribed than the original July 29 notice not just in the number of papers that took it up, but geographically as well: two of the reprintings were in other Philadelphia newspapers. In a delicious feedback loop that speaks to both the efficiency and inefficiency of postrevolutionary information networks, "Extract of a Letter from Boston" appeared in the Boston *Independent Chronicle and the Universal Advertiser* (which had been the first newspaper to replay the *Salem Mercury*'s original notice) more than two weeks after Belknap wrote his letter to Rush by way of a New York reprinting of the Philadelphia report.

3. Frances Theodora Apthorp (1766–1788), a young Boston woman whose story intersected with Whitman's in regional press. Having become pregnant twice by her older brother-in-law, a Boston politician named Perez Morton, Apthorp killed herself when her father convened a meeting to confront the lovers. Her story, like Whitman's, was taken up in William Hill Brown's *The Power of Sympathy*.

4. Curiosos, "For the Centinel," *Massachusetts Centinel*, Sept. 24, 1788, 12. For the poem's first appearance in print, see "To the Printers of the Herald of Freedom," *Herald of Freedom, and the Federal Advertiser*, Sept. 18, 1788, [6]. This initial publication also includes "A Letter in Characters Decyphered," as do all other newspaper printings of "Disappointment." The *Herald of Freedom* version, with an introductory letter signed "Z" that attributes the poem to "F——s T——e A——p," is reprinted under the heading "Heliconian Fount" in the [Portsmouth] *New-Hampshire Spy*, Sept. 23, 1788, 276, with a corrected attribution in the same issue on page 275; and under the heading "Pegasus of Apollo!" in the *Worcester Magazine*, Sept. 25, 1788, 4, with a corrected attribution on page 3: "The Printers of the Herald of Freedom, from whose paper we selected the poetry in the last page of this day's paper, appear to be mistaken in asserting it to have been written by the late Miss F.T.A. It is now known to be the production of the late unfortunate Miss Whitman, who lately died at the Bell tavern in Danvers." In response the *Massachusetts Centi-*

Mr. Russell,

The Publick curiosity having been excited respecting a young stranger Lady, who died at the Bell Tavern, in Danvers, in July last, I have collected the following account of her, for the information and improvement of your readers: I think it the more necessary, as a poetical production of hers (which is annexed—and which I have had in my possession some weeks) has been attributed, and published, as the performance of another person.

This young woman was brought to the Bell-Tavern, in a chaise by a young man who left her and drove off immediately. She said that she was married and expected there to meet her husband. She wrote *E. Walker.* on the door of the house, and when a gentleman who happened to come along the road stopped and read the name and went away, she said she was undone. She amused herself with reading, writing, and needle work, was agreeable, graceful and genteel in her deportment, and though in a state of anxiety, preserved a cheerfulness which seemed to be the effect not of insensibility, but of patience and firmness. After some time she was delivered of a lifeless child, and died in about a fortnight of puerperal fever, being supposed about 35 years of age.

It has since been discovered that she was an unmarried lady of a reputable family in Connecticut, of the name of Whitman. In her younger days she was admired for her beauty, good sense, and other engaging qualities. She was a *great reader of romances*, and having formed her notions of happiness from that corrupt source, became vain and coquettish, and rejected some very advantageous offers of marriage in hope of realizing something more splendid; until disappointed and past her bloom, she gave way to criminal indulgence, and the consequence becoming visible, she eloped from her friends, and terminated her career as is above related.

The sensibility and education of this young lady are evident from the following Poem written by her before her death—and mentioned as above. The decyphered letter which follows, is intelligible as it applies to her situation—and cannot be as applied to that of the person who is said to have wrote it.

Curiosos

---

nel printed Curiosos's original letter, followed by "Disappointment" and "A Letter in Characters Decyphered," under the general heading "Miscellany. For the Centinel," Sept. 20, 1788, 8. This version was repr. as "From the Massachusetts Centinel," *Middlesex Gazette*, Sept. 29, 1788, [4]; as "From the Boston Centinel," *New-York Packet*, Sept. 30, 1788, [2]; as "From the Massachusetts Centinel," *Pennsylvania Packet, and Daily Advertiser*, Sept. 30, 1788, [2]; and as "From the Boston Centinel," *Vermont Gazette or Freeman's Depository*, Nov. 3, 1788, [4]. Once again it seems significant that the Salem, Mass., newspapers chose not to reprint the item.

*DISAPPOINTMENT.

With fond impatience all the tedious day
I sigh'd, and wish'd the lingering hours away;
For when bright Hesper led the starry train,
My Shepherd swore to meet me on the plain;
With eager haste to that dear spot I flew,
And linger'd long, and then the tears withdrew:
Alone, abandon'd to love's tenderest woes,
Down my pale cheeks the tide of sorrow flows;
Dead to all joys that fortune can bestow,
In vain for me her future bounties flow;
Take back each envied gift ye pow'r divine,
And only let me call Fidelio mine.
Ah, wretch! what anguish yet thy soul must prove,
Ere thou canst hope to lose thy care in love;
And when Fidelio meets thy fearful eye,
Pale fear and cold despair his presence fly;
With pensive steps, I sought thy walks again,
And kiss'd thee smiling on the verdant plain;
With fondest hope, thro' many a blissful hour,
We gave the souls to fancy's pleasing pow'r;
Lost in the magick of that sweet employ,
To build gay scenes, and fashion future joy,
We saw mild peace o'er fair *Canaan* rise,
And show her pleasing from benignant skies;
On airy hills our happy mansion rose,
Built but for joy, no room for future woes;
Round the calm solitude, with ceaseless song
* * * * * * * *

Sweet as the sleep of innocence, the day,
By transports measur'd, lightly danc'd away;
To love, to bliss, the union'd soul was given,
But, ah too happy, ask'd no brighter heaven.
And must the hours in ceaseless anguish roll?
Will no soft sunshine cheer my clouded soul?
Can this dear earth no transient joy supply?
Is it my doom to hope, despair and die?
Oh! come, once more, with soft endearments come,
Burst the cold prison of the sullen tomb;
Thro' favour'd walks, thy chosen Maid attend,
Where well-known shades their pleasing branches bend;
Shed the soft poison from thy speaking eye,
And look those raptures lifeless words deny;
Still be, tho' late, re-heard what ne'er could tire,
But, told each eve, fresh pleasures would inspire;
Still hope those scenes which love and fancy drew;

But, drawn a thousand times, were ever new.
>    Can fancy paint, can words express;
>    Can aught on earth my woes redress;
>    E'en thy soft smiles can ceaseless prove
>    Thy truth, thy tenderness and love:
Once thou could every bliss inspire,
Transporting joy, and gay desire;
Now cold Despair her banner rears,
And pleasure flies when she appears;
Fond hope within my bosom dies,
And agony her place supplies:
O, thou! for whose dear sake I bear,
A doom so dreadful, so severe,
May happy fates thy footsteps guide,
And o'er thy *peaceful* home preside;
Nor let E——A's early tomb
Infect thee, with its baleful gloom.

### A LETTER IN CHARACTERS DECYPHERED

Must I die alone? Shall I never see you more? I know that
you will come, but you will come too late: This is, I fear, my
last ability. Tears fall so, I know not how to write.—Why
did you leave me in so much distress? But I will not reproach
you: All that was dear I left for you; but do not regret it.—
May God forgive in both what was amiss:—When I go from
hence, I will leave you some way to find me;—if I die, will
you come and drop a tear over my grave?

# WILLIAM HILL BROWN

## *From* The Power of Sympathy[†]

### LETTER XL.

### *Mrs.* HOLMES *to* MYRA.

BELLEVIEW.

I sit down to give you, my dear *Myra*, some account of the visitants
of to-day, and their conversation. We are not always *distinguished* by
such company, but perhaps it is sometimes necessary; and as it is a
relaxation from thought, it serves to give us more pleasure in return-
ing to the conversation of people of ideas.

---

[†] From *The Power of Sympathy: or, the Triumph of Nature* (Boston: Isaiah Thomas, 1789).

Mrs. *Bourn* assumes a higher rank in life than she pretended to seven years ago.—She then walked on foot—she now, by good fortune, rides in a chariot. Placed, however, in a situation with which her education does not altogether comport, she has nothing disagreeable but her over assiduity[1] to please—this is sometimes disgusting, for one cannot feast heartily upon honey: It is an errour which a candid mind easily forgives. She sometimes appears solicitous to display her mental accomplishments, and desirous to improve those of her daughter; but it is merely apparent. Notwithstanding a temporary wish may arise towards the attainment of this point, a habitual vacancy nips it in the bud.

Miss *Bourn* is about the age of fourteen—genteel, with a tolerable share of beauty, but not striking—her dress was elegant, but might have been adjusted to more advantage—not altogether awkward in her manners, nor yet can she be called graceful—she has a peculiar air of *drollery* which takes her by fits, and for this reason, perhaps, does not avail herself of every opportunity of displaying the modesty of her sex—she has seen much company, but instead of polishing her manners, it has only increased her assurance.

Thus much of the characters of our *company*. After some small chat which passed as we took a turn in the garden, we entered the Temple.

"What books would you recommend to put into the hands of my daughter?" said Mrs. *Bourn*, as she walked into the library—"it is a matter of some importance." "It is a matter of *more* importance," answered *Worthy*, "than is generally imagined; for unless a proper selection is made, one would do better never to read at all:—Now, Madam, as much depends on the choice of books, care should be taken not to put those in the way of young persons, which might leave on their minds any disagreeable prejudices, or which has a tendency to corrupt their morals."—"As obvious as your remark is," added Mr. *Holmes*, "it is evidently overlooked in the common course of education. We wisely exclude those persons from our conversation, whose characters are bad, whose manners are depraved, or whose morals are impure; but if they are excluded from an apprehension of contaminating our minds, how much more dangerous is the company of those books, where the strokes aimed at virtue are redoubled, and the poison of vice, by repeatedly reading the same thing, indelibly distains the young mind?"

"We all agree," rejoined *Worthy*, "that it is as great a matter of virtue and prudence to be circumspect in the selection of our books, as in the choice of our company.—But, Sir, the best things may be

---

1. Extreme carefulness.

subverted to an ill use. Hence we may possibly trace the cause of the ill tendency of many of the Novels extant."

"Most of the Novels," interrupted my father, "with which our female libraries are overrun, are built on a foundation not always placed on strict morality, and in the pursuit of objects not always probable or praiseworthy.—Novels, not regulated on the chaste principles of true friendship, rational love, and connubial duty, appear to me totally unfit to form the minds of women, of friends, or of wives."

"But, as most young people read," says Mrs. *Bourn*—"what rule can be *hit upon* to make study always terminate to advantage?"

"Impossible," cried Miss, "for I read as much as any body, and though it may afford amusement, while I am employed, I do not remember a single word, when I lay down the book."

"This confirms what I say of Novels," cried Mr. *Holmes*, addressing *Worthy* in a jocular manner, "just calculated to kill time—to attract the attention of the reader for an hour, but leave not one idea on the mind."

"I am far from condemning every production in the gross," replied *Worthy*; "general satire against any particular class, or order of men, may be viewed in the same light as a satire against the species—it is the same with books—If there are corrupt or mortified members, it is hardly fair to destroy the whole body. Now I grant some Novels have a bad tendency, yet there are many which contain excellent sentiments—let these receive their deserved reward—let those be discountenanced; and if it is impossible "to smite them with an apoplexy, there is a moral certainty of their dying of a consumption,"—— But, as Mrs. *Bourn* observes, most young persons read, I will therefore recommend to those who wish to mingle instruction with entertainment, method and regularity in reading. To *dip* into *any book* burthens the mind with unnecessary lumber, and may rather be called a disadvantage, than a benefit—The record of memory is so scrawled and blotted with imperfect ideas, that not one legible character can be traced."

"Were I to throw my thoughts on this subject," said my good father-in-law, as he began to enter more warmly into the debate— drawing his chair opposite *Worthy*, and raising his hand with a poetical enthusiasm—"Were I to throw my thoughts on this subject into an Allegory, I would describe the human mind as an extensive plain, and knowledge as the river that should water it. If the course of the river be properly directed, the plain will be fertilized and cultivated to advantage; but if books, which are the sources that feed this river, rush into it from every quarter, it will overflow its banks, and the plain will become inundated: When, therefore, knowledge flows on in its proper channel, this extensive and valuable field, the mind, instead of being covered with stagnant waters, is cultivated to

the utmost advantage, and blooms luxuriantly into a general efflorescence—for a river properly restricted by high banks, is necessarily progressive."

The old gentleman brought down his hand with great solemnity, and we complimented him on his poetical exertion. "I cannot comprehend the meaning of this matter," said the penetrative Miss *Bourn*. "I will explain it to you, my little dear," said he, with great good nature—"If you read with any design to improve your mind in virtue and every amiable accomplishment, you should be careful to read methodically, which will enable you to form an estimate of the various topicks discussed in company, and to bear a part in all those conversations which belong to your sex—you see, therefore, how necessary general knowledge is—what would you think of a woman advanced in life, who has no other store of knowledge, than what she has obtained from experience?"

"I think she would have a sorry time of it;" answered Miss.

"To prevent it in yourself," said Mrs. *Bourn* to her daughter, "be assiduous to lay in a good stock of this knowledge, while your mind is yet free from prejudice and care."

"How shall I *go to work*, Madam," enquired the delicate daughter.

Mrs. *Bourn* turned towards Mr. *Holmes*, which was hint enough for the good old man to proceed.

"There is a medium to be observed, continued he, in a lady's reading; she is not to receive every thing she finds, even in the best books, as invariable lessons of conduct; in books written in an easy, flowing style, which excel in description and the luxuriance of fancy, the imagination is apt to get heated—she ought, therefore, to discern with an eye of judgment, between the superficial and the penetrating—the elegant and the tawdry—what may be merely amusing, and what may be useful. General reading will not teach her a true knowledge of the world.

"In books she finds recorded the faithfulness of friendship—the constancy of *true love*, and even that honesty is the best policy. If virtue is represented carrying its reward with it, she too easily persuades herself that mankind have adopted this plan: Thus she finds, when, perhaps, it is too late, that she has entertained wrong notions of human nature; that her friends are deceitful—her lovers false—and that men consult interest oftener than honesty.

"A young lady who has imbibed her ideas of the world from desultory reading, and placed confidence in the virtue of others, will bring back disappointment, when she expected gratitude. Unsuspicious of deceit, she is easily deceived—from the purity of her own thoughts, she trusts the faith of mankind, until experience convinces her of her errour—she falls a sacrifice to her credulity, and her only consolation is the simplicity and goodness of her heart.

"The story of Miss *Whitman*[2] is an emphatical illustration of the truth of these observations. An inflated fancy, not restricted by judgment, leads too often to *disappointment* and repentance. Such will be the fate of those who become (to use her own words)

"Lost in the magick of that sweet employ,"
"To build *gay scenes* and fashion *future joy.*"

"With a good heart she possessed a poetical imagination, and an unbounded thirst for novelty; but these airy talents, not counterpoised with judgment, or perhaps serious reflection, instead of adding to her happiness, were the cause of her ruin."

2. This young lady was of a reputable family in *Connecticut*. In her youth she was admired for beauty and good sense. She was a great reader of novels and romances, and having imbibed her ideas of *the characters of men*, from those fallacious sources, became vain and coquetish, and rejected several offers of marriage, in expectation of receiving one more agreeable to her fanciful idea. Disappointed in her *Fairy* hope, and finding her train of admirers less solicitous for the honour of her hand, in proportion as the roses of youth decayed, she was the more easily persuaded to relinquish that *stability* which is the honour and happiness of the sex. The consequences of her amour becoming visible, she acquainted her lover of her situation, and a *husband* was proposed for her, who was to receive a considerable sum for preserving the reputation of the lady; but, having received security for the payment, he immediately withdrew. She then left her friends, and travelled in the stage as far as *Water-town*, where she hired a young man to conduct her in a chaise to *Salem*. Here she wandered alone and friendless, and at length repaired to the *Bell-Tavern*, in *Danvers*, where she was delivered of a lifeless child, and in about a fortnight after (in *July*, 1788) died of a puerperal fever, aged about 35 years.

Before her death she amused herself with reading, writing and needlework, and though in a state of anxiety, preserved a cheerfulness, not so much the effect of insensibility, as of patience and fortitude. She was sensible of her approaching fate, as appears from the following letter, which was written in characters.

"Must I die alone? Shall I never see you more? I know that you will come, but you will come too late: This is, I fear, my last ability. Tears fall so, I know not how to write. Why did you leave me in so much distress? But I will not reproach you: All that was dear I left for you; but do not regret it.—May God forgive in both what was amiss: When I go from hence, I will leave you some way to find me; if I die, will you come and drop a tear over my grave?"

In the following Poem, she, like the dying *Swan*, sings her own Elegy, and it is here added, as a sorrowful instance, how often the best, and most pleasing talents, not accompanied by virtue and prudence, operate the destruction of their possessor.

The description of her unfortunate passion, will remind the critical reader of the famous ode of *Sappho*. In genius and in misfortune, these poetical ladies were similar.

> *"DISAPPOINTMENT.*
> "With fond impatience all the tedious day
> I sigh'd, and wish'd the lingering hours away;
> For when bright *Hesper* led the starry train,
> My shepherd swore to meet me on the plain;
> With eager haste to that dear spot I flew,
> And linger'd long, and then with tears withdrew:
> Alone, abandon'd to love's tenderest woes,
> Down my pale checks the tide of sorrow flows;
> Dead to all joys that fortune can bestow,
> In vain for me her useless bounties flow:
> Take back each envied gift, ye pow'rs divine,
> And only let me call FIDELIO mine.
>     "Ah, wretch! What anguish yet thy soul must prove
> Ere thou canst hope to lose thy care in love;
> And when FIDELIO meets thy tearful eye,

"I conclude from your reasoning," said I, "and it is, besides, my own opinion, that many fine girls have been ruined by reading Novels."

"And I believe," added Mrs. *Bourn*, "we may trace from hence the causes of spleen[3] in many persons advanced in life."

"You mean old maids, Madam," cries the sagacious Miss, "like my aunt *Deborah*—she calls all the men deceitful, and most women, with her, are no better than they should be."

"Well said!" exclaimed *Worthy*, "the recollection of chagrin and former disappointment, sours one's temper and mortifies the heart—

> Pale fear and cold despair his presence fly;
> With pensive steps, I sought thy walks again,
> And kiss'd thy token on the verdant plain;
> With fondest hope, thro' many a blissful bow'r,
> We gave the soul to fancy's pleasing pow'r;
> Lost in the magick of that sweet employ,
> To build gay scenes, and fashion future joy,
> We saw mild peace o'er fair *Canäan* rise,
> And show'r her blessings from benignant skies;
> On airy hills our happy mansion rose,
> Built but for joy, no room for future woes;
> Sweet as the sleep of innocence, the day,
> (By transports measur'd) lightly danc'd away;
> To love, to bliss, the union'd soul was given,
> And each! too happy, ask'd no brighter heaven.
>   "And must the hours in ceaseless anguish roll?
> Will no soft sunshine cheer my clouded soul?
> Can this dear earth no transient joy supply?
> Is it my doom to hope, despair and die?
> Oh! come, once more, with soft endearments come,
> Burst the cold prison of the sullen tomb;
> Through favour'd walks, thy chosen maid attend,
> Where well known shades their pleasing branches bend,
> Shed the soft poison from thy speaking eye,
> And look those raptures lifeless words deny;
> Still be, though late, reheard what ne'er could tire,
> But, told each eve, fresh pleasures would inspire;
> Still hope those scenes which love and fancy drew;
> But, drawn a thousand times, were ever new.

>   "Can fancy paint, can words express;
> Can aught on earth my woes redress;
> E'en thy soft smiles can ceaseless prove
> Thy truth, thy tenderness and love.
> Once thou couldst every bliss inspire,
> Transporting JOY, and gay DESIRE:
> Now cold DESPAIR her banner rears,
> And PLEASURE flies when she appears;
> Fond HOPE within my bosom dies,
> And AGONY her place supplies:
> O, thou! for whose dear sake I bear,
> A doom so dreadful, so severe,
> May happy fates thy footsteps guide,
> And o'er thy *peaceful* home preside;
> Nor let ELIZA's early tomb
> Infect thee, with its baleful gloom."

[*Brown's note.*] See the accumulated details in "The Elizabeth Whitman Paper Trail" in this Norton Critical Edition, pp. 302–07.

3. Ill temper. Related to splenetic. In the medical theories of this era, an excess of spleen made one short-tempered or melancholy.

disappointment will be more or less severe in proportion as we ele-
vate our expectations; for the most *sanguine*[4] *tempers* are the
soonest discouraged; as the highest building is in the most danger
of falling."

"It appears from what I have said," resumed Mr. *Holmes*, "that
those books which teach us a knowledge of the world are useful to
form the minds of females, and ought therefore to be studied."

I mentioned *Rochefoucault's* maxims.—[5]

"Do they not degrade human nature?" enquired my father.

"This little book," answered *Worthy*, "contains much truth——
and those short sketches traced by the hand of judgment, present to
us the leading features of mankind." "But," replied my father, "that
*interest should assume all shapes*, is a doctrine, which, in my mind,
represents a caricature rather than a living picture." "It is the duty of
a painter to produce a likeness," said *Worthy*.—"And a skilful one,"
cried my father, continuing the metaphor, "will bring the amiable
qualities of the heart to light; and throw those which disgrace
humanity into the shade." "I doubt," rejoined *Worthy*, "whether this
flattery will answer the purpose you aim to accomplish—You enter-
tain a high opinion of *the dignity of human nature*, and are displeased
at the author who advances any thing derogatory to that dignity.
*Swift*, in speaking of these maxims, in one of his best poems, affirms,

> "They argue no corrupted mind
> "In him——the fault is in mankind."[6]

"As I began this subject," added I, "it shall be ended by one
observation—As these maxims give us an idea of the manners and
characters of men, among whom a young person is soon to appear;
and as it is necessary to her security and happiness that she be made
acquainted with them—they may be read to advantage."

"There is another medium," said Mr. *Holmes*, assenting to my
observation, "to be noticed in the study of a lady—she takes up
a book, either for instruction or entertainment; the medium lies
in knowing when to put it down. Constant application becomes
labour—it sours the temper—gives an air of thoughtfulness, and
frequently of absence. By *immoderate reading* we hoard up opinions
and become insensibly attached to them; this miserly conduct sinks
us to affectation, and disgustful pedantry; *conversation* only can rem-
edy this dangerous evil, strengthen the judgment, and make reading
really useful. They mutually depend upon, and assist each other.

4. Hopeful, confident.
5. François VI, Duc de La Rochefoucauld (1613–1680) published several editions of his
   famous volume *Réflexions ou sentences et maximes morales* beginning in 1665.
6. From Jonathan Swift, "Verses on the Death of Dr. S——, D.S.P.D. Occasioned by
   Reading a Maxim in Rouchefoucault" (1739).

"A KNOWLEDGE of HISTORY which exhibits to us in one view the rise, progress and decay of nations—which points out the advancement of the mind in society, and the improvements in the arts which adorn human nature, comes with propriety under the notice of a lady. To observe the origin of civilization—the gradual progress of society, and the refinements of manners, policy, morality and religion—to observe the progression of mankind from simplicity to luxury, from luxury to effeminacy, and the gradual steps of the decline of empire, and the dissolution of states and kingdoms, must blend that happy union of instruction and entertainment, which never fails to win our attention to the pursuit of all subjects.

"POETRY claims her due from the ladies. POETRY enlarges and strengthens the mind, refines the taste and improves the judgment. It has been asserted that women have no business with *satire*—now satire is but a branch of poetry. I acknowledge, however, much false wit is sent into the world, under this general title; but no critick with whom I am acquainted ever called satire false wit—for as long as vice and folly continue to predominate in the human heart, the satirist will be considered as a useful member of society. I believe *Addison*[7] calls him an auxiliary to the pulpit. Suffer me to enlarge on this *new idea.* Satire is the correction of the vices and follies of the human heart; a woman may, therefore, read it to advantage. What I mean by enforcing this point, is, to impress the minds of females with a principle of self correction; for among all kinds of knowledge which arise from reading, the duty of self knowledge is a very eminent one; and is at the same time, the most useful and important.

OUR ordinary intercourse with the world, will present to us in a very clear point of view, the fallacious ideas we sometimes entertain of our own self knowledge.—We are blinded by pride and self love, and will not observe our own imperfections, which we blame with the greatest acrimony in other people, and seem to detest with the greatest abhorrence; so that it often happens, while we are branding our neighbour for some foible, or vanity, we ourselves are equally guilty.

"Ridiculous as this conduct must appear in the eyes of all judicious people, it is too frequently practised to escape observation.

"I will drop this piece of morality, with a charge to the fair reader, that whenever she discovers a satire, ridiculing or recriminating the follies or crimes of mankind, that she look into her own heart, and compare the strictures on the conduct of others with her own feelings."

---

7. Joseph Addison (1672–1719), a popular English essayist, playwright, and politician. He is best known for editing the *Spectator* magazine with Richard Steele and for his play, *Cato: A Tragedy* (1712). See p. 20, note 2 in this Norton Critical Edition.

# ANONYMOUS

## A Pathetick Fragment.†

*By the late unfortunate Miss Whitman.*

\* \* \* Thy presents to some happier lover send,
Content thyself to be Lucindia's friend;
The soft expressions of thy gay design,
Ill suit the sadness of a heart like mine;
A heart like mine, forever doom'd to prove,
Each tender woe—but not one joy of love.
First from my arms a dying lover torn,
In early life it was my fate to mourn;
A father next by fate's relentless doom
With heart felt woe I followed to the tomb;
Now all was lost—no friends remain to guide,
My erring steps or calm life's boisterous tide.
Again the admiring youths around me bow'd,
And one I singled from the sighing crowd;
Well skill'd he was in every winning art,
To warm the fancy or to touch the heart;
Why must the pen the noble praise deny,
Which virtue, worth, and honour should supply.
O youth belov'd—what pangs this breast has borne,
To find thee false, ungrateful and forsworn;
A stygean¹ darkness o'er my prospects spread,
The damps of night and death's eternal shade;
The scorpion sting by disappointment brought,
And all the horrours of desparing thought:
Sad as they are I might perhaps endure,
And bear with patience what admits no cure:
But here my bosom is to madness mov'd,
I suffer'd by the faults of him I lov'd;
O had I died by pitying heaven's decree,
Nor prov'd so black, so base a mind in thee;
But vain the wish, my breast was doom'd to prove,
Each torturing pain, but not one joy of love;
Wouldst thou again fallacious prospects spread,
And woo me from the confines of the dead?
The pleasing scenes that charm'd me once, retrace,
Gay hours of rapture and perpetual bliss?
How did my heart admire the dear deceit,
And I myself request the pleasing cheat!

† From *Massachusetts Magazine; or Monthly Museum* (June 1792): 392.
1. Related to the river Styx in Greek mythology; hellish; infernal.

Delusive hope and wishes idly vain,
Unless to sharpen disappointment's pain!
Couldst thou in language like the blest above,
Paint to my views that paradise of love.

# The Nineteenth-Century Legacy

## J. HORATIO NICHOLS
### *From* The New England Coquette[†]

MEN.

Maj. Sanford, a libertine. C. Deighton.—Mr. Boyer. Eliza's lover.
Mr. Selby. Mr. Boyer's friend.

WOMEN.

Eliza, a coquette. Lucy, and Julia, her friends. Mrs. Wharton, Mrs.
Sanford.

✳   ✳   ✳

[Act II] Scene 2.        *Eliza and Lucy. Eliza sings.*

> Must I if jealous lovers frown,
> And in distraction fly the town,
>     Be sad and cry,
>     Be sick and die?
>     No, no not I.
> Die for a lover? not for four.
> If one goes, I'll conquer more,
>     Still, still be gay,
>     Whip time away,
>     Dance sing and play.
> In fashion's splendid circle sport,
> And smiling pleasure's favor court;
>     The merry swain
>     Shall sigh again,
>     And fly me, pain.

---

† From J. Horatio Nichols, *The New England Coquette: From the History of the Cele-*
*brated Eliza Wharton, a Tragic Drama in Three Acts* (Salem: N. Coverly, 1802).

> Ah sprightly Sanford, thee I love,
> Life's airy round we'll sweetly move
>     Love's note shall swell,
>     And song dispel
>     Our grief; farewel.

This affected happiness half deceives myself; once was I very happy but alas! I have been tossed on the waves of folly till shipwrecked on the shoals of despair. Oh Lucy, I am undone! Slighted by th' man who sought my hand; by him deserted, who has work'd my ruin! No he cannot wilfully neglect me.

LUCY.        Where, O Eliza Wharton, is that fund of sense and sentiment, which your engaging form once animated?

ELIZA.        Fled like a dream, like dew dissolved. Oh broken, broken hearted.

LUCY.        Why resign these valuable endowments, and suffer your self to be tossed and torn, in the raging elements of contending passions?

ELIZA.        To you great Gods, I make my last appeal;
>        O, clear my conscience, or my crimes reveal!
>        If wand'ring thro the paths of life I've run
>        And backward trod the steps I sought to shun.
>        Impute my errors to your own decree;
>        My feet were guilty, but my heart was free.

I would forget if possible, to think on my long lost Mr. Boyer; But no, frantic with grief; he dropt a tear upon my hand and left me; my eye marked the spot, and in a day full twenty times, I view it; and fondly imagine it still there remains. How could I give him pain? I hope his happy Mary never will! but I forbear, this melting theme dissolves my soul, and no wonder.        *weeps*.

LUCY.        Ah let me conjure you to dispel that gloom so dangerous to your peace; harrow not up sorrows half forgotten. You still have admirers, and yet may have a partner of your cares and joys, to walk with you the dull and flowery paths of life; whose talents and whose virtues may justly merit love esteem and confidence. With such a man, the hours glide so sweetly on, and my Eliza must be so happy that she would forget a loss, for which her charms cannot fail to make a reprisal. For when ambition fires the soft bossom[1] of a youthful female, what power is able to oppose, and when a woman conquers, there's a victory for you!

ELIZA.        The spirit of a slave is broken, nor dares rebel against the oppressor's force, because he thinks from habit, that he shall be

---

1. Bosom.

beat, so with me. I am the slave of disappointed love, and as the bloody despot props his throne from sinking, by making vassalage a habit; so sorrow, my tyrannic task master, sways in my heart, and will sway me to the tomb.

LUCY.          O fie Eliza! revolutionize that ill constructed government of habit in your temper, establish a republic, let its legislature be quite elective, let passion be the most inferior branch, while philosophy and reason sway the power, executive supreme; and were't not for being stigmatized a jacobine,[2] I would give your mind a new form of constitution, and guilotine despair and melancholy.          *Exit together*

### Enter Boyer and Selby.

BOYER.          Alas my friend, the hour at last is fixed, but O how differently, from what I long had wished, not the nuptial day, but day of final and eternal separation. Yes, she is lost to me for ever; I have torn myself from her, though it has torn my heart asunder, she was unworthy of love, a finished coquette; but thank heaven, I was not so blind, as not to see her faults, detect her artifices, nor so desperate in love, as when I saw the danger not to escape it.

SELBY.          O fie! for these love sick gentry! that love which borders on desparation, and terminates in womanish dejection, is not the sort for me; why my friend, if I were in love with a lady, who loved not me, yet to indulge her coquettish temper, had quite a mind to jilt, to smile upon, and jilt again, I would do as you have nobly done; leave her to her own mortification and chagrin; and find another, whose charms and virtue poize the scale alike; to her I would transfer my soul's affections, and in a return of honest love, be as happy as a prince, surrounded by all the dazling pomp and splendor of voluptuous courts!

BOYER.          O brave indeed! your philosophy arms my soul with double fortitude. Your theory I have adopted; I have weened my too fond heart from every thought of Eliza; and have transferred my love to another! one whose merits are not unworthy of a man's regard, virtue shines in all her looks, acts itself out in every thing she does, her soul is gentle as the summer's breeze, and her charms of person equal those of my forgotten, no longer mine! her sincerity deserves my confidence, and with her, if happiness is to the nuptial state attached, your Boyer will be blessed; you are amazed! your countenance! why does the colour fly your check? Say my worthy friend?

SELBY.          Ah my hopes! my dear Maria!

---

2. I.e., Jacobin, or a supporter of the most violent phase of the French Revolution. A radical democrat.

BOYER.          Your hopes? Did you hope, and have I your appro-
bation? Then am I doubly happy: brother, it is your lovely, your vir-
tuous sister, in whom the tendrest affections of my heart concentre.
That after a course of faithful friendship, we are no less faithful
brothers. Give me your hand, our hearts have long been one; let us
present ourselves to the lovely maid; join our hands and our society,
and solemnize the hymenial rites.          *Exit. Drop the scene.*

<div style="text-align:center">✳   ✳   ✳</div>

[ACT III, Scene 3.]
SANFORD.          Torment me not thus. (*Groans and rises suddenly.*)
It was she, her angel, all pale and ghastly. O horror! where has the
injured spirit fled? Where shall I again catch sight of her, to sacrifice
my murderous soul on the altar of atonement. O heaven! dost thy
chrystal walls contain the lovely angel! unfold the golden gate, dis-
close her to my view, let guardian seraphs, drawn up in regular bat-
talia escort her to this scene, and thou, O hell, suspend thy ponderous
jaws! pour forth a sulphurous train of hissing fires to seize upon your
prisoner, and "drag him to your torments!"[3] *Enter Deighton.*
DEIGHTON.          Surely the man is mad, or whence the horrable
soliloquy?
SANFORD.          O, Charles, I am undone! Eliza I am convinced,
no longer lives. Now as I slept, a spectre, rob'd in white, nor whiter
were her flowing robes than pallid countenance. She swiftly pass'd
me, with an agonizing look, and was gone. Yes, it was the injured,
lost, Eliza!
DEIGHTON.          O a ghost! well, I thought there might have
been a ghost here from the noise I heard. The constable, I suppose,
after his bonds, or pray is not that the ghost, and not gone so fairly
yet? (*pointing to a letter on the floor. Sanford stands amazed. Charles
takes the letter and reads.* To Major Sanford. *Sanford seizes the letter,
breaks the seal, and throws it on the floor again.*
SANFORD.          The fatal suspicion is hereby confirmed. She is
dead! Now is the measure of proscription full, and of all the victims
to my treacherous artifices, myself decreed the last! O could I call
her back to life again, or animate that once heavenly form, with its
former vivacity and happiness, how calmly would I consign myself
to the umbrian shades of grim Pluto. But thither now, O my dis-
tracted soul, thou hiest, without any palliation of thy crime, to
wail and weep in all the anguish of excruciating torture! Now will
the future votaries of levity and dissipation, learn that their crimi-
nal excesses rear the frightful precipice, from which themselves,
with fatal violence, like me, must fall, to mount the stage of life no

---

3. Shakespeare, *Richard III*, I.iv.57.

more, like me expire the victims of their guilt, if not by the ven-
geance of their own hands. *Stabs himself.*

※   ※   ※

# WILLIAM R. HAYDEN

*From* Clara Wharton; A Sequel to Eliza Wharton.[†]

### CHAPTER I.

> And while the rich tranquility we view,
> Hope's sweetest promises again renew,
> As if the twilight angel hovered there,
> To waft from nature's rest a balm for care.
>
> TUCKERMAN.

*The cottage—The widow—The beautiful portrait—The errand boy—
The letter—Story of little Willy.*

On a fine afternoon in the early part of October, in the year 18–,
amid the suburbs of the beautiful town of Hartford, stood a neat
little cottage, in which was an elderly lady, in deep mourning, reclin-
ing on a sofa. A close observer might have detected in her counte-
nance the recent marks of care and grief; yet there was that calm
resignation depicted in her countenance—always so beautiful in the
christian—and which lingers on the mind with pleasing recollec-
tion, and gives to us that respect and veneration which nothing else
can impart. Everything in the abode bespoke order, neatness and
quiet. The furniture, though plain, was arranged with the nicest
care and taste. Suspended from the wall, opposite the lady of whom
we have been speaking, was a fine portrait, in a gilded frame. It was,
indeed, a work of art, for those days; it was the likeness of a beauti-
ful girl of about twenty years of age. O! it was a sweet and heavenly
face to look upon,—the eyes were of a soft and melting blue, that
could not fail to fascinate and enchain the beholder to the spot. The
forehead was expansive and lofty, and bore the impress of more than
ordinary intellect; her features were of a fine oval cast—a dimple in
her cheek—with lips that looked as if they would open and speak to
you from the canvas,—hair of a dark brown, that fell over a neck and
shoulders of spotless beauty.

---

[†] From William R. Hayden, *Clara Wharton: or, The triumph of love over pride. A sequel
to Eliza Wharton* (Boston: National Pub. Co., 1851).

The lady of whom we have spoken would look long and fondly upon the portrait which we have so inadequately attempted to describe, and then she would turn her eyes down the road, as though she was anxiously awaiting the return of some one. But there was nothing to be seen but the children returning from school, who bowed and courtesied as they passed the house of one whom they had learned to love and respect. Next came the farmers' boys, slowly driving home the cattle from the pastures. Still she kept her eyes turned wistfully in the same direction.

The sun was fast sinking in the west, leaving a halo of golden light behind. The shades of evening were gathering around her, but she still continued to watch down the long road, overhung by lofty elms. The darkness seemed to gather faster on her face than on the sky. But now a sudden light illumines her pale features! In the dim and shadowy distance a boy is seen emerging from a bend in the road.

It is poor Willy, the village errand boy.

Though he has no one to provide for him, yet his goodness and the mildness of his disposition, have not failed to procure for him warm and generous friends who have supplied his wants. With his open, smiling countenance—ever willing to render his humble services to all who might require them. He was universally beloved by all who knew him, and many a little present—in money, clothing and books, had he received from the good people of the neighborhood. Although he was but eight years old, he had quite a little sum of money in the care of the Rev. Mr Boyer—a man who possessed a warm and generous heart. It mattered not in what part of the town Willy happened to be, there he had a home—for all knew his short but sad story. But the place which he called his home, and where he passed the most of his time, was with Mrs. Wharton—the lady who now stands at the gate, awaiting his arrival. As he came up to her she clasped his hand and imprinted a warm kiss on his cheek that made him feel that he was not wholly motherless.

'Well, Willy, have you brought any news for me?'

'Yes, mother, I have a letter for you and should have returned sooner, but the stage did not arrive till much later than usual, to-night,' replied Willy, handing Mrs. Wharton a letter.

'It was so late that I feared some accident might have befallen you,' replied Mrs. Wharton. 'Come in, Willy, and have your supper, while I read the letter.' Saying this, they went into the house, and while Willy partook of his evening repast, Mrs. Wharton broke the seal and read the following:

6 NEW HAVEN,———.

Mrs. M. WHARTON—*Dear Madam:*—

It is almost three months since I last took up my pen to address you. My only apology for my long silence must be the dangerous illness of my dear mother. But, thanks to a kind Providence, she is now past danger, and fast recovering her health. I now hope that in a few days I shall be able to leave New Haven for Danvers, and as soon as possible return to you with the little charge which the lost Eliza has left behind— bequeathed to your tender care and solicitude, which, I doubt not, it will receive, judging from your well known goodness and kindness of heart. May the child live to be an ornament to society—a blessing and consolation to you in your declining years. May she profit by her mother's sad experience, and avoid those snares and temptations into which she fell and was lost, through the arts of a designing villain—by the aid of the prevailing fault of many young women—*coquetry.*

Believe me, yours, as ever,

JULIA GRANBY.

After she had read the letter she sat for a few moments in silence—a tear started in her eye and rolled down her cheek. Willy, who was sitting at the table, raised his eyes to Mrs. Wharton, and observing that she seemed troubled, he sprang from his chair, and running up to her he said, in a voice choked with emotion,—

'Mother, is there any bad news in the letter?'

'No, my dear, it contains very good news indeed; but it brought fresh into my mind the recollections of the past, and I could not restrain my feelings. But it is past now, and I have some news with which I think you will be pleased. Miss Granby will be here in a few days, and bring little Clara with her.'

\*     \*     \*

'Clara,' said Alfred, 'I have just returned from the post office, and here is a large packet for you, it is sealed with black; I fear it must contain some unpleasant intelligence. Do you know the hand-writing?'

'No.'

'When you have perused its contents, I will return and talk with you,' continued Alfred as he passed into an adjoining apartment.

Clara broke the seal with a trembling hand, and opening the package she found several sheets of paper closely written. Taking up the first one she read as follows:

"———, *R.I.*

DEAR CHILD,—

You will pardon me for calling you by the sacred name, for though depraved and fallen in crime, my heart yearns to you with all the affection of a better parent. My life has been spent in worthless dissipation, and I must pay the forfeit for the indulgence of my unholy passions, and for breaking the divine laws, to violate which we are strictly forbidden.

'Dear Clara, O that I could look upon your innocent face once more before my eyes are closed in that sleep which knows no waking; for you are the image of your poor mother whom I must soon meet at the bar of divine judgment, to answer for my treachery to her and others; and may I receive that forgiveness of which I am so undeserving. But before I leave this world, which I now feel will be soon, let me reveal to you a secret which is of the utmost importance to your welfare.

Before I became acquainted with your mother, I had nearly squandered the larger portion of my property. I loved her truly, but was unable to support her, and my own extravagance. To retrench and settle down on what little I had left, my pride would not suffer. Your mother refused to keep my company unless I married her at once; I could not bear the thoughts of a separation; I therefore proposed a *secret marriage* which neither of us was to reveal without the consent of the other in life or death. Accordingly we set out for a distant town and were secretly married. There were but two witnesses to the ceremony, the clergyman and his wife, to whom I gave a liberal sum, and they solemnly promised me not to reveal the secret; they not knowing my motives. I think they are yet living, and can testify to the truth of this declaration. Shortly after our marriage, I informed your mother of the true state of my affairs; that my creditors were becoming clamorous, that I was bankrupt, and that unless I resorted to some extraordinary means, I should be ruined. I also told her that I had become acquainted with a lady who was worth a large amount of property in money and real estate, besides she was the sole heir of her parents, who were reputed to be immensely rich. She was in very delicate health and did not give promise of a long life. Eliza asked me what I proposed to do. I informed her that I meant to marry the young lady, and then pay my debts with the money I should receive with her; that our own marriage was unknown, and as soon as a year should pass away, and I had secured money sufficient, that we would go to some distant part of the country and pass the remainder of our days in peace. O, heaven! I shall never forget her look as I concluded. 'Major Sanford,' she exclaimed, 'have you the heart to betray an innocent girl, to rob

and embitter her life better that we beg our bread from door to door. But you surely cannot be serious, you will not be guilty of so great a sin.' But I was firmly resolved not to be shaken, and finding all her entreaties and expostulations in vain, she begged that she might be permitted to leave the place, but to this I would not consent until after my second marriage. Circumstances soon forbade her to remain longer in the neighborhood, and I sent her to a town near Salem, where, shortly after your birth, she died, broken-hearted. I was compelled to speak and write of her to my friends as only a female acquaintance, but the scandal became too general, and coming to Mrs Sanford's knowledge, she required an explanation, but I being unable to give a satisfactory one, and in endeavoring by evasion to answer some of her questions, I became entangled in falsehoods which she detested, and left me for her parents house. Thus in my wickedness was I doubly punished by the loss of both, though I only loved your mother. For a time after her death I was bereft of my reason, and when I recovered I went to Boston.—Having little besides my clothing, and no profession or other employment, I soon fell in with two skillful burglars and coiners; with them and others, with whom I became acquainted, have I passed many years in deeds of crime; but all is nearly over with me in this world, and ere you receive this, your poor father will have found a resting place beneath the charitable earth, which does not refuse to receive all, good and bad, within its impartial bosom.

It has been said truly, that all things are for our good, and by trial that we shall work out our own salvation. Had not a kind Providence sent you to Boston and led you into troubles, your father might have never become a repentant man, but have gone down to the grave without forgiveness in this world or that to come. Clara, I fear that you will become weary of these long letters, but I cannot lay down my pen, the desire is so strong within me to say all that is possible while I am permitted. In another sheet you will find the name of the clergyman and his residence, where you can go, and by showing him this paper he will be at liberty to divulge all. I have learned that you are in the hands of good friends—may you always remain so.

But oh, I must draw this sad history to a close, and should you ever pass through this place, will you not turn aside to the little village burying ground, and as you wander through the silent streets of the dead, you will observe a small slab on which will be only the single letter S. That stone will mark *your father's grave.*

'My own dear child, as I wrote the last line, I have been blest with that which I have been a stranger to for years; I have shed tears which have bedewed this paper; oh, what a relief, I feel

like an innocent child again. My heart swells within me, and chokes my utterance.

Farewell. Clara,—may we meet in Heaven where all sorrow is at an end. May God in his infinite mercy watch over and protect you through life, and keep you uncontaminated by the influence of the wicked, is the last dying prayer of your repentant father.

P. Sanford.

To his daughter *Clara Sanford*.

On reading the letter, Clara's eyes were filled with tears; although she had never experienced a father's care, yet for the humble repentant and yearning affection of a parent for a child, she felt as though he had ever been near and dear to her; and so wrapped up was she for a time in this feeling, that she entirely lost sight of the important secret which was of so great moment to her. Taking up another letter she read the superscription which ran thus—

"Miss Clara Sanford,—

Dear Madam, it becomes my painful duty to inform you, that your father, Peter Sanford, died in this place three days since, after a lingering illness of two months; during the greater part of which time I was with him. He made a confident of me, and entrusted these papers to my care, exacting a promise that I should send them to you after his death. He also left directions in regard to his tomb-stone and grave, which you will know by its bearing the single letter S. He died calm and happy, with a firm reliance on Him who is eternal life.

Allow me, Dear Madam, to sympathise with you in your affliction, and to close my unpleasant epistle by subscribing myself,

Yours, at command,
Henry P. Rumford.

As Clara concluded reading the letters, she sat lost in melancholy reverie, and indulging in her grief, when she was aroused by Mrs. Foster's entrance.

'Why, Miss Wharton, I am sorrow to find you in tears; I trusted that after what I had said to you this morning you would be more cheerful.'

Clara made no reply but by handing the letters which she had received. Mrs. Foster took them, and after carefully reading their contents, she turned to Clara with all a mother's affection, and kissed her and said—

'Clara, can you any longer doubt, if you ever did, the wise decrees of Providence?'

'I own that I am not sufficiently thankful for the blessings which I receive, or reconciled to those reverses which are intended for my good. But I trust in future to be more patient.'

'Remember Clara that after darkness comes light, and though the morning of life be overcast with clouds, the meridian and decline may be all the more brilliant and beautiful.'

\* \* \*

# ANONYMOUS

## Tragedy in Tale of Love[†]

### *What an Old Weather-Worn Peabody Gravestone Tells*

MYSTERY THAT HUNG ON THE LIFE OF ELIZA WHARTON;
SHE IS THOUGHT TO HAVE INSPIRED THE WRITING OF
THE "SCARLET LETTER."

"And the tears of strangers watered her grave." These few words upon the weather-beaten remnant of a brown gravestone in the burying ground of Peabody, Mass., are among the most conspicuous of the few clews to a great tragedy of love, the life of Eliza Wharton, from which claims are being made Hawthorne drew the inspiration of his famous romance, "The Scarlet Letter."

Like Eliza Wharton, Hester Prynne was a beautiful woman of extraordinary strength of character. Like Eliza Wharton, according to tradition, Hester Prynne sinned, Eliza Wharton, with her child, swiftly passed from the anguish of the mortal world, while Hester Prynne endured a living death, but, alike, they suffered the deepest pain of human hearts, unsoothed by tender care or consolation from dear ones, and both, with a wonderful devotion to their false lovers, keeping their secrets, Eliza Wharton confiding her mystery to the silence of that greater mystery, the grave.

The passing of a century has not lifted the veil from the life of Eliza Wharton, nor broken the silence of the grave. Hawthorne raveled the tangled skein of Hester Prynne's life, but the stern Puritans of Salem ever maintained the purity of the life of the Rev. Arthur Dimmesdale, according to the closing chapter of "The Scarlet Letter," so in New England tradition the mystery of Hester Prynne was as impenetrable as that of Eliza Wharton.

[†] *Boston Sunday Herald* (August 31, 1902): 40.

It is true some worldly judges recite to their own satisfaction the life of Eliza Wharton, but ever there rises up the stern command, "Judge not," and the defender of woman or thoughtful investigator of facts with a single truth or mass of unanswerable questions that convert the theories of self-commissioned judges into a mass of rubbish.

"Let candor throw a veil over her frailties" pleads an unknown who lovingly marked her last resting place; but those who knew of the great strength or the great frailties of this beautiful strange woman have long since joined her.

That Eliza Wharton was born, and that she died, appear to be the sole points agreed upon by those who have attempted to describe her life for the benefit of the public. The influences upon her life, her character, her loves and her acts are alike disputed by biographers, but above the snarling controversies rises clear and free the fact that Eliza Wharton loved, whether in purity or in guilt is unknown, but with a faith so great, even as she passed into the alley of the shadow, that for years afterward sweethearts of Peabody stood by her grave and vowed to love as truly as did she who lay beneath.

The unfortunate woman was born in Hartford, Ct., in 1752, the eldest daughter of the Rev. Elnathan Whitman, a graduate of Yale College and minister of the Second Congregational Church in that city. She grew to be a beautiful woman, both in person and mind, and she was well educated and of a warm, poetical mind, as her writings show. She seems to have been a beautiful flower ruthlessly trampled upon by fate, which has visited but few women so harshly.

Her first lover, the Rev. Joseph Howe, was considered a young man of talent and piety, was driven from his pulpit in the Green Church, Boston, by the outbreak of the revolution. He found shelter in the home of the Rev. Mr. Whitman, and fell in love with the beautiful Eliza. Her father approved his suit, and, like a dutiful daughter, Eliza obeyed her father's wishes, and accepted his love. But the young man sickened and died, Eliza tenderly caring for him for a long time. She did not love him with her heart, and she sorrowed little. From this remote point of view, it appears that the minister was too weak a man to hold firmly a place in the vigorous, burning heart of Eliza.

Eliza next went to visit the family of the president of Yale College, a friend of her father. While there a number of gallants sought her hand, chief among whom was the Rev. Joseph Buckminster, a tutor in the college. He also lacked the strength to meet the passion of this beautiful woman, but she consented to marry him to please her family.

Her marriage was especially urged because the revolution was drawing finances tight everywhere, and the minister's salary was suffering. Her friends protested against this match, and while she

was discussing it with a gentleman (tradition says her cousin, Judge Edwards, a married man) in the arbor of her garden, Buckminster surprised her, and in mad jealousy broke the engagement to settle over a church in Portsmouth, N.H.

Despite this cruel blow, Eliza continued a brave, cheerful woman, and she passed the bloom of her youth in pleasant, and often helpful and charitable, intercourse with her friends. But the record of her mature years is a sealed book, which several have vainly tried to transcribe. "The Coquette," a novel of a score of editions, first published in 1800, claims to relate the true story of Eliza Wharton's life, Mrs. Hannah Foster, its author, stating that she was a cousin to the unfortunate woman, and that she came into possession of her papers.

"The Coquette" relates that Eliza fell a victim to the passion of her cousin, Judge Pierrepont Edwards,[1] but the Rev. J. W. Hanson, a historian of the town of Peabody, refutes the book, saying of it: "The catchpenny volume of letters which pretends to give her history has but the figment of the imagination of the authoress to recommend it."[2]

Mrs. Foster holds up Eliza as a wanton and a coquette, but Mrs. Caroline H. Dall, a much later writer, who also claims to possess papers of the unfortunate woman, declares her faithful and strong and true loving. Mrs. Dall furthermore avers that Eliza's relations with Judge Edwards were most proper, and that she was married. Mrs. Dall says that Eliza, in her dying days, showed no sense of guilt, but showed perfect trust in God's love, and insisted that her wedding ring be buried with her.

Her death saddened and discouraged her family, which had been unfortunate in money matters, and none had the courage to deny Mrs. Foster's cruel allegations, hence her marriage was never verified, nor was the certificate brought to light. Be it remembered, however, that these statements were made by Mrs. Dall more than half a century after Eliza's death, and after "The Scarlet Letter" appeared.

It seems entirely just to dismiss "The Coquette" from the evidence of the case, because of its inaccuracies so plain to the reviewer. It deserves suppression more than many modern prohibited books, for it contains phrases and sentiments too unbridled to be allowed about with a halter. This condemns it.

The reader may judge the hidden period of Eliza's life as he may see fit, provided it is in a kindly spirit, and then pass to the true and open story. A bright June day brought to the old Bell Tavern in Peabody a woman who registered as Mrs. Walker, and who said she

---

1. Pierpont Edwards (1750–1826), youngest son of the famous Puritan minister Jonathan Edwards, was by the 1850s widely believed to have been the father of Whitman's child.
2. J. W. Hanson, *The History of the Town of Danvers* (1848), p. 206.

would await her husband, who was coming in a few days. She wore a wedding ring, and both received and posted letters to her husband, she claimed.

She was gentle and graceful in all that she did, and, as she passed along the street, an old chronicler says: "Old and young turned to look after the beautiful, strange lady."[3] She used to sit at the south window of her chamber, apparently watching for somebody, and she wiled away the hours playing her guitar, or plying her needle, and she is said to have possessed that marvelous skill in sewing which Hawthorne attributes to Hester. She won the sympathy of her sisters of the town, and they were of the strict Puritanical type, too, but whatever tale she told them, they have forever kept.

One day Eliza wrote with chalk the letters "E. W." before the door, but some children at play rubbed them out. At dusk, a soldierly looking man rode by, studied the door, failed to note the erased chalk marks, and passed on. Eliza exclaimed, "I am undone." Fate often rests upon trivialities.

Soon after Eliza gave birth to a dead child, and quickly she herself sank to her grave, of a broken heart, a kind friend has said. She was tenderly laid to rest by strangers in the little burying ground, just across the Salem line, and the townspeople, marveling at her beauty, and mourning her sad fate, followed, in large numbers, the body to the grave.

Soon after her death, an unknown person erected over her grave a sandstone tablet, bearing the following inscription:

"This humble stone, in memory of Elizabeth Whitman, is inscribed by her weeping friends, to whom she endeared herself by uncommon tenderness and affection. Endowed with superior genius and accomplishments, she was still more endeared by her humility and benevolence. Let candor throw a veil over her frailties, for great was her charity to others. She sustained the last painful scene far from every friend, and exhibited an example of calm resignation. Her departure was on the 25th of July, A.D., 1788, in the 37th year of her age, and the tears of strangers watered her grave."

For many years afterward the tears of strangers continued to water her grave, and occasionally, so tradition says, an old man wept upon it. Visitors chipped off and took away little bits of the headstone in remembrance of her whose love was strong even in death, and in apparent desertion, and today barely six inches of the weather-beaten stone, bearing the last few words of the inscription as quoted in the beginning, stands in the tall grass of the cemetery.

An examination of her papers, threw no light on the mystery, although it revealed her beautiful and strong character. One letter,

3. Ibid., p. 208.

in particular, said to be in cipher, was published in the Massachusetts Sentinel, Sept. 20, 1788, and it is as follows:

"Must I die alone? Shall I never see you more? I know that you will come, but you will come too late. This is, I fear, my last ability. Tears fall so, I know not how to write. Why did you leave me in so much distress? But I will not reproach you. May God forgive in both what was amiss. When I go from hence I will leave you some way to find me. If I die, will you come and drop a tear on my grave?"

A fragment from her poems, written in her chamber in Peabody Tavern, also shows more character than a few words can describe. It is as follows:

> O! Thou for whose dear sake I bear,
> A doom so dreadful, so severe.
> May happy fates thy footsteps guide,
> And o'er thy peaceful home preside.

In the long tiresome days of the year 1849 Hawthorne paced the floor of the Salem Custom House, being surveyor of the port of Salem, struggling to master the inspiration of a great romance. The daily life of his colleagues furnished him the introductory chapter, which brought down upon his head a storm of abuse from the retired shipmasters whom he pictured.

At this time the tradition of Eliza Wharton was still burning in the public mind, and her memory had not been cleaned of the taint of sin. This was a Salem, as much as a Peabody, tradition, for Peabody is a suburb of Salem. That the great romancer seized upon the beautiful and unfortunate life, and drew it and enlarged upon it with all the strength of his master mind, seems a reasonable statement.

He knew, as did every Salemite, of the old punishment for adultery, the wearing of the letter "A" upon the breast, for it had been several times inflicted, according to the colonial records. Indeed, he mentions the punishment in his story of "Endicott and the Red Cross." The romance, the emotions, the conflict of sentiments and facts to be found in the life of Eliza Wharton perhaps formed the base of the romance, and Hawthorne confessed in the midst of his work that he did not know how to end.

Hawthorne's best works are based on traditions of his native city. Critics still debate as to whether his "House of the Seven Gables" is that odd-looking structure standing at the foot of Turner street in Salem, but the general public accepts it as such. Other critics have vainly tried to find the original of the Rev. Arthur Dimmesdale in the Rev. Thomas Cobbett of Lynn, who preached the election sermon in 1649, the year in which Hawthorne set his story.

Certainly there is no other character in New England tradition or history so much like Hester Prynne as was Eliza Wharton, and if

Hawthorne drew his character from tradition, consciously or unconsciously, then Hester Prynne could be no other than the unfortunate Eliza.

# CAROLINE WELLS HEALEY DALL

## *From* The Romance of the Association[†]

\* \* \*

I found "Charlotte Temple"[1] and "Eliza Wharton"[2] on my father's book-shelves when I was a very little girl.[3] They were in a dusty corner by the side of Mackenzie's "Man of Feeling"[4] and "Dorcasina Shelton,"[5] the only representatives of what my father was pleased to call "works of *fiction*."

Charlotte's story seemed pitiful enough, yet uninteresting, because her own character offered neither points nor variety, but "Eliza Wharton" interested and perplexed me. Of course, I was too young to take in the whole meaning of her story: still I detected its inconsistencies; I wondered over its stilted sentiment, the severe rebukes she received, and the almost idolatrous love she inspired; and, the older I grew, the more perplexed I became.

It is no small tribute to the literary skill with which its heterogeneous material is welded together that I read this book several times, could not easily dismiss the troubled interest it excited, and finally went to the nursery with my questions.

"I cannot tell you any thing about her," said my mother. "When I went to stay with the Hackers in Salem, we used to walk out to her

---

† From Caroline Wells Healey Dall, *The Romance of the Association; or, One Last Glimpse of Charlotte Temple and Eliza Wharton. A Curiosity of Literature and Life* (Cambridge: Press of J. Wilson and Son, 1875), 31–39.

1. *Charlotte, A Tale of Truth*, most often reprinted under the title *Charlotte Temple*, by Susanna Rowson, was printed in London in 1791 and in Philadelphia in 1794. The story of a schoolgirl seduced and kidnapped by a British officer, it was reprinted dozens of times in the United States over the course of the nineteenth century.

2. *The Coquette* was often referred to by the heroine's name. Some editions were even bound with that title, rather than *The Coquette*, on the spine.

3. Caroline Wells Healey Dall (1822–1912) was a prolific essayist, novelist, and reformer. Her book *The Romance of the Association* (1875), from which this selection is drawn, purported to tell the true story of Elizabeth Whitman and included heavily edited versions of some of the letters collected in this Norton Critical Edition, pages 269–300. Dall hoped her book would clear Whitman's name; she rejected the version of events recounted in *The Coquette*.

4. *The Man of Feeling* (1771), a sentimental novel by Scottish author Henry MacKenzie, was popular on both sides of the Atlantic.

5. The heroine (and colloquial title) of Tabitha Tenney's popular 1801 novel *Female Quixotism: Exhibited in the Romantic Opinions and Extravagant Adventures of Dorcasina Sheldon*, which satirized female readers of sentimental novels. Tenney lived in Exeter, New Hampshire, and published her novel in Boston.

grave. Even in winter, there was always a foot-track to the very spot, and all the young people round about went to it to plight their troth. You must go to your grandmother. *She* was born in Danvers."

Now my grandmother was only my grandmother's cousin.

That is to say, my grandfather was twice married. His first wife, a beautiful and dainty creature from the old Essex family of Symonds, had died soon after my mother's birth. The far-off cousin who came to nurse her in her last illness, and to take care of the two babies she left, had been her roommate at Madame Rowson's,[6] and remained her most intimate friend. She was now my grandfather's second wife. She was born within a hundred yards of the spot where Eliza Wharton was laid. She was twenty years old when the deal coffin, borne by four kind-hearted strangers, was slowly carried past her mother's door; and this was her answer, delivered in Mrs. Rowson's stateliest way, and with due attention to the rhetoric of the occasion,—

"There is only one lesson for *you* to learn from 'The Coquette.' *You* are to mind your mother. If Eliza Wharton had done as her mother bade her, she would have died quietly in Hartford, and nobody would have called her hard names."

"But, grandmamma, was she a bad woman? If she was, what did you go to her grave for, and why do the young lovers like to talk of her?"

"I don't think she was," my grandmother reluctantly admitted. "She said she was a married woman with her dying breath, and her ring was buried with her. Her husband must have been a cruel man. She was always expecting him, but he never came. If he had loved her as he ought, she would not have died alone. But, whatever *he* was, *she* was true to him: she never gave the least hint of his name; she burned all her papers, and kept his secrets, and so perhaps some other woman loved him after she was dead. Her faithfulness was what the young lovers liked. Why, child, your own grandmother came home in tears from her grave the night she was promised to your grandfather!"

"Then the book can't tell the truth!"

"Can't it?" It was an old story to my grandmother, and she would not pursue it. But I thought of it all through my maiden life, never once accepting the conclusions of the novel, and always wishing that I could go to Danvers and stand upon her grave.

Soon after my marriage, I went to Portsmouth to live, and it happened that one of the dearest friends I found there was Mrs. Alexander Ladd, a lady nearly as old as my grandmother, yet as sweet

---

6. Susanna Rowson, author of *Charlotte Temple* and several other books and plays, also operated a Boston-area boarding school for young women.

and charming as a young girl of eighteen. We chanced one day to speak of Buckminster,[7] and she gave me one or two of his manuscript sermons.

"I think Eliza Wharton loved him," I said. "Why couldn't she make up her mind to marry him? Do *you* think she was a coquette?"

"Buckminster did not," said Mrs. Ladd, "and he ought to know. He would never allow any one to blame her in his presence. There were reasons enough why no woman should marry him. He was subject to terrible attacks of hypochondria even in college, and after Eliza's death they became still more prostrating. Mrs. Lee[8] said she would not dare unveil her father's journal to a generation that felt no sympathy with his religious convictions."

"But I have heard that he liked the novel," I continued: "the family of the author insist that he thought the letters written to Boyer so like those written to himself as to make it probable they were copies."

"It is possible that he may sometime have spoken on some particular point to the author's husband," answered my friend, "for Mr. Foster was his relative in just the same degree as Eliza herself;[9] but I can hardly conceive it. The book does him great injustice by representing him as discussing his love and her affairs with his friend. That is something he never would have done. As to the rest, I can tell you what happened in this very room. Just after the book was published, Mr. Buckminster came to call on my mother. She was not quite ready to receive him, and probably forgot that a fresh copy of the book, just received from Boston, lay upon the table.

"When she came down, she found the doctor thrusting something under the coals upon the hearth. As he turned round to greet her with flaming eyes, she saw its leather covers curling in the blaze. 'Madam,' said he, pointing to the spot, 'there lies your book. It ought never to have been written, and it shall never be read,—at least, not in my parish. Bid the ladies take notice, wherever I find a copy I shall treat it in the same way,' and so saying he stalked out of the room, leaving my poor mother speechless."

So, little by little, my first feeling gathered strength. The years went by, and my son, old enough now to have a romance of his own, was leaving me the second time for Alaska.

---

7. Joseph Buckminster (1751–1812), a Yale tutor and one of Elizabeth Whitman's suitors in the late 1770s, was widely believed to be the model for *The Coquette*'s Reverend Boyer. After 1778 he lived and preached in Portsmouth, New Hampshire.

8. Eliza Buckminster Lee (1792–1864) authored *Memoirs of Rev. Joseph Buckminster, D.D., and of his son, Rev. Joseph Stevens Buckminster* (1849).

9. Rev. John Foster, Hannah Webster Foster's husband, was a distant relative of Elizabeth Whitman. Though no evidence exists that they were well acquainted, many nineteenth-century readers seized on this fact to support the idea that the novel was founded in fact.

We parted as those part who know that all the issues of life lie between that moment and their next meeting. We asked nothing of each other, but from San Francisco he wrote back,—

"While I am gone, write briefly some record of your own life, and a few words about my ancestors. I don't believe I know the name of my great-grandfather, and I think that is disgraceful."

I read the letter to my mother.

"You ought to do it," she said: "you promised me long ago that you would go to Middleton[1] and look up the history of my mother's family. Do it now."

My mother's mother had been the last of her line. My mother had never seen any one of her blood. In the earlier part of her life she had thought little about it; but, as she grew older and came nearer to the veil which covered the past, she became restless and impatient of her own ignorance.

So it happened that for her sake I went to Middleton, and stood upon the lovely beech-covered knolls, and pursued the crystal brooks which had replaced to my ancestors the fertile fields and purling streams of Kent. But I could not work so fast as she faded, and her sweet eyes were closed in death when I first laid my hand upon the old register.

I stood there dreaming, my cheeks wet and a soft mist over all the distance, when the harsh voice of the old clerk jarred upon my ear.

"They burnt up the records,—some of the folks at the Hall. Perhaps you'll find 'em at Danvers. A great-aunt of your mother's was there when Eliza Wharton died. The Symondses owned the Bell Tavern once."

Even here this shadow of a shade pursued me!

The course of weeks brought me to Danvers, and there a lady well known to every kind and generous work drove me about in her own carriage, and helped me in my earnest quest.

"That is where the Bell Tavern stood," she said, as we drove, "my father owned that at one time."

"Not while Eliza Wharton was in it?" I cried breathlessly.

"No," she said "it was afterwards. He was building a house for himself, and bought the tavern to live in while it was building. It was a great deal larger than he needed, and so it sometimes happened that he kept a traveller overnight."

"Did you ever hear your mother talk of Eliza?"

"Oh, yes! very often, and I remember the Southwicks very well. Mrs. Southwick was with her to the end, and loved her so much!"

"Did she ever know who her husband was?" I asked, "or guess why he did not come to her in her last agony?"

---

1. Middletown, Connecticut.

"He did come," answered my friend, "but why he did not find her is still a mystery. Eliza had written to him and expected him; but it was after she was very feeble, and she took no one into her confidence. One afternoon, when the end was near, one of the Symonds boys was sitting at the door and saw some chalk letters on the flag. Thinking that they had been written in play, he stooped down and rubbed them out. Still later in the dusk, a man in a military dress, and of a distinguished appearance, came on horseback down the road. As he drew near the tavern, he looked carefully about, rode up close to the door-steps, and at the tavern itself dismounted and seemed to search for something.

"He made no inquiries: no one happened to be about the tavern door; and, although he was observed by some children and a few of the neighbors, no one thought to connect him with the dying woman until the following day, when the scattered chalk upon the door-stone still showed faint traces of the letters E. W., and the unconscious author of Eliza's disappointment owned that he had tried to wipe them out.

"No one told her what had happened, and it is certain that from that moment her spirits sank."

I could not speak for a few moments. I was thinking sadly of the disproportioned measure meted out to the sinners of the world.

Slight indeed compared to many, successfully concealed and never punished even by the reproaches of society, was the error of this rare and beautiful woman. Was it the love of God that so watched over her, and would not bear with the least backsliding from the good old way of her fathers?

While I was thinking, my friend spoke,—

"I wish you could tell me who it was that used to come every year, for many years after her death, to look at that lonely grave. Soon after the stone was put up, a lady and gentleman came in a chaise to look at it. My father was in the tavern at the time, and entertained them. No one thought of asking who they were. Every year at the same time, they appeared, growing older and sadder till both were white-haired and bent. They sought us out wherever we were. Leaving the horse to be cared for, they walked away to Eliza's grave, stayed there a while, dined with us, and then went away. They never gave us any names, and we never asked for any. Who were they?"

I could not tell her then, but I know now. How their hearts must have ached as they sat there, wondering who had robbed them of their treasure, trying in vain to penetrate the secret those sods had covered!

\*   \*   \*

This image appeared in the 1829 edition of *The Boarding School* with the label "Clara." It also appears in at least two other editions of *The Coquette* as Eliza Wharton (1831 edition, published in New York by J. P. Clusman; also the edition of 1833 by Charles Gaylord of Boston). It may be a reworking of a painting by John Jackson, English portrait painter, of Lady Georgina Agar-Ellis.

This image of Eliza Wharton appeared in the 1855 edition of *The Coquette.*

PORTRAIT OF ELIZA WHARTON.

# THE COQUETTE;
## OR, THE HISTORY OF
# ELIZA WHARTON.

This image of a saucy Eliza Wharton accompanied the novel's reprinting in *The Star-Spangled Banner* (September 20, 1851). Courtesy of the American Antiquarian Society.

PORTRAIT OF CLARA WHARTON.

Clara Wharton, from the title page of the novel of the same name (1851). Used by permission of the University of Missouri-Kansas City Libraries, Dr. Kenneth J. LaBudde, Department of Special Collections.

Original tombstone of Elizabeth Whitman in what was Danvers, Massachusetts, alongside a new version, erected by the Peabody Historical Society in 2004.

# CRITICISM

# CARROLL SMITH-ROSENBERG

## *From* Domesticating 'Virtue': Coquettes and Revolutionaries in Young America[†]

Read as a celebration of the values of commercial republicanism, this is just the novel we would expect to find written in the New England of the 1790s. But such a reading is too simple. *The Coquette* painstakingly and persistently complicates what should be clear-cut. First, Eliza is not a heroine like Pamela or Clarissa, virtuous to the core. Rather, as Cathy Davidson argues in her fine study of early American literature, *Revolution and the Word*, Eliza fuses talent and virtues with serious moral failings. Even more remarkably, her failings and her fall endear her to her friends within the novel and to her readers outside. Second, the novel persistently leads the reader to resist the prudent marriage and to root for the rake. Third, the moral spokeswomen of the novel end by warning the heroine that male ministerial texts can be as misleading and dangerous as women's romances and novels. Finally, *The Coquette* is not simply a fiction, but, as Davidson details, a rewriting of an earlier, male-authored historical text, the popular reporting of the scandalous death of Elizabeth Whitman.[1] * * * The men's reading of the event emphasized women's social and sexual vulnerability: woman's passion, uncontrollable when enflamed by novel and romance reading, easily overcame women's fragile hold on virtue.[2]

Hannah Foster's *Coquette* offers us a different narrative. Eliza Wharton's downfall, Foster tells us, was not lust but the desire for independence coupled with the wish to rise socially. As such she represented those within the emergent middle class, who, rejecting traditional norms, anxiously embraced individualism, risk, and the new capitalism.

---

[†] From Elaine Scarry, ed., *Literature and the Body: Essays on Populations and Persons* (Baltimore: Johns Hopkins UP, 1988), 169–78. Reprinted by permission. Parenthetical citations to the novel refer to the 1986 edition from Oxford UP, ed. Cathy Davidson. Page numbers in square brackets refer to this Norton Critical Edition.

This essay took form first as a paper at a conference on "American Democracy and *Democracy in America*: Tocqueville After 150 Years," University of California, Berkeley, November 1986. I am particularly indebted to the suggestions of Elaine Scarry, Alvia Golden, Toby Ditz, Phyllis Rackin, and Mary Poovey and most especially to those offered by Maureen Quilligan and by the literature graduate students at the University of Pennsylvania who were members of a graduate seminar on Language, Gender, and Power. Maureen Quilligan, assisted by those students, taught me the fundamentals of close reading. She contributed significantly to my analysis of *The Coquette*. [Smith-Rosenberg's note]

1. Cathy N. Davidson, *Revolution and the Word: The Rise of the Novel in America* (New York: Oxford UP, 1986), xi.
2. *Ibid.*

To be appreciated fully, *The Coquette* must be read as a gendered misprisioning of the political and economic discourses of its time. Just as the capitalist revolution problematizes "independence" and "virtue" as understood within classical republicanism, so *The Coquette* underscores the ways concepts of female "independence" and "individualism" further complicated the republican lexicon. The book's opening sentence alerts the reader to the significance of this issue. "An unusual sensation possesses my breast," Eliza writes her friend, Freeman, "a sensation which I once thought could never pervade it on any occasion whatever. It is *pleasure*, pleasure, my dear Lucy, on leaving my paternal roof. Could you have believed that the darling child of an indulgent and dearly-beloved mother would feel a gleam of joy at leaving her? But it is so" (5) [4]. Two events, Eliza continues, have freed her: the death of her father and the death of the man her father had chosen as her husband, another minister, whom she did not love. While both patriarchal figures lived, Eliza had exhibited behavior appropriate to her class and gender. "Both nature and education had instilled into my mind an implicit obedience to the will and desires of my parents. To them, of course, I sacrificed my fancy in the affair, determined that my reason should concur with theirs, and on that to risk my future happiness" (5) [4].

To read these statements in a political context, let us start by juxtaposing Eliza's comment, "determined that my reason should concur with theirs, and on that to risk my future happiness," to one drawn from that primer of American republican rhetoric, the Declaration of Independence. Here we find "certain inalienable rights" listed, "among these, life, liberty and the pursuit of happiness." *The Coquette* begins by telling us that the heroine, as a virtuous daughter, has resigned her *liberty* of choice and her pursuit of *happiness* in deference to parental wishes; she has agreed, that is, to link happiness to the sacrifice, not the assertion, of liberty. This pious sacrifice is then contrasted to the pleasure she now reports experiencing at resuming her lost independence, pleasure, a word that she twice repeats, and that Hannah Foster italicizes. Circumstances reversing her position, Eliza now associates liberty with pleasure—and with her ability to pursue happiness on her own.

The Declaration of Independence tells us that liberty and the pursuit of happiness are unalienable rights. Numerous other republican texts warn Americans that to relinquish them will endanger virtue. But the Declaration also insists that a passion for liberty be balanced by prudence. "Prudence, indeed, will dictate that Governments long established should not be changed for light and transient causes." But Eliza's very first sentence signals a subtle shift away from the hegemonical Declaration of Independence, a shift

that challenges the traditional relation among pleasure, happiness, and prudence. Eliza has called pleasure an "unusual" emotion, especially when associated with independence and liberty. To most eighteenth-century republicans, it was both an unusual and a dangerous emotion. Popular versions of moral philosophy, especially that most common to Puritan New England, pitted pleasure against both happiness and prudence.[3] For them, "happiness" signified contentment with one's place in life, "the attainment of what is considered good."[4] It was subservient to, indeed rooted in, social norms. "Pleasure," in contrast, implied delight in the sensations; it hinted at passion—an association reinforced when Eliza represents her pleasure in a physical, indeed, a sensual vocabulary. Pleasure, invoked by her newfound independence, she tells Freeman, "possesses my breast." It illuminates her with "a gleam of joy." When independence is absent in this text, so is sensuality. In acquiescing to her parent's will, Eliza tells Freeman, she had "sacrificed my fancy." "My heart" was not "engaged." "I never felt the passion of love." Eliza, in short, has invested her female independence and liberty of choice with desire. And with an equally dangerous emotion—individualism. Pleasure, especially in Eliza's usage, presumes individuals capable of fancying and privileging their own desires, of acting independent of society's approval in order to secure them. Eliza significantly ends her letter by underscoring this note of individualism. "This letter," she confesses to Lucy, "is all an Egotism" (5–6) [4–5]. What a significant beginning for a novel written in the shadow of the American Revolution!

Throughout the novel, Eliza Wharton will insist that pleasure can legitimately be wedded to a desire for independence and liberty, that marriage without such a "wedding" will destroy happiness.[5] Her family and friends will tell her virtue and happiness are tied to prudence and a socially appropriate marriage, that pleasure and fancy will endanger both. Throughout, Eliza will insist on her right as an independent woman to pursue happiness guided by her own standards.

---

3. See, for example, Clyde A. Holbrook, *The Ethics of Jonathan Edwards; Morality and Aesthetics* (Ann Arbor: U of Michigan P, 1973). For British usage, see Edward A. Bloom and Lillian Bloom, *Joseph Addison's Sociable Animal in the Market Place, on the Hustings, in the Pulpit* (Providence: Brown UP, 1971).

4. *The Compact Edition of the Oxford English Dictionary* (Oxford and New York: Oxford UP, 1971).

5. The comments in the Declaration of Independence concerning the purpose of a just government can also be read in relation to Eliza's concerns about the government of marriage and the family. The Declaration follows its initial sentence that states that life, liberty and the pursuit of happiness are inalienable rights with its definition of a just government. * * * A subversive reading of *The Coquette* (and of the Declaration) might suggest the question: if marriage and the family do not promote the liberty and happiness of women, do women have a right to alter or abolish them?

The following interchange between Eliza and the proper and prosperously married Ann *Richman* schematically presents the conflict. Eliza, rejecting Richman's advice to cut short her new-found liberty and marry the minister, replies: "I hope my friends will never again interpose in my concerns of that nature. A melancholy event has lately extricated me from those shackles which parental authority had imposed on my mind. Let me, then, enjoy that freedom which I so highly prize. Let me have opportunity, unbiased by opinion, to gratify my natural disposition in a participation of those pleasures which youth and innocence afford." Richman's response warns Eliza against conflating independence and pleasure, a conflation which Richman links to scenes of fashionable dissipation. "Of such pleasures, no one, my dear, would wish to deprive you," Richman insists, "but beware, Eliza! Though strewed with flowers, when contemplated by your lively imagination, it is, after all, a slippery, thorny path. The round of fashionable dissipation is dangerous. A phantom is often pursued, which leaves its deluded votary the real form of wretchedness" (13) [11].

The disruption of the easy relations between happiness and virtue which Eliza's desire for pleasure and independence affected underscores a second disjuncture which greatly troubled the eighteenth century, that between perception and reality. The eighteenth century desired mimesis and despaired of achieving it. They feared that fancy and passion, tied to individualism and to the twin paper revolutions of credit and printing, would disrupt the ability of words and the imagination to represent material reality. Reality would become a chimera, especially for the innocent and the inexperienced, especially, that is, for women and the young. In the particular dialogue just cited, for example, Eliza insists that female independence is not only legitimate and pleasurable but a real option. The married and thus mature and experienced Richman dismisses Eliza's words as immaterial, "phantoms" obscuring the bodily reality of "slippery, thorny paths," and the "real form of wretchedness" which female independence, fused with female pleasure, will bring. Eliza alarms rather than persuades the reader by her willful and defiant response: "I despise those contracted ideas which confine virtue to a cell" (13) [11].

Here, then, is the dilemma Foster presents. Independence endangers at the same time as it gives pleasure; domestic restraints destroy pleasure and liberty at the same time as they guarantee virtue and economic security. At all the key points in the novel two critical disjunctures appear. The imagination and the passions threaten to distort perception; virtue, independence, liberty, and happiness are divided against themselves. Eliza would like to unite all. Her virtuous advisers tell her this is no longer possible. Take the correspon-

dence between Eliza and Freeman in which Eliza contrasts social independence (which she depicts in corporeal and fanciful terms) to marriage and public service (which she associates with the loss of economic independence, social liberty—and pleasure). "My sanguine imagination paints, in alluring colors, the charms of youth and freedom, regulated by virtue and innocence," Eliza writes Freeman, "Of these I wish to partake." She tells of her fears of the stuffy minister who wants to carry her off to the wilderness of New Hampshire. "I recoil at the thought of immediately forming a connection which must confine me to the duties of domestic life, and make me dependent for happiness, perhaps, too, for subsistence, upon a class of people [the minister's parishioners] who will claim the right to scrutinize every part of my conduct, and, by censuring those foibles which I am conscious of not having prudence to avoid, may render me completely miserable." She then asserts her right to make her own decision. "You must either quit the subject, or leave me to the exercise of my free will" (29–30) [23]. Lucy Freeman, whose role in the novel is to express republican ideals, snaps back. Eliza's words and fancy have obscured Eliza's perceptions of reality.

Freeman's heated response underscores the opposition between pleasure and happiness, women and liberty, female independence and female virtue. "You are indeed very tenacious of your freedom, as you call it; but that is a play on words. A man of Mr. Boyer's honor and sense will never abridge any privileges which virtue can claim" (30–31) [24]. Indeed, liberty or "freedom" for women is so inconceivable to Freeman that it exists only "as a play on words." She replaces "freedom" with female "virtue" which can only claim privileges from a posture of dependence. And privilege, other republican texts tell us, is dangerous, tied to corruption, as in the unearned privileges of birth, which commercial republicanism scorns.[6]

If women's relation to liberty and freedom underscores the complexities and uncertainties of those words, women's relation to economic independence does the same. Indeed *The Coquette* quite pointedly spells out the ways women's relation to independence limits their right to liberty—and predetermines the boundaries of their happiness. The same characters that tell Eliza that her independence/freedom is a play on words, Freeman, Richman, and the Reverend Mr. Boyer, warn her that middle-class women lack the financial resources to support an independent social role. (Eliza stretches the limits of her mother's income when visiting Freeman in Boston and must compromise her independence by accepting presents [73] [57].) Freeman and Richman warn her not to overstep

6. Isaac Kramnick, "Republican Revisionism Revisited," *The American Historical Review* 87.3 (June 1982): 629–64.

her class in her ambition to make a fashionable show. A minister is just the right husband for her. "His situation in life," the prudent Freeman advises, "is . . . as elevated as you have a right to claim. Forgive my plainness, Eliza. . . . I know your ambition is to make a distinguished figure in the first class of polished society, to shine in the gay circle of fashionable amusements, and to bear off the palm amidst the votaries of pleasure" (27) [22].

It is Eliza's twin desires for the pleasures of social independence and social eminence that attract her to the rake, Major Sanford. When Mr. Boyer finally rejects Eliza, it is not her loss of chastity that motivates the minister, but her independence coupled with her extravagance in dress and her desire to rise above her father's social station. And, significantly, it is at this point that Boyer enters into a debate about the contested meanings of the word "virtue," defining it as far more than sexual propriety. In a letter to his friend and col-league, the Reverend Mr. T. Selby, Boyer writes, "I would not be understood to impeach Miss Wharton's virtue; I mean her chastity. Virtue in the common acceptation of the term, as applied to the sex, is confined to that particular, you know. But in my view, this is of little importance, where all other virtues are wanting!" (78) [61].

Boyer's denunciation of Eliza's assertion of social independence unsupported by economic independence is the turning point in the novel. Once the minister has rejected her as an appropriate wife for his class, no other man proposes. Eliza's passion for liberty and social independence has reached imprudent limits. It has propelled her into the classless state of the spinster, with only marginal rights to the economic resources of any man. Her independence has cost her what it at first promised: pleasure, happiness, free access to the world outside the home. It will ultimately cost her her sexual virtue as well. Though warned against the rake by friends and family, she insists on judging him by her own criteria and falls.

Foster's telling of Eliza's story contains significant discontinui-ties and silences. Foster splits Eliza's fall into two almost unrelated events: her rejection by the Reverend Mr. Boyer, her affair with the rake. Years separate the two. The second, the sexual fall, comes unaccompanied by either pleasure or passion.[7] The requisite physi-cal decay, in fact, rather than following from her sexual seduction, precedes it by approximately a year (105, 110) [82, 86]. If anything, Eliza's sexual seduction appears the formulaic conclusion demanded by the novel of seduction and needed to connect Hannah Foster's Eliza Wharton with Elizabeth Whitman, the woman who died of

7. The absence of sexual desire from the process of sexual seduction or, indeed, of any mention of sexuality is one of the most striking aspects of this novel. Davidson point-edly remarks on it (*Revolution*, 149), as do most other readers.

childbirth in a Massachusetts inn. We are drawn back to Cathy Davidson's suggestion that Hannah Foster deliberately wrote against an existing male narrative of sex and passion. Can the striking absence of sexual passion be explained, then, by the fact that Foster's Coquette, like Henry James's Daisy Miller, died not from lust but from the imprudent desire for an impossible social independence and the desire to assert her right to control her own body?[8]

Three letters that separate the two sections of the novel suggest an even more subversive reading—that Eliza's real seduction and fall occurred a year after Boyer's denunciation and long before her sexual fall with Sanford (101–6) [79–83]. At this point, realizing that no other man will propose, Eliza writes Boyer, acquiescing in his denunciation of her. He was right, she confesses; she had sinned. Indeed his letter of denunciation has led her to repent. She begs him to marry her. Boyer responds that he is pleased she now accepts his reading of her acts, but "Your letter came too late." He has chosen another, a "virtuous . . . amiable . . . accomplished" woman who will serve him better than the fanciful, extravagant, and independent Eliza. The tone of his letter is authoritative, judgmental, and assured (101–4) [79–82].

It is at this point that Eliza cries out to Freeman: "O my friend, I am undone. . . . O that I had not written to Mr. Boyer!" She then reaffirms her submission to his text. "I blame not Mr. Boyer. He has acted nobly." From this submission comes not inner peace but ruin, inner torment, and decline. For a second time in the book, Eliza misappropriates language traditionally used to describe the sexual to discuss the social. She writes Freeman: "I approve his conduct, though it operates my ruin . . . and what adds an insupportable poignancy to the reflection is self-condemnation. From this inward torture where shall I flee? Where shall I seek that happiness which I have madly trifled away?" Eliza has finally accepted the fragmentation of virtue, independence, and happiness. She has been seduced not by the rake but by the minister's text of individual (especially female) submission to social consensus. It is the relinquishing of her social and intellectual independence, not of her sexual virginity, that constitutes her true fall. It is this fall, not her later sexual seduction, that she reports with all the anguish of a sexual fall and in the appropriate formulaic language—even to a discussion of the decline of her health. "My bloom is decreasing. My health is sensibly impaired" (105) [83]. Without the pleasures of

---

8. Gayle Rubin argues that the most radical political assertion possible occurs when a young woman asserts her right to control the right of access to her body and her sexuality. Gayle Rubin, "Traffic in Women," in *Towards an Anthropology of Women*, ed. by Rayna Reiter (New York: Monthly Review Press, 1975).

independence and of "the exercise of my free will" Eliza's body wastes away.

It is at this point in Eliza's seduction by Boyer's text that the prudent Freeman, always Boyer's advocate, reverses her position. She chides Eliza on her fall from reason into sentimentality. To Eliza's lamentations, she sensibly responds: "Your truly romantic letter came safe to hand. Indeed, my dear, it would make a very pretty figure in a novel. A bleeding heart, slighted love, and all the *et ceteras* of romance enter the composition" (107) [84]. Eliza, she says, has given her heart to two imprudent texts—the text of religious prudery (Boyer's) and the text of the romance. Freeman recalls her to the better text of independence, reason, and strength, to the text of republicanism. It is that text that will lead her to happiness and virtue. "Where, O Eliza Wharton, . . . is that strength of mind, that independence of soul, that alacrity and sprightliness of deportment, which formally raised you superior to every adverse occurrence? Why have you resigned these valuable endowments and suffered yourself to become the sport of contending passions?" (107) [84]. Ironically, then, Foster does in the end agree with the male sermon and newspaper writers: reading romances led to Eliza's fall. Romances did so, however, not because they taught women sexual passion for men but because they taught women to renounce their own reason and independence. In this way, women lost their happiness. To cure Eliza from the excesses of male texts, Freeman tells her, a mutual friend, Julia, a sprightly, unmarried woman, will come to carry Eliza back to Boston and to her female friends. Freeman, in other words, in virtually her last letter in the novel, denounces the texts middle-class men use to construct gender and privileges the nontextual world of female friendship as a way back to the true text of republicanism.

But Julia comes too late. Eliza has already fallen victim, not to Sanford—he is secondary—but to the authoritative male discourse of her age. She has relinquished her quest to fuse independence and pleasure; she now accepts her community's definition of virtue. But such a definition, because it denies independence to women, brings neither happiness nor pleasure. "I frequent neither . . . the company [nor] the amusements of the town," she tells Julia. "Having incurred so much censure by the indulgence of a gay disposition, I am now trying what a recluse and solitary mode of life will produce. . . . I look around for happiness, and find it not. The world is to me a desart [*sic*]. And when I have recourse to books, . . . if novels, they exhibit scenes of pleasure which I have no prospect of realizing!" (135) [106]. Pallor, depression, an "emaciated form!" replace Eliza's gay independence (140) [110]. Only then, having lost indepen-

dence, pleasure, and happiness, does Eliza relinquish her virtue as well.

Cathy Davidson reads Hannah Foster's Eliza Wharton as Every-Woman who, during years marked by political and economic revolution, lusted for independence. She sees *The Coquette* as a subversive novel which encourages the reader, against her reason, to applaud Eliza's desires and mourn her death.[9] I embrace Davidson's reading but suggest an additional layering. Eliza Wharton is *Everyman* as well as Everywoman. Her career underscores the way economic change has transformed the independence of classical republicanism, making it highly individualized and economically risky. No longer securing social order, independence, tied to liberty and freedom, endangers the individual and society. Foster dramatizes the new impotence of family and community against the autonomy of youth and the power of the individual. Familial and community spokesmen have become spokeswomen, the feminized Greek chorus of Richman, Freeman, and Eliza's widowed mother, who, at the end, can only mouth hollow platitudes as Eliza is seduced in her mother's parlor and then disappears into the night.[1]

*     *     *

## CLAIRE C. PETTENGILL

## [Female Friendship in Foster's Novels][†]

*     *     *

Female friendship, expressed through letters, is a central theme of Foster's work. Important letters from Foster to her friends survive, and her two published works, *The Coquette* and the subsequent *The Boarding School* (1798), emphasize, largely through letters, the power of female connectedness. *The Coquette* consists almost entirely of letters between women friends; *The Boarding School* includes letters, parables, and lectures shared among the director and recent graduates of a finishing school for girls. Both works

---

9. Davidson, *Revolution*, 144–50.
1. Davidson points to Foster's construction of an impotent maternal figure in Mrs. Wharton. *Revolution*, 148–49.
† From "Sisterhood in a Separate Sphere: Female Friendship in Hannah Webster Foster's *The Coquette* and *The Boarding School*," *Early American Literature* 27 (1992): 187–94. Copyright © 1992 by the University of North Carolina Department of English. Used by permission of the University of North Carolina Press, www.uncpress.unc.edu. Page numbers in square brackets refer to this Norton Critical Edition.

deal explicitly with society's expectations of young women on the threshhold of adulthood, and both discuss female friendship as having a specific social function. Together, they powerfully evoke the complex ideology of sisterhood that helped shape the daily lives of young American women at the turn of the eighteenth century.

Social historians have convincingly documented the importance to postrevolutionary American women of a network of sisters and friends. Sibling attachment, especially between sisters, grew more intense in the wake of changes in work, the democratization of the family, and the emergence of institutions directed toward the young. Within the separate, domestic "sphere" to which women were more and more confined, girls turned to their sisters for "a sense of shared values, for understanding of their particular experience, for clarification of expectations about the future, and for recognition and support in attaining their goals" (Schiller-Chambers 128). Female friends outside the family were perhaps even more important:

> As time went on, the verbal distinction between family members and unrelated friends became clearer . . . language released "friendship" from blood ties so that it existed purely in elective relationships and became subject to idealization. (Cott 186)

Often, female friendship existed not in "isolated dyads," but in highly integrated, self-conscious networks sustained by social rituals (Smith-Rosenberg 417). As Nancy Cott observes, friendship among women "became a subject of . . . conversation, reading, reflection and writing" (160).

The role of sister and friend "mediated" in a positive way between the roles of daughter and independent woman—involving a kind of support network that helped a woman establish her identity in opposition to both social and parental authority in an era where both were increasingly challenged (Schiller-Chambers 147). "Sisterhood" included potentially negative, limiting connotations, inscribed by the constraining ideology of woman's separate sphere (155), but like "fraternity," it was a "term of crucial political, intellectual and social significance" (128). Both *The Coquette* and *The Boarding School*, I want to suggest, present female friendship in terms of this intense, culturally significant sisterhood.

That these two books make up Foster's entire canon, and deal with very similar themes, might seem reason enough to compare them. Surprisingly few critics have done so, however. One reason might be that *The Boarding School* is overwhelmingly didactic, apparently less complex and thus less interesting than *The Coquette*. Its title is apt; the book is portable pedagogy, setting forth unquestioned moral precepts in the thinnest fictional veil. Mostly a record of dis-

cussions about and parables illustrating virtuous behavior, *The Boarding School* lacks any coherent plot, any fully developed character, any "novelistic" complexity. Its heavy-handed moralizing has provoked at least one critic to dismiss it as "moral wish fulfillment" (Shuffelton 223).

Seen in the light of Foster's concern with sisterhood, however, and in comparison with *The Coquette*, *The Boarding School* acquires great interest. Both works portray women during the crucial transition in their lives from daughterhood to wife-and-motherhood, from parental to husbandly authority. But the boarding school set is younger, with school days still fresh in their memories, and the complications of courtship and marriage just coming into their range of vision. Only one of the graduates marries in the timespan covered by the book. The women in *The Coquette*, on the other hand, are farther along in life; when Eliza dies at age 37, only one of her friends, Julia Granby, remains single and a virgin. Whereas in *The Boarding School* the male world is shadowy and vague, in *The Coquette* it occupies the same space, jostling the women with demands that threaten even as they support the logical self-sufficiency of sisterhood and the female sphere. Together, the two books cover the prolonged "premarital state" described by Davidson, where socializing and "circulating" are productive labor, not only providing opportunities to choose a suitable mate (113), but also reinforcing ties between women.

Basically, then, *The Boarding School*'s presentation of the meaning and function of female friendship echoes and affirms that in *The Coquette*. But beyond this, the fact that *The Boarding School* is not a novel at all, but rather a work of didactic fiction—"conduct fiction," to use Sarah Emily Newton's phrase—means that it works according to different generic conventions, and can present Foster's vision of sisterhood in more explicit terms.

Newton describes *The Boarding School* as belonging to a "hybrid" genre: a "largely unexplored bridge between the dry female behavioral models found in the didactic book of advice and the more lively portrayal of female characters in early American fiction" (140). Conduct, or "usable" fiction, combines the powers of the novel and the didactic manual, engaging women emotionally in the cultural work of conforming to gender conventions while offering them a promise of "the good life" (which Newton describes as "women's entitlement through motherhood and self-control" [140]) if they comply.

Generically and politically, then, *The Boarding School* can be seen as lying in the middle of a continuum the endpoints of which are marked by the conduct manual on one hand and the novel on the other. If the conduct book is "hegemonic," inculcating constant self-regulation (Armstrong 120), and the novel can be "subversive,"

a medium that dramatizes conflict and thereby often works against the message it is assigned to convey (Davidson 128), books like *The Boarding School* might be described as "moderate," able to bridge cultural contradictions in an effective way.[1]

From this perspective, a comparison of the ideologies of sisterhood in *The Coquette* and *The Boarding School* becomes even more fruitful. Read as companion pieces, Foster's works serve as a two-part argument for the practical value of female friendship in a world of separate spheres, a world as familiar and troubling to young female readers as their own rapidly changing lives. Pressed into service by different but closely related genres, female friendship in these works also reveals itself as a complex, malleable and often contradictory source of meaning.

The first part of *The Boarding School* consists of a series of moral lessons and parables—a kind of "closing argument"—offered by Mrs. Williams, who runs a small finishing school and is the widowed mother of two girls, as her charges prepare to return to their families and get on with their lives. The second half comprises letters among the girls and Mrs. Williams, most of which interpret incidents in their new lives in the light of values inculcated at Harmony Grove, as the school is called. These letters echo the moralizing lectures of Mrs. Williams, seemingly unmediated, almost undigested.

Obviously, the "judicious Mrs. Williams" is the linchpin of this female circle; her authority is unquestioned. However, its nature is entirely appropriate to her "sphere":

> Where her judgment and prudence aided the useful acquisitions of the mind, a sprightly fancy and a cheerful disposition, regulated by experience and discretion, qualified her to enter, at once, with becoming dignity and condescending ease, into all their concerns; to participate [sic] their pleasures; while with candour and mildness, she reproved their errors, detected their follies, and facilitated their amendment. (6) [137]

Mrs. Williams is a perfect "republican mother," riding the crest of the historical circumstances which have produced her. Paternal (and not coincidentally, clerical) authority within the household has declined

---

1. Critics differ as to whether particular genres are "conservative" or "radical" by nature, just as they differ in their theoretical basis for argument. For example, conduct fiction has been read on a continuum of generic significance defined on one side by a disciple of Foucault (Armstrong) and on the other by a critic who takes a Bakhtinian view of things (Davidson). Armstrong would deny that domestic novels can in any way work against a culture's hegemonic forces (see, for example, *Desire and Domestic Fiction*). An exploration of the debate over the ideology of the novel would go far beyond the scope of this essay—what I want to suggest is only that different genres can highlight different aspects of ideologies which they seem to share, so that a comparison can help expose inherent contradictions, or unappreciated complexities, within the ideology itself.

in the most concrete way, with the death of her minister husband. Freed from the necessity for productive labor, Mrs. Williams's role is to educate, within the home, and to instill the appropriate virtues in those under her care: "she particularly endeavored to domesticate them: to turn their thoughts to the beneficial and necessary qualifications of private life" (7) [138]. In other words, Harmony Grove explicitly prepares daughters to function in a separate sphere.

Mrs. Williams's pedagogical methods are intriguing; of particular interest is her effort to mold female minds not only by serving as a model or a pattern, but also by unobtrusively "entering in" to her pupils' emotions in order to understand them. In a remarkable passage, she describes the breakfast hour at Harmony Grove as a time when the teacher habitually "suspended the authority of the matron" so that her charges would be "free from restraint. By this mean [sic] she had an opportunity of observing any indecorum of behaviour, or wrong bias" (9) [139]. By participating in the pleasures of younger women (and by refraining from public correction, saving her criticisms for later, private dialogue), Mrs. Williams demonstrates the terms of authority in a world of separate spheres. She is a "sister" as well as a mother, a friend as well as a teacher.

Jay Fliegelman has described the kind of education provided by Mrs. Williams as representative of an era in which "an older, patriarchal family authority was giving way to a new parental ideal characterized by a more affectionate and equalitarian relationship with children" (1), and which involved a "new pedagogical ideal of authority . . . that transformed coercion into conditioning" (31). With the development of the ideology of separate spheres, mothers became more and more responsible for educating their children, especially in the moral virtues previously considered the province of patriarchal authority (Davidson 134; Mintz ch. 3; Cott 84, 87). By locating this parental and pedagogical ideal in one character, the teacher-mother who acts as a friend, *The Boarding School* makes it both an essential component of the ideology of separate spheres as well as a means of reproducing that ideology, in an "empire of influence infinitely more powerful than the empire of force" (Fliegelman 16).

Mrs. Williams behaves toward her pupils just as she expects them to behave toward one another; the girls not only open themselves to her love and scrutiny, but imitate her relationship with them in their bonds with other women—foregoing all restraint with their friends. As Mrs. Williams observes, true friendship

> invariably seeks the permanent good of its object; and in so doing will advise, caution and reprove, with all the frankness of undissembled affection . . . flattery is utterly excluded. (92) [179].

In other words, openness and criticism are signs of true female friendship, or "sisterhood," and domestic rituals that exercise them (like breakfast) are the glue that holds the female circle together.

The ideal female bond thus requires the exercise of self-discipline and tenderness, a peculiar combination that Ruth Bloch identifies as key to essentially contradictory, gendered notions of virtue that placed civic virtue in the hands of mothers but required them to practice it only at home (52). In effect, Mrs. Williams is inculcating in her pupils, through her lectures and other female bonding rituals, the central contradictions of the notion of separate spheres, contradictions whose consequences are most apparent, not in *The Boarding School*, but in *The Coquette*.

Obviously, the boarding school is not only a school; it is a model family, better than a real one. This truth dawns on its students when they return to their homes. Significantly, they move from the rural utopia of Harmony Grove to more corrupt urban areas—what Mrs. Williams anticipates as "new scenes . . . which will call for the exercise of every virtue" (11) [140] and the inhabitants of which one young woman describes with disillusion as a "listless tribe of yawning mortals." Not only does this correspondent miss her "preceptress" and "amiable companions," but she finds her own family unequal to the elevated standards of Harmony Grove: her sisters sleep late and don't appreciate her early-morning piano playing (115–16) [191–92].

In the fallen world beyond the school, letter-writing replaces the rituals of female bonding exemplified by the Harmony Grove breakfasts. Evidently, the young women "need" to open themselves to their friends. They long for those "among whom I had been used to unbend every thought" (115) [191]; beg former schoolmates to visit "because your friendship is void of flattery" (135) [202]; and criticize new, less sincere acquaintances (148) [207–08].

Neither the school breakfasts nor these letters are private in the sense of isolated. Thoughts and letters are shared among all the friends. To give only one example: Harriot Henley sends Laura Guilford a letter from "the volatile Amelia Parr" (an outsider, of whom Harriot disapproves), as well as a copy of Harriot's reply to Amelia, so that Laura can see for herself Amelia's character flaws (and implicitly, Harriot's virtues) (155) [211]. Clearly, the letters do more than express private affection. They connect a series of American households in a female institution, a reading circle, the function of which is to maintain the highly integrated female network formed at Harmony Grove. The correspondents share thoughts, conversations, poems, letters, novels and other books, reading not only written works but incidents and people in their lives—including one another—in light of the moral standards of Harmony Grove, to be approved or disdained accordingly. Reading and writing, in this

work, serve not the institution of the self, but sisterhood and the structure of separate spheres which gives it so much force.

Despite *The Boarding School*'s emphasis on the importance of friendly criticism, however, it is significant that none of the Harmony Grove graduates ever finds occasion to criticize one of their own. Sometimes they recall (always with a sense of gratitude) Mrs. Williams's "judicious" admonitions (123) [191], but they tend only to exercise their own critical skills on works of literature, frivolous social practices, new acquaintances, or friends who did not attend the school. Thus, Caroline Littleton relates her "chagrin" on "reading Pope's letters" (126) [197] and bemoans "Absurd and expensive fashions" as "injurious to society at large" (130) [199]; Anna Williams attacks the "unbecoming levity of some of my sex" at an assembly (143) [206]; and Sophia Manchester condemns the conversation of some new and beautiful acquaintances for its "ludicrous insinuations, hackneyed jests, and satirical remarks upon others . . . who were absent" (149) [208].

Indeed there is no apparent need for the young women to criticize one another; not one is tempted by vice in any form. Even though stories of abandoned virtue and lurid consequences fill the pages of the book, providing occasions for moral reflection, they are always marked off in one of two ways from the experiences of the Harmony Grove graduates. First are the parables related by Mrs. Williams. These usually contrast patterns of virtue and vice, personified in females with symbolic and/or Romanized names like Elvira, Celia, Lucinda, Levitia, Florella, and so on. Second are the stories the young women themselves relate in their letters to one another about less-than-virtuous acquaintances. These are always women outside the immediate circle, like "the volatile Amelia Parr." The only real fallen women (that is, not overtly fictionalized like those in Mrs. Williams's stories) in *The Boarding School* are outsiders—an Irish servant girl rescued from infamy by Maria Williams (227–31) [247–49], and "the beautiful and admired Clarinda" (186) [226], who is apparently an acquaintance but not a close friend of Julia Greenfield's.

This didactic device—the fastidious separation of virtuous characters from fallen ones—is one of the plainest and most significant differences between *The Boarding School* and *The Coquette*. In *The Coquette*, Foster marks off one character as the site of the battle between virtue and vice, setting the stage for a more "realistic" exploration of the bonds of sisterhood. Eliza's story certainly bears an uncanny resemblance to *The Boarding School*'s parables and anecdotes about seduced women, and she is strongly attracted to fashion, the city, entertainment, and other pleasures associated in both books with vice. But far from being either a flat fictional symbol or a mere acquaintance, Eliza is a solid member of the

respectable female circle. Consequently, where rituals of female bonding in *The Boarding School* separate the subject of openness from the object of criticism (friends open their hearts to one another by frank criticism of outsiders), reinforcing solidarity by constructing sisterhood against the outside world, *The Coquette* requires the women to exercise both the positive and the negative "arms" of sisterhood within the female circle itself.

It is important to remember that Eliza is not the only character who completes a major transition in the novel. Her two best friends, Lucy Freeman and Mrs. Richman, also undergo critical changes—Lucy marries, and Mrs. Richman bears and loses a child. Implicitly, *The Coquette* deals with the possible breakdown of an established female circle as its members accept suitors, marry, and bear children, or—worst of all—fall prey to seduction. The novel explores the limits of female friendship, dramatizing not only predictable tensions between the ideology and practice of sisterhood, but also among the multiple, contradictory ideologies these women struggle to live by. Torn between loyalty to one another and to a patriarchal division of the world which simultaneously encourages and thwarts female friendship, Eliza and her friends face quandaries Foster never requires the protégées of Mrs. Williams to imagine. Sisterhood in this context takes on a more challenging task than parroting lessons learned at school: theory is put to the test.

From the start, friendship is "exercised" in *The Coquette*. Eliza's very first letter, to her friend Lucy Freeman, is extremely open; she admits that she does not really regret her fiancé's death, and that she is happy to leave her mother's house. Freed from the constraints of a loveless engagement, Eliza wants to enjoy herself, as she frankly acknowledges. Lucy's reply is not recorded, but from Eliza's next letter we learn that Lucy's notion of true friendship is a familiar one; she would feel at home in Harmony Grove: "I have received your letter; your moral lecture rather; and be assured, my dear, your monitorial lessons and advice shall be attended to" (7) [6]. Notable here is Eliza's gentle irony, an element largely absent from *The Boarding School*, and signalling the more complex view of sisterhood that informs this novel.

Throughout the story, Eliza's friends frankly criticize her thoughts and actions, almost always using true friendship to justify (and to soften) their words. "Forgive my plainness, Eliza," writes Lucy on one occasion, "It is the task of friendship sometimes to tell disagreeable truths" (27) [22]. Despite such "plainness," Eliza holds nothing back, remarking early on, "I must write to you the impulses of my mind; or I must not write at all" (8) [6], and later, "Pray write me impartially; let me know your real sentiment, for I rely greatly on your opinion" (53) [42].

Eliza's friends discuss her behavior openly. They share her letters among themselves and feel entitled to demand a complete account of her actions. Not only does she comply, but she makes certain that other friends learn of her compliance, even as she shares with them the information she imparts about her love affairs. For example, she writes Lucy Freeman about an encounter with Sanford (of whom everyone disapproves), as well as about a subsequent conversation with their mutual friend, Mrs. Richman:

> Come, I presume you are not interested to keep his secrets . . . Will you give me a little sketch of his conversation? Most willingly, said I; and accordingly, related the whole. When I had concluded, she shook her head, and replied, beware, my friend, of his arts. (38) [31]

Eliza's trust in the judgment of her friends is, I think, despite her occasionally flip tone, completely sincere. Although her behavior often contravenes strict *Boarding School* precepts, her faith in female friendship, at least, is the orthodox faith of *The Boarding School*, marked by strict observation of its forms (openness, receptivity to criticism), as well as its constant exercise (through letters and conversation). She often takes advice to heart; indeed, her fall into the arms of Sanford might have come much earlier, if she had not several times, on the strength of admonitions from her friends, almost overcome her attraction to him (38, 59, 91) [29, 47, 71]. For much of the novel, the ideology of sisterhood "works" for her.[2]

As the novel progresses, however, it becomes clear that the criticism, and to a large extent the openness, work only in one direction. Eliza expends great energy in relating numerous details of her private life, and her friends expend similar energy criticizing her behavior. They never go into detail about their own lives (beyond platitudes about their happiness), and she never presumes to criticize their personal decisions or actions. The emotional-disciplinary circuit that reinforces sisterhood is not operating at full (theoretical) capacity. Just as *The Boarding School* diverts the potentially destructive capacity of criticism into less threatening channels, so *The Coquette* situates Eliza in such a way that she provides almost all the openness and absorbs almost all of the criticism.

---

2. To appreciate the special importance of female friendship in Foster's work, one only has to compare *The Coquette* and/or *The Boarding School* to that other bestselling and influential seduction novel of the era, Susannah Rowson's 1794 *Charlotte Temple*. Centered on a heroine educated in a boarding school, who dies in childbirth after being seduced, Rowson's novel shares key features with Foster's works. But what is specifically missing from the life of the unfortunate Charlotte is trustworthy female friends. Encouraged in the path of vice by an immoral and unscrupulous French governess, she makes only one respectable friend after her "fall"—Mrs. Beauchamp, who is away with her husband at fateful moments in Charlotte's life.

The lopsided nature of the relationship between Eliza and her friends arises from several related factors, and has important consequences. First is the fact that Lucy and Mrs. Richman are several steps "beyond" Eliza in the crucial transition from daughter to wife to mother. As the novel opens, Mrs. Richman, already established in a "perfect union," is pregnant with her first child, and Lucy is engaged to be married in the near future. Both have successfully navigated the tricky passage, even as Eliza, following the death of her fiancé, begins the trip anew, leaving her "paternal roof" with "a gleam of joy" (5) [4]. For Mrs. Richman and Lucy, sisterhood has served its mediating purpose, and their primary focus is now on their own fledgling households. They still value their friends, but no longer need them so desperately. As Mrs. Richman observes,

> . . . we cannot always pay that attention to former associates which we may wish; but the little community which we superintend is quite as important an object; and certainly renders us more beneficial to the public. (25) [20]

In other words, she has become a votary of republican motherhood. Sisterhood retains its value, but only as a corollary to the main thesis—a function, like republican motherhood, of the greater ideology of separate spheres.

<p style="text-align:center">✳ ✳ ✳</p>

### WORKS CITED

Armstrong, Nancy. *Desire and Domestic Fiction: A Political History of the Novel.* New York: Oxford UP, 1987.

———. "The Rise of the Domestic Woman." In *The Ideology of Conduct: Essays in Literature and the History of Sexuality.* Ed. Nancy Armstrong and Leonard Tennenhouse. New York: Methuen, 1987. 96–141.

Bloch, Ruth H. "The Gendered Meanings of Virtue in Revolutionary America." *Signs* 13 (1987): 37–58.

Cott, Nancy. *The Bonds of Womanhood: "Woman's Sphere" in New England* 1780–1835. New Haven: Yale UP, 1977.

Davidson, Cathy N. *Revolution and the Word: The Rise of the Novel in America.* New York: Oxford UP, 1986.

Fliegelman, Jay. *Prodigals and Pilgrims: The American Revolution Against Patriarchal Authority, 1750–1800.* New York: Cambridge UP, 1982.

Foster, Hannah Webster. *The Boarding School.* Boston: I. Thomas, 1798.

———. *The Coquette.* Ed. Cathy Davidson. New York: Oxford UP, 1986.

Mintz, Steven. *Domestic Revolutions: A Social History of American Family Life*. New York: Free Press, 1988.

Newton, Sarah Emily. "Wise and Foolish Virgins: 'Usable Fiction' and the Early American Conduct Tradition." *Early American Literature* 25 (1990): 139–67.

Schiller-Chambers, Virginia Lee. *Liberty, A Better Husband: Single Women in America: The Generations of 1780–1840*. New Haven: Yale UP, 1984.

Shuffelton, Frank. "Mrs. Foster's Coquette and the Decline of the Brotherly Watch." *Studies in Eighteenth Century Culture* 16 (1986): 211–24.

Smith-Rosenberg, Carroll. "The Female World of Love and Ritual: Relations Between Women in Nineteenth Century America." In *The American Family in Social-Historical Perspective*. Ed. Michael Gordon. New York: St. Martin's, 1983. 411–35.

# JULIA A. STERN

## [Live Burial and the Tyrannies of Voice in *The Coquette*]†

✳   ✳   ✳

Foster encapsulates *The Coquette*'s most pertinent cultural themes in two evocative spectacles of leisure enjoyed by the privileged cohort of genteel republicans who constitute her dramatis personae; these emblematic tableaux refract in miniature the tragic double vision with which the author imagines the paradoxical nature and limits of liberty in post-Revolutionary America. The first scene involves a heated drawing-room debate in which members of both sexes argue the merits of female interest in the public sphere; in the course of this passage, one woman expropriates the voice of her ordinarily outspoken female companion in order to draw conclusions about the circumscribed prospects for women's political agency in the new nation. This episode, much commented on by recent scholars of the novel, pits dramatic against civic discourse but at the same time reveals that, from the moment of the Founding and into the Federalist period and beyond, politics function as America's primary form of national theater.

† From *The Plight of Feeling: Sympathy and Dissent in the Early American Novel* (U of Chicago P, 1997), 72–73, 75–77, 95–96, 126–28, 130, 138–39, 142, 147, 150–51. Copyright 1997 by the University of Chicago. All rights reserved. Reprinted by permission. Page numbers in square brackets refer to this Norton Critical Edition.

Unaccountably ignored by Foster's critics, the second tableau exposes the political underpinnings of theatrical expression itself. In this later episode, the female spokesperson of the republican chorus—the cohort of patriarchal women and men of feeling who constitute the heroine's community—unleashes a tirade against several types of public entertainment found in Boston in the mid-1790s. The objects of Lucy Freeman Sumner's moral indignation include a performance of Shakespearian tragedy and the self-display of female equestrians in the early national circus; in vivid contrast, Bowen's Museum, which exhibits wax effigies of prominent public figures of the late-eighteenth-century Anglo- and Franco-American world, receives her heartfelt endorsement.

Each of these tableaux foregrounds theatricality as a forum in which rival notions of fellow feeling vie for ascendancy in the new republic. Such clashing discourses of sympathy reflect the political divisions plaguing early national culture in the 1790s, as well as the attendant notions of sociality such competing visions suggest. The dominant mode of compassion the novel represents is connected to republican ideology and its constitutive components: the centrality of the community rather than of the individual, the idea of a material self-sufficiency that enables the transcendence of personal "interest," and a belief in collective sacrifice for the sake of the greater good. An exclusively public principle, such sympathy works along the lines René Girard elaborates in *Violence and the Sacred*: the cohesion of the republican community is predicated on the reality—indeed, the necessity—of a certain form of violence. Any individual who threatens the integrity of the group must be expelled in order to guarantee the hygienic purity and virtue of the collective.[1] We can identify this version of compassion with the practices of the feminized patriarchal chorus led by Lucy Freeman Sumner, the moral majority that controls the workings of the social milieu Foster's novel explores in detail.

The other form of sympathy *The Coquette* reveals to its readers commands far less influence among the fictive population and is related to then-emerging liberal modes of thought and their central tenets: a focus on the autonomous individual, the dedicated pursuit of economic advantage, and an understanding of the commonweal predicated on the well-being of solitary citizens. Such compassion is entirely a private matter; in this protoliberal version of fellow feeling, mutual understanding unfolds between independent persons who experience the social world largely as free agents rather

---

1. See René Girard, *Violence and the Sacred*, trans. Patrick Gregory (1972; Baltimore: Johns Hopkins UP, 1977). See also Susan L. Mizruchi, *The Science of Sacrifice: American Literature and Modern Social Theory* (Princeton: Princeton UP, 1997).

than as members bound in collective relation. Following the schema outlined by Adam Smith in his *Theory of Moral Sentiments*, such sympathy arises only when one is able to envision taking another's place in order to feel his or her part.² Such imaginative extension of humanity involves the exercise of the mind as well as the heart and requires that individuals function as mirrors of compassion for their suffering fellows. That Foster's fiercely independent heroine Eliza Wharton is the only character in the novel who exercises this version of sympathy is precisely the fact that spells her doom: in the absence of an empathic respondent to reflect much-needed compassion, this female practitioner of protoliberal fellowship remains ideologically isolated, socially invisible, and emotionally erased.³

\* \* \*

Eliza Wharton's protoliberal impulses are ultimately stillborn and her rebellious nature recontained because she cannot imagine a life beyond the very republican cohort that would stifle and bury alive her powerful desire for freedom. Foster's narrative form—the novel's dialectical expression and erasure of the female voice—reflects and replays this fact. The heroine's tragedy finally involves her failure to function as the sympathetic spectator of her own plight. When Eliza can no longer provide the mirror of compassion *for herself*, once she loses the capacity to see her dissent from the majority's tyranny as a valid desire, her interpellation into the ideology of republican fellow feeling becomes complete. Eliza moves from serving as the object of collective scrutiny to playing the victim in a public sacrifice; in the final ironic twist of her unhappy fate, the heroine orchestrates her own violent expulsion from the

2. I borrow this phrasing from David Marshall. See his *The Surprising Effects of Sympathy: Marivaux, Diderot, Rousseau, and Mary Shelly* (Chicago: University of Chicago Press, 1988), 3.
3. Eva Cherniavsky similarly asserts that Eliza "envisions her power to feel not as the medium of social interpellation, but as the medium of social relations between women." Cherniavsky's notion of social interpellation comes from Louis Althusser's formulation "that ideology 'acts' or 'functions' in such a way that it 'recruits' subjects among the individuals (it recruits them all), or 'transforms' the individuals into subjects (it transforms them all) by that very precise operation which I have called *interpellation* or hailing, and which can be imagined along the lines of the most commonplace everyday police (or other) hailing: 'Hey, you there!'" The Althussarian dynamic Cherniavsky identifies approximates my notion of "republican sympathy," while what she characterizes as social relations between women comes closer to what I term "protoliberal sympathy." The distinction, with all its attendant ideological freight, would suggest that republican sympathy is coercive and tyrannical, while protoliberal sympathy enables freedom. While such facile comparisons are to a large degree congruent with the general contours of Foster's novel, the brilliance of *The Coquette* inheres in is representation of the limits and dangers of liberty as well as of social restriction. See Cherniavsky, *That Pale Mother Rising: Sentimental Discourses and the Imitation of Motherhood in 19th-Century America* (Bloomington: Indiana UP, 1995), 39. See also Althusser, *Lenin and Philosophy and Other Essays*, trans. Ben Brewster (New York: Monthly Review Press, 1971), 174.

community. This act of self-immolation enables the female chorus to reconsolidate its hegemony over her recently buried corpse in gothically literal fashion. Indeed, as Eva Cherniavsky remarks, Eliza's "fall reintegrates [this] disembodied body as a body of mourners, which forms again around the locus of an absence, (re)assembles around a grave."[4] Having incorporated the majority's values as her valedictory act, the heroine offers her life in exchange for a sympathy that can exist for her only in theory precisely because it is predicated on her expedient demise. Eliza's death thus takes on a redemptive, if not a transformative, power for the feminized chorus. Renewed and reconstituted by the tragedy, the community must continue to disavow the transgressive reality of the pleasure, possibility, and imaginative freedom afforded them by Eliza Wharton's life and letters. In the ultimate transaction of republican sympathy, neatly mystified in the chorus's exorbitant exhibition of grief, the heroine proves more valuable to her peers as a fetishized corpse than she has as an animated and exuberant friend.

## Faction and Tyrannical Majority

In a scene that foregrounds the preoccupation in the early republic with who shall possess political voice, Foster pits the world of theater against the realm of politics:

> The general topic of conversation . . . was politics. Mrs. Richman and Miss Wharton judiciously, yet modestly, bore a part; while the other ladies amused themselves with Major Sanford, who was making his sage remarks on the play, which he held in his hand. General Richman at length observed that we had formed into parties. Major Sanford, upon this, laid aside his book. Miss Laurence simpered; and looked as if she was well pleased with being in a party with so fine a man; while her mother replied, that she never meddled with politics; she thought they did not belong to ladies. Miss Wharton and I, said Mrs. Richman, must beg leave to differ from you, madam. We think ourselves interested in the welfare and prosperity of our country; and consequently, claim the right of inquiring into those affairs, which may conduce to, or interfere with the common weal. We shall not be called to the senate or the field to assert its privileges, and defend its rights, but we shall feel for the honor and safety of our friends and connections, who are thus employed. If the community flourish and enjoy health and freedom, shall we not share in the happy effects? If it be oppressed and disturbed, shall we not endure our proportion of

4. See Cherniavsky, *That Pale Mother Rising*, 40.

the evil? Why then should the love of our country be a mascu-
line passion only? Why should government, which involves the
peace and order of the society, of which we are a part, be wholly
excluded from our observation?[5]

In this incident, the characteristically vocal heroine of *The Coquette*
is curiously silent. Stifled at the center of this scene is Eliza Whar-
ton, who is given body in Selby's epistolary tableau but deprived of
the voice we have come to identify as the most eloquent and imagi-
native force in Foster's novel. More precisely, during a conversation
about the proper relationship between American women and the
political realm, an exchange in which she is alleged to bear "a part,"
Eliza Wharton does not speak for herself but instead is spoken for.
Women's speech emanates from the centrally embedded narrative
core of this letter, but it is framed and recast at multiple removes.

Mr. Selby omits whatever Eliza might have expressed about poli-
tics in his missive reconstructing the tableau for Boyer; he effec-
tively reports that she has "judiciously, yet modestly," borne a part
in this conversation and then censors her contribution in an act of
nonrepresentation. What he chooses to depict is the point at which
another woman determines to *vocalize for Eliza*, the moment when
Mrs. Richman takes it on herself to *speak representatively* for a fel-
low member of the female sex. The enunciatory complexity of the
episode comes full circle as Mr. Selby relays Mrs. Richman's speech
in his written account of the incident, thus inscribing an act of ven-
triloquism by turning oral expression into epistolarity. Significantly,
it is a male voice (in the letter form, a male signature) that unfolds
this scene of vocal cooptation within the female community through
a transvestite mode of narrative. Foster, the female author, cloaks
herself in the persona of Selby, a male correspondent who does
surveillance by proxy for the Reverend Mr. Boyer, Eliza's straight-
laced suitor. In his epistolary report to Boyer, Selby relays the dia-
logue of General Richman, Mrs. Laurence, and Mrs. Richman with
a narrative ease that masks the intricate expressive dynamics that
have given rise to his writing.

The episode brings into focus issues central to the political debates
unfolding in the decade after the Founding: the dilemma of which
voices shall be enfranchised and questions about the nature of repre-
sentation itself. Translated into the fictive terms of *The Coquette*,
such concerns become an inquiry into the workings of narrative
transmission: Why does Foster choose to dramatize this charged

---

5. Hannah Webster Foster, *The Coquette*, ed. Cathy N. Davidson (1797; New York:
Oxford UP, 1986), 44 [35–36]. Hereafter, all citations will be to this edition of the
novel and will be noted parenthetically in the text.

discussion of female political agency in the words of a masculine cor-
respondent? Why does she deputize a male persona to filter the
exchange through reported speech, a stylistic maneuver that deprives
Mrs. Richman of immediate expression? Why is it that, within the
mimesis, Mrs. Richman does not utter her opinions on her own but
elects to appropriate the words of her ordinarily outspoken friend
in order to enter into the conversation at all? And, finally, why is
Eliza Wharton rendered silent in a scene that foregrounds women's
articulation as a form of political action?

Such instances of the dislocation and suppression of women's
political voices haunt *The Coquette*, extending from Eliza's mysteri-
ous silence and Mrs. Richman's vocal appropriation within the fic-
tive world to Mr. Selby's epistolary repetition of her gesture and
Foster's own transvestism at the level of narrative. The dynamics of
this scene anticipate and rehearse the way in which the novel's
patriarchal majority, figures who regardless of gender employ a
characteristic feminized discourse, annex women's language in
order to promote civic values—at the same time foreclosing on any
possibility for emerging liberal sympathy. This emblematic appro-
priation and erasure of female speech at the moment of enuncia-
tion, what Eve Sedgwick would call the "live burial" of the female
voice,[6] functions not only as the defining principle of *The Coquette*'s
narrative form. In fact, the gothicization of women's expression is
Foster's very subject.

*       *       *

Adam Smith views the need for sympathy as a problem produced
by people's essential isolation from each other, a challenge that
moral beings must surmount. In his *Theory of Moral Sentiments*,
Smith elaborates the difficulty of expanding the imagination in
order to envision and then feel for the troubles of an-*other*. Smith's
notion of compassion is a liberal, indeed a protodemocratic, impulse:
it imaginatively leaps toward and embraces the other, domesticating
differences under the larger umbrella of a common humanity. The
republican version of sympathy, in contrast, pointedly identifies
otherness and interdicts it from the affective circle, decidedly
rejecting Smith's premise that difference does not compel alien-
ation. Such understanding is what Eliza idealistically believes she
has enjoyed with her female companions before their marriages
made a "tomb of friendship" (24) [19–20], but, while the heroine's
language would suggest that women are only annexed by the patri-

---

6. Eve Kosofsky Sedgwick, *The Coherence of Gothic Conventions* (New York: Methuen,
1986), 5. Sedgwick notes that a constitutive relationship exists between formal dynam-
ics in gothic narrative and the issues of content that "haunt" the genre.

archal republican cohort at marriage, the example of the sparkling Julia Granby—Eliza's unattached doppelgänger—actually implies that interpellation begins far earlier in the female life-cycle, as soon as a young woman becomes eligible to enter the romantic lists. The model Julia plays powerful foil to Eliza, cultural counterexemplum.

Eliza's trenchant characterization of the losses women suffer in the ritual of matrimony emphasizes the link between the feminized chorus and the dead patriarchs whose voices it channels: the metaphor underscores the way in which marriage functions as a mechanism of live burial for the female homosocial cohort. It also underscores the alienation the heroine confronts in the face of such gothic affiliations; avoiding her own encryptment necessarily distances her from the moribund world of her married friends, whose emotional absence she keenly feels. Writing to the newly married Lucy Freeman Sumner, Eliza exclaims, "Oh that you were near me as formerly, to share and alleviate my cares' to have some friend in whom I could repose my confidence, and with whom I could freely converse, and advise, on this occasion, would be an unspeakable comfort!" (106) [83]. The heroine's lamentation operates on multiple levels. Literally, she is mourning over the geographical gap that now separates the married Lucy from her childhood friend, but the distance is also psychological: Eliza's wish for interchange and dialogue—for conversation itself—suggests that such sources of empathy have become remote, indeed, have dried up for her, and her use of the term "unspeakable" to communicate the cathartic relief she dreams of achieving through an uninhibited exchange points up the ways in which her feelings have already been made gothic by the misapprehension of the chorus.

\* \* \*

*Spectacle*

\* \* \*

In Lucy's assessment of Boston's popular entertainment in the Federalist period, both the tragic drama and the equestrian circus constitute deeply unruly if not actually transgressive cultural forms, but Bowen's Museum, the third and final place of resort mentioned in her letter on amusements, proves a genteel exception to this disturbing pattern: "With Mr. Bowen's museum, I think you were very much pleased. He has made a number of judicious additions to it, since you were here. It is a source of rational and refined amusement. Here the eye is gratified, the imagination charmed, and the understanding improved. It will bear frequent reviews without palling on the taste. It always affords something new; and for one, I am

never a weary spectator" (113) [89]. According to Lucy's narrative account, the local modes of mass entertainment break down into three important typologies that reflect late-eighteenth-century ideas about perceptual experience: that of sensibility, both head and heart, undone by tragedy; that of the gazing eye, outraged in its vision of the circus; and that of disembodied reason, elevated by the museum.[7] Both the theater and the circus are modes of spectacle that produce their generic effects through the articulation of physical sensation, but, while the drama calls for a visceral response that immediately translates into cerebral activity, the circus would seem to pander to the baser nature of its audience. Waxworks like those exhibited at Bowen's Museum, in contrast, make of embodiment an uncanny thing: existing on the middle ground between theater and painting, wax figures defamiliarize both the animation of dramatic performance and the stasis of the painted portrait. Such likenesses afford their beholders a greater emotional remove than do theatrical representations, because of their striking resemblance to human bodies that have been cosmetically transformed for viewing before burial. Indeed, as Marie-Hélène Huet suggests in the chapter on Mme Tussaud in *Monstrous Imagination*, evocatively titled "Family Undertaking," there exists a fascinating connection between the art of the mortician and that of the sculptor using wax as a medium. In her discussion of Tussaud's wax museum, Huet argues similarly that the wax figures occupy a transitional space between life and death; Tussaud crafts the faces for her chamber of horrors from death masks she casts from famous personages of the French Revolution.[8]

As an art form whose origin lies in mortuary practices, waxworks make particularly evocative objects of admiration in *The Coquette*, given the associations between the patriarchal majority and the clerical dead that Foster draws throughout. I will return to this connection shortly, but before doing so it is important to understand something more about the origins and nature of the cultural forum in which these waxworks are displayed.[9] Daniel Bowen's museum originates as a traveling exhibition that moves up and down the

7. See G. J. Barker-Benfield, *The Culture of Sensibility: Sex and Society in 18th-Century Britain* (Chicago: University of Chicago Press, 1992); and Janet Todd, *Sensibility: An Introduction* (London: Methuen, 1986).

8. See Marie-Hélène Huet, *Monstrous Imagination* (Cambridge, Mass.: Harvard UP, 1994), 212–14, and 188.

9. Lucy does not describe Daniel Bowen's museum as a display of waxworks; nor does she detail the contents of the collection. Such omissions suggest that Bowen's establishment is well known to Foster's audience, functioning as a part of its collective *mentalité*. Although the museum probably figures in what we might term eighteenth-century America's repertoire of cultural literacy, little information about it survives in the historical record. Those few remaining sources that however incompletely document por-

eastern seaboard in the post-Revolutionary period. Its growth and development, though given scant detail, are recorded briefly in histories of both the early American theater and the circus as well as in books on the origins of waxworks in the new nation. Amplifying on contemporary newspaper reviews that enumerate the contents of the collection in the 1790s, Isaac Greenwood provides a late-nineteenth-century account:

> In 1788 and '89, Mr. Bowen had a much more extensive exhibit at No. 74 Water street, opposite Crane Wharf [in New York City], with which he had come up from the Carolinas; it included the Royal Family, several of the prominent clergy of the city, some scriptural and humorous subjects, and the President, with a flying figure overhead crowning him with laurel.[1]

Late-eighteenth-century newspaper advertisements for the museum provide an extensive if hyperbolic catalogue of its curiosities (most likely composed by Daniel Bowen himself). A notice run on December 7, 1795, announces in somewhat less heightened language that

> BOWEN's Columbian Museum At the head of the Mall, BOS-TON, WAS opened (for the first time) on Thursday last, Containing a large and elegant collection of PAINTINGS, historical, theatrical, and fancy subjects; with portraits of some of the most distinguished characters in the United States; Landscapes, Drawing, &c. Wax figures in a detached room; a perfect representation of a man suffering under the guillotine. The assassination of John P. Marat by Miss Charlotte Carde [sic]. Baron Trench loaded with chains in a Dungeon. A great variety of more pleasing Wax Figures placed in the museum hall. *Curiosities*, natural, and artificial, among which, are a Glass Ship; a real Scalp of an Indian Chief, lately taken at the Westward; together with a Collection of Birds, in the highest state of preservation, &c.[2]

These historical facts allow us to make some informed speculations about the symbolic import of the curiosities Bowen displays to the public and to which Lucy makes general reference in *The Coquette*.

---

tions of Bowen's collection can be found scattered in Boston newspapers from the period as well as in early nineteenth-century histories of the American theater and circus and twentieth-century studies of wax sculpture in America. For an advertisement for Bowen's museum from the beginning of the 1790s, see *Columbian Centinel* [sic], June 1, 1791, 91. For an anonymous review of the collection that appears during the (roughly approximate) period in which the novel is set, see *Boston Gazette*, December 28, 1795, 3.
1. Isaac J. Greenwood, *The Circus: Its Origin and Growth* (1889; Washington, DC: Hobby House Press, 1962), 82.
2. See the *Boston Gazette*, December 7, 1795, 3.

372        Julia A. Stern

  In its elaborate totality, the exhibit constitutes a narrative repre-
sentation of early national identity formation at work. * * * The
effigy of Charlotte Corday telegraphs in elegantly economical fash-
ion a composite version of the loathed trio of American altierity:
the alien (she is French); the savage (like the Native Americans
who threaten the frontier, she too is a barbarous murderess); and
the female. While Bowen's waxen image of the guillotine reinforces
the impact of Mlle Corday's homicidal power and underscores the
Federalists' virulent hostility to the events, practices, and material
artifacts of the French Revolution, the scalp of the Native American
becomes not only an emblem of the vicious ferocity of the republic's
aboriginal enemies but also an index of early American colonial
prowess; in this fetishistic display of the scalp, early republicans
can disavow their own decided affinity for savage acts of violence,
behavior that unsettles any claims to moral and cultural superiority
attending the establishment of national identity and of individual
republican selfhood.[3]
  In light of the contents of the exhibition, patriarchal power—
incarnated in the figures of George the Third and his family, nota-
ble members of the local clergy, and George Washington being
crowned with laurel—would seem to be the prevailing theme of
Bowen's wax assemblage. This panorama is peopled by an idealized
if phantasmagoric gathering of the early republican elite who coex-
ist in odd array with their former political nemesis and his kin. The
characters of the two wax Georges, the literal (ex)-monarch of the
Anglo-American community and the figurative "father" of the new
nation, reflect two visions of authority existing in such close proxim-
ity in the Federalist imagination that their boundaries begin to blur;[4]
though his wreath is made of laurel rather than gold, the spectacle
nevertheless enacts the wish that Washington be crowned.[5] If we

3. See Carroll Smith-Rosenberg, "Dis-covering the Subject"; and "Subject Female: Autho-
   rizing American Identity," *American Literary History* 5.3 (fall 1993): 481–511. See also
   Jared Gardner, "Alien Nation: Edgar Huntly's Savage Awakening," *American Literature*
   66.3 (September 1994): 429–61.
4. Looby writes of anther instance in which George the Third is figuratively linked with
   George Washington. This is the moment when the King's visage transforms into the
   face of the American general, Founding Father, and first President on the sign in front
   of the local inn in Washington Irving's "Rip Van Winkle." Looby argues that what is
   "decisive" about this detail is "Rip's *recognition* of the change as one of semiotic substi-
   tution, his immediate demystification of the new order of signs of authority." See *Voic-
   ing America*, 43 and 94–96. In Foster's representation of Bowen's Museum, in contrast,
   there is no dissenting spectator from outside the Federalist majority who could demys-
   tify the reactionary, indeed the nostalgic, political aura that surrounds these doppel-
   gängers in wax. In fact, this contiguity carries a decidedly conservative ideological
   charge, suggesting that the differences between the two figures are easily collapsed.
5. Elkins and McKitrick note that "Adams laid himself open to charges, which he never
   fully lived down, of secretly favoring monarchy" (*Age of Federalism*, 46). Looby suggests,
   however, that "George Washington's construction as a charismatic symbolic presence

read the tableau as a narrative, the separate parts of which exist in syntactical relation to each other, the contiguity of these two Georges becomes significant. Despite the powerful and transformative reality of the American Revolution, these uncanny mirror figures signify that the republic's orientation lies as much in a patriarchal and auto-cratic past as it does in any rising liberal future.[6] The notable figures of the local clergy only reinforce this reading, and their presence in the display conjures the spectral patriarchs of Foster's book, the min-isters Wharton, Haly, and Boyer.

<p style="text-align:center">✻   ✻   ✻</p>

Projecting and affirming an idealized image of the world she actually inhabits, the museum is the perfect "place . . . of resort" for Lucy Freeman Sumner (113) [89]; it becomes not only a site of recre-ation or entertainment but also a refuge and a resource. In fact, Foster's word bears both meanings: deriving from the Old French term "to escape, ally," resort is related to the word "resource," which comes from the Latin for resurrection and means a "source of supply or support," "something to which one has recourse in difficulty," a "possibility of relief or recovery."[7] In the second half of the novel, the notions of resort and resource take on vital importance, as the letters that pass between the heroine and her community begin to chart the progressive disappearance of such forms of respite for Eliza in the face of her quest for freedom.

<p style="text-align:center">✻   ✻   ✻</p>

was largely a posthumous, retroactive phenomenon, part of a long and contested pro-cess of creating out of an ambiguous revolutionary past usable political myths and tradi-tions; and to the extent that the cult of Washington existed during Washington's life and during the immediate postrevolutionary consolidation, it was a deeply ambivalent phenomenon, marked by bombastic inflations and the widespread dissemination of his idolized image on the one hand, and on the other hand by such public demurrals as that of John Adams, who in Congress in 1777 said he was 'distressed to see some of our members disposed to idolize an image which their own hands have molten. I speak here of the superstitious veneration which is paid to General Washington'" (*Voicing America*, 43). See also Adams, quoted in Barry Schwartz, *George Washington: The Making of an American Symbol* (New York: Free Press, 1987), 22.

6. Liberalism as a political philosophy does not reject patriarchal authority; indeed, Car-ole Pateman, Joyce Appleby, Lynn Hunt, Margaret Jacobs, Smith-Rosenberg, and oth-ers have argued that the de facto liberal subject is a white male of the privileged classes. It is nevertheless true that the Lockean model of individualism is less inflected by gender than is the male homosocial republican formulation that originates in classi-cal theory. See, in particular, Appleby, *Liberalism and Republicanism in the Historical Imagination* (Cambridge, Mass.: Harvard UP, 1988). See also Pateman, *The Sexual Contract* (Stanford: Stanford UP, 1988).

7. *Merriam-Webster's Collegiate Dictionary*, 10th ed., sv "resort."

## Fetishism and Live Burial

> At the hour appointed, I went tolerably composed and resolute
> into the garden. I had taken several turns, and retired into the
> little arbor, where you and I have spent so many happy hours,
> before Major Sanford entered.
>
> (Eliza Wharton to Lucy Freeman, 91 [72])

As a space of resort, the female world of love and ritual that Eliza
nostalgically recalls in this letter haunts Foster's novel in two
important ways: within the fiction, a women's sphere exists only in
the girlhood of Eliza's past; and outside the book, in the world of
history, a sanctioned female homosocial realm does not come into
meaningful existence until the first quarter of the nineteenth
century.[8] By attempting to identify sisterhood as a redemptive
arena for women's action in Foster's book, critics such as Pettengill
seek to recuperate the novel from its melancholy ending, but, in the
present tense of *The Coquette*'s historical moment, a separate sphere
of adult women, living in meaningful relation to each other inside
but apart from patriarchal culture, is simply a fantasy. Pettengill is
attentive to the contradictions republican ideology presents to Amer-
ican women in the early national period, noting that Eliza is angry
at the "inadequacies of both sisterhood and republican motherhood,
which have promised so much and delivered so little" (197). But her
idealizing argument that homosocial bonds constitute a distinct
space of possibility for women ignores the fact that the female com-
munity, pointedly called "the whole *fraternity*" by Major Sanford
(158 [124], my emphasis), exists at no distance from the dominant
culture and in fact has been thoroughly penetrated by the patriar-
chal values for which it speaks.[9]

\*   \*   \*

\* \* \* From the time of her rejection by Mr. Boyer to the point at
which she succumbs to Major Sanford's sexual demands, Eliza
charts a trajectory of increasing social withdrawal, domestic con-

---

8. Although both Smith-Rosenberg and Lee Virginia Chambers-Schiller locate the ori-
gins of the dynamic at the turn of the eighteenth century, the bulk of the substantiat-
ing data derives from early nineteenth-century sources. It is my contention that the
dominant energies of Foster's novel, embodied in the feminized patriarchal chorus,
look backward to a real eighteenth-century ethos, while Eliza's desires point to the
opening possibilities of the nineteenth century. But, as much as the heroine would
revel in a female world of love and ritual, such a space is precisely what is missing in
Foster's novel. See Smith-Rosenberg, "Female World of Love and Ritual"; and see
Chambers-Schiller, *Liberty, a Better Husband, Single Women in America: The Genera-
tions of 1780–1840* (New Haven: Yale UP, 1984).
9. Scholars such as Harris, "Critiquing Franklin's America," Smith-Rosenberg, "Domesti-
cating 'Virtue,'" and Shuffelton, "Brotherly Watch," note the parallels that exist
between the chorus and the patriarchy. For the historical origins of this alliance, see
Douglas, *Feminization of American Culture*, 94–139.

finement, physical immobility, and epistolary silence. In her drive
to escape relegation to the world of domesticity by asserting her
sexual freedom as a last resort, she winds up as confined, home-
bound, and trammeled as the most docile of republican wives. Eli-
za's capitulation to Sanford under her mother's roof marks the final
enactment of her double-voicedness: an attack on the very heart of
domestic ideology, Eliza's defilement of maternal space at the same
time reveals that, despite her hostility to home and hearth, she can-
not escape their pervasive reach.[1] The immobility that overtakes
Eliza operates in direct contrast to her former propensity to remain
always in motion. Wayward desire has become paralyzed. In fact, it
is not an overstatement to say that Eliza begins to suffer the symp-
toms of agoraphobia (literally, fear of the marketplace) after having
been utterly exploited by market conditions: "I intended, this week,
to have journeyed to Boston with Julia Granby; but my resolution
fails me. I find it painful even to think of mixing again with the gay
multitude. I believe the melancholy reflections, by which I am
oppressed, will be more effectually, if not more easily, surmounted,
by tarrying where they are rendered familiar, than by going from
them awhile, and then returning" (126) [100]. Eliza's bad feelings
allow her space neither for dissent nor even for escape but render
her incapacitated and frozen; in contrast, having assumed Eliza's
former life and identity, Julia Granby is able to travel with full
mobility.

That we can locate Eliza's sexual fall in the period of Julia's ill-
timed visit to Lucy, when the heroine, sunk in the depths of despair,
needs the newcomer's companionship more than ever, suggests
how unmerciful the majority's adherence to republican ideology
can be. Despite the overpresence of the moralizing chorus and its
rhetoric of sororial care, the community's investment in "disinter-
est" becomes code for an inability to tolerate fanciful behaviors like
melancholic resignation. Such brutality is not unique to Julia. Both
Lucy and Sanford himself turn their backs on Eliza's predicament
at the end of the novel, the former in order to travel into the coun-
try with her husband and the latter so he can protect his property
from confiscation by angry creditors. The matron and the libertine
uphold, respectively, two defining attributes of the classical repub-
lican citizen: allegiance to republican wifehood and concern for
the preservation of financial independence; allowing such ideo-
logically driven considerations to supercede the claims of any pos-
sible "interest" in Eliza, both Lucy and Sanford show their

---

1. Fizer similarly notes that "Eliza's final acts of fornication" "mark at once the liberti-
nous nature of her sexuality and its redomestication" ("Signing as Republican Daugh-
ters," 244).

dispassionate colors while the heroine is sacrificed in the wake of their insensibility. * * *

* * * The community's posthumous celebration of Eliza's professions is thus perfectly congruent with its earlier disavowal of the gravity of the plaintive epistles she dispatched in her last year of life. Yet the chorus's consolation, the notion that the "regret occasioned by her absence" could really be "greatly alleviated" by her pious scraps of writing, remains a scandal of sympathy, for, while the heroine's earlier letters, faithfully mimetic effusions of her volatile nature, disturbed the propriety and equanimity of her friends, the funereal shards to which the grieving community clings conjure none of the living power of her "play about words." When Lucy mourns for "Not only the life, but what was still dearer, the reputation and virtue of the unfortunate Eliza" (163) [128], we see the fetishizing impulse at work. She notes that the heroine lives "still in the heart of her faithful Lucy; whose experience of her numerous virtues and engaging qualities, has imprinted her image too deeply on the memory to be obliterated" (167) [131]. Entirely erased from this hagiographic tableau is any recognition of the positive power of Eliza's fancy, which defined her charm as well as her unhappy fate; in the eyes of the community, the heroine's extravagant zeal for liberty casts her beyond the pale of sympathy,[2] leaving her isolated from decorous republican society. At such a sanitary distance, the chorus can disclaim the way in which her fall casts a shadow on their collective enterprise, tainting the purity of their ideas of independence, disinterest, and virtue itself.

* * *

Out of a gothic tragedy the community reconstruct a heroine of sentiment and inscribes itself for posterity. While Eliza's transgressive writing diminishes to the point of nonexistence, the chorus writes furiously *about* her.[3] If grammatical forms can be read for symbolic content, it is surely interesting that, in her final epistolary reports to Eliza's grieving mother, Julia Granby dispatches her information about the heroine's last days in the first-person plural voice (161) [126]. Although I have spoken of the feminized majority that dominates the discursive world of *The Coquette*, that term has been less literal than suggestive: in the final pages of Foster's book,

---

2. I here borrow the language of Christopher Castiglia, "In Praise of Extravagant Women: *Hope Leslie* and the Captivity Romance," *Legacy* 6 (1989): 3–16.
3. Pettengill notes, "Ironically, Eliza's friends continue busily to communicate with one another for and about Eliza. When she stops writing, her conversations and actions are reported at second hand, passed around from friend to friend" ("Sisterhood in a Separate Sphere," 198).

however, the most aggressive and self-righteous member of "the whole fraternity" (158) [128] begins to speak as "we," erasing any possible distinctions of perspective within or among the female friends. Thus, the wound to the social fabric created by Eliza's death has a perversely reparative effect on the majority left behind. The coherence and uniformity of the chorus have never been greater than at the moment when Julia proclaims to Mrs. Wharton, in the final letter of the novel, "I hope . . . that you will derive satisfaction from these exertions of friendship" (169) [133].

That such collective forms of relation are not all they purport to be, that communities based on a proudly held "disinterest" may in fact be destructive, is nevertheless the latent suggestion of the novel's penultimate epistle; in it, Lucy Sumner makes an uncanny statement about the impulses of affiliation: "to associate, is to approve; to approve, is to be betrayed" (168) [131]. On the surface, her statement alludes to Eliza's efforts to seek avenues of exchange outside conventional venues: Major Sanford is the obvious, though unmentionable, referent of her maxim. Yet it is precisely Eliza's wish to remain independent of associations that jeopardizes her relationship with the community. The price she pays for her reluctance to associate or approve of the feminized majority is nothing short of being betrayed by their indifference. In fact, it could be said conversely that the ultimate associations and betrayals Eliza faces come not at the hands of the libertine but from the heart of the majority of which *he* is a member. In her final moments, Lucy continues to insist that Eliza's troubles can be located outside the safety and security of the Federalist community. But the duality of her own aphorism suggests something far darker: that the sources of destruction lie within the very disinterested impulses of republicanism itself.

*The Coquette* is less a didactic or even a subversive novel than it is an early American palimpsest. Constructed of an ostensible panoply of voices, it tells the story of an outspoken republican woman who ultimately fails to be heard. The book unfolds as a dialectic of revelation and erasure, which becomes the author's subject and which also dictates her form. Foster's transvestite storytelling embodies at the level of narrative Eliza's impulse to venture into the linguistic terrain of the masculine public sphere, which is figured in the novel by the woman equestrian. Novelist, heroine, and minor character alike traverse this difficult border to make statements about women's freedom that will be audible above the roar of the feminized patriarchal discourse that characterizes post-Revolutionary culture. The significance of Foster's achievement, paradoxically, rests on its constitutive failure: in bypassing the discourse of sentiment for the vocabulary of politics, or more

precisely, by speaking the language of liberty but overlaying it with the rhetoric of moral feeling, she reaches for a level of expression foreclosed to republican women at the very moment she buries it alive. Thus, the auditory apparition of Eliza's voice as it takes form in her remarkable epistles resonates beyond the bleakness of *The Coquette*'s ending; raising haunting questions about the success of such efforts of entombment, its tones evoke the enormous cultural power available to women such as Foster when they presume to play about words.

# GILLIAN BROWN

## *From* Consent, Coquetry, and Consequences[†]

When Eliza Wharton, the heroine of Hannah Foster's best-selling novel *The Coquette,* frankly describes her engagement as the sacrifice of her own "fancy in this affair" (5) [4], she is voicing a standard criticism about the constraints on female and filial consent. Far from expressing her own desire, Eliza's consent represents the subordination of personal desire. In "obedience to the will and desires of my parents," Eliza discloses, she accepted "their choice" of a husband for her, the "esteemed" Reverend Mr. Haly (5) [4]. Her consent to this "alliance" signified no "passion of love for Mr. Haly," only her compliance with her parents' will (5) [4].

Eliza's situation appears to be the typical predicament of eighteenth-century novelistic heroines since Clarissa: woman's subjection to parental, which is to say patriarchal, authority. The scenario of a daughter compelled to follow her parents' will also evokes the republican rhetoric of violated filial rights that figured so urgently and effectively in American revolutionary politics.[1] Stories of compelled consent pervade late-eighteenth-century America, conveying an uncertain—if not antithetical—relation of consent to individual freedom.

[†] From *American Literary History* 9.4 (winter 1997): 625–28, 633–37, 640–43, 645. Reprinted by permission of Oxford University Press. Page numbers in square brackets refer to this Norton Critical Edition.
1. Readers could find in novels such as Samuel Richardson's *Clarissa* (1747–48) and Rousseau's *Julie, ou La Nouvelle Héloïse* (1761) evidence for if not advocacy of matrimonial republicanism. (For an informative account of matrimonial republicanism and early American women's actual experiences in courtship and marriage, see Mary Beth Norton's *Liberty's Daughters: The Revolutionary Experience of American Women, 1750–1800* [1980].) As Jay Fliegelman has noted in his exposition of "the American revolution against patriarchal authority," American editions of Richardson's novel altered the original title—*Clarissa or the History of a Young Lady. Comprehending the*

In Foster's novel, however, the image of female and filial subjection is both preceded and succeeded by a display of self-determination. At the opening of *The Coquette,* Eliza announces her "pleasure" "on leaving my paternal roof" (5) [4], a pleasure won by successfully gambling her consent. As Eliza then explains, she has strategically exercised her personal interests even as she followed her parents' wishes. For when she "determined that my reason should concur with theirs," she did so with a sense of the odds against this accord ever really posing a "risk" to her "future happiness" (5) [4]. Seeing, from their "first acquaintance, his declining health," Eliza "was the more encouraged" to chance the engagement to Haly (5) [4]. Her speculation proves successful when both her father and fiancé die before the marriage can take place.

Foster complicates the conventional portrait of consent as a form of female subjection with evidence of the operation of a woman's design in consent. The room for individual maneuvering that Eliza finds in her exercise of consent demonstrates what a woman can do for herself within the limits of her historical condition, a condition defined by gender, class, race, nationality, and geography. Presenting consent in a light potentially more favorable than unfavorable for women's self-determination, Foster underscores agency in consent, even when the consenting agent is at odds with the content of her consent.

For those without access to full social, economic, and political self-determination, the idea that they are agents in consent understandably may seem a mockery of freedom. But what Foster delineates in Eliza's practice of consent is the limits in which consent always operates. Locating agency in consent and, more significantly, locating agency in the consent of the disenfranchised, Foster demonstrates that freedom exists even within the limits that curtail the experience and scope of freedom. Dramatizing the possibilities as well as limits of women's freedom, the portrait of consent in *The Coquette* recapitulates the meaning of consent developed in liberal political theory and psychology.

---

*Most Important Concerns for Private Life and Particularly shewing, The Distresses that may attend the Misconduct Both of Parents and Children in Relation to Marriage*—by substituting *wherein the Arts of a Designing Villain and the Rigours of Paternal Authority, conspired to Complete the Ruin of a Virtuous Daughter* for the words following "private life" (Fliegelman, *Prodigals* 87). Instead of a mutual partner in "the misconduct both of parents and children," Clarissa now appears the victimized daughter. A similar brief for filial rights against parental tyranny could be found in *Julie,* wherein the heroine's unacceptable lover declares, "Are not the ties of marriage the most free, as well as the most sacred of all engagements? Yes, every law to lay constraint on them is unjust. Every father, who presumes to form or break them is a tyrant" (qtd. in Fliegelman, *Prodigals* 131). In this view, parental interference in the daughter's exercise of consent violates not just the daughter but the doctrine of individual liberty.

Under the concept of consent, society follows from and must fulfill the will of the individuals who compose it. As Locke so influentially reasoned, polities can legitimately exist only on the basis of the consent of the governed, who establish government for their own protection.[2] For the eighteenth century, and for America in particular, Lockean consent theory justified the establishment of republican governments. Consent theory supplied a story of the origins of society and governments that defined social and political institutions as emanating from, and thus subject to, the persons who constitute them.[3] From the sanction of the people comes (or should come) the conditions in which they find themselves. Their freedom consists in being voluntarily bound to their own determinations.[4] In the act of consenting to government, individuals choose and accept constraints upon themselves. Thus, though individuals in the act of consent freely determine their lives, forming states, contracts, and alliances, they also simultaneously embody cultural authority.[5]

2. Locke formulated the principle of political consent in his second of the *Two Treatises of Government* (1690), which he subtitled "An Essay Concerning the True Original, Extent, and End of Civil Government."

3. Ever since Hume dismissed the notion of originary social contracts, critics have noted the implausibility of founding moments in which persons consented to governments. Skepticism about consent as the origin of governments points to the mythic character of consent in conveying societies with founding stories. Consent is therefore a hypothetical but useful historical account, according to Hanna Pitkin, because it preserves the role of citizens in making their governments. As Elaine Scarry further elaborates, the fictiveness or "artifactuality" is precisely the point and power of consent. Scarry argues that consent expresses and may institutionalize an imaginative act of individual authority. I follow Scarry's attentiveness to and respect for the representational structure and operation of consent, as well as Pitkin's delineation of consent's necessarily hypothetical character. For Scarry, however, the performance of consent invokes and relies upon the body. But the body, I would point out, is alternately or contradictorily volitional and nonvolitional, certainly an uncertain source of authority. The body, moreover, is a representational as well as material entity, not a set frame of reference. Founding consent in the body enacts once again the myth of individual control that consent sponsors and exemplifies.

4. This understanding of consent as a point where free will and determinacy converge is congruent with Jonathan Edwards's formulation of the consistency of free will with determinism, though Edwards of course saw determinism as the natural system and expression of the deity. Perry Miller thus astutely recognizes in Edwards's exposition of *The Freedom of the Will* (1754) not a conservative Calvinistic attack on liberalism, but an incorporation of liberalism into Protestant theology (263). For an illuminating study of the influence of Calvinism on Locke's own thought, see Dunn, esp. 203–61.

5. Although consent theory furnishes a justification of revolution, it preserves the principle of cultural authority. So changing cultural authority, say from patriarchalism to republicanism, does not relieve consent of the presence of the conventional; rather, it redefines conventions. Thus the liberal republican principle of self-determination does not dispense with but rather relocates the source of authority for the individual. "The chief problem of the American revolution," Hannah Arendt observes, "turned out to be the establishment and foundation not of power but authority" (178). Contrary to J. G. A. Pocock's denigration of the significance of Lockean thought in early America, I am arguing, like John Diggins (esp. 347–65), for the persistence of Lockean consent doctrine in structuring all forms of republicanisms—conservative, moderate, liberal, radical—that appear in early American political and cultural life. That is, even what Pocock and others (e.g., Bailyn, Wood) have identified as Americans' retrospective

Lockean consent theory foregrounds the individual's response and relation to authority, delineating the psychology of subjects living in liberal societies. Arguing against patriarchal forms of government and power, Locke stressed individual authority, by which he meant an authority that develops by the internalization of parental strictures. The Freudian conception of the superego is thus anticipated in Lockean psychology: the liberal formulation of self presents the self as always under rule.[6] Thus the sense of the compulsory in consent, customarily identified with parents, can never be eliminated. Because Locke defines consent as a relation to authority, and more specifically as an affirmation of one's relation to authority, consent always includes the acknowledgment, however happy or unhappy, of one's subjection. Put another way, consent is a kind of self-dictation: consent is the subjection to our circumstances that we acknowledge when we are not rebelling from or objecting to them.

That individuals clearly do embody cultural authority, that consent is conventional, has always provoked doubts about and objections to liberal consent doctrine.[7] The limited citizenship of women in liberal societies, for example, would seem to preclude their consent from denoting any form of self-determination whatsoever. Yet the apparent deficiency in consent that the subjection of women exposes lies not in consent, but in the culture that consent affirms. In the case of subordinated populations such as women, Native Americans, and slaves, consent marks the limits (as well as the possibilities) of self-determination because consent expresses the individual's relation to authority and therefore the different relations of different individuals to authority and to their differing internalizations of authority.

---

appeal to classical republicanism can be read as part of a narrative of liberalism. The adventures of consent, documented in various forms, thus register the tangencies of as well as tensions between liberalism and republicanism. Though I am rejecting Pocock's elevation of an Atlantic republican tradition in early America, the prevalence of the term in early American letters cannot be denied * * * In my reading, consent is one of the forms through which republicanism or republicanism—and other interests—get articulated.

6. For Locke, individual freedom entails the individual's subjection to his own reason and rule. See his discussion of self-denial as the bedrock of child development (*Some Thoughts* 107). Charles Taylor similarly has noted that Locke's "theory of rational control of the self" and "ideal of rational self-responsibility" shapes and permeates modern psychology (174). This model of self-control is not the panoptical design of socially self-regulating individuals that Michel Foucault describes in *Discipline and Punish: The Birth of the Prison* (1977), but a vision of the power of individual agency within social limits. Fliegelman describes the role of social limits upon individuals in late-eighteenth-century America as "soft compulsion," a compulsion that sometimes generated anxieties about individual agency (*Declaring Independence* 35–62).

7. The history and bibliography of debate on consent theory are too vast to record here. A useful summary of the persistent issues in the debate can be found in Partridge; the most incisive account of these issues is furnished by Pitkin. Among the most cogent of recent critiques of consent doctrine are the works of Herzog, Walzer, and Pateman.

Far from female consent being a contradiction in terms, then, female consent epitomizes individual subjection in a liberal society. Eliza's manipulation of the terms of her subjection—her plot to elude the marital expectations placed upon her—causes her friends to call her "coquettish" (7) [6], a characterization already ascribed to her by the novel's title. By labeling Eliza "the coquette," Foster draws attention to the guile in Eliza's practice of consent. Eliza's artful use of consent suggests that individuals can appropriate consent for their own purposes. Once released from "those shackles, which parental authority had imposed on . . . [her] mind," Eliza is determined to suit herself and "gratify . . . [her] natural disposition in a participation of those pleasures which youth and innocence afford" (13) [11]. Her sense of achieving liberty, however, proves short-lived, as she soon finds herself being urged into another engagement to another unappealing minister. Her evasion of this alliance leads to another unsuccessful implementation of consent: her seduction, impregnation, and ultimate death.

Through the limited effectiveness of Eliza's coquetry, Foster examines the failure of coquetry as a critique and an appropriation of consent. Though coquetry exhibits as it exploits the potential agency of women in consent, Foster's narrative of the coquette's difficulties in pursuing her desires reveals that having agency is not enough. Women as well as men are agents, Foster emphasizes, but gender defines and maintains different spheres of agency. It is in the failure of Eliza's coquetry that the inequality in the compasses of agency becomes most glaring. Featuring agency as a bounded activity, *The Coquette* depicts the perimeter within which female consent in eighteenth-century America operated. Until that perimeter changes, Foster intimates, consent cannot effectively serve women. To make consent a constructive instrument for women, Foster recommends that women eschew coquetry because it only sustains the limited sphere of their self-determinations.

## 1. Consent and Coquetry

What makes coquetry a dubious tactic for women's self-determination is the disparity that it enacts between a woman and her word, or between her different self-representations. Eliza's calculated act of consent differentiates her public word from her private words and desires, creating at least two versions of herself. In doing so, she simply exhibits the potential discrepancy between self-representation and self that consent always comprises. Unfortunately for Eliza, though, a woman's exercise of representational vagaries signifies for her culture not an act of self-determination but a show of deceit

and, moreover, an example of a constitutionally feminine deceitful proclivity.

By characterizing Eliza as a coquette, Foster invokes a longstanding identification of women with deception. The imagery and vocabulary of coquetry in late-eighteenth-century America drew on the Enlightenment paradigm of femininity, most vividly delineated by Jean-Jacques Rousseau and most vigorously denounced by women's rights advocates such as Catherine Macaulay, Mary Wollstonecraft, and Judith Sargeant Murray, and, I suggest, by novelists such as Foster and Susanna Rowson. Writing the story of a coquette's failure at self-determination, Foster joins in the eighteenth-century feminist project of validating female consent by distancing it from coquetry.[8]

*   *   *

For this goal, the coquette's sovereignty had to be overthrown. Wollstonecraft identified this sovereignty with the immorality of monarchical power that she saw embodied in Marie Antoinette, whom she described as "an adept in all the arts of coquetry that debauch the mind" (*Historical* 29–30). From this association of coquetry with the corrupt economic and sexual practices of monarchy, the coquette emerged in the late eighteenth century as the antitype of republican virtue. Like Marie Antoinette, "a profound dissembler," the coquette seeks not alliance but tyranny. The young American man in a 1792 moral tale can therefore congratulate "himself that he has escaped from the smiles of a coquette," from social and sexual wiles that would subordinate him (qtd. in Lewis 698). These "insidious and deluding wiles of the coquette" also come under censure in the advice book for "the Young Ladies of America" that Hannah Foster published the year after *The Coquette*. "How disgusting must this character appear to persons of sentiment and integrity," Foster writes (*Boarding School* 98) [182]. What most bothers Foster and her feminist contemporaries about the coquette is

---

8. In calling Eliza a coquette, Foster follows the popular press's view of the woman upon whom Foster based her "history of Eliza Wharton," Elizabeth Whitman. Whether figuring Whitman as a failed social climber or a victim of reading romances, journalists characterized her behavior as coquettish (see Davidson). The term *coquette* "has an interestingly ambiguous gender in the eighteenth century." Derived from *coq*, the word *coquette* evokes masculine vanity, the image of "the preening barnyard rooster surrounded by a flock of admiring men. Hence coquetry is unfeminine. The masculine behavior it mimes, however, is generally regarded as foppish when observed in the salon rather than the barnyard, and hence it is strongly tinged with femininity. Thus coquetry can be imagined as doubly androgynous: it is practiced by women in imitation of effeminate men" (Gallagher 210). I would add that the gender ambiguity of coquetry is one form of the uncertain relation between persons and their self-representations that coquetry thematizes.

her use of deceit—her pretense of consent—to realize her ambition
to rule. She dallies with suitors, alternately intimating and revok-
ing her consent to a series of men. In effect the coquette takes on
the role of the seducer, engineering courtships to suit her pleasure.
Ambiguous in her language and her acts, the coquette obfuscates
the self-representational mission of consent. She further under-
mines consent's purpose as a vehicle of self-representation by
detaching it from consequentiality. Her word is not a warranty of
what can be expected from her. Coquetry takes the consequentiality
out of courtship and consent, leaving uncertain the aftermath of a
woman's acts.

It is in light of faulty self-representation that the coquette comes
to epitomize for Foster, Wollstonecraft, Macaulay, and other women
in the eighteenth century, not female defiance but female debility.
Indeed, from a feminist perspective the coquette's evasion of conse-
quentiality epitomizes the state of nonconsensuality in which per-
sons exercise no authority for their acts and therefore have no
accountability. From this standpoint Rousseau's pronouncement that
"to be a woman means to be coquettish" might stand as an accurate
account of woman's nonconsensual condition.

## 2. Consent and the Seduction Story

If Rousseau, in characterizing women as transparent coquettes,
provoked feminist anticoquetry, he also, in the textured, layered
quality of individuality that he imaged (and sought to eliminate) in
the coquette, suggested a novelistic model of female character and
consent. Taking a cue from Rousseau, eighteenth-century feminists
like Foster and Wollstonecraft found the novel a useful format in
which to analyze and reformulate masculinist accounts of femininity.
In the novel, the very complications in consent and self-representation
that Rousseau tried to eliminate through his elevation of the witness
can work to credit rather than invalidate an individual.[9] Since
women's words conspicuously circulated and mattered in the novel,
female consent in the novel could just as readily appear to bear and
retain consequentiality as it appeared to defy and deny consequen-

---

9. Ian Watt (in *The Rise of the Novel: Studies in Defoe, Richardson, and Fielding* [1957])
and subsequent critics have established the novel's integral relation to the project of
substantiating individual experience as well as the novel's feminization of that project.
For illuminating feminist expositions of that feminization, which eighteenth-century
women writers immediately grasped, see Nancy K. Miller's *The Heroine's Text: Read-
ings in the French and English Novel, 1722–1782* (1980) and Claudia L. Johnson's
*Equivocal Beings: Politics, Gender, and Sentimentality in the 1790s* (1995). Alexander
Welsh has recently advanced the thesis of the novel's representational purposes in his
compelling analysis of the relation of the novel's evidentiary techniques to British legal
and cultural formulations of circumstantial evidence in *Strong Representations: Narra-
tive and Circumstantial Evidence in England* (1992).

tiality in Rousseau's narrative. This is why women in eighteenth-century novels so often suffer so much: they bear the consequences of consent. In these novels' almost obsessive preoccupation with female responses to courtship and seduction, they register both the difficulties and advantages of representational acts that female consent so vividly typifies.[1]

*   *   *

The novel of seduction in particular portrayed both the inadequacy of female representation and measures by which to enforce or contain or empower or overcome that frailty. The seduction novels popular in early America employ the fate of seduced heroines to signify a variety of views on female consent, which in turn disclose different views on consent itself. In these seduction tales consent is regularly depicted as an act leading to invariable consequences. Seduction stories operate on the premise that agency inevitably leaves traces, and they supply those traces. The evidentiary abundance and conviction of the seduction story make it a perfect vehicle for conveying the ideal of self-determination. Foster accordingly finds the seduction tale an effective medium for her project of translating coquetry into consequentiality.

At the center of the seduction scenario is a woman who comes to a destined end. In the predictability of her sad story, the seduction heroine represents an ideal of consent as originary and effective.[2] Her exercise of consent, her affirmative or denial, can be seen to be con-

1. The novelistic obsession with the subject of female consent and chastity emerges from and exemplifies the eighteenth-century feminization of virtue (see, e.g., Lewis), which supplanted the classical republican identification of virtue with manliness (see Pocock 37–50 and Pitkin, *Fortune* 54, 237, 241). That actual sexual practices did not match sexual and gender ideals is clear from Nancy Cott's informative study of eighteenth-century Massachusetts divorce records. As late eighteenth-century republicanism feminized virtue—in the figures of the "republican mother" and "republican wife" described by Kerber (ch. 9) and Lewis—it also forwarded a misogynistic tradition of blaming women for social ills, inadequacies, and excesses. Carol Kay provocatively argues that the sentimentalization of virtue in republicanism in fact signifies a remasculinization of moral virtue. Whatever the influence or noninfluence of classical republican ideals on eighteenth-century America, the language of republicanism is prominent in early American literature as such scholars as Fliegelman and Davidson, for example, demonstrate. In this essay, I am analyzing the early American novelistic feminization of virtue as both an engine and effect of what might be called the modern republicanism generated by Lockean consent doctrine. Thus the term "republican" recurs in this essay as it does in early American literature, denoting antimonarchical principles. The term can both encompass and exclude the values of (Lockean) liberal individualism—rather than simply standing against it. I therefore find it more useful and accurate to characterize novelistic views of female virtue as falling within a spectrum of republicanism that ranges from radical to reactionary.
2. The idea that consent can ever serve women is an ongoing subject of feminist debates. Some feminist readers of Locke see his generational and familial model of consensuality as a paradigm that potentially includes and encourages the concept of female consent and citizenry (see Butler and Nicholson 133–66). Other feminists, such as Carol Pateman and Catharine MacKinnon (150), have developed provocative critiques of the androcentrism and misogyny of liberal consent theory. Pateman regards consent as a

sequential. In their generative capacity (all sexually active women in seduction stories seem to immediately conceive) women exemplify an inevitable sequential process of consent that consent theory can only fantasize. They produce evidence of consent and by that evidence consent becomes a truly originary act. Even as the political status of women suggests the imaginary—or at least imaginative—character of consent, women's reproductive capacity furnishes a seemingly irrefutable proof of consent (whether voluntary or involuntary).

Compacting the series of events that consent (theoretically) represents, the seduction scenario keeps effects closely connected to causes. The consequences of female desire stay within the compass of the female body. The seduction story's focus on a specific female biological destiny affords a view of consent as the immediate embodiment of personal desire—a spatial and temporal proximity between cause and effect. Generating children thus retells, as it results from, consent. Each generation is a chronicle of previous generations, testifying to prior acts of consent. Everybody is imagined to be the evidence of somebody else's consent. In this definitive portrait of consent, consent perfectly expresses and matches the individual. Not only does consent adequately represent persons but persons represent consent. A society formed on such an ideal standard of consent would be harmonious, composed of persons in complete accord with one another. This is why, as Rousseau's fantasy of a constant consensuality embodied in women indicates, liberal societies have a stake in denying rape or depicting rape as seduction (and thus portraying women as liars and seductresses).

By the seduction story formula in which desire leads to sex that results in pregnancy, and usually death in childbirth, consent creates and destroys bodies. The babies and corpses produced in the wake of consent become the standard proofs that consent has occurred. The feminization of consent that the novel of seduction reflects and conducts thus advances the evidentiary role women play in consent. In this arrangement of the liberal imagination, the reproductive labor of women makes consent material. Yet women also produce testimonies and therefore can complicate the reading of physical evidence. Seduction stories from a feminist point of view could question or rearrange or redefine or even throw out evidence. * * *

---

"hypothetical social contract" (*The Disorder of Women* 73) premised on the actual subordination and repression of women (*Sexual Contract* 109); she thus renames it "the sexual contract." From my perspective, in which consent is a hypothetical but functional construct, often identified with a certain hypothesis about female biology, consent represents a desire by men as well as women that could be masculinist or feminist. How persons choose to tell and use the consent story shapes the character of consent. Historically, of course, consent primarily has served masculinist interests though it also has figured prominently in the development of Anglo-American feminism since Wollstonecraft. For the deployments of liberal individualism by Wollstonecraft and twentieth-century anorexics and feminists, see Brown.

\* \* \* Foster's narrative of Eliza Wharton's history restages the question of female character as an alternating conflict and consensus about consent in the early years of American nationhood. Dedicated to choosing her way and her partners, Eliza appears something of a republican heroine. Her plea, "Let me then enjoy that freedom which I so highly prize" (13) [11], certainly invites this identification, which has become a standard premise of readings of *The Coquette* (see, e.g., Davidson, *Revolution* 140–50; Smith-Rosenberg). Eliza's insistence on following her "natural propensity" (7) [6] for enjoyment invokes the natural rights basis for self-determination prevalent in eighteenth-century republican theory. Her characterization of the change in her situation as a movement from subordination to freedom conspicuously echoes the rhetoric of filialism—the rights of each new generation over the claims of hereditary authority embodied in monarchy—that figured so urgently in American revolutionary polemics.

Yet in her unwise exercise and enjoyment of her freedom—she becomes impregnated by a notorious rake—Eliza can also appear more of a cautionary case than an exemplar of freedom. To her friends Eliza seems to have "wrong ideas of freedom, and matrimony" (30) [24], making them worry that she is as "seducible" (38) [30] as she turns out to be. Whether we take Eliza to typify the desirability or undesirability of the independent exercise of consent, both characterizations regard consent as an act producing some form of certainty. Consent in the radical republican ideal ratifies self-determination by representing it; that is, consent expresses and realizes individual desire. In the reactionary view, consent appears self-destructive. From this perspective the seduction story formula, in which desire leads to sex that results in pregnancy and usually death in childbirth, only confirms that consent inevitably leads to bad consequences.[3] Indeed, the reactionary formulaic vision of experience epitomizes the certainty of individual authority and efficacy to which the republican ideal of self-determination aspires.

The sheer familiarity and predictability of the seduction story make it the perfect vehicle for conveying the concepts of—indeed, commitments to—causality and generation embedded in the idea of consent, whatever attitude toward consent a writer may wish to promulgate. Eliza's story is not simply a seduction tale but also a retelling of a well-known story, as Foster's subtitle, *The History of Eliza Wharton, A Novel; Founded on Fact*, acknowledges. The fact

3. The sexual determinacy of the seduction story appears also in eighteenth-century medical and popular accounts of pregnancy and childbirth. See Stafford for eighteenth-century beliefs about pregnancy and childbirth as the expression not only of a woman's sexual desire (and pleasure) but of all her desires and feelings (ch. 4).

in this case was the 1788 incident of an unmarried woman named Elizabeth Whitman dying at a Massachusetts inn after giving birth to a stillborn child. Before Foster wrote her version of the story, numerous accounts of it circulated in newspapers, sermons, and other novels, notably in what most literary historians identify as the first American novel, William Hill Brown's *The Power of Sympathy: Or, The Triumph of Nature, Founded in Truth* (1789). And long after the publication of *The Coquette,* the Elizabeth Whitman story continued to be retold. The continual retelling of the story by successive generations demonstrates the way in which seduction stories are freighted with particular visions of consent. Between 1875 and 1912, Caroline Dall, Charles Bolton, and Mary Crawford published rebuttals of what they took to be Foster's distortion of Elizabeth Whitman's character. They argued that the young woman was, in fact, secretly married. She was thus telling the truth when she told the innkeeper that she was waiting for her husband to join her. As Dall insisted, there was no "evidence of that coquetry which [Foster's] novel has attached to her name" (17). Instead of a cautionary tale of a seduced and abandoned woman, the Elizabeth Whitman story in these retellings becomes an exemplum of faithful, enduring love. In keeping with this legend, the tombstone of Whitman in Peabody, Massachusetts, became a celebrated tourist attraction for lovers (Davidson, *Revolution* 149).

Besides extending the life of the Elizabeth Whitman story, these rehabilitations of her character attempt to legitimate her consent. That is, they adhere to all the details of the original affair but imagine a morally acceptable exercise of consent to have propelled the inevitable chain of events that the woman experienced. Purifying the seduction tale, however, alters nothing of the determinant and generative operations of consent. The same consequences follow for the heroine whether she is married or unmarried.

<p style="text-align:center">*   *   *</p>

### 3. Coquetry and Consequences

In telling the Elizabeth Whitman story as a rake's crusade against a coquette, Foster includes in her novel a feminist indictment of patriarchal determinism. That is, the novel invites us to consider Eliza's fate as fully determined and sealed by the rake who plots her destruction. Even as eighteenth-century feminists vilified the figure of the coquette, they regarded her male counterpart as more vicious and dangerous. "There are quite as many male coquets as female," Wollstonecraft noted, "and they are far more pernicious pests to society, as their sphere of action is larger, and they are less exposed

to the censure of the world" (*Thoughts* 28). In the world of Eliza Wharton, rakes do get their full due of censure. The moral that Eliza's friends draw from her history is to beware of rakes: "From the melancholy story of Eliza Wharton, let the American fair learn to reject with disdain every insinuation derogatory to their true dignity and honor. Let them despise, and for ever banish the man, who can glory in the seduction of innocence and the ruin of reputation" (168) [131]. Yet if the history of the coquette in Foster's treatment provokes an indictment of the rake, the novel does not hold the rake wholly and solely accountable. Eliza accords blame to herself as well as Sanford. In her last conversation with him, she condemns coquetry in both its female and male forms:

> May my unhappy story serve as a beacon to warn the American fair of the dangerous tendency and destructive consequences of associating with men of your character, of destroying their time, and risking their reputation by the practice of coquetry and its attendant follies! But for these, I might have been honorably connected; and capable, at this moment, of diffusing and receiving happiness! But for your arts, I might have remained a blessing to society, as well as the delight and comfort of my friends! (159) [125]

It is her own "practice of coquetry" as well as Sanford's arts that ruin Eliza. Eliza furthermore acknowledges her own fault "for disregarding the counsels, warnings and admonitions of my best friends" (159) [125]. Censuring all practices of coquetry, however gendered, the novel dramatizes an enmity between society and coquetry. Eliza's sense of her allegiances being caught between her friends on the one hand and male and female coquetry on the other hand reiterates Sanford's own account of his pursuit of Eliza as prompted as much by a desire for "revenge for . . . [Eliza's friends'] dislike and coldness" (158) [124] as by desire for Eliza.

Both rakes and coquettes set themselves against social conventions by seeking to evade the consequences of courtship. In Foster's novel, however, both come to suffer the repercussions of their behavior. Uttering the standard words of the seduced woman—"I am undone!" (164) [129]—Sanford finds himself in the very poverty that he had schemed to avoid by marrying an heiress instead of Eliza. Just as Eliza's friends wish that Sanford "ought for ever to be banished from human society" (163) [128], he recognizes that he "must become a vagabond in the earth" (165) [129]. As long as he lives, Sanford attests, "I must feel the disgraceful, and torturing effects of my guilt in seducing . . . [Eliza]! . . . Her friends, could they know the pangs of contrition, and the horror of conscience which attend me, would be amply revenged!" (165) [130].

With the biologically determined exits of coquettes and the socially decreed evictions of rakes, Foster's novel would appear to be making coquetry consequential with a vengeance. Yet as Eliza and Sanford come to their fates, their histories are strikingly revised. Lovelace-like Sanford reconstructs his actions into those of a lover toward his beloved. After ruining Eliza, he wishes he could legitimate their relation. Eliza does attain a form of legitimation through her friends. They rehabilitate, if not sanctify, her character in their memorial inscription on her tombstone:

> This humble stone, in memory of ELIZA WHARTON, is inscribed by her weeping friends, to whom she endeared herself by uncommon tenderness and affection. Endowed with superior acquirements, she was still more distinquished [sic] by humility and benevolence. Let candor throw a veil over her frailties, for great was her charity to others. She sustained the last painful scene, far from every friend; and exhibited an example of calm resignation. Her departure was on the 25th day of July, A.D.——, iin [sic] the 37th year of her age, and the tears of strangers watered her grave. (169) [133]

The epitaph converts the story of coquetry into the biography of a moral paragon. This posthumous transformation of Eliza, moreover, aligns consent with an image of virtuous and civic-minded women. With the end of the coquette, the character of consent as an expression of community affiliation prevails. Thus, the words on the tombstone recall less the history of Eliza Wharton than the "truly republican" creed of female consent espoused early in the novel by her friend Mrs. Richman (44) [35]. Women, Mrs. Richman asserts, have a voice in politics because they are affected by them. As members of the community, subject to its "happy effects" as well as its "evil," women must be "interested in the welfare and prosperity of our country." They therefore "claim the right of inquiring into those affairs, which may conduce to, or interfere with the common weal" (44) [35]. Mrs. Richman stops short of claiming political equality for women, accepting that "[w]e shall not be called to the senate or the field to assert its privileges" (44) [35]. Tracing women's role in the state, her argument relies on the cause and effect consent narrative in which effects signify, or are taken to signify, the intentions of persons. By this logic the present state of subjection to the state marks prior consent; the continued existence of a government manifests the authorization of its subjects. If women are subject to the state's authority, Mrs. Richman reasons, women are not just subjects but also interested agents of the state. Thus, the current state of American women in the eighteenth century can be conceived as the effect of women's participation in a social compact.

Republican womanhood retroactively gains authority as Mrs. Richman invokes a consensual origin for communal subjection.

To fortify this vision of consent, *The Coquette* accomplishes the eighteenth-century feminist goal of disengaging coquetry from female consent. Yet the novel's reconfiguration of consent to signify women's membership in the social contract remarkably refuses to celebrate Eliza's republican-minded friends. Mrs. Richman and Lucy and Julia appear most often as annoying exponents of gender and class proprieties rather than as advocates of the rights of individual women. The disparity between Eliza's desires and her friends' recommendations (a disparity sometimes internalized in her as her own conflicting desires), and between her life and her friends' posthumous account of it, remains at the novel's close. Women's participation in the social compact does not necessarily serve the rights of women, particularly when female members of society only espouse long-standing androcentric views of courtship, marriage, and family.

<p style="text-align:center">✳   ✳   ✳</p>

For women, this ontological burden includes—indeed demands—their reproductive labors: their production of the evidence of consent. By the liberal logic of seduction stories that I have been unfolding here, pregnancy proves the operation of consent, recognizing it even in its extralegal, extramarital or premarital, exercise. Indeed, as in Rousseau's portrait of consent, nonconsensuality barely seems an option for women when all their pregnancies, whatever the circumstances of insemination, signify consent. Hence the seductions ascribed to rakes and coquettes, and so often recounted in late eighteenth-century American literature, seem to suggest an extending franchise of consent. If women thus gain entitlements in a liberal society, they do so at the price of the suppression of their nonconsensuality. But Foster strikingly refuses to give generation the testifying function it usually has in seduction stories. If all offspring, legitimate or illegitimate, die, no one substantiates female consent. Without children the Lockean tradition of measuring consent by self-projection and self-retrospection halts.

In drawing attention to the mortality of the body, Foster dramatizes the fragility of this form of evidence for female consent. Eliza's removal from Foster's narrative, coincident with her impregnation and the progress of the pregnancy, thus signifies not only Foster's expulsion of coquetry but her refusal to yoke consent merely to physical evidence. Without the standard physical evidence of consent, the witnesses who confirm consent can present only anecdotal evidence: the final testimonial that they offer to Eliza's mother is quite literally anecdotal, the words borrowed from Elizabeth

Whitman's epitaph. What the end of *The Coquette* underscores, then, is not the consequences of Eliza's consent—"Let candor throw a veil over her frailties," the epitaph counsels (169) [133]—but the task of redefining the testimonials of consent.

WORKS CITED

Arendt, Hannah. *On Revolution*. London: Penguin, 1963.

Bailyn, Bernard. *The Ideological Origins of the American Revolution*. Cambridge: Belknap-Harvard UP, 1967.

Bolton, Charles Knowles. *The Elizabeth Whitman Mystery at the Old Bell Tavern in Danvers: A Study of "Eliza Wharton," the Heroine of a Famous New England Romance*. Peabody: Peabody Historical Society, 1912.

Butler, Melissa. "Early Liberal Roots of Feminism: John Locke and the Attack on Patriarchy." *Feminist Interpretations and Political Theory*. Ed. Mary Lyndon Shanley and Carole Pateman. University Park: Pennsylvania State UP, 1991. 74–94.

Cott, Nancy F. "Eighteenth-Century Family and Social Life Revealed in Massachusetts Divorce Records." *A Heritage of Her Own: Toward a New Social History of American Women*. Ed. Nancy F. Cott and Elizabeth H. Pleck. New York: Simon, 1979. 107–35.

Crawford, Mary C. *The Romance of Old New England Churches*. Boston: Page, 1904.

Dall, Caroline. *The Romance of the Association: Or, One Last Glimpse of Charlotte Temple and Eliza Wharton*. . . . Cambridge, 1875.

Davidson, Cathy N. Introduction. *The Coquette*. By Hannah Webster Foster. Ed. Cathy N. Davidson. New York: Oxford UP, 1986. vii–xx.

———. *The Revolution and the Word: The Rise of the Novel in America*. New York: Oxford UP, 1986.

Diggins, John P. *The Lost Soul of American Politics: Virtue, Self-Interest, and the Foundations of Liberalism*. New York: Basic, 1984.

Dunn, John. *The Political Thought of John Locke: An Historical Account of the Argument of the "Two Treatises of Government."* Cambridge: Cambridge UP, 1969.

Fliegelman, Jay. *Declaring Independence: Jefferson, Natural Language, and the Culture of Performance*. Stanford: Stanford UP, 1993.

———. *Prodigals and Pilgrims: The American Revolution against Patriarchal Authority, 1750–1800*. Cambridge: Cambridge UP, 1982.

Foster, Hannah. *The Boarding School: Or, Lessons of a Preceptress to Her Pupils.* Boston, 1798.

———. *The Coquette.* Ed. Cathy N. Davidson. New York: Oxford UP, 1986.

Gallagher, Catherine. *Nobody's Story: The Vanishing Acts of Women Writers in the Marketplace, 1670–1820.* Berkeley: U of California P, 1994.

Herzog, Don. *Happy Slaves: A Critique of Consent Theory.* Chicago: U of Chicago P, 1989.

Kay, Carol. "Canon, Ideology, and Gender: Mary Wollstonecraft's Critique of Adam Smith." *New Political Science* 15 (1986): 63–76.

Lewis, Jan. "The Republican Wife: Virtue and Seduction in the Early Republic." *William and Mary Quarterly* 3d ser. 44 (1987): 689–721.

Locke, John. *Some Thoughts Concerning Education.* Ed. John W. Yolton and Jean. S. Yolton. Oxford: Clarendon, 1989.

MacKinnon, Catharine. *Feminism Unmodified: Discourses on Life and Law.* Cambridge: Harvard UP, 1987.

Miller, Perry. *Jonathan Edwards.* New York: Meridian, 1959.

Nicholson, Linda. *Gender and History: The Limits of Social Theory in the Age of the Family.* New York: Columbia UP, 1986.

Partridge, P. H. *Consent and Consensus.* New York: Praeger, 1971.

Pateman, Carole. *The Disorder of Women: Democracy, Feminism, and Political Theory.* Stanford: Stanford UP, 1989.

———. *The Sexual Contract.* Stanford: Stanford UP, 1988.

Pitkin, Hanna. *Fortune Is a Woman: Gender and Politics in the Thought of Niccolo Machiavelli.* Berkeley: U of California P, 1984.

———. "Obligation and Consent." *American Political Science Review* 59 (1965): 990–99; 60 (1966): 39–52.

Pocock, J. G. A. *Virtue, Commerce, and History: Essays on Political Thought and History, Chiefly in the Eighteenth Century.* Cambridge: Cambridge UP, 1985.

Scarry, Elaine. "Consent and the Body." *New Literary History* 21 (1990): 868–95.

Smith-Rosenberg, Carroll. "Domesticating 'Virtue': Coquettes and Revolutionaries in Young America." *Literature and the Body: Essays on Populations and Persons.* Ed. Elaine Scarry. Baltimore: Johns Hopkins UP, 1988. 160–84.

Spurlin, Paul Merrill. *Rousseau in America, 1760–1809.* University: U of Alabama P, 1969.

Stafford, Barbara Maria. *Body Criticism: Imaging the Unseen in Enlightenment Art and Medicine.* Chicago: U of Chicago P, 1991.

Taylor, Charles. *Sources of the Self: The Making of the Modern Identity.* Cambridge: Harvard UP, 1989.

Unger, Roberto Mangabeira. *Knowledge and Politics*. New York: Free, 1975.

Walzer, Michael. *Obligations: Essays on Disobedience, War, and Citizenship*. Cambridge: Harvard UP, 1970.

Wollstonecraft, Mary. *An Historical and Moral View of the Origin and Progress of the French Revolution and the Effect It Has Produced in Europe*. 2nd ed. 1794. Delmar: Scholars' Facsimiles and Reprints, 1975.

———. *Thoughts on the Education of Daughters: With Reflections on Female Conduct, in the More Important Duties of Life*. 1787. New York: Garland, 1974.

Wood, Gordon S. *The Creation of the American Republic, 1776–1787*. Chapel Hill: U of North Carolina P, 1969.

Ziff, Larzer. *Writing in the New Nation: Prose, Print, and Politics in the Early United States*. New Haven: Yale UP, 1991.

## JEFFREY H. RICHARDS

## [Theater, Sexuality, and National Virtue in Foster's Novels]†

\*   \*   \*

In *The Coquette* and *The Boarding School*, Hannah Foster imagines a social world whose attractions women must resist, yet on whose stage women must know how to perform if they are to live in the world at all—a world that both is and is not a playhouse. Entering a society where theatricality governs much of what passes as interpersonal relations, and where going to the theater represents the most fashionable of amusements, Eliza Wharton and the other women in Foster's novels confront a dangerous loss of self-definition as they tread the uncertain space between republican mother and ruined coquette.

The problem for the protagonist of *The Coquette* is learning to understand the kind of acting that is required to make the right impression among virtuous people. From her first letters, however, Eliza Wharton writes against expectation. Though polite society assumes that she will mourn the loss of her betrothed, the minister

---

† From "The Politics of Seduction: Theater, Sexuality, and National Virtue in the Novels of Hannah Foster," in Della Pollock, ed., *Exceptional Spaces: Essays in Performance and History* (Chapel Hill: U of North Carolina P, 1998), 243–47, 249–51. Reprinted by permission. Parenthetical citations refer to Cathy N. Davidson's 1986 Oxford University Press edition of the novel. Page numbers in square brackets refer to this Norton Critical Edition.

Haly, she instead celebrates liberation from her "paternal roof" and chooses the path of honesty; for the late Haly she has felt the "sincerest friendship," but only obedience to parents could have led her to an engagement with a man so opposite her personality (pp. 5–6) [4]. This overt rejection of patriarchal authority would seem to be well inside the new Revolutionary American tradition. But by the internal conventions of sentimentalized virtue, Eliza would have to mask her own lack of heartfelt enthusiasm—something she has a hard time doing. For Eliza, other forces regulate her actions; she is, she tells Lucy Freeman, "naturally cheerful, volatile, and unreflecting"; and though she is excited to be reentering the "gay world" of visits and parties, she promises, "I shall never again assume those airs, which you term *coquettish*, but which I think deserve a softer appellation; as they proceed from an innocent heart, and are the effusions of a youthful, and cheerful mind" (p. 7) [5–6]. Youthful, cheerful, volatile, unreflecting, honest, sincere, and, above all, innocent, Eliza defines herself in ways that affirm bourgeois convention even as they deny the authority of social expectations to limit the freedom of her conduct.

Innocence by itself, then, cannot sustain a spotless character; thus, Eliza's innocent freedom makes her vulnerable, even in a republic of virtue, to corruption. Her female friends advise suspicion and modesty, even as they encourage her to avoid remaining long in melancholy—but Eliza by and large rejects such advice. When her friend, the wealthy and well-married Mrs. Richman, expresses concern that Eliza be "suitably and agreeably connected," the latter retorts with a statement of principles that, as it turns out, proves fatal in a world where appearances matter: "Let me then enjoy that freedom which I so highly prize." "But beware, Eliza!" Mrs. Richman responds; "The round of fashionable dissipation is dangerous" (p. 13) [11]. Yet as many recent critics have observed, Eliza finds the rules of determining the difference between freedom and dissipation to be unclear at best. From Mrs. Richman, she receives a more pointed warning later, about the roué, Major Sanford. He has earned "censure," Eliza's friend says, "by being a professed libertine; by having too successfully practised the arts of seduction; by triumphing in the destruction of innocence and the peace of families!" "Must I then become an avowed prude?" asks Eliza. "By no means" is Mrs. Richman's response; one can be polite, yet "forbidding"—that is, give the seducer entrance into the house of virtue but there resist his "arts" (p. 20) [16–17].

What *The Coquette* suggests, *The Boarding School*—a book that has received little comment and less praise—makes overt: the arts

of seduction must be fought by other arts, those of virtue.[1] Mrs. Williams, the schoolmistress of Harmony Grove, recognizes that young women even from the best homes may lack full education in the ways of the world; they require a complete course of instruction in self-defense, as it were, a school of martial as well as marital arts that teaches women how to walk confidently into areas hostile to virtue, repel all threats, and emerge with reputation intact. Unfortunately for Eliza, the haphazard schooling she gets from letters and conversations with her female friends does not fully prepare her for those who calculate and deceive—though perhaps had she had a woman with the method and character of Mrs. Williams to teach her first, those admonitory epistles from the sorority of the virtuous might have had greater effect. As it is, the other women in Eliza's life all play by different rules from those of "natural vivacity." Lucy Freeman urges the choice of Rev. Boyer for Eliza's suitor, for all the obvious reasons of virtue, honor, and stability, and repudiates Eliza's alleged desire "to shine in the gay circle of fashionable amusements" (p. 27) [22]. Mrs. Richman later draws the analogy between Richardson's characters Clarissa and Lovelace and her acquaintances Eliza and Sanford: "beware, my friend, of his arts. Your own heart is too sincere to suspect treachery and dissimulation in another." Yet she urges Eliza to be governed by "sincerity and virtue," telling her that one of the qualities that makes her vulnerable must also be used in her own defense (p. 38) [31].

In the social world that Eliza inhabits, one of parties and visits and cultural events, the sincere woman plays against a person who is seemingly all show but is undone when she cannot wear another face to meet the faces of fashion. For virtue to thrive, those who would be virtuous must know the rules of social behavior—a kind of theatricality where performers are also spectators—but resist the distractions of costume for entertainment's sake. Eliza, as the daughter of a virtuous but ineffective mother, and as a woman of small material resources, "confined to the rigid rules of prudence and economy," is, among the professionally wealthy—those like Sanford whose whole mode of being is dedicated to "show" and "equipage"—an amateur (pp. 61, 115) [48, 91]. She can, for instance, put on a socially correct front. In one scene, as she anticipates the

---

1. Even Cathy Davidson, in her "Hannah Webster Foster" article in the *Dictionary of Literary Biography*, vol. 37, edited by Emory Elliott (Detroit: Gale, 1985), pp. 161–63, remarks that *The Boarding School* "is didactic and prosaic, lacking in art and ingenuity." I would argue that though the book is indeed didactic, it is far more subtle than Davidson and less sympathetic readers have suggested. For a recent reevaluation of *The Boarding School* that puts Foster's novel in the context of friendship among women, see Claire C. Pettingill, "Sisterhood in a Separate Sphere: Female Friendship in Hannah Webster Foster's *The Coquette* and *The Boarding School*," *Early American Literature* 27 (1992): 185–203.

arrival of her righteous suitor, Boyer, she says, "I must begin to fix my phiz . . . and try if I can to make up one that will look *madamish*" (p. 61) [48]. But Eliza suffers from her sincerity as well. In the climactic scene, Boyer comes to press her for an answer to his marriage suit. Meanwhile, fearful of losing the object of his intrigues, the unsavory Sanford appears in the garden to make one last appeal before Eliza chooses the minister as her spouse. During his speech, "a consciousness of the impropriety of this clandestine interview" causes Eliza to blush; Boyer enters, catches the two in an agitated tableau—"mute as statues"—and, finding a woman whose sincerity exposes her consciousness of the impropriety of being alone with Sanford, storms off to tell Eliza's mother that he renounces the attachment to her daughter (pp. 91–92) [72]. Eliza has made him, he accuses, "the dupe of coquetting artifice," while she, with "no inclination to self defence," takes his accusations, all her "natural vivacity" departed (pp. 92–93) [73].

The natural is not so base here as foolish. Although many modern critics, including Davidson, Hamilton, and Smith-Rosenberg, denounce Boyer for his priggishness, the fact remains that by the rules of conduct that Foster upholds, he must react to the *appearance* of impropriety; and though modern readers may find his haughty epistolary rebuff to Eliza a smug and arrogant gesture, his abandoning Eliza is the mechanical consequence of her failure to perform appropriately, to look sufficiently *"madamish"* when Sanford has been present. Mrs. Williams, the doyenne of Harmony Grove, attacks both the "language of seduction" and the "insidious and deluding wiles of the coquette," urging instead "the dignity and decision of insulted virtue," a pose that comes directly from a "rational and discreet plan of thinking and acting" in securing from a suitor his "affection" (*The Boarding School*, pp. 103, 98–99) [184, 182].

Though virtue is touted in both of her books, Foster nowhere makes social action a completely moral issue. Rather, she asserts that all social relations are governed by plans, schemes, wiles—motives may differ, but no one can afford innocence where it is tied to naiveté. Eliza has only *appeared* to be "coquettish," as the intensity of her remorse and her abject letter to Boyer show; but in a world of calculation, even among the virtuous, all appearance is judged as if it is reality—a reality that includes some measure of expected artifice. To outfox the seducer, one must adopt the stance most repellent to him: a posture of virtue so assertively put forward that the "charms" of the seducer have no audience. What prevents Sanford from chasing after the "alluring" Julia Granby, for instance, as opposed to her friend Eliza, is "the dignity" of Julia's "manners" and "the very expression of her eye [that] blasts in the bud, every thought, derogatory to her honor" (*The Coquette*, p. 140) [131].

Unlike Eliza, Julia acts with all the certainty of a right-thinking female education, as if she has been tutored by someone of Mrs. Williams's character. In *The Boarding School*, the young women whom Mrs. Williams has been preparing for the world go forth and correspond with each other about the life they meet, their goals, follies, and fears, and their remembrance of their teacher's advice. Following the opening section—Mrs. Williams's lectures—the first letter, by Harriot Henly, notes that at her home in Boston, the streets are full of loud "Bachanalians" and her home full of persons who care nothing for such polite and uplifting entertainments as reading or singing hymns (p. 114) [191]. Well might she note the disjunction between a closed, harmonious society where performance is limited to one woman's reading aloud while the others work with needles and the more open, threatening society of the city, filled as it is with theatrical performances of all kinds: plays, professional singing and dancing, exhibitions. Mrs. Williams has told Harriot and the others that they need to be accomplished in such performing arts as music and dancing, but that those arts "sometimes allure their fond votaries from that purity and rectitude which are the chief embellishments of the female character" (p. 42) [155].

She illustrates her point with the story of Levitia, the daughter of parents who, while "not affluent," encourage her to develop her talents. The woman, however, becomes obsessed with performing. Glutting herself on flattery, she accepts a smooth-talking foreigner as guardian, who prepares her for a professional career. Ruin follows swiftly: "She made her appearance on the stage. She sung and danced, for which she was caressed, flattered, and paid. A licentious mode of life, quadrating with the levity of her heart, soon left her a prey to seduction. Her gaiety and beauty gained her many votaries, and she became a complete courtezan" (*The Boarding School*, p. 44) [156]. Further disasters succeed. Mother dies, lover flees, father grows ill; and though she returns to her father, she cannot recover her lost reputation: "She is now despised and avoided by all her former acquaintance, and must inevitably spend the remainder of her days in wretchedness" (p. 45) [156].

Theater threatens not entirely by its form. Indeed, the well-educated woman knows many of the same arts as those of the stage. Rather, it is as if knowing how to perform, albeit modestly, enables a woman to determine the rules and artifice of performance generally. Nevertheless, to escape censure, a woman must learn to reconcile knowledge of potential corruption with an appearance of innocence and behave with a restraint that cannot be scorned as prudish. In fact, the social circle that surrounds the stage has greater potency as a corrupting force than the entertainments themselves: "At the play, the ball, the card-table," young women expose themselves as "dupes

of adulation, and the votaries of coquetry," falling in love with men who are "all show" (*The Boarding School*, pp. 89–91) [177–78]. A woman must learn further to discriminate between virtuously informed criticism of plays and uninitiated abandonment to brilliant social surface.

<center>*   *   *</center>

*The Boarding School* helps us read *The Coquette* by seeing in the title of the latter a false lead. Like Flavia, Eliza falls from the pedestal of virtue without ever actively assuming the reality of a coquette. To be sure, she is not entirely naive; Eliza receives far more direction from women in what Mrs. Williams calls the "path of rectitude" than Flavia (*The Boarding School*, p. 48) [158]. Neither is Eliza entirely unsophisticated about plays and theater or even politics; nor is she beholden to a father of any sort, honorable or not. Nevertheless, without a will for self-defense, Eliza leaves herself every bit as exposed to loss of virtue and independence as Levitia, Flavia, or any other antiheroine in one of Mrs. Williams's cautionary tales.[2]

If what we have been discussing is essentially the theater of social life, where one ideally plays at virtue until one actually acquires it— or one mistakenly falls in love with the brilliant surfaces that make virtue look dull by comparison—there are, in essence, two more theaters in *The Coquette* to which Eliza must pay heed: the theater itself and its texts, and the metaphoric world stage on which people imagine their lives to be roles in a larger drama. For someone like Mrs. Williams, the well-educated, well-defended republican woman should be able to distinguish carefully among all three, recognize each for what it is, yet know when any theater absorbs too much of one's being for safety's sake. The problem with the world Foster creates, however, is that there is no space in which one can *be* without subjection to exacting standards of what constitutes an acceptable performance. Eliza knows her theaters, but she cannot always draw curtains between them or fully appreciate the dangers inherent in overindulgence. Despite the warnings she receives—sometimes couched in contradictory terms—Eliza acts as if it were possible for essence to supersede appearance.

Still, Foster makes it clear that Eliza's sentiments often conform to the Harmony Grove model. Boyer's friend Selby recounts a social gathering involving Eliza, Sanford, Mrs. Richman, and others in

2. Frank Shuffelton, "Mrs. Foster's *Coquette* and the Decline of the Brotherly Watch," *Studies in Eighteenth-Century Literature* 16 (1986): 211–24, sees Foster's novels as expressing the problem of a culture that has decriminalized sin and left the virtuous exposed without the protection of the "brotherly watch." For women, that is replaced, as in *The Boarding School*, with a "sorority of affection and care" (p. 222).

which the women divide into groups: one, involving most of the women, surrounds Sanford, who, with a play in his hand, makes "sage remarks" that the women seem witlessly to affirm; and another, engaging Selby, Eliza, and Mrs. Richman, debates the role of women in a republic. When the groups unite, Eliza stands with Mrs. Richman as the latter delivers a lecture to the other women: "We shall not be called to the senate or the field to assert its [the country's] privileges and defend its rights, but we shall feel for the honor and safety of our friends and connections who are thus employed. . . . Why, then, should the love of our country be a masculine passion only?" (*The Coquette*, pp. 91–92) [35]. With the crowd finally assenting that Mrs. Richman's speech is "truly Roman, and, what was more, they said, truly republican," Foster—despite the tacit acceptance of female disenfranchisement—asks us to see in the implied competition between play talk and political rhetoric an affirmation of the latter as the right arena for the new American woman (p. 92) [36].

Even so, Eliza finds that the world of plays has its own allure. While Boyer still pursues his marriage plans, Eliza puts him off by demanding the free use of her own time. This includes attending what she calls later "a favorite amusement of mine," the theater (*The Coquette*, p. 100) [79]. Boyer will have no part of it; but at the theater, Eliza writes to her mother, she sees "Major Sanford in the very next box" (p. 74) [58]. As Boyer later tells Eliza, no good can come from seeking "the adulation of coxcombs . . . nor could the fashionable amusements of brilliant assemblies, and crouded theatres furnish the mind with 'That which nothing earthly gives, or can destroy / The soul's calm sunshine, and the heart felt joy'" (p. 76) [59–60]. But after Boyer leaves her for good, Eliza asks the virtuous Lucy Sumner to tell her about the theater in Boston and to send her plays to get her out of her depression—requests to which her friend readily accedes.

Letter 52, in which Lucy describes the Boston theater, shows how carefully Foster discriminates among acceptable and unacceptable theatrical activities for a woman of sensibility. "Come and see whether they [performers] can afford you any entertainment," she urges Eliza, implying that the theater per se is an appropriate balm for a depressed republican woman (*The Coquette*, p. 112) [88]. But once in the theater, what can one see without harm? Lucy herself has just seen *Romeo and Juliet*: "Distressing enough to sensibility this! Are there not real woes (if not in our own families, at least among our own friends, and neighbors) sufficient to exercise our sympathy and pity, without introducing fictitious ones into our very diversions? How can that be a diversion, which racks the soul with grief, even though that grief be imaginary. The introduction of a

funeral solemnity, upon the stage, is shocking indeed!" (pp. 112–13) [88–89]. If one cannot "play" death, then surely lighter fare such as the circus would be acceptable. Yet this too gets attacked, largely on gender grounds. Lucy particularly belittles female equestrians: "To see a woman depart so far from the female character, as to assume the masculine habit and attitudes; and appear entirely indifferent, even to the externals of modesty, is truly disgusting, and ought not to be countenanced by our attendance, much less by our approbation." With tragedy and circuses (and cross-dressing/acting) ruled out, there remains one "rational and refined amusement"—museums (p. 113) [89].

But Eliza has already made it clear that she cannot be confined by such dull fare. She has kept Boyer at a distance, using the argument that their "dispositions" are different; yet she has concurred with Mrs. Richman that women ought to take an active role in the affairs of the republic. She defines her freedom as that of choosing her own companions and attending amusements of her choice, recognizing that what held for her mother—stoic acceptance of life's trials—cannot hold for her. As with the country as a whole, Eliza feels the need for the new, yet everywhere she is cautioned about leaving the old.

Foster implicitly argues for a greater role for women in national affairs but, at the same time, uses the voices of several characters to explain the need for clearly delineated, gender-defined limits to allowable behaviors in that role. At once recognizing the desire of women for autonomy and yet urging women to dispose their attentions and favors carefully in order not to lose all, Foster suggests that prudence must govern—but that continual restraint has its costs. Encouraged to read light plays and attend diverting amusements, yet cautioned against frivolity and associating with a man as familiar with the stage as Sanford, Eliza has few outlets for her impulse toward theater. As Lucy Sumner might say, why see *Romeo and Juliet* when one can watch the tragedy of Eliza Wharton firsthand?

Indeed, it appears that Foster has had Eliza on another stage all along, the metaphoric stage of tragic example, for which the novel in America is a new vehicle. Removed from the direct connection to flesh and blood that the theater maintains, the novel uses language that frames the lives of characters in theatrical terms yet seems to adopt a moral stance that questions the utility of the actual stage. Before the postwar reopening of the theaters, a like strategy appears in other texts: sermons, orations, and diaries, for example. And while those same texts continue to use theater metaphors, the novel—often linked in sermons and related tracts to the corrupting stage—both absorbs theatrical conventions and reexpresses experience in ways that convey the intensity of dramatic situation without some of

the ambiguities of representation that worry the moralists.[3] Thus Foster, unable to find a place for Eliza at the theater, and unwilling to allow her to act in the theater, exhibits her life on stage anyway—the stage of metaphorical preconceptions that says that every action in a (woman's) life has dramatic, national consequences.

\* \* \*

# GWENDOLYN AUDREY FOSTER

## [The Dialogics of Sisterly Advice in *The Boarding School*][†]

\* \* \*

Early American conduct texts exemplify the struggle for power over the female body. Though a body of critical studies in the area of conduct literature exists (Armstrong and Tennenhouse, Foster, and Sarah Emily Newton, and others), the intersection between the realm of the fictive narrative and the conduct manual needs to be more fully explored. In the dialogic struggle between the conduct manual and the newly crafted world of American fiction, one finds in *The Boarding School*, by Hannah Webster Foster, an example of the increasingly fluid boundaries contained within women's literature of the period. While *The Boarding School* presents itself to the reader as a fictional narrative, encoded within the diegesis of the text is a series of questions, yet also affirmations, of the standards and mores of Foster's world.

This creates a feminist dialogism, a fluid state in which Foster seemingly supports the standards of female virtue, while she simultaneously calls these standards into question. However, Janet Wilson James sees early women conduct authors as adherents to male standards of virtue and propriety, and she cites Hannah Webster Foster's *Boarding School* (1798) as a case in point (238–39). The *Boarding School* does not support this paradigm. In the first half of this epistolary novel, which takes the form of a valedictory address of a preceptress to her pupils, the narrator praises the domestic virtues: "piety, morality benevolence, prudence and economy. . . .

---

3. For a discussion of *theatrum mundi* metaphors in early American writing, see Jeffrey H. Richards, *Theater Enough: American Culture and the Metaphor of the World Stage, 1607–1789* (Durham, N.C.: Duke UP, 1991).
† From *Troping the Body: Gender, Etiquette, and Performance* (Carbondale: Southern Illinois UP, 2000), 47–53, 59–60. Reprinted by permission. Page numbers in square brackets refer to this Norton Critical Edition.

'Nothing lovelier can be found in woman, than to study household good'" (7) [138]. The dominant voice would seem to adhere to patriarchal constructs of virtue and deny the female public construction of self. The second half of *The Boarding School* consists of "A Collection of LETTERS, written by the Pupils, to their INSTRUCTOR, their FRIENDS, and each other." In this section, women speak to themselves in a manner that suggests a distinctive urge to create a new sense of the female self in a society dedicated to suppressing the female body.

\* \* \* A close textual analysis of *The Boarding School* reveals a decidedly subversive tone and disrupts the world view in which nothing lovelier can be found in woman than to study household good. Like Foster's more well known novel, *The Coquette*, in which Sharon Harris finds a sisterhood of "women acting in consort, as a community separate from, and in opposition to, the oppression of the patriarchal republic" (15), *The Boarding School*, in many ways, explores the possibility of female community beyond household ornamentation.

In 1722, Cotton Mather lauded women as "People, who make no Noise at all in the World; people hardly Known to be in the World; persons of the Female Sex" (*Ornaments* 34, 35). Foster's preceptress only stands as an obvious exemplification of a woman who speaks (for the first 113 [52] pages). Her address, in fact, takes a week in its entirety, and the collective response of the students reads as an audible song of female friendship and solidarity. These pupils make noise in the world, as their later letters will testify. The voices of the students "all united in testifying the sense they entertained of the advantage they had received from Mrs. William's tuition, the happiness they had enjoyed in each other's society, and their determination to remember her counsels, cultivate continued friendship among themselves, and endeavor to be worthy of hers" (113) [189]. The women of Harmony-Grove, a utopic sphere of female community, speak often and loudly, especially as they mature into activists and critics. The preceptress effectively "engraves" her voice on their memories (15) [142], as she has set out to speak herself and their collective response seals a bloodbond of unity of women who speak.

Among the pupils of *The Boarding School*, Laura Guilford stands as one loud voice calling for speech among women. In her verse, Guilford proclaims:

> Thoughts shut up, want air . . .
> Speech ventilates our intellectual fire;
> Speech burnishes our mental magazine;
> Brightens for ornament, and whets for use.
>
> (174) [220]

Matilda Fielding responds to Laura's letter with a recounting of a women's meeting in which she boasts the women found they could speak "without restraint, or the fear of criticism" (176) [221]. A letter from Amelia Parr interrupts the dialogue of the pupils of Harmony-Grove. In a strangely imperious tone, Amelia accuses Harriot Henly of having "strange ideas of the world," which she blames on the environment of the boarding school. Harriot responds with a cutting retort to her letter, saying that "your letter—your rattle, rather, came to hand yesterday" (157) [212]. For Foster, Amelia represents the embodiment of the ornamental female, a body that is both critiqued and catalogued in the text of her work. Foster's attitude toward the ornamental female is one of contempt and ridicule, both in *The Boarding School* and in *The Coquette*. Foster does extend some sympathy toward patriarchally defined women such as Amelia, whom she views as constructs of a male-defined education system. Even as Foster voices her disgust with women like Amelia, she employs the dialogics of the novel-conduct book to criticize the era's patriarchally defined education of women.

Harriot Henly dismisses Amelia's criticisms of Harmony Grove, which she praises as a place where "we have no card-parties, avowedly formed for the purpose of *killing time!*" (158) [213]. The need for a sphere in which women could speak and study freely is a consistent subtext of *The Boarding School*, which was written at a time in which rhetoric against female boarding schools emphasized their supposed "undomestication" of women. In 1795, the Reverend John Bennett attacked boarding schools on the basis that they discouraged domestification of the female body, whose finest qualities were, for Bennett, "innocence, simplicity and domestick worth" (109):

> Boarding schools wholly counteract these dispositions. They trample upon nature, and give us artificial creatures, artificial looks, and artificial smiles. In their formal walls, airs, gestures, syllables, articulation, all are studied, and are sure to disgust. Like hot beds, they give a forwardness to the fruits, but deprive them of their natural healthiness and flavour; and the fine ladies they send into the world, feel themselves ridiculously exalted above (what they conceive to be) the groveling offices of family economy, or domestick attentions. (109)

An exchange of letters between Sophia Manchester and Maria Williams displays a characteristic voicing of support for the female boarding school. "Restore me again to the native simplicity and sincerity of Harmony Grove!" (H. Foster 149) [208], writes Sophia, after criticizing the uneducated, overdressed women she finds in her new circle. "How vain then is this subterfuge?" she asks. "Beauty cannot

possibly maintain its sway over its obsequious votaries, unless the manners and the mind unitedly contribute to secure it" (148) [208]. Matilda Fielding responds with an admonishment designed to defend women: "Few, you should remember, have had the advantages which you have enjoyed. . . . Let charity then draw a veil over the foibles of others, and candour induce you to look on the best and brightest side" (150) [209]. Education itself is consistently praised in highly embellished, almost hyperbolic metaphors of female pleasure. Julia Greenfield and Cleora Partridge, for example, decide to read geography tests together. Julia implores Cleora in a tone of romantic sublime: "Come, then, my dear Cleora, and without fatigue or expense, we will make a tour of the globe together. . . . We will traverse the frozen wastes of the frigid zones, and the burning sands of the equatorial region; then return and bless the temperate and happy medium in which we are placed" (226) [246–47].

The rhetoric of *The Boarding School* not only actively supports the role of the education of women, but it provides a glimpse of early American feminist literary criticism. Sophia Manchester, for example, dismisses *Tristram Shandy*, dismisses the "obscene and vulgar ideas" of Swift (205) [235], and proclaims her preference for the history of women. Immersed in a text of American biography, she notes that "the native virtues of our sex suddenly reanimate our frame" (207) [236] and she shows decidedly more interest in Isabella than Columbus and in Pocahontas than Captain Smith. Laura Guilford is another budding literary critic. "I am not equally pleased with all Richardson's writings" (161) [214], writes Guilford, not missing an opportunity to criticize the male novel: "it dissipates the mind" (162) [215]. Pope's letters are artfully criticized by Caroline Littleton: "He, said I to myself, who bears the palm from all contemporary poets, and who is so consummate a master of this divine art, must surely furnish a source of superior entertainment. . . . The greater part of them have little other merit than what arises from the style" (126) [197].

*  *  *

Hannah Webster Foster emphasizes the scrutiny of reading materials far more often than the scrutiny of prospective husbands. Novels "are the most dangerous kind of reading, now adopted by the generality of young ladies," warns Foster, adding that "their romantic pictures of love, beauty, and magnificence, fill the imagination with ideas which lead to impure desires" (18) [143]. Foster urges her pupils to read good poetry, essays, and in a display of self-reflexivity, epistolary conduct books. Foster even encourages women to write epistolary novels, couching her feminist rhetoric in patriotic language:

"Thrice blessed are we, the happy daughters of this land of liberty, where the female mind is unshackled by the restraints of tyranni-cal custom, which in many other regions confines the exertions of genius to the usurped powers of lordly man!" (31) [149–50]. Foster embraced the power of the pen to reclaim the female body, and she understood its ability to span the course of time. "Always employ your pens upon something useful and refined," she wrote, adding the sage's wisdom: "'I am writing for futurity'" (33) [150]. On the choice of husbands, Foster provides ample advice, but she does this in a decidedly feminist manner. In *The Boarding School*, as in *The Coquette*, Foster warns her female audience: "'That reformed rakes make the best husbands,' is a common, and I am sorry to say, a too generally received maxim" (103) [184].

Foster stresses the importance of relying upon female friendship and maternal guidance in matters of the heart. In one of the many allegories presented in the valedictory address, Florinda "saves" her friend Narcssa from an attachment "to a man who was much her inferior" (94) [180]. The women exemplify "the bonds of true and generous friendship" (94) [180], and Florinda stops her friend from eloping by threatening to tell her parents. Foster stresses sisterly compassion and action in many of the allegories weaved into the patchwork of *The Boarding School*. Prudelia saves her sister, Myra, from ruin: when she hears that she has been seduced and aban-doned. Prudelia gives up her lifestyle of affluence to seek out her sister and helps her to reestablish herself, and reclaim her virtue. The subtext here implies that even the most "fallen" women can be saved through sisterhood: "[T]aking her reclaimed sister with her, she returned to her anxiously expecting family" (88) [177]. Prudelia is acting upon the words of the preceptress, whose final remarks in the novel stress the ideology of sisterhood: "Watch over your dear little sisters, with all the tenderness of fraternal affection; be their protector and friend; instil into their minds the principles of virtue and religion; arm them against the snares and temptations by which they will be surrounded; and lead them, by your own conduct, in the way of truth and peace" (251–52) [261].

In Hannah Webster Foster's ideological framework, for a woman to be praised is for her to act in union with her sisters. In Cotton Mather's *Ornaments for the Daughters of Zion*, "for a woman to be praised, is for her to be married" (32). Foster breaks with the tradi-tional view, then, of women as chattel and redefines the female body as an empowered vehicle of female friendship. Foster views marriage as less of a choice than a proscribement. In fact, her most favored status for women seems to be the single female. Further, Foster suggests that the optimum status for a woman in patriarchal early America is that of the married woman whose husband is con-

veniently abroad! "Look upon Elvira," urges the preceptress: "Her acquirements in a single state have qualified her for a shining pattern of matronal duties. Her husband's business abroad prevents him from attending to domestic avocations; nor need he be anxious respecting the management of household affairs" (27) [148]. The preceptress ends her complimentary incantation on the merits of Elvira's household situation with a telling remark: "But I flatter myself that each of you, my dear pupils, will be an Elvira" (28) [148]. One cannot but think that Foster's subtext here would read "Be an Elvira." In a disruption of the patriarchal order, Elvira enjoys the privilege of the economic support of the patriarchy without its bodily restraints. She is free to read, write, and enjoy sisterhood. She stands as a model of the capable female; capable in both spheres, she creates her own sphere of empowered status. Jane West, Foster's British counterpart, plainly questions whether marriage even involved choice or freedom of movement for women: "Moralists are as much inclined to prescribe rules for the choice of a husband, as of a friend. I am afraid that the very title they prefix to their admonitions is apt to mislead a young mind" (101). In West's view, then, women are decidedly cut off from the decision-making process in marrying. Without a net of sisterhood to rely upon, women are forced into alliances against their will. Foster prefers to paint an Edenic universe in which husbands conveniently die or live abroad, as in the case of Elvira. Female solitude is often a prescription for happiness in Foster's schema.

Julia Greenfield opts for a retreat from "the noise and bustle of the world," a place where we can "commune with our own hearts" (H. Foster 139) [204]. This letter, in which Julia Greenfield stresses retreat, sisterhood, and the values of education is in keeping with the themes of the novel. Outside of the boundaries of social discourse ("giddy amusements"), Julia experiences a sort of connubial bliss as she tastes the solicitude of the scholar: "Give me a mind to range the sylvan scene, and taste the blessings of the vernal day" (139) [203]. A preoccupation, then, with education replaces the preoccupation one would expect that these women would share about marriage. It seems as if incidences of marriage have been silenced by Foster, in favor of an alternate discourse of desire for education and filial affection.

Marriage is sometimes viewed as suspect territory in the course of the novel, especially in one letter of Harriot Henly. Having returned from a wedding, Harriot speaks plainly of her distaste for the occasion, and portrays its ghastly, doomed, false spectatorship. "I imagine such exhilarating scenes [are] designed to dispel the anxiety and thoughtfulness," she says of the participants, adding that if she were to wed, "I should choose to retire from the observa-

tion of those indifferent and unfeeling spectators" (134) [201]. Henly
implores Cleora to "look around the world and see the great many
unhappy marriages" (134) [201]. Married couples, in Harriot's view,
even those "contracted with the brightest prospects," end up in states
of "wretchedness for life" (134) [201].

<p align="center">*   *   *</p>

*The Boarding School* at times seems to adhere to male standards of
propriety, as seen mainly in the opening valedictory address of the
Preceptress. However, the epistolary letters speak of an artfully sub-
versive early woman writer fragmenting patriarchal ideology. Foster's
*Coquette* shares an equally fervent, if more covert, attempt to ques-
tion the dominant ideology. *The Boarding School* takes Foster's
agenda a step further. It presents a community of female voices
articulating suppressed desires for female education, sisterhood,
same sex union, celibacy, financial independence, and perhaps what
is most important, the desire for political equality and the reclaimed
female body.

### WORKS CITED

Bennett, John, Rev. *Strictures on Female Education.* Rpt. New York:
Source Book P, 1971.

Foster, Hannah Webster. *The Boarding School: or, Lessons of a Pre-
ceptress to Her Pupils: Consisting of Information, Instruction, and
Advice. Calculated to Improve the Manners, and Form the Char-
acter of Young Ladies, to Which Is Added a Collection of LET-
TERS, Written by the Pupils, to Their INSTRUCTOR, Their
FRIENDS and Each Other.* Boston: I. Thomas and E. T. Andrews,
1798.

Harris, Sharon M., ed. *Redefining the Political Novel: American
Women Writers 1797–1901.* Knoxville: U of Tennessee P, 1995.

James, Janet Wilson. *Changing Ideas about Women in the United
States.* New York: Garland, 1981.

Mather, Cotton. *Ornaments for the Daughters of Zion. Or the
Character and Happiness of a Virtuous Woman.* Rpt. New York:
Delmar, 1978.

West, Jane. *Letters to a Young Lady in Which the Duties and Char-
acter of Women Are Considered.* 3 Vols. Rpt. New York: Garland,
1974.

# ELIZABETH HEWITT

## [Foster's Epistolarity]†

\* \* \*

Scholarship on the British epistolary novel has noted that the epistolary mode becomes increasingly rare after the form becomes irrevocably associated with the revolutionary politics of the turn of the century.[1] This account substantially refutes the conventional understanding that the move away from epistolarity signaled the increasing sophistication and maturation of fictional narratives. But this conventional account continues to maintain its currency as an explanation for the history of the *American* novel, where we likewise find almost no epistolary fiction after 1830. Consequently, most scholars have tended to all but ignore the role of epistolarity to the literature of the early national period. By this I do not mean that there isn't substantial attention paid to the numerous epistolary novels that circulated among early American readers: thanks in large measure to Cathy Davidson's work on the sentimental fiction of the 1790s, Hannah Webster Foster's epistolary novel *The Coquette* has quickly become one of the most widely read and studied texts in early American literature. Instead, I am pointing to the failure to attend to the generic specificity of *The Coquette* (to name only one example) as an *epistolary* novel.[2] The tendency has instead been to treat the epistolary novel as proof of the nation's submission to European forms and therefore evidence of the young nation's puerile literary culture. Epistolary American novels are generally understood to be the least "original" of American fictional forms, merely an importation of European models (*Clarissa, Nouvelle Héloïse*, or *The Sorrows of Werther*, to cite the most popular examples). Yet, if American epistolary novels merely capitulate to outdated European conventions, then we might ask why it is that these

† From *Correspondence and American Literature, 1770–1865* (New York: Cambridge UP, 2004), 27–31. Copyright © 2004 Elizabeth Hewitt. Reprinted with the permission of Cambridge University Press. Page numbers in square brackets refer to this Norton Critical Edition.
1. See Mary Favret, *Romantic Correspondence: Women, Politics, and the Fiction of Letters* (New York: Cambridge UP, 1993); Nicola J. Watson, *Revolution and the Form of the British Novel, 1790–1825: Intercepted Letters, Interrupted Seductions* (New York: Oxford UP, 1994); and Elizabeth Heckendorn Cook, *Epistolary Bodies: Gender and Genre in the Eighteenth-Century Republic of Letters* (Stanford UP, 1996). Blythe Forcey also discusses the importance of the epistolary form in *Charlotte Temple* in her "Charlotte Temple and the End of Epistolarity," *American Literature* 63 (1991): 225–241.
2. The important exceptions here are Bruce Burgett's *Sentimental Bodies: Sex, Gender and Citizenship in the Early Republic* (Princeton: Princeton UP, 1999) and Julia Stern's *The Plight of Feeling: Sympathy and Dissent in the Early American Novel* (U of Chicago P, 1997).

410          ELIZABETH HEWITT

European novels are *not* themselves published in epistolary form in
their American editions. All of the numerous "abridged" editions
of Richardson's *Clarissa, Pamela*, and *Grandison* published in the
United States in the eighteenth century, for example, have been
"translated" out of epistolary form.[3]

The epistolary form in American literature operates according to
a somewhat different political logic than it does in England or
France. The American letter, unlike its European counterpart, is
not aligned with radicalism and, therefore, does not need to be dis-
ciplined in the same ways it does abroad. While the dominant strain
of much European epistolary fiction is the need to contain writing
that is aligned with a destabilization of national authority, the domi-
nant strain in American epistolary novels depicts the *breakdown* in
correspondence as signaling a breakdown in sympathetic attach-
ments and therefore the corrosion of republican virtue on which
national consolidation is forged.[4] Even in those epistolary novels in
which the protection of female virtue is prominent, the prophylac-
tic is found not in curbing female letter-writing, but in its proper
regulation. In Foster's *The Coquette*, for example, Eliza is seduced
*not* because she writes letters to the Lovelacian rake, Sanford, but
because she *stops* writing letters to her mother and to her female
friends. Only when she stops publishing her private sentiments
(and therefore is no longer subject to public scrutiny) can Sanford
gain access to her.[5]

Foster's second novel, *The Boarding School* (1798), likewise
insists on epistolary writing as social regulation.[6] A generic amalga-
mation of epistolary novel, conduct manual, and letter-writer, Fos-
ter's book is divided into two sections.[7] The first half introduces us
to Mrs. Mary Williams, the enterprising widow who has started a
boarding school affectionately named Harmony-Grove, and is dom-
inated by Mrs. Williams's lectures to her graduating class. The

3. The following American editions of Richardson's novels, for example, are all non-
epistolary: *The History of Pamela; or Virtue Rewarded. Abridged from the Works of
Samuel Richardson* (Worcester: Isaiah Thomas, 1794); *The Paths of Virtue Delineated;
or, the History in Miniature of the Celebrated Clarissa Harlowe* (Cooperstown: Phinney,
1795); *Clarissa; or the History of a Young Lady* (Boston: Samuel Hall, 1795).
4. See Stern, *The Plight of Feeling*, 16.
5. In Susanna Rowson's *Charlotte Temple*, ed. Cathy N. Davidson (New York: Oxford UP,
1986), Charlotte's downfall is caused by the interception of letters. *Reuben and Rachel*
also details the social and historical catastrophe caused when letters fail to be deliv-
ered. The American editions of *Clarissa* similarly emphasize that Clarissa's downfall
happens because her parent's tyrannical prohibition against her writing letters force
her into clandestine epistolary writing.
6. Hannah Webster Foster, *The Boarding School; or, Lessons of a Preceptress to her Pupils*
(Boston: Thomas & Andrews, 1798). Further citations will be given parenthetically in
the text.
7. Notably several letters from Foster's *The Boarding School* are included in letter writers.
For example, one sequence is anthologized in *The New Universal Letter-Writer* (Phila-
delphia: Hogan, 1800).

second half of the book consists of the correspondence between the boarding school girls after their departure from Harmony-Grove. Notably, then, we meet the young women who are students at the boarding school *after* they have already received their education. In this way, it would seem that we are to read the letters of the second half as illustrations of the kinds of instruction that Mrs. Williams had offered, and corroboration of the success of her teaching methods. That the novel opens with the departure of the girls from school also significantly emphasizes their teacher's absence, which is likewise insisted on by Mrs. Williams herself who tells her pupils that the period of separation will be "painful," but also essential, as it will release them into "new scenes of care, pleasures, of trials, and of temptations, which will call for the exercise of every virtue" (11) [140]. She suggests that the exile from the utopian Harmony-Grove is the ultimate test of the adequacy of their American education. Foster's text, in this way, fashions itself as part of a national correspondence class: it will circulate to the "young ladies of America," to whom it is dedicated, so that they too will be able to profit by Mrs. Williams's example, even if they are (necessarily) deprived of access to her literal presence.

One crucial strategy of Mrs. Williams's instruction is that she "suspend[s] the authority of the matrons" of the school, and, in so doing, she cultivates the "familiarity" of her pupils such that "they might be free from restraint . . . and appear in their genuine characters" (9) [139]. The cultivation of this "freedom," however, has the ultimate design of disciplining her students: "By this means she had an opportunity of observing any indecorum of behaviour, or wrong bias; which she kept in mind, till a proper time to mention, and remonstrate against it; a method the salutary effects of which were visible in the daily improvement of her pupils" (9) [139]. Mrs. Williams plays the friend so as better to discover the faults of her students and correct them. This method of moral education rivals Franklin's in its sophisticated technology of self-discipline: by making discipline coextensive with freedom, Mrs. Williams insures that her students will regulate themselves even in her absence. The success of the strategy seems proved by the frequent references in her pupils' letters to Mrs. Williams's monitoring of their epistolary correspondence, even if she has no access to the letters themselves.

Indeed, that all letters are potentially subject to public scrutiny forms one of the crucial lessons that Mrs. Williams imparts in her final days with her pupils. Describing the particular democratic value of the letter ("a species of writing . . . open to every capacity, and ornamental to every station"), she also insists that epistolary writing is characterized by "frankness, simplicity, and sincerity" (32) [150]. Yet the story that follows directly contradicts this emphasis

on free and honest expression. Instead, Mrs. Williams advises: "Suffer not the expectation of secrecy to induce you to indulge your pens upon subjects, which you blush to have exposed" (33) [151]. * * * Mrs. Williams asserts that while epistolary writing might be a site of freedom, it is *not* private. Even within the ostensibly private space of a familiar letter, the writer must assume a public audience; she must assume that anyone (including Mrs. Williams) might be looking over her shoulder.

To illustrate she tells the story of Celia and Cecilia, two young friends who, having recently left boarding school, "commence [ . . . ] an epistolary correspondence" (33) [151] that Mrs. Williams characterizes as one of "unlimited confidence; and, without the least reserve, to reveal every dictate of levity and thoughtless folly" (33–34) [151]. In short, she condemns their letters for presuming too much freedom; and, indeed, they are specifically castigated for imagining themselves "perfectly secure from the censure of the critic." Because they don't presume such a critical eye, Celia writes letters to her friend in which "[p]urity of sentiment, delicacy of thought, and refinement of taste were entirely laid aside" and in which Celia's suitor, Silvander, is discussed with too much "freedom . . . and familiarity" (34) [151]. Anxious to discover the subjects of Celia's letters to her friend, Silvander purloins them, and upon reading them, he immediately becomes the public critic "mortified, disgusted, and chagrined" in his discovery of "the lightness of mind exemplified in them!" (34) [151]. As retaliation, he copies Celia's letter (taking care to leave out "references to his own affairs") and then "circulated her letters among his acquaintance" (35) [151].

This circulation, Mrs. Williams sermonizes, "fixed the stamp of ignominy on the correspondents," and Celia never recovers from this assault on her character, her "reputation . . . materially injured" (35) [151]. Celia proceeds to follow the same tragic path of many a seduced young woman (at least in novels) and dies "in melancholy, regret, and obscurity." Mrs. Williams thus instructs her students that women "must not only be virtuous, but unsuspected" (74) [171], and one way to insure that you are unsuspected is to assume that your letters are always subject to public scrutiny. Thus, while she lightly censures Silvander's mail theft, she insists "no adequate excuse can be offered for the young ladies, who dishonored their pens and their talents by a most improper and unbecoming use of both" (35) [152]. We can only become good writers and good citizens, Mrs. Williams implies when we imagine ourselves subject to the critical eyes of others—when we presume that someone else is reading our private letters.

The emphasis of this particular moral lesson is found in the parallels between the two women in the story and the correspondence

that comprises the second half of Foster's novel. Like Celia and Cecelia, the young women who leave Harmony-Grove attempt to compensate for their "painful separation" by finding recourse in epistolary correspondence. In so establishing this parallel, Foster demands that we determine what constitutes the difference between the letters of Celia and Cecelia and the letters between Mrs. Williams's students. Although we are invited to assume that the letters in *The Boarding School* are intended as virtuous examples, it is not always entirely clear what distinguishes them from the letters according to which poor Celia was prosecuted.

The crucial difference is that Foster's "good" correspondent-citizens imagine a critic reading every word; and because this epistolary "freedom" is always monitored, the correspondence is necessarily also virtuous. One student's letter, for example, is stylistically far different from the others in its passionate tone and language: "You have left—you have forsaken me, Caroline! But I will haunt you with my letters; obtrude myself upon your remembrance; and extort from you the continuance of your friendship" (123) [195]. Here seems to be an instance of a letter "without the least reserve" that Mrs. Williams earlier condemned. Yet there is nothing to suggest that this letter is judged as inappropriate; indeed the author of this letter, Julia, while she admits her "eccentricities" and "gay disposition," also notably remarks, "Mrs. Williams's instructions were very seasonably interposed to impress my mind with a sense of virtue and propriety" (123) [195]. She goes on to describe the numerous times in which Mrs. Williams would "take me into her chamber, and reminded me of indecorums of which I was unconscious at the time." Here, then, is confirmation of the effectiveness of Mrs. Williams's method. Julia is "impressed" (as if she were a page proof) with Mrs. Williams's hidden and silent monitoring, and as such her "gay disposition" is firmly controlled by Mrs. Williams's disciplining hand.

Although the perfect union of Harmony-Grove is disrupted when the girls are separated, correspondence is a compensatory substitute, and indeed, much of the emphasis of the letters is on describing the incredible vigilance required to approximate the ideals of Harmony-Grove. Foster's idealized version of female education is essentially Federalist: perfect union between the governing preceptress and her constituent pupils is sustained, even as they necessarily move away from her direct influence. Moreover, as was the strategic political calculus of Federalism, Mrs. Williams's model assuages anxieties about her despotism as well as anxieties about her pupil's potential lawlessness, since her pedagogical method makes their obedience coextensive with "free[dom] from restraint."

Such a Federalist model seems also to be emphasized by the fact that the anthologized correspondence does not accentuate reciprocal communication between the individual young women. Of the forty letters, there are only five occasions in which Foster gives us both the letter and its reply. This lack of emphasis on reciprocity suggests that the exemplary significance of these letters is to demonstrate the ways in which correspondence unifies the community not by stressing relations between individuals, but by highlighting the centralized authority that controls and monitors their epistolary exchange. The complicated political work of *The Boarding-School* is that Foster interpellates her readers into this correspondence by turning her book into just another letter, and thereby making all virtuous American women graduates of Harmony-Grove.

\* \* \*

# RODNEY HESSINGER

## [Gender in the Seduction Tales of the Late Eighteenth Century][†]

\* \* \*

In the years following the Revolution, American popular novels and periodicals began to define manhood as inherently immoral. The seduction and abandonment of young women by young male predators was a plot line that late eighteenth-century American readers knew quite well. The regularity with which this theme was explored and the seriousness of tone used in such investigations suggest that there was a very real fear underlying these stories. Seduction fiction depicted the difficulties facing young women who had gained more freedom from parents and community but as a result were exposed to greater exploitation at the hands of mobile and unrestrained young men. While seduction fiction may be important as a window into late eighteenth-century American society—its northern and older regions in particulars—it is of even greater significance because of the formative role it had in shaping American culture. Such fiction not only depicted the seduction and abandonment of young women; it offered solutions to this perceived problem.

A variety of cultural strategies were explored in seduction literature to resolve the problem of unaccountable male youth. Some

† From *Seduced, Abandoned, and Reborn: Visions of Youth in Middle-Class America, 1780–1850* (Philadelphia: U of Pennsylvania P, 2005), 24, 30–32, 36–37, 42–43. Reprinted by permission. Page numbers in square brackets refer to this Norton Critical Edition.

writers held up an ideal of manhood that was steeped in the culture of sensibility. Young men were encouraged to be men of feeling who were not ashamed to shed a tear or to assist a vulnerable woman. Similarly, writers asked men to listen to their internal monitors or their consciences. Both concepts were gaining wider cultural currency, registering an ideological shift from more coercive patterns of social control. However, writers were not reluctant to double their chances by appealing to coercion as well. Visions of otherworldly punishment for male seducers populated seduction tales. Some writers also gave a measure of blame to women and asked them to avoid coquettish behavior that attracted suspect males.

These cultural strategies of controlling men, however, did not prove popular because, in part, at least, they contradicted the logic of the most popular message to emerge from the seduction tales. Above all else, these tales insisted that young men were immoral and that, as a result, young women would need to seek the protective guidance of parents in seeking prospective partners. It was to young women that these tales were most often addressed. This female audience was increasingly told that they were by nature virtuous and chaste.[1]

While scholars have fully explored the process whereby womanhood was redefined as virtuous, the transformation of the definition of manhood deserves closer attention.

\*     \*     \*

Some writers of seduction tales seem to have hoped to reach young male readers, in addition to the young women to whom they most obviously directed their stories. By depicting regret and doubt in the characters who committed seduction, authors strove to cultivate sensibility in these potential male readers. Hannah Foster, who has been credited with pushing the seduction story furthest as a vehicle for the cause of women's freedom—a subject to which we will return—may have been more atypical in her in-depth depiction of a seducer who was also, at times, a feeling man. In Foster's *The Coquette*, the seducer Sanford first entertains doubts about his plan of seduction and later experiences extreme regret in seeing its ill effects. After committing the crime, Sanford expresses the sentiments usually spoken by the ruined heroines: "Oh, Deighton, I am undone! Misery irremediable is my future lot! She is gone; yes, she

---

1. On the intended audience of seduction fiction, see Cathy N. Davidson, *Revolution and the Word: The Rise of the Novel in America* (New York: Oxford UP, 1986), 111–25. On the redefinition of womanhood as innately virtuous, see Ruth H. Bloch, "The Gendered Meanings of Virtue in Revolutionary America," *Signs* 13 (Autumn 1987): 37–58 and Nancy F. Cott, "Passionlessness: An Interpretation of Victorian Sexual Ideology, 1790–1850," *Signs* 4 (Winter 1978): 219–36.

is gone for ever! The darling of my soul, the centre of all my wishes and enjoyments is no more!"[2]

\* \* \*

Thus a few authors seem to have allowed their male characters, sometimes even their villain, to display sensibility. But only in these few novels is one likely to find such depictions; periodical stories, which stripped seduction scenarios down to the bare minimum, much less frequently explored such ideas. Moreover, in the novels discussed above, authors spent much more time depicting the evils and dangers of men rather than upholding a sentimental model for them. To the degree that they addressed male readers, seduction fiction writers were more willing to send another type of appeal to potential seducers: a message of fear. Appeals to conscience can be found in the periodicals, but more in the form of a threat rather than an extended hand. For example, in one magazine piece entitled "The Sorrows of Amelia," a direct warning to men is offered: "learn instruction from the fate of Alonzo . . . check the disposition which would prompt you to spread toils for unsuspecting innocence. Guilt will destroy the bliss of the seducer, intrude on his morning pleasure and damp his evening joys."[3] The threat of a guilty conscience could be heightened by depicting its ultimate result as suicide. In a story in *The Gentleman's and Ladies Town and Country Magazine*, which was presented as a letter from the "reformed" rake Edmund to his friend who still practiced the evil arts, the reader learns of the horrible consequences of seduction for the seducer. Edmund relates the story of a young man who felt intense guilt over his seduction of a young woman. This man went to a secluded cabin in the woods; there he worshiped a wax resemblance of the woman he had seduced (and who had died) and ultimately commited suicide.[4]

A heavy burden of guilt was not the only potential cost of seduction for men. Authors also used the threat of damnation. In a story in *The Key,* the reader is informed that the libertine will eventually pay for his crime: "But the thunders of heaven will not sleep; injustice will be visited by vengeance."[5] William Hill Brown in *The Power of Sympathy* dedicates an extended scene to a dream of Mr. Harrington, who visits a Dante-like hell where the worst station is reserved for the seducers:

2. Hannah W. Foster, *The Coquette,* ed. Cathy N. Davidson (New York: Oxford UP, 1986; 1st ed., Boston: Samuel Etheridge, 1797), 35, 72, 164 [27, 56–57, 129].
3. "Sorrows of Amelia," *The Baltimore Weekly Magazine,* July 5, 1800, 87.
4. "The Fatal Effects of Seduction," *The Gentlemen and Ladies Town and Country Magazine* (Boston), June 1789, 250–51.
5. "Matilda," *The Key* (Fredericktown, Md.), April 14, 1798, 106.

In their countenances were depicted more anguish, sorrow, and despair—I turned my head immediately from this dreadful sight . . . Quivering with horror, I inquired who they were—"These," answered my guide, with a sigh, "are the miserable race of SEDUCERS—Repentance and shame drive them far from the rest of the accursed. Even the damned look on them with horror, and thank fate their crimes are not of so deep a die."[6]

Melodramatic, perhaps, but the social fear of seduction is quite evident in such threats.

While authors appealed to the anxiety of potential male readers more than their sensibility, both strategies ultimately must have seemed futile if men were truly depraved. A story entitled "A Melancholy Tale of Seduction" that ran in the *Massachusetts Magazine* displays this tension extremely well. Addressed to a libertine, it begins by appealing to his sensibility, asking him to mend his ways: "I hope your mind has not lost all its sensibility, and that there may be a time when this letter shall prove a monitor." It goes on to tell him, in good sentimental fashion, how one of his victims has died of shame (a frequent fate for seduction victims). However, this address gradually seems to give up on any hope of his reform. The author first asks a series of rhetorical questions: "Were there never times when your heart checked you, and obliged you almost to revoke?—Could neither youth; nor beauty, nor innocence, find even a momentary friend in your thoughts? . . . Were your vices only permanent, all your better resolutions transitory?" After asking this final query, the author provides a gloomy response: "They were. To feel for another's wo[e] was a lesson you had never known." At the end of the article, the author warns the seducer that eventually he will be racked with guilt: "Pensive moments will come to make you wretched . . . Be assured, that the burden of misery which awaits yourself, is heavier far than any you have heaped on another."[7] Yet by this point the warning is quite hollow. It seems doubtful whether even the author could believe that this immoral youth, lacking conscience, would ever feel remorse. As manhood was constructed as immoral, it would seem pointless to ask men to mend their ways. Solutions to female vulnerability would have to be found elsewhere.

* * *

Seduction tales were not the only type of fiction to assert men's immorality. Mildred Doyle, in her comprehensive study of early

6. William Hill Brown, *The Power of Sympathy, or, The Triumph of Nature. Founded in Truth*, 2 vols. (Boston: Isaiah Thomas, 1789), 2: 105.
7. "Melancholy Tale of Seduction," *Massachusetts Magazine* (Boston), April 1795, 40–42.

American periodicals, noted that the second most popular theme, after seduction, was the abuse of wives by cruel husbands.[8] In this theme, as in seduction, virtuous female characters were constructed in opposition to the male figures. The characterization of male figures in the seduction tales had the potential to spill into larger cultural molds of gender that were taking form in American culture as a whole. Although some authors were careful to draw character distinctions between the male figures in their works, collectively their tales convey an image of male depravity. It is not surprising, then, that someone could have penned the lyrics that opened this chapter, which declared "men are all rovers alike." The slightly more circumspect judgment presented in "Almira and Alonzo" perhaps better represents the collective message of seduction fiction to its female readers: "Your spotless bosoms, the seat of honor, unsuspecting of deceit . . . admit too flattering ideas of men . . . Few—few indeed, are deserving the confidence they obtain."[9]

Imagined in this way, young men seemed hopeless. American authors were breaking with an essential component of the British tradition of sensibility by casting off the prospect of male reform. Samuel Richardson, whose mid-eighteenth-century British novels helped inspire American seduction tales, had held out the possibility of male reform in his 1740 novel *Pamela*. Resisting the sexual advances of her master Mr. B, the servant girl Pamela eventually won admiration and an offer of marriage from her pursuer. Richardson himself drew a less rosy picture in a subsequent novel, *Clarissa*, but many British writers on sensibility still continued to believe in cultivating virtue in men. Perhaps most emblematic of the tradition was Henry Mackenzie's 1771 novel *The Man of Feeling*, a tale in which the lead figure meets and assists a range of downtrodden characters. American seduction writers challenged the wisdom of Richardson's *Pamela*, and writings on sensibility more generally, by rejecting the possibility of reforming rakes. Lucy Freeman in *The Coquette* explicitly states what most tales implied in their emphasis on cautioning females rather than reforming males: " 'A reformed rake,' you say, 'makes the best husband;' a trite, but a very erroneous maxim, as the fatal experience of thousands of our sex can testify."[1]

It is uncertain how young men might have received such tales. It is certainly plausible that some might have reveled in the exploits of seducers. Correspondence uncovered from the late eighteenth-century does show rakish attitudes among some men engaged in

8. Mildred Doyle, "Sentimentalism in American Periodicals, 1741–1800" (Ph.D. diss., New York U, 1941), 50–55.
9. "Almira and Alonzo," *Massachusetts Magazine*, June 1789, 361–64.
1. G. J. Barker-Benfield, *The Culture of Sensibility: Sex and Society in Eighteenth-Century Britain* (Chicago: University of Chicago Press, 1992); Foster, *The Coquette*, 57 [45].

sexual liaisons.[2] Despite the strenuous efforts of authors to stabilize the meaning of their tales, there were in fact opportunities to read seduction tales subversively. For example, as Sanford confided his schemes of ruin to his friend Deighton, young men might have felt part of the circle, cheering Sanford on. Even the condemnations of libertines might have made seduction appear enticing because such warnings made sexual exploits seem dangerous.

\*   \*   \*

Ultimately in the American tales of seduction, young men could not be reformed. While these tales employed the devices of sensibility, and on occasion portrayed men as sensitive, they helped push sensibility into sentimentality by gendering empathy.[3] The gender-neutral model of sensitivity possible in eighteenth-century sensibility would yield to the feminized sensitivity of nineteenth-century sentimentalism. Faced with female vulnerability, authors had a range of responses available. By primarily choosing to define men as immoral, rather than asking men to assume responsibility, these writers participated in the construction of gender ideals that would come to dominate Victorian thinking. There was a certain, almost inexorable, logic to their decision. Fiction writers had to render complex social change into personal family dramas. Young men were already accorded more social freedoms than women in eighteenth-century society, so the easiest, and perhaps safest, path was to demand increasing self-control in women. In the emerging American ideology of domesticity, male immorality and female purity would continue to mutually reinforce one another as opposites. That dichotomy had been advanced with particular force in seduction tales. \*   \*   \*

# BLEVIN SHELNUTT

## *The Coquette* and Pseudonymous Attribution[†]

On August 22, 1797, the Boston newspaper *Massachusetts Mercury* announced: "*Just Published* (In 1 vol. neatly bound and lettered, price 1 Dollar,) *Sold by* E. LARKIN, *No. 47, Cornhill*, THE COQUETTE;

---

2. Godbeer, *Sexual Revolution in Early America*, 259–63.
3. On the rejection of the "man of feeling" in the early nineteenth-century, see Andrew Burstein, *Sentimental Democracy: The Evolution of America's Romantic Self-Image* (New York: Hill and Wang, 1999), 308–19. On sentimentalism as feminized, see Ann Douglas, *The Feminization of American Culture* (New York: Knopf, 1977).
† This essay is printed for the first time in this Norton Critical Edition. Used by permission of the author.

or, The History of ELIZA WHARTON, a Novel, founded on fact. By a
Lady of Massachusetts."[1] Printed by Samuel Etheridge in Newport
for Ebenezer Larkin, *The Coquette* joined William Hill Brown's
1789 novel, *The Power of Sympathy*, as a retelling of a local New
England scandal. Just more than nine years earlier, Elizabeth Whit-
man, the unmarried daughter of a respected Connecticut family,
gave birth to a still-born child in a Danvers, Massachusetts, tavern
and—without revealing her identity to any solicitous townspeople—
died soon thereafter of puerperal fever. As a new, thinly disguised
account of Whitman's well-known and sensational story, *The
Coquette* quickly found interested readers throughout New England,
becoming one of the most popular American novels of the eigh-
teenth century.

The first notice of Elizabeth Whitman's death, which appeared
in the *Salem Mercury* on July 29, 1788, refers to Whitman as an
anonymous "female stranger" while hinting that the paper pos-
sesses clues to her identity (copies of letters in her writing, for
example), which it withholds.[2] Subsequent circulating accounts of
Whitman in newsprint, such as the published "Extract of a Letter
from Boston," written by Jeremy Belknap to Benjamin Rush, repeat
the *Salem Mercury*'s simultaneous revelation and refusal of infor-
mation, functioning not only, as Bryan Waterman has argued, to
"generate suspense and readership," but also to present the publica-
tions "(and their mostly male editors and contributors) as trustwor-
thy sources of information and moral commentary, more fully
informed than the general citizenry."[3] As manuscript and print
versions of the controversial episode circulated and exchanged
places, at the same time reserving the privileged intelligence about
Whitman's identity of which they advertised possession, Whitman's
story, Waterman contends, "offered an opportunity to perform
one's access to accurate information, thereby elevating the status
of private male correspondence and newspapers alike" (330).
When, on September 20, 1788, the *Massachusetts Centinel* finally
revealed Whitman's name in a printed letter to the editor, the
paper secured for itself, according to Waterman, "a claim to more
accurate information than its competitors" and, by extension, a
claim to more accurate moral meanings of Whitman's story (340).
The author of the *Centinel* letter thus presents his discovery "for
the information and improvement of your readers," cautioning

1. "Just Published," *Massachusetts Mercury*, Aug. 22, 1797, 3.
2. "Salem, July 29," *Salem Mercury*, Jul. 29, 1788, 3.
3. "Elizabeth Whitman's Disappearance and Her 'Disappointment,'" *William and Mary
   Quarterly* 66 (2009): 330, 334. Further citations are parenthetical in the text.

them about the reasons for Whitman's undoing: "She was a *great reader of romances*, and having formed her notions of happiness from that corrupt source, became vain and coquettish, and rejected some very advantageous offers of marriage in hope of realizing something more splendid; until disappointed and past her bloom, she gave way to criminal indulgence . . . and terminated her career as above related."[4]

The contest for information and interpretative authority regarding Elizabeth Whitman's identity, which news networks played out in 1788, revived around a different object of interest in 1797 with the *Massachusetts Mercury*'s announcement of *The Coquette*. As the *Salem Mercury*'s death notice and Jeremy Belknap's published letter taunted readers with half-disclosures concerning the details of Whitman's life, the early title pages of *The Coquette* and eighteenth- and nineteenth-century advertisements for the novel worked both to evoke and to conceal the name of its author, Hannah Webster Foster, citing and elaborating on her pseudonym, "a Lady of Massachusetts." Foster's use of the pen name and the print world's insistence on maintaining the moniker—after Foster's authorship was publicly known and even after her death—suggest not only an entry point for considering the literary and cultural implications of pseudonymous female authorship in early American print but also the importance of Foster's adopted identity for reading and thinking about *The Coquette*. Drawing from the history of *The Coquette*'s reception and material texts, this essay examines the other unknown female figure in relation to the novel's early life, the (not so) mysterious "Lady of Massachusetts."

At the end of the eighteenth century, Foster's selected mark, "By a Lady," was still one of the most popular authorial sign-offs for women writers. Although a number of Foster's female contemporaries, such as Susanna Rowson and Helena Wells, saw their names on the title pages of their works, the tag of "By a Lady" or "By a Young Lady," as James Raven notes, appeared on nearly a third of the novels marketed in Britain in 1785.[5] In Lillie Deming Loshe's 1907 bibliography of early American novels, the designation occurs repeatedly, taking several personalized forms, including "By an American Lady," "By a Young Lady of the State of New York," "by a lady of Philadelphia," and "By a Young Lady of Worcester County,"

---

4. Curiosos, "Miscellany. For the Centinel," *Massachusetts Centinel*, Sep. 20, 1788, 8.
5. "The Anonymous Novel in Britain and Ireland, 1750–1830," *The Faces of Anonymity: Anonymous and Pseudonymous Publication from the Sixteenth to the Twentieth Century*, ed. Robert John Griffin (New York: Palgrave Macmillan, 2003), 145.

in addition to Foster's "By a Lady of Massachusetts."[6] As Margaret Ezell has demonstrated, however, the adoption of the pseudonym was far from being merely a compulsory move of convention or an assured means of maintaining anonymity and respectability. Troubling the long-held critical consensus that women writers developed such "authorial strategies to protect their reputations as socially acceptable females," Ezell asks: "[I]f cultural sanction against women being on public display in print was so encompassing and if the function of selecting anonymity of a pseudonym was to disguise the gender of the author to permit her to speak, what are we to make of the selection of 'By a Lady' as being one of the period's more popular solutions . . . ?"[7] Not simply refusing to identify a female author, the "Lady" alias foregrounds a writer's gender and often appears with additional clues, such as age, status, and regional identification, provoking readers to try to determine who the author may be. Like the newspaper accounts circling Elizabeth Whitman's anonymity, the "By a Lady" pseudonym only tenuously (and teasingly) withholds an author's identity.

Despite its attribution to "a Lady of Massachusetts," advertisements for *The Coquette* indicate that newspapers and booksellers had a notion of the novel's author within the first weeks of its release. The earliest newsprint accounts of the work, such as Ebenezer Larkin's announcement in the August 22nd *Massachusetts Mercury* and Isaiah Thomas's matching notice in the August 23rd *Massachusetts Spy*, refer to Foster in the language of the book's title page: "THE COQUETTE, or the History of ELIZA WHARTON, a Novel, founded on fact. By a Lady of Massachusetts."[8] The following week, however, Thomas issued a second notice indicating that he had more precise knowledge about the author's identity: "This work was written by a Lady near Boston, and is much admired."[9] Thomas qualifies Foster's residence, pinning her somewhere "near Boston," but stops short of revealing the specific town or city where she lives. In an echo of Thomas's tease, publisher Thomas Greenleaf advertised several weeks later in *Greenleaf's New York Journal*, "*An original, new, and excellent Novel*, INTITLED, THE COQUETTE, Or the history of ELIZA WHARTON—founded on fact, by the Lady of

---

6. *The Early American Novel* (New York and Lancaster, PA: New Era Printing, 1907), 107–11. The attributions correspond to *The Hapless Orphan* (1793), *The Fortunate Discovery* (1798), *Monima: or, the Beggar Girl* (1803), *Emily Hamilton, a Novel* (1803), and *The Coquette* (1797).

7. "'By a Lady': The Mask of the Feminine in Restoration, Early Eighteenth-Century Print Culture," *Faces of Anonymity*, 63–64. Further citations will be parenthetical in the text.

8. "Just Published," *Massachusetts Mercury*, Aug. 22, 1797, 3; "New Novel," *Massachusetts Spy*, Aug. 23, 1797, 4.

9. "This day published," *Massachusetts Spy*, Aug. 30, 1797, 4.

a Clergyman in Massachusetts."[1] While Greenleaf declares Foster to be "the Lady of a Clergyman," he does not say to which clergyman or family she belongs. Performing in miniature the concurrent presentation and denial of information that characterizes newsprint descriptions of Whitman—a move which other announcements for *The Coquette* perpetuate—Thomas's and Greenleaf's modified iterations of Foster's pseudonym offer new intelligence about her while paradoxically broadcasting that they do not tell all.

On November 8, 1797, bookseller John Fellows printed in the *Diary and Mercantile Advertiser* the most substantial description of Foster yet published. This "wife of a Clergyman of Massachusetts," Fellows divulges, is "a Lady whose literary talents are held in high estimation by those who have the pleasure of her acquaintance; and from whose pen the public may expect soon to be further gratified, by another work which is now preparing for the press." Repeating the suggestive reticence typical of other *Coquette* advertisements, the notice in the *Diary* reveals more about Foster than other publications but also directs attention to privileged information pointing to her identity, such as the names of the acquaintances who esteem her work, which Fellows continues to withhold.[2] He concludes with a critical assessment of the novel, more comprehensive and pointed than any Larkin, Thomas, or Greenleaf extend:

> As much . . . as truth is of more value than fiction, so much is this novel more estimable than romantic tales, the offspring of extravagant imagination, which bear no resemblance to real life. In this work the understanding is not insulted with an exhibition of enchanted castles, witches or ghosts, but possibilities and realities are presented to it, in that familiar and elegant language which is ever the characteristic of true taste.[3]

If the newspaper contributors providing the most information about Whitman present themselves as the authoritative moral arbiters of her behavior, then the bookseller introducing the most information about Foster figures himself as the authoritative reader of her work. Fellows's evaluation of *The Coquette* relies on the information he has uncovered about Foster—that she is well regarded, that her acquaintance is sought, that she is, in short, a woman of

1. "Just Published," *Greenleaf's New York Journal*, Nov. 11, 1797, 4.
2. In the same piece, Fellows revives the specter of Elizabeth Whitman's anonymity: Foster's novel, he argues, is, more accurately, a "compilation of facts respecting the History of Miss E. W.," the explanatory key to which "[it] would be improper to lay before the public." As if to draw from the excitement surrounding the question of Whitman's identity more than nine years earlier, Fellows refuses to name the real-life model for Foster's narrative and connects the obscurity of the "coquette" to the pseudonymity of the author.
3. "*The Coquette*," *Diary and Mercantile Advertiser*, Nov. 8, 1797, 3.

respectability, practicality, and taste, all of which are revealed in the "truth" and "familiar and elegant language" of her novel. Fellows's reading suggests, in other words, that knowledge of Foster's identity is important to understanding accurately *The Coquette*'s moral and sympathetic worth.

Although advertisements by booksellers show that the author of *The Coquette* was not, in fact, entirely anonymous as early as 1797, the pen name "By a Lady of Massachusetts" continued to appear on the title pages of subsequent editions of *The Coquette* as well as in newspapers, magazines, and literary reviews throughout the nineteenth century.[4] A weird embodiment of this phenomenon, the 1855 edition of *The Coquette*, printed fifteen years after Foster's death, actually reveals Foster's name in an appended "Historical Preface, including a Memoir of the Author," yet refuses to relinquish her pseudonym or admit her identity on the title page. The new 1866 edition and its 1874 reprint duplicate this discovery and omission; not until the first twentieth-century version of the text, Herbert Ross Brown's 1939 facsimile edition, does "Hannah Webster Foster" replace "a Lady of Massachusetts" beneath the title of the novel.

The persistence of Foster's adopted pen name in print and on the title pages of *The Coquette* after her identity had been made known and after her death indicates that something more was at stake in her pseudonym than modesty or reputation. Assuming, Ezell points out, "the intent of the design of the title page was to attract the browser to purchase and read the text," the announcement of gendered or localized authorship could have been meant as "an inducement to buy" (72). Foster's alias perhaps had a marketing value for *The Coquette*; conceivably, publishers and booksellers thought it was important for readers to know that the organizing force behind

4. Five years after releasing *The Coquette*, Etheridge and Larkin reunited to publish a second edition, of which *The Boston Weekly Magazine* observed in January 1803, "the rapid sale of the first edition, is a proof of its estimation by the moral, instructive and entertaining reader." "Literary Intelligence," *The Boston Weekly Magazine*, Jan. 29, 1803, 58. Third and fourth editions followed in 1811 and 1824, by Thomas & Whipple and Charles Whipple, respectively, and in 1828, Abel Brown of Exeter, New Hampshire, published what claimed to be the tenth edition of *The Coquette*. J. P. Clusman's 1831 edition announced itself as the twelfth, and, outdoing both, Charles Gaylord's 1833 edition declared itself the thirtieth. Tellingly, Gaylord's 1840 version of the novel maintains the thirtieth-edition designation on its title page, suggesting that it is a reprint of the 1833 edition. In 1855, Boston publisher W. P. Fetridge and Co. labeled its new edition simply a "New Edition." Finding still an interest in Foster's novel almost 70 years after its original publication, T. B. Peterson & Brothers of Philadelphia printed what was, at the least, the ninth edition of *The Coquette* in 1866. All of the eighteenth and nineteenth-century editions of the text display Foster's pseudonym, "By a Lady of Massachusetts," on their title pages. For periodicals repeating the pseudonymous attribution on subsequent editions, see, for example, "Literary Intelligence," *The Boston Weekly Magazine*, Jan. 29, 1803, 58; "Literary and Miscellaneous Intelligence," *The Panoplist, and Missionary Magazine*, Dec. 1811, 335; "New Editions," *The General Repository and Review*, Jan. 1, 1812, 227; "List of New Publications for December," *The United States Literary Gazette*, Jan. 15, 1825, 302; and "Quarterly List of New Publications," *The North American Review*, Apr. 1825, 474.

the narrative was a woman—and a woman of privilege—as well as a proximate witness to the incidents of Elizabeth Whitman's last days, someone close to and touched by Whitman's conduct.[5] Fore-grounding the author's gender, status, and state of residence, the sign-off, "By a Lady of Massachusetts," could have therefore lent more authenticity to the work than the designation of Foster's name.[6] The sometime print variation of Foster's pseudonym, "By a Lady of a Clergyman," further highlights her connection to Whitman, recalling Foster as a respected woman of a clergyman's family, like that which Whitman came from and into which she contemplated marrying. In her "Memoir" of Foster in the 1855 edition of *The Coquette*, Jane Ermine Locke more explicitly characterizes the author and her real-life subject as equals in sensibility, education, and class:

> Written as it was by one highly educated for the times,—the popular wife of a popular clergyman, connected in no distant degree, by marriage, with the family of the heroine, and one who by the very profession and position of her husband was, as by necessity, brought into the sphere of actual intercourse with the principal characters of the novel . . . it is not surprising that it thus took precedence in interest . . . of all American novels, at least throughout New England, and was found, in every cottage within its borders[.]

Locke claims that Foster's unique affinity with Whitman—the women's "similarity of positions and community of interests"—not only enabled Foster's sympathetic engagement with the sensational figure, "especially" qualifying her to write Whitman's history "with power and effect," but also worked to ensure the novel's lasting popularity in New England.[7]

---

5. Possibly out of a similar desire, New England readers for decades attributed William Hill Brown's *The Power of Sympathy* to Sarah Wentworth Morton, whose husband's affair with her sister is recounted in the novel.
6. The pseudonym's underscoring of gender can also backfire; in 1855, the *Spirit of the Times*, for example, condemned the author of *The Coquette*, which had been recently released in a new edition: "We have perused this work, and we regret that any woman could write such a book. It would be well if such scenes as are here described were never sent forth to the world, and we envy not the author, for there can be but little purity in the mind that can conceive and pen such sentences. Women should be chari-table towards each other, and not gloat over the ruin of a frail creature." "New Publica-tions, & c.," *Spirit of the Times*, Mar. 3, 1855, 36.
7. "Historical Preface, including a Memoir of the Author," in Hannah Webster Foster, *The Coquette; or, the Life and Letters of Eliza Wharton. A Novel: Founded on Fact. By a Lady of Massachusetts* (Boston: William P. Fetridge and Co., 1855), 4. Locke also focuses on Foster and Whitman's distant familial relationship: "[Foster] was daughter of Grant Webster, a well-known merchant of Boston, and wife of Rev. John Foster, of Brighton, Massachusetts, whose pedigree, but few removes backward in the line of her husband, interlinked, as has already been hinted, with that of the 'Coquette.' Thus did they hold towards each other that very significant relationship—especially in the past century—of 'cousins,' a relationship better heeded and more earnestly recog-nized and cherished than that of nearer kin at the present day" (4–5).

426          BLEVIN SHELNUTT

While there were many pieces produced by men explaining Whitman's fate, publishers and advertisers of *The Coquette* evidently perceived that it was important and desirable to represent Foster's novel as a text speaking in the voice of a woman close to Whitman's life—someone who might be able, as Waterman puts it, "to respond to her story with appropriate feeling" (343). In this case, Foster's mask of "a Lady" was not, as Ezell writes, "to disguise the identity of the author and to shield feminine modesty," but rather, it was to "serve more as a costume . . . a means to signify to the reader that a certain type of role was being performed, a type of personality was being staged" (68, 64). Foster's assumed name, in other words, casts the author of *The Coquette* as a particular player in its narrative—a neighbor, a peer in circumstance and class, and a woman, who represents her view of the events leading to Whitman's last days, promising to effect a different register of understanding with Whitman than the early newspaper reports about her actions and death.[8] The perpetuation of "By a Lady of Massachusetts" for nearly a century on *The Coquette*'s title pages and advertisements indeed suggests that those selling the book believed purchasers wanted to read such a view of Whitman's story.

Aligning her, to an extent, with her fictional heroine, Foster's pseudonym ironically re-enacts the coyness of which Eliza Wharton and her prototype are accused. Women writers' use of pen names, such as "By a Lady," Dorothy Mermin indicates, is "unavoidably duplicitous, with overtones of sexual coquetry, teasing withdrawal and self-display."[9] Like the newspaper editors who withheld Whitman's name, Foster's alias continually advances and retreats, taunting readers with a simultaneous suggestion and denial of the author's identity.[1] The "By a Lady" writer, Ezell contends, "'re-enacts' male expectations of femininity . . . in a heightened form, 'being on one's best behavior' so to speak, and thus fulfils the requirements of the

8. Cathy Davidson and Carroll Smith-Rosenberg have read Foster's *Coquette* as a more sympathetic and dignifying rewriting of the newspaper coverage of Whitman. See Smith-Rosenberg, "Domesticating 'Virtue': Coquette and Revolutionaries in Young America," *Literature and the Body: Essays on Populations and Persons*, ed. Elaine Scarry (Baltimore: Johns Hopkins, 1988), 160–84, especially 169, 175–77; Davidson, "Introduction," in Hannah Webster Foster, *The Coquette*, ed. Davidson (New York: Oxford UP, 1986), vii–xx; and Davidson, *Revolution and the Word: The Rise of the Novel in America* (New York: Oxford UP, 2004), 186–87, 221–32.
9. "Women Becoming Poets: Katherine Phillips, Aphra Behn, Anne Finch," *ELH* 57 (1990): 338, quoted in Ezell, 67.
1. In his reading of *The Coquette*, Grantland Rice argues that the genre of the early American novel itself engages in a coquettish performance, practicing, like Foster's pseudonym, a self-conscious and reflexive duality. While the figure of the coquette performed behind a veil of unaccountability and inscrutability in an effort to sustain her social value, freedom, and power," early American authors produced "a prose fiction that was divided against itself, and which identified with popular suspicions about the corrupting influence of novels . . . at the same time it denied the association." See *The Transformation of Authorship in America* (Chicago: U of Chicago P, 1997), 168–69.

viewer, all the while maintaining an ironic self-determination and control from behind the mask" (77). Foster's adopted designation, "By a Lady of Massachusetts," exploited, rather than acquiesced to, contemporary conventions of pseudonymous female authorship, manipulating the gendered standards of authorial attribution within a male-dominated print culture to advertise a female perspective on one of the most provocative and gender-relevant issues of her time.

# Hannah Webster Foster:
## A Chronology

1739    In July, Grant Webster of Haverhill confesses to and is convicted of fornication with Hannah Wainwright in advance of their May marriage. Pays a fine of 10 shillings each.

1758    Hannah Foster is born September 10, in either Amesbury or Salisbury, Massachusetts, to Grant Webster and Hannah Wainwright. Baptized September 17 in Salisbury's Second Church.

1765    Mother dies March 13. Grant Webster is by now established in Boston.

1775–83    American Revolution. One of Grant Webster's Boston properties is destroyed by fire on May 21, 1775.

1785    Marries Rev. John Foster, of the First Parish Church of Brighton, Massachusetts, on February 15; they take up residence at 15–17 Peaceable Street.

1789–96    Births of Foster's five surviving children.

1790    Moves to the new First Church Parsonage at 10 Academy Hill Road.

1797    *The Coquette* is published.

1797    Grant Webster dies August 30 and is buried in Mount Auburn Cemetery, Boston. Foster may have inherited a portion of her father's estate.

1798    *The Boarding School* is published.

1801    Funds the education of Phineas Adams, who graduates from Harvard this year.

1802    J. Horatio Nicols publishes the drama *The New England Coquette*, based on *The Coquette*.

1803    Phineas Adams founds *The Monthly Anthology or Magazine of Polite Literature*.

1808–09    John Foster oversees the building of a new church in Brighton.

1810    The Fosters build an impressive mansion on what becomes Foster Street.

1827    On October 31, John Foster retires following a factional dispute in his congregation; the Fosters are firmly Unitarian.

1829    *The Boarding School*'s second and only subsequent edition.

1829    In April, Foster is one of many women in attendance at the founding of the Brighton Ladies Association, the first Massachusetts Women's Club.

1829    John Foster dies September 16 and is interred in burying ground on Market Street.

1830    Bequest to Massachusetts Historical Society; soon after, Foster relocates to Montreal to live with two daughters, Eliza Lanesford Cushing and Harriet Vaughn Cheney. Also in Montreal is the family of deceased daughter, Hannah White Barrett. Foster's daughters were authors, editors, and Unitarian activists.

1840    Foster dies April 17; interred the following day at St. Andrew's Presbyterian, Saint Peter Street, Montreal.

1851    William R. Hayden first serializes then publishes *Clara Wharton. A sequel to The Coquette*, which resurrects the child born to Eliza Wharton as its heroine.

1855    Jane E. Locke composes introduction to *The Coquette*, including memoir of its author.

1861    Play *Eliza Wharton* is staged at Wyatt's Theatre, American Hall, Hartford, Connecticut.

# Elizabeth Whitman:
# A Chronology

| | |
|---|---|
| 1752 | Born to Abigail Stanley and Elnathan Whitman, pastor of the Second Church in Hartford, Connecticut. |
| 1775 | Fiancé Joseph Howe, of Boston's New South Church, dies August 25 at the Whitman house in Hartford after an almost three-week illness. |
| 1777 | Elnathan Whitman dies March 4 after a decline of some years. |
| 1778 | Elizabeth's acquaintance with poet Joel Barlow believed to begin late in year. Correspondence survives from 1779–82. |
| 1778–79 | Estimated period of presumed failed engagement to Joseph Buckminster. |
| 1781 | Joel Barlow and Ruth Baldwin secretly marry on January 26. |
| 1783 | New Year's Day poem dedicated to Joel Barlow. |
| 1786 | Remembered in the will of her uncle, William Stanley (1724–86), in recognition of "services done for me." |
| 1788 | Joel Barlow arrives in France, June 24. |
| 1788 | Late May or early June, departs Hartford, arriving in Danvers. Gives birth the second week of July, dying July 25, 1788. Buried in the Old South Burial Ground the following day. |
| 1788 | July 29, article appears in Salem paper asking for help in identifying mysterious woman. Soon Whitman's story and writings appear in other papers. |
| 1789 | Mentioned in William Hill Brown's novel *The Power of Sympathy*, published in January. |
| 1790 | Whitman family appears in the census for Hartford, with four residents total, one male, and three females. |
| 1797 | Abigail Stanley Whitman dies in November. |
| 1798 | Story fictionalized in Foster's novel, *The Coquette*. |
| 1827 | Whitman family home in Hartford destroyed by fire. Virtually everything is lost. |

1840 Fitch Poole claims to have found letters from Whitman and a series of artifacts belonging to her in the wall of the Old Bell Tavern. The discovery is later revealed to be a prank.

1855 Jane E. Locke composes an introduction to *The Coquette*, suggesting real counterparts to fictional characters.

1875 Caroline Wells Healey Dall publishes *The Romance of the Association; or, One Last Glimpse of Charlotte Temple and Eliza Wharton*, making a bowdlerized version of the Whitman-Barlow correspondence available for the first time.

1912 Charles Knowles Bolton publishes *The Elizabeth Whitman Mystery at the Old Bell Tavern in Danvers*.

2004 Series of events celebrating *The Coquette* and Whitman staged in Peabody, Massachusetts (a portion of which was formerly part of Danvers), culminating in unveiling of a new tombstone on March 24.

# Selected Bibliography

•indicates works included or excerpted in this Norton Critical Edition.

## HANNAH WEBSTER FOSTER

Davidson, Cathy. "Hannah Webster Foster." In *American Writers of the Early Republic*, ed. Emory Elliott. Detroit, MI: Gale Research Co., 1985, 161–63.
Marchione, William P. "Hannah Foster: Brighton's Pioneer Novelist." In *Allston-Brighton in Transition: From Cattle Town to Streetcar Suburb*. Charleston, SC: History Press, 2007, 27–30.
Pettengill, Claire C. "Hannah Webster Foster (1758–1840)." *Legacy: A Journal of American Women Writers* 12.2 (1995): 133–41.
Verhoeven, W. M. "Hannah Webster Foster." In *American Women Prose Writers to 1820*, ed. and intro. Carla Mulford, Angela Vietto, and Amy E. Winans. Detroit, MI: Gale Research, 1999, 122–31.

## ELIZABETH WHITMAN, *THE COQUETTE*, AND *THE BOARDING SCHOOL*

Baker, Dorothy Z. "'Detested Be the Epithet!': Definition, Maxim, and the Language of Social Dicta in Hannah Webster Foster's *The Coquette*." *Essays in Literature* 23.1 (1996): 58–68.
• Bolton, Charles Knowles. *The Elizabeth Whitman Mystery at the Old Bell Tavern in Danvers*. Peabody, MA: Peabody Historical Society, 1912.
• Brown, Gillian. "Consent, Coquetry, and Consequences." *American Literary History* 9.4 (1997): 625–52.
Cassuto, Leonard. "The Seduction of American Religious Discourse in Foster's *The Coquette*." In *Reform and Counterreform: Dialectics of the Word in Western Christianity since Luther*, ed. John C. Hawley. New York: Mouton de Gruyter, 1994, 105–18.
• Dall, Caroline Wells Healey. *The Romance of the Association; or, One Last Glimpse of Charlotte Temple and Eliza Wharton. A Curiosity of Literature and Life*. Cambridge: Press of J. Wilson and Son, 1875.
Dill, Elizabeth. "A Mob of Lusty Villagers: Operations of Domestic Desires in Hannah Webster Foster's *The Coquette*." *Eighteenth-Century Fiction* 15.2 (2003): 255–79.
Finseth, Ian. "'A Melancholy Tale': Rhetoric, Fiction, and Passion in *The Coquette*." *Studies in the Novel* 33.2 (2001): 125–59.
• Foster, Gwendolyn Audrey. "The Dialogics of Sisterly Advice: Hannah Webster Foster, *The Boarding School*." *Troping the Body: Gender, Etiquette, and Performance*. Carbondale: Southern Illinois UP, 2000, 47–60.
Hamilton, Kristie. "An Assault on the Will: Republican Virtue and the City in Hannah Webster Foster's *The Coquette*." *Early American Literature* 24.2 (1989): 135–51.
Harris, Jennifer. "Writing Vice: Hannah Webster Foster and *The Coquette*." *Canadian Review of American Studies* 39.4 (2009): 363–82.

Harris, Jennifer. "Wax Coquettes: Elizabeth Whitman, Henry Wadsworth Longfellow, and the Nineteenth-Century Traveling Waxwork Exhibition." *Canadian Review of American Studies* 40.3 (2010): 373–89.

Harris, Jennifer. "'Almost idolatrous love': Caroline Dall, Sarah Knowles Bolton, Mary C. Crawford and the case of Elizabeth Whitman." In *Women Writers and the Artifacts of Celebrity*, ed. Ann R. Hawkins and Maura Ives. London and Burlington, Vermont: Ashgate Press (2012): 119–32.

Harris, Sharon M. "Hannah Webster Foster's *The Coquette*: Critiquing Franklin's America." In *Redefining the Political Novel: American Women Writers, 1797–1901*, ed. Sharon M. Harris. Knoxville: U of Tennessee P, 1995, 1–22.

• Hessinger, Rodney. *Seduced, Abandoned, and Reborn: Visions of Youth in Middle-Class America, 1780–1850*. Philadelphia: U of Pennsylvania P, 2005.

• Hewitt, Elizabeth. *Correspondence and American Literature, 1770–1865*. New York: Cambridge UP, 2004.

Jarenski, Shelly. "The Voice of the Preceptress: Female Education in and as the Seduction Novel." *Journal of the Midwest Modern Language Association* 37.1 (2004): 59–68.

Korobkin, Laura H. "'Can Your Volatile Daughter Ever Acquire Your Wisdom?': Luxury and False Ideals in *The Coquette.*" *Early American Literature* 41.1 (2006): 79–107.

Mower, C. Leiren. "Bodies in Labor: Sole Proprietorship and the Labor of Conduct in *The Coquette*." *American Literature* 74.2 (2002): 315–44.

• Nichols, J. Horatio. *The New England Coquette: From the History of the Celebrated Eliza Wharton, a Tragic Drama in Three Acts*. Salem: N. Coverly, 1802.

• Pettengill, Claire C. "Sisterhood in a Separate Sphere: Female Friendships in Hannah Webster Foster's *The Coquette* and *The Boarding School*." *Early American Literature* 27 (1992): 185–203.

• Richards, Jeffrey H. "The Politics of Seduction: Theater, Sexuality, and National Virtue in the Novels of Hannah Foster." In *Essays in Performance and History*, ed. Della Pollock. Chapel Hill: U of North Carolina P, 1998, 238–57.

Schweitzer, Ivy. "Foster's Coquette: Resurrecting Friendship from the Tomb of Marriage." *Arizona Quarterly* 61.2 (2005): 1–32.

Shuffelton, Frank. "Hannah Webster Foster's *Coquette* and the End of the Brotherly Watch." *Studies in Eighteenth-Century Culture* 16 (1986): 211–24.

Shurter, Robert L. "Mrs. Hannah Webster Foster and the Early American Novel." *American Literature* 4 (1932): 306–08.

• Smith-Rosenberg, Carroll. "Domesticating 'Virtue': Coquettes and Revolutionaries in Young America." In Elaine Scarry, ed. *Literature and the Body: Essays on Populations and Persons*. Baltimore: Johns Hopkins UP, 1988, 169–78.

Sohn, Jeonghee. "Theory and Practice of Female Bonding in *The Coquette* and *Charlotte Temple*." *Feminist Studies in English Literature* 13.1 (2005): 87–107.

• Stern, Julia A. *The Plight of Feeling: Sympathy and Dissent in the Early American Novel*. Chicago: U of Chicago P, 1997, ch. 3.

Tassoni, John Paul. "'I Can Step Out of Myself a Little': Feminine Virtue and Female Friendship in Hannah Foster's *The Coquette*." In *Communication and Women's Friendships: Parallels and Intersections in Literature and Life*, ed. Janet Doubler Ward and JoAnna Stephens Mink. Bowling Green, OH: Bowling Green State U Popular P, 1993, 97–111.

Wakabayashi, Makiko. "Female Friendship in Hannah Webster Foster's *The Coquette*: A Legacy of the Seduction Novel." *Studies in English Literature* 47 (2006): 161–79.

Waldstreicher, David. "'Fallen under My Observation': Vision and Virtue in *Coquette*." *Early American Literature* 27.3 (1992): 204–18.

Waterman, Bryan. "Coquetry and Correspondence in Revolutionary-Era Connecticut: Reading Elizabeth Whitman's Letters." *Early American Literature* 6.3 (2011): 541–63.

Waterman, Bryan. "Elizabeth Whitman's Disappearance and Her 'Disappointment,'" *William and Mary Quarterly* 66.2 (2009): 325–64.

• Waterman, Bryan, ed. "The Letters of Elizabeth Whitman to Joel and Ruth Barlow, 1779–1783." *Early American Literature* 46.3 (2011): 565–600.

Weyler, Karen A. "Marriage, Coverture, and the Companionate Ideal in *The Coquette* and *Dorval*." *Legacy: A Journal of American Women Writers* 26.1 (2009): 1–25.

Wenska, Walter P., Jr. "*The Coquette* and the American Dream of Freedom." *Early American Literature* 12 (1977–78): 243–55.

## GENERAL

Barnes, Elizabeth. *States of Sympathy: Seduction and Democracy in the American Novel*. New York: Columbia UP, 1997.

Bloch, Ruth H. *Gender and Morality in Anglo-American Culture, 1650–1800*. Berkeley: U of California P, 2003.

Bontatibus, Donna R. *The Seduction Novel of the Early Nation: A Call for Socio-Political Reform*. East Lansing: Michigan State UP, 1999.

Brown, Gillian. *Domestic Individualism: Imagining Self in Nineteenth-Century America*. Berkeley: U of California P, 1990.

Lewis, Jan. "The Republican Wife: Virtue and Seduction in the Early Republic." *William and Mary Quarterly* 44 (1987): 689–721.

Rice, Grantland S. *The Transformation of Authorship in America*. Chicago: U of Chicago P, 1997.